THE
unofficial **GUIDE**®
ᵀᴼHawaii

6TH EDITION

THE *unofficial* GUIDE®
TO Hawaii

6TH EDITION

MARCIE *and* RICK CARROLL

Please note that prices fluctuate in the course of time and that travel information changes under the impact of many factors which influence the travel industry. We therefore suggest that you write or call ahead for confirmation when making your travel plans. Every effort has been made to ensure the accuracy of information throughout this book, and the contents of this publication are believed to be correct at the time of printing. Nevertheless, the publishers cannot accept responsibility for errors or omissions, for changes in details given in this guide, or for the consequences of any reliance on the information provided by the same. Assessments of attractions and so forth are based upon the author's own experience; therefore, descriptions given in this guide necessarily contain an element of subjective opinion, which may not reflect the publisher's opinion or dictate a reader's own experience on another occasion. Readers are invited to write the publisher with ideas, comments, and suggestions for future editions.

Published by:
John Wiley & Sons, Inc.
111 River Street
Hoboken, NJ 07030-5774

Produced by Menasha Ridge Press

Cover design by Michael J. Freeland

Interior design by Vertigo Design

For information on our other products and services or to obtain technical support, please contact our Customer Care Department within the United States at 877-762-2974, outside the United States at 317-572-3993, or by fax at 317-572-4002.

John Wiley & Sons, Inc., also publishes its books in a variety of electronic formats. Some content that appears in print may not be available in electronic formats.

ISBN 978-0-470-53325-3

Manufactured in the United States of America

5 4 3 2 1

CONTENTS

LIST *of* MAPS

ACKNOWLEDGMENTS

MAHALO NUI LOA, HAWAII.
For their generous research assistance on all six major islands of Hawaii, thus helping make *The Unofficial Guide to Hawaii*'s new edition a good read, we gratefully acknowledge and thank the following people and organizations: State Tourism Liaison Marsha Weinert; Kelii Brown, Maui Visitors Bureau; Kim Kessler, Ritz-Carlton, Kapalua; Dara Young, Hilton Hawaiian Village; Caroline Witherspoon, Becker Communications; Keith Vieira, Starwood Hotels & Resorts, Honolulu; Donna Jung Public Relations, Honolulu; Kaui Philpotts, Honolulu; Candy Aluli, Maui; Ruth Limtiaco, The Limtiaco Co.; David McNeil, McNeil Wilson, Honolulu; Sheila Donnelly & Associates; and Bonnie Friedman, Grapevine Productions, Maui.

—*Rick and Marcie Carroll*

ABOUT *the* AUTHORS

RICK CARROLL, author of many Hawaii books, is the creator of the best-selling *Hawaii's Best Spooky Tales* series and *Madame Pele: True Encounters with Hawaii's Fire Goddess.* A former daily journalist at the *San Francisco Chronicle,* Rick wrote award-winning travel and feature stories about Hawaii and the Pacific for *The Honolulu Advertiser* and United Press International. His best-selling book, *IZ: Voice of the People*—the biography of the late, legendary Hawaiian singer Israel Kamakawiwo'ole—was a Kiriyama Prize Notable Book of 2007. His new book, *Right Down Front: Ron Hudson Jazz Images,* is available on Amazon.com.

MARCIE RASMUSSEN CARROLL, freelance travel writer and former communications director for the Hawaii Convention and Visitors Bureau, wrote political, environmental, and other news for the *San Francisco Chronicle,* the *San Jose Mercury-News,* and United Press International in Atlanta. She was a journalism fellow in Asian studies at University of Hawaii and in energy studies at Stanford University.

Together, the Carrolls, who moved to Windward Oahu in 1983, collected and edited the anthology *Travelers' Tales Hawaii: True Stories of the Island Spirit,* which one reviewer praised as "the best collection of contemporary Hawaii travel stories." Their new book, *Three Centuries of Seafaring: The Maritime Art of Paul Hee,* is available on Amazon.com.

THE *unofficial* GUIDE®
TO Hawaii

6TH EDITION

INTRODUCTION

 ## MAKING *the* MOST *of* YOUR HAWAIIAN DREAM

HAWAII. HEAR THE WORD, and you're swept away by dreams of a tropical Eden, sensual swaying hula dancers, and visions of an endless, empty beach.

Can this place *really* be as magical as it seems? Or is it just an illusion? The right answers to those questions are yes and no, respectively. The tropical Eden is for real, hula is the heartbeat of the Hawaiian culture, and empty beaches stretch for miles on all the smaller islands. And volcanoes are still making Big Island beaches even more magical. This is, in all ways, a very special destination.

But it's more than a pretty place; it's an experience that can change your life, and that has to do with the people and their way of living. The lighthearted island attitudes, the warmth of people who go out of their way for you, and the sense of extended family soon begin to melt even the most resolute holdouts. Your stakes are huge in making the most of your visit to the Islands. If you get Hawaii right, the place will grab you by the heart and make you feel good. The best way to enjoy it is to loosen up and let Hawaii happen to you.

Approach Hawaii like you would another country, which it was not so long ago. Be prepared for exotic customs, serendipity, and unexpected disruptions of your plans. Be a good sport. Brief yourself by reading this book, prowling the Internet, and talking to friends. For those who come to the Islands with advance knowledge and plenty of patience, delightful encounters are bound to happen. Bring your children and elders. They'll have a good time, and the people of Hawaii cherish *keiki* (kids) and *kupuna* (wise older folks).

In Waikiki, don't expect idyllic huts by the sea (although you can find them elsewhere on the Islands). Expect high-rise hotels in an urban cityscape. Expect hustling on the sidewalks, although it's quite tame by big-city standards (most Waikiki hustlers want to hand you an ad). Don't expect to be met with a lei of flowers at the airport unless you have already paid for the greeting service or are being met by a friend who lives in the Islands. Brace yourself for hugs and kisses on the cheek when you meet effusive strangers, if you're lucky. Hawaii is one of the world's safer destinations, but don't be surprised if your wallet and camera are pilfered when you leave them on the seat of a rental car while you run to look at a mesmerizing view.

Strip away the veil of Hawaii's natural beauty and you'll find many of the same problems that burden other American communities: economic struggles, drugs, increasing crime, and traffic congestion. But you'll also find people who still smile at strangers and largely rely on kindness, respect, and humor when dealing with one another. You'll discover skies that are blue rather than gray, seawater that is clear and warm, air that is soft and fresh, and scenery that soothes the soul.

A visit to Hawaii is too precious to waste. So we're here to help you pursue your dream and along the way find some unexpected memorable experiences. Our purpose is to present a realistic view of contemporary Hawaii that helps you make the most of your Island holiday. We'll provide some of the details in advance, so that you'll be free to have fun.

In this guide you'll discover how to find the best deals on lodging, whether you want hotels, condominiums, or bed-and-breakfasts. You'll get an up-to-date review of the best adventures, attractions, beaches, hotels, clubs, and restaurants. And you'll gain insights into local customs and learn a few Hawaiian words and phrases to make you feel more like a *kamaaina* ("child of the land," a longtime or native-born Hawaii resident).

Along the way, we'll answer frequently asked questions like these:

- When is the best time to go?
- Which islands should we visit?
- Where are the best beaches?
- What hiking trails are recommended for families?
- Who are Hawaii's must-see entertainers?

You want to make the most of your time in the Islands. You want to be at the right place at the right time, enjoying the very best Hawaii has to offer, especially if it is your first trip. This book will help you. For those of you who have been to the Aloha State many times before and are ready to dig deeper, this book will suggest new possibilities. You may find a new discovery. So mix up a mai tai, put on your favorite Hawaiian music, and start your Hawaiian adventure with *The Unofficial Guide to Hawaii.*

E komo mai! Welcome.

ABOUT *This* **GUIDE**

WHY "UNOFFICIAL"?

JUST AS HAWAII INSPIRES UNCONVENTIONAL IDEALS and promotes individuality, so does the *Unofficial Guides* series. Most "official" guides to Hawaii tout the well-known sights, promote the local restaurants and hotels indiscriminately, and leave out the nitty-gritty. This one is different. We'll be up-front with you. Instead of nabbing you by the ankles in a tourist trap, we'll tell you if it's not worth the wait for the mediocre food served at a well-known restaurant. We'll complain loudly about overpriced hotel rooms that aren't convenient, and we'll guide you away from the crowds and congestion for a break now and then. If a museum is boring or a major attraction is overrated, we say so—and, in the process, make your visit exactly that: your visit. We got into the guidebook business because we were unhappy with the way travel guides make the reader work to get any usable information. Wouldn't it be nice, we thought, if we made guides that were easy to use?

OTHER GUIDEBOOKS

MOST GUIDEBOOKS ARE COMPILATIONS OF LISTS. This is true regardless of whether the information is presented in list form or artfully distributed through pages of prose. There is insufficient detail in a list, and with prose the presentation can be tedious and contain large helpings of nonessential or marginally useful information. Not enough wheat, so to speak, for nourishment in one instance, and too much chaff in the other. Either way, other guides provide little more than departure points from which readers initiate their own quests.

Sure, many guides are readable and well researched, but they tend to be difficult to use. To select a hotel, for example, a reader must study several pages of descriptions with only the names of the hotels in bold type breaking up the text. Because each description essentially deals with the same variables, it is difficult to recall what was said concerning a particular hotel. Readers generally have no alternative but to work through all the write-ups before beginning to narrow their choices. The presentation of restaurants, clubs, and attractions is similar except that even more reading is usually required. To use such a guide is to undertake an exhaustive research process that requires examining nearly as many options and possibilities as starting from scratch. Recommendations, if any, lack depth and conviction. By failing to narrow travelers' choices down to a thoughtfully considered, well-distilled, and manageable few, these guides compound rather than solve problems.

HOW *UNOFFICIAL GUIDES* ARE DIFFERENT

SOME HAWAII GUIDEBOOKS are full of pretty pictures. Others present a tedious stream of words with little practical advice. Many Hawaii guidebooks lead you only to a sugarcoated version of the Islands, but this book strives to be different.

Our goal at *Unofficial Guides* is to help you make informed decisions about topics like this: Anyone can find the Bishop Museum, but when is the best time to go? How much walking is involved? Is the museum really worth the price of admission?

Hawaii offers more to do and see than you could pack into a lifetime of vacations. If you have only a week or two and just want to relax on a palm-fringed gold-sand beach, no problem. We'll suggest that perfect beach and provide the information you need to enjoy it in a concise, easy-to-read format. Written for repeat and first-time visitors alike, this guide addresses typical planning concerns: "Can I leave my coat and tie at home?" or "Should I visit the Polynesian Cultural Center?" You'll find the answers to those questions and more in these pages.

Our philosophy: If it matters to you, then it matters to us. From the beginning, the people behind *Unofficial Guides* have worked diligently to deliver honest, straight-up reviews of major destinations. For this book, the authors are two former San Francisco daily-newspaper journalists who have lived in Hawaii and written about the Islands for two decades. They combine island knowledge with the ability to evaluate experiences from the visitor's point of view.

Special Features

This *Unofficial Guide* includes these special features:

- Insightful introductions to Hawaii's six main islands, highlighting the special appeal and character of each.
- A brief look at Hawaii's fascinating history, from its discovery by the first Polynesians, through the missionaries, to today's multicultural, mid-Pacific reality.
- Explanations of local customs and island styles.
- Candid opinions on the best and worst of Hawaii, including accommodations, beaches, restaurants, attractions, shows, clubs, and shops.
- Practical information on driving distances; how to avoid crowds, dodge traffic jams, and park cheaply; and how to get around Oahu without a car.
- Itineraries for families, honeymooners, seniors, and disabled travelers.
- A guide to the state's best golf courses.

COMMENTS AND SUGGESTIONS FROM READERS

WE WELCOME YOUR SUGGESTIONS AND COMMENTS about all our *Unofficial Guides*, including this book. Should you find any errors or omissions, we would appreciate hearing from you. Some of the best suggestions come from our readers.

How to Write the Authors

Rick Carroll and Marcie Carroll
The Unofficial Guide to Hawaii
P.O. Box 43673
Birmingham, AL 35243
unofficialguides@menasharidge.com

When you contact us by mail, put your return address on your letter as well as on the envelope. And remember, our work takes us on the road for long periods of time; please forgive any delayed response.

HOW INFORMATION IS ORGANIZED: BY SUBJECT AND BY GEOGRAPHIC AREAS

TO GIVE YOU QUICK ACCESS TO INFORMATION about the best Hawaii has to offer, we've organized material in several formats.

HOTELS So many Island hotels, condos, and bed-and-breakfasts seek your business that choosing the right one can be daunting. We offer easy-to-read charts, maps, and rating systems as well as pertinent information on room size, cleanliness, service, amenities, cost, and accessibility to the beach.

RESTAURANTS A highlight of every Hawaiian vacation is sampling the Islands' cuisine. The menu is vast and tasty, ranging from simple local favorites like plate lunches to gourmet repasts and Hawaii's own regional cuisine. We take you to Hawaii's best restaurants.

ENTERTAINMENT AND NIGHTLIFE Many visitors to the Islands enjoy live shows or nightspots during their stay. This is especially true of visitors to Oahu, where Waikiki is home to ongoing theatrical productions and plenty of hot spots. We've reviewed a few of the best live productions. We also check out the best nightclubs and lounges.

GOLF Golf is a major draw for many visitors. We detail vital stats of the state's top courses to help you choose the right one.

GEOGRAPHIC AREAS For added convenience, we've divided Hawaii into geographic areas. Perhaps you're interested in staying somewhere in Kapalua Resort on the island of Maui but aren't sure where it is. We'll note for you that Kapalua is in West Maui, and all other West Maui resorts, hotels, attractions, and restaurants will be in that vicinity.

Please note that the islands of Niihau and Kahoolawe, while technically among the main southernmost islands in the Hawaiian Island chain, are not included in our geographic areas, nor are the older Northwest Hawaiian Islands that stretch hundreds of miles into the North Pacific, now protected within the world's largest marine conservation area, the 140,000-square-mile Papahanaumokuakea Marine National Monument. Niihau is a private family-owned island and is, with few exceptions, inaccessible to visitors. For decades, Kahoolawe, was a target for United States Navy bombing practice. Now it is being transformed into a Hawaiian cultural preserve. The uninhabited island is off-limits, except by special invitation.

The Hawaiian Islands

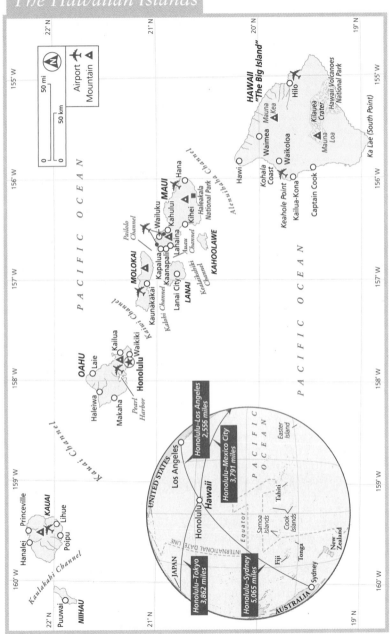

Molokai

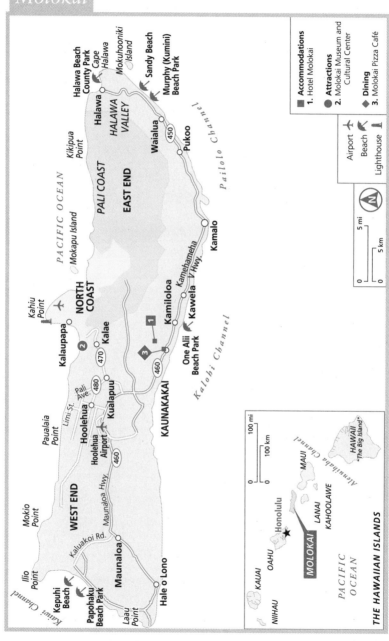

Accommodations
■ 1. Hotel Molokai

Attractions
● 2. Molokai Museum and Cultural Center

Dining
◆ 3. Molokai Pizza Café

✈ Airport
⚓ Beach
⚲ Lighthouse

N

0 ___ 5 mi
0 ___ 5 km

Halawa Beach County Park
Cape Halawa
Mokuhooniki Island
Sandy Beach
Murphy (Kumini) Beach Park
Halawa
HALAWA VALLEY
Waialua
450
Pukoo
Pailolo Channel
Kikipua Point
PALI COAST
EAST END
Mokapu Island
PACIFIC OCEAN
Kamalo
Kahiu Point
NORTH COAST
Kalae
Kamiloloa
Kamehameha Hwy.
Kawela
Kalaupapa
2
470
One Alii Beach Park
1
3
460
Kalohi Channel
KAUNAKAKAI
Pali Ave.
480
Limi St.
Kualapuu
Hoolehua
Hoolehua Airport
460
Paualaia Point
WEST END
Maunaloa Hwy.
Mokio Point
Ilio Point
Kaluakoi Rd.
Maunaloa
Hale o Lono
Kepuhi Beach
Papohaku Beach Park
Laau Point
Kaiui Channel

THE HAWAIIAN ISLANDS

KAUAI
NIIHAU
OAHU
Honolulu
MOLOKAI
LANAI
MAUI
KAHOOLAWE
HAWAII "The Big Island"
Alenuihaha Channel
PACIFIC OCEAN

0 ___ 100 mi
0 ___ 100 km

Oahu Orientation

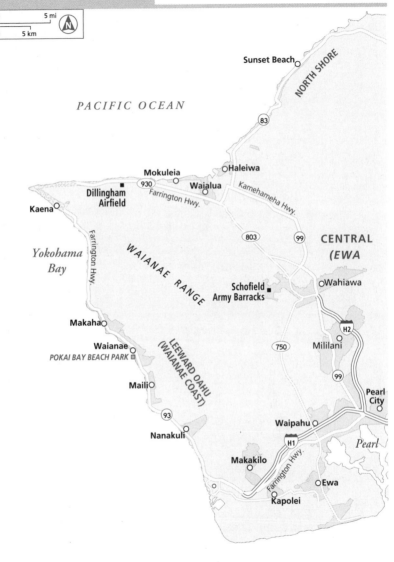

0 5 mi
0 5 km

PACIFIC OCEAN

Sunset Beach

NORTH SHORE

83

Mokuleia Haleiwa
930 Waialua
Dillingham Farrington Hwy. Kamehameha Hwy.
Airfield

Kaena

803 99 CENTRAL
(EWA

Yokohama
Bay

WAIANAE RANGE

Schofield Wahiawa
Army Barracks

Farrington Hwy.

Makaha

Waianae LEEWARD OAHU H2
POKAI BAY BEACH PARK (WAIANAE COAST) 750 Mililani

Maili 99

Pearl
City

93 Waipahu

Nanakuli H1 Pearl

Makakilo

Farrington Hwy. Ewa

Kapolei

PACIFIC OCEAN

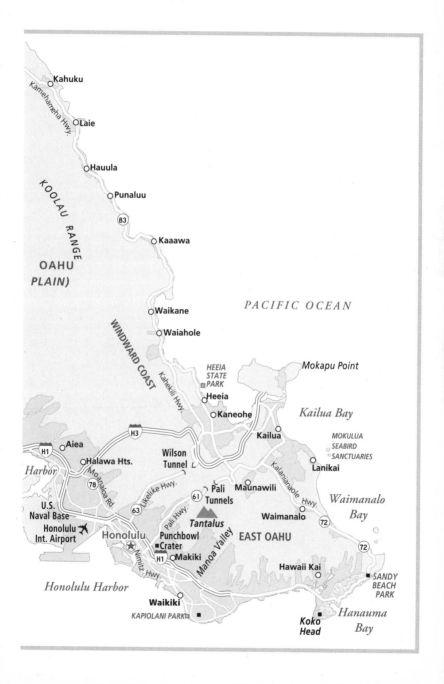

Waikiki Orientation

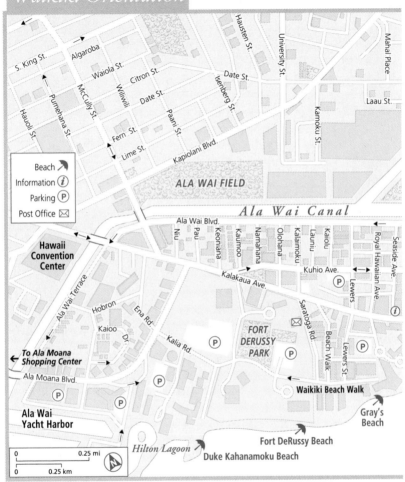

Beach 🏖
Information ⓘ
Parking Ⓟ
Post Office ✉

S. King St.
Algaroba
Waiola St.
Citron St.
Date St.
Date St.
Hausten St.
Isenberg St.
University St.
Mahai Place
Laau St.
Kamoku St.
Hauoli St.
Pumehana St.
McCully St.
Wiliwili
Fern St.
Lime St.
Paani St.
Kapiolani Blvd.

ALA WAI FIELD

Ala Wai Canal

Ala Wai Blvd.
Niu
Pau
Keoniana
Kaumoo
Namahana
Olohana
Kalaimoku
Launiu
Kaiolu
Royal Hawaiian Ave.
Seaside Ave.

Hawaii Convention Center

Ala Wai Terrace

Hobron
Ena Rd.
Kaioo Dr.
Kalia Rd.
Kalakaua Ave.
Kuhio Ave.
Lewers St.
Saratoga Rd.
Beach Walk
Lewers St.

FORT DERUSSY PARK

To Ala Moana Shopping Center
Ala Moana Blvd.

Ala Wai Yacht Harbor

Waikiki Beach Walk

Gray's Beach

0   0.25 mi
0   0.25 km

Hilton Lagoon
Fort DeRussy Beach
Duke Kahanamoku Beach

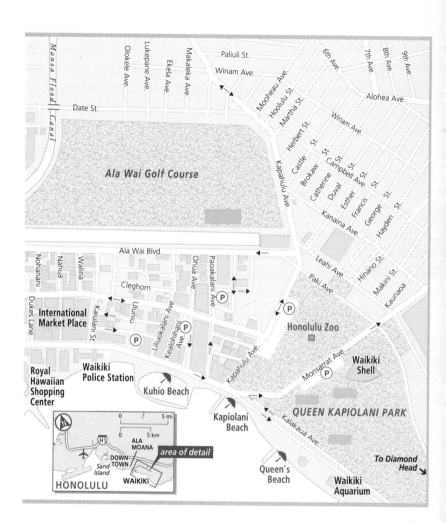

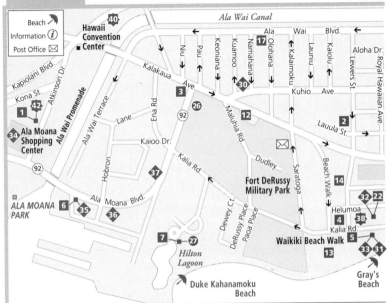

Waikiki

Accommodations
1. Ala Moana Hotel
2. Aston Waikiki Joy Hotel
3. Doubletree Alana Hotel Waikiki
4. Embassy Suites Waikiki Beach Walk
5. Halekulani Hotel
6. Hawaii Prince Hotel Waikiki
7. Hilton Hawaiian Village
8. Hilton Waikiki Prince Kuhio
9. Hyatt Regency Waikiki
10. Ohana Waikiki Beachcomber Hotel
11. Ohana Waikiki East Hotel
12. Outrigger Luana Waikiki Hotel
13. Outrigger Reef on the Beach
14. Outrigger Regency on Beachwalk
15. Outrigger Waikiki on the Beach
16. Pacific Beach Hotel
17. Royal Garden at Waikiki
18. Royal Hawaiian Hotel
19. Sheraton Princess Kaiulani
20. Sheraton Waikiki
21. Waikiki Beach Marriott Resort
22. Waikiki Parc Hotel
23. Westin Moana Surfrider

Attractions
24. Damien Museum
25. Honolulu Zoo
26. U.S. Army Museum of Hawaii

Dining
27. Bali by the Sea

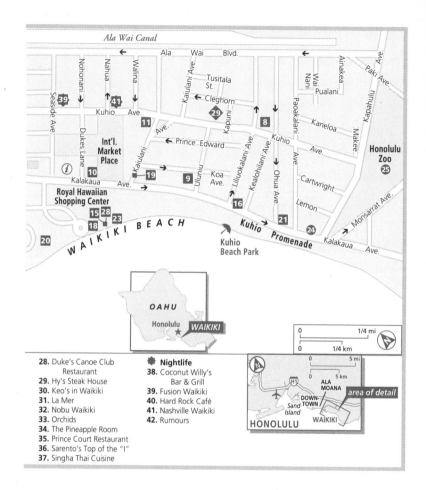

28. Duke's Canoe Club
    Restaurant
29. Hy's Steak House
30. Keo's in Waikiki
31. La Mer
32. Nobu Waikiki
33. Orchids
34. The Pineapple Room
35. Prince Court Restaurant
36. Sarento's Top of the "I"
37. Singha Thai Cuisine

🌺 Nightlife
38. Coconut Willy's
    Bar & Grill
39. Fusion Waikiki
40. Hard Rock Café
41. Nashville Waikiki
42. Rumours

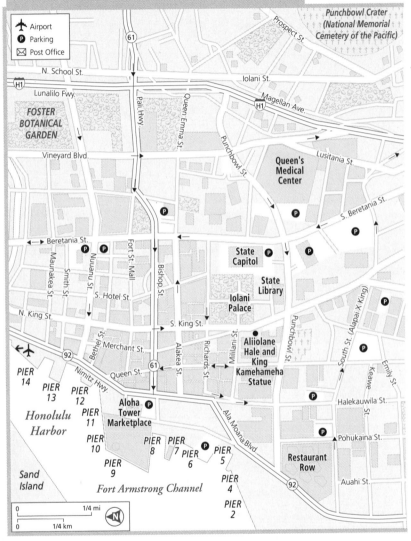

Downtown Honolulu Orientation

✈ Airport
🅿 Parking
✉ Post Office

Punchbowl Crater
(National Memorial
Cemetery of the Pacific)

Prospect St.

61

N. School St.

Iolani St.

H1

Lunalilo Fwy.

Magellan Ave.

H1

FOSTER
BOTANICAL
GARDEN

Pali Hwy.

Queen Emma St.

Punchbowl St.

Lusitania St.

Vineyard Blvd.

Queen's
Medical
Center

S. Beretania St.

Beretania St.

Fort St. Mall

Bishop St.

State
Capitol

State
Library

Maunakea St.

Smith St.

Nuuanu St.

S. Hotel St.

Iolani
Palace

N. King St.

S. King St.

Mililani St.

Punchbowl St.

South St. (Alapai-X-King)

Bethel St.

Merchant St.

Alakea St.

Richards St.

Aliiolane
Hale and
King
Kamehameha
Statue

Keawe

Emily St.

92

Nimitz Hwy.

61

Queen St.

Halekauwila St.

PIER
14

PIER
13

PIER
12

Aloha
Tower
Marketplace

Ala Moana Blvd.

Pohukaina St.

Honolulu
Harbor

PIER
11

PIER
10

PIER
8

PIER
7 PIER
6

PIER
5

Restaurant
Row

Auahi St.

PIER
9

Sand
Island

Fort Armstrong Channel

PIER
4

PIER
2

0   1/4 mi
0   1/4 km

N

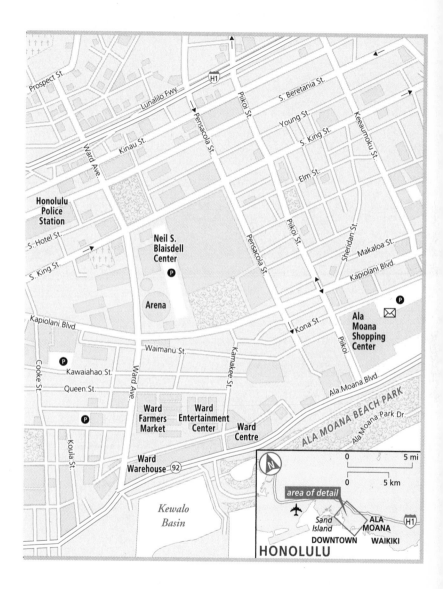

Prospect St.
Lunalilo Fwy.
H1
Pensacola St.
Piikoi St.
S. Beretania St.
Young St.
S. King St.
Keeaumoku St.
Kinau St.
Ward Ave.
Elm St.
Piikoi St.

**Honolulu
Police
Station**
S. Hotel St.
S. King St.
Pensacola St.
Sheridan St.
Makaloa St.
Kapiolani Blvd.

**Neil S.
Blaisdell
Center** P

Arena

Kapiolani Blvd.
Kona St.
Piikoi

**Ala
Moana
Shopping
Center** P ⊠

Waimanu St.
Kamakee St.
Kawaiahao St.
Queen St.
Cooke St.
Ward Ave.
Ala Moana Blvd.

**Ward
Farmers
Market**
**Ward
Entertainment
Center**
**Ward
Centre**

ALA MOANA BEACH PARK
Ala Moana Park Dr.

Koula St.
**Ward
Warehouse** 92

*Kewalo
Basin*

0   5 mi
0   5 km
area of detail
Sand
Island
✈
**ALA
MOANA**
H1
DOWNTOWN   **WAIKIKI**
HONOLULU

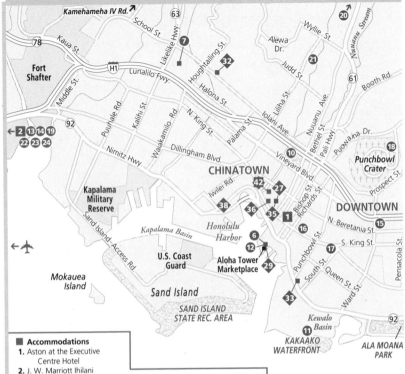

Honolulu Beyond Waikiki

■ **Accommodations**

1. Aston at the Executive Centre Hotel
2. J. W. Marriott Ihilani Resort and Spa
3. Kahala Hotel & Resort
4. Lotus at Diamond Head
5. New Otani Kaimana Beach Hotel

● **Attractions**

6. Aloha Tower
7. Bishop Museum
8. Contemporary Museum
9. Doris Duke's Shangri-La
10. Foster Botanical Garden
11. Hawaii Children's Discovery Center
12. Hawaii Maritime Center
13. Hawaii's Plantation Village
14. Hawaiian Railway
15. Honolulu Academy of Arts
16. Iolani Palace
17. Mission Houses Museum
18. National Memorial Cemetery of the Pacific
19. Pacific Aviation Museum
20. Queen Emma Summer Palace

21. Royal Mausoleum
22. USS *Arizona* Memorial
23. USS Battleship *Missouri* Memorial
24. USS *Bowfin* Submarine Museum and Park
25. Waikiki Aquarium

◆ **Dining**

26. Alan Wong's Restaurant
27. Brasserie du Vin
28. Chef Mavro Restaurant
29. Don Ho's Island Grill
30. Elua Restaurant & Wine Bar
31. Hau Tree Lanai
32. Helena's Hawaiian Foods
33. Hiroshi/Vino Eurasian Tapas
34. Hoku's
35. Indigo Eurasian Restaurant & Bar
36. Little Village Noodle House
37. Michel's at the Colony Surf
38. Sam Choy's Breakfast, Lunch, and Crab

39. Tango Contemporary Café
40. 3660 on the Rise

❀ **Nightlife**

41. Mai Tai Bar Honolulu
42. thirtyninehotel

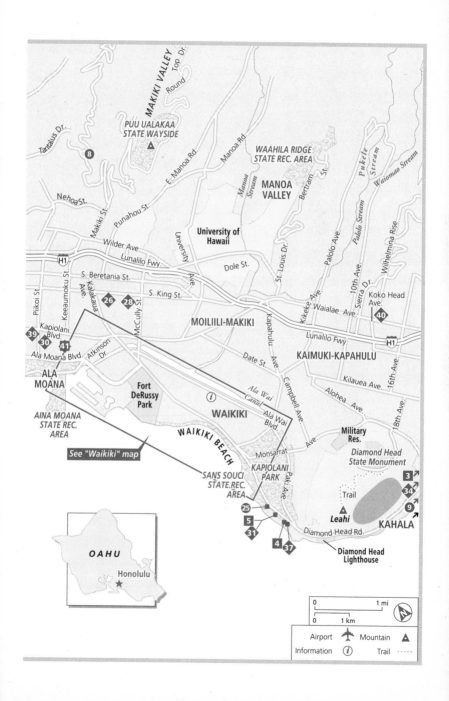

East Oahu

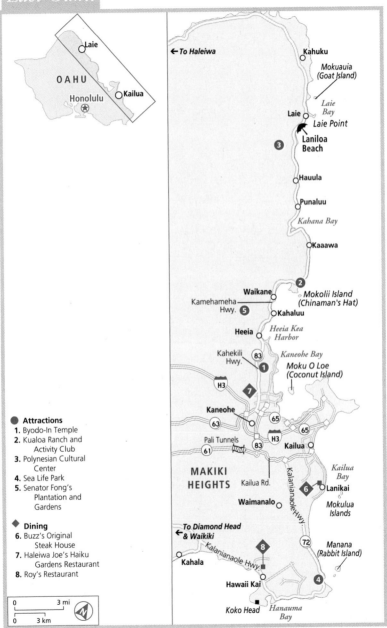

OAHU

Laie

Honolulu

Kailua

←To Haleiwa

Kahuku

Mokuauia
(Goat Island)

*Laie
Bay*

Laie

Laie Point

**Laniloa
Beach**

3

Hauula

Punaluu

Kahana Bay

Kaaawa

2

Waikane

Kamehameha
Hwy. 5

*Mokolii Island
(Chinaman's Hat)*

Kahaluu

Heeia

*Heeia Kea
Harbor*

Kahekili
Hwy.

83

1

Kaneohe Bay

*Moku O Loe
(Coconut Island)*

H3

7

Kaneohe

63

65

H3

65

Pali Tunnels

83

Kailua

61

**MAKIKI
HEIGHTS**

Kailua Rd.

*Kailua
Bay*

6

Lanikai

Waimanalo

*Mokulua
Islands*

*To Diamond Head
←& Waikiki*

Kalanianaole Hwy.

72

*Manana
(Rabbit Island)*

8

Kalanianaole Hwy.

Kahala

4

Hawaii Kai

Koko Head

*Hanauma
Bay*

● **Attractions**
1. Byodo-In Temple
2. Kualoa Ranch and
   Activity Club
3. Polynesian Cultural
   Center
4. Sea Life Park
5. Senator Fong's
   Plantation and
   Gardens

◆ **Dining**
6. Buzz's Original
   Steak House
7. Haleiwa Joe's Haiku
   Gardens Restaurant
8. Roy's Restaurant

0   3 mi
0   3 km

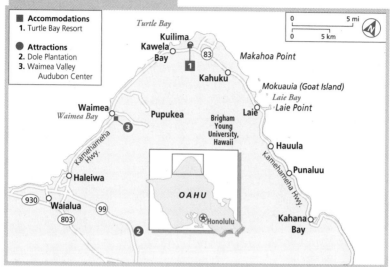

Oahu North Shore

Accommodations
1. Turtle Bay Resort

Attractions
2. Dole Plantation
3. Waimea Valley
   Audubon Center

Turtle Bay

Kuilima

Kawela
Bay

83

Makahoa Point

1

Kahuku

Mokuauia (Goat Island)
Laie Bay
Laie Point

Waimea
Waimea Bay

3

Pupukea

Brigham
Young
University,
Hawaii

Laie

Hauula

Haleiwa

Kamehameha Hwy.

Kamehameha Hwy.

Punaluu

930

Waialua

99

803

OAHU

Honolulu

2

Kahana
Bay

0   5 mi
0   5 km

Maui Orientation

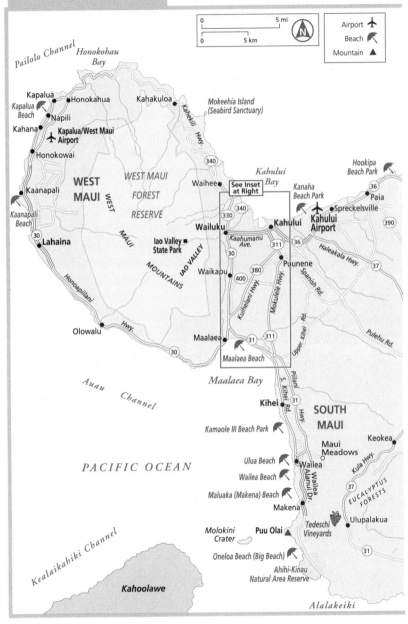

0 ____ 5 mi
0 ____ 5 km
N

Airport ✈
Beach 🏖
Mountain ▲

Pailolo Channel

Honokohau Bay

Kapalua ● Honokahua ● Kahakuloa ●

Kapalua Beach 🏖

Napili ●

Kahana ●

Kapalua/West Maui Airport ✈

Honokowai ●

WEST MAUI

WEST MAUI FOREST RESERVE

Kaanapali ●

Kaanapali Beach 🏖

Lahaina

WEST

MAUI

MOUNTAINS

IAO VALLEY

Iao Valley State Park ■

Olowalu ●

Honoapiilani Hwy.

Mokeehia Island (Seabird Sanctuary)

Kahekili Hwy.

(340)

Waihee ●

Wailuku

See Inset at Right

(340)

(330)

Kahului Bay

Kanaha Beach Park 🏖

Kahului

Kahului Airport ✈

(36)

Hookipa Beach Park 🏖

Paia ●

Spreckelsville ●

(390)

Kaahumanu Ave.

(30)

Waikapu ●

(400)

(380)

Puunene ●

Kuihelani Hwy.

Mokulele Hwy.

Maalaea ●

(30) (31) (311)

Maalaea Beach 🏖

Maalaea Bay

Haleakala Hwy.

(36)

(311)

Spanish Rd.

(37)

Pulehu Rd.

Auau Channel

PACIFIC OCEAN

Kihei

(31)

S. Kihei Rd.

Piilani Hwy.

SOUTH MAUI

Keokea ●

Kamaole III Beach Park 🏖

Maui Meadows ○

Ulua Beach 🏖

Wailea ○

Wailea Beach 🏖

Wailea Alanui Dr.

Kula Hwy.

(37)

Maluaka (Makena) Beach 🏖

Makena ●

EUCALYPTUS FORESTS

Ulupalakua ●

Tedeschi Vineyards 🍇

Molokini Crater

Puu Olai ▲

(31)

Oneloa Beach (Big Beach) 🏖

Ahihi-Kinau Natural Area Reserve

Kealaikahiki Channel

Kahoolawe

Alalakeiki

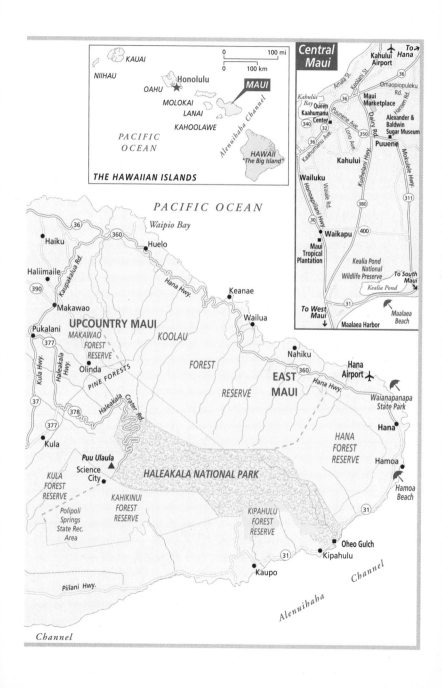

THE HAWAIIAN ISLANDS

KAUAI

NIIHAU

OAHU Honolulu

MOLOKAI
LANAI
KAHOOLAWE

MAUI

PACIFIC
OCEAN

Alenuihaha Channel

HAWAII
The Big Island

Central Maui

To Hana

Kahului Airport

36

Omaopiopuleku Rd.

Amala St

Keolani St

Hansen Rd.

Kahului Bay

Maui Marketplace

Queen Kaahumanu Center

Puunene Ave.

Lono Ave.

Dairy Rd.

Alexander & Baldwin Sugar Museum

340

32

Kaahumanu Ave.

350

Puunene

36

Kahului

Kuihelani Hwy.

Mokulele Hwy.

Wailuku

Waiale Rd.

Hoapililani Hwy.

30

380

Waikapu

400

311

Maui Tropical Plantation

Kealia Pond National Wildlife Preserve

To South Maui

Kealia Pond

To West Maui

31

Maalaea Harbor

Maalaea Beach

PACIFIC OCEAN

Waipio Bay

36

Haiku

360

Huelo

Haliimaile

Kaupakalua Rd.

Hana Hwy.

Keanae

390

Makawao

Wailua

UPCOUNTRY MAUI

MAKAWAO FOREST RESERVE

KOOLAU

Pukalani

377

Kula Hwy.

Haleakala Hwy.

Olinda

PINE FORESTS

FOREST

Nahiku

Hana Airport

360

Hana Hwy.

37

378

Haleakala Crater Rd.

RESERVE

EAST MAUI

Waianapanapa State Park

377

Kula

Puu Ulaula

Science City

KULA FOREST RESERVE

KAHIKINUI FOREST RESERVE

HALEAKALA NATIONAL PARK

Hana

HANA FOREST RESERVE

Hamoa

Hamoa Beach

Polipoli Springs State Rec. Area

KIPAHULU FOREST RESERVE

31

Oheo Gulch

Kipahulu

31

Kaupo

Piilani Hwy.

Channel

Alenuihaha

Channel

South Maui

MAUI

Kihei
Wailea
Makena

■ **Accommodations**
1. Fairmont Kea Lani Hotel Maui
2. Four Seasons Resort Maui
3. Grand Wailea Resort & Spa
4. Wailea Beach Marriott Resort & Spa

● **Attractions**
5. Maui Ocean Center

◆ **Dining**
6. Ko
7. Maalaea Waterfront Restaurant
8. Mala Wailea
9. Roy's Kihei Bar and Grill
10. Sansei Seafood Restaurant & Sushi Bar
11. Spago at Four Seasons Resort Maui at Wailea
12. Stella Blues Cafe

Kealia Pond National Wildlife Refuge

Maalaea Bay

Owapo Rd.

Kaiolohia St.

Kenolio Rd.

Ohukai Rd.

Piilani Hwy.

KIHEI

Kalepolepo Beach Park

Kaonoulu St.

Kihei Rd.

South

E. Lipoa St.

Waipuilani Rd.

PACIFIC OCEAN

Halama St.

E. Welakhao Rd.

Kalama Beach Park

KAMAOLE

Kanani Rd.

Kamaole Beach Park #1

Kamaole Beach Park #2

Kamaole Beach Park #3

Keonekai Rd.

Keawakapu Beach Park

Kilohana Dr.

Mokapu Beach

Maui Meadows

Okolani Dr.

Piilani Hwy.

Ulua Beach
Wailea Beach

WAILEA

Wailea Alanui

Wailea Point

Wailea 'Ike Dr.

Polo Beach

Kaukahi St.

Makena Rd.

Makena Alanui Dr.

Kalai Waa Dr.

Haloa Point

MAKENA

Nahuna Point

Makena Bay

Beach 🏖

0 ___ 1 mi
0 ___ 1 km

N

Kapalua–West Maui

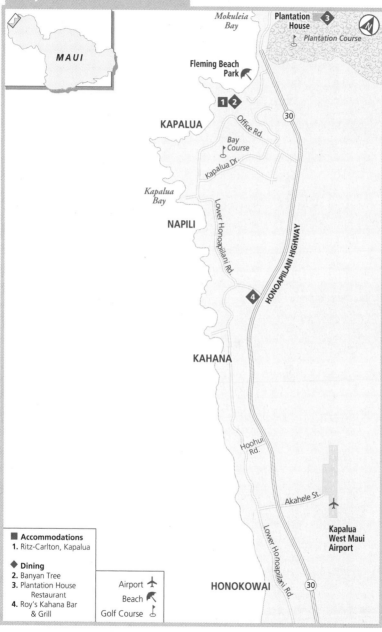

MAUI

Mokuleia Bay

Plantation House **3**

Plantation Course

Fleming Beach Park

1 **2**

KAPALUA

Office Rd.

30

Bay Course

Kapalua Dr.

Kapalua Bay

NAPILI

Lower Honoapiilani Rd.

HONOAPIILANI HIGHWAY

4

KAHANA

Hoohui Rd.

Akahele St.

Kapalua West Maui Airport

Lower Honoapiilani Rd.

HONOKOWAI

30

■ **Accommodations**
1. Ritz-Carlton, Kapalua

◆ **Dining**
2. Banyan Tree
3. Plantation House Restaurant
4. Roy's Kahana Bar & Grill

Airport ✈
Beach 🏖
Golf Course ⛳

Lahaina–Kaanapali Beach Resort

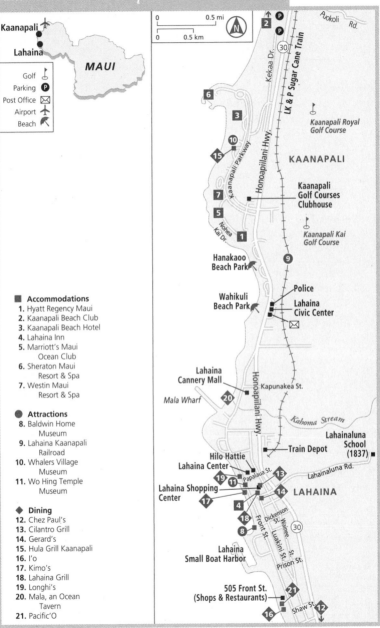

Accommodations
1. Hyatt Regency Maui
2. Kaanapali Beach Club
3. Kaanapali Beach Hotel
4. Lahaina Inn
5. Marriott's Maui
   Ocean Club
6. Sheraton Maui
   Resort & Spa
7. Westin Maui
   Resort & Spa

Attractions
8. Baldwin Home
   Museum
9. Lahaina Kaanapali
   Railroad
10. Whalers Village
    Museum
11. Wo Hing Temple
    Museum

Dining
12. Chez Paul's
13. Cilantro Grill
14. Gerard's
15. Hula Grill Kaanapali
16. I'o
17. Kimo's
18. Lahaina Grill
19. Longhi's
20. Mala, an Ocean
    Tavern
21. Pacific'O

Upcountry and East Maui

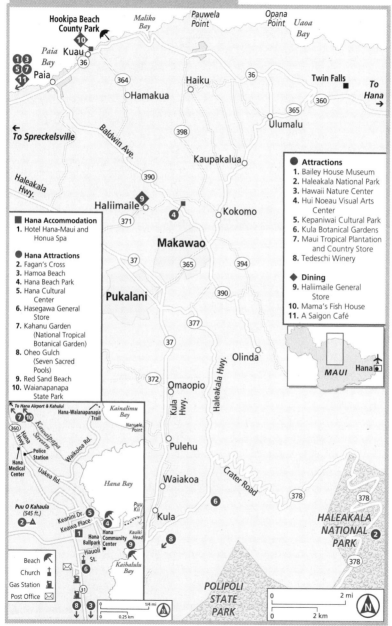

Hookipa Beach County Park 10

Maliko Bay

Pauwela Point

Opana Point *Uaoa Bay*

Paia Bay **Kuau** 36

1 3 5 7 11 **Paia**

Haiku

364

○**Hamakua**

36

Twin Falls ■ To **Hana** →

360

365

← To Spreckelsville

Baldwin Ave.

398

Ulumalu ○

Haleakala Hwy.

390

Kaupakalua ○

Attractions
1. Bailey House Museum
2. Haleakala National Park
3. Hawaii Nature Center
4. Hui Noeau Visual Arts Center
5. Kepaniwai Cultural Park
6. Kula Botanical Gardens
7. Maui Tropical Plantation and Country Store
8. Tedeschi Winery

Dining
9. Haliimaile General Store
10. Mama's Fish House
11. A Saigon Café

Haliimaile 9 ○

371

4 ■

○ **Kokomo**

Hana Accommodation
1. Hotel Hana-Maui and Honua Spa

Hana Attractions
2. Fagan's Cross
3. Hamoa Beach
4. Hana Beach Park
5. Hana Cultural Center
6. Hasegawa General Store
7. Kahanu Garden (National Tropical Botanical Garden)
8. Oheo Gulch (Seven Sacred Pools)
9. Red Sand Beach
10. Waianapanapa State Park

Makawao

37

365

394

Pukalani

390

377

37

Olinda ○

Haleakala Hwy.

372

Omaopio ○

Kula Hwy.

MAUI Hana ✈

↖ To Hana Airport & Kahului

7 10 Hana-Waianapanapa Trail

Kainalimu Bay

360

Kauaipapa Stream

Hana Hwy.

Police Station

Nanuele Point

Hana Medical Center

Waikoloa Rd.

Uakea Rd.

Hana Bay

Pulehu ○

Crater Road

Puu O Kahaula (545 ft.)

2 △

Keanini Dr. 5

Keawa Place

Hana Ballpark

1

Hana Community Center

4 ⛱

Puu Kii

Kula ○

Kauiki Head

Waiakoa ○

6

378

378

9

Hauoli St.

6

31

8 3

Kaihalulu Bay

8

Pulehu ○

Beach ⛱
Church ✝
Gas Station ⛽
Post Office ✉

0   1/4 mi
0   0.25 km

HALEAKALA NATIONAL PARK 2

378

POLIPOLI STATE PARK

0   2 mi
0   2 km

N

Hawaii (the Big Island) Orientation

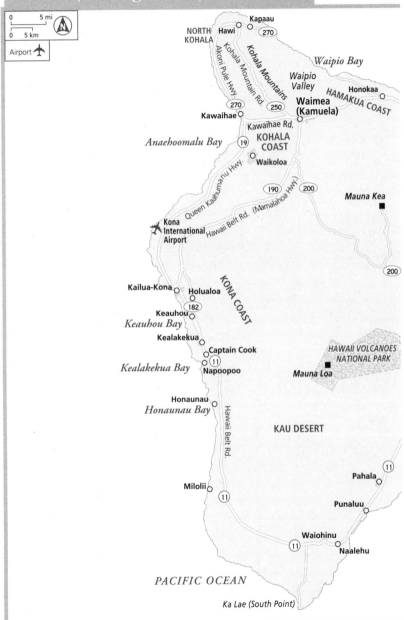

0   5 mi
0   5 km
Airport ✈

Kapaau
270
NORTH   Hawi
KOHALA
Akoni Pule Hwy.
Kohala Mountain Rd
Kohala Mountains
Waipio Bay
Waipio Valley
Waimea (Kamuela)
HAMAKUA COAST
Honokaa
270   250
Kawaihae
Kawaihae Rd.
KOHALA COAST
Anaehoomalu Bay   19
Waikoloa
Queen Kaahumanu Hwy.
190   200
Mauna Kea ■
Hawaii Belt Rd. (Mamalahoa Hwy.)
Kona International Airport ✈
200
Kailua-Kona   Holualoa
KONA COAST
Keauhou   182
Keauhou Bay
Kealakekua
Captain Cook
Kealakekua Bay   11
Napoopoo
HAWAII VOLCANOES NATIONAL PARK
Honaunau
Honaunau Bay
Mauna Loa ■
KAU DESERT
Hawaii Belt Rd.
Pahala   11
Milolii   11
Punaluu
Waiohinu   11
Naalehu
PACIFIC OCEAN
Ka Lae (South Point)

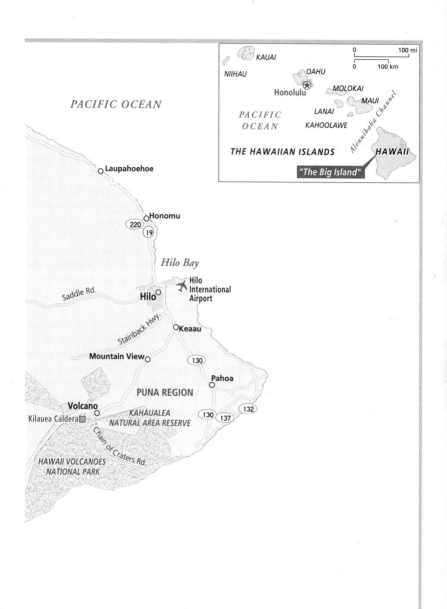

PACIFIC OCEAN

KAUAI

NIIHAU

OAHU

Honolulu

MOLOKAI

MAUI

PACIFIC
OCEAN

LANAI

KAHOOLAWE

Alenuihaha Channel

THE HAWAIIAN ISLANDS

HAWAII

"The Big Island"

0   100 mi
0   100 km

Laupahoehoe

Honomu

220

19

Hilo Bay

Hilo
International
Airport

Saddle Rd.

Hilo

Keaau

Stainback Hwy.

Mountain View

130

Pahoa

PUNA REGION

Volcano

KAHAUALEA
NATURAL AREA RESERVE

130 137

132

Kilauea Caldera

Chain of Craters Rd.

HAWAII VOLCANOES
NATIONAL PARK

Kona Coast

Kona
International
Airport

Keahole—Natural
Energy Laboratory
of Hawaii Authority
(NELHA)

To North Kohala

Kaimi
Nani Dr.

Queen Kaahumanu Hwy.

Kalaoa

To
Waimea

Mamalahoa Hwy.

19

190

Honokohau
Bay

OLD KONA
AIRPORT
STATE PARK

Pawai
Bay

Kailua Bay

KAILUA-KONA

180

See Kailua-Kona
Town Map

Holualoa

WAIAHA
SPRINGS
FOREST
RESERVE

187

Alii Dr.

Kuakini Hwy.

182

White Sands
Beach Park

Kahaluu Beach Park

Kahaluu

KAHALUU
FOREST
RESERVE

Keauhou Bay

Keauhou

Kuamoo Bay

11

Kealakekua

Keawekaheka
Bay

Mamalahoa Hwy.

Captain Cook

Captain Cook
Monument

Kealakekua Bay

Koa Rd.

Napoopoo

HONAUNAU
FOREST
RESERVE

Mokuakae Bay

Puuhonua Rd.

11

Honaunau
Bay

Honaunau

Waimea

Hilo

Kailua-Kona

HAWAII
(The Big Island)

South Point

■ **Accommodations**
1. Four Seasons Resort
   Hualalai
2. Kona Village Resort
3. Outrigger Keauhou
   Beach Resort
4. Sheraton Keauhou
   Bay Resort & Spa

● **Attractions**
5. Amy B. H. Greenwell
   Ethnobotanical
   Garden
6. Astronaut Ellison S.
   Onizuka Space
   Center
7. Kaloko-Honokohau
   National Historical
   Park
8. Ocean Rider Seahorse
   Farm
9. Puuhonua O Honaunau
   National Historical Park
10. Sadie Seymour Botanical
    Gardens

◆ **Dining**
11. Hualalai Grille by
    Alan Wong
12. Pahuia at Four Seasons

Airport ✈
Beach

Kailua-Kona Town

Accommodations
1. King Kamehameha's Kona Beach Hotel

Attractions
2. Ahuena Heiau
3. Hulihee Palace

Dining
4. Huggo's
5. O's Bistro

Parking P
Post Office ✉

To Kona Int'l Airport

Makala Blvd.
Kamakaeha Ave.
Kaiwi St.
Luhia St.
Alapa St.
To Old Airport Park
OLD INDUSTRIAL AREA
Kuakini Hwy.
Palani Rd.
Queen Kaahumanu Hwy.
19
190
11
5
To Waimea
Kuakini Hwy.
Henry St.
Alii Dr.
Hanama Place
Kalani St.
Kailua Pier
Sarona Rd.
Kailua Bay
To Holualoa
Hualalai Rd.
Kuakini Hwy.
Alii Sunset Plaza
Wailua Rd.
Kahakai Rd.
To Keauhou
To South Kona & South Point

Kailua-Kona
HAWAII (The Big Island)

North Kohala and Waimea

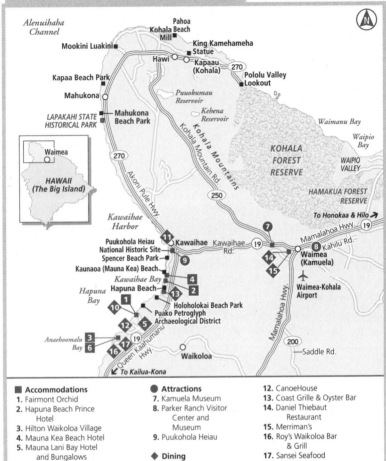

■ **Accommodations**
1. Fairmont Orchid
2. Hapuna Beach Prince Hotel
3. Hilton Waikoloa Village
4. Mauna Kea Beach Hotel
5. Mauna Lani Bay Hotel and Bungalows
6. Waikoloa Beach Marriott Resort & Spa

● **Attractions**
7. Kamuela Museum
8. Parker Ranch Visitor Center and Museum
9. Puukohola Heiau

◆ **Dining**
10. Brown's Beach House
11. Café Pesto
12. CanoeHouse
13. Coast Grille & Oyster Bar
14. Daniel Thiebaut Restaurant
15. Merriman's
16. Roy's Waikoloa Bar & Grill
17. Sansei Seafood Restaurant and Sushi Bar

Volcano Area

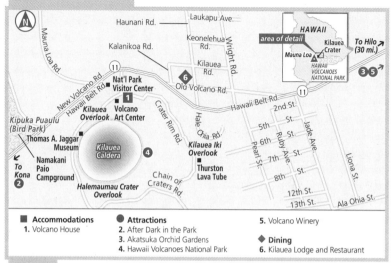

■ Accommodations
1. Volcano House

● Attractions
2. After Dark in the Park
3. Akatsuka Orchid Gardens
4. Hawaii Volcanoes National Park

5. Volcano Winery

◆ Dining
6. Kilauea Lodge and Restaurant

Hilo

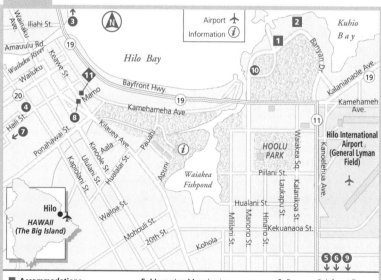

■ Accommodations
1. Hilo Hawaiian Hotel
2. Naniloa Volcanoes Resort

● Attractions
3. Hawaii Tropical Botanical Garden
4. Lyman Museum & Mission House

5. Mauna Loa Macadamia
   Nut Visitor Center
6. Nani Mau Gardens
7. Onizuka Center for International
   Astronomy and Mauna Kea
   Observatory
8. Pacific Tsunami Museum

9. Panaewa Rainforest Zoo
10. Suisan Fish Market and
    Auction

◆ Dining
11. Royal Siam Thai
    Restaurant

Kauai Orientation

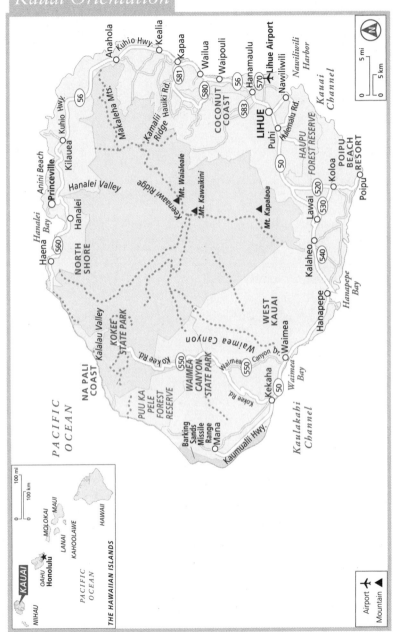

Airport ✈
Mountain ▲

Poipu

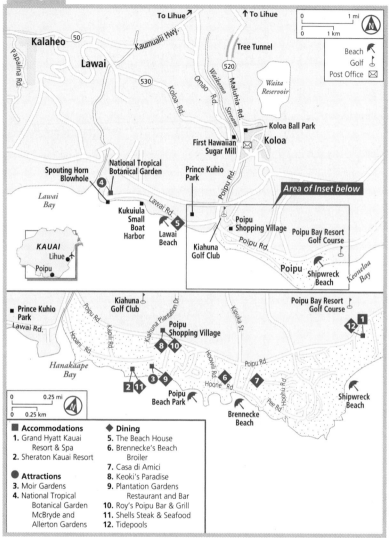

To Lihue↗   ↑ To Lihue

Kalaheo 50

Kaumualii Hwy.

Tree Tunnel

520

Papalina Rd.

Lawai

530

Koloa Rd.

Omao Rd.

Waikomo Stream

Maluhia Rd.

Waita Reservoir

Koloa Ball Park

First Hawaiian
Sugar Mill

Koloa

Spouting Horn
Blowhole

National Tropical
Botanical Garden

Prince Kuhio
Park

Poipu Rd.

*Lawai
Bay*

4

Area of Inset below

Kukuiula
Small
Boat
Harbor

Lawai Rd.

5

Lawai
Beach

Kiahuna
Golf Club

Poipu
Shopping Village

Poipu Rd.

Poipu Bay Resort
Golf Course

KAUAI

Lihue

Poipu

Poipu

Shipwreck
Beach

*Keoneloa
Bay*

0   1 mi
0   1 km

Beach
Golf
Post Office ⊠

Kiahuna
Golf Club

Poipu Bay Resort
Golf Course

Prince Kuhio
Park

Poipu Rd.

Hoaini Rd.

Kapili Rd.

Kiahuna Plantation Dr.

Poipu
Shopping Village

Kapika St.

1

12

Lawai Rd.

8 10

Hoowili Rd.

Poipu Rd.

*Hanakaape
Bay*

2 11

3 9

6

Hoone Rd.

7

Hoohu Rd.

Pee Rd.

Shipwreck
Beach

Poipu
Beach Park

Brennecke
Beach

0   0.25 mi
0   0.25 km

■ **Accommodations**
1. Grand Hyatt Kauai
   Resort & Spa
2. Sheraton Kauai Resort

● **Attractions**
3. Moir Gardens
4. National Tropical
   Botanical Garden
   McBryde and
   Allerton Gardens

◆ **Dining**
5. The Beach House
6. Brennecke's Beach
   Broiler
7. Casa di Amici
8. Keoki's Paradise
9. Plantation Gardens
   Restaurant and Bar
10. Roy's Poipu Bar & Grill
11. Shells Steak & Seafood
12. Tidepools

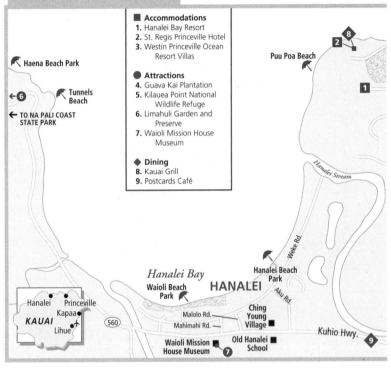

North Shore Kauai

■ Accommodations
1. Hanalei Bay Resort
2. St. Regis Princeville Hotel
3. Westin Princeville Ocean Resort Villas

● Attractions
4. Guava Kai Plantation
5. Kilauea Point National Wildlife Refuge
6. Limahuli Garden and Preserve
7. Waioli Mission House Museum

◆ Dining
8. Kauai Grill
9. Postcards Café

Haena Beach Park

Tunnels Beach

TO NA PALI COAST STATE PARK

Puu Poa Beach

Hanalei Stream

Hanalei Bay

HANALEI

Hanalei Beach Park

Waioli Beach Park

Weke Rd.

Aku Rd.

Hanalei   Princeville
Kapaa
KAUAI
Lihue

560

Malolo Rd.
Mahimahi Rd.

Ching Young Village

Kuhio Hwy.

Waioli Mission House Museum 7

Old Hanalei School

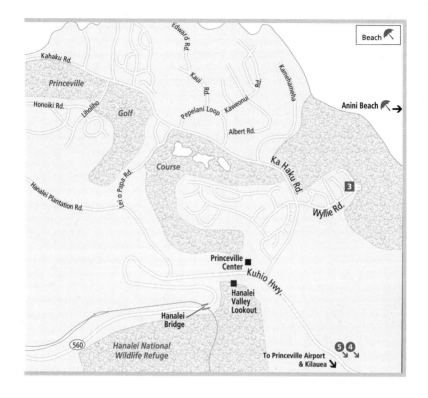

Lihue

To Kapaa & North Shore

56 Wilcox Memorial Hospital

Kuhio Hwy.
Akahi St.
Elua St.
Umi St.
570
Ahukini Rd.
Kapule Hwy.
1
51

Hardy St.

LIHUE

Puaole St.

Lihue Airport

Kaumualii Hwy.
Road
Haleko
4
Visitor Center
7
Rice St.
Hoolako St.
Halau St.
Haoa St.
Peleke St.
Vidinha Memorial Stadium

Old Nawiliwili Rd.
Kukui Grove Center
Pikake St.
Kaneka Rd.

5

To Poipu & Waimea

Police Station
Hoolako Rd.

Nawiliwili Rd.

Apapane St.
58
3
Kapena St.
51

KAUAI
Lihue

Nawiliwili
Lala Rd.
Nuhou Rd.
Rd.
Halelhaka
Wilcox Rd.
Kalapaki Rd.

Lagoons Golf Course
2
Kalapaki Beach
6
Kiele
Hulemalu Rd.
Waapa Rd.
Niumala
Nawiliwili Beach Park
Championship Golf Course
Nawiliwili Bay

HULEIA NATIONAL WILDLIFE REFUGE
Menehune Fishpond
Niumalu Beach Park
Nawiliwili Harbor
Huleia Stream

Accommodations
1. Hilton Kauai Beach Resort
2. Kauai Marriott Resort & Beach Club

● **Attractions**
3. Grove Farm Homestead
4. Kauai Museum
5. Kilohana Plantation

◆ **Dining**
6. Duke's Kauai
7. Hamura's Saimin Stand

Airport ✈
Information ⓘ
Post Office ✉

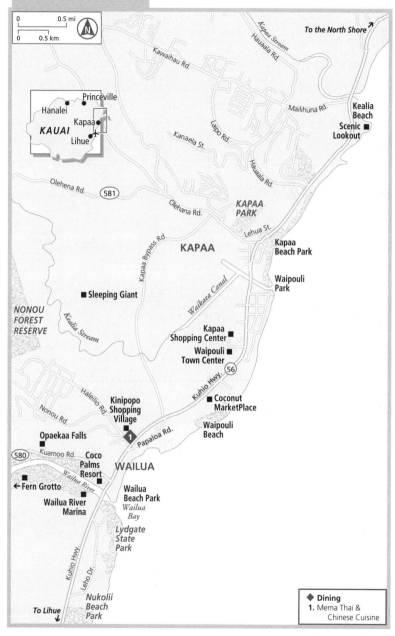

Coconut Coast

0 0.5 mi
0 0.5 km
N

To the North Shore ↗

Kawaihau Rd.

Kapaa Stream

Hauaala Rd.

KAUAI
Princeville
Hanalei
Kapaa
Lihue

Mailihuna Rd.
Kealia Beach
Scenic Lookout

Kanaela St.
Laipo Rd.
Hauaala Rd.

Olehena Rd.
581
Olehana Rd.

KAPAA PARK

Lehua St.

KAPAA
Kapaa Beach Park

Waipouli Park

Kapaa Bypass Rd.

Waikaea Canal

■ Sleeping Giant

NONOU
FOREST
RESERVE

Kealia Stream

Kapaa Shopping Center

Waipouli Town Center
56

Haleilio Rd.

Nonou Rd.

Kinipopo Shopping Village

Kuhio Hwy.

Coconut MarketPlace

Waipouli Beach

Opaekaa Falls

580
Kuamoo Rd.

Coco Palms Resort

1

Papaloa Rd.

WAILUA

Wailua River

← Fern Grotto

Wailua River Marina

Wailua Beach Park
Wailua Bay

Lydgate State Park

Kuhio Hwy.

Leho Dr.

Nukolii Beach Park

To Lihue ↓

◆ Dining
1. Mema Thai &
   Chinese Cuisine

Lanai

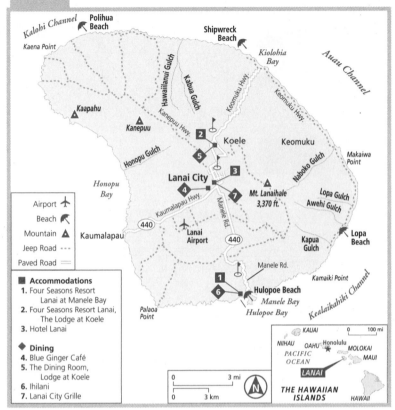

Kalohi Channel

Polihua Beach

Kaena Point

Shipwreck Beach

Kiolohia Bay

Auau Channel

Hawaiilanui Gulch

Kabua Gulch

Keomuku Hwy.

Keomuku Hwy.

Kaapahu

Kanepuu

Kanepuu Hwy.

2

Koele

Keomuku

Naboko Gulch

Makaiwa Point

Honopu Gulch

5

Honopu Bay

Lanai City

4

3

7

Mt. Lanaihale 3,370 ft.

Lopa Gulch

Awehi Gulch

Kaumalapau Hwy.

Manele Rd.

440

Lanai Airport

440

Kapua Gulch

Lopa Beach

Kaumalapau

Manele Rd.

Kamaiki Point

Kealaikahiki Channel

1

6

Hulopoe Beach

Manele Bay

Palaoa Point

Hulopoe Bay

Legend

Airport ✈

Beach 🏖

Mountain ▲

Jeep Road - - -

Paved Road ═

■ Accommodations
1. Four Seasons Resort Lanai at Manele Bay
2. Four Seasons Resort Lanai, The Lodge at Koele
3. Hotel Lanai

◆ Dining
4. Blue Ginger Café
5. The Dining Room, Lodge at Koele
6. Ihilani
7. Lanai City Grille

0 ___ 3 mi

0 ___ 3 km

N

KAUAI

NIIHAU

OAHU Honolulu

PACIFIC OCEAN

MOLOKAI

MAUI

LANAI

THE HAWAIIAN ISLANDS

HAWAII

0 ___ 100 mi

PART ONE

GETTING ACQUAINTED *with* HAWAII

ABOUT *the* ALOHA STATE

THE HAWAIIAN ISLANDS, in the middle of the sea and far removed from any continent, are an irresistible lure to anyone who's ever heard the word *aloha*. People from all over the world pay handsomely for the privilege of flying at least five hours to this jacks toss of islands in the tropical North Pacific. Hawaii is the most isolated population center in the world, 2,390 miles from California, 3,850 miles from Japan, 4,900 miles from China, and 5,280 miles from the Philippines. Only 7 of the 132 blips in the Hawaiian Islands archipelago are even inhabited, and one of those, Niihau, is a private ranch.

Despite the remoteness of the destination, more than 7.4 million people find their way annually to Hawaii to roam the sandy shores and volcanic peaks, enjoy the nearly perfect weather and easygoing lifestyle, gaze at the spectacular natural beauty, and dream of ways to drop out of sight and stay here forever.

Plenty of people have done just that. Since the Islands were discovered in about AD 650 by Polynesian seafarers, probably from the Marquesas, a wide range of folks have washed ashore—British and European explorers; field workers from Asia, Europe, and the Caribbean; German planters; Scottish merchants; American missionaries and whalers; South Pacific and other Polynesian Islanders; Southeast Asian refugees; and rogues of all nations who jumped ship and were unwilling, or unable, to leave. Some early-20th-century wayfarers ran out of fuel, crash-landed their planes in the sea, and swam ashore. It's a colorful history that led to the racial rainbow of people and cultures of which modern Hawaii is composed. These islands, America's only former royal kingdom complete with a fairy-tale palace, have been a state since 1959. In Hawaii's remarkable population, people of mixed blood outnumber other groups, no one is a majority, and the rarest soul of all is a pure Hawaiian.

In the beginning the Islands were empty slates, volcanic slopes in a beneficent climate rich with potential to sustain the good life. Creatures and plants blew in or were carried by the settlers, along with their heritage, customs, and languages. Imports mingled and thrived in the fecund tropical atmosphere, often at the expense of earlier arrivals. The riotous birds that wake the day and the fragrant flowers, lush plants, and towering trees that dress the landscape hail from India, the Americas, Asia, and still more distant regions. Subtle native plants and shy native birds were crowded into small corners or vanished altogether. As a result, Hawaii has the dubious reputation of being the endangered species capital of the world, with more than 75% of native birds extinct or threatened, and more than 250 species on the endangered list.

Without the enemies of their homelands, exotic species have a good life in the Islands. You don't often see the only native mammals, the hoary bat and the endangered monk seal, but men introduced hoofed cattle, pigs, donkeys, deer, and sheep that went wild and flourished, to the detriment of the fragile landscape. Houseplants got loose to climb tree trunks, where they sprouted leaves as big as your face. The ficus trees pampered in pots in many a mainland living room are two-story giants with massive canopies in Hawaii. The bright lantana blooming in the wild is said to have sprung from a single garden plant tossed into a garbage heap. Anything grows, larger than life, including the cityscape of Honolulu and the elaborate, world-famous beach resorts where each building component, investment dollar, computer, bedsheet, fork, vehicle, and tourist was shipped thousands of miles from another shore. Hawaii is not only a special place; for better or worse, it's a marvel.

You can look forward to an unforgettable experience in Hawaii, which is likely to call you back again. Hawaii enjoys one of the highest repeat-visitor rates of any destination.

Open your window shade on the plane when the final descent begins, after miles of open sea, and look for Mauna Kea and Mauna Loa looming through the clouds. Maui's Haleakala appears next, then the low red-dirt plains of Lanai across from moody Molokai. As the plane approaches Honolulu, the water seems to get bluer. Then Oahu appears, with the world's most remote and unlikely city sprawling along its southern shore. Excitement builds as you touch down and glide into Honolulu International Airport. You emerge into the open air, which smells of flowers, and feel the warm breeze on your skin. Welcome to Hawaii.

CHOOSING YOUR ISLAND

WHICH ISLAND SHOULD YOU SEE FIRST? It depends on what you want to do and who you're bringing along on this trip. Here's a thumbnail visitor's guide: The Big Island has active volcanoes, accessible cultural history, landscape diversity, and luxury golf resorts in the lava. Maui has wintering humpback whales, its own complement of big-time golf courses, and plenty of visitors to its sunny beach resorts, ranging from affordable condos to plush hotels. Molokai is the quietest and least oriented to tourism. Lanai is a virtually private former pineapple plantation with two classy hotels and golf courses. Oahu is the vibrant heart of the Islands, with the cosmopolitan city of Honolulu and the primary tourist destination Waikiki on one side, and unspoiled country all around the outskirts. Kauai is the lush green movie set where nature pulls out all the beauty stops.

Want to simply kick back at a beach resort and get spritzed with Evian by the pool or have a butler fix your mai tais? Hawaii offers at least two dozen upscale luxury choices, most of them clustered on South and West Maui and the Big Island's Kona-Kohala Coast, where you can be pampered in butlered bungalows for thousands of dollars per night.

Want to hike spectacular sea cliffs or green rain forests? You can't miss on Kauai, with pure wilderness on its Na Pali ("the Cliffs") Coast, or on the Big Island with its *kipuka,* oases of green forest amid black lava, and Hamakua Coast waterfall valleys. Equally spectacular are Maui's upcountry cloud forests, Oahu's sheer Koolau ridges, and Molokai's haunting fern-forested northeast coast.

Traveling with your family? Your kids, especially the teenagers, will love Waikiki. Maui's Kaanapali Beach Resort is a top family destination, but kids love Poipu Beach on Kauai too. And what could be more educational than watching a Big Island volcano in action? You'll find kids are welcome, even cherished, all over the Islands.

Golf doesn't get much better than the spectacular courses of Maui, Lanai, Kauai, and the Big Island. Oahu adds its share, including the busiest and most difficult courses in the nation.

You'd need more than a week to do justice to Oahu, but the trick is to hit the road. Rent a car or ride the bus, but do get out of town and see the beauty of the Koolau Mountains, the Windward Coast, the North Shore, the central plains and pineapple fields, and other destinations. Wear your swimsuit if you want to stop every now and then to go for a swim at a roadside beach. Spend a morning snorkeling at crowded Hanauma Bay, break for plate-lunch surfer chow, then go find your own choice of an empty near-shore reef to snorkel in the afternoon. Save another day for learning how to surf at Waikiki; a day for hiking or riding in the Windward hills or watching big waves on the North Shore; a day at the USS *Arizona* and USS *Missouri,* the Bishop Museum and Honolulu Academy of Arts; a day browsing the designer boutiques; a day exploring Honolulu's natural history; a day kayaking or windsurfing at Kailua Beach; and a day to rest after

unofficial **TIP**
Many of Hawaii's attractions and adventures will fill at least a day.

attending a Hawaiian music concert at Waikiki Shell and then boogie-ing all night. Pretty soon it adds up to a really good time.

If you're island-hopping, it's important to realize that many of Hawaii's attractions and adventures—including a visit to the Poly-nesian Cultural Center on Oahu, a Zodiac boat ride along Kauai's Na Pali Coast, coasting on a special bike from Maui's lofty summit of Haleakala down to the sea, a snorkel cruise to Lanai, and a mule ride down Molokai's sea cliffs—take up most of a day or more. You need more than a day to fully explore the natural wonders of Hawaii Volcanoes National Park, home of fire goddess Pele and her ever-erupting Kilauea Volcano.

To get the most out of your Hawaii visit, mix and match experi-ences: Combine the sparkle of Honolulu on Oahu with the meditative beauty of Hanalei, Kauai, or Hana, Maui. Supplement your big-game fishing adventure on the Big Island with a rugged trail ride down into Maui's Haleakala Crater. Soak up the sun in Wailea's luxury resorts on Maui, then sail across the channel to Lanai to cool off under the upcountry pines.

THE WEATHER REPORT

BLUE SKIES, TRADE WINDS, and sunshine with almost 12 hours of daylight every day of the year: There's no better climate than Hawaii's. The reason is geographic. The Hawaiian Islands are located in the North Pacific, 1,700 miles north of the equator, inside the Tropic of Cancer (stretching from 154 degrees 40 minutes to 179 degrees 25 minutes west latitude, and 18 degrees 54 minutes to 28 degrees 15 minutes north latitude, to be precise).

While the Islands share latitudes with Havana, Hong Kong, Calcutta, and the Sahara Desert, they enjoy a key advantage over those hot spots. Hawaii has natural air-conditioning. The Islands are 2,781 miles south of Anchorage, Alaska, across open sea. The cold northeast winds, which historically propelled merchants' ships to Honolulu from the West Coast to earn the name "trade winds," still sweep down the Pacific, softening as the water warms. The tamed breezes arrive in Hawaii as cooling trade winds, welcome whether gentle or blustery. Now and then, they die off in what is called *kona* (meaning leeward) weather, which is hot and still and fretful.

The coldest spot in Hawaii is atop Mauna Kea, where the Feb-ruary average is 31.1°F; however, a minimum temperature of 11°F was once recorded. The warmest spot is nearly 14,000 feet below at Puako, near Mauna Lani Resort on the Kohala Coast of the Big Island, with an August average of 80.7°F. Pahala, at the island's southern tip, once reached 100°F.

Hawaii's year-round average temperature of 77°F is judged the best in the United States. The difference between winter and summer, and between night and day, is about 5 to 10 degrees on the shorelines, where most people live. Daytime highs are usually somewhere in the 80s, although they can be lower in winter, when storms hide the sun, or rise to the low 90s in steamy August and September. Nights are in the 70s in summer and 60s in winter, with rare dips into the 50s. Winter nights at the coldest record in decades got down to 55°F in Honolulu, where summer

unofficial **TIP**
The temperature drops 3.5° for every 1,000 feet above sea level. If the heat gets you down, go up and cool off.

highs are unlikely to be higher than 94°F. The rest of the thermometer seems superfluous.

But it's not that easy. The Aloha State encompasses 21 of the 22 world climatic zones and features no fewer than 88 ecosystems, ranging from snowy mountaintops, rain forests, wetlands, and deserts to sea cliffs, beaches, and volcanoes.

Temperature zones vary with altitude, rather than with latitude. Around the coastlines, all of the islands are warm (highs in the 80s) and mostly sunny. As you gain altitude in the Upcountry, with 2,000- to 3,000-foot elevations, the weather cools off on all islands and is often wetter too. On the mountaintops, 10,000 feet and higher, the chill can be downright alpine, and the moisture turns to snow from time to time. You may need a jacket or sweater and a blanket at Kula, Maui; Waimea on the Big Island; Nuuanu on Oahu; Kokee State Park on Kauai; and Lanai City, Lanai.

All islands share another climatic trait: The weather is drier and hotter on the leeward sides and cooler, wetter, and windier on the windward sides. The line between is a northeast-southwest diagonal echoing the trade wind flow. Resorts tend to be located on the leeward coasts for the reliable sunshine: Waikiki and Ko Olina on Oahu; Makena, Wailea, Kihei, Lahaina, and Kaanapali on Maui; Kailua-Kona and the Kona-Kohala Coast on the Big Island; and the South Shore of Kauai around Poipu Beach.

Vacationers may not always agree, but rain is a good thing on islands too remote to import water. Hawaiians wrote chants about rain. And they created onomatopoeic words for water—*wai huihui* (cool water), *wai kapipi* (sprinkling water), *wai konikoni* (tingling water), *wai noenoe* (misty water), and *wai kai* (brackish water). And more familiar, Waikiki (spouting water) was named not for the ocean but for the fresh springs that gushed there. Oahu's municipal water is some of the best in the world, even better than the bottled designer kind because it is filtered through lava for a half-century before reaching the water table.

The average humidity level in the state ranges from 56 to 72%, but annual precipitation varies widely. Waikiki gets 25 inches of rain a year, but Manoa Valley, five miles inland, receives 158 inches.

Two of the wettest spots on Earth are found in Hawaii:

- Mount Waialeale on Kauai gets more than 400 inches of rainfall a year. Waialeale means "rippling or overflowing water," an apt title for the Kauai peak that one year received 950 inches of rain, nearly 80 feet.

unofficial **TIP**
If it rains, don't expect to get really wet—the shower will probably be gone in a minute or two.

• Puu Kukui, the 5,871-foot-high summit of the West Maui Mountains, gets 350 inches a year. In 1982, it had a record rainfall of 654.83 inches, or 54.5 feet.

Hilo, on the Big Island, meanwhile, has the soggy distinction of being the wettest city in the United States, averaging 128 inches of rain per year. A word about rain showers: Don't worry about getting wet. It feels good. No one wears a raincoat. Umbrellas are more often used to keep off the sun than the rain, and showers often come on winds that turn umbrellas inside out. If it rains while you're on the beach, get in the water or under a tree. If it rains during your alfresco brunch, put up the table umbrella and don't sit under the drip. The shower will probably be gone in a minute or two. With the ubiquitous Hawaiian "pineapple juice" showers that drift over while the sun shines brightly, everyone just gets wet one moment and dries off the next. Showers are considered blessings.

unofficial **TIP**
Locals don't use the familiar directions of north, east, south, and west. Instead, they use *ma uka* (inland, toward the mountains) and *ma kai* (toward the sea).

Weather can get extreme on these mid-Pacific pinpricks of land, but it's uncommon (see Perils of "Paradise" below).

A WORD ABOUT DIRECTIONS

THE FAMILIAR DIRECTIONS OF NORTH, east, south, and west won't be terribly helpful in Hawaii. Local usage has little to do with the compass. The words you want to know are *ma uka* (uphill, inland, toward the mountains) and *ma kai* (toward the sea). The other directions are known by a bewildering variety of local landmarks. In Honolulu, these are generally *Ewa* (west, or where the Ewa plantation used to be) and *Diamond Head* (that one's easy).

PERILS OF "PARADISE"

NO PLACE IS PERFECT, even this one, which is heavenly enough that many call it paradise. While nobody in Hawaii likes to "talk stink" (say anything bad), each island has certain drawbacks that you should be aware of.

Oahu suffers hellish chronic traffic congestion—too many cars and not enough roads—which is worst at rush hour and lunchtime. Traffic is much lighter in summer when school is out. If you drive, be patient and polite. Let cars merge in front of you. Remember that it's bad manners to honk in Hawaii unless you are signaling a friend, and rude gestures can get you in trouble. Don't worry unduly about mileage on your rental car. On Oahu, you run out of island in less than 50 miles between Honolulu and the end of the road at Mokuleia. Parking is inexpensive in downtown Honolulu compared to that in other big cities, but it can mount up unless you get validations from restaurants and offices you visit, or park in municipal lots. Hotels in Waikiki and Kaanapali Beach Resort on Maui charge for guest parking. Metered parking on the streets is inexpensive, so long as you pay attention to the hours and tow-away zones.

unofficial **TIP**
It's bad manners to honk at strangers in Hawaii, and rude gestures can get you in trouble.

Maui gets really windy most afternoons, when the breezes kick up whitecaps in the ocean, sling stinging sand in your face at the beach in Kihei, and make for bumpy landings at Kahului Airport. It's a natural phenomenon. Near-constant trade winds accelerate when they pass through Maui's funnellike isthmus.

Maui and Kauai both have traffic jams when big jets unload passengers around quitting time for local businesses. On Maui, the jam is worst between Lahaina and Kaanapali. On Kauai, it's worst between Lihue and Kapaa. You'll also encounter crowds at rental-car stands when DC-10s and 747s arrive. The best policy is to slow down and cool off. Allow more time. Strike up a conversation. Island pace just isn't as *wikiwiki* (speedy) as the stressful life you're vacationing from back home, so you might as well get used to it. It's called "Hawaiian time."

Kauai is nicknamed the Garden Island because it is so green, lush, and tropical. It thrives because it gets watered a lot, especially on the North Shore where short torrential downpours are common. The little one-way bridge over Hanalei River gets flooded at least once a year, briefly cutting off the North Shore from the rest of the world (there's no more celebrated excuse for being late for work). Residents put up with it because the old bridge guards their beautiful home ground from major bus and truck traffic and full-scale development. Lots of Hawaiian songs celebrate Kauai's beauty, but it takes rain, and sometimes lots of it, to make those triple rainbows and waterfalls. That's even more true of Hilo and the Hamakua Coast on the Big Island, where the verdant waterfall valleys and profusion of orchids, anthuriums, fruit, nuts, and other crops are a live giveaway to the moist climate.

The Big Island of Hawaii can thank its two active volcanoes, primarily Kilauea, for the hazy condition it often suffers, known as *vog.* That's short for "volcanic fog," which cloaks Kailua-Kona on many afternoons with a gray overcast that looks like doomsday. Sometimes a shift in the winds will carry the vog north to other islands. Something more acute, called *laze,* occurs close to active lava flows when volcano-produced sulfuric acid mixes with cool seawater and becomes hydrochloric acid, sometimes in a burst of steam. This is harmful to your health.

unofficial **TIP**
Vog, or volcanic fog, can pose a discomfort to asthma victims and make you drowsy or headachy.

Molokai's only hotel is the Hotel Molokai near Kaunakakai (luxury resort facilities on the West End have closed), but bungalows and condos still operate near Kaluakoi and along the East End's fishpond shore. The island receives milk and staples by once-a-week barge from Honolulu. If you shop the markets for food, you have to plan dinner around what there is to buy.

Clouds that delay takeoffs and landings often shroud the island of Lanai. You may spend more time on Lanai than you planned. Since the island is remote and there are only two resorts, everything is more costly, a fact of little concern to most of its high-budget visitors. An exception to the pricey picture is the small historic lodge, Hotel Lanai.

Besides the drawbacks we've mentioned, real perils are few, but be forewarned: Insects love tropical Hawaii—huge centipedes (and they bite, painfully); delicate, small scorpions (with a bite like a bee sting); several species of scary-looking cockroaches that don't bite; huge, fast, hairy but harmless cane spiders; several sizes of ants; your average fly and superfly; and mosquitoes that seem to prefer tender flesh from the mainland. You might see a bold fruit rat traveling on a power line.

But sunburn is a much bigger danger than bugs. Don't underestimate the power of tropical sun. It's strongest from 9 a.m. to 3 p.m. Do what you want when you want, but slather everyone with high-SPF, waterproof sunscreen, and use sunglasses and hats as well. If you get scorched, slather on even more aloe vera gel.

Shark attacks are rare in Hawaii, but sharks are not. Those clear blue waters harbor a variety of the creatures, which according to Hawaiian legend are more revered, as *aumakua* or family guardian spirits, than feared.

The Islands are subject to earthquakes, mostly small Big Island rumbles from Kilauea Volcano. Rogue waves can sweep you out to sea, and riptides can carry you off toward Tahiti. You can slip off a cliff trail or fall into the volcano. All of these awful things have happened to people on a holiday in normally benign Hawaii.

unofficial **TIP**
Sudden, heavy rains pose flash-flood danger. Go immediately to higher ground. If driving, park and wait an hour or two until the water flows out to sea.

Hawaii's most threatening perils are the occasional tsunami, high surf, and the temporary flash flooding that occurs when tropical cloudbursts, usually brief and intense, run off steep slopes. Sudden, heavy rains pose flash-flood danger, particularly in a downhill waterfall valley or on a road that briefly becomes a raging waterfall course. If you get caught by a squall while hiking by a stream, go immediately to higher ground.

The **ISLANDS** by **GEOGRAPHIC AREA**

OAHU: THE GATHERING PLACE

OAHU HAS A LOT TO BRAG ABOUT: two mountain ranges, natural beauty, world-class shopping, lots of sandy beaches, accommodations

OAHU FACTS

Flower Ilima	Color Yellow
State Capital, County Seat Honolulu	Area 608 square miles
Length 44 miles	Width 30 miles
Population 909,863	Coastline 112 miles
Highest Point Kaala Peak (4,025 feet)	

ranging from surf shacks to five-star hotels, sleepy country villages, international sophistication, a modern city and urban resort with clean air and water, open space, high-rise towers, a multicultural population, nightlife, a major university, and considerable wealth, drawn by the quality of life.

Small wonder everyone sooner or later ends up on Oahu, America's gateway to the Pacific and most-visited island in the chain. Ironically, an island famous for so much gets a bad rap from critics who complain of too many buildings and people. Perhaps they never left Honolulu. The truth is that the entire cityscape (including downtown), the urban resort of Waikiki, and the lion's share of suburban housing are squeezed into a narrow 26-mile-long corridor between the Koolau Mountains and the Pacific. Leave that corridor, and you have another Oahu. Within minutes of downtown, you could be hiking in a verdant waterfall valley. You need only cross over the mountains to the cool, scenic Windward Coast or head up the central valley between the Koolau and Waianae mountain ranges to the North Shore to discover Oahu's more natural side.

Waikiki

Historic leader among world beach resorts, Waikiki had been largely skidding on its laurels for many years, while swanky luxury resorts blossomed elsewhere in Hawaii and claimed increasing shares of the tourist dollar. Then Outrigger Hotels & Resorts Hawaii, the local chain which had opened Waikiki to the masses in the first place in the 1970s by building warrens of undistinguished, off-beach budget hotels, led an extreme makeover by private and public interests with the Waikiki Beach Walk project. Billions of dollars later, Waikiki looks to re-establish its command of international chic with the likes of Trump International Hotel & Tower, whose 464 luxurious condos sold in one day for more than $700 million; Embassy Suites' 421 all-suites hotel; Outrigger's own $100-million renovation and expansion of Outrigger Reef on the Beach; well-appointed 48-unit new Outrigger Regency boutique condo-hotel; and upgraded Ohana Islander Waikiki, as well as restaurants, shops, park-like greens, and other improvements. Just around the corner, a major face-lift of the low-rise concrete Royal Hawaiian Shopping Center on three blocks of Kalakaua Avenue aims to present a more Hawaiian facade with the small Royal Grove park and performance stage, with lush native gardens and trees. Neighboring hotels of all descriptions have been classing up, renovating buildings and surroundings, and acquiring enticing new restaurants.

Throughout the district, the streets of Waikiki sport new gardens, walkways, pools, and lighting, as well as an emphasis on projecting Hawaiian culture to guests in the un-Hawaiian environment of tall buildings and busy streets.

If you think of Waikiki as a lively urban resort where an incredible variety of people enjoy the most famous beach in the world, you'll love it, as public theater if nothing else. If you seek the good old days when cruise-ship passengers were met by maidens who jumped in the sea and swam to the boats, then escorted passengers to a handful of hotels where they resided royally for months, then you will surely be disappointed. You won't find grass shacks to sleep in—sadly, the Uniform Building Code outlaws even thatched roofs in most instances. You can see hula and Hawaiian arts and crafts; hear Hawaiian music; and watch surfers for free, as long as you want.

Waikiki packs into a square mile of space an average of 72,000 visitors per day in 33,000 units in 175 hotel and condo properties, plus apartments that house some 20,000 residents, restaurants, boutiques, theaters, nightspots, fast-food joints, museums, beaches, boats, churches, and just across the Ala Wai Canal, a major convention center. The district is a narrow peninsula between **Waikiki Beach** and the canal paralleled by Kalakaua Avenue, the main one-way inbound boulevard; secondary thoroughfare Kuhio Avenue, a block back from the beach; the one-way outbound Ala Wai Boulevard; and the canal, which defines the district on two sides. Kapahulu Avenue more or less defines the Diamond Head end. One big chunk of Waikiki at the beginning of the man-made peninsula is **Fort DeRussy,** the open spot along this end of the beach. This fortunately situated Army installation has a couple of high-rises for military visitors, plus low-rise buildings and lots of green. With even fewer buildings and more green, 170-acre **Queen Kapiolani Park** at the other end, the foot of Diamond Head, is a similar beachfront respite from congestion. King Kalakaua created the park in 1877 and named it for his queen. It is the home of the **Waikiki Band Shell,** an outdoor entertainment venue, and the **Honolulu Zoo.** It's a wonderful place for running, flying kites, having picnics, holding cultural festivals, and playing softball and tennis.

You could say Waikiki, where an estimated 100,000 people sleep on any given night, is the antithesis of urban sprawl. The compaction puts everything within walking distance or a short bus ride. Waikiki is like a city within a city, and while they might have done it better (no planners were used in the making of Waikiki), the resort accommodates, amazingly well, the millions who seek sun and sand, as well as a good time in a tropical urban setting.

Our suggestion is to visit Waikiki for at least two or three days, time enough to get your bearings, shake off jet lag, and press on, either elsewhere on Oahu or to a neighboring island.

At night, the sidewalks of Kalakaua and Kuhio are constant parades of passersby, including visitors from every corner of the globe. Plenty of free entertainment, such as hula performances and torch-lighting, competes with outstanding people-watching.

Waikiki is a safe area. The Honolulu Police Department maintains a strong and reassuring presence. After years of traffic congestion during Waikiki's face-lift, residents tend to avoid the tourist district, although the new developments court their attention. Venture outside Waikiki to experience the local lifestyle of Oahu.

Greater Honolulu

Honolulu has been the capital of Hawaii since 1850, when it was the heart of the kingdom. Today, its realms are financial, political, commercial, and cultural—during the daytime at least. The lively downtown shuts down at night, but an after-dark scene of hip bars, coffeehouses, galleries, and restaurants is replacing the old, sleazy nightscape of neighboring Chinatown. Retail continues unabated into the evenings in the out-of-downtown shopping centers.

The main downtown thoroughfare is Bishop Street, a continuation of the Pali Highway that goes one way *ma kai* all the way to Honolulu Harbor. The companion *ma uka*–bound thoroughfare is Alakea Street. The downtown area extends several blocks around them. Other boundaries are Ala Moana Boulevard, paralleling the harbor front, and Vineyard Boulevard on the uphill side, named for onetime wine vineyards planted long ago by a Spaniard, Don Marin. Through the middle, King and Beretania Streets, a pair of key one-way (through downtown) connectors, link neighborhoods for miles on either side of town. The downtown architecture is an interesting mix of historic buildings and new high-rises that speak of continued prosperity. Street trees and park areas, not to mention the mountain and ocean views at either end of the streets, make for a very attractive district. The government buildings and **Capitol District,** which includes **Iolani Palace** and other historic structures, are just *Diamond Head* of downtown, within easy walking distance.

unofficial **TIP**
In Honolulu, the directions locals use are *Ewa* (west, or where Ewa Plantation used to be) and *Diamond Head*.

Just *Ewa* of downtown is the historic Chinatown district, now populated more by Vietnamese than Chinese. Twice in the past, Chinatown burned to the ground and was rebuilt. Crime and drugs comprised the latest assault, but citizens banded together to salvage Chinatown. One key advance was the $30-million renovation of the 1,400-seat Hawaii Theatre, a masterpiece in gilt and 1920s style.

Windward Oahu

For peace and scenic splendor without high-rise canyons, go over the mountains to the Windward side to find **Kailua,** where hotels are banned but vacation rentals and bed-and-breakfasts offer affordable access to excellent beaches; **Haleiwa,** former plantation town and home of big-wave surfers on the North Shore; or **Ko Olina Resort,** the neighbor island–style luxury spread in west Oahu.

No signs point the way to Kailua, the quaint beach town at the other end of the Pali Highway from downtown. There's no tourist booth either, but tourists find their way over the mountain in search of boutique shopping, restaurants, and Kailua's great beaches, largely unknown to visitors until recently. **Kailua Beach** and **Lanikai Beach** rank as two of America's best. Kailua and neighboring Kaneohe, at the foot of the Likelike Highway through the Koolau, are bedroom communities of about 36,000 each and the bed-and-breakfast capital of Oahu.

unofficial **TIP**
Kailua Beach Park and Lanikai Beach are great for families with small kids, who can safely play in gentle waves.

Bed-and-breakfasts in Hawaii are most often rooms or suites in people's houses with breakfast or light kitchen facilities, rather than quaint inns. Many operate underground since the city and county of Honolulu, in a poor display of civic aloha, banned new bed-and-breakfasts years ago. Nonetheless, plenty of B&Bs and vacation rentals on or near beaches can be found on the Internet.

Windsurfing, kayaking, swimming, and snorkeling are the main water attractions here in the home of Robbie Naish, former world champion windsurfer who also pioneered kitesurfing (see details on page 295). The scenic **Mokulua,** two photo-op islets off Lanikai, are the most popular kayaking destinations. Rent all the gear you need right in Kailua Beach Park or at one of the shops in town.

Hikers scale 603-foot-high **Kaiwa Ridge** behind Lanikai for a panoramic view of the Windward side or hike other trails through the Koolau Rainforest along the Windward Coast. Fearless hikers with sheer-cliff experience can test their mettle on the spiky pinnacle of Olomana and the tougher backcountry Koolau hikes.

Opting for a vacation rental is one way to control expenses while maximizing exposure to local life—discovering unfamiliar foods in the supermarkets, for instance, or at the People's Market that moves from community to community around Oahu. Kailua is a favorite of many visitors seeking to live Hawaiian style. A rental car is necessary to make the most of it and to enjoy the surrounding Windward Coast. Farther up the reef-protected Windward shore, more than 50 miles of empty beaches (busier on weekends) are suitable for snoozing, swimming, shore fishing, spearfishing, learning to surf, or snorkeling.

Natural attractions include Kaneohe Bay, one of the most beautiful in the Pacific, with snorkel and dive trips departing from Heeia Pier; Kualoa Ranch, a 4,000-acre cattle ranch with 75 horses for trail rides and myriad other outdoor activities; and Hoomaluhia Botanical Garden, a 400-acre municipal garden with Hawaiian ethnic plants at the foot of the cathedrallike Koolau Mountain Range.

North Shore

Year-round, the sleepy North Shore sugar town of **Haleiwa** offers another alternative on Oahu, with its modest plantation-style buildings that house surf shops, clothing stores, art galleries, and restaurants.

The pace quickens considerably when the surf rises in winter, drawing the world's best wave riders and people who simply have never seen a 25-foot wave, much less someone surfing on it.

The North Shore has relatively few places to stay—a youth hostel; a few beach cottages, campgrounds, and private vacation rentals; plus the condo units and hotel rooms of Turtle Bay Resort. It is a great day-trip destination that shows Oahu's country face.

To the west from Haleiwa to road's end is **Mokuleia,** relatively undeveloped stretches of wild beach fronting old sugar lands. The road ends shortly after **Dillingham Airfield,** where gliders, skydiving, biplanes, and other aerial thrill rides are based. Oahu may have nearly a million residents, but it doesn't have a road that goes around the entire island. **Kaena Point Natural Area Reserve** (see below) is a wilderness area for hiking and other pursuits. You can walk or bike around to the Waianae Coast, but you can't drive there.

Agricultural landscapes still dominate the middle and upper central valley areas that culminate in the North Shore.

Leeward Coast

The hot, dry **Waianae Coast** is sheltered from view and separated from the rest of the island by the Waianae Range. The beach area of **Makaha,** long a popular surf break, remains relatively unexplored and nearly unknown to visitors since the lone resort hotel closed several years ago. Some condos and time-shares exist—you can find affordable lodging in condos like the Hawaiian Princess and Makaha Beach Cabanas and in vacation rentals listed on the Internet.

Makaha means "gate" in Hawaiian, and it serves as the entry to Oahu's last true shoreline wilderness area, **Kaena Point Natural Area Reserve,** a world removed from Waikiki. On this remote shore at Oahu's westernmost point, albatross nest in sand dunes, Hawaiian monk seals loll on empty beaches, and humpback whales cruise by in winter. Winter and spring bring the huge swells that draw surfers like magnets to this shore as well as to the North Shore communities around the point. But the paved road doesn't go through. You can drive to the end at **Yokohama Bay** (an old train used to stop here and drop off Japanese fishermen to fish the bay). Then it's a 90-minute walk down a dirt road to Kaena Point.

On the city end of the coast, the welcome mat will be out at the nearest resort hotel, **J. W. Marriott Ihilani Resort & Spa,** a luxurious retreat and elaborate spa with a man-made beach lagoon, beachfront suites, two fine-dining restaurants, and nearby, 18-hole **Ko Olina Golf Club.**

Central Oahu

The valley formed by Waianae Mountains on the west and Koolau Mountains on the east is a broad, scenic plain that from the sky resembles an avenue leading to **Pearl Harbor** and its war memorials. That's one path the Japanese warplanes took in 1941. On the way they bombed **Schofield Army Barracks** installation, halfway along the plain.

Aloha Stadium, the 50,000-seat facility that is home to annual NFL Pro Bowl games and other sports and entertainment events, neighbors **Pearl Harbor Naval Base.**

Today the Central Valley is still bucolic in the northern reaches, carpeted with gray-green rows of pineapple in the rich red dirt and wild cane where sugar plantations used to hold sway. You can stop at the **Dole Plantation** to learn about and taste the golden fruit, once a major Hawaii crop. Toward the southern end are the newer suburbs of housing and shopping centers, including **Waikele Premium Outlets.**

MAUI: THE VALLEY ISLE

MAUI FACTS	
Flower Lokelani (rose)	Color Pink
County Seat Wailuku	Area 729 square miles
Length 48 miles	Width 26 miles
Population 139,800	Coastline 120 miles
Highest Point Haleakala (10,023 feet)	

MAUI'S SUNNY RESORTS on its south and west coasts are mainly the reasons why just about everybody knows the name of this island, Hawaii's second largest. Maui is composed of two volcanic masses joined by a valley with golden beaches and blue sea on either end. Then there's 10,023-foot Haleakala, the dormant volcano whose sheer bulk forms more than half the island. But Maui seems to have more appeal than the sum of its parts. It combines a hint of the flash of Oahu with the genuine country attitudes of a rural plantation island and the sophisticated influence of its luxury spreads, as well as the people who frequent them.

Central Maui

Departing Kahului Airport, you may wonder why you came so far to see such familiar big-box landmarks (Costco and Walmart, for example). Wander farther into this amorphous waterfront town to find more shopping centers, neighborhoods, the port, and beaches. When you come to the shore, turn left or right—either way, you will discover why everyone raves about Maui.

The famous windsurfing areas, **Kanaha** and **Hookipa** beaches, are to the right, just beyond the airport on the way to Paia and Hana. They are justifiably famous for their beauty and wiggly route through myriad waterfall valleys. In the opposite direction, a small road wanders off toward Waihee and eventually around the whole northwest shoulder of Maui to Kapalua and the western resort coast. This is one of Maui's most scenic and unspoiled drives along sea cliffs and through large ranches, although housing developments are threatening to overtake parts of it. The pavement narrows to one lane often as it winds around the base of the **West Maui Mountains,** so watch the road.

Neighboring Kahului on the *ma uka* side is the quaint historic county seat of **Wailuku.** The countryside gets greener as you approach **Iao Valley State Park.**

When you face the opposite way, you see the isthmus valley, a sea of waving green sugarcane fields, a vanishing sight in the Islands. Above it pokes the smokestack of still functional **Puunene Sugar Mill.**

From Kahului Airport the main roads lead to resort areas: Follow the signs to Kihei/Wailea/Makena in South Maui, Maalaea in the middle, and Lahaina, Kaanapali Beach Resort, and Kapalua Resort in West Maui. The Haleakala Highway leads up the flank of the mountain, and the Hana Highway along the North Shore leads around the back of Haleakala to the ranch village of Hana, hiding near the end of this winding road.

South Maui

From Kahului Airport a 20-minute ride through the cane brings you to the resort coast. **Wailea, Makena,** and **Kihei** are the resorts of choice to the left in South Maui. Straight ahead is **Maalaea,** home of condo resorts, the **Maui Ocean Center Aquarium,** and the harbor where boats depart for many snorkel, whale-watching, and other cruise tours.

If you're on a budget, go to Kihei. When money's no object or you're pining for spectacular golf, go to **Kapalua** or **Wailea.** Got your sociable kids along? Go to **Kaanapali,** where they can enjoy the action. Or head to serene Makena at Maui's southern end for more solitude. When time is no object, go to **Hana** and stay awhile in the quaint seaside village with its singular low-key but pricey hotel.

Thrifty travelers find affordable condos in Kihei, a beachside strip lined with shops and malls. Kihei is also the home of many people who work in the neighboring resorts, as well as the U.S. Air Force Maui Supercomputing Center nearby. The town fronts a ten-mile coast indented by black lava reefs that frame some excellent gold-sand pocket beaches and broad strand beach parks. Most popular is **Kamaole Beach III,** in the heart of Kihei with a tree-shaded grass picnic area and park, views of Lanai and Kahoolawe, and free parking.

Hollywood celebrities, incentive winners, conference-goers, and honeymooners love **Wailea Resort,** a lush, groomed beauty spot where four luxurious hotels—**Grand Wailea Resort Hotel & Spa, Four Seasons**

Resort Maui, Marriott Wailea Beach, and Arabian fantasy–style **Fairmont Kea Lani**—share great beaches with plush waterfront condos, separated by park-like green spaces but united by a waterfront trail. The lower slope of Haleakala helps hide the mid-rise hotels and boutique shopping center from view. These temples of pleasure vary from refined retreat to swanky playground with a super-sized spa and elaborate water complex with water-powered elevator.

Find seclusion beyond Wailea at **Makena Resort,** where the **Maui Prince Hotel** stands alone amid 1,800 acres of dryland *kiawe* forest and several splendid beaches. South Maui is punctuated by Puu Olai, a cinder-cone peninsula that juts into the sea. Makena is an old village where cattle from the upland Ulupalakua Ranch were once herded into the water to swim for the ships that would take them to market. The tiny community has a picturesque Hawaiian-language church by the water. Haleakala's last eruption spilled down to the sea south of Makena in about 1790. It's now traversed by rough hiking trails across the lava after the road ends.

Wailea Resort has three scenic golf courses, and Makena adds two more. Horseback riding, a sporting-clay shooting range, hiking, a coastal trail, a competition tennis complex, the **Shops at Wailea** shopping village, and a shuttle bus to connect them are all part of the South Maui appeal.

West Maui

Head to the right from Maalaea around the foot of the West Maui Mountains, and you'll approach historic **Lahaina** town and **Kaanapali Beach Resort,** prize-winning progenitor of the planned resort complex popular in Hawaii and other destinations.

Lahaina, the old whaling capital, retains charm because of its quaint and preserved historic buildings. It's a happy, honky-tonk jumble of art galleries, coral jewelry and T-shirt boutiques, bars, restaurants ranging from David Paul's Lahaina Grill to waterfront Pacific'O to Cheeseburger in Paradise, and *Ulalena*, the best theatrical show on Maui (see page 454 for details). You can stay at the century-old **Pioneer Inn** for a real taste of history. It was once the hangout of lusty whalers on R&R, until the disapproving missionaries prevailed. Lahaina also has a variety of condo resorts, inns, vacation rentals, and B&Bs. In Lahaina many people stop what they're doing and gather to watch when the sun starts dropping like a fireball behind Lanai and the boats in Lahaina Harbor.

Kaanapali is a three-mile hop north of Lahaina, but when the traffic is heavy, it can take more than half an hour to get there. After more than 40 years, verdant Kaanapali continues to reinvent itself and remains a popular destination. The 600-acre resort has two golf courses, mid-rise blocks of deluxe and luxury hotels, time-shares and condos that line the four-mile beach and dot the hillside behind it, restaurants with a full range of open-air, ocean-view dining, and

Whalers Village Shopping Center. The shops include upscale European boutiques in an effort to attract Japanese shoppers. Kaanapali also features beachfront tennis, a boardwalk and beach parks, and a shuttle that connects to Kapalua–West Maui Airport (small aircraft).

*un*official **TIP**
If Kapalua is outside your budget, the resorts and condos of Napili Beach next door are a good alternative.

Farther north, the luxury coast culminates in **Kapalua Resort,** part of a 23,000-acre pineapple plantation with rows of spiky plants that stretch for miles in hilly fields below Puu Kukui, second tallest peak on Maui. This is the most beautiful part of West Maui, its wide-open vistas framed by Molokai offshore and wildlands to the north. A hotel, executive homes and luxury condos, two notable golf courses, and— for contrast—the tidy, prim red plantation buildings of the original pineapple plantation, still operated by Maui Land & Pineapple Company, share this setting. The roads are lined with signature Norfolk and Cook Island pines. Kapalua-bound guests can fly from Honolulu to nearby West Maui Airport and avoid the congestion of Kahului.

Upcountry Maui and Beyond

From central Kahului, a country road runs up Haleakala's lower slope and winds through the cool, pastoral community of **Kula,** where, at 3,000 feet, protea, roses, carnations, and blue jacaranda trees bloom. Visitors can stay at **Kula Lodge** or in a variety of bed-and-breakfast bungalows. Kula is on the way to **Haleakala National Park.** It's an escape from tropical heat sought by many of Maui's full-time residents, a fairly linear community on the shoulder of the mountain with wonderful views, botanical gardens, flower farms, and the winery at Ulupalakua, **Tedeschi Vineyards.** They sell a lot of pineapple wine, but you can also taste other vintages and sparkling wine at the tasting room. A cool, grassy setting under old avocado trees is fine for picnics. The road continues along the wide-open back side of Haleakala, seldom seen. You can drive all the way to Hana if you're a good, unflappable, and adventurous driver and the weather is good.

Maui's most famous road—the **Hana Highway**—gets to tiny Hana the other way, from Kahului and quaint little Paia. It winds by magnificent sea views, waterfalls, and botanical gardens on a skinny road for 53 miles to the ultimate tropical retreat. Count on three hours each way for the drive to Hana, more if you stop to swim in waterfall pools. The small coastal village is populated by Hawaiians (and a few celebrities) who wisely resist change. The rich and famous fly to Hana in small planes, and you can too. There is a small airport served by flights from Kahului.

A stay on Maui promises sunny beaches, great golf on championship courses, winter whale watching, snorkeling and sailing, hikes, sunrise viewing at Haleakala Crater, and a quiet nightlife outside of Kihei and Lahaina.

56   PART ONE GETTING ACQUAINTED WITH HAWAII

The island caters to the wealthy and free-spending corporate-incentive winners at many elegant hotels and resort condos, but it also offers some affordable bargains for budget travelers. Hikers and campers like Maui for its natural attractions and parks.

Folks who live on Maui have the motto *Maui No Ka Oi*, which means "Maui is the best." Readers of *Condé Nast Traveler* agree. For years in a row, they named Maui the "best island in the world."

HAWAII: THE BIG ISLAND

HAWAII FACTS

Flower Lehua	Color Red
County Seat Hilo	Area 4,028 square miles
Length 93 miles	Width 76 miles
Population 171,191	Coastline 266 miles
Highest Point Mauna Kea (13,796 feet)	

LONG BEFORE TOURISM became Hawaii's livelihood, the pluckiest visitors were those who journeyed high above Hilo more than a century ago to see a live, erupting volcano, one of the few in the world where observers could get fairly close in relative safety. That volcano shows no sign of stopping. In its current phase, **Kilauea Volcano** has been erupting since January 1, 1983, adding ever more real estate to the already big Big Island of Hawaii. **Mauna Loa,** the most voluminous structure on Earth, is quiet but still active. It last erupted in 1984.

If you have but one day to spend on the Big Island, see Kilauea at **Hawaii Volcanoes National Park.** Bring your children. The park is good even when the volcano is not cooperating.

The Big Island not only has five volcanoes (**Kilauea, Mauna Kea, Mauna Loa, Hualalai,** and **Kohala**) but it also has a sixth one, a work in progress named **Loihi,** now a seamount emerging from the ocean floor off the southeast coast. You can stargaze at the 9,000-foot-level visitor center of the 13,796-foot Mauna Kea, the tallest mountain in the tropical Pacific. There, the air is so clear and dark that scientists have set up a forest of high-tech telescopes to peer into deep space. If you are hardy, hike to the subarctic summit of slightly shorter 13,680-foot-high Mauna Loa. Both mountains rise more than 30,000 feet from the ocean floor, making them technically the tallest mountains on the planet.

Some visitors head for **Ka Lae** or **South Point,** the windswept southernmost point in the United States, where early Polynesians arrived around AD 650, according to carbon dating of ancient fishhooks. Others go to Holualoa, an artists' village amid backyard coffee farms on the hillside over Kailua-Kona. And lucky ones enjoy a sunny day in **Hilo,** gateway to the volcano park.

The Big Island is the only Hawaiian island big enough for a road trip of more than an hour or two. Plan on three days to see natural attractions like **Akaka Falls, Waipio Valley,** Hawaii Volcanoes National Park, the catch of the day at **Honokohau Harbor,** the coffee plantations of **Kona,** and **Puuhonua O Honaunau National Historical Park,** the ancient refuge where hapless victims and lawbreakers could find sanctuary. Nowadays, adventurers, vulcanologists, astronomers, marlin fishermen, and lovers of the outdoors share this singular island with golfers, international conferees, and the rich and famous.

Kona

Kona is the word for "leeward" in Hawaiian, and it usually means warm and still. The Big Island's Kona Coast is the area where several hulking volcanoes act to block the ever-blowing northeast winds and calm the sea. **Kailua-Kona** is the fishing village–turned–junior Waikiki that serves as headquarters for the Kona District. It's filled with affordable condos, hotel rooms, and suites (none of them terribly appealing), as well as shopping plazas, restaurants, and bars. Beaches are noticeably in short supply, although the **King Kamehameha's Kona Beach Hotel** has one. Instead, this is primarily a rocky shoreline where the waters are so dependably docile that walkways, restaurants, and rooms hang right over the floodlit waves in several places.

To the south of Kailua-Kona is the somewhat tonier **Keauhou Resort,** with a championship golf course, revamped Sheraton Keauhou Bay Resort & Spa (formerly Kona Surf) with a meetings-oriented layout, as well as deluxe condo complexes and the moderately priced **Outrigger Keauhou Beach Resort.** The Keauhou Beach has historic features (King Kalakaua's summer cottage and a small fishpond) on its grounds, and the hotel extends over a reef tide pool. Neighboring **Kahaluu Beach Park** and nearby **Disappearing Sands Beach** offer swimming, snorkeling, and surfing.

To the north of the airport and Honokokau Harbor, where the world-famous Kona Coast marlin fishing fleet is moored, the lava spilled by Hualalai Volcano some 200 years ago lines the highway in endless, desolate reaches of black. The first time we saw it, we had decided to hold green Kauai for another visit and opted instead for the raw island of big hot volcanoes. Somewhere north of Kailua-Kona, our hearts sank. Then we cut across the lava to find palm-edged oases by the sea and discovered some of the world's greatest beach resorts.

The first is the area of **Kaupulehu,** an ancient fishing village before it was overrun by lava and later metamorphosed into low-rise bungalow resorts. Honeymooners, CEOs, and families seek the **Kona Village Resort,** a casual but expensive enclave of traditional Polynesian-style private bungalows on the ancient village site between the beach and surrounding protective lava. Kona Village has petroglyph fields, a famous luau, a beautiful cove, tennis, and many other pluses, but it is the only resort along this stretch of coast without a world-famous championship golf course. Next door is its opulent and equally romantic modern neighbor, **Four Seasons Resort Hualalai,** which borders a golf course, exclusive condos and homes, and has several swimming pools, including one made to look like a natural lava tide pool, complete with tropical fish.

Up the highway at **Waikoloa Beach Resort,** the **Hilton Waikoloa Village** is a fantasy resort where you can swim with captive dolphins, ride a sleek silver tram to your tower, or take an Italian launch on a rail through a second-story waterway. The pools, falls, and waterslide are so elaborate that you can almost forget there's no natural beach. But a postcard-perfect beach is next door at **Anaehoomalu Bay,** fronting the completely revamped deluxe **Waikoloa Beach Marriott Resort & Spa.** Both hotels have spas, and the resort features two golf courses, the **Kings Village** shops, restaurants, and well-maintained historic features.

Next up the highway to the north is **Mauna Lani Resort,** with golf, tennis, walking trails, historic features, and the luxurious bungalows—butlered hideouts beside the beach. At **Orchid at Mauna Lani** you can bliss out with a massage in a tent by the sea at a "spa without walls."

Just north of Mauna Lani is **Mauna Kea Beach Resort,** home of the venerable **Mauna Kea Beach Hotel** and newer **Hapuna Beach Prince Hotel,** two golf courses, access to the two best beaches on the island (Kaunaoa, fronting the Mauna Kea, and Hapuna Beach), and all the amenities wealth can summon. Hotels and golf courses on sites carved from beachfront lava can be traced to 1965, when Laurance Rockefeller opened the Mauna Kea Beach Hotel on a prime beach that belonged to **Parker Ranch,** then the largest privately held cattle spread in the nation. The simple, elegant resort became a top choice of executives in search of a comfortable retreat, and their heirs kept up the tradition. ("Now I know where old Republicans go to die," once quipped Merv Griffin.) The art-filled hotel, with its signature architecture of soaring open spaces, ponds, and gardens under roof, set the tone for luxury Hawaii beach resorts to come.

History is right on the surface throughout this coast—Kona Village, Waikoloa, and Mauna Lani Resort all serve as stewards of petroglyph fields, lava beds that served as message boards for ancient travelers who carved them with thousands of primitive drawings. Mauna Lani and Waikoloa also boast well-kept historic fishpond complexes with signage to tell you how they work. Federal and state parks preserve cultural monuments throughout this area.

Vacation rentals and bed-and-breakfasts can be found in **Upcountry Holualoa,** the coffee country above Kailua-Kona, and in **Waimea,** Parker Ranch headquarters and a charming ranch town. Parker Ranch has a historic compound and rodeo grounds in addition to vast stretches of pastureland and open countryside.

Hilo and Volcano

Hilo tourism facilities were set up decades ago with great expectations for a tourism boom that didn't quite materialize. Some of the large hotels on Banyan Drive on **Hilo Bay** were transformed into residential dwellings. Reasonable rates predominate at the remaining ones, and some have been upgraded in recent years.

Hilo has a historic downtown district and a quiet charm. It gets plenty of rain and has the attributes of a wet, warm place—abundant flowers and tropical fruit (bananas hang in the lobbies of some hotels), huge shady trees, waterfalls and streams, and triple rainbows. Our recommendation is to stay a night or two at **Shipman House,** a restored Victorian bed-and-breakfast in a beautiful Hilo neighborhood, and to spend your days exploring Hawaii Volcanoes National Park and the nearby lava-watch area at Kalapana, where hot lava may still be rolling to the sea when you are there. Both are less than an hour's drive away. Stroll through one of Hilo's famous gardens, such as the **Hawaii Tropical Botanical Garden at Onemea Bay,** go for a swim in Hilo Bay, and enjoy the uncrowded pace. The **Lyman Museum & Mission House** in downtown Hilo is an excellent small facility whose exhibits will give you a feel for the life of early immigrants to the area.

Vacation rentals and bed-and-breakfasts make up the accommodations in upcountry Volcano, where you'll find charming lodging and tasty dinners at **Kilauea Lodge and Restaurant** in the misty fern forests.

If your goal is to get back to nature, the Big Island is your choice; there is too much to see and do in the great outdoors for just one week, including skiing on the occasionally snowcapped cinders. But if you only have a week, spend two days at Hawaii Volcanoes National Park, staying in Hilo or a nearby cottage, two days sightseeing or pursuing other activities, then splurge for three days at Kona Village Resort, Four Seasons Resort Hualalai, or Waikoloa Beach Marriott Resort & Spa, some personal favorites.

KAUAI: THE GARDEN ISLE
Kauai

KAUAI FACTS	
Flower Mokihana	Color Purple
County Seat Lihue	Area 549 square miles
Length 33 miles	Width 25 miles
Population 63,004	Coastline 90 miles
Highest Point Kawaikiki Peak (5,243 feet)	

The island's a beauty all right, where roadside forests are a riot of flowering vines and mangoes fall ripe to the ground. But it's not just a pretty place. It's tough and gritty and made for adventure. In modern times, it survived two monster hurricanes in a decade. In the late 1700s, it was the only island to resist Kamehameha the Great's military attempt to unite the kingdom, although its independent-minded chiefs gave up without a fight later. While the young Big Island is still black with lava in many spots and raw with new life, Kauai is the oldest major island, and its jagged peaks, mantle of green over steep cliffs, and shoreline of beaches are all testimony to the scenic inevitability of erosion.

The combination of rough nature and indulgent luxury is all the rage in Hawaii. When you go you can hang out at a fancy hotel in **Princeville on the North Shore** or **Poipu Beach** on the South Shore, or choose the so-called **Coconut Coast** in between, sipping Blue Hawaiis by the pool. Instead, you can get out and discover the island's true nature. Or enjoy both.

Some hike into the 3,000-foot-deep **Waimea Canyon,** a multicolored chasm, or brave the cliff-side 11-mile **Kalalau Trail** that winds along the remote **Na Pali Coast.** Some go up to **Kokee State Park** and venture into the cloud forests on the boardwalk trail into **Alakai Swamp,** last haunt of the Kauai Oo, a black bird with bright yellow thigh feathers. This 20-square-mile highland bog is home to rare plants, native birds, Hawaii's only native land mammal, the hoary bat, and a mosquito-eating plant.

Others angle for big-game fish off nearby **Niihau,** snorkel **Kee Beach's** fishy lagoon, and helicopter up to the 5,243-foot-high summit of **Mount Waialeale,** a crater ribboned with waterfalls as befitting one of the wettest spots in the world. Twenty inches of rain in a single day is common.

All that water refreshes Kauai's seven rivers (you can kayak on the **Huleia, Hanalei,** and **Wailua**) and keeps the Garden Island the great green place that it is.

Where to stay depends on the weather. Any place on Kauai can be sunny and hot, but showers are most likely to cool the moody green Hanalei (heavenly garland) area on the North Shore, a real-life version of movie land's Bali Hai (*South Pacific* was shot here). **Princeville Resort,** a development on a sea-cliff plateau with a spectacular view, has homes, condos, the luxurious St. Regis Princeville Hotel, shopping, restaurants, a spa, and world-famous golf at Princeville Golf Course. Part of it overlooks **Hanalei Bay,** the taro patches of the **Hanalei River Valley,** a mile-long beach, and the bowl of 4,000-foot cliffs creased by waterfalls that surrounds the valley. Seven miles beyond friendly, picturesque Hanalei town, the road ends at **Kee Beach** and an ancient footpath leads into Na Pali wilderness. No roads cross the northwest section of the island, a series of dramatic deep valleys carved by ancient streams.

Midway between Hanalei and Poipu is the Coconut Coast, including a number of small communities from **Kapaa** past the Wailua River to **Lihue,** the county seat and site of the airport. Affordable to deluxe beachfront condos and hotels share a golden beach. Water conditions can be rugged for all but surfers and body surfers. There is a sheltered swimming area at **Lydgate State Beach Park** by the river mouth. **Coconut MarketPlace** offers most of the shopping and restaurants.

Lihue, mostly devoted to commerce and county government, has a museum worth a stop—the small coral-block **Kauai Museum** on Rice Street. Kauai Lagoons by the airport was once a pinnacle of the fantasy resort movement. What's there now is the **Kauai Marriott Resort & Beach Club,** part hotel and part time-shares, with an opulent lobby and ballroom–conference complex, a seven-acre pool, an extensive art collection, two golf courses, and other amenities. Heading south, the highway passes a historic manor on the right known as **Kilohana,** which houses boutiques, galleries, and a restaurant. It will give just a taste of how sweet life was on Kauai for the onetime owners, the Wilcox family, when sugar was king.

Sunseekers and families like **Poipu Beach Resort,** a coastal complex with a good swimming beach, golf courses, a tennis complex, several notable restaurants, a wide range of plentiful condo resorts, and a hotel row redefined from time to time by hurricanes. Hotels never get too old on Kauai. Poipu features the **Grand Hyatt Kauai Resort & Spa,** a fine example of Hawaii-style Art Deco architecture, on the southern end and the **Sheraton Kauai Resort** on the northern end.

Children and adults enjoy **Spouting Horn Blow Hole,** a lava tube where surf sometimes shoots seawater 50 feet into the air. Inland is **Koloa,** where the Hawaiian sugar industry was born more than 150 years ago. Now it's a collection of restaurants, bars, and surf-n-sun shops that you pass through to get from the highway to the beach.

Looking for flowers on the Garden Isle? Serious green thumbs go to **Lawai** to visit **National Tropical Botanical Garden,** a congressionally chartered research facility. Its 186 acres include an important collection of rare tropical plants, tropical experimental gardens, and, for contrast, the finely trimmed formal gardens of a former royal estate. Honeymooners and couples seeking a romantic getaway will enjoy Kauai, as will those who come back with tiny shells in their pockets and red dirt on their hiking shoes.

MOLOKAI: THE FRIENDLY ISLE
Molokai

MOLOKAI FACTS

Flower White kukui blossom	**Color** Green
County Seat Kaunakakai	**Area** 260 square miles
Length 38 miles	**Width** 10 miles
Population 7,404	**Coastline** 88 miles
Highest Point Kamakou Peak (4,961 feet)	

If you crave bright lights and busy nights, avoid Molokai. One of Hawaii's main islands, Molokai can be described by what it doesn't have: traffic lights, shopping malls, nightclubs. The lifestyle is slow and unpretentious, and people pride themselves on being a traditional Hawaiian community.

For better or worse, Molokai has spurned, or been spared, "progress." Actually, the island has sustained a number of economic hits over recent years—sugar and pineapple production ceased, residents decided against new hotels and tourism, and federal officials ordered all the cows killed to stamp out an obscure ailment that had been around for decades.

Islanders grow prized produce: watermelons, sweet potatoes, boutique veggies, honey, coffee, and macadamia nuts. Molokai folks are uncommonly friendly and down-home. And honest. Once we left an airplane coupon ticket at the rental-car counter in Molokai's tiny airport. Three days later, it was still there—not far from the sign reminding passengers that airline rules prohibit carrying watermelons in the overhead racks.

The island is not a destination for everyone, especially those who like creature comforts. The beaches are wild and lengthy but not usually safe or desirable for swimming. The greatest natural feature, the world's tallest sea cliffs on the jungled North Shore, is virtually inaccessible. The most famous, and poignant, attraction is an isolated but still inhabited former leprosy colony and the mule ride down a steep switchback trail to get there. **Kalaupapa National Historical Park,** where victims of Hansen's disease were banished by royal edict in the 1860s, was the last home of famed Belgian priest Father Damien, who gave his own life treating the sick.

Why go to Molokai? There's plenty to do: hiking, snorkeling, diving, kayaking, and fishing. The Nature Conservancy runs preserves and offers hiking programs at **Moomomi Dunes,** where bones of flightless birds have been found, and at **Kamakou** in the high country, a cloud forest filled with rare native plants. Hikers have been known to trek through scenic **Halawa Valley** wilderness on the East End, although the ancient Hawaiian settlement was declared off-limits to visitors by the private owner. Check the status when you are on the island.

Sightseers find an odd assortment of natural and historic sites like ancient fishponds, the **Smith-Bronte Landing Site** (where the first airplane to Hawaii crash-landed in 1927), **Mapulehu Mango Grove,** and **Iliiliopae Heiau,** temple ruins of an ancient school of sacrificial rites.

The frontier-like town of **Kaunakakai** is a sleepy crossroads with a handful of stores and a beloved bakery. At Hoolehua Post Office, you can address, stamp, and send a Molokai coconut home like a postcard.

Turn left out of town onto Kamehameha V Highway and you'll soon find the **East End**—lush, green, and tropical with ancient fishponds lining the coco-palm coast where condo resorts, bed-and-breakfasts, and vacation beach houses are available.

Go right and you'll encounter the arid **West End,** spiked with cactus, roamed by cows, and home still to some condo resorts, although **Molokai Ranch** is closed and **Maunaloa** is virtually a ghost town. The Singapore-based owner of the ranch, which encompassed a third of the island, shut down the ranch, resort, and town operations after islanders vetoed a proposed upscale subdivision that might have offset some of the $80 million in ranch losses.

LANAI: THE PINEAPPLE ISLAND
Lanai

LANAI FACTS	
Flower Kaunaoa	Color Orange
County Seat Lanai City	Area 141 square miles
Length 18 miles	Width 13 miles
Population 3,193	Coastline 47 miles
Highest Point Lanaihale (3,366 feet)	

A short flight from Honolulu, Lanai is a world removed. On this smallest of Hawaii's six accessible islands, you can see most of the island chain from its loftier spots.

Buildings are dwarfed by the rolling terrain of what was the world's biggest pineapple plantation until the owners changed in the 1980s and planted resorts and upscale tourism instead. The quaint plantation cottages of **Lanai City** are still there, in remarkable contrast to the elegant **Four Seasons Resort Lanai, The Lodge at Koele** which resembles a British hill station, and the Mediterranean-style **Four Seasons Resort Lanai** at Manele Bay nestled on a coastal hillside.

When your plane lands in Palawai Basin, where pineapple grew as far as the eye could see, you discover an island of anomalies. It is rural yet sophisticated, with only three paved roads but a 100-mile network of red-dirt plantation lanes and a fleet of small SUVs to go four-wheeling on them for fun. In former times, the days started with a plantation whistle at 5 a.m. Now, days in the sun begin with more discreet wake-up calls.

Lanai is owned mostly by an American tycoon who acquired it incidentally in a corporate purchase. It is inhabited largely by Filipinos who immigrated to work the pineapple fields and stayed to retrain as luxury-hotel workers. Most plantation families still live there, sharing the streets of town with well-heeled world travelers and, increasingly, wealthy neighbors.

Golfers play either of the island's magnificent 18-hole courses—the ocean-side **Challenge at Manele** or the upland **Experience at Koele,** possibly the most beautiful course anywhere. Yet while visitors are signing up for substantial fees, locals choose the little nine-hole upland course where fees are paid on the honor system, a few bucks in a tin can.

When it was a plantation, nobody went to Lanai unless invited or fortunate enough to get one of the 11 rooms in the 1920s-era **Hotel Lanai.** Now the island appeals to those with means enough to enjoy peace and solitude. Pricey spreads are going up on the hillside so that vacationers can stay longer under their own roofs.

Honeymooners, this is your island. Bill and Melissa Gates took over the island to get married here. Outdoors lovers like it too. You can shoot clay pigeons or hunt real game like turkey, mouflon sheep, and axis deer. Lodge facilities include a riding stable and croquet on the lawns. Hiking trails lead off through the woods. Nightlife, however, is limited to whatever amusements the hotels have lined up.

Anyone who seeks peaceful surroundings with luxurious accommodations will want to visit Lanai, if only to explore a most atypical Pacific island. It is a combination of hot, dry coastal cliffs and cool uplands with Cook pine groves planted by a farsighted plantation manager long ago to trap clouds and bring water to the dry island. Lanai is no tropical wonderland; its deep gorges and eroded plains speak of a hard agricultural life. But there's beauty to its hinterlands, headlands, and wide-open red-dirt valley touched only by blue sky and puffy white clouds. While prowling the four-wheel roads, explorers can find historic sites like a crumbled sugar town and an ancient king's summer fishing residence.

On a clear day, from **Lanaihale,** the 3,379-foot island summit, you can see five of the seven main Hawaiian slands in a single glance. Only distant Kauai and Niihau remain over the horizon.

Lanai will appeal to anyone looking to get away from it all, whatever the price. In addition to a half-dozen bed-and-breakfasts, you have two swanky resort choices and the affordable, historic little Hotel Lanai with its appealing restaurant, and you can go back and forth by shuttle van. Four Seasons Resort, The Lodge at Koele sits on a 1,700-foot-high hill at the head of a lane lined with tall pines, and it looks so ostentatious that you think a king might greet you instead of a uniformed hostess with a flower lei. It is cooler here, especially at night, which is why the lodge is a favorite with weekending Honolulu residents who love to dress up in sweaters and sit by a roaring fire. Downhill, beside the only safe swimming beach at **Hulopoe Bay,** the Manele Bay simmers around its pool, a lobby full of Asian art, and tropical gardens around a man-made stream teeming with koi carp.

A drive into Lanai City is like entering a time warp. Most of the island's residents live in tidy little tin-roofed plantation houses with a riot of flowers, fruits, and vegetables growing in their front yards.

Stop and "talk story" with the locals about the not-so-good old days when pineapple farming dominated life. By all means, frequent the shops, restaurants, and art galleries in the tree-lined town square.

A BRIEF HISTORY

SCIENTISTS BELIEVE THE HAWAIIAN ISLANDS were formed millions of years ago, each rising from a single "hot spot" on the floor of the Pacific Ocean and then moving north with shifting tectonic plates. The Islands were barren until seeds carried by the wind or ocean currents took root and began to grow. Slowly but surely, birds and insects found their way to these islands, and humans too.

Historians believe seafaring Polynesian voyagers first discovered Hawaii in the fourth century AD and took residence along the coasts and valleys where fresh water was plentiful. They introduced dogs, pigs, chickens, and plants, including taro, coconut, breadfruit, banana, sweet potato, and sugarcane. A second wave of Polynesian seafarers, this time from Tahiti, arrived some 500 years later.

The early Hawaiians embraced a simple lifestyle. Taro was a chief food source: its root was pounded and mixed with water to make *poi,* the paste-like starch that remains a staple of Hawaiian diets and appears at every luau. Ahead of their time in understanding nature's ecosystem, early Hawaiians built and maintained large fishponds to ensure their chiefs an abundant supply of fish. Back then, a typical *hale* (house) was a wooden frame covered with pili grass; it looked like a haystack.

Hawaiians lived under a strict caste system, and high-ranking *al* (chiefs or rulers) wielded power by imposing many *kapu* (laws or prohibitions). In some cases, even to cross the shadow of a powerful *al* meant sure death. This system brought much bickering among the people, adding to the hostilities among chiefs eager to gain more territory under their rule.

Still, the Hawaiians thrived. When Captain Cook arrived in the Islands in 1778, an estimated 400,000 Hawaiians were living on Oahu, the Big Island of Hawaii, Maui, Kauai, Molokai, Lanai, Niihau, and Kahoolawe.

CAPTAIN COOK'S ARRIVAL

ON JANUARY 21, 1778, Captain James Cook, commander of Britain's HMS *Resolution* and HMS *Discovery,* became the first European to set foot on Hawaiian soil, landing at Waimea on the west coast of Kauai. Cook and his crew spent five days on Kauai before a short visit to Niihau, where they traded salt and yams for goats, pigs, and water.

Cook's second contact with the Hawaiians occurred a year later, this time at Kealakekua on the Big Island. As fate would have it, his arrival coincided with the Hawaiians' annual *makahiki* celebration, a four-month festival honoring Lono, the god of peace, agriculture, and fertility. (Today, this event is echoed in the statewide Aloha Festivals.) Historians believe the Hawaiians, seeing these strange vessels heading for shore, thought it was Lono himself returning to the island. Cook and his men were treated to the greatest welcome in Hawaii's history: Hawaiians greeted the ships by the thousands. Cook wrote: "I have nowhere in this sea seen such a number of people assembled in one place; besides those in the canoes, all the shore of the bay was covered with people, and hundreds were swimming about the ship like shoals of fish."

After the *makahiki* ended and Lono-like Cook began to act more human, however, the Hawaiians were no longer quite so hospitable. A scuffle broke out and more than 200 warriors attacked Cook's landing party. Five British marines were killed, including Cook himself. His remains were buried in the deep blue water of Kealakekua Bay.

THE KAMEHAMEHA DYNASTY

ONE BIG ISLAND WARRIOR who took great interest in the foreigners was Kamehameha I. He had been wounded by a gun during the fight, and he realized that any chief who possessed such powerful weapons would have a decided advantage during battles.

Kamehameha set out to conquer all the Hawaiian Islands and bring them under his rule. He secured Maui and Lanai in 1790, then conquered Maui again after losing it for a short time. He had his chief rival on the Big Island killed to claim sole leadership over the island. Then he conquered Molokai and Oahu, but two attempts to invade Kauai failed. In 1810 Kauai's chief peacefully surrendered his island (and the neighboring island of Niihau) to his persistent rival. The entire Hawaiian kingdom was finally unified under one ruler: King Kamehameha I.

Under Kamehameha's reign, trade with Europeans increased. Foreigners particularly valued Hawaii's sandalwood, and the king allowed the exportation of the precious wood to China until the forests were cut to the ground and the supply exhausted.

Kamehameha succumbed to a lengthy illness in 1819 in the area now known as Kailua-Kona on the Big Island. His bones were hidden at a secret location "known only to the moon and the stars," believed to be somewhere on the Kona Coast. Historians estimate he was in his early 60s when he died.

His son and successor, Liholiho (Kamehameha II), had a short but eventful reign. Kaahumanu, the favorite of Kamehameha's numerous wives, made herself the joint ruler, or queen regent, of the Hawaiian kingdom and almost immediately abolished the despised *kapu* system of religious prohibitions. She did so by persuading Liholiho to sit down with her at a feast (it was *kapu*, or forbidden, for men and women to eat together). Seeing that the gods did not punish the guilty parties, Hawaiians' faith in their system crumbled. Kaahumanu and Liholiho declared that all idols and temples be destroyed.

Without their places of worship, the Hawaiians experienced a gaping spiritual vacuum. They were ripe for conversion when fate intervened. In 1820, 14 American missionaries from New England arrived aboard the brig *Thaddeus*. They preached in Honolulu and in Kona for what was supposed to be a one-year trial period. They never left, marrying Hawaiian royals and gaining land and power.

Liholiho and his queen, Kamamalu, died of the measles in 1924 in London, where they had journeyed in hopes of meeting King George IV. Liholiho's successor was his younger brother, Kauikeaouli (Kamehameha III). Kaahumanu, meanwhile, embraced Christianity and announced a new system of laws based on the missionaries' teachings.

The missionaries' impact on Hawaii overwhelmed the old culture. They built churches and schools throughout the Islands and condemned the people for their manner of dress. Hula, regarded by the missionaries as lewd, was banned. Christianity became the new religion in Hawaii. The chiefs were converted first, and the commoners followed suit.

Kamehameha III took control of the kingdom in 1825. By then the whaling industry had replaced the exhausted sandalwood trade. From the mid-1820s through the 1850s, when whale blubber was replaced by oil as a source for light, the whaling industry was the kingdom's economic savior, and Lahaina became one of the most vital ports in the Pacific.

The king's 29-year reign was marked by several landmark events. The first came in 1843, when the Hawaiian kingdom fell to British control for a brief time. More significantly, in 1848 Kauikeaouli issued The Great Mahele, which divided Hawaii's lands among the monarchy, government, and common people. For the first time, the working class could own land. Just two years later, foreigners were also allowed to own land, and 40 years after the Great Mahele was decreed, two-thirds of all government lands belonged to foreigners.

By this time, the introduction of foreign diseases, including syphilis and smallpox, to the Hawaiians who had no immunity was taking a terrible toll. At the end of Kamehameha III's reign, the Hawaiian population had dropped to 70,000.

Sugar was fast emerging as the new lifeblood of the Islands' economy, and Kauikeaouli knew he had to find more laborers to work in the plantations. He turned to contract workers from other countries— the Chinese first, in 1852, when 293 laborers began working on the plantations for $3 a month. Then came the Japanese, Portuguese, Filipinos, Koreans, Puerto Ricans, Okinawans, Germans, Russians, and Spaniards. By the turn of the century, Polynesians no longer made up the majority of Hawaii's population.

Kauikeaouli died in 1854, and his nephew Alexander Liholiho ascended the throne as Kamehameha IV. He reigned for eight years before dying of an asthmatic attack at 29. His brother, Lot (Kamehameha V), served as king from 1863 to 1872, and upon his death, William Lunalilo was elected his successor. Lot's cousin, the Princess Bernice Pauahi, had been next in line to take the throne but adamantly refused. Lunalilo's reign was short-lived, however—he died after only a year as king.

THE "MERRIE MONARCH"

DAVID KALAKAUA WAS ELECTED to succeed Lunalilo, and his tenure as Hawaii's king proved to be as colorful as the man himself. Known as the Merrie Monarch because of his passion for Hawaiian music and dance, Kalakaua began to restore traditional culture. He commissioned construction of Iolani Palace, an extravagant masterpiece. With a fondness for the good life, he took a trip around the world, hosted gala balls, and bet on local horse races.

Kalakaua was the first reigning king to visit Washington, D.C., to meet with the president, Ulysses S. Grant, and Congress. The *New York Herald* reported, "[Kalakaua] is no common king, but one to whom we can give our allegiance with a clean conscience, for we believe him to be a good man who has the happiness of his nation at heart." Kalakaua returned home with a desirable reciprocity treaty giving Hawaii "favored nation" status and eliminating tariffs on sugar. While recognizing the benefits of a strong relationship with the United States, Kalakaua fought to maintain Hawaii's independence. The stronger the sugar industry grew, however, the more power shifted from the king to influential American businessmen. In 1887, an armed insurrection by this foreign political group forced Kalakaua to accept a new constitution that severely diminished his authority. The king's remaining years weren't happy ones, as he was relegated to a figurehead role in government. His health failing, he sought treatment in California in 1891. He died that year in San Francisco's Palace Hotel.

END OF THE MONARCHY

KALAKAUA'S SUCCESSOR, his sister Liliuokalani, was determined to restore the Hawaiian monarchy to power. But the queen was severely outmatched. In January 1893, pro-annexation forces struck. John B. Stevens, the United States minister in Hawaii, ordered American Marines from the visiting USS *Boston* to occupy Honolulu. It was a daring move that was not authorized by Washington, but it worked: The next day, a new government led by Sanford B. Dole was in place. Liliuokalani was forced to abdicate her throne.

President Grover Cleveland was dismayed by the action, calling it "an act of war against a peaceful nation." His attempts at reinstating Liliuokalani as Hawaii's ruler, however, were resisted by Congress. In 1894, the new government, the Republic of Hawaii, named Dole as its first president.

In January 1895, a group of royalists led by Robert Wilcox attempted a coup. The battle lasted for two weeks, with skirmishes erupting at Diamond Head Crater and at Manoa Valley, Punchbowl, and other sites on Oahu. Ultimately, the revolt failed, and the government arrested the royalists and the queen, charging them with treason. She was imprisoned at Iolani Palace—her own home—for nearly a year.

In 1898, members of the republic got what they had wanted all along: Hawaii was annexed to the United States. Two years later, it became a United States territory.

WORLD WAR II AND STATEHOOD

THE NEXT FOUR DECADES brought the birth of Hawaii's tourist industry, as well as the sweet days of pineapple and sugar, the backbone of the Islands' economic system. Then came December 7, 1941, when Japanese warplanes bombed Pearl Harbor. The bombs sunk the USS *Arizona* and sent 1,200 sailors aboard the 608-foot battleship to a watery grave. The air raid on Hawaii brought America to war with the battle cry: "Remember Pearl Harbor!"

Islands residents, devastated by the attack, enlisted and did what they could at home to support the U.S. war effort. In Waikiki, hotels were closed to visitors, then reopened to accommodate servicemen. The famed "Pink Palace," the Royal Hawaiian Hotel, was turned into an R&R center for military officers on leave. Barbed wire was strung all along the beach.

In the years following the war, Hawaii pursued statehood and finally won it on August 21, 1959. *The Honolulu Advertiser* reported, "A phone call from Governor Quinn in Washington today is expected to set off the biggest wingding in Island history to celebrate Statehood Day . . . the 52 air-raid sirens on Oahu will start screaming out the news . . . . Every church bell in town will begin pealing. Every ship in harbor will blow her whistle. Most folks will do a little shouting on their own, and, of course, there's nothing to stop you from hula-ing in the streets if you want to." And they did. President Dwight D. Eisenhower made it official, signing the proclamation welcoming Hawaii as the 50th state in the union.

Not all Hawaiians favored statehood, but they were too few to stand in the way of history, and a once-proud Polynesian nation became an American state.

HAWAII'S DIVERSE POPULATION

ONE OF THE OUTSTANDING FEATURES of Hawaii is the diversity of its people. In the 50th state, no single ethnic group represents a majority of the population, although, taken together, Asians and part-Asians make up an estimated 55%, the largest proportion of any state, says the U.S. Census Bureau. Native Hawaiians, Pacific Islanders, and part-Hawaiians or Pacific Islanders compose 21% of the state's total population. Ironically, of the 1 million Americans who claim Hawaiian and Pacific Island heritage, only about a quarter (269,000) live in Hawaii, according to the U.S. Census Bureau. The racial breakdown is as follows (U.S. Census Bureau 2008 estimates):

Asian (Japanese, Chinese, Filipino, Korean, Southeast Asians) 39.3%

Caucasian 24.9%

Mixed race (about half are part Hawaiian) 18.3%

Hawaiian and Pacific Islanders 9.1%

Hispanics 8.7%

African American 3.1%

Other .6%

Each ethnic group has made its mark on Hawaiian culture, contributing its foods, arts, music, customs, and political clout to Hawaii's melting-pot community. Many cultural groups hold annual festivals in Honolulu to celebrate their heritage—a great chance to sample the food, music, dance, national dress, and pride of the culture at hand. Several cultures share a passionate affinity for fireworks, which are more abundant in Hawaii than anywhere else in the country. Fireworks are big for western New Year, Chinese New Year, Japanese New Year, Fourth of July, and, for good measure, every Friday night at the Hilton Hawaiian Village in Waikiki.

The Chinese were the Islands' first immigrants. Nearly 300 workers from southeastern China came to the Islands in 1852 after signing five-year contracts to work the sugar plantations for food, clothing, shelter, and a salary of $3 per month. Most of the Chinese lived near Honolulu Harbor on Oahu and Lahaina on Maui. It was in Honolulu where Dr. Sun Yat-sen, regarded as the father of modern China, founded the Hsing Chung Hui, a revolutionary group instrumental in China's movement against foreign powers. The Chinese influence on the local community is visible today in the distinctively Hawaiian-style Chinese New Year celebrations, Chinese cuisine and arts, Chinese heritage of prominent citizens, and a little Chinese blood in many local residents.

The first Japanese immigrants arrived in 1868 to work on the plantations. Although the conditions were often miserable, more Japanese made their way to what they referred to as Tenjiku, or "heavenly place." By the beginning of the 20th century, more than 60,000 Japanese laborers and their families lived in Hawaii. Like all immigrants, Japanese faced racial prejudices, but far more so after Japan's attack on Pearl Harbor. Many Japanese Americans were taken away to internment camps on the mainland, and many more lost their family businesses, even though not a single case of Japanese American treason or sabotage was ever documented. But they rebounded strongly in Hawaii after the war, gained prominence in politics and education, and integrated Japanese customs and design into everyday life. Today, Japanese Americans are a major presence in Hawaii, and most residents embrace at least some degree of Japanese custom, including removing shoes before entering a home. Sushi, sashimi, mochi, and miso soup are served on the Hawaiian table.

In 1903, the first Koreans arrived to work on the plantations. Ambitious and hardworking, Koreans today have the highest education and income level per capita of any ethnic group on the Islands. Korean cuisine is extremely popular among Hawaiian residents, and you'll find Korean restaurants in every town. Try *kal-bi* (marinated beef) with rice and spicy *kimchi* (pickled vegetables).

A group of 15 Filipino laborers began working on Islands plantations in 1906; by midcentury, that number had swelled to 125,000. Every summer, the Filipino Fiesta festivals, held throughout the state, celebrate the colorful traditions and customs of the Filipino culture. Dishes such as chicken *adobo* and *lumpia* are favorites on local menus.

Samoans are among the newer ethnic groups in Hawaii, arriving from American Samoa shortly after the end of World War I. Most settled in the Mormon community in Laie on Oahu. Their many contributions to the Islands include the celebrated fire-knife dance that highlights most Polynesian luau. Local Samoans have also made their mark in the world of football: In the 1990s, Jesse Sapolu (San Francisco 49ers), Mark Tuinei (Dallas Cowboys), and Maa Tanuvasa (Denver Broncos) all played significant roles in helping their teams win Super Bowl championships.

In multicultural Hawaii, intermarriage is the norm rather than the exception, and a dizzying number of ethnic groups coexist at both the top and bottom of the economic scale. This tends to even things out. The ability to get along, born of necessity in plantation villages and perfected in the modern mix, may be Hawaii's most valuable contribution, far more lasting than a suntan and an aloha shirt.

In order to get along, plantation people from around the world had to communicate, so they developed Hawaiian pidgin—a true creole language according to many scholars, one that borrows words and grammar from several languages. Pidgin endures today, despite efforts of many inside and outside the education system to stamp it out, at least in school. Unofficially, it is lovingly cultivated as a kind of jive talk among kids, families, friends, and lovers. You'll see graffiti in pidgin. It's also still useful, since myriad ethnic immigrants continue to arrive. (See page 180 for a quick lesson in pidgin basics.)

Most people are proud of their diversity, but ethnic prejudices and stereotypes still exist. Caucasians can be the targets of slurs and jokes, along with everybody else. The word *haole* (foreigner) is widely used to refer to Caucasians, usually in a descriptive way. When using words to describe Islanders, beware of a linguistic minefield. Don't call us "Hawaiians" unless you mean native Hawaiians, not just residents of the Islands. Don't call anyone a "native" unless you're wearing your pith helmet, although "native Hawaiian" is still acceptable to distinguish the cultural group. "Local" is a somewhat more loaded word in Hawaii than elsewhere, applying to the multicultural people with broader antecedents who were born here. It's more neutral when it means the opposite of "just visiting." *Kamaaina* (child of the land, as described earlier) and *malahini* (newcomer) refer to length of stay rather than race or culture. Now you see why the most popular pidgin phrase is *da kine* (as in "the kind"), a handy catchall to refer to anything you can't or don't want to name specifically.

LOCAL CUSTOMS
and PROTOCOL

- When going to the *lua* (restroom) make sure you know the difference between *kane* (man) and *wahine* (woman), since many restrooms are only identified in Hawaiian.
- Close your middle three fingers of either hand while keeping your thumb and pinkie finger fully extended. Shake your hand a few times in the air. That's the *shaka* sign, a hand gesture expressing acknowledgment, goodwill, or appreciation. It's like *mahalo* (thank you).
- Every Friday is Aloha Friday, when residents wear aloha shirts and *muumuu* in celebration of Islands culture and lifestyle. Aloha wear is so in these days that it is worn any day. The first aloha shirt was sold in the mid-1930s in Honolulu. Boys during the time had been wearing similar shirts made from Japanese prints, and the idea caught on. The origin of the first muumuu traces to missionary days when the missionary wives sewed "Mother Hubbard" nightgowns to clothe the half-dressed Hawaiian women.
- If you get lucky and are invited to a *kamaaina* home, remember that most follow the custom of removing shoes before entering the house. The forest of shoes in front of the door is your reminder.
- Local people of all kinds profess a deep reverence for the *aina* (land), although all that litter along Hawaii's roads can't be from visitors alone. This is a beautiful place that deserves respect. Please don't trash it.

PART TWO

PLANNING YOUR VISIT

BEST TIME *to* GO

IT'S HARD TO THINK OF A BAD TIME to go to Hawaii, but some times are better than others, depending not so much on the weather as on your own plans. Seasonal changes are subtle, and the tourism industry is largely a year-round operation.

Hawaii has winter of a sort, when the daily highs lurk down around 80°F, sometimes even lower. It's the season of higher hotel and condo rates, when the weather where you live is more likely to be awful and more snowbirds flock to the tropics to escape. It's also the time to see migrating humpback whales, big surf, major golf events, squalls rolling across the horizon, and (perhaps) snow at nearly 14,000 feet atop Mauna Kea and occasionally down at 10,000 feet atop Haleakala. It's the rainier, slightly cooler, often less breezy time between late November and late March when bright amaryllis lilies spring up wild by the roadsides, the hills are particularly green, and at dusk you might need a windbreaker. Room rates peak from mid-December through March. In our first year on Oahu, we were anxious to see what winter would bring. One late afternoon everyone got cold, rummaged around for a sweatshirt, and checked the thermometer: 74°F. Everything's relative.

unofficial **TIP**
If you're on a budget, visit between September and Christmas or from mid-March to mid-June (excluding Easter), when rates dip.

The land of perpetual good weather has a summer, too. It starts in June, the time of ripe mangoes, calmer seas on north shores, bigger surf on south shores, hurricanes and tropical storms marching west across the Pacific, somewhat warmer and drier weather, and an explosion of flowers (not that there weren't plenty in winter too). The Southern Cross and Perseid meteor showers appear in the skies in late summer. Summer is a busy time in Hawaii since school is out and families head for fun in the sun.

Spring in Hawaii has the added advantage, like autumn, of lower rates and lesser crowds. To see the world's finest hula dancers, come the week after Easter for the annual Merrie Monarch Festival in Hilo—if you are lucky enough to get tickets. If not, Hawaii television carries the colorful contests live.

If you just want to kick back under the tropical sun, watch the ads and the Internet and catch the next plane that suits your purse and schedule. The weather's not much of a deterrent any time of year.

GATHERING INFORMATION
before **YOU LEAVE**

KNOW WHERE YOU'RE GOING before you get there: Get a map. The best Hawaiian Islands maps are created by cartographer James A. Bier and published by the University of Hawaii Press. Each topographic map includes island highways, roads, and trails as well as large-scale inset maps of population centers. The maps include points of natural, cultural, and historic interest; parks and beaches; sea channels; peaks and ridges (with altitudes); and Hawaiian words spelled with all their accent marks. These maps are inexpensive, printed on heavy paper, and fit easily into a carry-on bag or backpack.

If your bookstore doesn't carry them, order directly from the Marketing Department, University of Hawaii Press, 2840 Kolowalu Street, Honolulu 96822. Contact the University of Hawaii Press at ☎ 808-956-8255 or visit **www.uhpress.hawaii.edu.** You can also request a free catalog of books about Hawaii and the Pacific.

If you plan to camp at national or state parks and other popular spots, you may have to compete long before you arrive for reservations. (See "Camping in the Wilds," page 311.)

SURF THE INTERNET

FOR CENTURIES HAWAIIANS were master chanters, orators, song-writers, and storytellers. In the 1800s, when missionaries put the sounds into letters and words and taught Hawaiians to read them, the literacy rate in Hawaii was higher than in any other part of the world. The overthrow of the Hawaiian monarchy in 1893 brought a ban on the Hawaiian language in public schools. Over the next century, the language was nearly extinguished.

Now mellifluous Hawaiian is making a comeback, with attention to proper pronunciation, spelling, and marking of its words. It is being resurrected in language courses and special language-immersion schools designed to teach young children in Hawaiian, on street signs, in the media, and on the Internet. *Oiwi: A Native Hawaiian Journal,* a contemporary online anthology, features the work of Hawaiian writers and artists. The Web site (**www.hawaii.edu/oiwi**) presents stories in both Hawaiian and English. Surf over to bilingual **www.olelo .hawaii.edu** to find the University of Hawaii Hilo's Kualono page, which contains links to Hawaiian-language dictionaries and books.

CHINATOWN, HONOLULU STYLE It's easy to solve the mysteries of Chinatown by visiting its home page at **www.chinatownhi.com.** Tour the historic 17-block district, visit open markets, pick up Alan Lau's herbal remedy for the common cold at Tak Wah Tong in the Chinese Cultural Center, and even read about the adventures of Charlie Chan.

VISIT MAUI The Maui Visitors Bureau home page (**www.visitmaui.com**) makes you want to go there now. It offers lots of solid information and useful links, including seven remote cameras with scenes of the island (one focuses on Hookipa windsurfers). Check out the surf report and daily temperatures, order a free vacation planner, book a B&B, and tour resorts.

"MIGHTY MO," WORLD WAR II DREADNOUGHT The battleship USS *Missouri,* upon whose deck Japan surrendered in Tokyo Bay to end World War II, is now anchored in Pearl Harbor next to the USS *Arizona* Memorial and also in cyberspace at **www.ussmissouri.com** (where you can take a virtual tour).

"Mighty Mo" was saved from mothballs and towed across the Pacific to Hawaii to commemorate peace. The relics are bookends to World War II—the attack on the *Arizona* during the surprise air raid on Pearl Harbor launched the American entry in the war; the surrender aboard the *Missouri* came 3 years, 9 months, and 25 days later.

SURF MOLOKAI For such an atavistic island, Molokai has a big Internet presence, with at least 50 home pages, including Monkeypod Records (**www.monkeypod.com**), which promotes local musicians. One notable site details the somber history of the Kalaupapa Peninsula, where victims of leprosy were once banished. Now it's a national historic park, reached by way of air, sea, or the island's most famous attraction, the Molokai Mule Ride (**www.muleride.com**).

VISITORS AND CONVENTION BUREAUS

SEVERAL HOTELIERS IN HAWAII formed a tourist-information bureau in the early 1900s to attract those who had previously only dreamed of visiting the Islands. Their earliest marketer went to San Francisco to foster those dreams and drew crowds with a stereo optical lecture. The boosters later hired Mark Twain to extol the virtues of a Hawaiian vacation, mailed out enticing photos and postcards, and sent Hawaiian entertainers on the road to deliver aloha in person, a practice that continues today as the next best thing to being here. Today, the Hawaii Visitors and Convention Bureau spends millions of dollars globally to promote Hawaii as a top travel destination. Part of that job is to disperse information on islands, activities, accommodations, restaurants, and a calendar of festivals, cultural celebrations, sporting events, and activities.

Hawaii's Visitors Bureaus

Hawaii Visitors and Convention Bureau

2270 Kalakaua Avenue, 8th Floor, Suite 801
Honolulu 96815
☎ 808-923-1811 or 800-GO-HAWAII (464-2924); **www.gohawaii.com**
Request a free copy of *The Islands of Aloha*, the bureau's vacation planner.

Oahu Visitors Bureau

733 Bishop Street, Suite 1520
Honolulu 96813
☎ 808-524-0722 or 877-525-OAHU (6248)
www.visit-oahu.com or link from **www.gohawaii.com**

Big Island Visitors Bureau (Hilo)

250 Keawe Street
Hilo 96720-2823
☎ 808-961-5797 or 800-648-2441
www.bigisland.org or link from **www.gohawaii.com**

Big Island Visitors Bureau (Kamuela)

65–1158 Mamalahoa Hwy, Suite 27B
Kamuela 96743
☎ 808-885-1655 or 800-648-2441
www.bigisland.org or link from **www.gohawaii.com**

Maui Visitors Bureau

1727 Wili Pa Loop
Wailuku 96793-1250
☎ 808-244-3530 or 800-525-MAUI (6284)
www.visitmaui.com or link from **www.gohawaii.com**
View *Maui*—a travel planner featuring the Maui County destinations of
Maui, Molokai, and Lanai—online, or call to request a free copy.

Kauai Visitors Bureau

4334 Rice Street, Suite 101
Lihue 96766-1801
☎ 808-245-3971 or 800-262-1400
www.kauaidiscovery.com or link from **www.gohawaii.com**

RECOMMENDED MAGAZINES

HAWAII IS FEATURED OFTEN in magazines like *Condé Nast Traveler*, *National Geographic Traveler*, and *Travel + Leisure*, as well as airline in-flight magazines. Only a few feature magazines devote full coverage to the Islands:

- *Hawaii Magazine,* ☎ 808-537-9500 or **www.hawaiimagazine.com**
- *Honolulu Magazine,* ☎ 808-537-9500 or **www.honolulumagazine.com**
- *Maui No Ka Oi Magazine,* ☎ 808-242-8331 or
  www.mauimagazine.net

Molokai Visitors Association

2 Kamoi Street, Suite 200
Kaunakakai 96748
☎ 808-553-3876 or 800-800-6367
www.molokai-hawaii.com or link from **www.gohawaii.com**

Lanai Visitors Bureau

431 Seventh Street, Suite A
Lanai City 96763
☎ 808-565-7600 or 800-947-4774
www.visitlanai.net or link from **www.gohawaii.com**

International Contacts

UNITED KINGDOM

Hawaii Tourism Europe

Colechurch House, 1 London Bridge Walk
London SE19EU, England
☎ 44-207-367-0900
hawaii-tourism.co.uk

AUSTRALIA

Hawaii Tourism Australia

Level 6, 117 York Street
Sydney, NSW 2000, Australia
☎ 61-2-9286-8951
hawaiitourism.com.au

NEW ZEALAND

Hawaii Tourism New Zealand

Level 7, Citibank Building
23 Customs Street East
Auckland, New Zealand
☎ 64-9977-2234
hawaiitourism.com.au

◼◼ PACKING WISELY

EVERYONE BRINGS TOO MANY of the wrong kinds of clothes to Hawaii. Californians, most of your wardrobe is too warm. East Coasters, think summer, year-round. For packing purposes, it's always summer here.

If you're planning to ride horses, bring covered footwear and jeans and hang onto your hat. If you're going camping, you can bring or rent gear, according to your preference and the percentage of your trip you plan to camp. A night or two? Rent. A month? You might prefer your own stuff. Hiking or running? Bring the right shoes.

What men need: Shorts, T-shirts and informal tops, favorite Hawaiian shirts, swim trunks, lightweight slacks, a light jacket or sweatshirt for going upcountry, and sandals, sports shoes, or loafers. Don't even bring a tie. If you're hanging out at stuffy fancy restaurants, bring a jacket or be forced to wear one of theirs for dinner.

What women need: sundresses, swimsuits, cover-ups, shorts, tops, a light sweater or jacket, sandals, and maybe a muumuu for the luau (it's best to buy one here). Lose the hose and heels and other banes of your wardrobe. Unless you're staying in butlered digs, minimize the high-maintenance wear of wrinkle-prone silk and linen. Many hotel rooms come equipped with an iron and a board, if you insist.

Tennis shoes and athletic socks turn into hot, sweaty foot sponges in the tropics and are heavy to pack. Local folks prefer to wear sandals or airy flip-flops, known as "slippers."

Unless you're heading for Mauna Kea's 13,976-foot summit, you won't need any apparel heavier than a sweatshirt.

If you pack wisely for Hawaii's climate, you can put all your lightweight clothes in one case and bring an empty one for all you'll probably buy.

GETTING *to* HAWAII

THE FLIGHT TO HONOLULU INTERNATIONAL AIRPORT is about 5 hours from the West Coast, 8 from Dallas, 9 from Atlanta, and 11 from New York. Most major U.S. and international airlines serve Hawaii, along with charters from other countries. Hawaii-based Hawaiian Airlines connects the Islands with various western cities, including Las Vegas (Hawaii residents' favorite destination).

Honolulu International Airport (HNL) on Oahu is one of the nation's busiest airports, with service by more than 40 airlines handling more than 20 million passengers a year—many of them traveling

DOMESTIC AIRLINES	
Air Canada	☎ 888-247-2262, **www.aircanada.com**
Alaska Airlines	☎ 800-252-7522, **www.alaskaair.com**
American Airlines	☎ 800-433-7300, **www.aa.com**
Continental Airlines	☎ 800-523-3273, **www.continental.com**
Delta Airlines	☎ 800-221-1212, **www.delta.com**
Hawaiian Airlines	☎ 800-367-5320, **www.hawaiianair.com**
United Airlines	☎ 800-864-8331, **www.united.com**
US Airways	☎ 800-428-4322, **www.usairways.com**

to and from Asian, European, and Pacific destinations. The airport has three terminals: main terminal for worldwide flights, interisland terminal for in-state flights, and commuter terminal for small-craft flights to smaller island airports.

Although the majority of Hawaii-bound flights land in Honolulu, some fly direct to Neighbor Islands airports, including international service from Japan and Canada to Kona International Airport at Keahole (KOA) on the Big Island.

Call the toll-free numbers or contact Web sites on the previous chart for updated information.

TRAVELER ADVISORY

PUBLIC AIRPORTS ON THE NEIGHBOR ISLANDS include Kona International Airport at Keahole (KOA) in Kona and Hilo International Airport in Hilo (ITO) on the Big Island; Kahului Airport (OGG), Hana Airport (HNM), and Kapalua Airport (JHM) on Maui; Lihue Airport (LIH) on Kauai; Molokai (MKK) Airport on Molokai; and Lanai Airport (LNY) on Lanai. You can't fly directly to all of these, but all are used by island-hoppers (see "Interisland Flights," page 81).

Booking your vacation through a travel agent may save you time and money, as the agent can plow through myriad fares and rates to find you the best airfares, lodgings, and car rentals, and take advantage of specials offered only to agents.

If you make the arrangements on your own, here are some tips for finding a good deal on airfares:

- To get the lowest possible fare, be flexible in your travel plans. The best deals are usually limited to travel on certain days of the week or hours of the day. Ask the reservations agent how you might save money by leaving a day earlier or later or by taking a different flight. Check carefully into fare restrictions and penalties if you change plans after purchase. Check various travel-related sites on the Internet. You can hold your telephone reservation on some airlines for a day or so before you commit to the ticket. In some cases you may have to call to cancel. In others you have to call to activate the reservation.

- If your travel itinerary falls into a busy flight period, book early. Flights during holidays may sell out months ahead of time.

- Many discount fares are nonrefundable and nontransferable. If you want to change your discounted booking, you will pay more if that fare is not available on the new flight.

HOW TO AVOID JET LAG

START TO COMBAT JET LAG before you depart. Jet lag, known in scientific terms as circadian desynchronization, occurs after flying across several time zones. It is not a state of mind; it is a condition with physical and mental ramifications, lasting anywhere from a few hours to a few days. You feel sleepy, disoriented, and a little out of sync.

Several books offer remedies to ease jet lag. One of the best is *Jet Smarter* by Diana Fairechild, a veteran former flight attendant whose 21 years of experience took her often to and from the Hawaiian Islands.

Here are some practical tips:

- Avoid coffee for a day or two before and after your flight, and drink water rather than coffee, sodas, or alcohol on the plane. Alcohol can sharply intensify jet lag. Drink lots of water to prevent dehydration—an 8-ounce glass for each hour of flight, according to our doctor.
- Remove your shoes during flight to improve circulation. Flex your feet, ankles, and legs often. If possible, stroll through the cabin and stand for a while.
- Adjust your watch to Hawaii Standard Time (see the following section) as soon as you board the plane. This mentally prepares you as you adjust to Hawaiian time. Think of the time it is where you're going, not where you've been. On the ground, get acclimated to local time as soon as possible. Stay up until bedtime in the Islands if you can.
- Take a long soak in a bathtub or a warm pool or ocean. Not only will it replenish moisture lost during your flight, it will also relax your nervous system. Don't attempt too much on the day or night of your arrival.
- Try to spend some time outside while it's sunny, as bright daylight helps the body adjust its internal clock. Take care, however, to avoid overexposure; a sunburn is a miserable way to start your vacation.

WHAT TIME IS IT IN HAWAII?

ON STANDARD TIME, when it's noon in San Francisco, it's 10 a.m. in Honolulu. Hawaii is two hours behind the West Coast and five hours behind the East Coast. Hawaii doesn't change to daylight saving time, so when it's daylight saving time on the mainland, then Hawaii is three hours behind the West Coast and six hours behind the East Coast.

With an average of 12 hours of sunshine daily, year-round, Hawaii doesn't need to save daylight. Hawaii's longest day, June 21, is 13 hours and 26 minutes long. Its shortest day, December 21, is 10 hours and 50 minutes. Hawaii's time zone is known as Hawaii Standard Time, or HST.

WHAT NOT TO BRING

- The U.S. Department of Agriculture bans many animals and plants from Hawaii.
- Importation of unchecked flora and fauna can have a negative impact on Hawaii's fragile ecosystem. The U.S. Department of Agriculture also restricts shipping of most fruit, plants, and other items from Hawaii to the mainland to prevent the spread of fruit flies and other insects.

For inquiries, contact the Hawaii Department of Agriculture, Plant Quarantine Branch at ☎ 808-832-0566 (**www.hawaii.gov/hdoa**) or Animal Quarantine Branch at ☎ 808-483-7151.

INTERISLAND FLIGHTS

THE ISLANDS ARE LINKED by frequent, efficient jet service all day from sunrise into evening by Honolulu-based Hawaiian Airlines, which uses the interisland terminal at Honolulu Airport. *go!* Airline operates 50-passenger corporate-style jets from the Honolulu commuter terminal next door. *go!* and Hawaiian also serve Kona and Hilo on the Big Island; Kahului, Maui; Lihue, Kauai; and Molokai and Lanai. *go!* flies to Kapalua, Maui, and the other Neighbor Island airports. Fierce competition often prompts frequent fare specials, so it pays to shop the Internet sites.

Island Air flies smaller twin-engine planes to smaller airports, including Kapalua and Hana on Maui and Kalaupapa on Molokai.

Hawaiian has a small first-class seating area, but the flights only take half an hour or so, and the chief advantage, besides bigger seats and personal service, is that you can board and deplane first.

Check with the airlines for their carry-on baggage rules. Boogie boards, surfboards, full coolers, skateboards, and strollers are not allowed in the cabin.

CAR RENTALS

ONCE YOU'VE LANDED ON AN ISLAND, renting a car provides the greatest flexibility and mobility in Hawaii. On Oahu, a car can also put you right in the middle of the biggest traffic jam in the Pacific.

It's fun to cruise Hawaii in a shiny convertible, but it's no fun to sit sweating in gridlock while heading back from the beach. Watch your timing to avoid rush-hour traffic, which runs early in the Islands, a legacy from plantation

unofficial **TIP**
Rush-hour traffic runs until 8:30 a.m. on weekday mornings and 4 to 6 p.m. in the afternoon.

HAWAII'S AIRLINES

Hawaiian Airlines

TOLL FREE: ☎ 800-367-5320
Oahu: ☎ 808-838-1555
Maui: ☎ 808-871-6132
Big Island: ☎ 808-326-5615
Kauai: ☎ 808-245-1813
Molokai: ☎ 808-553-3644
Lanai: ☎ 808-565-7281
www.hawaiianair.com

go! **Airline**

☎ 888-I-FLY-GO2 or 888-435-9462;
www.iflygo.com

Island Air

TOLL FREE: ☎ 800-652-6541
Oahu: ☎ 808-484-2222
www.islandair.com

Pacific Wings

TOLL FREE: ☎ 888-575-4546
Maui: ☎ 808-873-0877
www.pacificwings.com

Car-rental Agencies

ALAMO RENT A CAR
  Toll free: ☎ 877-222-9075
  www.alamo.com
  OAHU
  Honolulu International Airport:
    ☎ 808-833-4585
  Ilikai Waikiki:
    ☎ 808-947-6112

  MAUI
  Kahului Airport: ☎ 808-872-1470
  Kaanapali Transportation Center:
    ☎ 808-661-7181

  BIG ISLAND
  Keahole-Kona International Airport:
    ☎ 808-329-8896
  Hilo International Airport:
    ☎ 808-961-3343

  KAUAI
  Lihue Airport: ☎ 808-246-0645

AVIS RENT A CAR
  Toll free: ☎ 800-331-1212
  www.avis.com
  OAHU
  Honolulu International Airport:
    ☎ 808-834-5536
  MAUI
  Kahului Airport: ☎ 808-871-7575
  Kaanapali: ☎ 808-661-4588
  Kihei: ☎ 808-874-4077
  BIG ISLAND
  Keahole-Kona International Airport:
    ☎ 808-327-3000
  Hilo International Airport:
    ☎ 808-935-1298

  KAUAI
  Lihue Airport: ☎ 808-245-7995
  Princeville Airport:
    ☎ 808-826-9773
  Grand Hyatt Kauai:
    ☎ 808-742-1627

BUDGET RENT A CAR
  Toll free: ☎ 800-527-0700
  www.budget.com
  OAHU
  Honolulu International Airport:
    ☎ 808-836-1700
  Hyatt Regency Waikiki:
    ☎ 808-921-5808

  MAUI
  Kahului Airport: ☎ 808-871-8811
  Kaanapali: ☎ 808-661-8721

  BIG ISLAND
  Keahole-Kona International Airport:
    ☎ 808-329-8511
  Hilo International Airport:
    ☎ 808-935-6878

  KAUAI
  Lihue Airport:
    ☎ 808-245-9031

DOLLAR RENT A CAR
  Toll free: ☎ 800-800-3665
  www.dollarcar.com
  OAHU
  Honolulu International Airport:
    ☎ 866-434-2226
  Dispatch Office:
    ☎ 808-952-4264

unofficial **TIP**
Do not leave valuables in your car, especially at Pali Lookout or the South Shore lookouts, such as the Blow Hole.

days. Plan to leave later than 8:30 a.m. on weekday mornings and avoid the highways in the late afternoons, roughly from 4 to 6 p.m. Listen to the radio for updates on particular problems. Summer driving is much easier because school's out.

DOLLAR RENT A CAR (*continued*)

MAUI
Kahului Airport: ☎ 866-434-2226
Kaanapali Transportation Center:
☎ 808-667-2651

BIG ISLAND
Keahole-Kona International
Airport: ☎ 866-434-2226

KAUAI
Lihue Airport: ☎ 866-434-2226

LANAI
Lanai Airport: ☎ 808-565-7227

HARPER CAR AND TRUCK RENTALS
Toll free: ☎ 800-852-9993
www.harpershawaii.com
BIG ISLAND
☎ 808-969-1478

HERTZ RENT A CAR
Toll free: ☎ 800-654-3131
www.hertz.com
OAHU
Honolulu International Airport:
☎ 808-529-6800
Hyatt Regency Waikiki:
☎ 808-971-3535
Waikiki Beach Marriott:
☎ 808-924-1681

MAUI
Kahului Airport: ☎ 808-893-5200
Wailea Beach Marriott Resort:
☎ 808-891-1383
Hyatt Regency Maui:
☎ 808-661-4368

BIG ISLAND
Keahole-Kona International Airport:
☎ 808-329-3566
Hilo International Airport:
☎ 808-935-2898

KAUAI
Lihue Airport: ☎ 808-245-3356

NATIONAL CAR RENTAL
Toll free: ☎ 877-222-9058
www.nationalcar.com
OAHU
Honolulu International. Airport:
☎ 808-834-6350
Kahala Resort: ☎ 808-733-2309

MAUI
Kahului Airport: ☎ 808-871-8851
Kaanapali Transportation
Center: ☎ 808-667-9737

BIG ISLAND
Keahole-Kona International Airport:
☎ 808-329-1674
Hilo International Airport:
☎ 808-935-0891

KAUAI
Lihue Airport:
☎ 808-245-5636

Carry as little as possible in your rental car that might appeal to thieves. We usually leave our car empty and open; there's no sense in paying for a broken window. Whatever you do, don't leave your valuables in the car while you dash out to view the Windward side from the Pali Lookout or the Blow Hole on the South Shore. These are favorite rip-off sites.

You can get by without a car on Oahu, which has a highly praised municipal bus system (TheBus), one of the best in the United States, as well as taxis, private transit, and (often) free shuttle vans. But it is a lot easier to explore the Windward Coast and North Shore and enjoy museums, botanical gardens, adventure areas, and vacant beaches with a car. One solution is to rent a car just for a day or two.

On Maui, Hawaii, Kauai, and Molokai, where beaches and natural attractions are all over the Islands, renting a car is a must unless you plan to hole up at your resort and commute on foot or by resort shuttle between your room and the beach or golf course.

On Lanai, a resort shuttle will take you to most sites. But one of Lanai's more popular activities is exploring the back roads in a rented four-wheel-drive vehicle, allowing you to discover backcountry and Island history on your own.

Car rentals are available on all islands. Rental-car rates are lower in Hawaii than in the rest of the nation as a whole. Shop for rates by telephone or on the Internet, if making your own arrangements. Most major car-rental firms offer special rates frequently and include car rentals in money-saving travel packages with airfare and accommodations. Check with your travel agent or call the car-rental agencies for details before you go.

When making interisland flight reservations, ask the airlines for any special deals on rental cars. They often partner with car agencies in promotional fly-and-drive packages. You may get a break of 5 to 15% for association memberships, credit cards, frequent-flier clubs, and coupons. Agency Internet sites (listed on pages 82–83) can offer up to 20% off regular rates.

All the major car-rental agencies are located at or near the airports, and many have reservations desks at various resorts or stores. On Maui, besides Kahului Airport and the hotels, many car-rental agencies operate at the Kaanapali Transportation Center (30-1 Halawai Drive), a five-minute ride from the Kapalua Airport in West Maui (linked by free shuttle service).

unofficial **TIP**
Transactions taking place at an airport, including car rentals, are subject to an additional concession fee of up to 10%.

As with car rentals in any destination, you can rent a car after you arrive, presuming one is available. Courtesy phones and free shuttles in airport terminals connect you to nearby car-rental offices.

However, you'd do better to reserve a car with the national agency before you go, usually a week or more ahead for the best rate. Rental rates are based on the number of cars available, so they constantly fluctuate. Because you don't have to pay up front, you can always recheck rates.

Expect to see that rental fee jump by the time you do pay. Car rentals on all islands are subject to a $3-per-day state surcharge and a nominal vehicle license tax (up to 60 cents per day). In addition, transactions that take place at an airport are subject to an airport concession fee of 11.11% of the rental fee per day on Oahu and 8.1% on the Neighbor Islands. Car rentals will also be charged sales tax of 4.712% on Oahu and 4.166% elsewhere in the state.

Optional insurance rates vary by car-rental agency. It's a hard-sell situation when you're picking up the car, but remember that your own car insurance and often your major credit card provide insurance coverage when you're driving rental cars. Check before you leave.

Gas prices will be higher in Hawaii than at almost any mainland location, particularly the East Coast. The Islands are small enough, though, that you seldom burn up a whole tank.

About island driving: Hawaii (even Oahu) doesn't have a lot of roads. Most roads are two lanes, and speed limits are lower than in other states. Oahu has three short "interstate" highways that absorb much of the traffic. Mainland

unofficial **TIP**
Leave your aggressive driving habits at home. Hawaii is a no-fault-insurance state.

drivers will find the entry and exit setups otherworldly. But island driving manners are such that people will let you in if you landed in the wrong lane. Just take it slow, signal, look, smile a lot, and wave your thanks.

People talk of driving "around the island," but you can't really do that around the entire coastline of any of the islands. You cannot circle the Big Island as motorists once could do, because Kilauea Volcano interrupted Chain of Craters Road with an impassable lava flow.

SO MANY ISLANDS, SO LITTLE TIME

BECAUSE HAWAII HAS SIX MAJOR ISLANDS to see, two weeks wouldn't be enough time to do it all. This keeps visitors coming back again and again to revisit favorite sites and sample new ones.

We suggest that newcomers spend the first two or three days in Waikiki or elsewhere on Oahu, slowing down enough to enjoy the pace of the Islands. But that's just a suggestion. We have a friend who comes to Waikiki at least once a year and never goes anywhere else. Other visitors shun Waikiki completely.

unofficial **TIP**
Newcomers will enjoy spending the first two or three days in Waikiki or elsewhere on Oahu.

All the ingredients of a grand tropical holiday can be found on Oahu—sunny days, warm water, great beaches, stunning scenery, a wide range of accommodations (mostly hotels, from budget to upscale), museums and cultural events, stimulating atmosphere, cuisines of many cultures, excellent shopping, and great nightlife. If you want quiet, check into a B&B or vacation rental outside of Waikiki, or pick another island and spend the rest of your time there.

Maui is the next most popular choice after Oahu, followed by the Big Island of Hawaii, Kauai, Lanai, and Molokai.

TO HOP OR NOT TO HOP?

FIRST-TIME VISITORS may have ambitions of island-hopping from one end of the Hawaiian chain to the other. One word of advice: Don't. You may think you can see them all in a single week—after all, you can *see* most of them in 20 minutes at 20,000 feet on the way in. But clearly, that's not enough. This is too fine a place to gloss over, so most people spend their trips on one or two islands and return later to see more. Although the interisland flights are brief, airport transfers and security are time consuming. Below are some factors to consider before island-hopping:

unofficial **TIP**
Plan to spend time on one or two islands on each trip to Hawaii rather than trying to stay on all six on one trip.

- Most Island flights are to and from Honolulu. You will likely have to go through Honolulu to fly between the islands. Each leg of a flight is an additional cost.
- Expect to spend several hours commuting from place to place—you'll have to pack, check out, get to the airport, return your rental car if you have one or go early in a transit vehicle, check in and go through security, wait for the plane, board and fly, deplane, get your luggage, get another rental car, drive to another hotel, register, and unpack. Phew!
- Many hotels offer a free night's stay when you book four to six consecutive nights.

With costs (in money and time) in mind, however, you can make a day trip to another island for an activity, such as a round of golf or a look at the volcano, and return to your hotel.

The quickest way to see all islands is a scenic flight on a twin-engine airplane. Several companies offer low-altitude, half-day, and full-day scenic air tours over the main islands. One is Pacific Wings: call ☎ 808-873-0877 or e-mail info@pacificwings.com.

Passenger ferry service is available between Maui and Lanai (Expeditions, **www.go-lanai.com**) or Maui and Molokai (Lahaina Cruise Company, **www.mauiprincess.com**).

Cruise lines offer interisland voyages with port calls in Honolulu and on Maui, Kauai, and the Big Island of Hawaii. (See "Cruising Hawaii," page 203.)

HAWAII FROM ABOVE

HAWAII IS FILLED WITH REMOTE, roadless wilderness that remains rugged and largely hidden. How to see it? Perhaps a helicopter flight that reveals glorious scenery and also lands for a close-up view of a beautiful spot or another activity.

- **Alexair** lifts off from busy Kahului Airport, Maui, up, up, and over Haleakala Crater with a descent back in time along the Hana Coast to old Hawaii, flight-seeing the Hana Rainforest and hovering at waterfalls before landing at a black-sand beach for a snack and respite.

- **Sunshine Helicopters** will show you the sights of Maui or the Big Island and combine your air tour with an adventure on the ground—such as a horseback ride on the remote Mendes Ranch, where the West Maui Mountains seem to fall like rumpled green velvet into the sea—or sub-sea level snorkel or submarine adventure off the Kona Coast. You can arrange a helicopter charter. If the agenda includes a proposal or other special occasion, they'll pack a picnic and iced flutes for your champagne.

- **Makani Kai Helicopters** reveals Oahu with tours ranging from a 15-minute peek to an hour-long indulgence in the otherwise inaccessible splendors of this island. If you want, the flight can be yours alone. Makani Kai will also charter a daytime flight with a landing in a secret scenic spot in the hinterlands.

- Float over all in Hawaii's only seaplane tour. **Island Seaplane Service** takes off from Keehi Lagoon near the Honolulu Airport for flight-seeing over Waikiki, the cityscape and scenic rural Windward Coast before returning over Pearl Harbor—an airy way to get a sense of this complex city and country island.

SUGGESTIONS *for* SPECIAL TRAVELERS

Singles

BEST ISLAND TO VISIT Oahu

OTHER RECOMMENDED ISLANDS Maui, Big Island

THINGS TO SEE AND DO On Oahu join the crowd on Waikiki Beach, catch a ride on an outrigger canoe, and have a beer and listen to live Hawaiian music at Duke's Waikiki Restaurant at the Outrigger Waikiki. Check out the *pau hana* (after-work) action at the open-air pubs of Aloha Tower Marketplace, shop at Ala Moana Shopping Center. Discover local food—an instant picnic of inexpensive plate lunches or *mana pua* (stuffed Chinese steamed buns, otherwise known as *char siu bao*) from downtown lunch wagons. Explore Hawaii's history at the Bishop Museum or Hawaii Maritime Center. Climb Diamond Head Crater. Boogie in Waikiki or Chinatown nightclubs and indulge yourself the next day with a spa extravaganza at Spa Halekulani, the newest addition to the spa lineup.

On the Big Island, don't miss the volcano, and have a drink at the Volcano House, which overlooks a steaming live crater. Explore Waimea and Parker Ranch country. Share a fishing charter at Honokohau Harbor. Join a pickup golf group and play a round on a course you'll never forget.

If you choose Maui, ride with a bike tour down Haleakala or take a snorkel tour to Molokini or Lanai. Drive to Makawao and Paia and poke around the villages. Head further upcountry to Kula and taste

Tedeschi wines at the winery at Ulupalakua Ranch. The places to party are Lahaina and Kihei.

COMMENTS Oahu has the most things to do and places to see and will keep your itinerary filled. If you're hoping to meet new friends during your trip, Oahu is the island with the most dance clubs and best nightlife.

Couples

BEST ISLAND TO VISIT Kauai

OTHER RECOMMENDED ISLANDS Lanai, Maui, Big Island

THINGS TO SEE AND DO Hang out in Hanalei, a naturally romantic setting you'll never want to leave; swim or body surf in Hanalei Bay; get to know some of the local citizenry at Tahiti Nui or neighboring spots. Go for a trail ride at Princeville Ranch Stables. Kayak down the Hanalei River to the bay and try to catch a wave on the way back. If the moon is full, go down to the beach to see if anyone is dancing hula in the moonlight, and join them. See for yourself what inspired Bob Nelson to write "Hanalei Moon," a well-known song describing a tropical moonrise.

Stay at Princeville, which provides gorgeous views of Hanalei Bay and the surrounding mountains. Pick a new North Shore beach to discover every day, and don't forget your snorkel gear. Take the boat ride up Wailua River to Fern Grotto. Walk up the Kalalau Trail the first two miles to the unforgettable Hanakapiai Valley, and return. Go south to Poipu Beach for at least a day, ride horses by the beach near the Grand Hyatt Kauai Resort & Spa (a honeymoon hotel), and don't miss dinner at Tidepools.

On Lanai, divide your time between Four Seasons' two plushy resorts—the seaside Manele Bay, where you can wake up to spinner dolphins in the waters, and upland The Lodge at Koele, where evenings in the romantic environs are chilly enough for cuddling. Hike or drive out to the hinterlands, or ride a horse through the woods. Witness a green flash, that magical prism phenomenon that sometimes happens when the sun meets the sea at the horizon.

On Maui, get up early to see the spectacular sunrise over Haleakala, then relax with massages for two in tents by the sea and take a stroll on Wailea Beach. Then go to Hana to discover Maui's true cultural heart. On the Big Island, stay at Kona Village Resort or Four Seasons Resort Hualalai, but save a day, and possibly a night, for spectacular discoveries at Hawaii Volcanoes National Park, such as hiking in a *kipuka* (oasis of green amid the black-rock desert) and, if you're lucky, witnessing fiery ribbons of lava on the move after dark.

COMMENTS Kauai is *the* choice for Hawaii's most romantic island, offering a combination of awesome scenery and wilderness settings.

Hikers

BEST ISLAND TO VISIT Kauai

OTHER RECOMMENDED ISLANDS Big Island, Maui

THINGS TO SEE AND DO Hike Kalalau Trail on Na Pali Coast (a difficult 12-mile trek each way)—this is a round trip for fit, experienced hikers with a stopover of at least one night in a state wilderness park in the valley. Or hike one way and arrange to catch a ride off the breathtaking coast on a Zodiac raft the other way.

Take the boardwalk on a sunny day through a highlands bog, Alakai Swamp, up at Kokee State Park. Explore the trails of 4,000-acre Kokee Forest, or see how the goats hang onto the precipitous ledges in Waimea Canyon. Hike the ridgeline above Kapaa to the Sleeping Giant.

On the Big Island, hike across simmering Kilauea Iki Crater and cool off by walking through Thurston Lava Tube. Hike the summit of Mauna Loa, but only if you're in shape for the thin air and high-altitude walking and are very experienced. On Maui: Hike the falls and forest at Kipahulu, beyond Hana.

COMMENTS Hikes on Kauai are the most dramatic because of the natural landscape, from thin ledges along the seacoast to miles of trails in a cloud forest.

Bikers

BEST ISLAND TO VISIT Big Island

OTHER RECOMMENDED ISLANDS Maui, Kauai

THINGS TO SEE AND DO Maui invented the sport of coasting down a volcano, but you can bike down a lower slope of Mauna Kea as well. Touring the Big Island in three or four days on a bike remains a challenge, so head for the wide, open spaces. One way is to proceed clockwise from Kona on the Upper Highway to Waimea, then along the lush, green Hamakua Coast to Hilo. From there, it's about 40 miles straight up to the village of Volcano and Hawaii Volcanoes National Park, where an errant lava flow cuts across Chain of Craters Road and sends you back the way you came. From Waimea this time, take a right on Kohala Mountain Road (250) out to Hawi, then loop around the North Kohala Coast and continue on across the open lava fields of the Kohala Coast before reaching your starting point at Kona.

On Maui, you will always remember the thrill of coasting down 10,000-foot-high Haleakala 38 miles to the sea on a specially built bicycle on a guided cruise, the only sensible way to descend the mountain on two wheels. Mountain bikers should head for Kauai and Oahu.

COMMENTS Bike enthusiasts test their stamina against the Big Island, the best all-around cycling island in the Pacific, because of its many challenging features: terrain that varies from lava desert to rain forest, steep inclines, and radically different temperatures from one area to the next.

Nature Lovers

BEST ISLAND TO VISIT Kauai

OTHER RECOMMENDED ISLANDS Big Island, Maui

THINGS TO SEE AND DO Snoop on boobies and goonies (Pacific seabirds) at Kilauea Point National Wildlife Refuge. See 600 species of palm trees and other tropicals at 300-acre National Tropical Botanical Garden. Wander in Waimea Canyon, the "grand canyon" of the Pacific. Spend the day in Limahuli Gardens, a botanical refuge for endangered native plants.

On the Big Island, explore Hawaii Volcanoes National Park, hike Chain of Craters Road to watch red-hot lava flow into the Pacific, cool your heels in lush Hawaii Tropical Botanical Garden on Onomea Bay near Hilo. Watch for rarely seen native Hawaiian forest birds. On Maui, look for rare silversword plants and endangered Hawaiian nene geese at Haleakala National Park, or the tropical Kahanu Garden hideaway on the Hana Coast.

COMMENTS   Hawaii's natural beauty is legendary; its wildlife (monk seals and native Hawaiian birds) may be endangered, but you will not be disappointed by the great outdoors, especially on Kauai, a botanical wonder all its own. The diverse nature of the Big Island with its lava-rock coasts and highland rain forests is like nowhere else on Earth. Maui's fabled town of Hana is a prime destination for people who like to feel overwhelmed by the majesty of nature. If you're lucky you may win admission to the Puu Kukui Nature Preserve atop the West Maui Mountains.

Beachcombers

BEST ISLAND TO VISIT Oahu

OTHER RECOMMENDED ISLANDS Kauai, Maui

THINGS TO SEE AND DO With 50 miles of sandy shore, Oahu has the most beaches in Hawaii. People-watch at Waikiki beaches. Windsurf Kailua Beach. Snorkel Hanauma Bay Beach. Search for shells at Malaekahana Beach in spring and summer and at Pupukea Beach on the North Shore. Watch big winter waves at Waimea Beach. Explore empty Yokohama Beach. Hide out and swim at Lanikai Beach. Have a picnic at Kualoa Ranch or any of a string of beach parks, such as Kaaawa or Hauula. Take a break from shopping at Ala Moana Beach, beyond the park just across the street from the mall.

unofficial TIP
The best and safest beaches are found on Oahu, the beach capital of Hawaii.

On Kauai, go body boarding at Poipu Beach, summer swimming at Hanalei Beach, snorkeling at Kee Beach and Tunnels Beach, or camping on 17-mile Polihale Beach, longest in Hawaii. Maui's best beaches include golden Wailea Beach and scenic Kapalua Beach, as well as remote black-sand Hamoa Beach in Hana.

COMMENTS The best, safest, and most dramatic beaches of Hawaii are found on Oahu, where the abundance of choice suits almost everyone's style. Plenty of beautiful beaches are found on Kauai and Maui, but Oahu is the beach capital of Hawaii.

Families

BEST ISLAND TO VISIT Oahu

OTHER RECOMMENDED ISLANDS Maui, Big Island

THINGS TO SEE AND DO If you enjoy paid attractions, take the family to Sea Life Park, the Honolulu Zoo, Waikiki Aquarium, and Bishop Museum. See beneath the sea without getting wet with Atlantis Submarines. Enjoy some sun, surf, and sand at Waikiki Beach and Ala Moana Beach Park, the most popular beaches in Hawaii.

Let the kids learn about the Islands and make new friends at supervised children's programs at the many hotels (the one at the Hilton Hawaiian Village is outstanding), while Mom and Dad get to enjoy some time on their own. Or, see if Hawaii Nature Center programs coincide with your visit so the kids can discover what's in the forested hills behind Honolulu. A visit to the USS *Arizona* Memorial and the USS Missouri will help your family understand what World War II was about.

On Maui, don't miss the Maui Ocean Center, Hawaii Nature Center, and Whalers Village Museum, all family-oriented attractions designed to educate as well as entertain.

On the Big Island, science prevails: The world's most restless volcano is always acting up within an excellent national park system that features strange sights and a vulcanology museum. The world's highest astronomers peer into deep space atop Mauna Kea, while kids glimpse the night skies at the high-altitude visitor center below. At the shore, aquaculture farms and energy researchers pipe up cold water from the ocean depths. Plenty of Hawaiian sites bring ancient culture to the mix.

COMMENTS Maui's Kaanapali Beach is the most popular family destination after Waikiki, but Oahu offers more family-oriented attractions and activities. Budding scientists will never forget the Big Island.

Active Seniors

BEST ISLAND TO VISIT Oahu

OTHER RECOMMENDED ISLANDS Big Island, Kauai, Maui

THINGS TO SEE AND DO Visit Oahu's historical attractions, including the Bishop Museum, Iolani Palace, Aloha Tower, Hawaii Maritime Center, and the Mission Houses Museum. Hike up Diamond Head Crater. Ride the open-air Waikiki Trolley. Learn Hawaiian crafts, like stringing lei, dancing hula, or playing the ukulele. Swim in the comfort of the warm and salty Pacific, even if you're not comfortable in a bikini. Many couples renew their wedding vows on the beach at sunset.

Seniors will find excellent tours by Elder Hostel that probe the Islands' interesting and educational facets at affordable rates. Contact Elderhostel at **www.elderhostel.org** or ☎ 800-454-5768.

On the Big Island, a functioning volcano is a prime draw for the awestruck of all ages. Don't miss this sight. If you love gardens, you will be intrigued by Honolulu's five municipal botanical gardens, including Foster Botanical Garden downtown with its array of towering exotic trees. On Maui, the Maui Tropical Plantation gives a glimpse of sample fields of island crops, plus a produce market. The only federally chartered research gardens, the National Tropical Botanical Garden, are definitely worth a visit on Kauai, at Lawai near Poipu Beach and Limahuli on the North Shore. On Maui, the Kahanu Garden of Pacific Island plants includes the state's largest archaeological site, Piilanihale Heiau. Plenty of privately operated botanical gardens are sprinkled throughout the Islands.

COMMENTS Anyone with gray in their hair is viewed with respect in Hawaii. You are considered a wise *kupuna* (elder), and doors are not closed to you. The healthy seniors who live in the Islands surf, dance, play golf, swim daily, and do anything else they want. So can you. Many visitor attractions and some stores offer discounts for seniors.

Visitors with Disabilities

BEST ISLAND TO VISIT Oahu

OTHER RECOMMENDED ISLANDS Maui, Big Island

THINGS TO SEE AND DO Take in a concert, film, or dance performance at the historic Hawaii Theatre in Honolulu, which provides special seating areas for the disabled.

Visit Iolani Palace, Sea Life Park, Polynesian Cultural Center, Honolulu Zoo, Hawaii's Plantation Village, and Mission Houses Museum on Oahu; Haleakala National Park, Maui Tropical Plantation, and Maui Ocean Center on Maui; Hawaii Volcanoes National Park, Panaewa Rainforest Zoo & Gardens, Nani Mau Gardens, and Puuhonua O Honaunau on the Big Island; and the Kauai Museum, Fern Grotto, and Kilauea Point National Wildlife Refuge on Kauai—all of which accommodate disabled visitors.

On Oahu, curb-to-curb transportation service is provided by the city and county of Honolulu via the Handi-Van (call ☎ 808-456-5555 for reservations and customer service). A sister company to TheBus, the Handi-Van transports some 2,000 passengers daily, operating from 5:30 a.m. to 11 p.m. Fares are $2 each way. City buses have elevator lifts for wheelchairs.

COMMENTS *The Aloha Guide to Accessibility,* published by the State Disability and Communication Access Board, provides detailed information on accessibility features of Island hotels, attractions, beaches, parks, theaters, shopping centers, transportation services, and medical and support services. Special transportation services are limited on the Neighbor Islands, but this free brochure covers that information as well. Write to the commission at 919 Ala Moana Boulevard, Suite 101, Honolulu 96814, or call ☎ 808-586-8121; you can also visit them online at **www.hawaii.gov/health/dcab.**

Hawaii Centers for Independent Living has a Web site that provides useful information for the disabled at **www.pacificil.org.**

Art Aficionados

BEST ISLAND TO VISIT Oahu

OTHER RECOMMENDED ISLANDS Maui, Big Island

THINGS TO SEE AND DO The Honolulu Academy of Arts and the Contemporary Museum, both in Honolulu, are the state's two best art museums. Doris Duke's Shangri La, a $100-million oceanfront mansion east of Honolulu, is now open to tours by small groups through the Honolulu Academy of Arts. A work of art itself, the house on five acres is filled with America's most extensive collection of Islamic art, collected globally over six decades by one of the world's richest women, the late tobacco heiress. Maui has a thriving arts community, with galleries in Lahaina, the Maui Arts & Cultural Center, and Hui Noeau Visual Arts Center. When you visit the Big Island, don't miss Volcano Art Center, housed in a historic building by the entrance of Hawaii Volcanoes National Park.

COMMENTS You can see and buy handicrafts by Hawaiian artisans at various craft fairs held throughout the Islands year-round, especially in November and December.

Hawaiian-Culture Seekers

BEST ISLAND TO VISIT Oahu

OTHER RECOMMENDED ISLANDS Maui, Kauai, Big Island

THINGS TO SEE AND DO Hawaiian culture is on display year-round but is especially in the spotlight during the Aloha Festivals, the biggest annual cultural celebration in the state. Colorful parades and pageantry, demonstrations of arts and crafts, and performances of music and dance are among the features. Aloha Festivals take place September through October, and each island has its own nine- or ten-day program. The Aloha Festivals Committee sets festival dates years in advance; contact ☎ 808-589-1771 or visit **www.alohafestivals.com** for a schedule.

The multiple ethnic groups that contributed to the Hawaii of today have heritage events throughout the year on all islands, but particularly on Oahu. The University of Hawaii often features its own cultural series of indoor and outdoor performances—showcasing contemporary Hawaiian music and dance, Chinese opera, and Japanese Noh theater, among others. The Bishop Museum, repository of more than 20 million Pacific Islands cultural artifacts, is the best place to explore Hawaii's rich past. The museum's new Waikiki annex at Hilton Hawaiian Village Beach Resort & Spa offers a preview. A must-visit spot for art lovers is the Luce Pavilion at the Honolulu Academy of Arts, where guests can see ink sketches by John Webber (who sailed with Captain Cook), Maui landscapes by Georgia O'Keeffe, and fiery canvases of Volcano School artists Jules Tavernier, Charles Furneaux, and D. Howard Hitchcock, who painted Madame Pele's volcanoes.

COMMENTS Look for *hula halau* (school) fund-raisers, slack key festivals, talk story events, and quilt shows; all offer a glimpse into the Hawaiian culture. You can also turn on the radio to an all-Hawaiian music station and get in the groove.

Gourmets and Gourmands

BEST ISLAND TO VISIT Oahu

OTHER RECOMMENDED ISLANDS Maui, Big Island, Lanai

THINGS TO SEE AND DO Superb fine-dining establishments can be found on every island. The best concentration of great restaurants, however, is in Honolulu on Oahu. Many of Hawaii's top regional cuisine chefs—including Roy Yamaguchi, Alan Wong, Sam Choy, and George Mavrothalassitis—have restaurants on Oahu. In addition, Honolulu enjoys pure ethnic and fine fusion versions of Japanese, Chinese, Thai, Vietnamese, Swiss, Korean, French, Italian, American, and other favorite cuisines.

The enthusiasm for creative chefs burns on other islands, too, fed by the notable kitchens of luxury hotels that gather talented staffs and excellent fresh local foods.

COMMENTS Be sure to treat your palate to a dinner of Hawaii regional cuisine at Roy's, Alan Wong's, or Chef Mavro's, featuring fresh ingredients produced or grown in the Islands. Not surprisingly, these restaurants are run by a trio of James Beard Award–winning chefs: Roy Yamaguchi, Alan Wong, and George Mavrothalassitis.

History Buffs

BEST ISLAND TO VISIT Oahu

OTHER RECOMMENDED ISLANDS Big Island, Maui, Lanai

THINGS TO SEE AND DO The greatest concentration of historical attractions is in a two-block area of downtown Honolulu, where the Iolani Palace, the State Capitol, the Governor's Mansion, Mission Houses Museum, Kawaiahao Church, and the Hawaii State Library are within easy walking distance of each other. Waikiki has a long history, but you have to look very closely to find it or go with a knowing guide—such as the intrepid *kupuna* (elders) of the Native Hawaiian Hospitality Association who lead free "talk story" walks that reveal the resort through native eyes. The Waikiki Historic Trail's surfboard-shaped trail markers lead a path through Waikiki's high-rise hotels. The two three-hour history walks encompass 23 historic sites that help explain how the area's original mosquito-choked fishponds, gold-sand beach, and famous surf attracted ancient Hawaiian kings and queens in old Hawaii and evolved into a world-class beach resort. Tours are held twice daily except Sunday. The Queen's Tour starts at the information kiosk at Kalakaua and Kapahulu avenues. The Kalia Tour starts on the second floor of Kalia Tower, Hilton Hawaiian Village. Contact the Native Hawaiian Hospitality Association, ☎ 808-628-6370 or **www .waikikihistorictrail.com.**

But in the tropics, where history vanishes quickly in the hot sun, salt air, and bug-laden environment, heritage sites are not always buildings. Rock platforms are all that's left of most *heiau*, or temple ruins, all over the Islands. They are still sacred to many, however.

On the Big Island, clues to the somewhat mysterious past are every-where if you care to search. The Kona-Kohala Coast resorts feature fields of ancient carvings and examples of early Hawaiian aquaculture techniques still in use today. Out in the nearby lava, the C-shaped rock shelters built by early soldiers are visible. In many places, including Wai-koloa, you can make out the pathway through the lava worn by bare human feet of royal messengers centuries ago.

On Maui, ambitious plans are proceeding in a multimillion-dollar effort to unearth a particularly prized cultural treasure—Mokuula, the royal palace of King Kamehameha III—which lies buried beneath a county ballpark in Lahaina but will one day be revealed by the restora-tion project. The huge Piilanihale Heiau dig near Hana will appeal to archaeology buffs.

On Lanai, you can drive and hike up to petroglyph rocks on a hill over Palawai Basin, or pilot a vehicle over rough roads to Kaunolu, King Kamehameha I's summer fishing camp.

COMMENTS Spend a day in the Bishop Museum, the best place to get a handle on Hawaii's history; it's in Kalihi at the Likelike Highway exit from H-1, a 20-minute drive from Waikiki.

Sports Fans

BEST ISLAND TO VISIT Oahu

OTHER RECOMMENDED ISLANDS Maui, Big Island

THINGS TO SEE AND DO Football fans have something to cheer about each winter on Oahu, scene of the annual Hula Bowl (college football all-stars), and collegiate Sheraton Hawaii Bowl featuring top NCAA teams. In December, the University of Hawaii hosts the prestigious Outrigger Hotels Rainbow Classic, an eight-team college basketball tournament. Other major Oahu sporting events include the Honolulu Marathon and Sony Open Golf Tournament, the Triple Crown of Surfing, the Kenwood Cup, Transpacific and other sailing races, annual lifeguard competitions, and a full schedule of outrigger canoe–paddling contests.

Maui hosts the annual EA Sports Maui Invitational (nationally tele-vised college basketball tournament), Wendy's Champions Skins Game at Wailea, and Kapalua's annual Mercedes-Benz Championship golf tournament, as well as several world windsurfing competitions and the Maui Marathon.

The Big Island is home to the world's most famous triathlon, the annual Ironman triathlon—which includes a 2.4-mile ocean swim, a rug-ged 112-mile bike ride, and a hot 26.2-mile run—and its one-up cousin, the Ultraman, which raises the bar to a 6.2-mile swim, 261.4-mile bike ride, and 52.4-mile run.

COMMENTS Sports teams may not be able to swing a regular Hawaii playing schedule, but collegiate all-star champions wouldn't miss their reward trip to Hawaii to end a stellar season with the Hula Bowl and Aloha Bowl games. For Hula Bowl tickets, see **www.hulabowlhawaii.com** or contact the Aloha Stadium box office, ☎ 808-486-9300, for information.

Business Travelers

COMMENTS The Aloha State is the only place in the world where you can con-duct business live with major financial centers in New York, Japan, China, and Hawaii all on the same day. The Islands are a good place to do busi-ness, especially when transactions involve linking U.S. concerns with Asia and the Pacific Rim. Honolulu boasts a large convention center as well.

The Islands are a great place for corporate groups to meet for fun and profit, rewarding top performers, top customers, and top prospects. The extensive choice of luxury resorts, outdoor sports and team-building events, alfresco parties, and other only-in-Hawaii fea-tures draws groups back year after year. Hawaii's remote setting, high degree of international air service, controlled access, and relatively safe and secure environment make it a favored choice for diplomats, scientists, political and economic leaders, and other international visi-tors. Hotels increasingly cater to business needs with office and fitness centers, in-room data ports, competent staffs, and a hip-to-technology attitude. The fiber-optic system linking the Islands to the West Coast is one of the best in the world, thanks to the presence of an Air Force supercomputer on Maui.

The Hawaii Convention Center Located on the edge of Waikiki, the Hawaii Convention Center combines high-tech wizardry with a Hawaiian sense of place. Designed by Hawaii architectural firm Wimberly Allison Tong & Goo, the airy four-story center opened to wide acclaim in the summer of 1998. The center has 100,000 square feet of meeting space, 200,000 square feet of exhibit space, a 36,000-square-foot ballroom, a 35,000-square-foot registration and lobby area, and an 800-space parking garage.

The ground floor houses the lobby area and exhibit hall, which is large enough to accommodate a reception for some 28,000 attendees. The second floor is reserved for parking; the third level features meeting rooms; and the fourth (top) floor houses the grand ballroom and rooftop garden terrace. A two-story glass wall enhances the lobby, where palms and tropical plants grow inside and out.

High-tech features include fiber-optic cables providing speedy, state-of-the-art communication; a pressroom with global links to any nation in the world; a built-in, six-station simultaneous translation room, allowing translators to view the speakers through a video monitor; a meeting room capable of hosting 400 computers working simultaneously; and an auditorium with built-in projection room and concert-quality sound system.

More than 30,000 hotel rooms and condominium units are within a one-mile radius of the center. The nearest, the Ala Moana Hotel, is across the street. Plenty of restaurants are within an easy walk. Nearby Ala Moana Shopping Center offers a range of restaurants and a food court. The older area around the convention center is still something of a surfeit of girlie bars, Korean bars, and just plain bars.

For more information, call the Hawaii Visitors and Convention Bureau at ☎ 808-923-1811 or visit **www.hvcb.org.**

▌ TYING *the* KNOT

HAWAII IS ONE OF AMERICA'S FAVORITE PLACES to get married and go on a honeymoon. Lovers can get married on the beach (check out **www.beachweddingshawaii.com** for information), by waterfalls, underwater amid tropical fish, in churches old and new, on sailboats, on offshore islets, and up in the air while skydiving.

In old Hawaii marriage ceremonies were reserved only for high-ranking citizens, or *alii*. The first Christian marriage took place in 1822, two years after the arrival of American missionaries. For a time, it was illegal for non-Christian marriages to be held in the Islands. Today, more than 10,000 out-of-state couples are wed here every year. For a time, legal same-sex marriages drew couples to Hawaii. However, voters amended the state constitution in 1998 to classify

Romantic Places to Get Married in Hawaii

- **Oahu** Kawaiahao Church, downtown Honolulu. This landmark coral-block church, designed by New England missionary Hiram Bingham and dedicated in 1842, is one of Oahu's most popular and stately venues for couples seeking a formal church wedding. Contact Kawaiahao Church at ☎ 808-522-1333, 957 Punchbowl Street.

- **Waikiki Beach** Just walk out on the gold sand at sunset, adorned in flowers with your intended mate and your officiator, and say "I do" before lots of witnesses, who may join you in singing the "Hawaiian Wedding Song" as you dance across the *lanai* (patio) at the House Without a Key. Don't forget to hire a photographer to capture the moment. Meanwhile, the Moët & Chandon is chilling up in your Halekulani honeymoon suite. Contact Halekulani Hotel at ☎ 808-923-2311 or **www.halekulani.com.**

- **Maui** Waterfall Garden, Maui Prince. At the waterfall pool in the open-air atrium where golden Japanese carp splash in black lava tide pools, many couples get married every weekend in peaceful Makena. Contact Maui Prince Hotel at ☎ 808-874-1111.

- **Big Island of Hawaii** Anaehoomalu Beach, Waikoloa This beach framed by palms and serene ancient fishponds, one of Hawaii's most romantic locations, appeals to many wedding couples as the place to recite vows. Contact Waikoloa Beach Marriott at ☎ 800-228-9290.

- **Kauai** On Kauai's North Shore, the Princeville Hotel overlooks the Bali Hai image you dream about: Hanalei Bay, with jagged, waterfall-creased volcanic peaks in the background. *Akamai* (with-it) couples wait for the golden hour around sunset when the blue sky is streaked with red and gold rays. Contact St. Regis Princeville Hotel at ☎ 808-826-9644.

- **Lanai** At the Conservatory on Lanai, exchange vows amid thousands of exotic orchids in the misty, glass-paned conservatory, then dance your wedding waltz in the Four Seasons Resort Lanai, The Lodge at Koele, a very romantic setting for weddings and honeymoons. Call ☎ 808-565-4000.

- **On the Ocean Blue** If your shipboard romance becomes the love of your life and you can't wait to tie the knot, have a wedding at sea. There's a little chapel aboard the *Pride of America* and special wedding packages so that you can get hitched and be on your tropical honeymoon in the time it takes to say, "I do." Contact Norwegian Cruise Lines at ☎ 866-234-0292.

marriage as pertaining to male-female relationships, and the state's supreme court upheld that in 1999. The long tradition in Polynesian culture of tolerance toward the "third sex," or *mahu*, still means that gay-oriented travel companies and commitment ceremonies are commonly accepted in the Islands.

HOW TO GET MARRIED

TO GET MARRIED IN HAWAII, you'll need a valid marriage license. You can obtain one at the Hawaii State Department of Health, Marriage License Office, 1250 Punchbowl Street, Honolulu 96813; ☎ 808-586-4545. The office is open from Monday to Friday, 8 a.m. to 4 p.m. (closed on holidays). Both bride and groom must be present when the license is issued. The license is valid statewide for 30 days.

On the Neighbor Islands, you can get a license from a marriage license agent (ask your hotel concierge or wedding coordinator to direct you to the nearest agent).

Both the bride and groom must be at least 18 years of age to be married without parental consent. If either partner has been married before, he or she is required to provide the date, county, and state (or country) in which the divorce was finalized for each previous marriage. The names of each person's parents and place of birth must also be provided.

A free "Getting Married" pamphlet is available from Hawaii's Marriage License Office. Write to the address above or call ☎ 808-586-4545. In addition, the Hawaii Visitors and Convention Bureau has a list of wedding planners on all islands at **www.gohawaii.com.**

PART THREE

ACCOMMODATIONS

 # WHERE *to* STAY

ON THE SIX MAIN ISLANDS in Hawaii, you can choose the lodging that's just right for you from among more than 72,500 hotel rooms, suites, condos and condo-hotel units, apartments, bungalows, and private homes—from budget surfer shacks to first-rate palaces, with prices to match. Most are on or near a beach.

You'll find the familiar names of international hotel-management firms—such as Westin, Sheraton, and other Starwood brands; Hilton, Hyatt, Marriott, Prince, Ritz-Carlton, Four Seasons, Embassy Suites, and Fairmont; plus the newest famous name on the Waikiki scene, Trump International—as well as locally owned Outrigger Hotels and Resorts, Aston Hotels & Resorts, and smaller independents. New players are entering the Hawaii scene, although some plans have been delayed pending more favorable national economic conditions:

- The Walt Disney Company is building its first freestanding hotel (without a neighboring theme park) at Ko Olina Resort in West Oahu, an 800-unit hotel-and-time-share property slated to open in 2011.
- Plans are suspended for Maui's Wailea Resort to gain the most glittering new hotel name of all–Baccarat Hotels and Resorts. The proposed 193-unit Baccarat Wailea Hotel & Residences, would be built on the 15-acre site of the closed Wailea Renaissance, according to former hotelier Barry Sternlicht, who also controls the renowned French crystal firm.

Many of the hotel giants have recently made huge investments in renovation and, in some cases, demolishing and rebuilding of existing hotel structures. After a long hiatus, Waikiki's billion-dollar construction renaissance is in full swing, with a new look for many venerable landmarks on and near acclaimed Waikiki Beach, foremost of which is the Royal Hawaiian Hotel, recently redone and reopened.

Our advice is to call properties for details before you make your plans, as some hotels are closed for face-lifts and others may offer construction-zone bargains.

With the same spectacular settings as their hotel neighbors, other lodging choices—condos, executive vacation homes, and, increasingly, time-share units—offer families and small groups private, relaxed alternatives to multiple hotel rooms and high-cost hotel meals. Particularly on Maui and Kauai, portions of large luxury hotels have been remade into "vacation club" time-shares run by firms like Westin, Embassy Suites, and Marriott. Fractional ownership and full private ownership of hotel units are also showing up in luxury digs such as Kapalua Resort on Maui. Existing hotel rooms have been combined into larger efficiency units which devoted returning guests can buy for a week or a month or more each year.

unofficial **TIP**
If you are a smoker, you may want to quit. Most public areas and hotel units are no-smoking zones in Hawaii. Hawaii has enacted a strict law that bans smoking in enclosed public areas, including bars, restaurants, lobbies, meeting rooms, and stores. It also requires hotels to limit smoking rooms to 20% or less of their total rooms; however most larger chains, such as Westin, Marriott, Hilton, Aston, and Outrigger Hotels and Resorts, have banned smoking completely. Some properties levy a stiff cleaning fee if someone cheats.

Kauai is home to more than a third of Hawaii's growing time-share market. Time-shares, with their up-front financing, helped Kauai properties recover from lingering physical and legal ravages of Hurricane Iniki, which devastated the island in 1992. Time-share owners have already paid for their lodging and tend to be less likely to cancel for faraway wars and other travel threats. What difference does it make to visitors' experience whether their rooms are hotel or time-shares? Probably not much. The larger units may be a better deal, minus some hotel services and plus a hard-sell pitch if guests agree to "free" time-share marketing offers. (Don't want the hassle? Just say no.)

Rooms with a view range from average to breathtaking. In Waikiki, "ocean" views can be a peek of blue between high-rises or a mesmerizing wall-to-wall panorama of the beach and the sea framed by Diamond Head on one side and sunset behind the Waianae Mountains in the distance. If you're off the beach, you could have a mountain view that reveals the haunting beauty of the Koolau Range, the twinkling neighborhood lights halfway up the slopes at night, and the busy paddlers on the Ala Wai Canal below. Garden rooms usually deliver tropical garden views. Most rooms have sliding-glass doors that open to outdoor lanai for balmy breezes.

The chief factors we used to rate hotels are: location (on the beach or nearby), views, service, amenities, character, price, and value. When you choose your lodging—whether through a travel agent or on your own—ask about nearby construction, recent room renovations, balcony or patio availability, airport transfers, and any extras included in the rate (such as daily paper, movies, Internet access, microwave and fridge, or breakfast). Most deluxe and luxury rooms come with coffeemakers, hair dryers, irons and boards, and safes; some also come with CD players.

If you're going upscale, inquire about the club floors. Rooms on these floors have keyed elevator access, a lounge with free drinks, continental breakfast, light buffet lunch, evening *pupu* (appetizers), and sinful fresh-baked cookies, plus a concierge to call their own. The rates are higher, but the buffets take care of breakfast, lunch, snacks, and cocktails, which are costly at resorts.

You don't have to go first class to get great service. Usually service at Hawaii hotels is friendly and courteous at every level, from maids to general managers. Staff members exhibit lots of aloha spirit and wear flowers and tropical uniforms. They may not all speak your language, but they will find someone who does, and they are anxious to please you.

Hawaii has a dynamic tourism industry, always changing to update facilities and respond to changing trends. Most prominent among current makeovers are a pair of projects in Waikiki:

- A cluster of older, funky budget hotels on Lewers Street has vanished, to be transformed into Outrigger Enterprises' ambitious billion-dollar Waikiki Beach Walk development. Much of it is in place and when complete, scheduled in 2010, the Beach Walk will feature not only a 90,000-square-foot retail-and-entertainment complex with 40 stores, six restaurants and bars, and a large pedestrian plaza, but also four new or rebuilt hotels— most spectacular among them, the 38-story, $350-million Trump International Hotel & Tower (Trump Tower Waikiki) marking Donald Trump's brand debut in Hawaii. The Trump condo-hotel's 464 units, at prices ranging up from $450,000 studio units, broke world records in November 2006, by selling out within eight hours for $700 million—despite the little advertised fact that while the ocean views will be smashing, none will be beachfront (**www.waikikibeachwalk.com**).

- Nearby, the three blocks of uninspiring concrete buildings and parking lots that make up Royal Hawaiian Shopping Center are glistening after a Hawaiian-izing face-lift to soften the facade and create a tropical outdoor entertainment glen.

Waikiki gets the lion's share of visitors from around the world, but the high-energy urban resort is not for everyone. When you seek a quieter getaway on Oahu, plan to stay at J. W. Marriott Ihilani Resort & Spa at Ko Olina on the Leeward side, Kahala Resort in suburban Kahala southeast of Waikiki, Turtle Bay Resort on the North Shore, or a B&B or vacation rental on the Windward side, where there are no hotels.

On Maui, Kapalua Resort underwent substantial redesign, which included demolishing the former Kapalua Bay Hotel to make way for an interval-ownership operation and adding more private homes and condos, new private golf course, and beach club. Historic Honolua Store and nearby shops and restaurants remain open to the public, along with existing vacation villas and condos, two golf courses (Bay and Plantation courses; former Village course was shut down), a tennis complex, and the Ritz-Carlton, Kapalua. The Ritz-Carlton underwent a $180-million face-lift to renovate 363 hotel units and create 107 "residential suites" with kitchen facilities for private sale. The expanded Spa at the Ritz-Carlton offers authentic Hawaiian spa treatments using Hawaiian healing therapies and ingredients. Kapalua events, including sports tournaments and Hawaiian cultural performances, continue.

Elsewhere on Maui, Kaanapali Beach Resort, like Waikiki, handles the greatest number of people very well, but the quieter resorts of Wailea, Kapalua, and Makena top our recommended list. Our favorite Big Island hotels are on the Kona-Kohala Coast. On Kauai, Poipu Beach and Princeville resorts are our favorites. Lanai has two fine hotels and a small lodge.

All Hawaii tourist accommodations are subject to an 8.25% room tax (9.25% after June 30, 2010) plus excise tax, which is 4.712% on Oahu and 4.166% on other islands.

GREAT PLACES TO STAY

SOME OF THE WORLD'S GREATEST beach hotels and resorts are in Hawaii, from traditional favorites, like the century-old Westin Moana Surfrider Hotel on Waikiki Beach, to newer stars, like the Four Seasons Hualalai Resort on the Big Island, that seem to define the Hawaiian experience for visitors of different eras. Some, like the Kahala Hotel & Resort on Oahu, Four Seasons Resort Maui at Wailea, Mauna Kea Beach Hotel on the Big Island, and St. Regis Princeville Resort on Kauai, are elegant retreats; others are fantasies come true, like Grand Wailea Resort Hotel & Spa on Maui, Marriott Waikoloa Beach Resort on the Big Island, and Kauai Marriott Resort & Beach Club. A precious few recall old Polynesia, such as Kona Village Resort or the Mauian at Napili Beach. Here's our list of favorites by category:

Hopelessly Romantic

HALEKULANI, OAHU No finer hotel exists on Waikiki Beach for lovers or for anybody who can handle the tab. If you don't care about the tab, show it by reserving the new 2,135-square-foot Vera Wang Suite ($5,500 per night for one bedroom) furnished with the designer's signature touch and goods for home, bath, and gifts. You can throw in the suite next door for another $1,500 if you insist on bringing company. The Vera Wang Suite comes with terrific views, giant lanai, signature decor and appointments, limo airport transfers, access to a Maserati Granturismo or a Lotus Elise for cruising Kalakaua, free Champagne if you can resist sipping special drinks like a Cupid's Arrow or Kiss of Venus—did someone say "honeymoon?"—butler service, in-suite spa services, VIP passes to Honolulu arts museums, and substantial pampering, like all Halekulani guests expect. Many Halekulani guests will find they can watch the sunset reflect on Diamond Head from their in-room tub. Anyone can enjoy a drink at sunset at the House Without a Key, Halekulani's outdoor lanai terrace, while a hula dancer sways gracefully to old songs. Then settle into a private booth at five-diamond restaurant La Mer for French Champagne and haute cuisine. ☎ 800-367-2343 or **www.halekulani.com.**

RITZ-CARLTON, KAPALUA, MAUI Hawaii's only Ritz commands the last outpost of resort life in West Maui. Its caring management and celebrations of Hawaiian culture and art add to this romantic oasis on an old pineapple plantation at the foot of the West Maui Mountains. You can get married in the historic little church on the grounds. You can buy a hotel suite-like unit of your own to return to year after year for anniversaries. ☎ 800-262-8448 or **www.ritzcarlton.com.**

kids **KONA VILLAGE RESORT, BIG ISLAND** Sleep under thatch in a private island *hale* (house) at Kona Village, created in the mid-1960s before there was road access. Guests flew or sailed into this retreat. Now you can drive from the airport in a few minutes across the lava field, but the sense of seclusion continues. The ultimate escape, this exclusive beach retreat is a collection of coastal huts in various Pacific Islands styles of architecture. When you seek genuine peace and quiet, stay here. When you want privacy, put your coconut out by the door. This is one of the few island resorts where rates include three meals a day. ☎ 800-367-5290 or **www.konavillage.com.**

HOTEL HANA-MAUI, MAUI This inn by the sea offers private Sea Ranch cottages for two with a bubbly hot tub and thick Turkish towels. Explore the neighborhood on foot or horseback—this sleepy area is all part of a large ranch. ☎ 800-321-HANA or **www.hotelhanamaui.com.**

GRAND HYATT KAUAI RESORT & SPA On one of Kauai's wild beaches, this hotel echoes island architecture of the 1920s, creating a romantic setting with gardens, pools, and intimate restaurants often frequented by hand-holding couples, not all of them honeymooners. ☎ 888-591-1234, 808-742-1234, or **www.kauai.hyatt.com.**

KILAUEA LAKESIDE ESTATE, KILAUEA, KAUAI A private lakeside estate for lovers or families seeking escape, Steve Hunt's Island Retreat has its own 20-acre lake, beach, tropical gardens, boats, kayaks, boat dock, and putting green and a three-bedroom, three-bath house. ☎ 310-379-7842 or **www.kauailakeside.com.**

kids Great for Families

HILTON HAWAIIAN VILLAGE BEACH RESORT & SPA Flamingos, peacocks, penguins, a lagoon, five pools (including Oahu's largest, 10,000-foot superpool), weekly fireworks, and more than 3,400 rooms on 22 acres on Waikiki Beach: What more could a kid want? A busy children's program full of daily surprises keeps everyone happy. Plenty of grown-up entertainment is available too, as well as a spa-and-wellness center, 20 restaurants and lounges, and a whole village full of (nearly 100) shops. The Village includes seven towers, three of them with time-share units. Guests can speed through check-in and checkout with several options, including self-service kiosks in the lobby that also print airline boarding passes. Other amenities include the $6-million Ocean Crystal wedding chapel, Waikiki's first. ☎ 800-949-4321 or **www.hiltonhawaiianvillage.com.**

WESTIN MAUI RESORT & SPA, KAANAPALI This open, airy beachfront hotel looks like a Disney fantasy jungle, with tropical foliage, water-falls, and parrots everywhere inside the open atrium and Kaanapali outside. Kids love the aquatic playground with a 128-foot slide, the easy-breezy feeling, and year-round summer camplike fun. It's a big hit with big kids, too. ☎ 866-500-8313 or **www.westinmaui.com.**

FAIRMONT KEA LANI, WAILEA, MAUI Like something out of *Arabian Nights,* the luxurious Fairmont Kea Lani hotel delivers more than just fantasy. All the units are well-equipped suites with high-tech stereos and kitchens, except for the special villas with two or three bedrooms and private plunge pools. It offers a scenic beach, great restaurants, separate pools for kids and adults. This is the southern end of Wailea Resort's 1.5-mile coastal trail linking neighboring hotels, shops, and restaurants. ☎ 800-659-4100, 866-540-4457, or **www.kealani.com.**

Great Historic Traditions

WESTIN MOANA SURFRIDER Enter this century-old hotel, and ghosts of old Waikiki surround you. That could be Queen Liliuokalani's carriage at the porte cochere. You can almost hear Webley Edwards broadcasting *Hawaii Calls* from the Banyan Court. The graceful grande dame of the beach was rescued and revived with a historic renovation some years ago, then freshened up in 2007 with a new look in the lobby and rooms and a new beachfront spa. Now in its second century, Waikiki's oldest hotel is on the National Register of Historic Places. ☎ 866-325-3535 or **www.moana-surfrider.com.**

ROYAL HAWAIIAN HOTEL They call it the "Pink Palace," a flamingo pink landmark by the blue sea. The Royal Hawaiian, the bright spot in Waikiki's bland concrete jungle, was inspired by a Rudolph Val-entino movie and built by Matson Steamship Lines in 1927 during Waikiki's golden age. After a renovation closure in 2008, the Royal is back and better than ever with a sensitive remodel of its rooms, lobby, public areas, and entry. It was worth waiting for. ☎ 866-500-8313 or **www.royal-hawaiian.com.**

PIONEER INN, LAHAINA, MAUI Overlooking Lahaina Harbor, the Pio-neer Inn turned 100 years old in 2001, holding on after a $5-million face-lift. This once-rowdy sailors' haunt is now a charming relic fit for all who "collect" old hotels and prefer tradition over trend. ☎ 800-457-5457, 808-661-3636, or **www.pioneerinn-maui.com.**

MAUNA KEA BEACH HOTEL, BIG ISLAND Laurance Rockefeller started a trend of secluded tropical luxury in 1965 when he arranged for this classic, gracious hotel and its world-famous golf course to be built beside a beautiful beach and invited the captains of industry to come relax. Now their grandchildren carry on the tradition. He filled the hotel with Asian and Pacific art and triggered a renaissance in Hawaiian quilting arts by commissioning handmade quilts for wall hangings. A path was blasted through the lava to reach the hotel. The soaring indoor-outdoor architecture befits the climate and was named one of the top 100 iconic buildings in the United States by the American Institute of Architects. ☎ 808-882-7222 or **www.princeresortshawaii.com.**

SHIPMAN HOUSE BED & BREAKFAST INN, HILO, BIG ISLAND Here's a rare, wonderful old Victorian family mansion built in 1899, restored and registered as a national and state historic treasure—and you can stay here, just as writer Jack London once did, as well as Hawaiian Queen Liliuokalani at the turn of the last century. Three bedrooms in the big house and two in a separate cottage are available at $219 to $259 per night for a two-night minimum, less for longer stays. The fee includes breakfast and access to the tropical gardens first assembled long ago by the Shipmans, who collected plants and were the first to bring orchids to the Orchid Isle. ☎ 800-627-8447, 808-934-8002, or **www.hilo-hawaii.com.**

WAIMEA PLANTATION COTTAGES, WAIMEA, KAUAI This is a resort comprised of restored tin-roof sugar shacks moved from former plantations and gathered in a palm grove by the sea. History buffs will be delighted. Cottages are named for families who lived in them. Dating from the 1880s to the 1930s, the charming cottages are updated with modern kitchens and baths, and furnished with period wicker and rattan. Some are on the beach. The setting, near the Waimea River in West Kauai, is off the beaten track, but it is near the place where Captain Cook stepped ashore nearby more than 200 years ago and "discovered" Hawaii. ☎ 877-997-6667, 808-338-1625, or **www .waimea-plantation.com.**

Great for High Rollers

FOUR SEASONS RESORT LANAI, THE LODGE AT KOELE, LANAI Live like a grand poobah, if only for a few days, in this highland inn on a nearly private, red-dirt island of abandoned pineapple fields. It's deliciously decadent, outrageously expensive, and captivating. You won't ever want to leave. It begins to feel like a friend's country estate. ☎ 800-321-4666, 808-565-4000, or **www.fourseasons.com/koele.**

FOUR SEASONS RESORT HUALALAI, BIG ISLAND Under dormant Hualalai Volcano, this is a series of clusters of handsome private bungalows arranged around pools by the beach, with outdoor shower gardens, tasteful decor, and oceanfront restaurants a step off the sand. From the thatched roofs over its outdoor whirlpool tubs to the natural amphitheater in a lava formation, Four Seasons Hualalai is wonderfully different, with rates ranging up from $500 a night for bungalows by the sea. The resort is surrounded by golf greens, ranks of swanky condos, villas, and private home lots. ☎ 888-340-5662, 808-325-8200, or **www.fourseasons.com/hualalai.**

Some private Hualalai villas are rented by their owners, such as a second-story, three-bedroom ocean-view villa for $1,850 per night. ☎ 808-443-0386, or visit **www.hualalailuxuryvillarental.com.**

MAUNA LANI BAY HOTEL AND BUNGALOWS, BIG ISLAND Fishponds, lava caves, petroglyphs—the physical evidence of early habitation is abundant on this shore. But it's doubtful they lived as well as current guests do, even though this was once a retreat for Hawaiian royalty. The Mauna Lani is the namesake hotel of Mauna Lani Resort, a 3,200-acre Kohala Coast retreat favored by Hollywood royalty who like to retreat to the $3,300 to $4,500-per-night bungalows by the sea. Difficult economic times caused the bungalows to lose their butlers (rates went to $7,500 per night with butlers), but a spokeswoman says the bungalows have been booked since the prices dropped. Butler services can be added à la carte. The Fairmont Orchid, two spectacular golf courses, plush condos, and private homes also share the resort, which is secluded by a lava wasteland. ☎ 800-628-7815 or **www.maunalani.com.**

HAPUNA BEACH PRINCE HOTEL, BIG ISLAND Built by a Tokyo tycoon, the Hapuna Beach Prince celebrates a spectacular ocean view, from the lobby as well as the rooms, on a cliff beside Hapuna Beach. The beauty is in the materials—burnished wood and slate with minimal interior decor. Critics call it stark, but think of the Hapuna Beach public and private rooms as mere frames for the marine-scene painting beyond. The huge pool awaits those reluctant to take on the golden sands and little-known snorkeling cove below. A $7,000-per-night, four-bedroom, 8,000-square-foot, butlered, attended, and fully party-equipped rental estate known as Hapuna Suite awaits VIPs. The golf course is a spare intrusion on the natural setting, a links-style natural course with native plants and par-busting views. ☎ 888-977-4623 or **www.princeresortshawaii.com/hapuna suite.**

Great Bargains

NEW OTANI KAIMANA BEACH HOTEL, OAHU Under Diamond Head, this small hotel with a big attitude, and an even better vantage point, is far enough away from the heart of Waikiki to have a great view of it—as well as Diamond Head, the Waianae Mountains, city of Honolulu, neighboring Kapiolani Park, and the Koolau Mountain Range behind the cityscape. And, of course, the great Pacific Ocean spread out in front. In short, it's hard to beat the views from the corner suites and rooms, no matter which corner, and the prices (ranging up from $190, with the views going for about $350, to a large penthouse suite for $1,350 a night). Some rooms are small; those pesky palms might interrupt your view from lower floors. But its beachfront location, gentle hospitality, famed Hau Tree Lanai (where Robert Louis Stevenson read poems to Princess Kaiulani), and decent rates make New Otani an old and valued favorite of repeat guests. Ask for the corner you want—ocean or Kapiolani Park view with Diamond Head or city-and-sunset exposure. On a budget, get a regular room and enjoy your peaceful perch surrounded by the park instead of the traffic, pavement, and crowds of central Waikiki. ☎ 800-356-8264 or **www.kaimana.com.**

WAIKOLOA BEACH MARRIOTT RESORT & SPA, BIG ISLAND In this ritzy neighborhood of high-end beach hotels, the updated, deluxe Waikoloa Marriott, with the best beach location, is the best value on the Kohala Coast. Features include a beach-view restaurant, spa, and special units. The hotel commands a spectacular site by a huge fishpond complex and palm-fringed Anaehoomalu Beach, one of Hawaii's best. ☎ 800-228-9290, 808-886-6789, or **www.waikoloamarriott.com.**

GARDEN ISLAND INN, KAUAI Kalapaki Beach and Nawiliwili Harbor (where freight and cruise ships call), plus shops and restaurants are all across the street from your spacious, third-floor suite, starting at $145 per night, with kitchen, wet bar, and private lanai, plus free tree-ripe papayas daily. ☎ 800-648-0154 or **www.gardenislandinn.com.**

THE MAUIAN HOTEL ON NAPILI BEACH Centered on an ideal golden beach where swimming is good and views even better, the 44 boutique studio condos come with a breakfast buffet, kitchen, lanai, comfortable furnishings, and warm Hawaiian atmosphere as only a local family can provide. Check Internet special rates. ☎ 800-367-5034 or **www.mauian.com.**

HOTEL LANAI, LANAI If you want to explore Lanai without spending a fortune on the two luxury resorts, stay in this quaint ten-room historic upland lodge plus cottage overlooking Lanai City (the two-block village that was once the heart of the island pineapple plantation). It was built in the 1920s to house plantation VIPs; today, even its separate cottage can be your hideaway for a moderate rate. Country-style rooms come with private baths and continental breakfast. ☎ 808-565-7211 or **www.hotellanai.com.**

DOLPHIN BAY HOTEL, HILO, BIG ISLAND The stalk of ripe bananas hanging by the lobby for all to enjoy sets the tone for this little budget-priced and friendly, not fancy, place to stay in Hilo when you're volcano-bound. Lots of lush gardens are the outdoor attraction, with walkways through a flower and fruit jungle making up for a lack of view or waterfront. Units have kitchens; ask early if you want the two-bedroom unit, which has a two-night minimum. ☎ 877-935-1466 or **www.dolphinbayhotel.com.**

GETTING *a* GOOD DEAL
on a ROOM

NOW THAT YOU'VE HAD A PREVIEW of some of Hawaii's great places to stay, here's how to get the best deal. In this difficult economic year, it's hard not to get a good deal on a Hawaii hotel or condo. Go to the Web sites of the hotels and condos that interest you to find special packages and rates that are slashed by a third or more, even for prime-time winter bookings.

- Book early.
- Go during fall and spring months (September through early December, April, May, and early June).
- Educate yourself on what you want, and where and when you want it before you go shopping or talk to a travel agent. They may have suggestions that alter your plans, but they'll surely do a better job for you if you narrow the search. Most agents now charge a fee for their services, as well as collect a percentage of the booking as their commission. Ask about your agent's fee policies in advance.
- If you use a travel agent, ask them to research package rates and other specials that combine your room with sports, spa, rental car, and other trip features. They may have access to information you won't find as a consumer.
- Call the hotel to see what rate you can negotiate. Ask for the best rate they offer, not the published rack rate. Often rates and fares are cheaper if you book via the Internet.
- Pursue discounts for corporate travel, seniors, kids staying free in your room, military personnel, travel clubs, and other special-status travel. See what frequent-flier mileage you may gain from your hotel stay.

Several factors—including demand, location, season, availability, view, grade of room, proximity to the beach, shopping centers, and entertainment—determine a hotel room rate.

Hawaii room rates are highest from late December through late March, when everyone wants to escape winter. Rates rise again in summer, when school's out and families flock to the Islands from the West Coast.

Hawaii's visitor industry provides one quarter of the gross state product, one quarter of the state's tax revenues, and one-third of the jobs. Hawaii's dependency on tourism means competitive rates and good deals for you.

WHERE THE DEALS ARE

CHECK TRAVEL SECTIONS of major newspapers for good room deals and combinations with airfare, hotel or condo rentals, and car rentals. Surf the Internet to preview islands, beaches, golf courses, hotels, condos, and vacation rentals. Try your luck with Internet brokers, such as **priceline.com, hoteldiscount.com, travelocity.com,** and others dedicated to travel bargains.

Other Money-saving Suggestions

Many hotels offer their own periodic package deals with value-added amenities like free rental car, food and beverage credits, rounds of golf, spa treatments, extra-special treatment for honeymooners (chocolates and Champagne) and for families, and free or cheaper second rooms when you book the first room. Many hotels offer a free extra night if you book a room for a certain number of nights (usually four to seven). Hotels off the beach are cheaper; so are mountain- or garden-view rooms. Ask if kids can stay in your room free.

Travel Packages

Those travel packages featured in the newspaper are the choice of many Hawaii vacationers. The plans, assembled by tour wholesalers for sale to travel agents or directly to the public, offer plenty of flexibility in price and places to stay, and often include extras like lei greetings, luau, scuba dives, or golf rounds. Hotels, condos, and B&Bs offer packages too, featuring lodging combined with activities. Package travelers may be part of a large flock on the same schedule, but it's by chance, and their arrangements are independent. Packages differ from traditional group tours, which are conducted en masse and shepherded by guides who take care of all the details and charge accordingly. Dozens of tour wholesalers offer Hawaii travel packages, including these:

- Classic Vacations: ☎ 866-267-1934 or **www.classicvacations.com**
- Creative Leisure International: ☎ 800-413-1000 or **www.creative leisure.com**
- Pleasant Holidays: ☎ 800-742-9244 or **www.pleasantholidays.com**

If You Make Your Own Reservation

If you hunt your own bargains, call the hotel directly instead of the chain's toll-free number. The clerk at a central site may not know about special local rates. The quoted, or rack, room rates—the ones printed once a year for brochures to be placed in a rack—are flexible. Virtually no one pays the full rack rate, except perhaps at peak travel times or for last-minute bookings. Don't be shy about inquiring about lower rates, especially during the low season, when your bargaining position is improved. Inquire about any other special deals. Hotels would rather fill rooms at discounted prices than leave them empty. Do your bargaining, however, when you reserve a room, not after your arrival.

Corporate Rates

Many hotels provide corporate rates (up to 20% off regular rack rates). Ask your hotel about them. Generally, you do not need to work for a large company or have a special relationship with a hotel to obtain corporate rates. Some hotels require a written request on company letterhead or some other verification of your employment status, but others will guarantee the rate over the phone.

Travel Clubs

Travel clubs offer discounts of up to half off participating hotels' rack rates, but with restrictions. They generally apply on a space-available basis and are not available in blackout periods (usually during peak travel times). Some may apply only on certain days of the week. Not all hotels offer a true 50% discount. Some base their discount on an exaggerated rack rate. Before joining a discount program, compare the rates offered to members with those available elsewhere.

Most travel clubs or half-price programs charge an annual fee, up to $125 or more. When you join, you receive a membership card and directory of participating hotels, including about 100 in Hawaii. Evaluate your long-term travel plans when considering membership in a travel club, as you may not recoup the membership fee in a single trip. Clubs work best for frequent travelers and travelers with flexible schedules.

Travel Advisory

The following advice applies to each of the money-saving methods of booking a room described above.

- Be wary of deals that seem too good to be true.
- Don't be pressured into accepting a deal on the spot. A good offer today should be a good offer tomorrow. Do not send money by messenger or overnight mail. Question any requests for you to send money immediately. Do not provide your credit card number or bank information over the phone unless you know the company.
- Ask questions. Find out what's covered in the total cost. Ask if there are additional charges. Ask about cancellation policies and refunds.
- Get all the information in writing before you agree to purchase a tour or travel package, and read it.

OTHER WAYS *to* STAY

CONDOMINIUMS

CONDOS CAN BE THE PERFECT SOLUTION for family trips, two couples traveling together, or one couple seeking more space, privacy, convenience, and value than a hotel room might offer.

Hawaii condo resorts are not your bare-bones ski units. They range from standard to first-rate with all the comforts home may not have. They come in small clusters or large buildings, by the beach or not, often with lobbies, front desks, maid service, and other hotel services. Frequently, they are located in major resort areas with the full menu of extras available to hotel guests, including golf, tennis, pools, restaurants, and shuttle service. The difference between some resort condos and hotels is hard to discern as a guest, other than the larger units and homelike facilities of condos. The units are individually owned, but the rentals are managed in a group. Units in one complex may be managed by several different companies, some of them hotel firms—just to confuse it further—and individual owners may rent out their own units too.

Units normally range from 700 to 800 square feet for a one-bedroom unit to 2,000 square feet or more for a two-bedroom unit. Three-bedroom units and villas are larger still. With kitchens, you have the option of cooking all meals or just putting together breakfast or lunch at home and having dinner in restaurants. This gives you the chance to indulge in fresh tropical fruit, Kona coffee, and other Hawaii specialties. Condo and villa unit prices can range from under $100 per night to more than $1,000 per night, depending on the type of accommodation, location, and dates of stay.

One choice is to book your condo through one of the dozens of central condo reservations agencies around the Islands and the nation (some are listed below) to find Hawaii units that suit your needs. State your preferences on location, unit size, price range, amenities, ambience, and the number in your party, and you'll receive a list of properties from which to choose. Some condo representatives offer extra services, like car rentals and lei greetings, and some handle private resort home rentals as well.

Kapalua Resort on Maui is one of several luxury resorts that has an on-site management operation handling some 200 luxury units and homes in several areas of the resort. Destination Resorts Hawaii at Wailea Resort, also on Maui, is another, handling a wide variety of condo units at Wailea.

If you shop for travel deals on your own, you'll find plenty of condo travel packages are available in the same way that hotel packages are offered. Watch the ads, use the Internet, ask your friends, and keep on top of special offers.

Terms and policies differ. A deposit is usually required, payable by a major credit card. Be sure to check on the cancellation policy. It's wise to book at least three months in advance, although late reservations are entirely possible. Again, holidays and other high-demand periods will mean more competition for the unit you want.

Recommended Condominiums

Here are some favorite condos, selected for their location, facilities, and the good times we had:

CASTLE RESORTS & HOTELS, WAIKIKI SHORE, OAHU The only resort condo on the sands of Waikiki Beach, this is a true find, right next door to the open Fort DeRussy beachfront. Beach, ocean, city, and mountain views in studios, one-bedroom, and two-bedroom, moderately priced units (best rates on the Internet). For more information,

2161 Kalia Road, Honolulu 96815; ☎ 800-367-5004 or 808-952-4500; www.castleresorts.com.

THE KAPALUA VILLAS, MAUI Luxurious, spacious villas in low-rise clusters with views and proximity to the beach and golf course. One- to three-bedroom units are available. For more information, 500 Office Road, Kapalua 96761; ☎ 800-545-0018 or 808-669-8088; www.kapalua.com.

OUTRIGGER AINA NALU This quiet oasis of leafy greens and decorous contemporary interiors is hidden away, a block off the main drag of hot, noisy, crowded Lahaina, waiting to surprise you. Two-story studio and one- and two-bedroom condos cluster around pools and palms, just walking distance from busy Front Street. For more information, 660 Wainee Street, Lahaina, 96761 Toll-free reservations: 800-688-7444 or 808-667-9766; www.outrigger.com.

HANALEI COLONY RESORT, KAUAI Take seven one-lane bridges past Princeville on the North Shore to find this low-rise hideaway of 48 two-bedroom units in an incredibly beautiful and remote location at Haena.

Get groceries at Princeville or Hanalei on the way, because commerce comes to a halt before you arrive, leaving only the breathtaking beachfront setting. Step off your lanai onto sand. The two-bedroom, two-bath units are well cared for and well managed. Amenities include a spa, coffee shop and restaurant next door, with celebrities' homes just beyond that. The road soon ends in wilderness at Na Pali Coast. Best rates and incentives are on the Internet. For more information, P.O. Box 206, Hanalei 96714; ☎ 800-628-3004 or 808-826-6235; **www.hcr.com**.

OUTRIGGER KANALOA AT KONA, BIG ISLAND Palatial bathrooms are a key feature of these one-, two-, and three-bedroom units. The low-rise units sprawl over a rocky headland at Keauhou Resort, south of Kailua-Kona, with a restaurant, tennis, three pools, and lots of lanai ambience. Some are on the waterfront. They're great for families. For more information, 78-261 Manukai Street, Kailua-Kona 96740; ☎ 866-733-0601 or 808-322-9625; **www.outriggerkanaloaatkonacondo.com**.

PANIOLO HALE, MOLOKAI Wrapped in former golf greens beside golden Kepuhi Beach, this is an architecturally appealing ranch-style retreat and the most interesting of several small low-rise condo complexes next to defunct Kaluakoi Resort on Molokai's west end. Paniolo Hale operates independently, and units are independently rented. For more information, P.O. Box 190, Maunaloa 96770; ☎ 800-367-2984; **www.paniolohale.org**.

BED-AND-BREAKFASTS AND VACATION RENTALS

A HAWAII-STYLE BED-AND-BREAKFAST or vacation rental can offer a satisfying personal island experience much like staying in a friend's home. Some B&B guests stay year after year in the same spot, and indeed, become friends of the family. They find that staying at B&Bs gets them out of the artificial resort atmosphere and into real Hawaiian life.

Vacation rentals are even more independent accommodations that provide a true slice-of-life experience and put visitors in touch with residents as neighbors. When you shop the weekly farmers' markets for produce and flowers, or gossip over the fish counter about the price of ahi, your Hawaii sojourn takes on a whole new dimension. Vacation rentals can range from humble cottages to elaborate estates, some with monthly minimums, with charges from affordable to astronomical. But there'll be plenty of room for the nanny.

On the mainland, "bed-and-breakfast" usually means a refurbished mansion or historic house. In Hawaii, it's usually a cottage, studio, or guest room in a private home. Most prevalent are studios with kitchenettes or full kitchens. There are true traditional-inn exceptions, such as **Holualoa Inn** on an upland Kona coffee estate on the Big Island (76-5932 Mamalahoa Highway, Holualoa; ☎ 800-392-1812 or 808-324-1121; **www.holualoainn.com**); **Old Wailuku Inn** on Maui (2199 Kahookele Street, Wailuku; ☎ 808-244-5897; **www.mauiinn.com**); or **Manoa Valley**

RECOMMENDED HAWAII B&BS

OAHU

**Hawaiian Islands Bed & Breakfast/
Lanikai Bed & Breakfast**
1277 Mokulua Drive
Kailua 96734
☎ 808-261-7895
www.lanikaibb.com

Ke Iki Beach Bungalows
66–250 Kamehameha Hwy., D-100
Haleiwa 96712
☎ 808-638-8229 or 866-638-8229
www.keikibeach.com

Pat's Kailua Beach Properties
204 S. Kalaheo Avenue
Kailua 96734
☎ 808-261-1653
www.patskailua.com

KAUAI

Kauai Country Inn
6440 Olohena Road
Kapaa 96746
☎ 808-821-0207
www.kauaicountryinn.com

Poipu Inn Bed & Breakfast
2720 Hoonani Road
Koloa 96756
☎ 808-557-1576
www.poipuinn.com

BIG ISLAND (Hilo/Volcano/Honokaa)

**Shipman House Bed &
Breakfast Inn**
131 Kaiulani Street
Hilo 96720
☎ 808-934-8002 or 800-627-8447
www.hilo-hawaii.com

Chalet Kilauea
19–4178 Wright Road
Volcano Village 96785
☎ 808-967-7786 or 800-937-7786
www.volcano-hawaii.com

Waipio Wayside Inn
Highway 240
Honokaa 96727
☎ 808-775-0275 or 800-833-8849
www.waipiowayside.com

BIG ISLAND (South Kona Coast)

**Dragonfly Ranch Tropical Fantasy
Lodging**
84-5146 Keale O Keawe Road
Captain Cook 96704
☎ 808-328-2159 or 808-328-9570
www.dragonflyranch.com

Holualoa Inn
76-5932 Mamalahoa Highway
Holualoa 96725
☎ 808-324-1121 or 800-392-1812
www.holualoainn.com

Kalaekilohana B&B
94–2152 South Point Road
Naalehu 96772
☎ 808-939-8052
www.kau-hawaii.com

LANAI

Lanai Plantation Home
1168 Lanai Avenue
Lanai City 96763
☎ 808-565-6961 or 800-566-6961
www.dreamscometruelanai.com

Inn, in Honolulu near the University of Hawaii campus (2001 Vancouver Drive, Honolulu; ☎ 808-947-6019; **www.manoavalleyinn.com**).

You probably won't get home-cooked breakfast at most of the in-house B&Bs, due to restrictive laws. But you can expect a basket of tropical fruit, breads, and Kona coffee. Most operators require a minimum three-night stay. Ask about private baths and entries.

Search the Internet to preview and reserve a B&B among several hundred B&B operations in Hawaii. Beach properties rent quickly and are often booked year-round by returning guests. Plan to make reservations two or three months in advance, longer for holiday periods. Ask about cancellation policies for these as well as all accommodations. Prices start at about $75 a night for a B&B room in a private home. Call the hosts directly or use a reservation service. You'll find both choices online. Pacific Islands Reservations offers hundreds of listings throughout the state; 571 Pauku Street, Kailua, Oahu; ☎ 808-262-5030; **www .pacificislandsreservations.com.** Bed & Breakfast Hawaii is the oldest of the reservation services; P.O. Box 449, Kapaa, Kauai; ☎ 800-733-1632 or 808-822-2723; **www.bandb-hawaii.com**. Bed & Breakfast Inns Online markets various choices but does not make reservations; ☎ 800-215-7365; **www.bbonline.com/Hi.**

At most bed-and-breakfast agencies, a 20% deposit plus tax is required to hold a reservation. A portion of the deposit is retained by the agency as a fee. Otherwise, deposits are generally refundable, but ask what the policy is before you commit yourself. Personal checks and credit cards are accepted for deposits. The balance is usually paid in cash to the host family, though some agencies require full payment before you arrive. You will generally receive a confirmation shortly after your deposit is received, followed by a welcome letter and a map.

▌ HOTELS RATED *and* RANKED

WE'VE RANKED MORE THAN 60 HOTELS in Hawaii, based on room quality (cleanliness, spaciousness, views, amenities, visual appeal), value, service, and location. These factors are combined into an overall rating, which is expressed on a five-star scale. These are our ratings, independent of any travel organization or club. The evaluations are relative to properties on the Islands. See the hotel profiles later in this section for more details. These descriptions will help you understand the reasoning behind a hotel's rank.

The overall rating takes into consideration all facets of a hotel. A property with a prime location, excellent restaurants, or a gorgeous lobby might rank highly despite mediocre rooms. Conversely, a property with elaborate rooms and little else may rank lower overall. Hence, the one- to five-star room-quality ratings. Obviously, a room's size, the quality of its furnishings, and its level of cleanliness are prime factors in room quality. However, *Unofficial Guide* researchers also take careful note of the things most guests notice only when something is awry: noise levels, lighting, temperature control, ventilation, and security.

The value ratings—also given on a five-star scale—are a combination of the overall and room-quality ratings, divided by the cost of an average guest room. They indicate a general idea of value for money. If getting a good deal means the most to you, choose a property by value

How the Hotels Compare in Hawaii

HOTEL	OVERALL RATING	QUALITY RATING	VALUE RATING	COST
OAHU				
Halekulani	★★★★★	★★★★★	★★★	$$$$$
J. W. Marriott Ihilani Resort & Spa	★★★★★	★★★★★	★★★	$$$$$
Hilton Hawaiian Village Beach Resort	★★★★½	★★★★½	★★★★	$$$
Hyatt Regency Waikiki Resort & Spa	★★★★½	★★★★½	★★★	$$$
The Royal Hawaiian Hotel	★★★★½	★★★★½	★★★★	$$$$$
Hawaii Prince Hotel Waikiki	★★★★½	★★★★	★★★	$$$$$
Kahala Hotel & Resort	★★★★½	★★★★	★★★	$$$$$
Westin Moana Surfrider	★★★★½	★★★★	★★★	$$$
Aston at the Executive Centre	★★★★	★★★★	★★★	$$$
Embassy Suites Waikiki Beach Walk	★★★★	★★★★	★★★★	$$$
Lotus at Diamond Head	★★★★	★★★★	★★★	$$$
Outrigger Reef on the Beach	★★★★	★★★★	★★★★	$$$
Outrigger Regency on Beachwalk	★★★★	★★★★	★★★★	$$$
Sheraton Princess Kaiulani	★★★★	★★★★	★★★	$$
Sheraton Waikiki	★★★★	★★★★	★★★	$$$
Turtle Bay Resort	★★★★	★★★★	★★★	$$$
Waikiki Beach Marriott Resort & Spa	★★★★	★★★★	★★★	$$$
Waikiki Parc Hotel	★★★★	★★★★	★★★½	$$$
Aston Waikiki Joy Hotel	★★★★	★★★½	★★★	$$$
New Otani Kaimana Beach Hotel	★★★★	★★★½	★★★★	$$$
Hilton Waikiki Prince Kuhio	★★★½	★★★★	★★★	$$$
DoubleTree Alana Hotel Waikiki	★★★½	★★★½	★★★	$$

WHAT THE RATINGS MEAN

★★★★★	Best of the best	★★★	Average
★★★★½	Excellent	★★½	Below average
★★★★	Very good	★★	Poor
★★★½	Good		

rating. Otherwise, room and overall ratings are better indicators of a satisfying experience. If a wonderful property is fairly priced, it may only get an average or ★★★ value rating, but you still might prefer the experience to an average property with a ★★★★★ value rating.

The chart on the next page indicates the symbols used in the hotel table and profiles to correlate with various hotel prices. The rates used here are based on the rack rate for a standard ocean-view

HOTEL	OVERALL RATING	QUALITY RATING	VALUE RATING	COST
OAHU (CONTINUED)				
Ohana Waikiki East	★★★½	★★★½	★★★	$
Outrigger Luana Waikiki	★★★½	★★★½	★★★★	$
Outrigger Waikiki on the Beach	★★★½	★★★½	★★★	$$
Pacific Beach Hotel	★★★½	★★★	★★★	$$
Ala Moana Hotel	★★★	★★★★	★★★½	$$$
Ohana Waikiki Beachcomber Hotel	★★★	★★★	★★½	$$
Royal Garden at Waikiki	★★★	★★★	★★★	$
MAUI				
Four Seasons Resort Maui	★★★★★	★★★★★	★★★★	$$$$$
Ritz-Carlton, Kapalua	★★★★★	★★★★★	★★★★	$$$$$
Hotel Hana-Maui and Honua Spa	★★★★½	★★★★★	★★★	$$$$$
Grand Wailea Resort Hotel & Spa	★★★★½	★★★★½	★★★	$$$$$
Fairmont Kea Lani, Maui	★★★★½	★★★★	★★★	$$$$$
Hyatt Regency Maui Resort & Spa	★★★★	★★★★	★★★½	$$$$
Marriott's Maui Ocean Club	★★★★	★★★★	★★★	$$$$
Sheraton Maui Resort & Spa	★★★★	★★★★	★★★★	$$$$$
Wailea Beach Marriott Resort & Spa	★★★★	★★★★	★★★	$$$$
Westin Maui Resort & Spa Kaanapali	★★★★	★★★★	★★★	$$$$
Kaanapali Beach Club	★★★★	★★★	★★★★	$$$
Lahaina Inn	★★★★	★★★	★★★½	$$
Kaanapali Beach Hotel	★★★	★★★	★★★	$$$

COST INDICATORS			
$$$$$	Above $500	$$	$200–$300
$$$$	$400–$500	$	$200 and below
$$$	$300–$400		

room (or suitable equivalent) during high season (December through March). Don't be intimidated by the cost indicators, which are simply a gauge of relative prices. Lower and higher prices (depending on the room category) are available at each hotel. Always check the Internet rates first. This year we have dropped the cost ratings for many hotels because of their lowered rates that reflect the financial times. Be prepared for those rates to rise again when the economy improves.

How the Hotels Compare (continued)

HOTEL	OVERALL RATING	QUALITY RATING	VALUE RATING	COST
THE BIG ISLAND				
Four Seasons Resort Hualalai	★★★★★	★★★★★	★★★	$$$$$
Hilton Waikoloa Village	★★★★½	★★★★½	★★★	$$$
Mauna Lani Resort	★★★★½	★★★★½	★★½	$$$$$
The Fairmont Orchid	★★★★½	★★★★	★★★	$$$$
Hapuna Beach Prince Hotel	★★★★½	★★★★	★★★	$$$$
Kona Village Resort	★★★★½	★★★★	★★★★	$$$$$
Mauna Kea Beach Hotel	★★★★½	★★★★	★★★	$$$$$
Sheraton Keauhou Bay Resort & Spa	★★★★	★★★★	★★★	$$$$
Waikoloa Beach Marriott Resort & Spa	★★★★	★★★★	★★★★	$$$
King Kamehameha's Kona Beach Hotel	★★★½	★★★★	★★★★	$$
Hilo Hawaiian Hotel	★★★½	★★★½	★★½	$$
Naniloa Volcanoes Resort	★★★	★★★	★★★	$
Outrigger Keauhou Beach Resort	★★★	★★★	★★½	$
Volcano House	★★★	★★★	★★★	$$

▌▐ HOTEL PROFILES

DETAILS ON HOTELS AND RESORTS follow, alphabetically by island:

OAHU

Ala Moana Hotel $$$

OVERALL	★★★	QUALITY	★★★★	VALUE	★★★½

410 Atkinson Drive, Honolulu 96814; ☎ 800-367-6025 or 808-955-4811; FAX 808-944-6839; www.outrigger.com

IT DOESN'T FRONT WAIKIKI BEACH, but it does have a great central location, close to everything. A sky bridge leads you to Ala Moana Shopping Center; the Hawaii Convention Center is across the street, and it's a five-minute walk to Ala Moana Beach Park. Traffic in this area is always busy and views might be disappointing, but everything is handy.

SETTING AND FACILITIES
Location On the fringe of Waikiki. **Dining** Options include Royal Garden (Chinese) and Tsukasa (Japanese). The Plantation Café serves international cuisine for breakfast, lunch, and dinner. **Amenities and services** Room service, laundry facilities (coin-operated), ice and soda machines, meeting facilities, ATM machine,

HOTEL	OVERALL RATING	QUALITY RATING	VALUE RATING	COST
KAUAI				
Grand Hyatt Kauai Resort & Spa	★★★★½	★★★★½	★★★★	$$$$$
St. Regis Princeville Resort	★★★★½	★★★★	★★★	$$$$$
Hilton Kauai Beach Hotel & Resort	★★★★	★★★★	★★★½	$$
Kauai Marriott Resort & Beach Club	★★★★	★★★★	★★★	$$$$
Sheraton Kauai Resort	★★★★	★★★★	★★	$$$$$
Westin Princeville Ocean Resort Villas	★★★★	★★★★	★★★	$$$$
Hanalei Bay Resort	★★★½	★★★½	★★★	$$
MOLOKAI				
Hotel Molokai	★★★	★★★	★★★	$$
LANAI				
Four Seasons Resort Lanai, The Lodge at Koele	★★★★½	★★★★½	★★½	$$$$$
Four Seasons Resort Lanai at Manele Bay	★★★★½	★★★★	★★★	$$$$$
Hotel Lanai	★★★½	★★★	★★★★	$$

business center, fitness center, lounge and nightclub, beauty salon, sundry shop, shopping arcade, concierge, self-parking, valet parking, swimming pool.

ACCOMMODATIONS

Rooms 1,058. Includes 67 suites; 28 rooms equipped for the disabled. **All rooms** AC, flat-screen TV, pay movies, free high-speed Internet access, clock radio, in-room safe, two double beds, direct-dial phone system, data port, in-room coffee, hair dryer, voice mail. **Some rooms** King and two doubles, concierge services, in-room steam and Jacuzzi unit, iron and board, *yukata* robes. **Comfort and decor** Very clean, well maintained, newly renovated. Rooms small to medium, decorated with light colors and Hawaiian-accented artwork, airy and bright ambience.

PAYMENT, RESERVATIONS, AND RESTRICTIONS

Family plan Children age 17 and under stay free in room with parents if using existing bedding. Each additional adult, $40 per night. Maximum of 4 people per room (maximum of 3 per room in Kona Tower). Rollaway bed, $25 per night; cribs free. **Deposit** To guarantee a reservation, a deposit of 1 night's room rate is required within 10 days of confirmation. Cancellation notice must be given at least 72 hours prior to scheduled arrival for refund. **Credit cards** All major credit cards accepted. **Check-in/out** 3 p.m./noon. Early check-in possible if the room is available.

Aston at the Executive Centre Hotel $$$

OVERALL ★★★★	QUALITY ★★★★	VALUE ★★★

1088 Bishop Street, Honolulu 96813; ☎ 877-997-6667 or 808-539-3000; FAX **808-523-1088; www.astonhotels.com/**

STYLISH ALL-SUITE HOTEL FOR THE BUSINESS TRAVELER who must be handy to Honolulu's downtown Bishop Street. The service staff is friendly and professional, and the swimming pool and fitness center are welcome amenities. Don't expect a resort atmosphere. Though downtown Honolulu is populated by an intriguing mix of people by day, the streets are fairly deserted at night, but lively bars and restaurants are a stroll away at Aloha Tower Marketplace and in Chinatown. If you're here on business, this downtown hotel is the best choice.

SETTING AND FACILITIES

Location In the heart of the downtown business district. **Dining** Hukilau Sports Bar & Grill Restaurant serves a local-style breakfast, lunch, and dinner but is closed on weekends. **Amenities and services** Swimming pool, fitness center, parking facilities, laundry and dry-cleaning services.

ACCOMMODATIONS

Rooms 116. All suites. **All rooms** AC, TV, partial kitchen, Continental breakfast, free local calls, free high-speed Internet access, newspaper. **Some rooms** Full kitchen, washer and dryer, fax machines, ocean view. **Comfort and decor** Well-appointed, spacious suites. The decor is elegant but subdued. Floor-to-ceiling windows provide superb views of downtown Honolulu.

PAYMENT, RESERVATIONS, AND RESTRICTIONS

Rates based on up to 4 occupants per unit. **Deposit** 2-night deposit will be charged, refundable if cancellation notice is given at least 72 hours prior to scheduled arrival (30 days for year-end stays); cancellation fees waived in exceptional circumstances such as severe weather. **Credit cards** All major credit cards accepted. **Check-in/out** 3 p.m./noon. Early check-in and late checkout may be available.

Aston Waikiki Joy Hotel $$$

OVERALL ★★★★	QUALITY ★★★½	VALUE ★★★

320 Lewers Street, Honolulu 96815; ☎ 877-997-6667 or 808-923-2300; FAX **808-924-4010; www.astonhotels.com/**

THIS IS ONE OF WAIKIKI'S BEST OFF-BEACH BOUTIQUE HOTELS. Its location puts you near the action in Waikiki, but the beach is a couple of blocks away. The Italian marble open-air lobby sets the tone, but what makes it special are lavish touches in the rooms, half of which are suites with kitchenette facilities. Music lovers will appreciate the impressive stereo entertainment systems. Free Continental breakfast served daily to guests on the veranda.

SETTING AND FACILITIES

Location In the center of Waikiki, one block *ma uka* of Kalakaua Avenue, 10-minute walk to the beach. **Dining** Cappucinos Café serves coffees, lunch, and dinner; G. S. Studio karaoke center features 16 private rooms and more than 4,000 songs. **Amenities and services** Laundry service, Continental breakfast, pool, sauna and fitness center, valet parking.

ACCOMMODATIONS

Rooms 94. Includes 47 suites, 2 wheelchair-accessible rooms, and 1 room with roll-in shower. **All rooms** AC, lanai, stereo entertainment center, TV, spa tub with jets, mini-fridge, hair dryer, data port, voice mail, high-speed Internet access. **Some rooms** Full kitchen. **Comfort and decor** Spacious, luxurious, and clean. Rooms have their own marble entries, entertainment system with Bose speakers, and private Jacuzzis.

PAYMENT, RESERVATIONS, AND RESTRICTIONS

Family plan Children age 18 and under stay free in room with parents if using existing bedding. **Deposit** Credit card required, 2-night deposit will be charged. Cancellation notice must be given at least 72 hours prior to scheduled arrival for a refund (30 days for Christmastime cancellations), except in special circumstances such as severe weather. **Credit cards** All major credit cards accepted. **Check-in/out** 3 p.m./noon. Early check-in and late checkout may be available.

DoubleTree Alana Hotel Waikiki $$

OVERALL ★★★½	QUALITY ★★★½	VALUE ★★★

1956 Ala Moana Boulevard, Honolulu 96815; ☎ 800-222-TREE or 808-941-7275; FAX 808-949-0996; www.doubletree1.hilton.com

THIS BOUTIQUE HOTEL IS A SHORT WALK of a few blocks from the beach, the convention center, and Ala Moana Shopping Center. What the hotel lacks in beach access, it makes up for in convenience. Service is friendly and efficient, and there's a level of charm and comfort here that you won't find in larger hotels, particularly if you splurge just a little and get a suite. Alana Bistro serves three meals daily. Room views are cityscapes, because most of Diamond Head is obscured by other hotel properties. Decorator suites are exceptional, especially two penthouse suites with outdoor lanai that wraps much of the building.

SETTING AND FACILITIES

Location On the fringe of Waikiki, 15-minute walk to the beach. **Dining** Breakfast, lunch, and dinner at J Bistro. **Amenities and services** Room service, deep furo bathtubs, valet parking, rental-car desk, dry-cleaning and laundry services, 24-hour business center, 4,000 square feet of meetings space, multilingual staff, conference services, high-speed Internet access available, remote guest room printing, daily newspaper, iron and board, hair dryer, fitness center, swimming pool, wine bar.

ACCOMMODATIONS

Rooms 268. Includes 45 suites and two penthouse suites. **All rooms** AC, private lanai, TV, mini-cooler, in-room safe, MP3 docks, coffeemaker, hair dryer, iron and board. **Some rooms** Living room with sofa bed. **Comfort and decor** Very spacious suites, tastefully appointed with plush sofas and chairs. Hawaiian-themed artwork adorns the walls.

PAYMENT, RESERVATIONS, AND RESTRICTIONS
Deposit Credit-card guarantee with a 1-night deposit. **Credit cards** All major credit cards accepted. **Check-in/out** 3 p.m./noon. Early check-in and late checkout available by request.

Embassy Suites Waikiki Beach Walk $$$

| OVERALL ★★★★ | QUALITY ★★★★ | VALUE ★★★★ |

201 Beachwalk Street, Honolulu 96815; ☎ 800-EMBASSY or 808-921-2345; www.embassysuiteswaikiki.com

WAIKIKI'S NEW ALL-SUITE TWIN TOWERS rise 21 stories into the blue Hawaiian sky overlooking all near neighbors, except the new Trump tower, which is even taller. The views are commanding, the units spacious, comfortable, and well equipped, and the breakfast-to-order by the broad pool deck is a fulfilling start to the day. The manager's nightly reception assures a pleasant start to the evening. The beach is half a block away, and the Waikiki Beach Walk complex of shops and restaurants, with daily cultural events in an entertainment plaza, adjoins the hotel. Embassy Suites units are two rooms for the price of one hotel room elsewhere.

SETTING AND FACILITIES
Location Across the street from Waikiki Beach. **Dining** Roy's Waikiki is located at street level; Waikiki Beach Walk restaurants offer other options. **Amenities and services** Pools, business center, fitness center, coin laundry, valet parking, outdoor whirlpool, concierge, meeting rooms, catering, and ADA suites available.

ACCOMMODATIONS
Rooms 369 one- and two-bedroom suites with separate living rooms. **All rooms** Room service for lunch and dinner; AC; microwave and small refrigerator; coffeemaker; free domestic, Canadian, and local telephone calls; data port; clock radio with CD and MP3 players; flat-screen HDTV; pay movies; free high-speed internet; newspaper; in-room safe. **Some rooms** Lanai, 2 bedrooms, partial or full ocean views. **Comfort and decor** Suites are khaki and cream with a Hawaiian retro theme carved in golden woods and woven in the smart tropical prints on black bedspreads; wet bars with granite counters; sleeper sofa, dining table, and chairs.

PAYMENT, RESERVATIONS, AND RESTRICTIONS
Family plan Children age 18 and under stay free in room with parents if using existing bedding. **Deposit** Credit card guarantees reservation. Cancellation notice must be given at least 72 hours prior to scheduled arrival to avoid penalty. **Credit cards** All major credit cards accepted. **Check-in/out** 3 p.m./noon. Hospitality room available for early arrivals and late departures. Early check-ins and late checkouts based on availability.

Halekulani $$$$$

| OVERALL ★★★★★ | QUALITY ★★★★★ | VALUE ★★★ |

2199 Kalia Road, Honolulu 96815; ☎ 800-367-2343 or 808-923-2311; FAX 808-926-8004; www.halekulani.com

THE HALEKULANI IS THE BEST HOTEL IN WAIKIKI, the best on Oahu (at least until Trump Tower Waikiki gets built and then, who knows), and the only hotel in Hawaii to have won the prestigious AAA Five Diamond Award for both hotel and restaurant. It lives up to its reputation.

Amid the hustle and bustle of Waikiki, the Halekulani remains a peaceful, elegant oasis with a postcard view of Waikiki Beach and Diamond Head. It is more famous for its signature orchid pool and terrace than for its pocket beach.

No experience recalls old Waikiki more than sunset cocktails at the House Without a Key, where a dancer performs the hula to live Hawaiian music as the sun sinks in the Pacific.

Service is impeccable, and the rooms are spacious and well appointed—all with an ocean view. The two restaurants, La Mer and Orchids, are open-air and face the sea. The cuisine is outstanding and the service, gracious. A weekly manager's reception serves complimentary hors d'oeuvres.

Geared more toward well-to-do couples than large families, the hotel has gained a loyal following, and many guests return every year.

SETTING AND FACILITIES

Location On Waikiki Beach. **Dining** The Halekulani has notable fine-dining establishments, including the AAA Five Diamond Award–winning La Mer, which serves neoclassic French cuisine. Orchids serves breakfast, lunch, and dinner, featuring Hawaiian regional cuisine. House Without a Key serves breakfast, lunch, and cocktails outdoors and under roof. **Amenities and services** Fresh fruit bowl and chocolates on arrival, newspaper, twice-daily turndown service, valet parking, self-parking, full-service, award-winning spa incorporating Pacific Islands healing traditions, fitness center, in-house laundry and dry cleaning, free high-speed Internet access, MP3 dock and DVD player, florist, business center, heated swimming pool. Guests can indulge in a bit of luxury cruising in the hotel's fleet of fancy cars—a Maserati, Bentley, and two Lotus models—which are complimentary for those staying in the more exclusive suites, à la carte to other guests.

ACCOMMODATIONS

Rooms 453. Includes 42 suites, 16 rooms for the disabled. **All rooms** AC, lanai, 3 phones, TV, mini-fridge, clock radio. **Some rooms** 2 bedrooms. **Comfort and decor** Spacious, stylishly appointed decor with light colors and tasteful furnishings, high ceilings, and plenty of drawer space. Large balconies include table, two chairs, and an adjustable folding chair.

PAYMENT, RESERVATIONS, AND RESTRICTIONS

Family plan Children age 17 and under stay free in room with parents if using existing bedding. **Deposit** Credit card guarantees reservation with 1-night deposit within 14 days of confirmation. Cancellation notice must be given at least 72 hours prior to scheduled arrival for refund; prior to November 1 for holiday reservations. **Credit cards** All major credit cards accepted. **Check-in/out** 3 p.m./noon. Hospitality room available for early arrivals and late departures. Early check-ins and late checkouts based on availability.

Hawaii Prince Hotel Waikiki $$$$$

OVERALL	★★★★½	QUALITY	★★★★	VALUE	★★★

100 Holomoana Street, Honolulu 96815; ☎ **800-321-6248 or 808-956-1111;** FAX **808-946-0811; www.princeresortshawaii.com**

AN UPSCALE PINK MARBLE MONUMENT overlooking Ala Wai Yacht Harbor, the Hawaii Prince offers exceptional service and proximity to Ala Moana Shopping Center, Ala Moana Beach Park, and the Hawaii Convention Center, all within easy walking distance. The hotel's business facilities and services are excellent. All 521 hotel rooms provide yacht harbor and ocean views. The expansive Italian marble lobby features a tuxedo-clad piano player. The fifth floor is often windy, but is still a favorite hangout, with a swimming pool, sun deck, and terraces for sunset cocktails. If you're looking for a tee time, the Hawaii Prince Golf Club isn't anywhere near the hotel (it's a 40-minute drive away on the *Ewa* side of Oahu), but this is the only Waikiki hotel with a golf course to call its own. Guests of this hotel receive preferred tee times and shuttle service.

SETTING AND FACILITIES

Location On the outskirts of Waikiki at Ala Wai Yacht Harbor, 15-minute walk to Ala Moana Beach. **Dining** Two restaurants of note are the Prince Court, which features Hawaiian regional cuisine, and Hakone, specializing in exquisite Japanese fare. **Amenities and services** Hot towels on check-in, valet parking, business facilities, fitness center, in-room safes, babysitting services, daily newspaper.

ACCOMMODATIONS

Rooms 521. Includes 57 suites; 10 rooms for the disabled. Nonsmoking rooms available. **All rooms** AC, TV with pay movies, mini-fridge, in-room safe, hair dryer, robes. **Some rooms** Extra bedroom and bath. **Comfort and decor** Very spacious, with lavish decor and floor-to-ceiling windows that partially open, but no lanai. Floral-themed artwork adorns walls in well-lit rooms with warm colors.

PAYMENT, RESERVATIONS, AND RESTRICTIONS

Family plan Children age 17 and under stay free in room with parents if using existing bedding. Maximum occupancy is 3 adults or 2 adults and 2 children per room; extra adult, $40 per night. **Deposit** 1-night deposit due 14 days within booking. Cancellation notice must be given 72 hours prior to scheduled arrival for refund. **Credit cards** All major credit cards accepted. **Check-in/out** 2 p.m./ noon. Early check-in and late checkout available on request.

kids Hilton Hawaiian Village Beach Resort & Spa $$$

OVERALL	★★★★½	QUALITY	★★★★½	VALUE	★★★★

2005 Kalia Road, Honolulu 96815; ☎ **800-445-8667 or 808-949-4321;** FAX **808-951-5458; www.hiltonhawaiianvillage.com**

HAWAII'S LARGEST HOTEL, THIS BEACHFRONT VILLAGE epitomizes the term "self-contained resort." You really don't have to leave. Expect crowds here, because the Hilton is a top choice for tour and convention groups, and it is the state's largest hotel with 3,433 rooms and units. The hotel rooms are currently housed in four separate towers: Tapa, Rainbow, Diamond Head, and upscale Alii towers. Hilton Grand Vacations Club offers time-share units in the Kalia Tower, which includes a health and wellness spa and four floors of retail shops, the Lagoon Tower, renovated extensively to offer condo units ranging from studios to three bedrooms, and the new 38-story Grand Waikikian with 331 more time-share units.

The HHV also has 14 restaurants and 5 lounges (with nightly entertainment), more than 90 shops and services, spa and preventive medicine center, and activities ranging from undersea submarine rides to wildlife tours. This hotel is terrific for young families, and it offers one of Hawaii's best year-round children's programs (including excursions to nearby attractions such as the Honolulu Zoo and Waikiki Aquarium). Lei-making, hula, and ukulele lessons are daily activities. Every Friday, the King's Jubilee and Fireworks show features a precision rifle drill team, Hawaiian music, and fireworks.

SETTING AND FACILITIES

Location Fronting Duke Kahanamoku Beach (part of Waikiki Beach) and newly restored Duke Kahanamoku Lagoon, near gateway to Waikiki. **Dining** Of the restaurants here, Bali by the Sea, an oceanfront restaurant serving innovative cuisine with an island accent, stands out among the finest restaurants on Oahu. **Amenities and services** 5 outdoor swimming pools, valet parking, parking garage, travel services, laundry and dry cleaning, wedding chapel, physicians on call, beauty and barber shops, post office and express-mail pickup and delivery, extensive meeting and banquet space, business services, children's program, florist.

ACCOMMODATIONS

Rooms 2,860. Includes 363 suites, 75 rooms for the disabled. **All rooms** AC, TV with pay movies, in-room safe, refreshment center. **Some rooms** Evening *pupu*, concierge service, robes, sparkling water, in-room fax, upgraded bathroom amenities, valet laundry service. **Comfort and decor** Moderate space, well lit, with airy, attractive Hawaiian decor that includes wicker furnishings and floral bedspreads.

PAYMENT, RESERVATIONS, AND RESTRICTIONS

Family plan Children age 17 and under stay free in room with parents if using existing bedding. **Deposit** 1-night deposit due within 10 days after confirmation. Cancellation notice must be given at least 72 hours prior to scheduled arrival for refund. **Credit cards** All major credit cards accepted. **Check-in/out** 2 p.m./11 a.m. Early check-in may be available (confirmed on arrival).

Hilton Waikiki Prince Kuhio $$$

OVERALL ★★★½	QUALITY ★★★★	VALUE ★★★

2500 Kuhio Avenue, Honolulu 96815; ☎ **800-HILTONS or 808-922-0811;** FAX **808-921-5507; www1.hilton.com**

CENTRALLY LOCATED PRINCE KUHIO is a short hike to Waikiki Beach. The Ala Wai Canal, Honolulu Zoo, and Kapiolani Park are also nearby. Kuhio Avenue can be just as busy as Kalakaua Avenue, and the area tends to get noisy at night. The lobby area is attractive, open-air, and inviting. Rooms are newly renovated.

SETTING AND FACILITIES

Location On Kuhio Avenue in Waikiki, 2 blocks from beach. **Dining** MAC (Modern American Cooking) 24–7 really serves MAC all day every day, something to keep in mind for late appetites. MAC 2-GO is a breakfast-and-lunch takeout operation with espresso. Hang 10 pool bar serves breakfast, lunch, and dinner; Lobby **Bar** serves evening *pupu* (appetizers) and drinks. **Amenities and services** Room service, activities desk, free high-speed Internet access, valet-only parking, coin laundry, swimming pool.

ACCOMMODATIONS

Rooms 601. Rooms for the disabled available. **All rooms** Nonsmoking, AC, HDTV, refrigerator, laptop safe, marble and stone baths, clock radio/MP3 dock, premium bedding, hair dryer, coffeemaker. **Some rooms** Balcony, kitchenette, concierge/club floor. **Comfort and decor** Rooms are small to medium, tastefully appointed, and very clean, with floor-to-ceiling windows, Hawaiian artwork, and comfortable furnishings.

PAYMENT, RESERVATIONS, AND RESTRICTIONS

Family plan Children age 17 and under stay free in room with parents if using existing bedding. **Deposit** 1-night deposit or credit-card guarantee required. Cancellation notice must be given 72 hours prior to scheduled arrival for refund. **Credit cards** All major credit cards accepted. **Check-in/out** 3 p.m./noon. Early check-in and late checkout available on request.

kids Hyatt Regency Waikiki Resort & Spa $$$

OVERALL	★★★★½	QUALITY	★★★★½	VALUE	★★★

2424 Kalakaua Avenue, Honolulu 96815; ☎ 800-233-1234 or 808-923-1234; FAX **808-926-3415; info@hyattwaikiki.com; www.hyattwaikiki.com**

EVERYTHING, INCLUDING THE BEACH, is just a short walk away. The Hyatt is composed of twin 40-story towers connected by the open-air Great Hall and has three-story arcade of shops. The lobby features free entertainment by Harry's Bar and a ten-story atrium with a waterfall; guests can enjoy drinks by the pool at the Elegant Dive. The Hyatt also has a full-service spa and a children's program, Camp Hyatt, which provides kids ages 3 to 12 with fun and educational activities. The neighborhood is noisy at night.

SETTING AND FACILITIES

Location Across the street from Kuhio Beach. **Dining** The Colony offers fresh steaks and seafood and Ciao Mein tests your tastes with Italian and Chinese menu. **Amenities and services** Room service, valet parking and self-parking, full-service spa, meeting and banquet facilities, children's program.

ACCOMMODATIONS

Rooms 1,229. Includes 18 suites; 24 rooms for the disabled. **All rooms** AC, flat-screen TV, lanai, windows that open, refrigerator, minibar, stereo with iPod dock, hair dryer, iron and board, in-room laptop safe, coffeemaker. **Some**

rooms Connecting parlor. **Comfort and decor** Spacious, well maintained. Decor is spare but gracious, with rattan furnishings and Hawaiian print accents against subdued colors.

PAYMENT, RESERVATIONS, AND RESTRICTIONS

Family plan Children age 17 and under stay free in room with parents if using existing bedding. **Deposit** 1-night deposit required within 10 days of confirmation. Cancellation notice must be given at least 72 hours prior to scheduled arrival for refund. **Credit cards** All major credit cards accepted. **Check-in/out** 3 p.m./noon. Early check-in and late checkout available on request.

J. W. Marriott Ihilani Resort & Spa $$$$$

OVERALL ★★★★★	QUALITY ★★★★★	VALUE ★★★

92-1001 Olani Street, Kapolei 96707; ☎ 800-626-4446 or 808-679-0079; FAX 808-679-0080; reservations@ihilani.com; www.ihilani.com

THE IHILANI, WHICH TRANSLATES TO "HEAVENLY SPLENDOR," was built by the Japanese for Tokyo moguls on holiday. Today it's a favorite of Oahu visitors seeking an alternative to Waikiki, only an hour but seemingly a world away.

Situated on one of four man-made lagoons, Ihilani overlooks a gold-sand beach. The resort's full-service spa, which uses seawater therapies, is regarded as one of the finest in the world. Six state-of-the-art tennis courts and nearby Ko Olina Golf Club make this a favorite for sports-minded visitors.

SETTING AND FACILITIES

Location At the Ko Olina Resort in Kapolei, on the Leeward side of the island. **Dining** Of 5 restaurants, Azul is Ihilani's signature dining spot and an award-winning restaurant with an extensive menu that blends the flavors of the Mediterranean and Hawaii. **Amenities and services** Twice-daily maid service, turndown service, daily ice delivery, 24-hour room service, full-service spa, tennis club, beauty salon, year-round children's program. Self-parking and valet parking.

ACCOMMODATIONS

Rooms 351. Includes 36 luxury suites; 14 rooms equipped for the disabled. **All rooms** AC, ceiling fan, TV, in-house movie library, in-room safe, high-speed Internet access, AM/FM radio with CD player, minibar, 3 phones, private lanai, hair dryer, robes. **Some rooms** Whirlpool spas, walk-in closets, large-screen TV, 2 bathrooms. **Comfort and decor** Very spacious (rooms average 640 square feet) and clean, rooms are decorated with local art and teak furnishings. One amenity allows you to turn lights on and off, adjust the room temperature, and find the current time anywhere in the world from your phone, which has instructions in six languages.

PAYMENT, RESERVATIONS, AND RESTRICTIONS

Family plan Children age 17 and under stay free in room with parents if using existing bedding. Rollaway bed, $35. **Deposit** To guarantee reservation, a 1-night deposit is required within 14 days of booking. Cancellation notice must be received at least 72 hours prior to scheduled arrival for refund. **Credit cards** All major credit cards accepted, except Discover. **Check-in/out** 3 p.m./11 a.m. Early check-in available by request.

Kahala Hotel & Resort $$$$$

| OVERALL | ★★★★½ | QUALITY | ★★★★ | VALUE | ★★★ |

5000 Kahala Avenue, Honolulu 96816; ☎ 800-367-2525 or 808-739-8888; FAX 808-739-8800; www.kahalaresort.com

OLD-TIMERS RECALL THIS GRAND BEACH HOTEL as the Kahala Hilton. It's still a good choice, particularly if you are a security-conscious golfer. This hotel sits between a private golf course and the ocean, so presidents and kings, who do stay and tee off here, sleep well.

Complimentary shuttle service transports you to and from major shopping destinations: Kahala Mall, Ala Moana Shopping Center, and Royal Hawaiian Shopping Center. The Kahala has its own reef-protected beach, exotic gardens, waterfall, turtle ponds, man-made dolphin lagoon, and beachfront lawn.

SETTING AND FACILITIES

Location In the upscale Kahala neighborhood, about 15 minutes from Waikiki. **Dining** Oceanfront Hoku's is a popular restaurant, serving fine international cuisine with fresh local ingredients. **Amenities and services** Room service, laundry service, valet parking, meeting and banquet facilities, business facilities, fitness center, children's program, 24-hour medical services.

ACCOMMODATIONS

Rooms 306. Includes 32 suites. ADA-approved rooms available. **All rooms** AC, flat-screen TV, CD player, clock radio, high-speed wireless Internet access, video games, 3 phones, minibar, computer outlets, data port, hair dryer, in-room safe, bathrobes. **Some rooms** Upgraded amenities. **Comfort and decor** Spacious, luxurious, and clean, rooms have a stylish turn-of-the-20th-century motif, with mahogany furnishings, teak parquet floors, and an inviting and comfortable appeal.

PAYMENT, RESERVATIONS, AND RESTRICTIONS

Family plan Children age 17 and under stay free in room with parents if using existing bedding. Rollaway bed, $40. **Deposit** All reservations guaranteed by credit card. Cancellation notice must be given at least 72 hours prior to scheduled arrival for refund. **Credit cards** All major credit cards accepted. **Check-in/out** 3 p.m./noon. Early check-in and late checkout available on request.

Lotus at Diamond Head $$$

| OVERALL | ★★★★ | QUALITY | ★★★★ | VALUE | ★★★ |

2885 Kalakaua Avenue, Honolulu 96815; ☎ 800-367-5004 or 808-922-1700; FAX 808-545-2163; www.castleresorts.com

THIS SMALL HOTEL (formerly a W Hotel) is a hidden gem nestled at the foot of Diamond Head. The setting is not beachfront, but it is peaceful and calm—as opposed to the nonstop action of central Waikiki. The service is personal and friendly. The views are eye-catching no matter what room you're in. Waikiki Shell, Waikiki Aquarium, and Honolulu Zoo are nearby in leafy, green Kapiolani Park.

SETTING AND FACILITIES

Location Diamond Head end of Waikiki, short walk to beach. **Dining** Diamond Head Grill serves "flavors of Hawaii" cuisine. The Living Room has Internet access. **Amenities and services** Room service, night club, high-speed Internet access, meeting and banquet facilities, laundry service, valet parking.

ACCOMMODATIONS

Rooms 48. All rooms AC, radio, TV, refrigerator, lanai, iPod dock/clock radio, minibar, coffeemaker, hair dryer. **Some rooms** 2 bedrooms. **Comfort and decor** Spacious and clean, with understated whites-and-woods Balinese furnishings that focus on natural materials. Accents in bright, sunny colors add to the overall style.

PAYMENT, RESERVATIONS, AND RESTRICTIONS

Family plan Rollaway bed, $45. **Deposit** Credit card guarantees reservation. Cancellation notice must be given 72 hours prior to scheduled arrival for refund. **Credit cards** All major credit cards accepted. **Check-in/out** 3 p.m./noon. Early check-in and late checkout may be available.

New Otani Kaimana Beach Hotel $$$

OVERALL ★★★★	QUALITY ★★★½	VALUE ★★★★

2863 Kalakaua Avenue, Honolulu 96815; ☎ 800-356-8264 or 808-923-1555; FAX 808-922-9404; rooms@kaimana.com; www.kaimana.com

WHAT WE LIKE BEST ABOUT THE KAIMANA BEACH is its location. It's on the edge of Waikiki, yet removed from its congested traffic and noise and wrapped in the leafy peace of Kapiolani Park. This small, low-key hotel with stylish touches and fabulous views from some rooms and suites fronts Sans Souci Beach with Kapiolani Park in its backyard, and Diamond Head on its flank. The Hau Tree Lanai Restaurant is popular with residents who meet for breakfast, lunch, or sunset cocktails on the terrace overlooking the beach and sea, with the Waianae Mountains framing the distant western vista. Robert Louis Stevenson noted more than a century ago, "If anyone desires lovely scenery, pure air, clear sea water, good food, and heavenly sunsets, I recommend him cordially to Sans Souci." We second the motion. This is Oahu's best small hotel bargain.

SETTING AND FACILITIES

Location On Sans Souci Beach, at the foot of Diamond Head, across from Kapiolani Park. **Dining** The oceanfront Hau Tree Lanai, one of Hawaii's most romantic settings, offers Hawaii regional cuisine. Miyako serves traditional Japanese fare. **Amenities and services** Room service, laundry and dry-cleaning service, valet parking, fitness center, business facilities.

ACCOMMODATIONS

Rooms 124. Includes 5 suites and 3 ADA-approved rooms. **All rooms** AC, TV, VCR, lanai, refrigerator, in-room safe, hair dryer; coffeemaker available on request. **Some rooms** Minibar. **Comfort and decor** Corner-suite views are hard to match anywhere else because of the location that allows you to see Waikiki and Diamond Head. Rooms are befitting their waterfront perch with blue and white decor and bright, warm accents. **Some rooms** are small but clean and well maintained, with a contemporary island-themed decor.

PAYMENT, RESERVATIONS, AND RESTRICTIONS
Family plan Children age 12 and under stay free. Rollaway bed, $30. **Deposit** Credit-card guarantee or 1-night deposit required. Cancellation notice must be given at least 72 hours prior to scheduled arrival for refund. **Credit cards** All major credit cards accepted. **Check-in/out** 2 p.m./noon. Hospitality room available for early arrivals and late departures.

Ohana Waikiki East $

OVERALL	★★★½	QUALITY	★★★½	VALUE	★★★

150 Kaiulani Avenue, Honolulu 96815; ☎ 800-462-6262 or 808-922-5353; FAX 808-926-4334; www.ohanahoteleast.com

THE OHANA EAST IS A GOOD BARGAIN CHOICE if you don't require unobstructed ocean views. The beach is just a few minutes' walk away. Ohana East is situated near the International Market Place. Some suites have kitchenettes for visitors on extended stays. Nothing exceptional, but nothing subpar, either.

SETTING AND FACILITIES
Location At Kuhio and Kaiulani avenues, 2 blocks from beach. **Dining** Keoni by Keo's (Thai), Chili's **Bar** & Grill (Southwest), and Chuck's Cellar (prime rib and seafood specialties). **Amenities and services** Room service (7 a.m. to 9:30 p.m.), meeting rooms, activities desk, fitness room, pool, parking, coin-operated washer and dryer.

ACCOMMODATIONS
Rooms 441. Includes 25 suites; 5 rooms for the disabled. **All rooms** AC, TV, high-speed Internet access, refrigerator, in-room safe, coffeemaker. **Some rooms** Lanai, kitchenette. **Comfort and decor** Recently renovated rooms are small to medium sized, with island-accented art and furnishings.

PAYMENT, RESERVATIONS, AND RESTRICTIONS
Family plan Children age 17 and under stay free in room with parents if using existing bedding. **Deposit** Credit-card guarantee or 1-night deposit required. Cancellation notice must be given at least 72 hours prior to scheduled arrival for refund. **Credit cards** All major credit cards accepted. **Check-in/out** 3 p.m./noon. Early check-in and late checkout available on request.

Ohana Waikiki Beachcomber Hotel $$

OVERALL	★★★	QUALITY	★★★	VALUE	★★½

2300 Kalakaua Avenue, Honolulu 96815; ☎ 877-424-6423 or 808-922-4646; FAX 808-923-4889; www.ascendcollection.com/hotel-honolulu.com

ALTHOUGH NOT AS WELL KNOWN as many of Waikiki's hotels, the Beachcomber has a lot going for it, including a renovation and new management

(Choice Hotels International). One asset is its front-and-center location in the heart of Waikiki, next to the International Market Place, where you can find bargains on all kinds of souvenirs and gifts, and directly across Kalakaua Avenue from the upscale Royal Hawaiian Shopping Center. The beach is also across the street, about a block away. We like the second-floor pool deck overlooking Kalakaua Avenue. The Beachcomber is the home of the *Magic of Polynesia* live stage show (see page 453) and Jimmy Buffett's at the Beachcomber, a new 400-seat casual restaurant.

SETTING AND FACILITIES

Location In the heart of Waikiki, about a block from the beach. **Dining** Hibiscus Café serves everything from burgers and pizzas to a wide selection of international specialties. **Amenities and services** Maid service, parking, fitness room, washer and dryer, swimming pool, ice machine.

ACCOMMODATIONS

Rooms 495. Includes 7 suites, 7 wheelchair-accessible rooms. **All rooms** AC; flat-screen TV with in-room movies; lanai; refrigerator; in-room safe; voice mail; free wireless high-speed Internet access; free local, domestic, and Canadian phone calls; business center; newspaper; coffeemaker; hair dryer; iron and board. **Some rooms** 2 TVs, 2 balconies, king-sized bed. **Comfort and decor** Spacious and clean, newly redone. Soft tropical colors add to a soothing and relaxing atmosphere. Decor is simple but pleasant, with Hawaiian paintings adorning the walls.

PAYMENT, RESERVATIONS, AND RESTRICTIONS

Family plan Children age 17 and under stay free in room with parents if using existing bedding. Rollaway bed, $30 per night. Maximum of 4 people per room. **Deposit** 1-night deposit due no later than 10 days after confirmation. Cancellation notice must be given 72 hours prior to scheduled arrival for refund. **Credit cards** All major credit cards accepted. **Check-in/out** 3 p.m./noon.

Outrigger Luana Waikiki $

OVERALL	★★★½	QUALITY	★★★½	VALUE	★★★★

2045 Kalakaua Avenue, Honolulu 96815; ☎ 800-688-7444 or 808-955-6000; FAX **808-943-8555; www.outrigger.com**

THREE BLOCKS FROM THE BEACH, this affordable hotel neighbors Fort DeRussy and the King Kalakaua Plaza shopping and restaurant complex. The Outrigger Luana recently renovated its hotel rooms, studios, and one- and two-bedroom condo units. Service is friendly and enthusiastic, and the atmosphere is comfortable. Overall, this is a good off-beach value.

SETTING AND FACILITIES

Location At the gateway to Waikiki, next to Fort DeRussy, 10-minute walk to the beach. **Dining** The Eastern Garden serves breakfast, lunch, and dinner. **Amenities and services** Room service, laundry and dry cleaning, swimming pool, Jacuzzi, business center, fitness center, parking.

ACCOMMODATIONS

Rooms 205. Includes 2 suites, 7 ADA-approved rooms. **All rooms** AC, free high-speed Internet access, TV, mini-fridge, lanai, in-room safe, hair dryer. **Some**

rooms Kitchenettes or full kitchens, extra bedroom, extra bathroom. **Comfort and decor** Medium-sized rooms are clean and comfortable, with soft colors and contemporary island decor.

PAYMENT, RESERVATIONS, AND RESTRICTIONS

Family plan Children age 17 and under stay free with parents. **Deposit** Credit-card guarantee or 1-night cash deposit due within 10 days of booking. Cancellation notice must be given 72 hours prior to scheduled arrival for refund. **Credit cards** All major credit cards accepted. **Check-in/out** 3 p.m./noon. Early check-in and late checkout available on request.

Outrigger Reef on the Beach $$$

OVERALL ★★★★	QUALITY ★★★★	VALUE ★★★★

2169 Kalia Road, Honolulu 96815; ☎ 800-688-7444 or 808-923-3111; FAX 808-924-4957; www.outriggerreef-onthebeach.com

FOLLOWING A $100 MILLION UPGRADE of all guest rooms and public areas, the Outrigger Reef is transformed, with a fresh and newly refined appeal, especially for beachgoing families. Rooms are larger, and more suites are offered in various sizes. Decor is handsome and reflects Hawaiian traditions and modern techy features. A "stream" meanders through the lobby, which features a collection of Polynesian canoe art by renowned historian Herb Kane and gives an architectural nod to Pacific heritage with a soaring-roofed canoe-house entry. It also includes 15 specialty shops, a library, and a quiet sitting room. This beachfront hotel serves to anchor Outrigger's extensive new Waikiki Beach Walk redevelopment, and all the project's restaurants and stores are close at hand. The Outrigger Reef provides all the island hospitality this *kamaaina* chain is known for, plus an incomparable location—not only right on Waikiki Beach but next to the wide open beaches of Fort DeRussy.

SETTING AND FACILITIES

Location On Waikiki Beach near Fort DeRussy. **Dining** A quartet of eateries, including Kani Ka Pila Grill with live Hawaiian music nightly and Shore Bird Restaurant & Beach Bar, as well as the Ocean House, serving Pacific Rim cuisine, and a Starbucks. **Amenities and services** Room service; spa; seated, personalized check-in; pool; children's program; business center; Hawaiian Airlines check-in desk; meeting facilities; daily Hawaiian activities; fitness center; activities desk; valet parking; coin-operated laundry; and the Outrigger catamaran ready to take you for a ride.

ACCOMMODATIONS

Rooms 639. Includes 44 suites; 10 rooms for the disabled. **All rooms** Lanai, AC, TV, mini-refrigerator, in-room safe, clock radio/MP3 dock, coffeemaker. **Some rooms** Kitchenette, whirlpool baths, chaise lounge sleeper. **Comfort and decor** Medium-sized (340 square feet and up), well-lit rooms are redone in soothing neutrals with subdued Hawaiian tapa patterns on fabrics, and framed artifacts such as feather lei. Suites have flexible configurations, so that up to three additional bedrooms can be arranged around a central living area.

Family plan Children age 17 and under stay free in room with parents if using existing bedding. **Deposit** 1-night deposit or credit-card guarantee. Cancellation notice must be given 72 hours prior to scheduled arrival for refund. **Credit cards** All major credit cards accepted. **Check-in/out** 3 p.m./noon. Early check-in and late checkout available on request.

Outrigger Regency on Beachwalk $$$

OVERALL	★★★★	QUALITY	★★★★	VALUE	★★★★

255 Beach Walk. Honolulu 96815; ☎ 800-688-7444 or 808-922-3871; FAX **808-922-3887; www.outriggerregencycondo.com**

OUTRIGGER HAS INTRODUCED ITS FIRST BOUTIQUE condo resort as part of the Waikiki Beach Walk redevelopment. Think hardwood floors with bright accents and tropical urban chic. Waikiki Beach is just far enough away for all the sand to fall off on the walk back to enjoy Waikiki's newest, cushy condo comforts.

SETTING AND FACILITIES
Location Off-beach; Beach Walk at Kalakaua, shopping central. **Dining** Arancino di Mare features Italian cuisine for lunch and dinner; Matsugen specializes in Japanese soba noodle dishes. **Amenities and services** Daily maid service, 24-hour front desk, parking, coin-operated laundry, dry cleaning and laundry valet, free newspaper, children's program.

ACCOMMODATIONS
Rooms 48 units, nonsmoking throughout. Includes 1- and 2-bedroom units. **All rooms** Gourmet kitchens, marble vanities, flat-screen TV with cable, AC.

PAYMENT, RESERVATIONS, AND RESTRICTIONS
2-night minimum during Christmas holidays. **Family plan** 4-person maximum in 1-bedroom units; 6 persons in 2-bedroom units. No additional person charge. Rollaway bed, $25 per night. **Deposit** 1-night cash deposit within 10 days or credit-card guarantee. Cancellation notice must be given at least 72 hours prior to scheduled arrival for refund. **Credit cards** All major credit cards accepted. **Check-in/out** 3 p.m./noon.

Outrigger Waikiki on the Beach $$

OVERALL	★★★½	QUALITY	★★★½	VALUE	★★★

2335 Kalakaua Avenue, Honolulu 96815; ☎ 800-688-7444 or 808-923-0711; FAX **808-921-9749; www.outrigger.com**

THIS HAS TRADITIONALLY BEEN CONSIDERED OUTRIGGER'S flagship property, and here's why: It's got the best location on Waikiki Beach. A short stroll around the second-floor lobby tells you right away you're in Hawaii, with soft Hawaiian music, floral-motif carpeting, island artwork, a seashell-shaped chandelier, and, most telling, the soothing sounds of the sea and beach. Not only is the Outrigger Waikiki front-and-center, right on the beach, but it is also next door to Waikiki's largest shopping complex, the Royal Hawaiian Shopping Center, and across the street from the International Market Place. Duke's Waikiki Restaurant, the hotel's best-known restaurant, is worth a visit just to peruse the memorabilia paying tribute to Duke Kahanamoku, Hawaii's surfing legend. The atmosphere is informal, colorful, and friendly.

SETTING AND FACILITIES

Location On Waikiki Beach, between the Royal Hawaiian Hotel and Moana Surfrider. **Dining** Duke's Waikiki Restaurant is a Waikiki favorite, serving breakfast, lunch, and dinner. Hula Grill Waikiki offers breakfast and dinner. **Amenities and services** Room service, lanai, parking, valet parking, pool, child care, fitness center, conference facilities, daily cultural activities, high-speed Internet access, activities desk, coin-operated laundry, Hawaiian Airlines check-in kiosk in lobby.

ACCOMMODATIONS

Rooms 497. Includes 30 suites. Rooms for the disabled are available. **All rooms** AC, TV, refrigerator, in-room safe, daily newspaper, coffeemaker. **Some rooms** Kitchenettes, lanai. **Comfort and decor** Medium-sized rooms with subdued colors and tropical woods are clean and well maintained.

PAYMENT, RESERVATIONS, AND RESTRICTIONS

Family plan Children age 17 and under stay free in room with parents if using existing bedding. **Deposit** 1-night deposit or credit-card guarantee. Cancellation notice must be given at least 72 hours prior to scheduled arrival for refund. **Credit cards** All major credit cards accepted. **Check-in/out** 3 p.m./noon. Early check-in and late checkout on request.

Pacific Beach Hotel $$

OVERALL	★★★½	QUALITY	★★★	VALUE	★★★

2490 Kalakaua Avenue, Honolulu 96815; ☎ 800-367-6060 or 808-923-4511; FAX 808-922-0129; www.pacificbeachhotel.com

EVERY WAIKIKI HOTEL TRIES TO DISTINGUISH itself from the others in some fashion, and the Pacific Beach Hotel makes a big splash with its three-story, 280,000-gallon oceanarium, featuring hundreds of marine plants and animals. The oceanarium is the centerpiece of the hotel's dining establishments. A busy hotel with friendly service and a prime location, it's across Kalakaua from the beach.

SETTING AND FACILITIES

Location Across the street from Waikiki Beach. **Dining** Oceanarium, whose star attraction is not the food but the fish in its 280,000-gallon saltwater tank. Shogun is a popular Japanese restaurant, and Neptune's Garden serves seafood, steaks, and continental fare. **Amenities and services** Swimming pool and whirlpool, full spa, tennis, parking, laundry service, room service, travel desk, 24-hour fitness center, business facilities, meeting rooms.

ACCOMMODATIONS

Rooms 837. Includes 8 suites; 13 rooms for the disabled. **All rooms** AC, HDTV, lanai, coffeemaker, in-room safe, mini-fridge, high-speed Internet access, hair dryer. **Some rooms** Bathrobes, iron and board, vanity kit. **Comfort and decor**

Rooms are small to medium. Soft, pastel colors help brighten them. Lanai open to scenic mountain or ocean views.

PAYMENT, RESERVATIONS, AND RESTRICTIONS

Family plan Children age 18 and under stay free in room with parents if using existing bedding. Maximum of 4 people per room. **Deposit** 1-night deposit required within 14 days of confirmation. Cancellation notice must be given at least 72 hours prior to scheduled arrival for refund. **Credit cards** All major credit cards accepted. **Check-in/out** 3 p.m./noon. Early check-in and late checkout based on availability.

Royal Garden at Waikiki $

OVERALL	★★★	QUALITY	★★★	VALUE	★★★

440 Olohana Street, Honolulu 96815; ☎ 800-731-4820 or 808-943-0202; FAX 808-946-8777; www.royalgardens.com

IT'S A DECENT WALK TO THE BEACH from this property—about 20 minutes—but the boutique Royal Garden is still a great choice. Everything is first-class, from the service to the amenities. The setting is one of quiet refinement, with interiors inspired by Hawaii's natural beauty. Lush gardens surround two swimming pools. Shopping nearby. Jogging along nearby Ala Wai Canal is pleasant.

SETTING AND FACILITIES

Location In Waikiki, near Ala Wai Canal, 20-minute walk to beach. **Amenities and services** Laundry facilities, business center, fitness center, sauna, Jacuzzi, swimming pool, soda machines, shuttle service. Hair dryer, iron and board, and crib available.

ACCOMMODATIONS

Rooms 220. Includes 19 suites. Rooms for the disabled available. **All rooms** AC, TV, free wireless high-speed Internet access, lanai, refrigerator, coffeemaker, voice mail, iron and board, wet bar, in-room safe. **Some rooms** Separate shower and Jacuzzi. **Comfort and decor** Luxurious, with marble bathrooms, extra closet space, and tropical plants.

PAYMENT, RESERVATIONS, AND RESTRICTIONS

Family plan Children age 12 and under stay free in room with parents if using existing bedding. Extra person, $25 daily. **Deposit** 1-night deposit required within 10 days of confirmation. Cancellation notice must be given at least 72 hours prior to scheduled arrival for refund. **Credit cards** All major credit cards accepted. **Check-in/out** 3 p.m./noon. Early check-in and late checkout may be available.

The Royal Hawaiian Hotel $$$$$

OVERALL	★★★★½	QUALITY	★★★★½	VALUE	★★★★

2259 Kalakaua Avenue, Honolulu 96815; ☎ 866-716-8109 or 808-923-7311; FAX 808-931-7098; www.royal-hawaiian.com

HOW DO YOU TAME A FLAMINGO? Very lovingly, if the Royal is any example. The famed "Pink Palace" opened in 1927 as a Moorish fantasy inspired by a Rudolph Valentino movie. Now after a year-long renovation, it has emerged again, tastefully updated and somewhat muted from its former screaming-pink interiors and exterior. It's still the centerpiece of the Waikiki waterfront, a small green-and-pink oasis among hulking high-rise towers. Over the years, the Royal has hosted numerous dignitaries and celebrities, from presidents to pop stars. The Royal Hawaiian has aged well, and its new do recalls Waikiki's elegant golden years, but with a modern approach to luxurious interiors. The hotel, surrounded by lush gardens and shady lawns in front, is now oriented more gracefully to its parklike setting. A stroll to the rear of the structure reveals a dreamlike beach view with gold sand and azure waters. The new Azure Restaurant welcomes diners where the Surf Room once held sway, but its fabulous beach view has been somewhat usurped by six new luxury cabanas—also known as the Royal Beach Club—on a beachfront-tented lanai in the decadent grand-poo-bah-of-the-desert tradition, with special servers, couches, tables, and privacy drapes that are sun shelters by day and dinner lounges by night.

SETTING AND FACILITIES

Location On Waikiki Beach, behind the Royal Hawaiian Shopping Center, between the Sheraton Waikiki and Outrigger Waikiki on the Beach. **Dining** Azure Restaurant for seafood and Surf Lanai for breakfast and lunch. **Amenities and services** Full-service spa and spa suites, lei greeting and banana bread amenity, multi-level pool and water complex, children's program, meeting and banquet facilities, business center, complimentary limo service within Waikiki, parking and valet parking, twice-daily maid service, high-speed Internet access.

ACCOMMODATIONS

Rooms 529, including 34 suites, in a 6-floor historic building and a 17-story tower. 6 are ADA-approved. **Comfort and decor** Medium-sized bedrooms have high ceilings, chandeliers, and Old World glamour, re-interpreted with a bit of hip by kamaaina interior design firm Philpotts and Associates. **All rooms** AC, flat-screen TV, refrigerator, iron and board, hair dryer, in-room safe.

PAYMENT, RESERVATIONS, AND RESTRICTIONS

Family plan Children age 17 and under stay free in room with parents if using existing bedding. Rollaway bed, $25 per night. **Deposit** Credit-card guarantee or 1-night deposit required within 10 days of booking to guarantee reservation. Cancellation notice must be given 72 hours prior to scheduled arrival for refund. **Credit cards** All major credit cards accepted. **Check-in/out** 3 p.m./noon. Early check-in and late checkout possible; hospitality suite available.

Sheraton Princess Kaiulani $$

OVERALL ★★★★	QUALITY ★★★★	VALUE ★★★

120 Kaiulani Avenue, Honolulu 96815; ☎ 800-782-9488 or 808-922-5811; FAX **808-931-4577; www.princess-kaiulani.com**

NAMED AFTER HAWAII'S BELOVED PRINCESS VICTORIA KAIULANI, last heir to the Hawaiian throne, this hotel is situated on the site of her garden estate, Ainahau, where the princess spent her childhood.

The Princess Kaiulani faces extensive renovations and the demolition of two of its three towers, to be replaced by a single tall tower and other facilities in 2010, although a spokesperson said no date has yet been set. Currently the hotel has 1,150 rooms surrounded by lobby areas, specialty shops, and gardens. The lobby area is bright, airy, and busy during the day. Original artwork and mementos from the era of Princess Kaiulani are displayed throughout the hotel. Arts and crafts demonstrations occur daily, and poolside entertainment is provided nightly. The hotel offers *Creation: A Polynesian Journey* dinner show in Ainahau Showroom (see page 453).

SETTING AND FACILITIES

Location In Waikiki, next to the International Market Place, across the street from Waikiki Beach. **Dining** Momoyama serves Japanese specialties in a traditional setting and features a sake menu. Lotus Moon features a Chinese menu. **Amenities and services** Room service, swimming pool, valet parking, self-parking, and coin-operated laundry machines.

ACCOMMODATIONS

Rooms 1,150. Includes 12 suites; 13 ADA-approved rooms and 6 rooms with roll-in showers. **All rooms** AC, TV, mini-fridge, in-room safe, coffee and tea, hair dryer. **Some rooms** Lanai. **Comfort and decor** Spacious, very clean. Simple but pleasant decor reflects island accents.

PAYMENT, RESERVATIONS, AND RESTRICTIONS

Family plan Children age 17 and under stay free in room with parents if using existing bedding. Maximum of 4 people per room. **Deposit** 1-night deposit or credit-card guarantee. Cancellation notice must be given by 6 p.m. on date of scheduled arrival for refund. **Credit cards** All major credit cards accepted. **Check-in/out** 3 p.m./noon. Early check-in and late checkout available.

Sheraton Waikiki $$$

OVERALL	★★★★	QUALITY	★★★★	VALUE	★★★

2255 Kalakaua Avenue, Honolulu 96815; ☎ **800-782-9488 or 808-922-4422;** FAX **808-923-8785; www.sheraton-waikiki.com**

WITH ITS ENTIRE SECOND FLOOR DEDICATED to meeting rooms and Waikiki's largest ballroom (26,000 square feet), this busy beach hotel is one of the state's largest—a 30-story wall of rooms often full of conventioneers. The main lobby centerpiece is a striking collection of colorful, ocean-themed glass sculptures, from fish and sharks to sea turtles. It personifies the hotel as a whole: pleasant but not stuffy. Hawaiian entertainment is provided nightly.

SETTING AND FACILITIES

Location On Waikiki Beach. **Dining** Up on the 30th floor, the Twist at Hanohano is renowned for its incredible views (with the highest vantage point on Waikiki Beach) and new "twist" on Island cuisine. Other restaurants include Yoshiya, serving traditional Japanese cuisine; Ingredients, where you can compose your own made-to-order breakfasts, lunch, and gourmet meals; and Kai Market by the pool for breakfast and dinner. **Amenities and services** Valet and self-parking, airport transfers, meeting facilities, secretarial business services, nightly poolside entertainment, fitness center, travel services, daily program in children's center.

ACCOMMODATIONS

Rooms 1,695. Includes 214 suites; 10 rooms for the disabled. **All rooms** AC, special bedding, flat-screen TV, high-speed Internet access, clock radio, minibar, refrigerator, electronic in-room safe large enough for a laptop, in-room video message and checkout facilities, room service, hair dryer, iron and board, coffeemakers. **Some rooms** Private lanai, ocean views from the bath, kitchen. **Comfort and decor** Rooms feature high ceilings, spacious bathrooms, and stylish furnishings with island-accented decor.

PAYMENT, RESERVATIONS, AND RESTRICTIONS

Family plan Children age 17 and under stay free in room with parents if using existing bedding. **Deposit** Credit-card guarantee or 1-night deposit required. Cancellation notice must be given before 6 p.m. on scheduled day of arrival for refund. **Credit cards** All major credit cards accepted. **Check-in/out** 3 p.m./noon. Hospitality suite available for early arrivals and late departures.

Turtle Bay Resort $$$

OVERALL	★★★★	QUALITY	★★★★	VALUE	★★★

57-091 Kamehameha Highway, Kahuku 96731; ☎ 800-445-8667 or 808-293-6000; FAX 808-293-9147; www.turtlebayresort.com

SITUATED ON THE NORTH SHORE OF OAHU, the Turtle Bay sprawls over a scenic peninsula that juts into the Pacific. With 880 acres and five miles of beach and waterfront, it is as far removed from Waikiki as you can get, on the laid-back side of the island.

Atmosphere is comfortable and relaxed. A choice spot for golfers and tennis players, the resort also offers a surfing school, trails for mountain-bike riding, snorkeling, and horseback riding.

SETTING AND FACILITIES

Location On Oahu's North Shore, at the tip of Kuilima Point. The hotel is near the North Shore's best surfing spots and beaches, including the legendary Sunset Beach. **Dining** 21 Degrees North features contemporary Island cuisine, extensive wine pairings, and breathtaking ocean views. Ola features Hawaiian regional style lunch and dinner at Bay View Beach. Lei Lei's Bar and Grill, overlooking tropical golf greenery, serves breakfast, lunch, and dinner. Palm Terrace serves breakfast, lunch, and dinner buffets. Hang Ten Bar & Grill features lunch and memorable mai tais outdoors by the sea. The weekly Voyages of Polynesia Luau is held on Friday nights outdoors on the lawn overlooking Kuilima Bay. **Amenities and services** Room service, laundry service, valet parking and self-parking, full spa, fitness center, golf, swimming pools and Jacuzzi, activity desk.

ACCOMMODATIONS

Rooms 375 plus 31 suites, 42 beach cottages and ocean villas; includes 5 rooms for the disabled. **All rooms** AC, TV, refrigerator, in-room safe, coffeemaker, wireless Internet access. **Comfort and decor** Comfortable, spacious, and clean, with light marine colors, Hawaiian artwork, and tropical plants.

PAYMENT, RESERVATIONS, AND RESTRICTIONS

Family plan Children age 17 and under stay free in room with parents if using existing bedding. **Deposit** 1-night deposit or credit-card guarantee required. Cancellation notice must be given 48 hours prior to scheduled arrival for refund. **Credit cards** All major credit cards accepted. **Check-in/out** 3 p.m./11 a.m. Early check-in and late checkout available.

Waikiki Beach Marriott Resort & Spa $$$

OVERALL ★★★★	QUALITY ★★★★	VALUE ★★★

2552 Kalakaua Avenue, Honolulu 96815; ☎ 800-848-8110 or 808-922-6611; FAX **808-921-5255; www.marriottwaikiki.com**

ONE OF HAWAII'S LARGER HOTELS, the former Hawaiian Regent is now the Waikiki Beach Marriott Resort & Spa, with a fresh look. Public areas and rooms have been redone in a tropical style with new art and furnishings. Friendly hospitality warms the reception in the hotel's two monolithic towers. The location at the far end of Waikiki's central district is family friendly: Kuhio Beach Park is just across the street, the small Damien Museum is next door, and Kapiolani Park and the Honolulu Zoo are also nearby.

SETTING AND FACILITIES

Location Across the street from Waikiki Beach, 1 block from Honolulu Zoo. **Dining** 6 restaurants include Sansei Seafood Restaurant and Sushi Bar, serving outstanding contemporary Pacific Rim cuisine, and d. k. Steak House. **Amenities and services** Room service, laundry, valet service, parking, business center, fitness center, spa, 2 pools, extensive meeting facilities.

ACCOMMODATIONS

Rooms 1,294. Includes 16 suites; 18 ADA-approved rooms. **All rooms** Non-smoking, AC, TV with movies, in-room safe, special bedding, high-speed Internet access, refrigerator, lanai, hair dryer, coffeemaker, iron and board. **Some rooms** More space, upgraded amenities. **Comfort and decor** Tastefully appointed, small-to medium-sized rooms have island-accented furnishings and decor.

PAYMENT, RESERVATIONS, AND RESTRICTIONS

Family plan Children age 17 and under stay free in room with parents if using existing bedding. **Deposit** Credit-card guarantee; cancellation notice must be given 72 hours prior to scheduled arrival for refund. For Christmas holiday reservations, 3-night deposit required within 10 days of booking; cancellation notice must be given 60 days in advance for refund. **Credit cards** All major credit cards accepted. **Check-in/out** 3 p.m./11 a.m. Early check-in and late checkout available on request.

Waikiki Parc Hotel $$$

OVERALL ★★★★	QUALITY ★★★★	VALUE ★★★½

2233 Helumoa Road, Honolulu 96815; ☎ 800-422-0450 or 808-921-7272; FAX **808-923-1336; www.waikikiparc.com**

THE HALEKULANI'S LITTLE SISTER, this boutique hotel is crammed in among neighboring properties, but it has charm and many advantages, including a central location with proximity to the beach, Spa Halekulani, and the new Waikiki Beach Walk shops and restaurants; stylish "Waikiki chic" decor inside; and a world-class restaurant, Nobu Waikiki, in its lobby.

SETTING AND FACILITIES

Location In Waikiki, across from Halekulani, 100 yards to the beach. **Dining** Innovative Japanese cuisine by renowned Chef Nobu Matsuhisa and sushi bar at Nobu Waikiki; Parc a.m. serves breakfast. **Amenities and services** Rooftop pool, room service, surfing lessons, laundry service, parking, business lounge.

ACCOMMODATIONS

Rooms 297. ADA-approved rooms available. **All rooms** AC, flat-screen TV, 2 phones, mini-fridge, in-room safe, hair dryer; coffeemaker, high-speed Internet access, iron and board. **Some rooms** Lanai, ocean view. **Comfort and decor** Spacious and well-maintained rooms have tile floors with plush carpeting, plantation shutters, ebony woods, white bedding, illuminated glass walls, and bold artwork.

PAYMENT, RESERVATIONS, AND RESTRICTIONS

Family plan Children age 17 and under stay free in room with parents if using existing bedding. Maximum of 4 people per room. **Deposit** Credit-card guarantee or 1-night deposit due within 14 days of booking. Cancellation notice must be given 72 hours prior to confirmed arrival for refund. **Credit cards** All major credit cards accepted. **Check-in/out** 3 p.m./noon. Early check-in and late checkout may be available.

Westin Moana Surfrider $$$

OVERALL ★★★★½	QUALITY ★★★★	VALUE ★★★

2365 Kalakaua Avenue, Honolulu 96815; ☎ 800-782-9488 or 808-922-3111; FAX 808-924-4799; www.moana-surfrider.com

OPENED IN 1901, THIS IS WAIKIKI'S OLDEST HOTEL. Nicknamed the "First Lady of Waikiki," the venerable Moana is still gracious and now newly refreshed by a substantial renovation of rooms and lobby that includes a spa, new Beachhouse Restaurant, and Westin Kids Club. We like the beachfront veranda where you can relax beside the shady banyan and watch the half-clad world go by. Ocean and beach views are excellent. The staff is efficient and courteous. Visit the mini-museum for a look at the golden age of the Moana and Waikiki. Memorabilia include historic photos, postcards, room keys, stock shares, sheet music, menus, and old brochures. A historic outdoor focus is the old 75-foot-high, 150-foot-wide banyan tree, where *Hawaii Calls* was broadcast for 40 years. The central portion of the Moana is listed on the National Register of Historic Places.

SETTING AND FACILITIES

Location On Waikiki Beach. **Dining** The contemporary Beachhouse at the Moana serves steaks and seafood; the Beachside Café offers breakfast, lunch, and dinner in a casual setting; the Veranda serves breakfast, afternoon tea, cocktails, and an evening buffet. **Amenities and services** 24-hour room service, full-service spa, valet service, self-parking, fitness center, concierge, children's program.

ACCOMMODATIONS

Rooms 793. Includes 46 suites; 18 ADA-approved rooms. **All rooms** AC, flat-screen TV, in-room safe, hair dryer, slippers, bathrobe, coffeemaker. **Some rooms** Oceanfront lanai, wet bar, refrigerator, high-speed Internet access, pullout sofa. **Comfort and decor** Historic rooms are small to medium in size, with high ceilings, oversized windows, and great views.

PAYMENT, RESERVATIONS, AND RESTRICTIONS

Family plan Children age 17 and under stay free in room with parents if using existing bedding. Maximum of 4 people per room. **Deposit** 1-night deposit or credit-card guarantee within 10 days of placing reservation. Cancellation notice must be given 72 hours prior to scheduled arrival for refund. **Credit cards** All major credit cards accepted. **Check-in/out** 3 p.m./noon. Early check-in and late checkout available on request.

MAUI

Fairmont Kea Lani, Maui $$$$$

OVERALL ★★★★½	QUALITY ★★★★	VALUE ★★★

4100 Wailea Alanui Drive, Wailea 96753; ☎ 866-540-4457 or 808-875-4100; FAX 808-875-1200; www.fairmont.com/kealani

WITH ITS WHITE TOWERS AND TURRETS, like something out of *Arabian Nights*, the luxury beachfront Fairmont Kea Lani Maui hotel delivers far more than fantasy. All the rooms are spacious, well-equipped suites with entertainment systems and kitchenettes, and the townhouse-style private villas add more bedrooms, full kitchens, and private plunge pools. Kea Lani has a great beach and interesting, varied restaurants. Kids are so welcome that they get their own pools with a slide; there's also a pool for adults only. Children ages 5 to 12 can participate in Keiki Lani, the hotel's year-round children's program, which features hula and lei-making lessons and swimming. The hotel has marvelous swimming lagoons that are connected by a 140-foot waterslide and swim-up beverage bar. Readers of *Condé Nast Traveler* voted the Kea Lani one of the top five resorts in the Pacific region, among many accolades for this popular retreat.

SETTING AND FACILITIES

Location On Polo Beach. **Dining** 5 restaurants, including Nick's Fishmarket Maui, a popular seafood bistro, and Ko, which celebrates Maui's plantation heritage through cuisine. Kea Lani Resaurant features alfresco breakfast and lunch. Caffe Ciao Deli is the place to assemble a gourmet picnic or food for the flight home, packaged in a keepsake canvas cooler. Polo Beach Grille and Bar offers casual poolside lunch and a swim-up bar. **Amenities and services** Spa and fitness center, 3 swimming pools, tennis, golf, children's program, indoor and outdoor meeting/conference space, free resort shuttle, room service, parking, wedding services.

ACCOMMODATIONS

Rooms 413. All suites. Includes 37 oceanfront villas; 11 suites for the disabled. **All rooms** AC and ceiling fans, 2 or more rooms, 2 TVs, stereo entertainment center (with CD player, VCR, and DVD, as well as an iPod dock), high-speed Internet access, mini-fridge, microwave, sleeper sofa, coffeemaker, marble bath with twin sinks and deep tub, private lanai. **Some rooms** Private villas with private plunge pool, gourmet kitchen, sun deck, barbecue grill, luxury-car rental, extra bedrooms. **Comfort and decor** Soft tropical colors provide cheerful ambience to very spacious suites, with separate living rooms.

PAYMENT, RESERVATIONS, AND RESTRICTIONS

Family plan Children age 18 and under stay free in room with parents if using existing bedding. Rollaway bed, $30. **Deposit** 2-night deposit due at booking. Cancellation notice must be given 21 days prior to scheduled arrival for refund. **Credit cards** All major credit cards accepted. **Check-in/out** 4 p.m./noon. Early check-in and late checkout available on request.

Four Seasons Resort Maui $$$$$

OVERALL ★★★★★	QUALITY ★★★★★	VALUE ★★★★

3900 Wailea Alanui Drive, Wailea 96753; ☎ 800-311-0630 or 808-874-8000; FAX **808-874-2244; www.fourseasons.com/maui**

Condé Nast Traveler MAGAZINE NAMED THE FOUR SEASONS the "Top Tropical Resort in the World" in 1993, and this luxurious resort continues to rate highly among travel experts and patrons, including the Hollywood set that frequents it. Four Seasons Maui is the perennial winner of the AAA Five Diamond Award (since 1991, the year it opened) and Mobil Five-Star resort, among other plaudits. In 2007, Zagat Surveyors named Four Seasons Maui among the top three destination spas in the world. A $50-million renovation should help keep this hotel on top of the Maui resort scene.

A honeymoon favorite, this gracious place makes a fine art of pampering, with special touches such as the famed Evian spritzes to cool off sunbathers by the pool and room service to the lounge chairs on the beautiful beach below. The Spa at Four Seasons offers indoor treatments and outdoor ocean-view massage huts. The breezy, open lobby is testament to the resort's island-oriented architectural design, which includes commissioned reproductions of early Hawaiian furniture as well as Hawaii paintings, sculptures, and other artwork. On-site features include a children's program, health club, spa, game room, and salon. The service is warm, professional, and courteous, never stuffy. The location is awesome—you can watch humpback whales spouting in the winter whale season from your ocean-view lanai, or from tees on Wailea Resort's three championship golf courses, or possibly from the top of the gallery at the 11-court Wailea Tennis Center (known as Wimbledon West). Overall, the Four Seasons rates as one of the best resorts, if not the very best, on Maui.

SETTING AND FACILITIES

Location On Wailea Beach. **Dining** 3 restaurants: Wolfgang Puck's Spago, featuring Puck's own brand of Hawaii-California fusion cuisine; DUO, for breakfast and later, for steak-and-seafood dinner; and Ferraro's Bar e Ristorante, serving Italian specialties for lunch and dinner under the stars. **Amenities and services**

24-hour room service, laundry, pools, workout facilities, full-service spa, salon, golf, tennis, business center, children's program, game room, free resort shuttle.

ACCOMMODATIONS

Rooms 370. Includes 74 suites. ADA-approved rooms available. **All rooms** AC, flat-screen TV, clock radio, DVD player, iPod or MP3 players, high-speed Internet access, Tassimo coffee-tea-latte-hot chocolate maker, lanai, in-room safe, minibar, hair dryer, data port, robes. **Some rooms** Fax machines, extra bedroom, club-floor concierge, lounge and refreshments. **Comfort and decor** Very spacious, exceptionally comfortable and well maintained. Soft neutrals let the Technicolor view take over the decor accented with sunset hues. Cushy tropical furnishings, large marble bathrooms with dual vanities, and island-themed artwork add to the luxurious atmosphere.

PAYMENT, RESERVATIONS, AND RESTRICTIONS

Family plan Children age 17 and under stay free in room with parents if using existing bedding. **Deposit** 2-night deposit due at booking. Cancellation notice must be given 21 days in advance of confirmed arrival for refund on most rooms, 30 days on some suites. Shortened stays may result in 1 night penalty. **Credit cards** All major credit cards accepted. Hospitality lounge for early arrivals and late departures. **Check-in/out** 3 p.m./noon.

 Grand Wailea Resort Hotel & Spa $$$$$

| OVERALL | ★★★★½ | QUALITY | ★★★★½ | VALUE | ★★★ |

3850 Wailea Alanui Drive, Wailea 96753; ☎ 800-888-6100 or 808-875-1234; FAX 808-879-4077; www.grandwailea.com

EVEN IF YOU DON'T STAY HERE, this $600-million opulent spread, the ultimate Hawaii fantasy resort, is worth a tour (and they conduct garden and art tours). Stroll through the 40-acre property to enjoy its $30 million in artwork that decorates public areas, including an exceptional collection of huge lounging Botero bronze sculptures in the lobby and an impressive collection of bronzes and other works by Hawaiian artists commissioned for the resort. The open-air lobby alone boasts 10,000 tropical plants. Even the elevators have painted ceilings. Among the features are Camp Grande, a 20,000-square-foot children's facility; the 50,000-square-foot Spa Grande; a wedding chapel complete with stained-glass windows; and a 2,000-foot-long river pool that includes valleys, waterslides, waterfalls, caves, grottos, white-water rapids, a Jacuzzi, a sauna, and the world's only "water elevator," which lifts swimmers from the lower-level pool to the higher-level pool. It's all very grand—indeed, even over the top—but lots of fun as well. It was created in the 1980s to appeal to incentive and meeting groups, honeymooners, families, and others who like to be amused and amazed with their beach vacation digs. Now it is part of Hilton's Waldorf-Astoria Collection. Is it still a hit? Apparently so—the resort runs its own frequent-guest membership program. And yes, there is a fabulous real beach, just beyond the man-made one.

SETTING AND FACILITIES

Location On Wailea Beach. **Dining** 5 restaurants and two bars. Bistro Molokini offers Hawaii-California fare for lunch and dinner. Cafe Kula serves imaginative and healthy spa fare. Humuhumunukunukuapuaa (named for the Hawaii state fish), or Humu for short, specializes in fresh seafood in a romantic open-air atmosphere with live music. It is built in a pond, with tropical fish and its own set of bronze sculptures commissioned by Hawaiian artists. **Amenities and services** Room service, full-service spa and fitness center, wedding chapel, extensive conference facilities with a separate entrance, 3 championship resort golf courses, extensive shopping area, complimentary scuba lessons, squash and racquetball court, self-parking and valet parking, free resort shuttle, children's program, high-tech water complex, and Hawaii's largest swimming pools (one with a man-made beach). A $25 daily resort fee includes free use of fitness facilities and Internet access.

ACCOMMODATIONS

Rooms 761. Includes 52 suites; 10 rooms for disabled. **All rooms** AC and ceiling fans, clock radio and CD player, TV with movies and games, lanai, in-room safe, 3 phones with free local calls, high-speed Internet access, honor bar, coffeemaker, hair dryer, robes, slippers. **Some rooms** Larger accommodations, extra baths, 3-bedroom suite, club privileges. **Comfort and decor** Very spacious, luxurious in furnishings and decor with large marble baths

PAYMENT, RESERVATIONS, AND RESTRICTIONS

Family plan Children age 17 and under stay free in room with parents if using existing bedding. $50 for additional adult, $100 in club rooms. Maximum 4 people per room. **Deposit** 2-night deposit required with cancellation notice 14 days prior to scheduled arrival for refund in nonholiday periods; increases during spring, Thanksgiving, and Christmas holidays. **Credit cards** All major credit cards accepted. **Check-in/out** 4:30 p.m./noon. Early check-in and late checkout may be available on request.

Hotel Hana-Maui and Honua Spa $$$$$

| OVERALL ★★★★½ | QUALITY ★★★★★ | VALUE ★★★ |

P.O. Box 9, 5031 Hana Highway, Hana 96713; ☎ 800-321-4262 or 808-248-8211; FAX 808-248-7202; www.hotelhanamaui.com

THIS COZY, SMALL HOTEL EXCELS in peace and privacy, charm, location, and Hawaiian service. Hana sits on 66 acres of landscaped gardens, and the ocean and mountain views are, like Hana, heavenly. Remote, quiet, and romantic, this is the epitome of a honeymoon hotel (if needed, you'll find television and Internet service in the club room). A weekly luau is held on the beach. Available outdoor activities include horseback riding, hiking, snorkeling, bike riding, and historical tours. A full-service spa-and-wellness center offers everything from massages to hydrotherapies to a lava-rock whirlpool to yoga. A favorite celebrity haunt, the Hotel Hana-Maui was built in 1946, which makes it Maui's oldest hotel. With its fine spa, handsome suites, and individual cottages sprinkled across the sloping seaside bluff and pastures, it also one of the most special and most expensive.

SETTING AND FACILITIES

Location In Hana, east end of Maui, shuttle to Hamoa Beach. **Dining** Kauiki, the dining room, serves breakfast, lunch, and dinner with live music and hula most nights and a Hawaiian show on Friday nights. Paniolo Lounge offers lighter fare. Hana Ranch Restaurant nearby serves à la carte lunches and, on Wednesday and Friday nights, dinners. **Amenities and services** Room service (breakfast only), daily yoga, bicycles, tennis, pools, laundry service, parking, wellness center, private beach facilities at Hamoa Beach, computer and Internet access in club room (and dial-up data port available in rooms).

ACCOMMODATIONS

Rooms 65 suites and cottages. **All rooms** Wet bar, lanai, coffeemaker, organic cotton linens, welcome amenities with tropical fruit and bread, robes, hair dryer, iron and board, in-room safe. **Some rooms** Deck Jacuzzis, shower gardens; one is a plantation manager's home. **Comfort and decor** Spacious units are comfortable and elegant with bleached hardwood floors, wicker and bamboo furnishings, handmade designer quilts, and private patios.

PAYMENT, RESERVATIONS, AND RESTRICTIONS

Family plan Children age 17 and under stay free in room with parents if using existing bedding except in September, when the resort is adults-only. **Credit cards** All major credit cards accepted. **Check-in/out** 4 p.m./noon. Early check-in and late checkout available on request.

kids **Hyatt Regency Maui Resort & Spa** $$$$

OVERALL ★★★★	QUALITY ★★★★	VALUE ★★★

200 Nohea Kai Drive, Lahaina 96761; ☎ 800-233-1234; FAX 808-667-4498; www.maui.hyatt.com

The HYATT REGENCY MAUI WAS THE FIRST of Hawaii's celebrated, larger-than-life "fantasy hotels," complete with an elaborate water playground with waterfall grotto, enclosed "lava tube" waterslide, a suspended rope bridge, and other features designed to appeal to the kid in everyone. The hotel's nightly *Tour of the Stars* program gives guests a guided peek at the Hawaiian skies through a state-of-the-art, computer-controlled, 16-inch reflector telescope. A wildlife tour brings visitors face-to-face with the resort's menagerie of penguins, swans, parrots, macaws, flamingos, and koi. You can also tour the tropical gardens (a two-mile walk) or browse the $2-million art collection. This hotel offers something for travelers of all ages and interests, including a spa. It's a favorite with meeting groups.

SETTING AND FACILITIES

Location On Kaanapali Beach. **Dining** 5 restaurants, 6 lounges. Omalu features an eclectic menu for lunch, dinner, or in-between. Son'z Maui at Swan Court features fresh local fish and Maui products prepared with flair beside a pool with stately swans swimming up for a handout. Cascades Grill and Sushi Bar has fresh seafood and steak. **Amenities and services** Full-service spa, fitness center, tennis, golf, outdoor dinner theater and luau, room service, shops, water playground, high-speed Internet access, free resort shuttle, activities desk, parking and valet parking, children's program, shops, meeting and convention facilities, rooftop astronomy program (fee). Daily resort fee, $15.

ACCOMMODATIONS

Rooms 807. Includes 31 suites; 4 rooms for the disabled. **All rooms** AC, lanai, TV, special bedding, iron and board, in-room safe, minibar, high-speed Internet access, hair dryer, robes, coffeemaker. **Some rooms** Living room, dining area, wet bar, refrigerator, club floor. **Comfort and decor** Spacious and clean rooms have plantation-style wood furniture, Hawaiian quilt wall hangings, comfortable furnishings, and light neutral color schemes.

PAYMENT, RESERVATIONS, AND RESTRICTIONS

Family plan Children age 17 and under stay free in room with parents if using existing bedding. Maximum 4 people per room. **Deposit** 2-night deposit due within 14 days after booking. Cancellation notice must be given 72 hours prior to scheduled arrival for refund. **Credit cards** All major credit cards accepted. **Check-in/out** 3 p.m./noon. Early check-in and late checkout based on availability.

Kaanapali Beach Club (formerly Embassy Suites) $$$

OVERALL ★★★★	QUALITY ★★★	VALUE ★★★★

104 Kaanapali Shores Place, Lahaina 96761; ☎ 877-696-6284 or 808-661-2000; www.kaanapali-beach-club.com

BACK IN 1988, THIS WAS THE FIRST HAWAII property to offer all-suite accommodations; now it is a time-share resort. Ninety percent of the suites have views of the ocean and the islands Molokai and Lanai. A popular feature is the 42-foot waterslide, which plops you into a one-acre swimming pool. A miniature golf course is also on the premises, although serious golfers will head for the championship courses located elsewhere at Kaanapali Beach Resort.

SETTING AND FACILITIES

Location On Kaanapali Beach. **Dining** 2 restaurants and a bar. **Amenities and services** Laundry and housekeeping service, workout room, sauna, parking (fee).

ACCOMMODATIONS

Rooms 395 1-bedroom suites; 12 ADA-approved rooms. **All rooms** AC, sofa sleeper, TV, VCR, microwave, refrigerator, coffeemaker, dishes and dishwasher, in-room safe, hair dryer, high-speed Internet access, iron and board. **Comfort and decor** Expansive suites (more than 800 square feet) have separate living rooms, soaking tub, walk-in closets, dual marble vanities, and big-screen TV. Decor has cool tropical appeal; cheerful and airy.

PAYMENT, RESERVATIONS, AND RESTRICTIONS

Family plan Children age 17 and under stay free in room with parents if using existing bedding; maximum of 4 adults per suite. **Deposit** 1-night deposit due at booking. Cancellation notice must be given 72 hours prior to scheduled arrival for refund. **Credit cards** All major credit cards accepted. **Check-in/out** 4 p.m./11 a.m. Hospitality suite available for early arrivals and late departures.

Kaanapali Beach Hotel $$$

OVERALL ★★★	QUALITY ★★★	VALUE ★★★

2525 Kaanapali Parkway, Lahaina 96761; ☎ 800-262-8450 or 808-661-0011; FAX 808-667-5978; www.kbhmaui.com

LOCATED ON ONE OF THE WIDEST STRETCHES of Kaanapali Beach, the independently operated Kaanapali Beach Hotel calls itself Maui's "most Hawaiian" hotel. The management and staff, schooled in Hawaiian hospitality, pride themselves on dispensing aloha spirit, and the smiles and friendliness are downright contagious. A variety of Hawaiian activities—including hula lessons, lei-making, lauhala weaving, and leaf-skirt making—are held daily. Employees provide Hawaiian entertainment three days a week. The spirit is wonderfully down-home Hawaii, and that is what keeps guests returning.

SETTING AND FACILITIES

Location On Kaanapali Beach; 4 separate wings form a semicircle around a ten-acre courtyard. **Dining** The Tiki Terrace Restaurant serves Pacific Rim cuisine. Kaanapali Mixed Plate features self-service buffets three meals a day, Island-style; Sunday brunch is lavish. *Kupanaha Dinner Show* at 4:30 p.m. Sunday through Thursday, is a Polynesian show with magicians Jody and Kathleen Baran. **Amenities and services** Laundry service, valet parking and self-parking (fee for both), children's program.

ACCOMMODATIONS

Rooms 430. Includes 15 suites. Rooms for the disabled available on request. **All rooms** AC, lanai, TV, in-room safe, refrigerator, coffeemaker, hair dryer, iron and board, robes. **Some rooms** More space, upgraded amenities. **Comfort and decor** Spacious, clean, and well maintained. Tropical green or golden-sand hues accentuate the Hawaiian mood, along with Hawaiian design bedspreads, tropical furniture, and local artwork.

PAYMENT, RESERVATIONS, AND RESTRICTIONS

Family plan Children age 17 and under stay free in room with parents if using existing bedding. Rollaway bed, $20. **Deposit** 1- to 5-night deposit due within 10 days of booking, depending on season. Cancellation notice must be given 3–14 days prior to scheduled arrival for refund, depending on dates. **Credit cards** All major credit cards accepted. **Check-in/out** 3 p.m./noon. Early check-in and late checkout available on request.

Lahaina Inn $$

OVERALL ★★★★	QUALITY ★★★	VALUE ★★★½

127 Lahainaluna Road, Lahaina 96761; ☎ 800-669-3444; FAX 808-667-9480; www.lahainainn.com

THIS 12-ROOM BOUTIQUE HOTEL is proof that good things can come in small packages. Rick Ralston, founder and owner of Crazy Shirts, restored this historic inn and drew from his personal collection to furnish each individually decorated room. Because of the value of the furnishings, children under age

15 are not allowed. A complimentary continental breakfast is served every morning. The inn's proximity to Front Street is close to the action, but tends to get noisy. The inn has no TVs. Lahaina is entertainment enough.

SETTING AND FACILITIES

Location In the heart of Lahaina, across from the waterfront, no beach. **Dining** Lahaina Grill, one of Maui's best restaurants, serves New American cuisine. **Amenities and services Parking** (fee), complimentary coffee.

ACCOMMODATIONS

Rooms 12. Includes 3 suites. All are nonsmoking. Several 1- to 3-bedroom cottages and condos also available for families or groups. **All rooms** AC, ceiling fans, high-speed Internet access, hair dryer, beach towels, iron and board. **Some rooms** Lanai, full bath and shower, king-sized bed. **Comfort and decor** Rooms are smallish and dimly lit, but well maintained and clean. Antique furnishings include restored brass and wood beds, period wall decorations, and wooden armoires.

PAYMENT, RESERVATIONS, AND RESTRICTIONS

Family plan No children under 15 allowed. **Deposit** 1-night deposit required for inn; cancellation notice must be given 2 days prior to scheduled arrival for refund minus $25 fee. Cottages require $300 deposit, full payment within 60 days before confirmed arrival; changes or cancellations will be charged at least a $150 fee. **Credit cards** All major credit cards accepted, except Discover. **Check-in/out** 3 p.m./10 a.m.

Marriott's Maui Ocean Club (*formerly* Maui Marriott Resort) $$$$

OVERALL ★★★★	QUALITY ★★★★	VALUE ★★★

100 Nohea Kai Drive, Lahaina 96761; ☎ 800-845-5279 or 808-667-1200; FAX **808-667-8300; www.marriott.com**

THIS IS NOW A TIME-SHARE RESORT, with a casual, family-oriented atmosphere and friendly service. Waterfalls, koi ponds, and tall coconut palms adorn the grounds.

SETTING AND FACILITIES

Location On Kaanapali Beach. **Dining** Longboards Kaanapali serves American food for dinner. **Amenities and services** Valet parking and self-parking, pool, Jacuzzi, fitness center, coin-operated laundry service, high-speed Internet access.

ACCOMMODATIONS

Rooms 442, nonsmoking. **All rooms** AC, TV, lanai, refrigerator, microwave, in-room safe, coffeemaker, hair dryer, DVD player, Internet access, iron and board. **Some rooms** Sofa sleeper, larger lanai, separate dressing area, dishwasher, table and chairs, second bedroom, third bath. **Comfort and decor** Spacious one-bedroom/two-bath and two-bedroom/three-bath units with gourmet kitchenettes, tasteful furnishings and art.

PAYMENT, RESERVATIONS, AND RESTRICTIONS

Family plan Children age 17 and under stay free in room with parents if using existing bedding. Maximum of 2 adults and 2 children per room. **Deposit**

1-night, credit-card guarantee. Cancellation notice must be given 72 hours prior to scheduled arrival for refund. **Credit cards** All major credit cards accepted. **Check-in/out** 4 p.m./10 a.m. Early check-in and late checkout available on request (no guarantees).

kids Ritz-Carlton, Kapalua $$$$$

| OVERALL ★★★★★ | QUALITY ★★★★★ | VALUE ★★★★ |

One Ritz-Carlton Drive, Kapalua 96761; ☎ 800-241-3333 or 808-669-6200; FAX 808-669-1566; www.ritzcarlton.com

THE RITZ, REFRESHED AFTER A $180-MILLION RENOVATION in 2008, which added a new kind of unit and doubled the size of the spa, is a AAA Five Diamond Award recipient, and it's not hard to understand why. Everything here, from service to rooms to dining, is perfect, with the exception of the Windward Coast weather, which can be blustery and cool. The atmosphere is one of blissful luxury. Set on 50 acres amid a century-old pineapple planta-tion, the Ritz features two six-story wings that step down the seaside slope, sheltering pools that step down as well, with waterfalls in between. Public areas are enhanced by historic artwork as well as large murals, paintings, and ceramics created by famed local artists. The Ritz Kids program intro-duces children (ages 5 to 12) to Maui's culture, nature, art, and ecology. Evening entertainment is provided at the Terrace Restaurant and Banyan Tree. Kapalua Resort has two championship golf courses and ten tennis courts, shopping, restaurants, and some wonderful beaches and snorkeling prospects. The Ritz hosts several notable annual events, including the PGA Tour SBS Championship, Celebration of the Arts, Kapalua Wine and Food Symposium, and the Earth Maui Nature Summit. The Ritz-Carlton Kapalua is the world's first Audubon Heritage Cooperative Sanctuary Resort Hotel.

SETTING AND FACILITIES
Location At Kapalua Resort in West Maui, a short but steep walk to the beach. **Dining** 6 restaurants, including the signature Banyan Tree with regional cuisine; The Terrace serves a breakfast buffet, lunch, and dinner; and Kai Sushi Bar. **Amenities and services** 24-hour room service, twice-daily maid service, laundry service, yoga studio and fitness center, spa treatments, multilevel swimming pool, hydrotherapy pools, business facilities, children's program that includes Jean-Michel Cousteau's Ambassadors of the Environment program, other nature programs, parking, valet parking, golf, tennis, ocean activities, free West Maui airport shuttle.

ACCOMMODATIONS
Rooms 463 remodeled rooms and suites. ADA-approved rooms available. **All rooms** AC, flat-screen TV with pay movies, 3 phones, lanai, in-room safe, minibar, hair dryer, iPod dock and clock, free high-speed Internet access, marble baths, robes. **Some rooms** Twice the size (new residential suites are 900 square feet and up), fully equipped kitchen, extra bedroom, additional lanai, club floor, personal concierge service, and complimentary food and beverages. **Comfort and decor** Oversized rooms feature dark wood floors, earthy, vibrant colors,

tropical furnishings, Hawaiian artwork, and a large private lanai (80% of rooms have ocean views).

PAYMENT, RESERVATIONS, AND RESTRICTIONS
Family plan Children under age 18 stay free in their parents' room (age 13 on the club floor); third person charge, $50. **Deposit** 2 night's room and tax charged 3 days after reservation confirmed; cancellation permitted 21 days in advance of arrival for refund. **Credit cards** All major credit cards accepted. Resort fee, $20. **Check-in/out** 3 p.m./noon. Early check-in and late checkout available on request (no guarantees).

kids Sheraton Maui Resort & Spa $$$$$

OVERALL ★★★★	QUALITY ★★★★	VALUE ★★★★

2605 Kaanapali Parkway, Lahaina 96761; ☎ 866-716-8109 or 808-661-0031; FAX 808-661-0458; www.sheraton-maui.com

THE SHERATON MAUI, A LUXURIOUS FULL-SERVICE RESORT, has the premier position on Kaanapali Beach, because it was the first hotel to be built at the resort. Front and center, it incorporates the volcanic landmark Black Rock into its architectural design (the New Spa at Black Rock is among the facilities built atop the headland). The hotel's elevated lobby opens to a wide panorama of the Pacific Ocean and a spectacular 147-foot-long oceanfront swimming lagoon. Children ages 5 to 12 can participate in the Keiki Aloha Club (in summer), beach activities, and field trips to historic sites. Legendary Black Rock, a place where Hawaiians believed spirits of the dead depart this world, is considered one of the best snorkeling areas on Maui. At sunset, torch-lighting and cliff-diving ceremonies bid aloha to another sunny day.

SETTING AND FACILITIES
Location On Kaanapali Beach. **Dining** 3 restaurants, including Teppan-yaki Dan, which offers a noteworthy blend of European and Pacific cuisines and showmanship (chefs wielding knives prepare your meal on a grill at your table as you watch), plus 3 lounges and Sunset Luau at Black Rock four nights a week. **Amenities and services** Swimming pool, room service, laundry facilities, valet parking, self-parking, resort shuttle, fitness center, spa, night-lit tennis courts, meeting and banquet facilities, children's summer program, "arrive and dine" service—order anything from a snack to a four-course dinner to arrive at your room just after you do.

ACCOMMODATIONS
Rooms 508. Includes 44 suites; 15 rooms for the disabled. **All rooms** AC, TV, in-room safe, mini-fridge, coffeemaker, iron and board, hair dryer, robes, high-speed Internet access. **Some rooms** Microwave, second TV, parlor. **Comfort and decor** Spacious and well-maintained rooms have custom bedspreads, tropical furnishings, and large lanai. Hawaiian artwork adorns the walls, and fine Hawaiian crafts are displayed throughout the public areas.

PAYMENT, RESERVATIONS, AND RESTRICTIONS
Family plan Children age 17 and under stay free in room with parents if using existing bedding. **Deposit** 1-night deposit due 10 days after booking.

Cancellation notice must be given 72 hours prior to scheduled arrival for refund. **Credit cards** All major credit cards accepted. A $25 daily resort fee is added to the room charge. **Check-in/out** 3 p.m./noon. Early check-in and late checkout available on request.

Wailea Beach Marriott Resort & Spa $$$$

OVERALL ★★★★	QUALITY ★★★★	VALUE ★★★

3700 Wailea Alanui Drive, Wailea 96753; ☎ 800-228-9290 or 808-879-1922; FAX **808-874-7888; www.marriott.com**

THIS LOW-RISE OCEANFRONT RESORT, built in 1976 and spreading along 22 prime acres of Wailea shoreline, has undergone extensive renovation, including the addition of a new Mandara Spa, an ocean-view restaurant, and an adult pool. Lei-making classes and crafts demonstrations are offered regularly, and Hawaiian entertainment is provided nightly. Luau is staged four nights a week on the lawn. Arcade games, billiards, darts, and air hockey are among the diversions offered at Paani, a game bar. A shuttle provides transportation to the Maui Ocean Center, half an hour away in Maalaea, and other destinations.

SETTING AND FACILITIES

Location At Wailea Resort, on the waterfront and beach. **Dining** Kumu Bar & Grill serves lunch and dinner with entertainment nightly; poolside Mala Wailea serves breakfast and Pacific Rim cuisine at dinner. *Honua Ula Luau Dinner Show* is held on the spreading lawns overlooking the sea. **Amenities and services** Spa, infinity and other pools, golf, tennis, children's program, parking, business facilities, game room, meeting facilities, golf, tennis.

ACCOMMODATIONS

Rooms 499 nonsmoking. Includes 47 suites; 10 rooms for the disabled. **All rooms** AC, lanai, flat-screen TV, in-room safe, CD player, special bedding, refrigerator, coffeemaker, hair dryer, high-speed Internet access, iron and board, robes. **Some rooms** Oceanfront, more space, sleeper sofa. **Comfort and decor** Spacious, bright, well-appointed rooms have cream, white, and golden wood interiors, and private lanai.

PAYMENT, RESERVATIONS, AND RESTRICTIONS

Family plan Children age 17 and under stay free in room with parents if using existing bedding. **Deposit** 1-night deposit required. Cancellation notice must be given 72 hours prior to scheduled arrival for refund. **Credit cards** All major credit cards accepted. **Check-in/out** 4 p.m./noon.

kids Westin Maui Resort & Spa Kaanapali $$$$

OVERALL ★★★★	QUALITY ★★★★	VALUE ★★★

2365 Kaanapali Parkway, Lahaina 96761; ☎ 866-500-8313 or 808-667-2525; FAX **808-661-5764; www.westinmaui.com**

THE WESTIN HAS AN ELABORATE WATER COMPLEX, sculpture and art displayed throughout, parrots and macaws stationed by the flagstone walkways, and a breezy casual atmosphere overall. The most notable physical feature is the 87,000-square-foot aquatic playground with five pools, three joined together by a pair of waterslides, and two divided by a swim-through grotto with twin waterfalls and a hidden Jacuzzi. One of the pools is designated for adults only and features a swim-up bar. The Westin Kids Club provides supervised fun and games. Island-style entertainment is provided nightly. Weekly luau features expert fire dancers. For night owls, it's just a five-minute drive away from Lahaina, where most of West Maui's after-dark action takes place.

SETTING AND FACILITIES

Location On Kaanapali Beach. **Dining** Tropica serves breakfast and dinner with live music nightly; OnO Bar & Grill serves three meals plus tapas, Hawaiian style, and kids under 12 eat free with paying adults. Wailele Polynesian Luau is performed twice weekly. **Amenities and services** Room service, spa, laundry and valet service, parking, business center, meeting facilities, health club, children's program, golf, tennis, resort shuttle. Daily resort fee, $25.

ACCOMMODATIONS

Rooms 758 nonsmoking units. Includes 27 suites; 14 rooms for the disabled. **All rooms** AC, TV, balcony, high-speed Internet access, minibar, special bedding, in-room safe, coffeemaker, iron and board, hair dryer. **Some rooms** Sofa bed in living room, separate dining area, Bose radio and CD player, upgraded amenities. **Comfort and decor** Spacious and clean rooms feature light neutrals and dark woods in a modern setting. The ambience is classy without being stuffy.

PAYMENT, RESERVATIONS, AND RESTRICTIONS

Family plan Children age 17 and under stay free in room with parents if using existing bedding. Maximum of 4 people per room. **Deposit** 2-night deposit due within 15 days after booking. Cancellation notice must be given 72 hours prior to scheduled arrival for refund. **Credit cards** All major credit cards accepted. **Check-in/out** 3 p.m./noon. Early check-in and late checkout if available.

THE BIG ISLAND OF HAWAII

The Fairmont Orchid $$$$

OVERALL	★★★★½	QUALITY	★★★★	VALUE	★★★

One North Kaniku Drive, Kohala Coast 96743; ☎ 800-845-9905 or 808-885-2000; FAX **808-885-5778; www.fairmont.com/orchid**

WHEN RITZ-CARLTON ORIGINALLY OPENED THIS PROPERTY, they built a beautiful European hotel but forgot the Hawaiian touches. When people come to Hawaii they want something that looks like Hawaii. Now the Orchid delivers a Hawaiian "sense of place" and a first-class experience. Exquisite Hawaiian quilts and original artwork adorn the walls. Hawaii's native koa wood is used prominently. Other physical features at this U-shaped hotel include a 10,000-square-foot swimming pool, a gold-sand beach, and a jogging and walking trail. Children ages 5 to 12 can make new friends at the Keiki Aloha Program; adults can relax at the Centre for

Well-Being. As part of Mauna Lani Resort, The Orchid shares access to two famous championship golf courses, a competition tennis complex, the Puako petroglyph field, and other historic features.

SETTING AND FACILITIES

Location On the Kohala Coast, a short walk to the beach. **Dining** 4 restaurants, 3 lounges. Brown's Beach House serves fresh island seafood and produce. The Orchid Court serves California cuisine and American favorites. **Amenities and services** Room service, twice-daily maid service, spa and wellness center, business facilities, meeting facilities, concierge, swimming pool, golf, tennis, child care, daily newspaper, self-parking or valet parking (both for fee).

ACCOMMODATIONS

Rooms 540. Includes 54 suites. **All rooms** AC, TV, lanai, 3 phones, iron and board, hair dryer, coffeemaker, honor bar, robes. **Some rooms** Living room, extra bath, pullout sofa. **Comfort and decor** Spacious and clean rooms have large Italian marble bathrooms, Hawaiian-accented decor with neutral tones and handcrafted quilts, and private lanai.

PAYMENT, RESERVATIONS, AND RESTRICTIONS

Family plan Children age 18 and under stay free in room with parents if using existing bedding. **Deposit** Credit-card guarantee only. Cancellation notice must be given 7 days prior to scheduled arrival for refund. **Credit cards** All major credit cards accepted. **Check-in/out** 3 p.m./noon. Early check-in and late checkout (up to 2 p.m.) may be available.

Four Seasons Resort Hualalai $$$$$

OVERALL ★★★★★	QUALITY ★★★★★	VALUE ★★★

72–100 Kaupulehu Drive, Kailua-Kona 96740; ☎ 888-340-5662 or 808-325-8000; FAX **800-325-8200; www.fourseasons.com/hualalai**

THIS FABULOUS RESORT IS LESS A HOTEL than an exclusive hideaway. The service is top-notch here, so relax and let yourself be pampered. Sitting on a dramatic landscape formed by eruptions from Hualalai volcano some 200 years ago, this AAA Five Diamond property features clustered low-rise, ocean-view bungalows strategically organized to ensure quiet and privacy. Hawaiian works of art—some dating back to the 18th century—are displayed throughout the resort. Located below the lobby is one of our favorite features at Hualalai: the Kaupulehu Cultural Center, which presents Hawaii's culture and history through artwork, exhibits, video and audio recordings, and hands-on educational programs. An additional special plus is the sports club–fitness center–spa facility, and yet another is the natural amphitheater formed by lava.

Enjoy swimming and snorkeling in the King's Pond, a large black lava pool inspired by the natural tide pools and brackish onshore lava ponds of this coast. You'll share it with some 3,500 colorful reef fish. The pond was sculpted from an ancient lava flow and is fed by natural artesian springs as well as water from the sea. It's one of several pools around which the bungalows are gathered. Ocean swimming here is limited by rough, shallow, rocky conditions.

SETTING AND FACILITIES

Location Beachfront at Kaupulehu on Kona-Kohala Coast, beachfront. **Dining** Pahuia serves contemporary Pacific cuisine from its spectacular setting on the beach. The Hualalai Grille by Alan Wong overlooks the golf course, offering Hawaii regional cuisine by one of Hawaii's most renowned chefs. **Amenities and services** Valet and laundry service, self-serve washer and dryer, valet parking and self-parking, concierge service, Hawaiian cultural center, golf, tennis, full-service spa, 3 swimming pools, children's program.

ACCOMMODATIONS

Rooms 243. Includes 51 suites; 14 rooms for the disabled. **All rooms** AC, flat-screen TV, refrigerated private bar, lanai, in-room safe, walk-in closets, fax line. **Some rooms** Second bedroom; private, lava-rock shower gardens that afford the option of bathing indoors or out. **Comfort and decor** The suites are our favorite rooms of any luxury hotel, done up in beautiful woods, warm-colored slate, plantation shutters, and plenty of Indo-Pacific tropical chic. Bathrooms feature large tubs and separate showers, as well as windows looking into a private garden.

PAYMENT, RESERVATIONS, AND RESTRICTIONS

Family plan Children age 18 and under stay free in room with parents if using existing bedding. **Deposit** 3-night deposit due at booking. Cancellation notice must be given from 3 to 6 weeks in advance of arrival, depending on room type and date of stay. Greater deposit required during the Christmas holidays. **Credit cards** All major credit cards accepted. **Check-in/out** 3 p.m./noon. Early check-in and late checkout available on request.

Hapuna Beach Prince Hotel $$$$

OVERALL ★★★★½	QUALITY ★★★★	VALUE ★★★

62-100 Kaunaoa Drive, Kohala Coast 96743; ☎ **800-866-774-6236 or 808-880-1111;** FAX **808-880-3142; www.princeresortshawaii.com**

THE HAPUNA BEACH PRINCE HOTEL is located next to its sister property, the Mauna Kea Beach Hotel. The layout of the property includes a large number of suites intermixed with well-designed guest rooms in buildings that ensure that every room has ocean views, a signature of Prince Hotels in Hawaii. Built with a contemporary design, the hotel includes an open foyer and lobby that provide a stunning view of Hapuna Beach, the most popular Big Island beach and one of the best beaches in Hawaii. The hotel has a competition-sized pool, championship golf course, and a 13-court tennis facility. Ocean activities include swimming, snorkeling, scuba diving, sailing, and whale watching.

SETTING AND FACILITIES

Location On the Big Island's Kohala Coast, overlooking Hapuna Beach. **Dining** Coast Grille Restaurant & Oyster Bar specializes in fresh island seafood. Hakone Steakhouse Sushi Bar features flame-broiled Kobe steaks and an East-meets-West menu. The Ocean Terrace offers a wide menu of breakfast selections, including an extensive buffet. **Amenities and services** Freshwater pool, Jacuzzi, welcome amenities, golf, tennis, water sports, beauty salon, fitness room, spa services, business services, complimentary valet and self-parking.

ACCOMMODATIONS

Rooms 350. Includes 36 luxury suites; 10 rooms for the disabled. One suite is a separate 8,000-square-foot, 4-bedroom estate. **All rooms** AC, TV, lanai, refrigerators, in-room safes. **Some rooms** Sitting rooms, upgraded amenities. **Comfort and decor** Spacious and attractive, all rooms have ocean views, soft tropical colors, island-accented furnishings, and artwork.

PAYMENT, RESERVATIONS, AND RESTRICTIONS

Family plan Children age 17 and under stay free in room with parents if using existing bedding. Maximum 2 adults and 2 children or 3 adults per room (third adult is $80 per night). **Deposit** 1-night deposit due at booking. Cancellation notice must be given 72 hours prior to scheduled arrival for refund. **Credit cards** All major credit cards accepted. **Check-in/out** 3 p.m./noon. Early check-in and late checkout available on request.

Hilo Hawaiian Hotel $$

OVERALL ★★★½	QUALITY ★★★½	VALUE ★★½

71 Banyan Drive, Hilo 96720; ☎ 800-367-5004 or 808-935-9361; FAX 808-961-9642; www.castleresorts.com

THE HILO HAWAIIAN DOESN'T QUALIFY AS A LUXURY RESORT, but it still rates as one of the best hotels in Hilo. Its sloping arc design blends well with its surroundings, including Hilo Bay. Built in 1974 and renovated in 1992, the hotel has attractive rooms, a friendly staff, and a popular prime-rib and seafood buffet (it's even a favorite among locals), but nothing stands out as extraordinary. This is a good choice for travelers who plan to spend most of their time exploring the volcanoes and the island and want a comfortable, clean, and affordable place to stay.

SETTING AND FACILITIES

Location At Hilo Bay, no beach. **Dining** Queen's Court serves nightly buffets. **Amenities and services** Free parking, coin-operated laundry, pool, beauty salon, gift shop.

ACCOMMODATIONS

Rooms 286. Includes 18 suites; 7 wheelchair-accessible rooms. **All rooms** AC, TV, refrigerator, coffeemakers; hair dryers and iron and board available on request. **Some rooms** Lanai, high-speed Internet access, extra space. **Comfort and decor** Spacious, mostly clean and well-maintained rooms have simple furnishings with a few island-inspired artworks but dim lighting.

PAYMENT, RESERVATIONS, AND RESTRICTIONS

Family plan Children age 17 and under stay free in room with parents if using existing bedding. **Deposit** credit-card guarantee at booking. Cancellation notice must be given 72 hours prior to scheduled arrival, 60 days in advance for holiday bookings. **Credit cards** All major credit cards accepted. **Check-in/out** 3 p.m./noon. Early check-in and late checkout available on request.

Hilton Waikoloa Village $$$

OVERALL	★★★★½	QUALITY	★★★★½	VALUE	★★★

69-425 Waikoloa Beach Drive, Waikoloa 96738; ☎ 800-445-8667 or 808-886-1234; FAX **808-886-2900; www.hiltonwaikoloavillage.com**

THINK OF THIS 62-ACRE RESORT AS AN ISLAND-STYLE Disneyland dedicated to vacation fun, complete with boat rides, lush tropical gardens, and encounters with some exotic but friendly creatures (ranging from parrots and macaws to Atlantic bottlenose dolphins). The Hilton Waikoloa, the ultimate creation of Hawaii's fantasy resort era of the late 1980s, has been updated with a $90-million renovation. Its three towers surround a beautiful five-acre lagoon where the dolphins live and play. A daily lottery determines which lucky guests can get into the water, pet the dolphins, and learn about these ocean mammals from a marine specialist. You can explore the hotel via canal boats or Swiss trams, or by hoofing it on the mile-long museum walkway, which is adorned with a multimillion-dollar collection of Asian and Pacific replicated art. A "self-contained resort," the Hilton Waikoloa has something for everyone: plentiful restaurant choices, pools with waterfalls and waterslides, swimming and beach activities at neighboring Anaehoomalu Beach, shops, sports club and spa, children's programs, luau, entertainment, golf, and tennis. Families with children, in particular, will love this resort.

SETTING AND FACILITIES

Location In Waikoloa Beach Resort, oceanfront (no beach). **Dining** The Palm Terrace offers a wide range of international specialties. Kirin serves dim sum at lunch and other Chinese cuisine at dinner. Imari features traditional Japanese fare. Kamuela Provision Company serves steak and seafood. **Amenities and services** Room service, laundry service, valet and self-parking (fee), business center, spa, children's program, Dolphin Encounter program, golf, tennis.

ACCOMMODATIONS

Rooms 1,240. Includes 57 suites. Rooms for the disabled available. **All rooms** AC, TV, lanai, honor bar, refrigerator, coffeemaker, in-room safe, hair dryer, iron and board. **Some rooms** Second bedroom, upgraded amenities. **Comfort and decor** Spacious rooms (standard rooms are 530 square feet) have bright atmosphere, lavish furnishings, and tasteful Hawaiian artwork.

PAYMENT, RESERVATIONS, AND RESTRICTIONS

Family plan Children age 18 and under stay free in room with parents if using existing bedding. **Deposit** 1- or 2-night deposit due at booking. Cancellation notice must be given 72 hours prior to scheduled arrival for refund. **Credit cards** All major credit cards accepted. **Check-in/out** 3 p.m./noon. Early check-in and late checkout may be available.

King Kamehameha's Kona Beach Hotel $$

OVERALL	★★★½	QUALITY	★★★★	VALUE	★★★★

75-5660 Palani Road, Kailua-Kona 96740; ☎ 800-367-2111 or 808-329-2911; FAX **808-329-4602; www.konabeachhotel.com**

KING KAMEHAMEHA'S KONA BEACH HOTEL sits next to historic grounds once home to royalty. In old Hawaii, high-ranking *alii* used this site as a summer retreat. Kamehameha the Great himself made this his royal residence nearly two centuries ago. The focal point of this historic area is the Ahuena heiau, which dates back to the 15th century and was used for human sacrifices. The hotel is centrally located in the seaside town of Kailua-Kona, on a small, protected gold-sand beach, within easy walking distance of restaurants and shops. The hotel has a very Hawaiian feel, with cultural artifacts and paintings of Hawaiian royalty displayed in the lobby and public areas, and is also popular among *kamaaina* visiting from other islands. Rooms are newly renovated, with a striking decor designed around Big Island themes of lava (black and red blanket trim on white bedding), tapa and tattoo, and native flora.

SETTING AND FACILITIES

Location In the heart of Kailua-Kona, on the (only) beach. **Dining** The Kona Beach Restaurant serves breakfast and dinner buffets, plus Sunday Champagne brunch. **Amenities and services** Parking (fee), room service, laundry facilities, swimming pool, Jacuzzi, tennis, sauna, beauty salon, luau.

ACCOMMODATIONS

Rooms 460. Includes 12 suites; 10 rooms for the disabled. **All rooms** AC, flat-screen TV with pay-per-view movies, free high-speed wireless Internet, mini-fridge, in-room safe, coffeemaker, hair dryer, iron and board available on request. **Comfort and decor** Medium-sized rooms with bold accents and Hawaiian artwork.

PAYMENT, RESERVATIONS, AND RESTRICTIONS

Family plan Children age 18 and under stay free in room with parents if using existing bedding. **Deposit** 1-night deposit required at booking. Cancellation notice must be given at least 72 hours prior to scheduled arrival for refund. **Credit cards** All major credit cards accepted. **Check-in/out** 3 p.m./11 a.m. Late checkout available until 6 p.m. for a fee of half a day's rack rate.

Kona Village Resort $$$$$

OVERALL ★★★★½	QUALITY ★★★★	VALUE ★★★★

Queen Kaahumanu Highway, Kailua-Kona 96740; ☎ 800-367-5290 or 808-325-5555; FAX 808-325-5124; www.konavillage.com

THE ULTIMATE RETREAT. Set between black lava fields and the blue Pacific, isolated, tranquil Kona Village offers the quintessential tropical escape to private, thatched-roof bungalows near the sea. No other place comes close, except maybe neighboring Four Seasons Hualalai, but there, the atmosphere is more obviously modern and upscale. Here you'll pay handsomely, too, for well-appointed but less-fancy digs, but with meals included. This venerable resort, built in the mid-1960s when access was by boat or plane only, still has a sense of being a world apart, buffered by the lava. It more closely echoes the old fishing village that once thrived on the same site, its crumbling foundations still visible today. Kona Village boasts a petroglyph field depicting symbols of life by the sea, including sailing and fishing, unique in the area. It has an ancient fishpond and ruins of the original village among its guest bungalows, and enough specimen trees and Hawaiian medicinal plants to warrant a botanical tour. Lava fields on the *ma uka* side keep the 21st century at a safe distance, but you can cross them in minutes via a gated road. No one cares whether the guests are CEOs (many are), famous authors (some write novels there), movie producers, or just folks. Kona Village offers the kind of hang-loose peace and quiet that restores souls. Kids are cherished in this camplike compound, but discouraged (with a daily rate for toddlers who are usually free) in May and September, when no kids' programs are offered. This place is incredibly romantic any time of year, kids or no kids.

Huts in various Pacific Island architectural styles, strewn in clusters along the coast, come without televisions, radios, phones, or air-conditioning (phones are available by the office.) Each *hale*, or house, is a thatched-roof bungalow with king-sized beds, mini-fridge, lanai, and other choice amenities. Some have a hot tub on the lanai.

Upon arrival, you're greeted with a fresh-flower lei and a cold tropical drink. Then you're set for an extraordinary holiday of total relaxation. Beach activities, guided kayak tours, snorkeling, diving, windsurfing, sailing and outrigger canoe rides, as well as a spa, tennis, and a renowned luau are recreational options. Rates include three meals daily and many of the activities and amenities for which other resorts charge extra (including the luau). Less is more here; you will know what we mean on the day you leave, reluctantly.

SETTING AND FACILITIES

Location In Kaupulehu, 14 miles north of Kailua-Kona, fronting a beach cove. **Dining** Hale Moana serves a wide variety of international and American favorites for breakfast, lunch, and dinner; the more formal Hale Samoa specializes in Pacific Rim cuisine. **Amenities and services** Fitness center, spa, beach facilities, tennis, complimentary programs for children ages 6 to 12, transportation to and from airport.

ACCOMMODATIONS

Rooms 125 *hale*. Rooms for the disabled available. **All rooms** Ceiling fan, lanai, mini-fridge stocked with free drinks, hair dryer, in-room safe, coffeemaker with pure Kona coffee. **Some rooms** Private whirlpool spa. **Comfort and decor** Spacious, with high ceilings; furnishings are comfortable and simple, with a tropical motif in rich earth tones and tasteful island-themed art.

PAYMENT, RESERVATIONS, AND RESTRICTIONS

Family plan Children age 5 and under stay free (except in May and September, when regular daily rates are charged). **Deposit** 2-night deposit due at booking; full payment required by September 1 for Christmas holiday stays. Cancellation notice must be given 30 days prior to scheduled arrival for refund (60 days for holidays other than Christmas, mid-April for the Christmas period). **Credit cards** All major credit cards accepted. **Check-in/out** 3 p.m./noon. Hospitality room available for early arrivals and late departures.

Mauna Kea Beach Hotel $$$$$

OVERALL ★★★★½	QUALITY ★★★★	VALUE ★★★

62-100 Mauna Kea Beach Drive, Kohala Coast 96743; ☎ 888-977-4623 or 808-882-7222; FAX 808-882-5700; www.princeresortshawaii.com

MAUNA KEA BEACH HOTEL, born again after a complete overhaul for earthquake repairs, is back welcoming the faithful. The exhaustive renovation resulted in fewer but larger rooms—two for every three in the former configuration—and more luxurious baths, which now have golf or ocean views. The hallowed dash of orange is again prominent in room decor (prior attempts to wash out the trademark shade of the Mauna Kea plumeria logo were upsetting to many returning guests).

The oldest Big Island resort—it opened in 1965—remains a favorite, for many very good reasons, not the least of which is its site on the island's best swimming beach. The Mauna Kea keeps its loyal, graying clientele and adds their junior replacements with babes in arms. Three generations of guests have checked in to enjoy this grand old lady of the Kohala Coast. The open-air architectural design, art-stuffed halls, perfect gold-sand crescent beach, and old-fashioned Hawaiian hospitality all contribute to the enduring success of this luxury hotel. The Mauna Kea steadfastly rejected modern gadgets like TVs until this current renovation, when the 21st century with its flat-screen HDTVs, iPod docks, and wireless Internet quietly entered the rooms. Golfers have their choice of the Mauna Kea Golf Course (also newly renovated) or the Hapuna Golf Course; tennis players can serve and volley at the oceanside Tennis Park, which features 13 Plexi-pave courts. Mauna Kea Stables offers Parker Ranch trail rides. The weekly luau and clambake are both back in force. After dinner, it's customary to wander down to the floodlit platform by the water where manta rays glide in for their evening meal, the smaller fry attracted by the lights.

SETTING AND FACILITIES

Location On the Big Island's Kohala Coast, fronting Kauna Oa Beach. **Dining** 4 restaurants including Manta, for breakfast, Sunday brunch, and Island cuisine at dinner. **Amenities and services** Swimming pool, Jacuzzi, new fitness center, shopping area, spa, golf, tennis, horseback riding, meeting facilities, beauty salon, museum-quality art display, resort shuttle, children's program.

ACCOMMODATIONS

Rooms 258. Includes 10 suites; 10 rooms for the disabled. **All rooms** AC, flat-screen TV, private lanai, clock radio/iPod dock, wireless Internet access, coffeemaker, mini-fridge, hair dryer, iron and board, robes and slippers. **Some rooms** 2 full baths, sitting room. **Comfort and decor** Very spacious. Warm woods in wainscoting and built-ins, beige fabrics with orange and black accents. Original watercolors are among the island-themed artworks.

PAYMENT, RESERVATIONS, AND RESTRICTIONS

Family plan Children age 17 and under stay free in room with parents if using existing bedding. **Deposit** 1-night deposit due at booking. Cancellation notice must be given 14 days prior to scheduled arrival for refund. **Credit cards** All major credit cards accepted. **Check-in/out** 3 p.m./noon. Early check-in and late checkout may be available.

Mauna Lani Resort $$$$$

OVERALL ★★★★½	QUALITY ★★★★½	VALUE ★★½

68-1400 Mauna Lani Drive, Kohala Coast 96743; ☎ **800-628-7815 or 808-885-6622;** FAX **808-885-1484; www.maunalani.com**

FOR ALL-AROUND LUXURY AND SECLUSION, the Mauna Lani is one of our favorite resorts—especially the bungalows.

Service is friendly, island-style hospitality gracious, and the site ideal for a beach resort. And if you're fortunate, you can a stay at one of the resort's five world-class oceanfront bungalows, for only $4,500 a night. Each 4,000-square-foot bungalow has two bedrooms and a private swimming pool. The former prime draw of butler service fell victim to the economy.

The hotel's main structure directly faces the ocean and has an atrium-style design with waterfalls, ponds, trees, and flora. Golf, tennis, and water sports are among the outdoor diversions available here, and kids ages 5 to 12 can participate in Camp Mauna Lani, which offers lei-making, hula dancing, history tours, and other activities. Don't miss the Puako petroglyph field beside the resort or the self-guided history tour of the ancient dwelling caves and fishpond by the hotel.

SETTING AND FACILITIES

Location On Big Island's Kohala Coast, fronting beach. **Dining** The Canoe House serves Pacific Rim cuisine. The poolside Ocean Grill features salads, gourmet pizza, fresh seafood. **Amenities and services** 24-hour room service, twice-daily maid service, laundry and dry-cleaning service, concierge service, meeting and banquet facilities, secretarial assistance, golf, tennis, spa, sports and fitness club, pools, complimentary self-parking and valet parking, children's program.

ACCOMMODATIONS

Rooms 343. Includes 5 exclusive bungalows, 28 villas; 12 rooms for the disabled. **All rooms** AC, TV, VCR, private lanai, honor bar, in-room safe, refrigerator, clock radio, wireless Internet access, hair dryer, ceiling fan, flashlight, umbrella, robes, slippers. **Some rooms** Bungalows have private pool, steam showers, large-screen TV, iMac and iPod, whirlpool spa. **Comfort and decor** Spacious (more than 600 square feet), well-kept rooms have tasteful island decor and furnishings. Cool tones of white and beige, large private lanai (more than 90% of the rooms have ocean views), atrium gardens, and pools lend a peaceful, tropical atmosphere.

PAYMENT, RESERVATIONS, AND RESTRICTIONS

Family plan Children age 12 and under stay free in room with parents if using existing bedding. Maximum of 2 adults and 2 children or three adults per room. **Deposit** 2-night deposit required to guarantee reservation. Cancellation notice must be given at least 14 days prior to scheduled arrival for refund. **Credit cards** All major credit cards accepted. **Check-in/out** 3 p.m./noon. Early check-in and late checkout available on request.

Naniloa Volcanoes Resort $

OVERALL ★★★	QUALITY ★★★	VALUE ★★★

93 Banyan Drive, Hilo 96720; ☎ **808-969-3333;** FAX **808-969-6622;**
www.hottours.us

THIS OLDER HOTEL HAS A PICTURESQUE setting on the bay and is open while undergoing an extensive (and long overdue) renovation (be sure to request a renovated room). Redone rooms boast crisp, minimalist decor with blond woods, simple lines, and neutral tones, plus an occasional splash of color in tropical wall hangings and bed covers. The renovated bathrooms feature stylish fixtures and tile. All in all, the new guest rooms have the feel of a trendy, boutique hotel. Oceanfront rooms face the bay—cruise ships, fishing boats, and paddlers glide in and out of the harbor just beyond your private lanai. With renovated-room rates starting at a little over $100, the Naniloa is a good value. The hotel is also the headquarters of the Merrie Monarch Festival, the world's most prestigious hula competition.

SETTING AND FACILITIES

Location Fronting Hilo Bay, no beach. **Dining** Hoomalimali Restaurant and **Bar** features prime rib and continental fare. **Amenities and services** Courtesy airport transfer service, free parking, spa and fitness center (under renovation), 9-hole golf course, pool, banquet facilities.

ACCOMMODATIONS

Rooms 383. Includes 19 suites; 1 floor for the disabled. Renovated rooms have AC, TV, coffeemaker, mini-fridge, microwave, hair dryer. **Comfort and decor** Rooms are small to medium, with attractive decor and tasteful furnishings.

PAYMENT, RESERVATIONS, AND RESTRICTIONS

Family plan Children age 17 and under stay free in room with parents if using existing bedding. **Deposit** 1-night deposit due within 10 days of confirmation. Cancellation notice must be given at least 72 hours prior to scheduled arrival for refund. **Credit cards** All major credit cards accepted. **Check-in/out** 3 p.m./noon. Early check-in and late checkout available on request.

Outrigger Keauhou Beach Resort $

OVERALL ★★★	QUALITY ★★★	VALUE ★★½

78-6740 Alii Drive, Kailua-Kona 96740; ☎ **800-688-7444 or**
808-322-3441; FAX **808-322-3117; www.outrigger.com**

THIS TEN-ACRE OCEANFRONT PROPERTY has a lovely setting, with a portion of the building jutting over a tide pool and lush tropical gardens onshore. Extensive renovations have been underway for rooms and public areas; be sure to ask for a new room. A favorite for *kamaaina* visiting from other islands, the resort features several prominent historic Hawaiian sites, including *heiau* and a replica of King Kalakaua's vacation *hale*. Children are welcome to explore several on-site tidal pools, and adults can enjoy snorkeling, scuba diving, or tennis on six courts.

SETTING AND FACILITIES

Location Oceanfront, next to the beach at Kahaluu Bay. **Dining** Kamaaina Terrace serves local favorites and seafood. **Amenities and services** Daily maid service, fitness center, activities and travel desks, parking, salon and spa, tennis, pool, sundry shop.

ACCOMMODATIONS

Rooms 310. Includes 6 suites; 14 rooms for the disabled. **All rooms** AC, TV, private lanai, clock radio, crib on request, hair dryer, iron and board, refrigerator. **Comfort and decor** Spacious, with Hawaiian-style decor.

PAYMENT, RESERVATIONS, AND RESTRICTIONS

Family plan Children age 17 and under stay free in room with parents if using existing bedding. **Deposit** Credit card guarantee, or one night cash deposit within 10 days. Cancellation notice must be given at least 72 hours prior to scheduled arrival for refund. **Credit cards** All major credit cards accepted. **Check-in/out** 3 p.m./noon. Early check-in and late checkout may be available.

Sheraton Keauhou Bay Resort & Spa $$$$

OVERALL	★★★★	QUALITY	★★★★	VALUE	★★★

78-128 Ehukai Street, Kailuau-Kona 96740; ☎ 808-930-4900; FAX 808-930-4800 www.sheratonkeauhou.com

SHERATON RESCUED THE FORMER KONA SURF RESORT with a $70-million renovation in 2004. In 2009, the property was rescued from foreclosure when its bank purchased it. The effects of this financial change on hotel operations were not known at press time. The 22-acre resort covers an ancient lava flow that spills into the sea as a rocky promontory south of Kona—the result is spectacular (but beachless), with fantasy pools and an open-air spa, as well as a wedding chapel. Manta rays live along this coast, and guests can enjoy a "Manta Experience," a night snorkel or dive, to swim with the rays.

SETTING AND FACILITIES

Location Oceanfront at Keauhou Bay, south of Kailua-Kona. **Dining** Kai serves breakfast buffet and dinner, with the spotlight on seafood; Manta Ray Bar & Grill serves sandwiches and salads; Crystal Blue offers hors d'oeuvres and cocktails; Kamahao luau-style dinner and show twice a week. **Amenities and services** Oceanfront fitness center, babysitting, concierge, business services, complete meeting and convention facilities including a 10,000-square-foot ballroom, room service, dry cleaning and valet, game room, shops, spa, parking, multilevel fantasy swimming pool and stream with 200-foot lava-tube waterslide, children's program, tennis and basketball courts, jogging and bike path. Located next to Kona Country Club championship golf courses.

ACCOMMODATIONS

Rooms 521. Includes 10 suites, plus oversized family rooms for up to 6 and 13 rooms specially equipped for the disabled. **All rooms** Open-air lanai, AC, TV with pay-per-view movies, special beds, coffeemaker, iron and board, hair dryer, wireless high-speed Internet access, clock radio, data port, mini-fridge, in-room safe. **Some rooms** Most rooms have some ocean view, some oceanfront. **Comfort and decor** Spacious rooms, historic art, sand-gold and sea-green with warm wood tones.

PAYMENT, RESERVATIONS, AND RESTRICTIONS
Family plan Children age 17 and under stay free in room with parents if using existing bedding. Maximum of 4 people per room. **Deposit** credit-card guarantee at booking. Cancellation notice must be given 72 hours prior to scheduled arrival for refund. **Credit cards** All major credit cards accepted. **Check-in/out** 3 p.m./ noon. Early check-in and late checkout available on request.

Volcano House $$

OVERALL ★ ★ ★	QUALITY ★ ★ ★	VALUE ★ ★ ★

P.O. Box 53, Hawaii Volcanoes National Park 96718; ☎ 808-967-7321; FAX 808-967-8429, www.volcanohousehotel.com

AT THE EDGE OF A VOLCANO, inside Hawaii Volcanoes National Park, this funky lodge, Hawaii's oldest continuously operated hostelry, is filled with history and lore and is a good place to stay if you plan to spend a lot of time at the park or watching the fireworks at night. The lobby features a warm fireplace—tradition has it that the fire has not gone out for the hotel's 135 years of existence—for those chilly nights, and the walls are covered with nostalgic photographs and paintings of Hawaiian royalty. The hotel's lone restaurant fills quickly with busloads of tourists during lunch hour, but the view of Halemaumau Crater is one of a kind.

SETTING AND FACILITIES
Location Inside Hawaii Volcanoes National Park ($10 entry fee is valid for 7 days). **Dining** Ka Ohelo Dining Room specializes in prime rib, and also features breakfast and lunch buffets. **Amenities and services** Free parking, snack shop.

ACCOMMODATIONS
Rooms 42. Includes 1 wheelchair-accessible room. **All rooms** Portable heater, telephone. No TV. **Comfort and decor** Spacious, with koa furnishings, Hawaiian comforters, and tasteful decor. Ten, more rustic cabins also available.

PAYMENT, RESERVATIONS, AND RESTRICTIONS
Family plan Children age 12 and under stay free in room with parents if using existing bedding. **Deposit** 1-night deposit due at booking. Cancellation notice must be given at least 72 hours prior to scheduled arrival for refund. **Credit cards** All major credit cards accepted. **Check-in/out** 3 p.m./noon. Early check-in and late checkout available on request.

Waikoloa Beach Marriott Resort & Spa $$$

OVERALL ★ ★ ★ ★	QUALITY ★ ★ ★ ★	VALUE ★ ★ ★ ★

69-275 Waikoloa Beach Drive, Waikoloa 96738; ☎ 800-228-9290 or 808-886-6789; FAX 808-886-3602; www.waikoloamarriott.com

THE WAIKOLOA BEACH MARRIOTT, after a $50-million renovation, boasts refurbished rooms and a new infinity pool, ballroom, fitness center, and Mandara Spa. It has the best location at Waikoloa Beach Resort, over-looking Anaehoomalu Bay's fishponds and a picturesque gold-sand crescent beach framed by palm trees.

The 19-acre property's open-air lobby overlooks the pool and gardens, with the Pacific in the backdrop. Cultural sites, including the extensive petroglyph field near the hotel front and large ancient Hawaiian fishpond in back, add a sense of relevance and history. The King's Shops complex is just across the road, and golfers can play one (or all) of three nearby Waikoloa courses.

SETTING AND FACILITIES

Location Anaehoomalu Bay, on the Big Island's Kohala Coast. A short walk to the beach. **Dining** Hawaii Calls serves breakfast, lunch, and dinner, featuring Pacific-Asian cuisine. **Amenities and services** Room service, laundry service, 2 pools, business center, spa and fitness center, tennis, golf, children's program, parking (fee); resort fee of $20 per day.

ACCOMMODATIONS

Rooms 533. Includes 22 suites and 15 rooms for the disabled. **All rooms** AC, flat-screen TV with pay-per-view movies, high-speed Internet access, lanai, in-room safe, coffeemaker, hair dryer, refrigerator, iron and board, robes, special bedding. **Some rooms** Oversized rooms, concierge service. **Comfort and decor** Well appointed, spacious, and clean. Dark tropical woods contrast with peach walls, white bedding, and blue-and-yellow trim fabrics echoing the beach-inspired color scheme.

PAYMENT, RESERVATIONS, AND RESTRICTIONS

Family plan Children age 17 and under stay free in room with parents if using existing bedding. **Deposit** Credit card guarantee required. Cancellation notice must be given at least 72 hours prior to scheduled arrival for refund. **Credit cards** All major credit cards accepted. **Check-in/out** 3 p.m./noon. Early check-in and late checkout available on request.

KAUAI

Grand Hyatt Kauai Resort & Spa $$$$$

OVERALL ★★★★½	QUALITY ★★★★½	VALUE ★★★★

1571 Poipu Road, Koloa 96756; ☎ 866-567-7834 or 808-742-1234;
FAX **808-742-1557; www.kauai.hyatt.com**

KAUAI'S BEST BEACH RESORT, the Grand Hyatt Kauai Resort & Spa is an architectural treat, recalling the 1920s nostalgia of Hawaii's golden age. The open-air lobby is one of the most beautiful of a galaxy of luxurious and opulent Hawaiian hotel offerings that include ocean views, gardens, and waterfalls. View settings are dressed with Art Deco finishes, brilliant tropical flowers, koa-wood furnishings, and handsome Italian marble. In terms of amenities and services, the Hyatt, last of the fantasy-oriented hotel boom, pulls out all the stops. The splashy centerpiece is a huge playground of saltwater lagoons and freshwater pools, complete with waterslides.

Among the highlights are a creative program of cultural and ecotourism activities, a children's program, a health spa, great dining, and nightly entertainment. We like Stevenson's Library as a place to sip something special. Of course, it doesn't hurt that Poipu is a marvelous resort destination with a beautiful gold-sand beach–but at the Hyatt, stick to the pools for safe swimming.

SETTING AND FACILITIES

Location Fronting Keoneloa Bay in Poipu, a short walk to beach. **Dining** Tidepools features Pacific Rim specialties; Dondero's serves award-winning northern Italian cuisine. **Amenities and services** 24-hour room service, parking, laundry service, business center, spa, fitness center, babysitting service, beauty salon, meeting and banquet facilities, cultural activities, children's program, tennis, and golf. $15 daily resort fee.

ACCOMMODATIONS

Rooms 602. Includes 37 suites, 26 rooms for the disabled. **All rooms** AC, TV, lanai, marble baths, coffeemaker, stereo with iPod dock, wireless Internet access, iron and board, hair dryer, beverage chiller, robes. **Some rooms** Continental breakfast and snacks. **Comfort and decor** Spacious (standard rooms are 600 square feet) and well-maintained rooms have a comfortable ambience with retro-print accents, a teal-and-coral color scheme pulled from natural surroundings, handsome wood furnishings, and Hawaiian-themed art.

PAYMENT, RESERVATIONS, AND RESTRICTIONS

Family plan Children age 18 and under stay free in room with parents if using existing bedding. **Deposit** 2-night deposit due at booking. Cancellation notice must be given at least 72 hours prior to scheduled arrival for refund. Some Internet rates require prepayment in full and have special cancellation penalties. **Credit cards** All major credit cards accepted. **Check-in/out** 3 p.m./noon. Early check-in and late checkout available on request.

Hanalei Bay Resort $$

OVERALL	★★★½	QUALITY	★★★½	VALUE	★★★

5380 Honoiki Road, Princeville 96722; ☎ 800-827-4427 or 808-826-6522; FAX 808-826-6680; www.hanaleibayresort.com

THIS 22-ACRE RESORT, with some hotel rooms but mostly one-, two- and three-bedroom time-share rentals, has spectacular Hanalei Bay and ocean views and a gold-sand beach down a steep cliff. Carved into a hillside and featuring lush tropical landscaping, the resort offers privacy and solitude ideal for honeymooners. A tennis pro and eight paved tennis courts are located on the premises, and a pair of world-class golf courses beckon nearby.

SETTING AND FACILITIES

Location In the Princeville Resort area on North Shore. **Amenities and services** Free parking, coin-operated laundry, dry-cleaning service, 2 swimming pools, outdoor gas grills, hot tub with sand bottom, high-speed Internet access, tennis, golf, children's programs (seasonal), babysitting.

ACCOMMODATIONS

Rooms 137. Includes hotel rooms, studios, and 1- to –3-bedroom units. **All rooms** AC, TV, lanai, refrigerator, in-room safe, coffeemaker, maid service. **Some rooms** Full kitchens, washer and dryer, extra bedrooms and bathroom. **Comfort and decor** Spacious and tastefully appointed with island-themed art and furnishings and cool, tropical colors.

PAYMENT, RESERVATIONS, AND RESTRICTIONS

Family plan Children age 17 and under stay free in room with parents if using existing bedding. **Deposit** 1-night deposit or credit-card guarantee due within 10 days after booking. Cancellation notice must be given at least 7 days prior to scheduled arrival for refund. **Credit cards** All major credit cards accepted. **Check-in/out** 4 p.m./ 10 a.m. No early check-ins. Hospitality room available.

Hilton Kauai Beach Hotel & Resort $$

OVERALL ★★★★	QUALITY ★★★★	VALUE ★★★½

4331 Kauai Beach Drive, Lihue 96766; ☎ 800-HILTONS or 808-245-1955; FAX 808-246-9085; www.hiltonkauairesort.com

JUST A FEW MINUTES AWAY FROM LIHUE AIRPORT by complimentary shuttle, this 25-acre property, which recently became a Hilton, offers everything you want in a deluxe hotel, including spa, dining, business center, meeting space, and a great beach for walking (but unsafe for swimming). The open design promotes a relaxing and refreshing atmosphere, and its central location on the island's east side makes the property a good starting point for adventure. Golfers can tee off at adjacent Wailua Golf Course, Hawaii's best municipal course. Reasonable rates, especially if you take advantage of Internet offers or ask for special rates, make this recently renovated hotel a very good value.

SETTING AND FACILITIES

Location In Lihue, minutes from the Lihue Airport. **Dining** Naupaka Terrace serves breakfast and dinner, featuring American favorites. **Amenities and services** Room service, business center, meeting facilities, airport shuttle, 4 pools and flume waterslide; nightly Polynesian show and guest cocktail party included in $12.95 daily resort fee.

ACCOMMODATIONS

Rooms 350 nonsmoking rooms and suites. **All rooms** AC, TV, lanai, voice mail, mini-fridge, in-room safe, wireless high-speed Internet access, parking, valet parking, coffeemaker, special bedding. **Some rooms** Separate parlor, upgraded amenities; club floor with concierge service. **Comfort and decor** Small but attractive (recently renovated), with warm colors and comfortable atmosphere.

PAYMENT, RESERVATIONS, AND RESTRICTIONS

Family plan Children age 17 and under stay free in room with parents if using existing bedding. **Deposit** 1-night deposit or credit-card guarantee due within 10 days after booking. Cancellation notice must be given at least 72 hours prior to scheduled arrival for refund. **Credit cards** All major credit cards accepted. **Check-in/out** 4 p.m./noon.

Kauai Marriott Resort & Beach Club $$$$

OVERALL ★★★★	QUALITY ★★★★	VALUE ★★★

3610 Rice Street, Kalapaki Beach, Lihue 96766; ☎ 800-220-2925 or 808-245-5050; FAX 808-245-5049; www.marriotthawaii.com

THIS WELL-SITED RESORT ON 800 ACRES (a mile from the airport on a sheltered beach by the harbor) has toned down its glitzy former self—it was one of the last 1980s fantasy resorts—but remains a world-class destination offering excellent service. The sprawling hotel, half of it now a time-share operation, offers a seven-acre swimming pool for a focal point, lavish furnishings and artwork, and a major ballroom and conference facility. Tranquil lagoons and elevated waterways are traversed via mahogany launches, and horse-drawn carriages provide a leisurely exploration of the resort grounds. Golfers are advised to play at least a round at one of the resort's two championship Jack Nicklaus courses.

SETTING AND FACILITIES

Location On Kalapaki Beach. **Dining** 5 restaurants, including Duke's, which serves steak, fish, and seafood specialties. The poolside Kukui's Restaurant & Bar features Pacific Rim cuisine. Cafe Portofino offers Italian fare. **Amenities and services** Room service, coin-operated laundry, maid service, valet service, business center, golf, tennis, free airport transportation, fitness center, day spa, meeting facilities, pools, children's program, self-parking and valet parking (fee).

ACCOMMODATIONS

Rooms 356 nonsmoking rooms. Includes 11 suites; 10 rooms for the disabled. **All rooms** AC, TV, minibar, in-room safe, high-speed Internet access, coffeemaker, hair dryer, iron and board, special bedding, robes and slippers. **Some rooms** Kitchenette, microwave. **Comfort and decor** Rooms are small to medium and pleasant, with subtle tropical decor and artwork.

PAYMENT, RESERVATIONS, AND RESTRICTIONS

Family plan Children age 17 and under stay free in room with parents if using existing bedding. **Deposit** One-night deposit due within 10 days of booking. Cancellation notice must be given at least 72 hours prior to scheduled arrival for refund. **Credit cards** All major credit cards accepted. **Check-in/out** 4 p.m./noon. Early check-in (from 2 p.m.) and late checkout (until 2 p.m.) available on request.

Sheraton Kauai Resort $$$$$

OVERALL ★★★★	QUALITY ★★★★	VALUE ★★

2440 Hoonani Road, Poipu Beach, Koloa 96756; ☎ 866-716-8109 or 808-742-1661; FAX 808-742-9777; www.sheraton-kauai.com

HALF OF THE SHERATON KAUAI EMBRACES Poipu Beach, and the other half explodee in a garden of ginger, anthurium, heliconia, and bamboo. No building is taller than a coconut tree, which adds to the sense of seclusion at this 20-acre resort. The 394 rooms are housed in a trio of four-story buildings, each identified by major views (ocean, beach, garden). Amenities include a children's program, swimming pools, and a fitness center.

SETTING AND FACILITIES

Location On Poipu Beach. **Dining** Shells serves a variety of international cuisine for breakfast, lunch, and dinner. Naniwa is a fine-dining Japanese restaurant. A beachfront luau is available. **Amenities and services** Room service, self-parking and valet parking (fee), fitness center, laundry facilities, tennis, business facilities, children's program, 2 pools and 2 children's pools, championship golf nearby. A $15-per-day resort fee is added to the room charge.

ACCOMMODATIONS

Rooms 394. Includes 8 suites; 11 rooms for the disabled. **All rooms** AC, TV, radio, refrigerator, in-room safe, hair dryer, iron and board, robes, coffeemaker, special beds, private lanai. **Some rooms** Larger space, fresh flowers. **Comfort and decor** Spacious and bright, rooms have warm earth tones and handsome wood furnishings.

PAYMENT, RESERVATIONS, AND RESTRICTIONS

Family plan Children age 17 and under stay free in room with parents if using existing bedding. **Deposit** Credit card guarantee at booking. Cancellation notice must be given at least 72 hours prior to scheduled arrival for refund. **Credit cards** All major credit cards accepted. **Check-in/out** 3 p.m./noon. Early check-in and late checkout available on request. Hospitality room available.

St. Regis Princeville Resort $$$$$

OVERALL	★★★★½	QUALITY	★★★★	VALUE	★★★

5520 Ka Haku Road, Princeville 96722; ☎ **808-826-9644;**
FAX **808-826-1166; www.princevillehotelhawaii.com**

St. Regis Princeville is the first St. Regis in Hawaii. With the best view in the Islands, Princeville Resort is a Versailles by the sea. The hotel sets a high standard of excellence and has made every effort to incorporate Hawaiian culture in the guest experience.

It's all here: shopping, fine dining, a swimming pool, nightly Hawaiian entertainment, a small gold-sand beach, and that incredible view of Hanalei Bay. Come here to be pampered in the clubhouse spa and play the challenging Prince Course, ranked number one in the Islands.

SETTING AND FACILITIES

Location At St. Regis Princeville Resort on Kauai's North Shore, rooms are set into a sea cliff overlooking spectacular Hanalei Bay and the broad, blue sea. Elevators handle most of the grade in the short walk down to the beach. **Dining** Kauai Grill is the signature restaurant, by Chef Jean-Georges Vongerichten. **Amenities and services** 24-hour room service, laundry service, concierge desk, butler service, spa, golf, tennis, meeting and banquet facilities, health and fitness center, swimming pool, business center.

ACCOMMODATIONS

Rooms 252. Includes 51 suites; 7 rooms for the disabled. **All rooms** AC, TV, honor bar, safe, oversized bathroom, hair dryer, iron and board, robes, most with no lanai but with large windows that drink in the view. **Some rooms** Lanai, second TV. **Comfort and decor** Very spacious, with custom-designed furnishings and original artwork.

PAYMENT, RESERVATIONS, AND RESTRICTIONS

Family plan Children age 17 and under stay free in room with parents if using existing bedding. **Deposit** 2-night deposit required within 14 days of booking. Cancellation notice must be given at least 7 days prior to scheduled arrival for refund. **Credit cards** All major credit cards accepted. **Check-in/out** 3 p.m./noon. Early check-in and late checkout available on request.

Westin Princeville Ocean Resort Villas $$$$

| OVERALL | ★★★★ | QUALITY | ★★★★ | VALUE | ★★★ |

3838 Wyllie Road, Princeville 96722; ☎ 800-937-8461 or 808-827-8700; FAX 808-827-8701; www.westinprinceville.com

FEW PLACES IN THE WORLD MATCH THE BEAUTY of this mystical area. Princeville Resort offers horseback riding stables, world-famous golf, tennis, helicopter tours of the Na Pali Coast, and easy access to the restaurants and shops of Hanalei and the gardens and beaches at the north end of the road. This property offers spacious new condo-style time-share units fully equipped and ready for the family.

SETTING AND FACILITIES

Location On a cliff overlooking Hanalei Bay and the blue Pacific. **Dining** Nanea restaurant offers breakfast, lunch, and dinner, as well as a bar. **Amenities and services** 4 pools, fitness and steam/sauna facilities, barbecue grills, business center, children's program, Princeville Market with deli, golf, tennis, beaches, and resort shuttle to shopping, Anini Beach, golf clubhouses, and other points.

ACCOMMODATIONS

Rooms 346; half studios, half 1-bedroom units; 2-bedroom units on request. **All rooms** AC, flat-screen TV, DVD player, stereo, high-speed Internet access, fully equipped kitchen, washer and dryer, sleeper sofa, special bedding. **Comfort and decor** Dark woods, cream walls with island-inspired art, and decorative touches.

PAYMENT, RESERVATIONS, AND RESTRICTIONS

Family plan Unit prices based on 4 occupants. **Deposit** Credit-card guarantee at booking, with deposit of 1 night's stay. Cancellation Notice must be given at least 3 days prior to scheduled arrival for refund. **Credit cards** All major credit cards accepted. **Check-in/out** 4 p.m./10 a.m.

MOLOKAI

Hotel Molokai $$

| OVERALL | ★★★ | QUALITY | ★★★ | VALUE | ★★★ |

Kamehameha V Highway, P.O. Box 120, Kaunakakai, HI 96748; ☎ 808-553-5347; www.hotelmolokai.com

MOLOKAI'S ONLY HOTEL, after the 2008 shutdown of Molokai Ranch and its luxury lodge and beach tent camp, makes the most of its beach setting on Molokai's east end, close to the town of Kaunakakai. Dark brown A-framed bungalows with steep Polynesian roofs contain newly repainted and upgraded units (condos; some are also rented by owners). This is a mixed bag—the retro architecture, waterfront locale, and down-home Molokai style can be charming, but the restaurant is iffy and the music from the popular bar wafts in on the breeze, causing some guests to bring ear plugs in order to sleep. Ask for oceanfront units, and kitchen facilities if you want to make your own meals. The beachfront location has broad lawns and appealing views, but the water is shallow and the bottom is reef, so you'll need to drive farther east to find swimming beaches.

SETTING AND FACILITIES
Location Beachfront, near Kaunakakai. **Dining** Hula Shores Restaurant and Bar is a popular open-air waterfront restaurant and bar with live music nightly. Amenities and Services Free parking, coin laundry, small pool, high-speed Internet access, meeting room.

ACCOMMODATIONS
Rooms 37; 1 suite. **All rooms** Ceiling fans, cable TV, lanai, high-speed Internet access, coffeemaker, small refrigerator, microwave, iron and board, hair dryer, kitchen or kitchenette. **Some rooms** Oceanfront, AC (honeymoon suite). **Comfort and decor** Low-key atmosphere with open-air design to catch the trade winds for cooling, island-style decor.

PAYMENT, RESERVATIONS, AND RESTRICTIONS
Family plan Unit prices based on 3–4 occupants. **Deposit** Credit-card guarantee at booking, with deposit of 1 night's stay. Cancellation Notice must be given at least 3 days prior to scheduled arrival for refund. **Credit cards** All major credit cards accepted. **Check-in/out** 4 p.m./11 a.m.

LANAI

Four Seasons Resort Lanai at Manele Bay $$$$$

OVERALL ★★★★½	QUALITY ★★★★	VALUE ★★★

1 Manele Bay Road, Lanai City 96763; ☎ 800-321-4666 or 808-565-2000; FAX 808-565-2483; www.fourseasons.com/manelebay

PERCHED ATOP WINDSWEPT SEA CLIFFS, the Manele Bay overlooks Lanai's magnificent coastline and Hulopoe Bay, a favorite playground of spinner dolphins (Manele Bay is actually next door, where the boats dock). A blend of Mediterranean and Hawaiian designs, the Manele Bay is full of exotic artifacts and grand murals, some hand-painted by local residents. Lush tropical gardens add color to the otherwise arid landscape, but still fall short of the spectacular ocean views. It's just a short stroll downhill to Hulopoe Beach, one of the best beaches in Hawaii, with excellent water clarity for snorkeling and scuba diving. Great golf awaits you at The Challenge at Manele. Like The Lodge at Koele, Manele delivers a memorable experience.

SETTING AND FACILITIES
Location Overlooking Hulopoe Bay; short walk to the beach. **Dining** Ihilani serves fine Italian cuisine. Ocean Grill features fresh seafood four nights a week and lunch daily. **Amenities and services** Room service, valet parking and self-

parking, spa, golf, tennis, concierge service, children's program, fitness center, live entertainment nightly, pool, beach and pool amenities such as chilled towels and fruit skewers, meeting facilities, babysitting.

ACCOMMODATIONS

Rooms 236. Includes 21 suites; 6 rooms for the disabled. **All rooms** AC, TV, VCR, CD player, high-speed Internet access, radio, in-room safe, lanai, minibar, hair dryer, robes, twice-daily housekeeping, sitting area. **Some rooms** Butler service. **Comfort and decor** Large (averaging 700 square feet), comfortable rooms have refined furnishings, a restful cream, gold, and beige color scheme with a tropical motif, and accessories collected from around the world.

PAYMENT, RESERVATIONS, AND RESTRICTIONS

Family plan Children age 18 and under stay free in room with parents if using existing bedding. Maximum of 3 people per room. Extra person, $100. **Deposit** 2-night deposit due at booking. Cancellation notice must be given 21 days prior to scheduled arrival to avoid fees. **Credit cards** All major credit cards accepted. **Check-in/out** 3 p.m./noon. Early check-in and late checkout may be available.

Four Seasons Resort Lanai, The Lodge at Koele $$$$

OVERALL ★★★★½	QUALITY ★★★★½	VALUE ★★½

1 Keomoku Highway, Lanai City 96763; ☎ 800-321-4666 or 808-565-4000; FAX 808-565-4561; www.fourseasons.com/koele

NESTLED ON THE ISLAND'S CENTRAL HIGHLANDS, The Lodge at Koele is reminiscent of an English hill station, complete with manicured lawns, cozy fireplaces, croquet, and afternoon tea. Paintings, sculptures, and artifacts adorn the resort's interiors. Paths meander through flower gardens, past a conservatory filled with ferns and orchids, to an inviting swimming pool. The atmosphere is calm and relaxed, providing a welcome escape, but there is plenty to do: work out at the new fitness center; explore the rugged countryside astride a horse or a mountain bike, on foot, or by four-wheeler; play tennis; or enjoy a round at one of Lanai's two award-winning championship courses. There's not much nightlife on this quiet island.

SETTING AND FACILITIES

Location Upcountry, on the island's central uplands; beach is a 25-minute shuttle ride away. **Dining** The award-winning Dining Room showcases Pacific Rim cuisine with local ingredients. **Amenities and services** Room service, concierge, laundry service, fitness center, swimming pool, golf, children's programs, free shuttle service.

ACCOMMODATIONS

Rooms 102. Includes 14 suites; 2 rooms for the disabled. **All rooms** Ceiling fans, TV, VCR, CD player, high-speed Internet access, private lanai, minibar, coffeemaker, in-room safe, twice-daily housekeeping, robes, slippers. **Some rooms** Fireplaces, larger space, upgraded amenities, butler service. **Comfort and decor** Very spacious and comfy, with country-chic, chintz interiors, hand-carved poster beds, ceiling fans, and oil paintings by local artists.

Family plan Children age 18 and under stay free in room with parents if using existing bedding. Maximum of 3 guests per room. Extra person, $100. **Deposit** 2-night deposit due at booking. Cancellation notice must be given 21 days prior to scheduled arrival for refund (30 days for suites). **Credit cards** All major credit cards accepted. **Check-in/out** 3 p.m./noon.

Hotel Lanai $$

OVERALL	★★★½	QUALITY	★★★	VALUE	★★★★

828 Lanai Avenue, Lanai City 96763; ☎ 877-665-2624 or 808-565-7211; FAX 808-565-7377; www.hotellanai.com

OPENED IN 1923 FOR VISITING DOLE PINEAPPLE EXECS, the little upcountry lodge known as Hotel Lanai has always attracted a loyal following. Rooms are comfortable, service is friendly, and you'll probably meet some interesting local characters at *pau hana* time. If you can't afford to stay at The Lodge at Koele or Manele Bay, or if you prefer down-home charm to opulence, this is your alternative.

SETTING AND FACILITIES
Location In village of Lanai City; beach is a 20-minute shuttle ride away. **Dining** Lanai City Grille, with a dinner menu created by Maui celebrity chef Bev Gannon working with executive chef Mike Davis, offers Pacific Rim dining and comfort food. An open-air tent behind the restaurant area becomes an entertainment and dancing venue on weekends, or a special event area, with heaters and seating for 50. **Amenities and services** Free parking, free wireless Internet access. No room service or laundry service.

ACCOMMODATIONS
Rooms 11; 10 in the lodge and 1 adjacent cottage (ask about additional 2- and 3-bedroom cottages in village for larger groups). **All rooms** Nonsmoking. Ceiling fans, private bath, hair dryer, iron and board, phone, Continental breakfast. **Some rooms** TV, bathtub, lanai, separate living room, additional bedrooms, kitchen. **Comfort and decor** Medium-sized rooms with classic plantation-era decor: pine floors, hala mats, ceiling fans, custom Hawaiian appliqued quilts, and original photographs depicting the island's early days.

PAYMENT, RESERVATIONS, AND RESTRICTIONS
Family plan Children age 8 and under stay free in room with parents if using existing bedding. **Deposit** Pay deposit of half of total stay in advance on booking. Cancellation notice must be given 14 days prior to scheduled arrival for refund. Cancellations are charged a $20 processing fee. **Credit cards** ae, MC, V. **Check-in/out** 2 p.m./11 a.m. Early check-in and late checkout available on request.

PART FOUR

ALOHA!
Welcome to Hawaii

WHEN YOU ARRIVE

ARRIVING IN HAWAII IS A SENSUAL EXPERIENCE. You smell exotic flowers, hear ukulele and people singing Hawaiian music, and feel the tropical warmth and trade winds. If you walk to baggage claim outdoors rather than taking the free Wikiwiki Shuttle, look beyond the airport to the moody mountains ahead of you and the city and Diamond Head off to your right for your big-picture view.

Honolulu International Airport, one of the busiest in the United States, is simple to navigate. Gates have numbers; just follow the signs. Baggage-claim areas are designated by letters of the alphabet in the primary mainland arrival terminals, and by numbers in the interisland terminal. Note that mainland flights by the local carrier, Hawaiian Airlines, use the interisland terminal for ticketing and baggage. Latest arrival and departure times appear on the video monitors. Upon arrival, follow the clearly marked signs to baggage claim on the street level. The wait only seems long because you're anxious to hit the beach.

In baggage claim, you will find car-rental agencies and courtesy phones. Outside, you will find taxis, buses, Waikiki shuttles, car-rental shuttles, and private or hotel limousines.

If you arrive on an international flight, the first to wish you "aloha" in their fashion are U.S. Customs and Border Protection agents. Honolulu is today a far better staffed and more efficient port of entry than it was in the past.

FLYING INTERISLAND

WE'VE NOTICED THAT INTERISLAND AIRLINES and airports tend to be very efficient at handling the constant loads of passengers and bags—much more so than most commuter connections on the mainland. For people who live on the Islands, this process replaces public transit. Neighbor Islands airports are smaller, less formal, and easier to navigate. An exception is Maui's main Kahului Airport, where the extra security measures of the post–September 11 era can cause an exasperating jam-up with long, slow lines and demands extra time to navigate. Plan accordingly.

Of Maui's three airports, Kahului Airport, at the island's center, is the main terminal for interisland and mainland flights. Car-rental desks and taxi service are available outside baggage claim. Most people take a shuttle to the car compound a few minutes away. Kapalua–West Maui Airport serves only interisland flights on smaller aircraft but is handy to West Maui resorts and towns. Car rentals are available nearby, and resort shuttles serve the airport. Tiny Hana Airport serves small-plane traffic.

The Big Island of Hawaii has two major airports. Kona International Airport at Keahole is a full-service, open-air facility carved from the lava fields of the Kona Coast, eight miles from Kailua-Kona. Landing on this black landscape below a dormant volcano is a bit like landing in a barbecue pit. You get used to it, especially after you notice explosions of neon-colored bougainvillea and palm trees growing out of the cinders. You take a shuttle to get to the rental-car compounds, located a few minutes away.

Hilo International Airport at General Lyman Field serves the east side of the island. Hilo's airport is much larger than you might expect. It was designed and built a few decades ago when Hilo was expected to become a major port of entry into Hawaii because it's closest to the U.S. mainland. Car-rental agencies are on site.

The Lihue Airport is the main airport on Kauai, a modern air-conditioned facility. Princeville Airport on the North Shore serves general aviation and helicopters.

Molokai's airport is an older, island-style, open-air facility located mid-island near Kaunakakai. Lanai's airport is a new, modern facility below Lanai City. Arriving guests are met by resort staff and transported by shuttle van.

GROUND TRANSPORTATION

Oahu: Honolulu International Airport

RENTAL CARS Five car-rental agencies—Avis, Budget, Dollar, Hertz, and National—have customer-service desks in most baggage claim areas at street level. Other car-rental agencies (Alamo, Enterprise, Thrifty, Advantage, Tradewinds, and JN Rentals) are located in the vicinity of the airport and have courtesy phones inside the baggage-claim area. See car rentals on pages 81–85 for more details.

AIRPORT–WAIKIKI EXPRESS From the baggage-claim area, head outside and look for any ticket agent wearing a blue aloha shirt; the agent will direct you to the nearest pickup point. The cost is $9 per person one way and $15 per person round-trip (cash only), with extra charges for golf bags, surfboards, bikes, and windsurf gear. The 18-seat, air-conditioned red-white-and-blue shuttle—marked "Airport–Waikiki Express"—arrives every 25 to 30 minutes from 6 a.m. to 10 a.m.; after 10 a.m. every 20 to 25 minutes. Call ☎ 808-539-9400 for more information or see **www.airportwaikikishuttle.com.**

TAXIS Cabs are available just outside the baggage-claim area. Look for a dispatcher wearing a mustard-colored shirt. The fare from the airport to Waikiki ranges from $30 to $35, excluding tip.

THEBUS TheBus is the cheapest airport transfer, if you are traveling light. The fare is $2.25 per adult and $1 per child over age 6 or senior over age 65, exact change required. Luggage is limited to one bag measuring no more than 24 by 18 by 12 inches that must fit under your seat or in your lap.

Look for the number 19 and number 20 buses marked Waikiki Beach & Hotels. Bus stops—two at the main terminal and one at the interisland terminal—are located on the second-floor (departures) level.

Buses arrive every 30 minutes depending on the route number. In the evening, only the number 19 bus serves the airport. For more information, call ☎ 808-848-5555 or check **www.thebus.org.** The bus takes about 30 minutes to reach Waikiki, depending on traffic.

Maui: Kahului Airport

RENTAL CARS Alamo, Avis, Budget, Dollar, Hertz, and National desks are just outside the main terminal (turn right as you leave the baggage area). Thrifty and Aloha (formerly Word of Mouth) have courtesy phones at the airport information board inside the baggage-claim area.

TAXIS Maui Airport Taxi has a dispatcher inside baggage claim. Or you can just walk directly across the street and hail a cab at the curb. Typical fares range from $40 for Wailea to $50 for Lahaina and $70 for Kapalua.

SHUTTLES You can use the courtesy phones to contact SpeediShuttle, or for Kapalua, call the Kapalua Executive Transportation Service (☎ 808-833-2303). The wait for Speedi is usually less than 15 minutes; costs vary depending on the destination. To reserve a shuttle in advance, call SpeediShuttle at ☎ 808-875-8070.

Roberts Hawaii at ☎ 866-898-2519 also provides transportation to the Kaanapali Beach Resort area from 9 a.m. to 4 p.m. daily, with an evening run between 6:30 and 7 p.m. Look for the customer-service desk marked Airport Hotel Shuttle in the baggage-claim area (directly across from carousel number 4). Shuttles depart every half hour.

Maui: Kapalua Airport

RENTAL CARS AND TAXIS Use the courtesy phone at the baggage-claim area for a free shuttle van to car-rental offices. Taxis are curbside outside baggage-claim area.

SHUTTLES Various hotel shuttles will pick up arriving guests with advance notice. Be sure to let them know your arrival time.

The Big Island of Hawaii: Kona International Airport at Keahole

RENTAL CARS The car-rental counters for Avis, Alamo, Budget, Dollar, Harper, Hertz, National, and Thrifty are all accessible via shuttle service fronting the baggage areas.

TAXIS Cabs are parked across the street from the baggage-claim area.

PUBLIC TRANSPORTATION No public transportation service is available at the airport.

SHUTTLES Various hotel shuttles will pick up arriving guests with advance notice. Be sure to let them know your arrival time. You can also call for a pickup at the information booth, just outside the baggage-claim area.

The Big Island of Hawaii: Hilo International Airport

RENTAL CARS Car-rental pickups for Alamo, Avis, Budget, Dollar, Hertz, and National are located directly across the street from the airport restaurant, near the main gates.

TAXIS Taxis are available curbside near the baggage-claim area.

PUBLIC TRANSPORTATION No public transportation service is available at the airport.

Kauai: Lihue Airport

RENTAL CARS Car-rental desks for Alamo, Avis, Budget, Dollar, Hertz, National, and Thrifty are conveniently located directly across the street from the airport security entrance.

TAXIS Use the dispatch phone by the visitors information desk in the baggage area to summon a cab.

PUBLIC TRANSPORTATION No public transportation service is available at the airport.

SHUTTLE The neighboring Kauai Marriott and Hilton Kauai resorts offer free shuttle service for guests. At the visitors information desk, phone the hotel and request a pickup.

Molokai: Molokai Airport

RENTAL CARS Budget and Island Kine rent cars at customer-service desks located by the baggage-claim area.

TAXIS Molokai Off-Road Tours & Taxi (call ☎ 808-553-3369) serves the airport. Look outside the baggage-claim area to spot a taxi van or call for a pickup.

Lanai: Lanai Airport

RENTAL CARS Dollar is the only car-rental agency on Lanai. Upon arrival, walk to the reception desk and use the red courtesy phone. A van will pick you up and transport you to Dollar's pickup location, about three miles away.

SHUTTLE A convenient way to get around is Island Transportation's shuttles. For guests of the two Four Seasons resorts, the $35-per-person charge (half for children age 3 to 11) includes round-trip airport transportation and unlimited use of shuttles between the island's two resorts and golf courses for the duration of the stay. For visitors who are not guests of the Four Seasons, there is an $11 round-trip fee for transportation from the airport or the Expeditions Ferry to Dollar, Hotel Lanai, or the two resort golf courses. Shuttle vans are located to the right outside the airport's baggage-claim area.

THINGS *the* LOCALS
Already KNOW

THE LEI TRADITION

A HAWAIIAN FLOWER LEI is one of the most extravagant presents in the world. Some lei take more than a thousand flowers and quite a bit of time and artistry to make. They fade and perish within hours or days of their creation. Often they are worn only once.

Lei-giving is one of the most colorful traditions in Hawaii. You'll see it first at the airport. But it isn't an embarrassing designation of a newly arrived tourist. Lei are a sign of honor, for a family member, friend, or special guest, of either gender.

 Having a garland placed around your neck is a special welcome, farewell, or congratulations, usually followed by a hug or kiss on the cheek, especially if you know the donor. A lei greeting remains Hawaii's most tangible expression of aloha. Local tradition is to drape loved ones up to their noses with lei at graduations; they are also given for anniversaries, birthdays, and other special celebrations. They're great icebreakers with local strangers, who want to admire the lei and congratulate you on your special occasion. It's also customary to share the lei around after you wear it for a while (take it off and give it to someone else to wear).

Hawaiian language advisory: The word *lei* is singular and plural; there is no *s* in the Hawaiian language.

The tradition of lei-giving may have originated with Hawaii's earliest settlers, who brought flowering plants to use for adornment. Early Hawaiians offered lei to their gods during religious ceremonies.

Today, long lei are also draped over the statues or images of important people in Hawaiian history, or over the bows of victorious racing canoes, or on anything worthy of commemoration. Each June the Kamehameha Day Celebration kicks off with a colorful lei-draping ceremony at the King Kamehameha statue in downtown Honolulu.

Writer-poet Don Blanding initiated Lei Day, an annual May 1 celebration held since 1928. The biggest event is held at Kapiolani Park in Waikiki, where floral creations by the state's top lei makers are displayed.

Fresh-flower lei can be purchased throughout Hawaii, at every major airport and many supermarkets, as well as florists. Home style is to make your own, and many families still do. You'll find lei made of all kinds of flowers, including plumeria, gardenias, ginger, orchids, pakalana, roses, ilima, and carnations, as well as fragrant maile leaves, braids of ti leaves, kukui nuts, seashells, flowers made of dollar bills, and, for the kids back home, even candy and gum.

Many high-quality, lower-priced lei stands are concentrated in Honolulu's Chinatown. Costs range from a few dollars for a simple crown flower or sweet-smelling tuberose lei to around $40 for an intricately crafted rope lei. One of the most popular lei is the cristina, an expertly sewn garland made of purple dendrobium orchids ($25 to $30).

Often people try to keep a lei alive by refrigerating it. Here's another suggestion: Drape it over a doorknob or lamp shade in your hotel room or some other place where it cheers you to see the flowers and smell the fragrance.

A TIP ABOUT TIPPING

MANY SERVICE WORKERS in Hawaii depend on tips for their living. At the airport, tip a porter $2 per bag, unless they arrange and ease your entire check-in, then another $10 is a small price for the convenience. Taxi drivers receive a 15% tip of the total fare plus 25 cents per bag or parcel. At the hotel, tip the bellhop $5 for transporting your luggage to and from your room, and give the parking valet a couple of dollars. Tip your room housekeeper $2 for each day of your stay. For dining, tip 15% to 20% of the bill.

STATE HOLIDAYS

IN ADDITION TO ALL MAJOR U.S. HOLIDAYS, Hawaii celebrates three state holidays.

- **Kuhio Day** (March 26). This holiday honors Prince Jonah Kuhio Kalanianaole (1871–1922), a statesman and member of the royal family who served in the U.S. Congress in the early 1900s.
- **King Kamehameha Day** (June 11). Hawaii's great king, Kamehameha I, united the Islands into a kingdom under one rule. An imposing figure—some reported him as tall as eight feet—the Big Island–born monarch died in May 1819, when he was believed to be in his early sixties, and his bones are believed to be hidden in a secret location on the Kona Coast. Modern Islanders celebrate the life of Kamehameha with colorful festivities, including lei-draping ceremonies, parades, and hoolaulea (public parties).
- **Admission Day** (third Friday in August). On August 21, 1959, U.S. President Dwight D. Eisenhower signed the proclamation welcoming

Hawaii as the 50th state, following a long, often emotional campaign for statehood that originated more than a century earlier. Many expected Hawaii to be named the 49th state, but that distinction went to Alaska in 1958. Today, "Hawaii—49th State" memorabilia, ranging from record labels to buttons, is highly prized by collectors.

SAYING IT IN HAWAIIAN

IN HAWAII, ENGLISH AND HAWAIIAN are both official languages. The Hawaiian alphabet has only 12 letters—the vowels *a, e, i, o,* and *u* and the consonants *h, k, l, m, n, p,* and *w.* A diacritical mark called the *okina,* pronounced as a glottal stop, is almost as vital as a letter, so that those vowels can do extra duty. The language takes practice and patience.

Here are some general rules of thumb for you to remember:

- Vowels are pronounced this way: *a* as "uh," as in the second *a* in "lava"; *e* as "ay," as in "hay"; *i* as "ee," as in "fee"; *o* as "oh," as in "low"; and *u* as "oo," as in "moon."
- All consonants are pronounced as in English except for w, which is usually pronounced as "v" when it follows an i or e. Example: *Ewa* Beach is pronounced as "Eva" Beach. When following a *u* or *o*, *w* is pronounced as "w." When it is the first letter in the word or follows an *a* there is no designated rule, so the pronunciation follows custom. Which means "Hawaii" and "Havaii" are both acceptable.
- Some vowels are slurred together in a diphthong, forming single sounds. Examples: *ai* as in "Waikiki," *au* as in "ma uka," *ei* as in "lei," *oi* as in "poi," *ou* as in "kou," and *ao* as in "haole."
- Some are separated by a glottal stop, or *okina,* an upside-down and backward apostrophe that emphasizes a separate vowel sound, acting like another consonant, and keeps identically spelled words from being confused. For instance, *pau* means "finished," but *pa'u* is a skirt worn by women horseback riders. *Pau* is pronounced as "pow," and pa'u is pronounced as "pah-oo." For simplicity, we left the *okina* out of this guide.
- A macron, or *kahako,* designates a long vowel. A macron is marked as a line directly over the vowel. Logically enough, long vowels last longer than regular vowels. The macron isn't needed often to distinguish between words. This book, like most English publications from Hawaii, excludes macrons. However, don't be surprised if you see them over the *i*'s in Waikiki. They indicate that the word is correctly sounded "why-kiki" rather than "why-kee-kee."
- Every Hawaiian syllable ends with a vowel. Therefore, every Hawaiian word ends with a vowel. Which means the word *Hawaiian* isn't a Hawaiian word.
- If a word contains no macrons, the accent usually falls on the next-to-last syllable. Examples: a-**LO**-ha, ma-**HA**-lo, ma-li-**HI**-ni, and o-**HA**-na.

In our opinion, the most authoritative Hawaiian language book is the *Hawaiian Dictionary,* by Mary Kawena Pukui and Samuel H. Elbert.

Commonly Used Pidgin Words and Phrases

An den?	So? And then?
Braddah	Brother or friend
Brah	Short for "braddah"
Bumbye	Do it later
Bummahs!	That's unfortunate!
Da kine	The kind of, that thing
Fo' real?	Really?
Garans	Guaranteed
Geev um!	Go for it!
Go fo' broke	Give it your all (*famous motto of the 442nd battalion in WW II*)
How you figgah?	How do you think that happened?
Howzit?	How are you?
Laytahs	See you later
Li'dat	Like that
Minahs	Minor; no problem; don't worry about it
Mo' bettah	Better
No shame	Don't be shy or embarrassed!
'Nuff already!	That's enough!
Shaka	Greetings; good job; thank you
Small keed time	Childhood
Soah?	Does it hurt?
Stink eye	Disapproving glance, a dirty look
Talk story	Converse, talk, or gossip
T'anks, eh?	Thank you
Whatevahs	Whatever
Who dat?	Who is that?
Yeah, no?	That's right!

PIDGIN

YOU MAY HEAR PEOPLE TALKING in what sounds like abbreviated English, except that it's more colorful. Hawaii-style pidgin, the local patois, is the third language of the Islands. It combines words and syntax of several languages and was developed so that multicultural plantation people could communicate. Although it is a true Creole language and not simply slang, it's definitely not an official tongue.

The pros and cons of pidgin have long been debated by local educators and cultural experts. Some say that the practice is not an acceptable manner of speech, whereas others insist that pidgin is a treasured cultural asset that should not be looked down upon. In Hawaii, it's not uncommon for a *kamaaina* to speak perfect English in an office setting, then pick up the phone and speak pidgin to a friend. See the previous page for some commonly used pidgin words and phrases you might hear during your stay.

TWENTY WORDS EVERY HAWAII VISITOR SHOULD KNOW

IF YOU CAN PRONOUNCE *Aiea, Kalanianaole, Keeaumoku,* and *Anaehoomalu* correctly, know hapa from *hapai,* then you are *akamai, brah.* No need to read *da kine.* If you no can understand a word of this, *mo' bettah you read da kine.*

Da kine is one of 20 words or phrases every Hawaii visitor should know. So are *akamai* and *pau.* When you go *pau* reading *da kine,* you will be *akamai, li'dat.*

Welcome to Hawaii, the linguistically rich and confusing Islands with not one but two official languages—Hawaiian and English—and everybody speaks a little of the unofficial third language, pidgin.

You probably can get by with a now-and-then *aloha* and a mumbled *mahalo,* but to understand what's really going on in Hawaii, you need to know a few basic words like: *huhu, da kine, humbug,* and *mo' bettah.*

Everyone knows *wahine* from *kane* and *ma uka* from *ma kai,* but what about *kokua* and *holoholo?* Most *haole* (that's you, *seestah* and *blahlah*) have trouble saying Hawaiian words because they are repetitive, have too many vowels, and look like the bottom line of an eye chart, for example, *Kaaawa, Kuliouou,* and *Napoopoo,* or *humhumunu-kunukapuaa,* the state fish.

To *haole* eyes honed on brittle consonants, Hawaiian looks impossible. When spoken the way Hawaiian was intended, the soft, round, soothing vowels are music to your ears. Banned after the monarchy was toppled at the turn of the last century, the native tongue survived underground to carry a nation's culture down through generations in warrior chants, hula lyrics and "talk story," or storytelling.

And then there is pidgin, the local Creole attributed to Chinese immigrants, said to have created it in order to do business without a common lingo. The root word of pidgin is, in fact, business.

A caveat: Before you go to Hawaii and put your foot in your mouth, it's probably a good idea to clip and save this lexicon for future review. Or, as any local might put it: *Good t'ing, brush up on da kine, brah, so no make A* (polite shorthand for making an ass of yourself).

Here are 20 Hawaiian words in everyday usage that you should know. Fo' real.

Commonly Used Hawaiian Words and Phrases

HAWAIIAN	ENGLISH
Aina	Land, earth
Aloha	Love, kindness, or goodwill; can be used as a greeting or farewell
E komo mai	Welcome!
Hale	House
Hana hou	Do again, repeat, or encore
Haole	Formerly any foreigner, now primarily anyone of Caucasian ancestry
Holoholo	To go out for a walk, ride, or other activity
Hoolaulea	A big party or celebration
Hooponopono	To correct or rectify a situation
Ikaika	Strong, powerful
Ilima	A native shrub bearing bright yellow or orange flowers; used for lei
Kahuna	Priest, minister, expert
Kala	Money
Kamaaina	Native-born or longtime island resident
Kanaka	Person, individual
Kane	Male, husband, man
Kapu	Taboo
Keiki	Child
Kohola	Humpback whale
Kokua	Help, assistance, cooperation
Kolohe	Mischievous, naughty; a rascal
Kupuna	Grandparent

1. **kokua** (ko-coo-ah) *noun or verb;* help, as in assist, (please *kokua*), or contribute (*kokua luau*), or a gentle reminder, ("Your *kokua* is appreciated.") A *kokua* barbecue, should you be invited to one, is a potluck. Bring something to grill and share.

2. **pau** (pow) *adverb;* finished, all gone, quitting time (*pau hana*). Politely as dishes are removed when you finish kaukau ("*All pau?*"), when your car or other mechanical object breaks down ("Eh, dis buggah *pau.*"). Not to be confused with *make* (mah kay) which means dead, a permanent form of *pau.*

3. **malihini** (mah lee hee nee) *noun;* non-derisive term for newcomer, opposite of *kamaaina.* If it's your first time to come to Hawaii, that's you, *brah,* a stranger, someone who wears socks and shoes instead of rubbah slippahs and eats rice with a fork instead of chopsticks.

HAWAIIAN	ENGLISH
Kuuipo	My sweetheart
Lanai	Porch, verandah
Lua	Toilet, bathroom
Luna	Foreman, boss, leader
Mahalo	Thank you
Makahiki	Ancient Hawaiian harvest festival with sports and religious activities
Ma kai	Toward the ocean; used in directions
Malihini	Newcomer
Mana	Spiritual power
Ma uka	Inland direction, toward the mountain
Me ke aloha pumehana	With warm regards
Mele	Song
Menehune	Legendary small people who worked at night building fishponds, roads, and temples; according to legend, if the work was not completed in one night, it was left unfinished
Ohana	Family
Ono	Delicious
Pau	Finished, done
Pupu	Hors d'oeuvre, appetizer
Tutu	Grandmother
Wahine	Female, wife, woman

4. **mo' bettah** (mow bedder) *adjective;* contemporary pidgin, for preferable or even outstanding, as in *"Dis beach mo' bettah."* Sometimes spelled "moah bettah."

5. **no ka oi** (no cuh oy) Hawaiian *adjective phrase* for superlative or the best, as in *"Maui no ka oi."* Maui is the best; a stage just beyond *mo' bettah.*

6. **hana hou** (huh nuh ho) *verb phrase* for do it again; Hawaiian equivalent of encore, most often heard at music concerts.

7. **to da max** (to dah macks) *adverbial phrase* for boundless enthusiasm, no limits, or another famous pidgin phrase, *go fo' broke,* the motto of the 442nd Battalion in World War II. Also title of popular book, *Pidgin to Da Max.*

8. **akamai** (ah kah my) *noun* for clever, common sense as opposed to intelligence. *"Many are smart but few are akamai."* Name of high-tech Internet outfit.

9. **chance 'em** *verb* for give it a try. Often heard in Las Vegas at 21 tables in California Hotel and in Honolulu at Aloha Stadium late in fourth quarter when Warriors are behind. Fourth and inches on the five; coach says, "Chance 'em."

10. **chicken skin** *adjective phrase* for goose bumps, frisson, shiver of excitement; title of best-selling local spooky book by favorite author (also of this book). *"Oh, da spooky kine gives me chicken skin."*

11. **laters** *adverb* for good-bye, sayonara, adios.

12. **howzit**? (houze it) *phrase of greeting,* always a question; contraction of "how is it?" or "how's by you?" Preferred response is, "'s good, brah!" Or, maybe not so good if feeling *junk* (poorly).

13. **shaka brah** (shah kah brah) *pidgin gesture* with phrase for hang loose. A *shaka* is a hand signal with thumb and pinkie extended; index, middle, and ring fingers closed; then a brisk flip of wrist or horizontal—a public sign that everything is cool, no problem. "Life is good, brah," followed by *shaka*. Made famous by entertainer Don Ho; seen daily on local TV news sign-off. *Brah* (braw), noun for brother, not to be confused with bra.

14. **holoholo** (hoe low hoe low) *adverb* with "go," old Hawaiian word for going around on pleasure trips. Not to be confused with similar sounding *halohalo,* (hah low hah low), the classic Filipino dessert made with ice cream and chopped fruit.

15. **wikiwiki** (wee key wee key) *adverb* meaning quickly; name of Honolulu International Airport shuttle bus. This is also a concept missing on the islands of Molokai and Lanai, as in to move rapidly or to hurry, not to be confused with *hele* (hell lay), which means to go or let's continue, as in "Hele on."

16. **ma uka/ma kai** (mao cah/mah kigh) *adjectives* for two of four key directions, i.e., up and down. *Ma uka* and *ma kai* are used on all Hawaiian Islands. *Ma uka* means toward the mountain, or inland; *ma kai* means toward the ocean. Where it gets tricky is the other two directions on circular islands with little use for western compass points. In Honolulu or Waikiki, they are *Ewa* (eh vah), generally toward the airport and the Ewa Plantation that used to be there and no longer is, and *Diamond Head,* for the Waikiki crater known in Hawaiian as *Leahi* (lay ah hee) or *tuna brow.* Other local landmarks define the side-to-side directions on other islands and other parts of Oahu. On Maui, the term in English *upcountry* (uhp-kuhn-tree) means same t'ing, *ma uka, brah.*

17. **kapu** (kuh poo) *adverb* corresponding to taboo or forbidden; means off-limits, or keep out. Often seen on signs in danger spots, or religious sites and geothermal plants.

18. **hapa haole** (hapa hawlee) *adjective* or *noun* describing many modern-day citizens of the Islands. *Haole* is what early Hawaiians called the first European visitors who looked pale as death, or breathless. *Hapa* is Hawaiian for "half," not to be confused with *hapai* (hah pie) which is "one and a half," or pregnant. *Hapa-haole* is "half white," or "part dis and dat," "li'dat," or "not quite chop-suey" (lots of antecedents). *Haole* may be considered derogatory if prefaced by "stupid" or "dumb."

19. **da kine** (dah kyne) literally "the kind of something"; perfectly understood but not defined, a one-size-fits-all generic expression used when two or more people know what they are talking about but nobody can think of the right word. "Cannot explain, you know, *da kine.*"

20. **li'dat** (lye daht) *adverbial existential pidgin phrase,* that's the way it is, like that. Agreement or confirmation that an idea, concept, or statement is what it is. It is, *li'dat.* Similar to English *uh-huh* and Japanese *honto desu.*

Note: All definitions of Hawaiian words are based loosely on original interpretations by Mary Kawena Pukui and Samuel H. Elbert, authors of the *Hawaiian Dictionary.*

IMPORTANT PHONE NUMBERS

ON THE FOLLOWING PAGE are phone numbers that may come in handy during your stay. For interisland calls, use the area code 808 before the number. Be aware these calls generally are charged long-distance rates.

NEWSPAPERS

LOCAL DAILY NEWSPAPERS INCLUDE *The Honolulu Advertiser* and *Honolulu Star-Bulletin* on Oahu; the *Hawaii Tribune-Herald* and *West Hawaii Today* on the Big Island of Hawaii; *The Maui News* on Maui; and *The Garden Island* on Kauai.

A key source for entertainment news and listings is the *Honolulu Advertiser*'s "TGIF" section, published each Friday.

SAFETY TIPS

YOU WON'T FIND STATE, CITY, OR TOURISM spokespeople bragging about this, but *Money* magazine calls Honolulu the safest large city in the United States, according to an analysis of FBI crime statistics. Hawaii is a peaceful state with few violent crimes. Much is invested in the safety of tourists, the state's biggest industry, but the state is not crime free. We urge you to use the same common sense and self-protective measures you would at home.

- Carry only as much cash or traveler's checks as you need for the day.
- Never leave your luggage unattended until you arrive at your hotel.
- Never display large amounts of cash during transactions or at automated teller machines.
- Beware of pickpockets, especially in crowds.
- Carry your purse close to your body.
- Carry your wallet in a front pocket rather than back pocket.
- Avoid waiting alone at a bus stop after dark.
- Leave nothing valuable in your rental car.
- If your vehicle is bumped from behind at night, do not stop; instead, call 911 for assistance.
- Leave your hotel-room key at the front desk when going out.

Important Phone Numbers

ALL ISLANDS

Police, fire, ambulance: 911

Directory assistance: 411

OAHU

Weather forecast: 973-4380, 973-4381

Marine conditions: 973-4382

Time of day: 983-3211

Honolulu International Airport: 836-6413

Honolulu Physicians Exchange: 524-2575

Hawaii Dental Association Hotline: 593-7956

Information and complaints: 523-4385

Office of Consumer Protection: 586-2630

Better Business Bureau: 536-6956

MAUI *(Note:* Maui County also includes Molokai and Lanai*)*

Weather forecast: 877-5111

Marine conditions: 877-3477

Time of day: 242-0212 (Maui), 643-8463 (Molokai and Lanai)

Kahului Airport: 872-3803, 872-3893

Kapalua Airport: 669-0623

Hana Airport: 248-8208

Molokai Airport: 567-6140

Kalaupapa Airport: 567-6331

Lanai Airport: 565-6757

Office of Consumer Protection: 984-8244

THE BIG ISLAND OF HAWAII

Weather forecast: 961-5582, 935-8555 (Hilo)

Marine conditions: 935-9883

Time of day: 643-8463

Volcano eruption information: 985-6000

Kona International Airport at Keahole: 329-3423

Hilo International Airport: 934-5838

Office of Consumer Protection: 933-0910

KAUAI

Weather forecast: 245-6001

Marine conditions: 245-3564

Time of day: 643-8463

Lihue Airport: 245-7995

PART FIVE

GETTING AROUND

TRANSPORTATION CONSIDERATIONS

IT'S EASY TO GET AROUND Hawaii when you know how.

Only Oahu is busy enough to pose a problem, and that's only during Honolulu's morning and evening commute hours, when traffic chokes freeways and city streets. Traffic in and out of Waikiki is congested on weeknights and weekends. Hawaiian street names are difficult to read and recall, and gas is expensive. Fortunately Oahu is also the island with an outstanding municipal bus system. It's called TheBus.

You can ride TheBus, take shuttle vans, or hail a taxi to get almost anywhere you want to go. An open-air, motorized Waikiki Trolley tour stops at visitor attractions and shops.

What you won't find in the Islands are trains or subway systems, although a light-rail mass transit system is in the works.

Before choosing your primary mode of transportation, weigh the factors of convenience, flexibility, time, and cost. For example, catching a taxi from Waikiki to the *Arizona* Memorial may be the fastest and most convenient option, but it will also set you back $35 or more. Catching TheBus is the cheapest way to go, but it will take longer and you won't have as much flexibility.

The newest highway, so-called Interstate H-3, links Pearl Harbor on the west side of Oahu with Kaneohe Bay Marine Corps Air Station on the Windward side of the island. This highway, most expensive in the nation at the time, topping $1 billion a mile, triggered controversy because its route violated a sacred area and an ancient temple site. The roadway today is underused, very scenic, and worth a spin if only for the dramatic views.

TRAFFIC ADVISORY

IF YOU DECIDE TO EXPLORE the island by car, remember that Oahu reputedly has more cars per capita than any city in the United States.

unofficial **TIP**
On Oahu, avoid H-1 and H-2 freeways as well as the Pali and Kalanianaole highways during morning and evening weekday rush hours.

Traffic is worst on school days, particularly when classes start in August and September, and tends to jam up around downtown Honolulu at lunchtime. Roadwork is as big a cause of traffic backup as anything. The truth is that even Oahu's traffic looks tame next to many a big mainland city's problems. Drivers regularly exceed the posted speed limit here, but be aware that the Honolulu Police Department uses radar to nail offenders, mostly on the H-1 Freeway, Pali Highway, and Kalanianaole Highway when congestion eases.

GETTING AROUND NEIGHBOR ISLANDS

YOU WON'T HAVE TO WORRY about major traffic jams on most of the Neighbor Islands, where the population is a small fraction of Oahu's. Barring accidents, traffic backups are nonexistent on Molokai and Lanai and the Big Island. (The one traffic snarl on the Big Island occurs during morning and afternoon rush hours in Kailua-Kona.) Maui and Kauai have developed their own commuter traffic, with the busiest times being 6:30 to 8:30 a.m. and 3:30 to 5:30 p.m. Road congestion intensifies on Maui and Kauai when jumbo jets and other planes land at once, coinciding with shift change and commute hours, and in Kapaa on Kauai during lunch hour.

Hawaii's road system is simple but arcane, with posted signs (white lettering against a dark-green background) providing directions. Considering the number of vehicles, particularly on Oahu where the number of registered vehicles doubled in the past two decades, Hawaii's roadways and streets are in relatively good repair. You may hit rough spots along the H-1 (eastbound) near the Aiea exit and on Kamehameha Highway on Windward Oahu and the island's North Shore.

Island-style caveat: Big waves lash ashore, flash floods inundate roads, especially on Kauai, rock and landslides are common on Maui, red-hot lava closes Chain of Craters Road on the Big Island, and ghostly nightmarchers (spirits of alii) are blamed for all manner of mysterious accidents after dark.

DRIVE TIMES

SEE THE FOLLOWING PAGES for estimated drive times from popular resort areas to specific points of interest. The estimations are given for periods outside rush hour.

PARKING

FINDING A PARKING SPOT ISN'T A PROBLEM IN MOST AREAS. Waikiki hotels and downtown Honolulu offices charge the highest parking rates in Hawaii. Your hotel is likely to charge you a daily rate of at least $15 to park your car. Many Neighbor Island resorts now charge a daily fee for self- or valet parking, but others still offer free self-parking lots.

Parking rates in private lots in Honolulu's main business district start at $3.25 per half hour, but banks, stores, restaurants, and most professional offices validate.

There are two city-operated affordable parking structures to keep in mind: the Alii Place lot at Alakea and Hotel streets (enter off of Alakea) charges $1 per half hour for the first two hours and $2 per each following half hour. On weekends and evenings, the rate is only 50 cents per half hour, with a $3 maximum. The Chinatown Gateway Plaza lot at King and Bethel streets (enter off of Bethel) also charges 50 cents per half hour for the first two hours and $1 per each additional half hour.

In the downtown area near Iolani Palace, your best bet is finding a metered parking spot on the street, either Richards or Punchbowl Street. There is no metered parking available on King Street.

You can also try to find a metered parking spot on Bethel, Merchant, and Nuuanu streets in Chinatown. The best times to find an empty space are midmorning and midafternoon.

If you're catching a show at the Hawaii Theatre downtown, consider parking at the Macy's underground lot at King and Bethel (enter off Bethel Street). It's a flat rate after 4 p.m.

In Waikiki, the best option is to leave the car in your hotel parking garage and explore the area on foot. If you're driving into Waikiki, however, the best parking option is the multilevel IMAX garage located on Seaside Avenue (on the right immediately after turning left from Kalakaua Avenue). This parking garage is centrally located and has the most affordable rate. In the Honolulu Zoo and Kapiolani Park area, street parking becomes much easier to find. Metered stalls there cost only 50 cents per hour, with a four-hour limit at Kapiolani Park and a three-hour limit near the zoo.

On Neighbor Islands, finding an available parking space is most difficult in Maui's congested Lahaina. The best option is to park at the Lahaina Center (enter from either Papalaua or Wainee Street). If you purchase anything from a shop—even a single postcard—they'll validate your parking, up to four hours.

Currently, no parking meters exist on the Neighbor Islands except near a few public office buildings. Downtown Hilo had meters, but they recently discontinued them.

All parking lots are fairly well lit, almost always filled to near capacity with frequent turnover (particularly in Waikiki), and considered safe for your person if not your valuables. Do not leave valuables in your car, even in the trunk.

Drive Times

OAHU

FROM CENTRAL WAIKIKI TO:	TIME TO TRAVEL
Ala Moana Shopping Center	7 minutes
Aloha Tower Marketplace	15 minutes
Arizona Memorial	30 minutes
Bishop Museum	20 minutes
Chinatown Honolulu	15 minutes
Haleiwa	1 hour
Hanauma Bay	30 minutes
Honolulu International Airport	25 minutes
Polynesian Cultural Center	1 hour, 15 minutes
Sea Life Park	40 minutes
University of Hawaii–Manoa	15 minutes

MAUI

FROM KAHULUI AIRPORT TO:	TIME TO TRAVEL
Haleakala National Park	1 hour, 45 minutes
Hana	2 hours, 30 minutes
Kaanapali	50 minutes
Kapalua	1 hour
Kihei	25 minutes
Lahaina	45 minutes
Makena	40 minutes
Wailea	35 minutes
Wailuku	10 minutes

BIG ISLAND

FROM KONA TO:	TIME TO TRAVEL
Hilo	2 hours, 15 minutes
Volcano	2 hours, 30 minutes
Waimea (Kamuela)	50 minutes

PUBLIC TRANSPORTATION

USING THEBUS

THEBUS IS THE INEXPENSIVE WAY to get from here to there on Oahu. It is safe, friendly, and efficient and has twice been recognized by the American Public Transit Association as the best in the nation. Each day, the fleet of buses collectively transports 260,000 passengers and travels 60,000 miles, equal to two and a half trips around the world.

The advantages of riding TheBus go beyond cost. This is an excellent opportunity to mingle with local residents (chances are you'll want to ask their help in figuring out which stop you want). Strike

BIG ISLAND

FROM HILO TO:	TIME TO TRAVEL
Volcano	45 minutes
Waimea (Kamuela)	1 hour, 15 minutes

KAUAI

FROM LIHUE TO:	TIME TO TRAVEL
Kilauea	40 minutes
Kokee	1 hour, 30 minutes
Poipu	30 minutes
Princeville	45 minutes
Waimea Canyon	1 hour, 15 minutes

MOLOKAI

FROM MOLOKAI AIRPORT TO:	TIME TO TRAVEL
Halawa Valley	2 hours
Kaunakakai	15 minutes
Kepuhi Beach	25 minutes
Mapulehu	35 minutes
Maunaloa	15 minutes
Papohaku Beach	30 minutes

LANAI

FROM LANAI AIRPORT TO:	TIME TO TRAVEL
Garden of the Gods	45 minutes
Hulopoe and Manele bays	25 minutes
Lanai City	5 minutes
Munro Trail	15 minutes
Shipwreck Beach	35 minutes

up a conversation and, hopefully, enjoy a sampling of Hawaii's aloha spirit. Outside rush-hour traffic, the buses are usually uncrowded and the ride is pleasant. Tell the driver where you want to go, and he or she will help make sure you get off at the right place.

The exact-change, one-way fare on TheBus is $2.25 for adults and $1 for students (age 6 through high school); exact change, please, dollar bills accepted; child sitting on adult lap, free (max age 6). You can request a free transfer, which entitles you to board up to two other buses where routes intersect, at the time you pay your fare. Stopovers or picking up a bus again in a continuous direction is not permitted, and there is a time limit to the transfer. You can ride around the whole circle-island route, which takes about four hours.

thebus

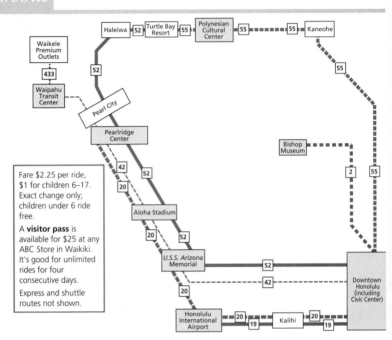

Fare $2.25 per ride, $1 for children 6–17. Exact change only; children under 6 ride free.

A **visitor pass** is available for $25 at any ABC Store in Waikiki. It's good for unlimited rides for four consecutive days.

Express and shuttle routes not shown.

Common Bus Routes:

Ala Moana Shopping Center: Take bus #19 and #20 AIRPORT. Return via #19 WAIKIKI, or cross Ala Moana Blvd. for #20.

Bishop Museum: Take #2 SCHOOL STREET. Get off at Kapalama St., cross School St., walk down Bernice St. Return to School St. and take #2 WAIKIKI.

Byodo-In Temple: Take bus #2 to Hotel-Alakea St. (TRF) to #55 KANEOHE-KAHALUU. Get off at Valley of the Temple Cemetery. Also #19 and #20 AIRPORT to King-Alakea St., (TRF) on Alakea St. to #55 KANEOHE-KAHALUU.

Circle Island: Take a bus to ALA MOANA SHOPPING CENTER (TRF) to #52 WAHIAWA CIRCLE ISLAND or #55 KANEOHE CIRCLE ISLAND. This is a 4-hour bus ride.

Chinatown or Downtown: Take any #2 bus going out of Waikiki to Hotel St. Return, take #2 WAIKIKI on Hotel St., or #19 or #20 on King St.

The Contemporary Museum & Punchbowl (National Memorial Cemetery of the Pacific): Take #2 bus (TRF) at Alapai St. to #15 MAKIKI–PACIFIC HGTS. Return, take #15 and get off at King St., area (TRF) #2 WAIKIKI.

Diamond Head Crater: Take #22 HAWAII KAI–SEA LIFE PARK to the crater. Take a flashlight. Return to the same area and take #22 WAIKIKI.

Dole Plantation: Take bus to ALA MOANA SHOPPING CENTER (TRF) to #52 WAHIAWA CIRCLE ISLAND.

Foster Botanical Garden: Take #2 bus to Hotel-Riviera St. Walk to Vineyard Blvd. Return to Hotel St. Take #2 WAIKIKI, or take #4 NUUANU and get off at Nuuanu-Vineyard. Cross Nuuanu Ave. and walk one block to the gardens.

Aloha Tower Marketplace and Hawaii Maritime Center: Take #19 and #20 AIRPORT and get off at Alakea–Ala Moana. Cross the street to the Aloha Tower.

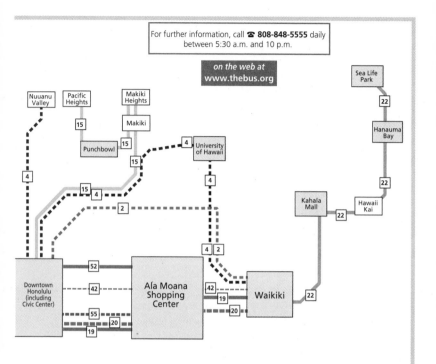

For further information, call ☎ **808-848-5555** daily between 5:30 a.m. and 10 p.m.

on the web at **www.thebus.org**

Honolulu Zoo: Take any bus on Kuhio Ave. going DIAMOND HEAD direction to Kapahulu Ave.

Iolani Palace (also **state capitol, Honolulu Hale, Kawaiahao Church, Mission Houses, Queen's Medical Center, King Kamehameha Statue, State Judiciary Bldg.**) Take any #2 bus and get off at Punchbowl and Beretania St. Walk to King St. Return #2 WAIKIKI on King St.

Kahala Mall: Take #22 HAWAII KAI–SEA LIFE PARK to Kilauea Ave. Return, #22 WAIKIKI.

Pearl Harbor (*Arizona* Memorial): Take #20 AIRPORT. Get off across from Memorial, or take a bus to ALA MOANA SHOPPING CENTER (TRF) to #52.

Polynesian Cultural Center: Take a bus to ALA MOANA SHOPPING CENTER (TRF) to #55 KANEOHE CIRCLE ISLAND. Bus ride takes 2 hours one-way.

Queen Emma Summer Palace: Take #4 NUUANU, or board a bus to ALA MOANA SHOPPING CENTER (TRF) to #55 KANEOHE.

Sea Life Park: Take #22 HAWAII KAI–SEA LIFE PARK. #22 will stop at Hanauma Bay en route to the park.

University of Hawaii: Take #4 NUUANU. The bus will go to the University en route to Nuuanu.

Waimea Valley Adventure Park: Take a bus to ALA MOANA SHOPPING CENTER (TRF) to #52 WAHIAWA CIRCLE ISLAND or #55 KANEOHE CIRCLE ISLAND.

Waikele Premium Outlets: Take bus #42 from Waikiki to Wapahu Transit Center, then bus #433 to Waikele.

ABBREVIATED LIST OF BUS NUMBERS AND THEIR DESTINATIONS	
Note: Routes and numbers are subject to change.	
3	Kaimuki
4	Nuuanu/Punahou
6	Pauoa/Woodlawn (University of Hawaii)
8	Waikiki/Ala Moana
19	Waikiki/Airport and Hickam
20	Airport/Waikiki
23	Hawaii Kai/Sea Life Park
43	Waipahu
52	Wahiawa/Circle Isle
55	Kaneohe/Circle Isle
57	Kailua/Waimanalo/Sea Life Park
88A	North Shore Express

If you plan on using TheBus frequently during your stay, we recommend purchasing a $25 visitor pass, which allows you unlimited rides for four days, or a $50 monthly pass ($25 for students). These passes are available at all ABC stores in Waikiki.

For bus route information, call ☎ 808-848-5555 between 5:30 a.m. and 10 p.m. daily. Be sure you have a pencil and paper handy, and be ready to provide the following information: your current location, your desired destination, and the time of day you need to arrive at that destination. TheBus also has an informative Web site, **www.thebus.org,** with a complete schedule you can download.

Also, you can get recorded route information from Waikiki to some of the most popular visitor attractions by calling ☎ 808-296-1818, entering code number 8287, and then following the directions. If you want to take TheBus to the Polynesian Cultural Center, for example, select option 13 and listen to the recording, which will instruct you to board any *Ewa*-bound bus numbered 8, 19, 20, 47, or 58; ride to Ala Moana Shopping Center; then transfer to the #55 bus, which will take you to the cultural center. It's that simple. For customer-service information, call ☎ 808-848-4500.

RIDING THE WAIKIKI TROLLEY

TAKE THE WAIKIKI TROLLEY for a fun and pleasant way to get around Waikiki and Honolulu. You can choose the **Red Line, Blue Line,** or **Yellow Line.** You'll get a good look at Oahu as you go.

The trolley's **Red Line** covers all of Waikiki and Honolulu, stopping at the Honolulu Zoo, Waikiki Aquarium, Bishop Museum, Chinatown, Aloha Tower, and Iolani Palace (26 stops in all).

The **Blue Line** traces Oahu's scenic southern coast, including stops at Hanauma Bay and Sea Life Park (11 stops in all).

The **Yellow Line** takes passengers on a shopping and dining excursion, with stops at Ala Moana Shopping Center, Ward Warehouse, Ward Center, DFS, and other locales (20 stops in all).

Four-day passes are available at the following rates: $52 per adult ($25 per child ages 4 to 11) for unlimited rides on either the Red and Yellow or Blue and Yellow routes, and $45 per adult ($18 per child) for unlimited rides on all three routes. For a one-day pass, the cost is $25 per adult ($18 per child) for either the Red and Yellow or Blue and Yellow routes, and $30 ($12 per child) for all three routes. Passes may be purchased at all major hotel tour desks or from service representatives at selected stops.

The **Waikiki Trolley,** operated by E Noa Tours, runs daily from 8:30 a.m. to 11 p.m. on four lines with more than 30 stops. Red Line trolleys arrive at and depart from at appointed stops every 20 minutes; Blue Line trolleys every 60 minutes; and Yellow Line trolleys every 10 to 30 minutes. All routes originate from the Royal Hawaiian Shopping Center depot in Waikiki on Royal Hawaiian Avenue.

E Noa Tours also operates tours via trolleys and air-conditioned vans to popular visitor attractions, such as the *Arizona* Memorial. Call ☎ 800-824-8804 for more information.

TAXIS

A TAXI IS PROBABLY the best way to travel through Honolulu when you don't know your way around. Taxis are not cheap, but they will save you time and frustration. If you are staying in Waikiki for only three days and have no plans to leave the beach resort, your best bet may be to take a taxi.

A fare from the Honolulu International Airport to Waikiki will be from $30 to $40, depending on which end of Waikiki your hotel is located. A few taxi companies provide sightseeing excursions at a fixed rate. At the airport, curbside attendants assign taxis to riders on a first-come, first-served basis outside baggage claim.

Of the 30 taxicab companies on Oahu, you may choose those with a flat rate or metered rate, or hire a limo for sightseeing trips..

If you need to call a cab, we recommend **Charley's Taxi & Limousine,** one of the oldest, locally owned companies at ☎ 808-531-1331.

RESORT AND SHOPPING SHUTTLES

TAKE A SHUTTLE VAN, which is often free or inexpensive. Shuttles are air-conditioned vans or buses that go to and from a specific destination. Many hotels and resorts operate shuttles of their own, while private operators, who pick up passengers by request or at multiple designated sites, tend to offer more elaborate routes. Ask your hotel concierge for any shuttles that serve your hotel. A listing of some widely used shuttle services follow the taxi chart on the next page.

TAXI COMPANIES

OAHU

Aloha State Cab ☎ 808-847-3566

Americabs ☎ 808-591-8830

Charley's Taxi & Limousine
  ☎ 808-531-1331

City Taxi ☎ 808-524-2121

Royal Taxi & Tour ☎ 808-944-5513

TheCab ☎ 808-422-2222

MAUI

AB Taxi ☎ 808-667-7575

Alii Cab ☎ 808-661-3688

Maui Central Cab ☎ 808-244-7278

Classy Taxi ☎ 808-661-3044

Kahului Taxi Service ☎ 808-877-5681

Kihei Taxi ☎ 808-879-3000

La Bella Taxi ☎ 808-242-8011

Royal Sedan and Taxi Service
  ☎ 808-874-6900

Wailea Taxi & Tour
  ☎ 808-874-5000

BIG ISLAND

A-1 Bob's Taxi ☎ 808-963-5470

Ace One Taxi ☎ 808-935-8303

Aloha Taxi ☎ 808-325-5448

BIG ISLAND (continued)

Alpha Star Taxi ☎ 808-885-4771

C&C Taxi ☎ 808-329-6388

Hilo Harry's Taxi ☎ 808-935-7091

Kona Airport Taxi ☎ 808-329-7779

Paradise Taxi ☎ 808-329-1234

Percy's Taxi ☎ 808-969-7060

KAUAI

Ace Kauai Taxi ☎ 808-639-4310

Akiko's Taxi ☎ 808-822-7588

City Cab ☎ 808-245-3227

Kauai Taxi ☎ 808-246-9554

MOLOKAI

Molokai Off-Road Tours & Taxi
  ☎ 808-553-3369

Kukui Tours and Limousines
  ☎ 808-336-0944 or
  808-553-4227 after 5 p.m.

LANAI

No full-time taxi companies serve Lanai. **Dollar Rent A Car** provides taxi service on a driver-available basis. Call ☎ 808-565-7227.

Oahu

A trolley service between Waikiki and the Aloha Tower Marketplace is available daily from 9:15 a.m. (departing the Hilton Hawaiian Village) to 9 p.m. (departing the Marketplace). Pickup–drop-off points in Waikiki include the Hilton, the Duke Kahanamoku Statue, Honolulu Zoo, Waikiki Aquarium, Hilton Waikiki Prince Kuhio, Ohana Waikiki West, ResortQuest Waikiki Beach Hotel, and Waikiki Parkside. The one-way fare is $2 for adults and $1 for children. ☎ 808-528-5700.

Maui

Free shuttles offer visitor transportation within Wailea Resort, with stops at the Grand Wailea Resort, Four Seasons Resort Maui at Wailea, Wailea Beach Marriott Resort & Spa, and the Wailea golf courses and (on request) tennis facilities. The shuttle operates daily from 6:30 a.m., with the final drop-off at 8:30 p.m. ☎ 808-879-2828.

In Kaanapali, a shuttle transports guests between the Whaler's Village Shopping Center and hotels within the resort area. The service is provided daily from 9 a.m. to 11 p.m. ☎ 808-669-3177.

Guests staying at Kapalua Resort can take a free shuttle that stops at the hotel, golf courses, tennis facilities, and shops in the area. The daily service runs from 6 a.m. to 11 p.m. ☎ 808-669-3177.

Big Island of Hawaii

Hawaii County's free Hele-On Bus can get you around the island from any of the major resort areas. ☎ 808-961-8744.

Lanai

For the duration of their stay and a fee of $33 per person, guests at either of the two Four Seasons resorts on Lanai can enjoy unlimited shuttle service between the hotels, the airport, and the island's two championship golf courses: The Experience at Koele and The Challenge at Manele. Other shuttles transport non–Four Seasons guests to and from the airport, Expeditions Ferry, Lanai City, or the two golf courses for $11 per person round-trip. ☎ 808-565-3000.

THE LAHAINA–LANAI FERRY

VISITORS TO MAUI AND LANAI can take advantage of Expeditions' Lahaina–Lanai Passenger Shuttle, which makes five round-trips daily between the two islands.

Departure times from Lahaina Harbor on Maui are 6:45 and 9:15 a.m. and 12:45, 3:15, and 5:45 p.m. Departure times from Lanai are 8 and 10:30 a.m. and 2, 4:30, and 6:45 p.m. The fare is $28.80 each way for adults, $20 for children age 11 and under. Each trip takes between 45 and 55 minutes. If you're prone to motion sickness, take your Dramamine ahead of time, as the cruise across the Auau Channel is often choppy. ☎ 808-661-3756.

PART SIX

EXCURSIONS

ADVENTURES *on* YOUR OWN

EXPLORING DOWNTOWN HONOLULU

DOWNTOWN HONOLULU is small enough to conquer on your own, on foot, with an abundance of historic buildings linked by cool and leafy, parklike greens. In between are busy streets, so try to avoid rush hour as well as the heat of the day for a more relaxed experience.

You'll see the Mission Houses Museum, Kawaiahao Church, the gilded statue of King Kamehameha, the justice hall Aliiolani Hale behind it, Honolulu Hale (city hall), Iolani Palace, Washington Place (the Governor's Mansion), the State Capitol, and a total Capitol District route of a few large blocks. You are bound to gain insights about Hawaii (especially if you take a tour of Iolani Palace) like the sad tale of how it came to be that Hawaii's last queen, Liliuokalani, was imprisoned in her own palace while her kingdom was taken away. Call a day or two in advance to reserve space on palace tours, led by docents (see contact and schedule information on the next page).

If you're in town on the third Wednesday in January, head for the state capitol for the cultural and culinary extravaganza that traditionally marks opening day of the legislature. You'll never see the likes of it elsewhere. The nation's youngest legislature is in business through April in the state's volcano-shaped capitol building.

Take TheBus

In Waikiki, catch the number 2 or number 13 bus on Kuhio Avenue and get off at Punchbowl Street. The drivers are friendly; ask them to let you know when to get off for the Capitol District. You can drive into town and pay to park in lots under the capitol or city hall complexes or the inexpensive city lot in Alii Plaza on Alakea Street (on the right just before Hotel Street).

What to Wear and Bring

This downtown is tropical, so sundresses, shorts, and aloha shirts are acceptable. Wear comfortable walking shoes, sunglasses, and sunscreen. Don't forget your camera.

What It Will Cost

Bus fare is $2 per adult and $1 per child ages 6 to 18. Admission for the Grand Tour to Iolani Palace is $20 for adults and $5 for children ages 5 to 17 (children ages 4 and under not admitted to the palace); Gallery self-guided tour is $6 for adults and $3 for children ages 5 to 17 (children age 4 and under free). Mission Houses Museum admission is $10 for adults; $8 for seniors and military; $6 for high school and college students; and free for children ages 5 and under.

If You Get Hungry

Snacks and restaurants (a bonanza of ethnic eateries) are a short walk away in the main business district along Bishop and Alakea streets.

Sights to See

IOLANI PALACE (*ma uka* [mountain] side of King Street) The most unusual downtown sight you'll see outside of Europe is Iolani Palace. The Italianate architectural gem is the only royal palace on American soil and a far cry from the grass shacks of early Hawaii kings. (The docent may tell you that the kings actually lived in a grass shack nearby and kept the palace for affairs of state.) Built in 1882, Iolani was the official residence of the last two monarchs, King Kalakaua (who had it built for $360,000, which nearly bankrupted the kingdom) and Queen Liliuokalani. The queen surrendered the throne under hostile pressure from American businessmen in 1893 and later was imprisoned in her own rooms at the palace. Guided tours last about 45 minutes and are scheduled at 15-minute intervals. Pick up your tickets at Iolani Barracks, located on the palace grounds. The palace is open Tuesday through Saturday, from 9 a.m. to 2 p.m.; the new basement galleries containing the crown jewels and other relics operate from 9 a.m. to 4 p.m. ☎ 808-522-0832.

HAWAII STATE CAPITOL BUILDING Behind the palace, linked by a walkway through shady grounds, is the Hawaii State Capitol, designed to reflect the Islands' volcanic and oceanic origins. On the *ma kai* (seaward) side of the building is a bronze statue of Queen Liliuokalani. On the *ma uka* side is a statue of Father Damien, the Belgian priest who dedicated his life to ministering to leprosy patients on Molokai.

WASHINGTON PLACE (Governor's Mansion) Across busy Beretania Street on the Richards Street or downtown end of the capitol complex is the historic governor's residence, slated to become a museum when enough funds are raised. Banyan trees with giant roots shade the grounds.

THE MISSION HOUSES MUSEUM From the corner of Punchbowl and South King streets, walk in the Diamond Head direction to the Mission Houses Museum, a complex of missionary-era buildings located on the *ma kai* side of King Street. This is where the first American missionaries established their headquarters in 1820. The structures are the oldest surviving Western-style buildings in the state. The first printed works in the North Pacific were produced in the Coral House. Guided tours are scheduled from 9:30 a.m. to 3 p.m. The museum is open Tuesday through Saturday, from 9 a.m. to 4 p.m. ☎ 808-531-0481.

KAWAIAHAO CHURCH From the museum, head Ewa (west) to nearby Kawaiahao Church. Dedicated in 1842, this historic church was a favorite place of worship for many Hawaiian monarchs. This handsome coral-block structure was the setting for Kamehameha IV's coronation and wedding. Listed on the state and national historic registers, Kawaiahao is one of the few churches left in Hawaii that still offers services in the Hawaiian language.

THE KING KAMEHAMEHA STATUE Cross Punchbowl Street and walk on King Street until you reach the King Kamehameha statue, one of Hawaii's most photographed. The king is shown holding a spear in his left hand, and his right arm is outstretched in a welcoming gesture.

HAWAII STATE LIBRARY Cross King Street, return to the palace, and walk right, toward Diamond Head, passing by the Hawaii State Archives building. The next big building is the Hawaii State Library. Its Hawaii and Pacific section houses the state's largest collection of Hawaii-related books, periodicals, and documents. Library hours vary, but it usually opens at 9 a.m. on weekdays. ☎ 808-586-3500.

kids **HONOLULU HALE** Across Punchbowl Street is Honolulu Hale, otherwise known as city hall. This California Spanish–style structure, built in 1927, is worth a visit with the kids at night during the Christmas season, when the grounds are a festive display of oversized cartoon characters and other holiday adornments.

From Honolulu Hale, cross South King Street and Punchbowl to the bus stop nearest the main intersection. Catch the number 2 or number 13 bus back to Waikiki.

DINNER CRUISES

FOR THOSE WHO WANT TO ENJOY views from the sea, Hawaii offers several nightly dinner cruises, daily sunset sails, and other short cruises. The scenery, especially at sunset, is mesmerizing, and most of the boats and crews provide state-of-the-art facilities and cheerful service. On Oahu, **Atlantis Adventures** (☎ 800-548-6262) operates the 141-foot *Navatek 1*, a smooth-riding vessel that uses SWATH (Small Waterplane Area Twin Hull) technology to minimize motion sickness; the ship glides above the surface while twin submarine-like hulls ride below the waves. Rates are $106 to $127 for adults and $67 for children ages 2 to 12.

Also on Oahu is **Star of Honolulu Cruises & Events** (☎ 800-334-6191 or 808-983-7827; **www.starofhonolulu.com**), which operates the *Star of Honolulu,* a 232-foot, four-deck ship that offers daily and nightly cruises. The dinner cruises are $39 to $179 per adult and $25 to $65 per child ages 3 to 11.

Both these ships sail from Honolulu Harbor and cruise waters off Honolulu and Waikiki.

Cruise providers on the Neighbor Islands include **Maui Princess** (☎ 877-500-6284) and Windjammer Cruises (☎ 808-661-8600) on Maui; **Captain Bean's Dinner Cruise** (☎ 808-329-2955) and **Body Glove Cruises Hawaii** (☎ 800-551-8911) on the Big Island; and **Captain Andy's** (☎ 808-335-6833) and **Liko Kauai Cruises** (☎ 888-732-5456) on Kauai. Call for a schedule of trips, which may range from morning excursions and whale-watching tours to sunset cruises. Lunch and sunset meals are usually served buffet style; evening dinners are typically sit-down affairs with a set beef-and-seafood menu.

At Wailua State Park on Kauai, you can putter up the Wailua River on a boat ride to the famous stop of Fern Grotto. **Smith's Motor Boat Service** (☎ 808-821-6892) offers the 90-minute cruises daily.

HELICOPTER TOURS

HELICOPTER "FLIGHTSEEING" RIDES aren't for everyone, and they are not without risk, particularly in the tricky flying conditions they sometimes encounter. Helicopters are a good way to see the big picture, especially in roadless wilderness areas like Na Pali Coast, the rainy summit of Waialeale, or the active lava pool of Kilauea Volcano.

We've seen several adventurers returning to terra firma needing a place to lie down. For those for whom motion sickness is not a problem, the best views of Hawaii are from the air aboard a chopper.

Schedule flightseeing tours early in your vacation; if the weather doesn't cooperate on the day of your tour, you'll have an opportunity to reschedule. Try to book a few days in advance—tours are often filled if you wait until the last minute, especially during high-season holidays.

Prices generally are $99 per person for a 20-minute flight, $179 for a 45-minute flight, and about $210 for a full-hour adventure. There are no age restrictions, but passengers weighing more than 250 pounds are assessed an additional charge (usually 50%) because an extra seat will be blocked off for added comfort. Only a few operators offer ground transportation to and from hotels.

Passengers are weighed before the tour, and seats are assigned based on body weight to balance the helicopter. Generally, every other passenger is assigned a window seat. Most tours, however, use the new A-Star aircraft, which provides better viewing conditions than previous helicopters from interior seats. Accommodating up to six passengers, the A-Star is comfortable, air-conditioned, and fully enclosed.

Helicopter tours provide dramatic panoramas of such locales as Pearl Harbor, Punchbowl National Memorial Cemetery of the Pacific,

HELICOPTER OPERATORS

OAHU

Hawaiian Odyssey	☎ 808-833-4354
Magnum Helicopters	☎ 808-833-1133
Makani Kai Helicopters	☎ 808-834-5813
Rainbow Pacific	☎ 808-834-1111

MAUI

ALEXAIR Helicopters	☎ 888-418-8455
Blue Hawaiian Helicopters	☎ 808-871-8844
Hawaii Helicopters	☎ 808-877-3900
Sunshine Helicopters	☎ 808-871-0722

THE BIG ISLAND

Blue Hawaiian Helicopters	☎ 808-961-5600
Safari Helicopters	☎ 808-969-1259

KAUAI

Blue Hawaiian Helicopters	☎ 808-245-5800
Inter-Island Helicopters	☎ 808-335-5009
Jack Harter Helicopters	☎ 808-245-3774
Safari Helicopters	☎ 808-246-0136
Will Squyres Helicopter Tours	☎ 808-245-7541

and Diamond Head on Oahu; Kilauea Volcano and the steep rain-forest valleys of the Big Island; Haleakala National Park and the West Maui Mountains on Maui; and the rugged Na Pali and Mt. Waialeale Crater on Kauai. You'll get to see some spectacular hidden spots—waterfalls, black-sand beaches, lava fields, and cinder cones—that are otherwise inaccessible. And some helicopters land for short stops.

Each tour is fully narrated by the pilot, adding to the music humming in your specially equipped headset. Many pilots are certified tour guides, providing insights on history, geology, and nature, and adding an educational facet to the tour.

The pilot also operates a multicamera system within the helicopter, capturing the scenery (and sometimes you!) on tape. You can buy the video at the end of your journey, usually for about $25.

About motion sickness: In addition to over-the-counter and prescription drugs that may help prevent motion sickness, you may want to try elastic wristbands that are designed to stimulate an acupuncture point on your wrist and counter air- or seasickness without drugs. Ginger is a favorite local remedy to prevent motion sickness; try drinking real ginger ale or snacking on ginger shortly before the flight.

A caveat: Choppers, like any aircraft, crash. It's a fact. Bad weather, mechanical failure, and pilot errors all cause helicopters to go down. While the safety record in Hawaii is excellent, it's not faultless. Each year at least one helicopter crashes somewhere in the Islands. Keep an eye on weather conditions, especially on Kauai, and postpone your tour if the weather is unsettled. Go early in the day, when the air is still and calm. If you're flying over water, make sure your bird has pontoons, and you have a life vest.

🍍 kids MOLOKAI MULE RIDE

IN TODAY'S ERA OF HIGH-TECH ATTRACTIONS and showbiz wizardry, it's heartwarming to see that this rugged mule ride remains a favorite tourist activity. The Molokai Mule Ride to Kalaupapa stars sure-footed mules that carry their riders down (and back up) a hair-raising, 26-switchback trail. The 90-minute excursion includes breathtaking views of Molokai's northern coast. Kalaupapa is the historic settlement where Father Damien ministered to leprosy patients from 1873 to 1889. Offered daily except Sunday, the $165-per-person tour includes a picnic lunch. Flights in to Kalaupapa can also be arranged. ☎ 800-567-7550 or **www.muleride.com**.

🍍 kids SUBMARINE RIDES

IF YOU CAN'T BRING YOURSELF to put your face in the water to snorkel, there is another way to admire the undersea beauty off Hawaiian shores. Atlantis Submarines offers narrated, air-conditioned tour rides on three islands in which you never get wet but can observe coral reefs teeming with yellow tangs, parrot fish, moray eels, and many other types of colorful sea life. On Oahu, catch the sub ride at Hilton Hawaiian Village, where you board a shuttle boat and transfer to large (48- to 64-passenger) vessels. On Maui, shuttle boats depart from Lahaina and take you to a 48-passenger sub that explores the ocean channel between Maui and Lanai. In Kailua-Kona on the Big Island, Atlantis's 48-passenger sub examines a large natural coral reef.

Rates are $79 to $84 for adults and $39 to $42 for children. ☎ 800-548-6262 or **www.atlantissubmarines.org**.

CRUISING HAWAII

IF YOU HAVEN'T SAILED AMONG the Hawaiian Islands, you've missed one of the best cruising experiences in the Pacific. A seven-day cruise reveals the essence and natural beauty of the Islands. You can lounge on the sundeck with a good book, but there's much to see: sunsets, rainbows, and whales. Shore excursions offer the chance to sample the sights, nature, and culture of the Islands.

Norwegian Cruise Line (NCL) has made a major investment in luxury steamships in Hawaii for interisland voyages since 2001, taking over from defunct American Hawaii Cruises and United States Lines operations.

Pride of America was the first passenger ocean liner built to sail under the American flag in nearly half a century. The ship runs seven-day itineraries with lots of time for passengers to enjoy shore excursions in the Islands, and a choice of departure port (Honolulu, Oahu or Kahului, Maui).

kids Norwegian Cruise Line
(☎ 866-234-0292; www.ncl.com)

TYPE OF SHIP New luxury ocean liner.

TYPE OF CRUISE Destination, family oriented, casual and flexible.

COMMENTS The 921-foot-long *Pride of America* has a crew of 920 and passenger capacity of 2,002, housed on 13 decks, with nine restaurants, seven lounges and bars, a theater, art gallery, kids center, and shops. Cruise line officials have gone to some lengths to assure that *Pride of America* will reflect the culture through crew and decor. That local focus, plus attractive prices, makes these cruises appealing. The ship has a Kumu Cultural Center designed by Hawaii designer Mary Philpotts to reflect Island heritage and history.

CRUISING, PRO AND CON

IF YOU'VE NEVER VISITED HAWAII and want to see two or more islands, a cruise is a good solution. A slow boat between the Islands is relaxing. You'll avoid repacking and changing lodging and save time and money, but there's a trade-off. Because a sea cruise usually allows only a day or two in each port, you'll only get of a hint of each island. Think of a cruise as a scouting expedition.

You can sign up for shore excursions offered by the cruise line or strike out on your own on foot, by taxi, or by rental car. If you have a place in mind that you simply must see, rent a car and go. You can reserve a car while still on board ship.

Otherwise, check out the full roster of shore excursions offered by the cruise line—golf (plan it right and you can get eight rounds of golf in on your cruise), helicopter tours of Kauai, hikes and kayaking tours, Kona deep-sea fishing, snorkeling and dive trips—all easily booked on board.

All meals are included in the price, which means you will miss the best of the Islands' regional cuisine. Food aboard is abundant, but it's not the same as dining at Alan Wong's restaurant.

If you love the beach, you're out of luck at Island ports except on Kauai, where Kalapaki Beach is a five-minute walk from Nawiliwili Harbor, the anchorage.

OTHER TOURING SUGGESTIONS

OAHU

HAWAII'S MOST FAMOUS LANDMARK, Leahi Crater, was renamed Diamond Head in the early 1800s by British sailors who claimed to see diamonds glittering on the crater. (The "diamonds" turned out to be merely sparkling calcite crystals.)

Waikiki Beach is actually a collection of small beaches, some with imported sand (from Molokai's empty beaches). The hotels block all ocean views from Kalakaua Avenue until Kuhio Beach, site of the Honolulu Police Department's Waikiki precinct house, surfboard racks, and the larger-than-life statue of Duke Kahanamoku, Hawaii's legendary sports hero.

Kahanamoku was a record-setting swimmer (he captured gold medals in the 1912 and 1920 Summer Olympics) who set the 100-meter freestyle world record in 1911. In later years, Kahanamoku traveled the world, staging surf exhibitions to popularize the sport. He died in 1968 at the age of 77.

In 1850, **Honolulu** became the capital of the kingdom. Today it is a 26-mile-long urban strip, but the city and county of Honolulu not only encompasses all of Oahu but also extends 1,400 miles northwest up the island chain to Kure Atoll. In Hawaii, folks call Honolulu "town" and everything else that lacks a building over three stories tall "country." Waikiki is Waikiki.

Drive up Ala Moana Boulevard to **Honolulu Harbor.** Until Pearl Harbor was made navigable in the early 1900s, Honolulu Harbor was the only protected body of water of its size in Hawaii. In 1794, the English ship *Butterworth*, led by Captain William Brown, became the first foreign vessel to enter the harbor.

The centerpiece of the harbor remains the ten-story **Aloha Tower,** the tallest building in Honolulu when it opened in 1926. Its tenth-floor observation deck provides views of Oahu's southern coastline.

From the 1930s to the 1950s, steamships carrying dreamy-eyed visitors radioed their arrival schedule to harbormasters at the tower. And as luxury liners such as the Matson Line's SS *Lurline* and SS *Monterey* pulled into port, a festive celebration—"Boat Day"—took place, as residents welcomed *malihini* (newcomers) with Hawaiian music, hula, and sweet-smelling flower lei. A modern version of Boat Day occurs when interisland steamships depart the harbor from the area of **Aloha Tower Marketplace,** a retail-restaurant complex with open-air waterfront restaurants that offer a seat on the busy harbor plied by tugboats and in- and outbound ships.

From the harbor, take Alakea Street up to get on the Pali Highway and head to **Nuuanu Valley,** gateway to the Koolau Mountains and Oahu's Windward side.

At the top of the Pali in 1795, Kamehameha I and his army drove 300 Oahu defenders over the cliff to their deaths. You can still see the squared outline of a gun rampart on top of the mountain from the highway, a reminder of the battle.

Today, the **Pali Lookout** is one of the island's most visited spots, as evidenced by the parking lot full of tour buses. Stop to be blown by the wind and admire the striking views of haunting Windward Oahu.

Travelers Advisory: Pali Lookout is a prime area for *cockaroaches,* the pidgin term for thieves who smash car windows and grab purses, cameras, or anything in sight. You can lock your car doors and trunk and still lose. It is best to take all items of value with you and leave the car empty, open, and unlocked.

Up behind Waikiki is misty **Manoa Valley,** formed in part by the 2,013-foot **Mount Tantalus.** The rainbow-laced valley is home to **University of Hawaii–Manoa,** with an enrollment of 20,000 students. The sprawling campus, shaded by specimen tropical trees, is a mix of disparate architecture, with Korean temples beside World War II–like barracks. The most graceful building is the East West Center, a think tank begun by President Lyndon B. Johnson with congressional funds to foster alliances in Asia and the Pacific.

Back in Waikiki, drive east on the H-1 to find the tony neighborhood of **Kahala** and the **Kahala Hotel & Resort,** surrounded by grandiose estates from the Japanese property-buying heyday of the 1980s, a tradition now carried on by other owners. Continuing on Kalanianaole Highway, you enter suburban **Hawaii Kai,** home to Roy's Restaurant, where foodies worship nightly at one of Hawaii's first regional cuisine restaurants. **Koko Head Crater** looms over the suburban homes and marks the spot where Oahu at last begins to reveal its raw, natural self along the Kaiwi Coast with its rocky shoreline, sandy beaches, famous spouting **Halona Blowhole** (a geyser-like phenomenon caused when big waves hit an L-shaped coast hole in the rocks), pocket beaches, and view of Molokai 26 miles across the sea. The 2,000-foot-deep Kaiwi Channel between Oahu and Molokai, considered one of the world's most dangerous because it funnels open ocean currents between the Islands, is the course for the celebrated Molokai Hoe outrigger canoe race each year, featuring daring paddlers from around the Pacific battling the seas and each other from Molokai to Waikiki Beach.

The main attraction here is not the crater (which you can climb on a steep trail) but **Hanauma Bay,** a coastal crater with a blown-out sea wall; the reef is a tropical fish preserve and the most popular snorkel spot in Hawaii, attracting 3,000 visitors a day.

Windward Oahu

Continuing east from Koko Head crater affords you a scenic drive along Oahu's southeastern coastline. To your right you will spot **Makapuu Beach Park** and the crashing waves beyond. Note also a pair of offshore islands; the larger one (67 acres) is **Manana Island,** or Rabbit Island. In the late 1800s, its owner, John Cummins, used the island to raise European hares, and a small population of rabbits still resides there, although the island is mainly a seabird sanctuary.

Ahead is Sea Life Park, an old-fashioned marine attraction where captive creatures like dolphins jump through hoops. The park also serves as a rehabilitation center for injured sea life.

Rising up 2,000 feet and more, the jagged spine of the majestic **Koolau Mountains** begins here, providing a dramatic backdrop to the Windward towns of Waimanalo, Kailua, and Kaneohe. Geologists believe the sheer precipice of the Koolau may have been formed when a huge portion of the coast dropped off into the sea, leaving a vertical wall now cloaked in rain-forest green.

In **Waimanalo,** a country settlement with a great bodysurfing beach, farmers grow abundant food and flower crops in the broad fertile plain below the cliffs. Nearby, the U.S. military has maintained a 1,500-acre seaside retreat beside an airfield known as Bellows. The first Japanese prisoner of war was captured on **Bellows Beach** shortly after the December 7, 1941, raid on Pearl Harbor, when his small submarine struck the reef in Waimanalo Bay and sank.

With nearly 60,000 residents, **Kailua** is the second largest town in the state. Kailua sits between the **Kawainui Marsh** and the Pacific Ocean. The marsh, the largest body of freshwater in Hawaii, is slowly becoming a meadow. But Kailua is blessed with splendid beaches, a picturesque bay, natural vistas, and a strong sense of community. **Kailua Beach** is one of the state's best beaches, famous as a windsurfing spot (onshore trade winds blow nearly all the time). Nearby, **Lanikai Beach** is becoming a kind of Malibu West with celebrities like cookie magnate Wally "Famous" Amos in residence, and others such as Robin Williams and Mel Gibson among the frequent visitors.

Neighboring Kaneohe, an undistinguished strip mall of a town surrounded by incredibly gorgeous mountains and sea, borders one of the world's most beautiful azure bays, **Kaneohe Bay,** dotted with islets and surrounded by steep cliffs.

Farther up the Windward Shore, bound for the North Shore, you'll come to Kaaawa, home to **Kualoa Ranch,** a working cattle ranch that has turned to tourism to make ends meet and to share its magnificent setting. You have seen Kualoa in movies like *Jurassic Park* and the television series *Lost.* Activities offered here include horseback riding, helicopter tours, scuba diving, all-terrain-vehicle (ATV) riding, Jet Skiing, shooting range, hiking, an ancient fishpond, and a hidden beach.

About 600 yards off **Kualoa Beach Park** stands one of Hawaii's most photographed little islands: **Mokolii Island** known as Chinaman's Hat. Ancient Hawaiians fancied the island looked like a lizard's tail. Modern folks gave it the nickname Chinaman's Hat because its conical shape resembles the straw coolie hats once favored by immigrant workers.

The best and safest way to take its photo is to leave the highway, either to enter the park or to pull off along one of the beaches.

North Shore

Laie is where you'll find the **Polynesian Cultural Center,** one of the state's notable attractions.

Driving on around the northern point of the island, you approach the famous North Shore surfing beaches. Gone are the sweet-smelling scents of coconut oil and suntan lotion, replaced by the aroma of fresh salt air. Gone is the jungle of hotels and condominiums, replaced by surfer cottages and homes frequently threatened by massive winter surf. Gone are the friendly ocean waves of Waikiki, replaced by gigantic swells that have helped the North Shore gain worldwide notoriety as the undisputed capital of surfing.

Each winter, the world's top professional and amateur surfers make their annual pilgrimage to such renowned surf spots as **Sunset Beach, Alii Beach,** and **Ehukai Beach** (and its famous Banzai Pipeline).

The heart of Oahu's North Shore is **Haleiwa,** a funky village of surf shops, art galleries, mom-and-pop shops, shaved ice stands, and small main-street bistros like Kua Aina Sandwich Shop and Café Haleiwa, where surfers stoke up when waves are flat. Jameson's by the Sea is an irresistible but crowded steak-and-seafood restaurant with an always-popular lanai at sundown.

The best attraction is the **Haleiwa Surf Museum,** which traces the origins and history of the sport with photographs, artifacts, and memorabilia from Hollywood to Haleiwa.

Leeward Oahu

Here on the **Waianae Coast** in towns like Nanakuli and Makaha, pit bulls guard plantation houses with rusty pickups in the yard. This is one of the last enclaves of Hawaiians on Oahu. In general, the western side of Oahu turns its hot, dry back on tourists. Seldom (if ever) featured in travel magazines, this side of Oahu has, however, some spectacular unspoiled places.

Once you get comfortable with the local scene, you'll begin to enjoy the reef-fringed, 20-mile-long stretch of coast that ends in exclamation at needle-nosed **Kaena Point,** Oahu's westernmost point and a popular fishing spot.

Though Kaena "points" toward Kauai, early Hawaiians believed the point was one place where human souls departed Earth—good souls to the right, less virtuous to the left.

Kaena means "heat" in Hawaiian. You'll understand why when you take the hike to the point that "throbs in the sun," according to a chant. Sunsets here are red hot. Bring plenty of water.

Heading back toward Honolulu, you'll arrive at **Makaha,** site of a popular longboard-surfing contest, emphasizing the surfing style favored in the 1950s and 1960s. The North Shore attracts worldwide attention, but true surfing insiders know Makaha as one of Hawaii's hottest surf spots. Here you'll find some of the finest surfers in the state, from young prodigies to legendary old-timers.

Beyond Makaha and Nanakuli is **Waianae,** a place often ignored by visitors. However, this may soon change. Recently, community leaders have talked about boosting Waianae's economic potential through cultural tourism, recognizing visitors' desires to learn about Hawaii's culture. One realization of these discussions is the **Na Hana Lima** store, a cooperative of a dozen Waianae-area artisans, located at Waianae Mall Shopping Center. The store includes Hawaiian jewelry, sculptures, woodwork, kapa, prints, pottery, and other items.

Nearby is **Ko Olina,** a lavish resort area featuring J. W. Marriott Ihilani Resort & Spa, a 387-room luxury retreat. The resort's eye-catching man-made lagoons are now open to all for swimming.

MAUI

ON A MAP, MAUI LOOKS ALMOST like a person. It's easy to make out a head, a neck, and a body. The **West Maui Mountains** form the head, the neck is the isthmus of the Valley Isle, and **Haleakala** is the body. Such diverse geographical anatomy makes it Hawaii's second most popular island, attracting more than two million visitors a year.

Most arrive at the airport in Kahului, the trafficky center of commerce, and head straight to one of the main resorts in Wailea, Kihei, Kapalua, or Kaanapali. A lucky few avoid the crowds and fly from Honolulu directly to Kapalua–West Maui Airport or to the lush tropical retreat of Hana. Wherever you choose to stay on Maui, go for a ride at least once to get a glimpse of the rest of the island, outside the resort zone. Here are some day trips to consider.

At Maui's "chin" is **Maalaea,** a small waterfront community with a boat harbor, condos, a surfing area, and a stop worth your attention, the **Maui Ocean Center.** It features a 600,000-gallon aquarium with hundreds of ocean creatures, including rays, sea turtles, reef fish, and sharks.

South Maui

Driving south, you reach **Kihei,** a busy beach town with more than 100 small hotels and condos, shops, restaurants, and businesses. Kihei has nightlife, a rarity on the Neighbor Islands, in nightclubs, sports bars, and karaoke bars.

South of Kihei is the master-planned resort of **Wailea** ("water of Lea," goddess of canoes), a 1,500-acre oasis of luxury hotels and condos set on five crescent beaches. After Wailea, the paved road ends at the isolated resort and old community of **Makena,** where the elegant Maui Prince Hotel sits amid 1,800 acres of rugged, natural dryland slope and two championship golf courses. Beyond the Prince, the road continues past beachfront homes until it ends on an old lava flow.

Driving west from Maalaea, two-lane Highway 30 passes through a tunnel on the coastal route; there's a whale-watch lookout nearby at **McGregor Point,** as well as miles of open coastline and small tree-shaded beach parks, old graveyards, and views of Lanai and Molokai.

West Maui

Turn left into **Lahaina** (it means "the heat") to discover its historic buildings, harbor, and Front Street hangouts, popular day or night. The entire town is designated a National Historic Landmark, and Lahaina's storied past lives on in its restored relics that cluster around a mammoth banyan tree in the town square.

In the 18th century, Maui's ferocious high chief Kahekili, said to have built houses out of the skulls of defeated warriors to keep his enemies terrified, declared Lahaina his capital. He favored the area for its weather, lush thickets of banana and breadfruit trees, and defensible location between steep West Maui slopes and the sea, where it afforded a natural harbor. Kahekili, whose name was given to a nearby beach, survived all his foes and died in Waikiki in his 80s.

Lahaina was the focal point of the whaling industry in the mid-19th century; at the height of the whaling era, more than 100 whaling ships dropped anchor at the town's harbor. Along with the ships came hundreds of pleasure-seeking sailors, the bane of the disapproving Christian missionaries. In 1825, a mob of British sailors threatened to kill missionary settler William Richards and set his house on fire unless a law forbidding prostitution and alcohol was repealed. Two years later, a cannon struck Richards's home from a visiting whaler.

A short drive up from Lahaina is **Kaanapali Beach Resort,** where decades ago Alexander and Baldwin converted sugarcane fields into one of the world's first master-planned resort—a parklike setting on a four-mile gold-sand beach with two championship golf courses, deluxe and luxury hotels, condos and homes, and an open-air, beachfront mall with shops and restaurants.

Beyond Kaanapali other communities of condos and apartments dot the shoreline, but at the northwest end of the resort coast, **Kapalua Resort,** a picturesque resort with five exquisite bays, puts an end to human work and lets nature take over. For hiking enthusiasts, the Kapalua Nature Society offers guests hikes in the West Maui Mountains. The road continues on to Kahului, paved but still tortuous, skinny, and slow going. It's a great drive through a relatively unspoiled area of the island.

North Shore

Heading toward Hana from Kahului on Highway 36 takes you to **Paia,** a breezy former sugar plantation town full of quaint, brightly painted shops and bistros that look more Caribbean than Hawaiian. Paia is unofficial headquarters for nearby windsurfing favorite **Hookipa Beach.** Hookipa's strong year-round winds and ideal wave conditions draw the world's top windsurfers, dubbed the Maui Air Force for their aerial antics. It is a sight to see these daredevils hit waves head-on and gain "hang time" up in the air before splashing down in the sea. Nearby, **Haiku** has inexpensive lodging in B&Bs and vacation rentals.

Upcountry

From Paia, you can head inland up through the open fields to the cooler heights of Maui called Upcountry. The drive up the foothills of Haleakala, a dormant volcano, takes you to **Makawao.** This *paniolo* (cowboy) town has avoided becoming a ghost town by becoming a kind of arts center. It's the scene of an unforgettable July 4 parade and rodeo.

Farther upcountry is **Kula,** a scenic community that clings to Haleakala's side at 3,000 feet and is known for its cool climate, its thriving flower farms (growing the strange South African flowers known as protea), its sweet onions, and **Ulupalakua Ranch.** The 20,000-acre ranch, a nearly vertical spread where the volcano last erupted around 1790, raises cattle and elk and grows wine grapes.

Drop by the tasting room at **Tedeschi Vineyards** to sample pineapple wine. Better yet, bring a picnic basket, pair it with a Maui vintage, and enjoy the afternoon in the cool uplands.

From Kula you can take the road up to the island's greatest natural spectacle, **Haleakala National Park.** According to Hawaiian legend, the demigod Maui captured the sun with his magic lasso on Haleakala. He convinced the sun to slow down its travels, lengthening the days and giving his mother, Hina, more time to dry her tapa cloths.

Haleakala is one of only two places in the world—the Big Island is the other—where you may see the exotic silversword, an odd-looking plant with silvery leaves and tall spikes of yellow and violet florets, from June through October.

Hana

Taking a different route from Paia starts you on the long drive to **Hana,** a three-hour trip, that crosses 56 one-lane bridges and takes 617 twists and turns (about 12 curves a mile). The rental car parade goes slowly so everyone can ogle Maui's natural beauty: crashing surf, steep green hills, waterfalls, and flowers.

Hana is a small community of about one thousand residents. The lifestyle here is slow and unpretentious. Highlights include the **Hana Cultural Center,** which retells area history, **Hana Coast Gallery, Hana Gardenland,** and **Hasegawa General Store,** where "you'll find a baseball bat and a piano hat, sunburn creams and the latest magazines, muumuu and mangoes and ukuleles, too," according to the lyrics by Paul Weston, who wrote the 1961 hit song "The Hasegawa General Store." Best of all, you can buy the sheet music and, if you're lucky, a cassette recording of this song by Arthur Godfrey, Hilo Hattie, and local residents Jim Nabors and Carol Burnett. The other noted local musician, the late George Harrison of Beatles fame, frequently shopped at Hasegawa's, but he somehow never got around to recording the song.

Hana also has a single resort hotel, Hotel Hana-Maui (owned by the Californians who developed Big Sur's Post Ranch Inn), a few condos, and B&Bs that provide limited lodging.

Ten miles south of Hana is **Kipahulu,** where Charles Lindbergh is buried in the backyard of a cliff-side church. The famed American aviator—in 1927, he became the first person to fly solo across the Atlantic Ocean—first visited Kipahulu in the 1950s. "I love Maui so much, I would rather live one day in Maui than one month in New

York," a cancer-stricken Lindbergh told his doctor. The "Lone Eagle" died on August 26, 1974, at age 72. Lindbergh's grave lies near **Palapala Hoomau Congregational Church.**

THE BIG ISLAND OF HAWAII

YOUNGEST OF THE HAWAIIAN ISLANDS, the Big Island of Hawaii, which lends its name to the entire archipelago, is by far the largest—twice the size of all other Hawaiian Islands combined, with a grand total of 4,028 square miles. And of the 13 climatic regions on Earth, the Big Island has all but the two most extreme: Arctic and Saharan. Birthplace of Hawaii's greatest king, Kamehameha I, the island is full of history, legend, and spirits.

The easiest way to plan your vacation itinerary here is to take a Big Island map and draw a vertical line right down the middle of the island. Locals refer to the left half of the island as the "Kona" side, and the right half as the "Hilo" side. Both sides are well worth a visit, necessitating a rental car.

Kona Side

The hub of visitor activity is on the Kona side, particularly at the seaside village of **Kailua-Kona.** American humorist Mark Twain, who fell in love with the Hawaiian Islands during his visit in March 1866, once described Kailua-Kona as "the sleepiest, quietest, Sundayest-looking place you can imagine."

If Twain were alive today, perhaps he would put on his brightest aloha shirt and join the parade of people walking and driving along **Alii Drive.** His "Sundayest" place now is a Friday-night kind of place. Although few landmarks from Twain's day remain, the town is now a busy jumble of hotels, condominiums, bars, restaurants, and shops.

Each August, Kailua-Kona hosts the **Hawaiian International Billfish Tournament,** a prestigious fishing event luring the world's top anglers. The largest fish caught during the event was a 1,166-pound marlin in 1993.

Five miles and 1,400 feet uphill from Kailua-Kona sits **Holualoa,** a village of coffee groves and artists' studios and galleries on the slopes of Hualalai.

South of Kailua-Kona and down the slope to the sea is mile-wide **Kealakekua Bay,** a state marine conservation district and favorite place to snorkel. A 27-foot white obelisk marks the spot of Captain Cook's death in 1779. The British sea captain and four of his men were killed in a skirmish with Hawaiians (four Hawaiian chiefs and 13 commoners were also killed in the battle).

Farther south, 22 miles from Kailua-Kona, is **Puuhonua O Honaunau National Historical Park,** which in old Hawaii was a sanctuary where anyone who violated *kapu* (religious taboo) could escape a death sentence, if he ran fast enough. The hapless could seek absolution and do penance, then be forgiven and allowed to return home safely.

Hawaiians of old strongly enforced their laws, believing that sins left unpunished would incur the wrath of their gods in the form of earthquakes, tidal waves, famines, and volcanic eruptions. They pursued violators relentlessly and killed them. Puuhonua O Honaunau is the best preserved of all Hawaii's places of refuge. More than 400,000 visitors come to see this 180-acre site each year. Each summer, the park hosts a cultural festival of Hawaiian arts and crafts, with *lauhala*-weaving demonstrations, games, hula performances, and food.

Traveling all the way down the South Coast is a full-day outing that ends at the southernmost part of the island—of the nation, in fact—**Ka Lae** (South Point).

Kohala Coast

Go north from Kailua-Kona to find the sunny Kohala Coast and its luxury resorts, hiking trails, and gold-sand beaches. Historical points of interest are also prevalent here. The area has several ancient fishponds, where fish were raised for royalty. The fish would be wrapped in *ti* leaves and delivered by servants to their *alii* in Kailua-Kona. Parts of this "King's Trail" are still visible from the coast.

Inland from the north end of the Kohala Coast, in the foothills of Mauna Kea, is **Waimea** (also called Kamuela), the peaceful village where the *paniolo* (cowboy) lifestyle still thrives on rolling emerald hills and lush pastures that disappear in the often misty distance. These cool uplands are the home of the 175,000-acre Parker Ranch, one of the largest cattle ranches in the United States, and the site of a major rodeo held every July 4. The nearby **Parker Ranch Visitor Center and Museum** recites the history of the ranch, as that of six generations of the Parker family.

North Kohala, the peninsula that forms the northernmost tip of the Big Island and ends in the village of Hawi, is the birthplace of Kamehameha I. His birthplace is near the giant **Mookini Heiau,** Hawaii's first National Historic Landmark. The stones used for the construction of the *heiau* (temple) were supposedly passed hand to hand for nine miles from the coastline.

Hamakua Coast

Heading east from Waimea, toward Hilo, is **Waipio Valley** a chasm of 2,000-foot cliffs laced with 1,000-foot Hiilawe Falls and carpeted with taro patches that run down to a black-sand beach. Once a thriving community and favorite retreat of Hawaiian royalty, the valley is accessible via a steep cliff, by shuttle tour, by four-wheel-drive vehicle, or on foot. It's easy going down, but a tough pull back up, so take the shuttle.

Hilo is the island's county seat and largest town, with a population of 47,639. Yet it never outgrew its small-town feel. Most years, Hilo ranks as the wettest city in the United States. The average annual rainfall at the Hilo International Airport is 131 inches; that's more than ten feet, and the result is a profusion of tropical flowers, trees, and fruit.

Hilo was once the center of trade. The activity heightened with the arrival of Westerners, as Hilo Bay gave foreign vessels safe harbor. In August 1881, however, a lava flow from neighboring Mauna Loa cut a path straight toward Hilo, threatening to consume the growing town. On August 9, an auspicious day in Hawaii history, Princess Ruth Keelikolani—an imposing figure at six feet tall and 400-plus pounds—arrived from Honolulu and, standing at the edge of the lava flow, prayed and presented offerings of *ohelo* berries, tobacco, flowers, red silk, and brandy to the goddess Pele. Hilo was spared.

Hilo was not as fortunate when it came to tidal waves. On April 1, 1946, the Hawaiian Islands were struck by devastating tidal waves, the result of an Alaskan earthquake. Hilo was the hardest hit, with nearly 100 deaths. In 1960, another tsunami struck Hilo, killing 61 residents.

When in Hilo, go downtown and walk around the restored historic buildings to find interesting shops and restaurants, and the twice-weekly Hilo Farmers Market.

Other Hilo highlights include the **Panaewa Rainforest Zoo & Gardens,** the **Lyman Museum,** and the new **Pacific Tsunami Museum,** which recalls the waves that almost wiped out Hilo.

It's nearly an hour's drive uphill from Hilo to **Volcano,** an upcountry art community in a fern forest just outside **Hawaii Volcanoes National Park,** the top visitor attraction in the state. Volcano-viewing conditions depend on the weather and lava activity. Call ☎ 808-985-6000 for recorded updates.

KAUAI

THE NORTHERNMOST MAJOR ISLAND and the oldest is also the most beautiful. Many believe that it was the first to be populated, rather than the Big Island. It is certainly the most independent, located on the remote end of the cluster of main islands, about 70 miles across the water from Oahu. It's proven to be quite the movie star, serving as a setting for more than 50 films, including *South Pacific, Blue Hawaii, King Kong, Raiders of the Lost Ark,* and *Jurassic Park.*

The beauty runs deep. Kauai recently suffered and survived devastating damage from two major hurricanes, Iwa in 1982 and Iniki in 1992. But Kauai's 63,000 residents and abundant attributes recovered.

South Shore

You land in **Lihue,** a onetime plantation town with an airport surrounded by cane fields and sea on the southeastern part of the island. A drive along Rice Street takes you to the **Kauai Museum,** where the island's history is retold with artifacts, artwork, photographs, and other exhibit items. Also in Lihue is the island's major seaport, **Nawiliwili Harbor,** and the **Alekoko** (Menehune) Fish Pond farther up the Huleia River. The Menehune, legendary elfin people, are credited with great feats of engineering overnight to create fishponds, roads, and temples. Just beyond Lihue are **Grove Farm Homestead,** a plantation-era home turned into a museum, and, a few miles farther, **Kilohana Plantation,** another plantation manor.

To the west, just after the 520 turnoff toward Koloa and Poipu Beach Resort, is Lawai, home of the **National Tropical Botanical Garden,** a 186-acre Eden that maintains the largest collection of tropical flora in the world.

West Kauai

Farther leeward at the mouth of the Waimea River are the rocky remains of **Fort Elizabeth,** built in 1816 by Anton Schaeffer in an unsuccessful attempt to claim Kauai for the Russian crown.

In the town of **Waimea** stands a statue of Captain James Cook, who first set foot on Hawaiian soil at Waimea Bay on January 20, 1778.

Nearby is 3,600-foot-deep **Waimea Canyon,** a 15-mile-long gorge with waterfalls, wild goats, and colorful striations that glow in fading light. Mark Twain dubbed it "the Grand Canyon of the Pacific." You can hike or ride horses in the canyon.

Just north of Waimea is the **Pacific Missile Range Facility.** Check in at the gate and head to **Barking Sands Beach,** so named because of the "barking" sounds the sand makes as you hotfoot across the beach. The beach is a safe distance from the still-active missile range.

Beyond lies 17-mile **Polihale Beach,** the longest beach in Hawaii, which ends on the island's northwest shore where Na Pali begins.

Driving uphill from Waimea, you'll come to **Kokee State Park,** a favorite spot for camping and hiking, with 45 miles of trails into the **Alakai Swamp,** last stand of Kauai's endangered native birds. In old Hawaii, Kokee was revered as a sanctuary for the gods.

Coconut Coast (East Kauai)

The Wailua River and **Wailua River State Park** mark an ancient historic area, with prominent *heiau* and birthing stones. High-ranking ancient women gave birth on such stones because they believed the children would grow up to be powerful chiefs. The baby's umbilical cord would be placed in a cloth and hidden in or under the navel stone (or *piko* stone), a practice continued very privately in some places today.

North Shore

When you pass the busy town of Kapaa, the crowds and buildings fall away and the road leads to the fabled North Shore. On the way, turn right at Kilauea and stop at the **Kilauea Point National Wildlife Refuge,** home to the largest seabird nesting areas and historic **Kilauea Lighthouse.** Spinner dolphins, humpback whales, sea turtles, monk seals, and albatross often can be seen here.

In another ten miles or so, you approach Princeville Resort on a high cliff marking one side of **Hanalei River Valley,** a green patchwork of taro ponds along the river surrounded by a bowl of mountains. It's worth stopping at the overlook. Then the road leads down to the valley floor, through Hanalei and on around the next mountain base, past seven one-lane bridges and several narrow valleys cut by streams. This is the scenery of your tropical dreams. Keep on until the road ends at the base of the magnificent **Na Pali Coast.** Na Pali ("the cliffs") is a dramatic 25-mile stretch of wind- and wave-worn precipices and hanging valleys cloaked in green. It is accessible only by foot on the ancient 11-mile Kalalau Trail, or by boat during summer months.

MOLOKAI

MOLOKAI, WHERE LESS IS MORE, is always described in negatives: Molokai has no Disneyesque fantasy resorts, no fancy restaurants, no stoplights, no malls or fast food, no freeways, and no buildings taller than a coconut tree. The beaches are too small or too dangerous for swimming; fishponds are muddy and mostly off-limits, one-third of the island is a private ranch now off limits due to hard times, and the main tourist attraction is a leper colony. So what's the big deal about Molokai? The simple life and absence of contemporary Americana landmarks is what attracts those in search of old Hawaii.

You arrive at Molokai Hoolehua Airport, the small, open-air lava-rock terminal with rental cars and a lunch counter serving chili rice and Spam *musubi,* Which way you leave the airport depends on whether you like it hot and dry or lush and tropical. The 38-mile-long island divides at **Kaunakakai,** the funky main town, into two different climate zones, known locally as the West End and the East End. The West End looks like Mexico. The East End resembles Tahiti.

"The Cockeyed Mayor of Kaunakakai," a *hapa-haole* song performed by Hilo Hattie, put Molokai's biggest town on the map in the 1940s. The song was written in 1934 by the late, great R. Alex Anderson. His other songs included "Lovely Hula Hands" and "I Will Remember You." FYI: There is no mayor of Kaunakakai.

A sun-faded, three-block town with harbor and pier, Kaunakakai looks more like an old western movie than a tropical village. Molokai's chief settlement includes a bank, post office, drugstore and grocery store, medical center, and family-run businesses: **Molokai Drive-Inn, Oviedo's Filipino Restaurant,** and **Kanemitsu Bakery,** where 19 different types of bread are baked fresh daily. The brightest lights in town shine on **Mitchell Pauole Center,** site of softball games, hulihuli chicken roasts, and community events.

Above Kaunakakai, defunct **Kamakou Volcano,** the island's tallest mountain, is home to a virgin forest of native trees, including rare sandalwood. The Nature Conservancy runs the 2,774-acre Kamakou Preserve, home to native Hawaiian birds and 200 indigenous plants, which you can see on monthly tours given by the Nature Conservancy. Call ☎ 808-553-5236 or e-mail **hike-molokai@popmailnc.org** to take part in tours of this or other preserves on the island.

East of Kaunakakai, you'll find the top edge of the world's highest sea cliffs, which rise 3,250 feet from sea level and stretch 14 miles on the island's corrugated North Shore. On the way, you pass coffee plantations, the **Ironwood Hills Golf Course,** and **Molokai Museum and Cultural Center** in a restored sugar mill.

Nearby, on a plateau of Mauna Loa, is **Kaana,** a hill setting where Molokai tradition holds that *Laka,* the goddess of the hula, created the native Hawaiian dance. Molokai celebrates the birth of the hula at the annual Molokai Ka Hula Piko, held each May at **Papohaku Beach Park,** a shady seaside grove on the island's West End. The day-long festival features hula performances, Hawaiian music, food, and local arts and crafts.

As you head to the East End, the island becomes lush, green, and tropical. Fishponds like 54-acre Keawanui Pond line the shore for 20 miles. Take a swim at **Waialua Beach** at Mile Marker 19, one of the island's best beaches, or **Mile Marker 20 Beach** for snorkeling.

At the **Mapulehu Mango Grove,** where 2,000 mango trees flourish by the sea, you can hitch a ride on the Molokai Horse and Wagon Ride to one of the spookiest places in Hawaii: **Iliiliopae Heiau,** a school of sacrifice where *kahuna* taught final rites in the massive temple of doom that's three stories high and bigger than a football field. More than 700 years old, the *heiau,* legend has it, was built of car-sized boulders passed hand to hand from Molokai's opposite side in exchange for shrimp. (*Iliili* means rounded rock and *opae* means shrimp in Hawaiian.)

On Kamehameha V Highway you'll discover affordable seaside condos, like Wavecrest Resort, and perfectly sited vacation rentals like Dunbar Beachfront Cottages and the Country Cottage at Puu O Hoku Ranch. The highway turns to hairpins on the far eastern end. After scenic vistas of pocket beaches, offshore islets, and dense jungles, it dead-ends at **Halawa Valley.**

Inundated by a tsunami in 1946, Halawa Valley, an ancient settlement, was abandoned. Now privately owned, the valley is closed, and the trailhead to 250-foot Moaula Falls is posted with no trespassing signs. Observe the *kapu,* but enjoy **Halawa Beach County Park** and its black-sand beach with the island's only decent surf break.

People stricken with leprosy in 1860 were banished to **Kalaupapa Peninsula,** a lava shelf down below the famous sea cliffs. The victims were literally pushed from a boat into the waters off the peninsula and had to swim to shore. Father Damien, a Belgian priest, arrived in 1873 and embraced the outcasts, cared for them, and sought medicine, food, shelter, and clothing for them. It was an exhausting labor of love, and Father Damien was mostly alone in his efforts. Any contributions by visiting doctors were left on a fencepost to avoid physical contact with patients. By the end of the 1870s, approximately 1,000 people had been exiled to Kalaupapa. On April 15, 1889, Damien himself died of leprosy at age 49. Some 60 patients, their disease controlled by modern medicine, still live at the settlement and serve as tour guides. Damien is a sainthood nominee.

LANAI

LONG AGO HAWAIIANS BELIEVED LANAI was haunted by spirits so wily and vicious that no human who went there could survive. Today, nearly everyone who goes there not only gets a good night's sleep but leaves reluctantly. Spirits still haunt the island, but they are thought to be benign.

In 1904, American businessman Charles Gay began purchasing various parcels on Lanai; four years later he owned the entire island. Gay sold it in 1922 to James Dole, who quickly turned his $1.1-million investment into the pineapple capital of the world. For the next six decades, pineapple was king on Lanai. Today, Lanai survives by cultivating a few privileged visitors seeking peaceful surroundings, luxurious hotels, outstanding golf, and one of the best dive spots in the Pacific. The sweet and juicy pineapple once covered more than 19,000 acres of the island's red-dirt Palawai Basin; all that remains is a relic field so visitors can see what pineapple looks like.

Most people will never know the taste of a fresh-plucked Hawaiian pineapple, which 1930s poet laureate Don Blanding wrote "tastes like champagne and honey . . . the most delicious fruit grown in any Garden of Eden." Neither pine nor apple, nor Hawaiian in origin, the South American import that became the symbol of the Islands is now grown and harvested in Third World tropical nations (Honduras, Costa Rica, Dominican Republic, Mexico, Thailand, and the Philippines) where labor is less costly. Sweet and juicy, the king of fruit ruled the island of Lanai for a half-century; inspired its nickname, "The Pineapple Island"; provided wages, shelter, and jobs for plantation workers (also imported to Hawaii); and made global conglomerate Dole Foods a household name. Now an exhibition crop in most of Hawaii, pineapple on Lanai is represented in two thin rows of spiky gray-green specimen plants that line the lane to Lanai's little airport in Puuwai Basin, where rows upon rows once filled the old volcanic crater. Today, a lone golden painted pineapple looms larger than life on the pediment arch of the Lodge at Koele; the mural, too, is fading in the tropic sun.

In 1987, California tycoon David Murdock bought a controlling interest in Castle & Cooke, owners of Dole, and found that the deed to 98% of Lanai came with the deal, along with plans for hotel development. He envisioned an island resort like no other, and in the early 1990s, The Lodge at Koele and the Manele Bay Hotel (now the Four Seasons resorts) opened. Visitors content with less palatial properties might enjoy the venerable 1920s-era Hotel Lanai in the center of town.

Golf is the sport of choice on Lanai, at two 18-hole championship courses: **The Experience at Koele,** designed by golf superstar Greg Norman and architect Ted Robinson, and **The Challenge at Manele,** designed by Jack Nicklaus.

The chief landmark is 3,366-foot **Mount Lanaihale,** the highest point on the island.

A hike or drive up **Munro Trail** to the summit on a clear day will afford a rare five-island view of Maui, Molokai, Kahoolawe, Oahu, and the Big Island. Historians believe Lanaihale served as a strategic vantage point so that chiefs could keep an eye on canoe traffic in the sea lanes.

Lanai is regarded as a five-star locale among divers. *Skin Diver Magazine* rated **Cathedrals,** two large underwater caves near Hulopoe Bay, as Hawaii's top diving spot. On the opposite end of the island is **Shipwreck Beach,** where the rusted remains of the *Helena Pt. Townsend,* a World War II liberty ship, are still stuck on the reef.

On the slopes of Lanaihale overlooking the broad Palawai Basin, you can find Stone Age art known as petroglyphs on 20 boulders. The best time to search is midafternoon, when the declining sun lights up the pecked and incised stick figures. It's a most amazing cast of characters unlike any others on Lanai, or any other island for that matter. You can see a canoe sailing across a gigantic red boulder, a curly-tailed dog barking at a centipede, two turtles inching along, and a horseman with a hat riding a thin steed while two V-chested men walk down a trail.

The most significant historic site is **Kaunolu,** where once there was the summer retreat for King Kamehameha I, who tried his hand at fishing with the blessing of Kunihi, a three-foot stone fish god, filled with *mana* (power). The idol is believed to still exist somewhere on Lanai. If you spot it, think twice before touching it. The last person to touch the idol is said to have died as a result.

NIIHAU: THE "FORBIDDEN" ISLAND

YOU CANNOT GO EASILY TO NIIHAU, Hawaii's other privately owned island, because ranch owners want to preserve the old ways in this last Hawaiian enclave where about 150 to 200 residents still speak Hawaiian and pay little heed to the world beyond.

Long off-limits to visitors without an invitation, the forbidden island can sometimes be seen by travelers like us whose curiosity gets the best of them. It takes written permission from the owners. You can go to beachcomb, fish, hunt wild pigs and goats, or just see a mostly raw island. You may not see any of the Hawaiians who live there. Interest in Niihau, for most of us, began when we first read about this strange island bought for $10,000 in gold from a king more than 100 years ago and inhabited only by a "lost" tribe of 200 Hawaiians who are said to choose a pure and simple life over 21st-century trappings.

It all sounds wonderfully arcane, the stuff of *Swiss Family Robinson:* a 6-by-18-mile, late-18th-century island, 17 miles northwest of Kauai. It's actually owned now by a man named Robinson. Cattle-ranching is Niihau's primary business, along with helicopter tours, pig-hunting safaris, and its precious shell necklaces once worn by queens.

To visit Niihau, fax a written request to the Robinson family at ☎ 808-338-1463 or sign up for a helicopter tour of its beaches.

KAHOOLAWE: THE TARGET ISLAND

FROM MAUI OR LANAI, the island of Kahoolawe appears forbidding and bleak, forgotten in time. Its huge red scars show where U.S. Navy pilots, who for nearly half a century practiced air-raid skills here.

The bombing was halted in 1990 by President George H. W. Bush, who was shocked to learn the U.S. Navy was still bombing one of the Hawaiian islands. The 45-square-mile island, about the size of San Francisco, was returned to native Hawaiians to become a cultural retreat someday, after the unexploded ordnance is all cleaned up. A $400-million U.S. Navy cleanup sweep then commenced.

Kahoolawe variously served in the past as penal colony in the monarchy period, as a cattle ranch during territorial days, and as the staging zone for World War II–era U.S. forces preparing for the invasion of Okinawa. In 1965, the U.S. Navy dropped a 500-ton TNT bomb on Kahoolawe to simulate an atomic explosion; the impact irreparably cracked a submarine water lens and turned the island's fresh water brackish.

TOUR COMPANIES

FOR MORE ASSISTANCE in planning your Hawaii trip, one option is to set up a tour through a local company. Each offers an extensive menu of sightseeing excursions. The destination descriptions in this chapter and the profiles of specific attractions which follow in Part Seven will help you to determine what you most want to do in Hawaii. You can determine if a guided tour suits your agenda. Tours operate according to set itineraries, so flexibility is limited; however, they can also provide a very efficient day of sightseeing. Day tours range in price from $20 to $75, with extras such as luau and meals increasing the price. Interisland day and overnight tours are pricier, but may appeal to travelers who want a look at another island despite time or budgetary constraints.

TOUR COMPANIES

OAHU, MAUI, BIG ISLAND, KAUAI

Polynesian Adventure Tours
- ☎ 808-833-3000 (Oahu)
- ☎ 808-877-4242 (Maui)
- ☎ 808-329-8008 (Big Island)
- ☎ 808-246-0122 (Kauai)
- ☎ 800-622-3011 (toll free)
  www.polyad.com

Roberts Hawaii
- ☎ 808-954-8652 (Oahu)
- ☎ 808-871-6226 (Maui)

- ☎ 808-245-9101 (Kauai)
- ☎ 866-898-2519 (toll free)
  www.robertshawaii.com

OAHU

E Noa Tours   www.enoa.com
- ☎ 808-591-2561; ☎ 800-824-8804

KAUAI

Hawaii Movie Tours
- ☎ 808-822-1192; ☎ 800-628-8432
  www.hawaiimovietour.com

PART SEVEN

ATTRACTIONS

YOU CAN WATCH A VOLCANO ERUPT, hold a seahorse in your hand, toss a snowball high atop Mauna Kea, watch night-blooming cereus unfold at midnight, see the Southern Cross, ride a mule down the world's tallest sea cliffs, or snorkel a tropical lagoon with long-nose butterfly fish. And that's just the beginning.

Choosing which attractions to visit during your Hawaii vacation is daunting. So much to see and do—and so little time! Most of Hawaii's top visitor attractions, from museums and gardens to historic sites, have a nominal fee, but many are free. Refer to the maps in the introduction to locate the attractions.

The following profiles provide basic information on Hawaii's attractions, such as location, hours of operation, and cost. Each also features a rating for five age groups and a brief description. Given on a five-star scale, the ratings don't guarantee that a certain segment of visitors will love or hate the attraction, but they do provide a reliable evaluation of each group's typical reaction. For example, some teenagers want to visit historical sights, but more want to go to the beach. Together, the information, ratings, and descriptions will help you plan an itinerary pleasing to all members of your family or group.

■ ATTRACTION PROFILES

OAHU

Aloha Tower GREATER HONOLULU

APPEAL BY AGE	PRESCHOOL ★	GRADE SCHOOL ★½	TEENS ★★★
YOUNG ADULTS ★★★	OVER 30 ★★★½	SENIORS ★★★½	

Aloha Tower Marketplace, Pier 9 at Honolulu Harbor; ☎ 808-528-5700; www.alohatower.com

Admission Free. **Hours** Daily, 9 a.m.–sunset. **When to go** Anytime. **How much**

time to allow 20 minutes. **Author's rating** ★★★; go to the top, look around, come down.

DESCRIPTION AND COMMENTS Now dwarfed by high-rises in downtown Honolulu, Aloha Tower was once the tallest building in Hawaii. The slender, square ten-story tower was erected in 1926. Now the centerpiece of the Aloha Tower Marketplace shopping-and-restaurant complex, the historic tower is perhaps the most recognized man-made structure in the Islands, with its large clock with faces on each side, the huge letters A-L-O-H-A, and the 40-foot flagstaff. In 1997, the tower closed for two years, undergoing an extensive renovation (among the additions were disabled-accessible restrooms, security cameras, and emergency exits). It reopened to visitors in April 1999. Ride the elevator to the tenth floor and take in 360-degree views of Honolulu. You'll have sweeping views of the downtown area, Honolulu Harbor, and the leeward and Koolau mountains.

TOURING TIPS Bring your camera or video camera.

OTHER THINGS TO DO NEARBY Aloha Tower Marketplace features shops, live entertainment, and restaurants. The tower is a short walk away from the Hawaii Maritime Center.

kids Bishop Museum GREATER HONOLULU

| APPEAL BY AGE PRESCHOOL ★★★ GRADE SCHOOL ★★★★★ TEENS ★★★★★ |
| YOUNG ADULTS ★★★★★ OVER 30 ★★★★★ SENIORS ★★★★★ |

1525 Bernice Street; ☎ 808-847-3511; www.bishopmuseum.org

Admission $14.95 for adults; $11.95 for seniors 65 and over and children ages 4–12. **Hours** Daily (except Christmas), 9 a.m.–5 p.m. **When to go** Anytime. **How much time to allow** 2½ hours. **Author's rating** ★★★★★; don't miss the best cultural-history museum in Hawaii and the Pacific, now expanded to include an exciting new Island science center.

DESCRIPTION AND COMMENTS The Bernice Pauahi Bishop Museum boasts the world's largest collection of Hawaiian and Pacific artifacts. But with the addition of its new $40 million Science Adventure Center exhibit, the Bishop also makes a much-needed foray into natural sciences, especially Hawaii's volcanoes, oceans, and biodiversity. The 16,500-square-foot, state-of-the-art interactive exhibit sends visitors along a Hawaii-origins tunnel to operate submersible robots in a deep-ocean zone, where a replicated Loihi is growing into a new volcano, and enables them to interact with live insects and explore island evolution in the Living Islands Gallery. They are also able to climb up to a tree house perch, go down through a lava tube for a view of a 26-foot-high, periodically erupting volcano, and even experiment with actual molten rock. The exhibit is laid out in a circle like a caldera, and future additions are planned to study Hawaii's oceans, skies, plants, and animals. The museum is a public science center in a state with a natural environment unique in the world.

But save time for the riveting cultural exhibits in the rest of the Bishop that suggest the history of the Pacific. Literally thousands of cultural treasures are housed here, including ancient weaponry, feather cloaks, clothing, jewelry, koa bowls, photographs, illustrations, and even a re-created Hawaiian grass *hale* (house). At the entrance to the museum, you'll see the gift shop to the left (be sure to pay a visit before you leave, as the shop carries an impressive line of Hawaiian books, artwork, crafts, and souvenirs) and a small exhibit on Hawaii's political history. From the ticket office, proceed to Hawaiian Hall, the stone building that houses the bulk of the museum's Hawaiian artifacts. The galleries here provide a powerful look into Hawaii's past, with items such as chiefs' feather capes, weapons made of sharks teeth, and the finely decorated *kapa* cloth Hawaiians of old made from mulberry bark. The planetarium tells how ancient Polynesian voyagers used the stars to navigate their arduous journeys throughout the Pacific.

Also, sports fan should seek out the Hawaii Sports Hall of Fame, located in the Paki Building, which pays tribute to Hawaii's most storied athletes, coaches, promoters, and other sports figures. Among them are Olympic Gold Medal swimmer-surfer Duke Kahanamoku, Alexander J. Cartwright (the father of baseball, who lived in Hawaii for much of his life), sumo pioneer Jesse "Takamiyama" Kuhaulua, and legendary female surfer Rell Sunn.

TOURING TIPS Guided tours of the museum's Hawaiian Hall are scheduled daily at 10 a.m. and noon. A garden tour is held at 12:30 p.m. The Journey by Starlight program at the planetarium is conducted daily at 11:30 a.m.

Byodo-In Temple WINDWARD OAHU

| APPEAL BY AGE | PRESCHOOL ★★ | GRADE SCHOOL ★★ | TEENS ★★ |
| YOUNG ADULTS ★★ | | OVER 30 ★★ | SENIORS ★★★½ |

Valley of the Temples Memorial Park, 47-200 Kahekili Highway; ☎ 808-239-8811

Admission $2 for adults; $1 for senior citizens and children ages 6–12. Hours Daily, 9 a.m.–4 p.m. When to go Anytime. How much time to allow 45 minutes. Author's rating ★★; a peaceful spot to visit.

DESCRIPTION AND COMMENTS Nestled at the foot of the scenic Koolau Mountains, the Byodo-In Temple is a replica of the famous 900-year-old temple in Japan. A stroll of the temple grounds leads you to an immaculate Oriental garden, a colorful carp pool, a nine-foot-tall Buddha statue, and a stately teahouse. Peacocks, swans, ducks, and shimmering waterfalls add to the scenery.

Contemporary Museum GREATER HONOLULU

| APPEAL BY AGE | PRESCHOOL ★★ | GRADE SCHOOL ★★½ | TEENS ★★★½ |
| YOUNG ADULTS ★★★½ | | OVER 30 ★★★½ | SENIORS ★★★½ |

2411 Makiki Heights Drive; ☎ 808-526-1322; www.tcmhi.org

Admission $5 for adults; $3 for students with valid ID and senior citizens; free for children under age 12. Hours Tuesday–Saturday, 10 a.m.–4 p.m.; Sunday, noon–4 p.m.; closed Mondays and major holidays. **When to go** The museum is free to all on the third Thursday of each month. **How much time to allow** 75 minutes. **Author's rating** ★★★; if you love modern art, you'll enjoy this.

DESCRIPTION AND COMMENTS Originally built in 1925 as a residence of a wealthy socialite, the Contemporary Museum opened its doors in 1988 as a modern-art collection. The small museum features 1,300 works, dating from 1940 to the present, on rotating exhibits. A special highlight is a permanent walk-in multimedia exhibit by David Hockney, inspired by Maurice Ravel's opera *L'Enfant et les Sortileges*.

You'll probably spend as much time outside the museum as you will inside. The museum's 3.5-acre garden is dotted by a variety of bronze, ceramic, stainless-steel, copper, and aluminum sculptures. The garden was originally created in the 1930s by a Honolulu reverend with a passion for landscape design, and it remains a blissful retreat. The Contemporary Café is a favorite spot for lunch, and shoppers will want to visit the museum's gift boutique.

OTHER THINGS TO DO NEARBY Continue your drive up Mount Tantalus to see sweeping views of Honolulu.

Damien Museum WAIKIKI

APPEAL BY AGE	PRESCHOOL ★	GRADE SCHOOL ★	TEENS ★★½
YOUNG ADULTS ★★		OVER 30 ★★	SENIORS ★★

St. Augustine by the Sea Church grounds, 130 Ohua Avenue;
☎ **808-923-2690**

Admission Free, donations welcomed. **Hours** Monday–Friday, 9 a.m.–3 p.m.; plus every 3rd and 4th Sunday of the month. **When to go** Anytime. **How much time to allow** 30 minutes. **Author's rating** ★★½; make a pilgrimage to this shrine before you go to Molokai and Kalaupapa.

DESCRIPTION AND COMMENTS This minimuseum houses several artifacts belonging to Father Damien de Veuster (1840–1889), the Belgian priest who dedicated his life to caring for leprosy patients at Kalaupapa settlement on Molokai. Among the displays are some of Father Damien's possessions, including books, tools, candlesticks, and personal letters. A 20-minute video, available for $25, highlights the minister's life and reflects on this sad chapter in Hawaiian history.

OTHER THINGS TO DO NEARBY The Honolulu Zoo and Kapiolani Park are a block away, and Waikiki Beach beckons just across Kalakaua Avenue.

Dole Plantation CENTRAL OAHU

APPEAL BY AGE	PRESCHOOL ★½	GRADE SCHOOL ★★★★	TEENS ★★★
YOUNG ADULTS ★★★		OVER 30 ★★★	SENIORS ★★★

64-1550 Kamehameha Highway, Wahiawa; ☎ **808-621-8408;**
www.doleplantation.com

Admission Plantation free; Pineapple Express: $7.50 for adults, $5.50 for children; Pineapple Garden Maze: $4.50 for adults, $2.50 for children; free self-guided tour of the plantation. **Hours** Daily, 9 a.m.–5:30 p.m. **When to go** Anytime. **How much time to allow** 90 minutes. **Author's rating** ★½; the maze is more popular than the pineapple.

DESCRIPTION AND COMMENTS Situated just outside the town of Wahiawa, the Dole Plantation features outdoor displays on Hawaii's pineapple history as well as the life of the plantation's founder, Jim Dole. Sample some pineapple juice and stroll through the Pineapple Garden, which features 21 different varieties of the prickly fruit. Since its debut in 1998, the biggest attraction here (and the one the children most want to see) is the Pineapple Garden Maze, which covers nearly two acres and has a path length of 1.7 miles. The maze was built from 11,400 Hawaiian plants, including varieties of the state flower, the hibiscus. In 1998, the *Guinness Book of World Records* dubbed it the world's largest maze.

Doris Duke's Shangri-La GREATER HONOLULU

| APPEAL BY AGE | PRESCHOOL ★ | GRADE SCHOOL ★★ | TEENS ★★★ |
| YOUNG ADULTS ★★★★ | OVER 30 ★★★★ | SENIORS ★★★★★ |

Honolulu Academy of Arts, 900 South Beretania Street;
☎ **808-532-8701; www.shangrilahawaii.org**

Admission $25. **Hours** Tuesday–Saturday, 10 a.m.–4:30 p.m. **When to go** Wednesday–Saturday. **How much time to allow** Up to 3 hours for tour and round-trip from Honolulu to Black Point. **Author's rating** ★★★★★; a unique palace of art, history, and culture.

DESCRIPTION AND COMMENTS Inspired by the Taj Mahal and built by the late Doris Duke, the "richest little girl in the world," Shangri-La is a $100 million Islamic-style palace on five oceanfront acres at exclusive Black Point. Once a private enclave, it is now open to the public on limited tours by the Honolulu Academy of Art. Inside the seldom seen or photographed 14,000-square-foot palace is one of the most extensive collections of Islamic art, paintings, ceramics, and textiles in the United States, more than 3,500 objects collected by Duke over six decades.

The mansion itself is a work of art, with painted ceilings, elaborately carved doorways, inlaid stone, and mosaic-tile panels set amid lush gardens and a saltwater swimming pool at the edge of the Pacific.

A part-time Oahu resident, the tobacco heiress died in 1993 at age 80 at her Beverly Hills estate, Falcon's Lair. Born November 22, 1912, in New York City, Duke was the daughter of James Buchanan "Buck" Duke, the tobacco tycoon who founded American Tobacco Company, maker of Lucky Strike cigarettes. When her father died in 1925, the 13-year-old Duke inherited $30 million. Educated in Europe, she founded Duke University in North Carolina, funded the Doris Duke Foundation, and became an orchid grower and patron of New York City's Metropolitan Museum of Art. In her will, she created the Doris Duke Foundation for Islamic Art to "promote the study and understanding of Middle Eastern art and culture" and to manage her Honolulu home as an art center open to the public.

TOURING TIPS The $25 tour, conducted Wednesday through Saturday, originates at the Honolulu Academy of Arts, where tour participants get an orientation through educational programs and exhibits on Islamic art and culture before their visit to Shangri-La. Visitors are shuttled to and from Shangri-La and escorted though the estate in small groups. Make reservations far in advance at **www.honoluluacademy.org**.

OTHER THINGS TO DO NEARBY Black Point is one of Honolulu's most private, upscale neighborhoods; you will ooh and ahh at the houses and may even spot someone rich and famous out walking their dog or working on their tan. The ocean view from the Duke mansion is one in $100 million.

Foster Botanical Garden GREATER HONOLULU

APPEAL BY AGE	PRESCHOOL ★★	GRADE SCHOOL ★★½	TEENS ★★★
YOUNG ADULTS ★★★	OVER 30 ★★★½		SENIORS ★★★½

50 North Vineyard Boulevard; ☎ 808-522-7066

Admission $5 for adults; $1 for children ages 6–12. **Hours** Daily, 9 a.m.–4 p.m. **When to go** In the morning, when it's coolest. **How much time to allow** 1 hour. **Author's rating** ★★★; a thoroughly pleasant outing.

DESCRIPTION AND COMMENTS One of Oahu's most popular tropical gardens, on the edge of downtown Honolulu, is a beautiful 14-acre oasis. Foster Botanical Garden boasts one of the nation's largest collections of tropical plants, including many rare and endangered species. Among the highlights are an exquisite orchid garden, several rare and endangered trees, an herb garden, and an "economic" garden, which displays plants that are used for food, fabrics, dyes, and medicine. Foster Botanical Garden was placed on the Hawaii Register of Historic Places in 1988 and has been the setting for several Hollywood films and TV shows. It is the best known of Honolulu's five municipal botanical gardens.

TOURING TIPS Guided tours are available weekdays at 1 p.m. Call for reservations.

Hawaii Children's Discovery Center
GREATER HONOLULU

APPEAL BY AGE	PRESCHOOL ★★★★	GRADE SCHOOL ★★★★★	TEENS ★★★★
YOUNG ADULTS ★★★½	OVER 30 ★★★		SENIORS ★★★

111 Ohe Street; ☎ 808-524-5437; www.discoverycenterhawaii.org

Admission $10 for adults and children; $6 for seniors. No strollers permitted in the exhibit area. **Hours** Tuesday–Friday, 9 a.m.–1 p.m.; Saturday and Sunday, 10 a.m.–3 p.m. **When to go** Anytime. **How much time to allow** 2 hours. **Author's rating** ★★★★; excellent children's museum; the kids will love it.

DESCRIPTION AND COMMENTS Originally opened in 1989 as the Hawaii Children's Museum at Dole Cannery, the $10 million Children's Discovery Center reopened in 1998 at a larger, 37,000-square-foot location. Four separate galleries—Fantastic You, Our Town, Hawaiian Rainbows, and Your Rainbow World—are featured on three floors, each with a variety of hands-on, interactive galleries designed for children. Our favorites were

Fantastic You, which helps children understand their bodies and organs, and Our Town, which features a working television station that lets children take on roles as news anchors and camera technicians. A gift shop sells a variety of toys, games, and books. A spokesperson once explained its mission this way: "The museum isn't really to educate children. Instead, it's to motivate them, stimulate them, to arouse their curiosity about things, and to give them an excitement and joy about learning."

OTHER THINGS TO DO NEARBY Kakaako Waterfront Park, directly across the street, provides a great picnic setting.

Hawaii Maritime Center GREATER HONOLULU

| APPEAL BY AGE | PRESCHOOL ★★ | GRADE SCHOOL ★★★ | TEENS ★★★ |
| YOUNG ADULTS ★★★½ | OVER 30 ★★★½ | SENIORS ★★★½ |

Pier 7, Honolulu Harbor; ☎ 808-536-6373; www.holoholo.org/maritime

Admission $15.95 for adults; $12.95 for seniors age 65 and over and for children ages 6–17. **Hours** Daily, 8:30 a.m.–5 p.m. **When to go** Anytime. **How much time to allow** 75 minutes. **Author's rating** ★★★; if you love ocean history and messing around with boats, see this shipshape museum.

DESCRIPTION AND COMMENTS Hawaii's colorful ocean history is the story line, from ancient Polynesian voyagers and rowdy whalers to the legendary Waikiki beach boys and luxury liners of the 1920s and 1930s. Take an audio tour and browse through 50 displays, including a skeleton of a humpback whale (one of only two such displays in the world). Two major attractions here are the Falls of Clyde (built in 1817) and the well-traveled Polynesian voyaging canoe Hokulea. You can board the Falls of Clyde, which is the last four-masted, full-rigged ship in the world and a National Historic Landmark. The Hokulea is a double-hulled sailing canoe in which modern Hawaiians retraced the voyages of ancient Polynesians in the 1970s and 1980s using only the stars and ocean currents to guide them.

OTHER THINGS TO DO NEARBY The Aloha Tower Marketplace is next door.

Hawaii's Plantation Village CENTRAL OAHU

| APPEAL BY AGE | PRESCHOOL ★ | GRADE SCHOOL ★★ | TEENS ★★½ |
| YOUNG ADULTS ★★★ | OVER 30 ★★★ | SENIORS ★★★ |

94-695 Waipahu Street; ☎ 808-677-0110;
www.hawaiiplantationvillage.org

Admission $13 for adults; $10 for seniors; $7 for military personnel; $5 for children ages 5–17. **Hours** Monday–Saturday, guided tours every hour, 10 a.m.–2 p.m. **When to go** Anytime. **How much time to allow** 90 minutes. **Author's rating** ★★★; best place to learn about Hawaii's plantation history.

DESCRIPTION AND COMMENTS Located in the former plantation town of Waipahu, this outdoor museum pays tribute to Hawaii's plantation era. Included are artifacts, household items, photos, and documents representing the cultures and lifestyles of eight different ethnic groups that labored on the sugar plantations: Japanese, Chinese, Okinawans, Filipinos,

Koreans, Puerto Ricans, Portuguese, and Hawaiians. Nearly 30 replicated dwellings dot the village's three acres, including a Chinese cookhouse, a plantation store, and a community bath. The different types of architecture illustrate the cultural differences of those workers and how they had to figure out how to get along while living together so closely.

Hawaiian Railway LEEWARD OAHU

APPEAL BY AGE	PRESCHOOL ★★	GRADE SCHOOL ★★★	TEENS ★★★
YOUNG ADULTS ★★★	OVER 30 ★★★		SENIORS ★★★

91-1001 Renton Road; ☎ 808-681-5461

Admission $10 for adults; $7 for seniors and children ages 2–12; $20 per seat in parlor car. **Hours** Sundays only, 1 p.m. and 3 p.m. (charter groups can schedule weekday rides). **When to go** Anytime. **How much time to allow** 2 hours. **Author's rating** ★★½; for train buffs.

DESCRIPTION AND COMMENTS These old tracks and locomotives used to transport sugarcane, but now they haul Sunday passengers, with an ocean view from the open cars or a taste of Victorian style in the restored parlor car. In the heyday of Hawaii's plantation era, more than 40 sugar plantations utilized private railway systems to transport their crops. Today, Hawaiian Railway Society members strive to preserve what's left of Hawaii's railroad history on Oahu. They restored this 6.5-mile stretch of track, three vintage diesel locomotives, and the fancy parlor car, built for Oahu Railway and Land Co. founder Benjamin Dillingham in 1900, decked with iron grillwork and fluted awnings outside and wood paneling, rugs, and leather chairs inside. Queen Liliuokalani and other royals were guests in those days; now the royal treatment is enjoyed by charter groups and travelers on the second Sunday of the month. The 90-minute ride begins at the Ewa station and travels at a leisurely pace of 15 miles per hour. Trained narrators tell of Hawaii's railway history, explain how the trains were used by plantations, and point out sites along the way. The end of the line, literally, is scenic Kahe Point, where passengers can spend a few minutes enjoying views of the Pacific Ocean.

Honolulu Academy of Arts GREATER HONOLULU

APPEAL BY AGE	PRESCHOOL ★½	GRADE SCHOOL ★★½	TEENS ★★★
YOUNG ADULTS ★★★½	OVER 30 ★★★★		SENIORS ★★★★

900 South Beretania Street; ☎ 808-532-8701 or 808-532-8700; www.honoluluacademy.org

Admission $10 for adults; $5 for students, seniors, and military personnel; free for children age 12 and under. **Hours** Tuesday–Saturday, 10 a.m.–4:30 p.m.; Sunday, 1–5 p.m.; docent-guided tours are free; a new audio tour is $5 additional. **When to go** Anytime. **How much time to allow** 2 hours. **Author's rating** ★★★★; the biggest and best Hawaiian art museum.

DESCRIPTION AND COMMENTS Founded by Anna Rice Cooke, the Hawaiian-born daughter of New England missionaries, the Honolulu Academy of

Arts opened in 1927 with 4,500 donated works of art. That number has grown to more than 34,000 pieces, ranging from paintings and textiles to sculptures and prints. With 32 galleries and 34,000 works of art from cultures around the globe, Honolulu Academy of Arts long ago achieved its reputation as the premier East-West art center. Now the academy presents the best at last: the art of Hawaii. Hawaii-themed artworks are a primary feature of the new two-story, $9 million Henry R. Luce Pavilion Complex. The complex welcomes visitors with a skylight by contemporary American glass artist Dale Chihuly and four outdoor sculptures called *Dangos* (a Japanese word for dumpling) by Japanese artist Jan Kaneko. Once inside you discover two 4,000-square-foot galleries, one for traveling exhibits and the other dedicated to Hawaii. Unrivaled anywhere, the Hawaii gallery (named for John Dominis and Patches Damon Holt) chronicles the history of the Islands from pen-and-ink sketches of John Webber (1752–1793), who accompanied Captain James Cook on his voyages to Hawaii and gave the Western world its first glimpses of exotic Hawaiians and island lifestyle, to erotic works by Georgia O'Keeffe (1887–1986), who came to Hawaii to paint pineapples in 1939 for the Hawaii Pineapple Company (later Dole Corporation), but grew bored and began painting vaguely suggestive waterfalls and tropical flowers. On display are some of Hawaii's most vivid works of art—*Hawaiian Fisherman* by Dutch portrait artist Hubert Vos (1855–1935); triptych *Egrets and Pandanus* by Hilo-born Lloyd Sexton (1912–1990); and *The Lei Maker* by San Francisco painter Theodore Wores (1859–1939). The fiery canvases of the Volcano School artists—a self-titled group of artists and friends who painted volcanoes and included Jules Tavernier (1844–1889), Charles Furneaux (1835–1913), and D. Howard Hitchcock (1862–1943)—are worth the price of admission. Funded by the late Clare Boothe Luce, a Honolulu resident and former Secretary of the Treasury, the Luce Pavilion is named for her husband, Henry Luce, the late co-founder and editor in chief of *Time* magazine.

The Western art collection includes Roman, Greek, and Egyptian works that date as far back as the third millennium BC and American and European works of the 1990s. The academy's collection of Asian works is among the most highly regarded in the country and includes paintings, sculptures, ceramics, lacquer ware, and prints. Of special note is the sizable collection—more than 8,000 works in all—of Japanese wood-block prints, most of which were donated by the famous American novelist James Michener. The collection represents the wood-block printmaking masters of Japan in the 18th and 19th centuries. Also, the academy's collection of Chinese works includes more than 100 paintings, some of which date back to the Ming dynasty.

TOURING TIPS Guided tours are scheduled at 11 a.m. Tuesday through Saturday and 1:15 p.m. on Sunday. The museum is fairly large, and the tour will likely make your visit here more enjoyable.

OTHER THINGS TO DO NEARBY The academy's Pavilion Café is an ideal place for lunch. Across the street is Thomas Square Park, a leafy green space where arts-and-crafts fairs are frequently held on weekends.

kids Honolulu Zoo WAIKIKI

APPEAL BY AGE	PRESCHOOL ★★★★	GRADE SCHOOL ★★★★★	TEENS ★★★½
YOUNG ADULTS ★★★½	OVER 30 ★★★		SENIORS ★★★★

151 Kapahulu Avenue, Kapiolani Park; the entrance is on the *ma kai* side of the zoo; ☎ 808-926-3191; www.honoluluzoo.org

Admission $12 for visitors age 13 and over; $3 for children ages 4–12; free for children under age 4. **Hours** Daily, 9 a.m.–4:30 p.m., closed on Christmas and New Year's Day; special "Moonlight Walks" are offered from 6:30 to 8:30 p.m. once a month, before the full moon. **When to go** Anytime. **How much time to allow** 2 hours. **Author's rating** ★★★; a zoo is a zoo, but why not if you've had enough sun?

DESCRIPTION AND COMMENTS Set on 42 acres at Kapiolani Park, the Honolulu Zoo is the largest zoo for 2,300 miles. It is also big on history: the land for the zoo was donated in 1876 by King Kalakaua, Hawaii's "Merrie Monarch." The zoo began exhibiting animals in 1914; a monkey, a bear, and a few lion cubs were among the first furry occupants. Today, the roster of wildlife has expanded to include more than 120 different species divided into four separate exhibits. The African savanna includes lions, hippos, gazelles, rhinoceroses, giraffes, zebras, cheetahs, chimpanzees, crocodiles, warthogs, hyenas, flamingos, tortoises, pelicans, and more. The tropical rain forest features tigers, monkeys, sun bears, gibbons, alligators, black swans, Amazon parrots, king vultures, toucans, Burmese pythons, iguanas, and the zoo's biggest (literally) attractions: Mari and Vaigai, a pair of Indian elephants. A popular spot for the kids is the Children's Zoo, with a variety of donkeys, sheep, llamas, potbellied pigs, and farm animals. The Islands of the Pacific exhibit spotlights a few indigenous bird and reptile species. The zoo has several spots for picnicking, and food stands and strollers are available. Also, the Zootique gift shop carries an impressive selection of wildlife-related merchandise that stresses education as well as fun.

TOURING TIPS The zoo holds twilight tours every Saturday from 5:30 p.m. to 7:30 p.m. ($12 for adults, $8 for kids 4–12) to reveal what the animals do when the sun goes down and the zoo gates close. Purchase tickets in advance at the zoo's front desk.

OTHER THINGS TO DO NEARBY The zoo is located at Kapiolani Park, a great place for picnicking. The Waikiki Aquarium is within easy walking distance, as is Waikiki Beach.

Iolani Palace GREATER HONOLULU

APPEAL BY AGE	PRESCHOOL —	GRADE SCHOOL ★★½	TEENS ★★★½
YOUNG ADULTS ★★★★½	OVER 30 ★★★★½		SENIORS ★★★★½

364 South King Street; ☎ 808-522-0832; www.iolanipalace.org

Admission Grand tour: $20 for adults; $5 for children ages 5–17; children under age 5 are not allowed in the palace. **Reservations** are suggested. **Hours**

Tuesday–Saturday, 9 a.m.–2 p.m. Gallery tour: $6 adults, $3 kids over 5. **Hours** Tuesday–Saturday, 9 a.m.–4 p.m. **When to go** Anytime. **How much time to allow** 1–2 hours. **Author's rating** ★ ★ ★ ★ ½; this fairy-tale Italianate structure is the only true palace in America, the last monument to the Hawaiian Monarchy Period and one of Hawaii's architectural treasures.

DESCRIPTION AND COMMENTS Built in 1882, Iolani Palace, the only royal residence on American soil, was the official home of Hawaii's last two monarchs, King Kalakaua and later Queen Liliuokalani (although it is reported the royals actually preferred living in a grass house near the elaborate Western-style palace). In its brief heyday, the palace was the scene of spectacular galas, including the fun-loving Kalakaua's extravagant 50th-birthday jubilee. Sadly, it was also the site of political chaos, which led to the downfall of the kingdom in the late 1890s when it was usurped by American sugar planters who imprisoned the queen in her own bedroom. From then until 1969, when the adjacent State Capitol was completed, the palace served as the capital of the republic, territory, and finally the State of Hawaii, and it suffered extensive deterioration. Iolani was brought back to museum quality in the 1970s, and efforts to embellish and care for the palace continue.

After a $1 million restoration, new galleries have been created in the palace basement to showcase the Hawaiian Crown Jewels—the king's and queen's gold, gem-encrusted crowns and the royal scepter and sword of state—as well as historic photographs and portraits, ancient and Western royal regalia, and relics, including a magnificent ancient yellow-and-red-feather cloak worn by King Kamehameha.

Operated by the nonprofit Friends of Iolani Palace, this remarkable building is open five days a week for docent-guided public tours. The inside is striking, with a large koa-wood staircase serving as a stately centerpiece. The Throne Room, adorned in maroon and gold, was the setting for royal audiences, receptions, and events of state. The Blue Room was the site of informal gatherings and parties. The Dining Room is beautifully appointed with portraits of various world leaders of the past. The second floor includes the King's Suite, the Queen's Room, two guest rooms, and the Music Room.

A royal uproar of more recent vintage occurred in 1998, when the president of Friends of Iolani Palace sat on one of the thrones for a photo session with a magazine photographer. Her faux pas caused some damage to the fabric. Bishop Museum officials later said the throne's silk material was in such deteriorated condition that any touch would have caused damage. The damage was repaired, but the modern-day royal, a great-grandniece of King Kalakaua, was forced to resign.

TOURING TIPS Grand tours include a video presentation and orientation, a docent-led palace tour, and then a self-guided look at the Palace Galleries, the newly created museum in the palace basement. The docent tours are scheduled at 15-minute intervals, each lasting about 45 minutes. Tours with signing for the hearing impaired can be arranged in advance. The gallery tour is self-guided, so that you can see the crown jewels, regalia, and historic photographs at your own pace. Pick up tickets at Iolani Barracks, located on the palace grounds, 15 minutes before your docent tour, then sit down to don paper booties over your shoes to avoid damaging palace floors. The palace is wheelchair accessible; call ahead for special requirements.

OTHER THINGS TO DO NEARBY The Mission Houses Museum, Kamehameha Statue, Hawaii State Archives, Hawaii State Library, and the State Capitol are all within easy walking distance from the palace, and so is downtown Honolulu.

Kualoa Ranch and Activity Club WINDWARD OAHU

| APPEAL BY AGE | PRESCHOOL ★★½ | GRADE SCHOOL ★★★ | TEENS ★★★★ |
| YOUNG ADULTS ★★★★★ | | OVER 30 ★★★★ | SENIORS ★★★ |

49-560 Kamehameha Highway; ☎ 808-237-8515 or 800-231-7321; www.kualoa.com

Admission Rates for individual activities range $15–$87. Hours Daily, 9 a.m.– 5 p.m. When to go Anytime. How much time to allow 2–6 hours. Author's rating ★★★★; offers myriad activities, with something for every age group, outdoors in one of the world's most beautiful settings.

DESCRIPTION AND COMMENTS One of Oahu's best attractions, this 4,000-acre working cattle ranch with six miles of mostly open coastline offers more than 15 outdoor activities. You can spend an entire day here enjoying horseback riding, hiking, all-terrain vehicles, snorkel tours, jet skis, target shooting, canoeing, volleyball, helicopter rides, tennis, a petting zoo, a garden tour, badminton, kayak rides, and a ride around the ranch in an open-sided wagon that includes a narrated ranch and movie-set tour. Kualoa Ranch was the setting for dozens of television shows and Hollywood films, including *Windtalkers, Jurassic Park, Mighty Joe Young,* and *Godzilla*. In addition to its scenic mountainside headquarters and broad coastal valleys, it includes an ancient fishpond, plant nursery, and aquaculture ponds. Our favorite activity here? Relaxing at Secret Island, a remote beach where you can nap in a hammock, play volleyball, go snorkeling, play table tennis, and more.

TOURING TIPS Numerous tour packages are available, most including a buffet lunch and transportation to and from your hotel. You can also go directly to the ranch and sign up for whatever activities interest you.

Mission Houses Museum GREATER HONOLULU

| APPEAL BY AGE | PRESCHOOL ★ | GRADE SCHOOL ★½ | TEENS ★★ |
| YOUNG ADULTS ★★★ | | OVER 30 ★★★ | SENIORS ★★★ |

553 South King Street; ☎ 808-531-0481; www.missionhouses.org

Admission $10 for adults; $8 for seniors and military personnel; $6 for students ages 6 and over. Hours Tuesday–Saturday, 10 a.m.–4 p.m. When to go Anytime. How much time to allow 1 hour. Author's rating ★★★; a good bet for history buffs, but boring for kids.

DESCRIPTION AND COMMENTS This is where the first American Protestant missionaries established their headquarters in 1820. Built between 1821 and 1841, these structures—the oldest surviving Western-style buildings in all of Hawaii—house such original artifacts as furniture, books, quilts, and other household items belonging to missionary families. Visit the white-frame house, which served as home to several of Hawaii's most prominent missionaries; the Chamberlain House, which was used as a storehouse and separate home; and the Coral House, where the first-ever printing in the Pacific was done. The missionaries also introduced the art of New England quilting to Hawaiian women, and this museum has a sizable collection of some early Hawaiian quilts.

TOURING TIPS Guided tours are scheduled at 11 a.m., 1 p.m., and 2:45 p.m.

OTHER THINGS TO DO NEARBY The museum is next to historic Kawaiahao Church and near the Hawaii State Library, Iolani Palace, the State Capitol, Kamehameha Statue, and the State Archives.

National Memorial Cemetery of the Pacific
GREATER HONOLULU

APPEAL BY AGE	PRESCHOOL ½	GRADE SCHOOL ★	TEENS ★
YOUNG ADULTS ★★½	OVER 30 ★★★½		SENIORS ★★★★

2177 Puowaina Drive; ☎ 808-532-3720

Admission Free. Hours Daily: March 2–September 29, 8 a.m.–6:30 p.m.; September 30–March 1, 8 a.m.–5:30 p.m.; Memorial Day, 7 a.m.–7 p.m. When to go Anytime. How much time to allow 1 hour. Author's rating ★★★; a poignant experience for all.

DESCRIPTION AND COMMENTS Also known as Punchbowl (the 112-acre site sits inside Punchbowl Crater), this national cemetery is the final resting place for more than 40,000 war veterans (and their family members) who served the United States in World War II, the Korean War, and the Vietnam War. It is a solemn sight, with rows of small, flat, white headstones stretching far across the crater floor. Among those buried here is famed war correspondent Ernest Taylor "Ernie" Pyle. (While serving as a correspondent with the 77th Infantry Division, Pyle was killed on April 18, 1945, by Japanese gunfire on the small Pacific islet of Ie Shima.) Panoramic views of Waikiki, Honolulu, and Pearl Harbor add to the experience here. Each Easter morning, thousands of Hawaii residents and visitors attend the Sunrise Service.

Pacific Aviation Museum GREATER HONOLULU

APPEAL BY AGE	PRESCHOOL ★★	GRADE SCHOOL ★★★½	TEENS ★★★½
YOUNG ADULTS ★★★★	OVER 30 ★★★★		SENIORS ★★★★

Pearl Harbor Hangar 37, Ford Island, 319 Lexington Boulevard; ☎ 808-441-1000; www.pacificaviationmuseum.org

Admission $14 for adults; $7 for children ages 4–12; Aviator's guided tour: $7; Military, Kama'aina, and school group discounts available. Hours Daily, 9 a.m.–

5 p.m.; ticket office: 8 a.m.–4 p.m.; closed Christmas Day, Thanksgiving Day, and New Year's Day. **When to go** Anytime. **How much time to allow** 1 hour. **Author's rating** ★★★.

DESCRIPTION AND COMMENTS This shrine to military aviation in the Pacific opened on the 65th anniversary of the aerial attack on Pearl Harbor that launched the United States into World War II. It encompasses three hangars on this island in the middle of Pearl Harbor, in which visitors can view aircraft such as a WW II B25 bomber, MIG-15, F-86 Sabre jet from the Korean War, Huey and Cobra helicopters from the Vietnam War era, the Boeing Stearman that former President George H. W. Bush flew as the youngest pilot in WW II, and the little Aeronca biplane that was in the air with a student pilot and civilian instructor when the Japanese attacked.

kids Polynesian Cultural Center THE NORTH SHORE

APPEAL BY AGE	PRESCHOOL ★★	GRADE SCHOOL ★★★★	TEENS ★★★★½
YOUNG ADULTS ★★★★½	OVER 30 ★★★★½		SENIORS ★★★★½

55-370 Kamehameha Highway; ☎ 800-367-7060 or 877-722-1411; www.polynesia.com

Admission General admission is $45 for adults and $35 for children ages 3–11 and includes admission to 7 Polynesian villages, canoe rides, the Pageant of Long Canoes, and a tram tour. Special deluxe packages featuring an IMAX film, a buffet, and the evening show *Horizons* are as follows: Ambassador Package, $120 for adults and $85 for children; Super Ambassador Package, $225 for adults and $175 for children; Luau Package, $100 for adults and $78 for children; Twilight Luau, $88 for adults and $64 for children. Evening show with no dinner option is offered for $60 for adults and $45 for children. **Hours** Monday–Saturday, 12:30–9 p.m.; villages close at 6 p.m. **When to go** Anytime; if you enjoy watching Samoan fire-knife dancers, however, be sure to come during the World Fire-Knife Dance Championships, which are held each year in April or May. **How much time to allow** All day, including 2½ hours' driving time to and from Waikiki. **Author's rating** ★★★★½; most popular paid visitor attraction in Hawaii.

DESCRIPTION AND COMMENTS Set on 42 acres in Laie, home of Brigham Young University–Hawaii, the Polynesian Cultural Center delivers a cultural experience that includes re-created villages representing the cultures of Samoa, Fiji, Tahiti, Tonga, New Zealand, Marquesas, and Hawaii.

Friendly native Pacific Islanders, dressed in traditional attire, share their arts, crafts, songs, and dances. Most of them are students at the neighboring campus. They work part time at the PCC in exchange for tuition, room, board, and books. Hands-on demonstrations include coconut husking, wood carving, *lauhala* weaving, *poi* pounding, and *tapa* making. Waterways and lush gardens are the settings for canoe rides, a tram tour, and a colorful pageant of canoes.

A variety of buffet-and-show packages culminates in an impressive evening show featuring a cast of more than 150 dancers and musicians. Alcohol is not part of the program at this Mormon institution.

Queen Emma Summer Palace GREATER HONOLULU

APPEAL BY AGE	PRESCHOOL ½	GRADE SCHOOL ★★	TEENS ★★½
YOUNG ADULTS ★★½	OVER 30 ★★½		SENIORS ★★½

2913 Pali Highway; ☎ 808-595-3167

Admission $6 for adults; $4 for seniors; $1 for children under age 15. **Hours** Daily, 9 a.m.–4 p.m. **When to go** Anytime. **How much time to allow** 1 hour. **Author's rating** ★★★; worth a visit for Hawaiian history students.

DESCRIPTION AND COMMENTS Maintained and operated by the nonprofit Daughters of Hawaii, this charming white-frame house served as a summer retreat for Queen Emma, consort to Alexander Liholiho (King Kamehameha IV). Many of the queen's possessions are on display here, including an opulent gold necklace and various wedding and baby gifts presented to Emma by England's Queen Victoria. This was among the first Hawaiian properties to be listed on the National Register of Historic Places.

OTHER THINGS TO DO NEARBY Behind the palace, off Puiwa Road, is Nuuanu Valley Park, a serene hideaway favored for its shady trees.

Royal Mausoleum GREATER HONOLULU

APPEAL BY AGE	PRESCHOOL ½	GRADE SCHOOL ★½	TEENS ★★
YOUNG ADULTS ★★	OVER 30 ★★		SENIORS ★★

2261 Nuuanu Avenue; ☎ 808-587-0300

Admission Free. **Hours** Monday–Friday, 8 a.m.–4:30 p.m. **When to go** Anytime. **How much time to allow** 45 minutes. **Author's rating** ★★½; not your typical visitor attraction.

DESCRIPTION AND COMMENTS Considered the most sacred burial ground in the entire state, this three-acre site is the resting place for six of the eight Hawaiian monarchs: Kings Kamehameha II, III, IV, and V; King Kalakaua; and Queen Liliuokalani. (The bones of Kamehameha I were hidden at a secret location on the Kona Coast of the island of Hawaii; William Lunalilo, or Kamehameha VI, per his wishes, was buried in a private tomb on the grounds of Kawaiahao Church.) This current site was prepared in 1865 by Kamehameha V to replace the original royal burial tomb on the grounds of Iolani Palace.

TOURING TIPS Call ahead to arrange for guided tours.

kids Sea Life Park WINDWARD OAHU

APPEAL BY AGE	PRESCHOOL ★★★★	GRADE SCHOOL ★★★★★	TEENS ★★★★
YOUNG ADULTS ★★★★	OVER 30 ★★★★		SENIORS ★★★★

41-202 Kalanianaole Highway; ☎ 866-365-7446; www.sealifeparkhawaii.com

Admission $29 for adults; $19 for children ages 4–12; free for children under age 4. **Hours** Daily, 9:30 a.m.–5 p.m. **When to go** Anytime. **How much time to**

allow 3–4 hours. **Author's rating** ★★★½; even if you have similar attractions back home, this is a family fun spot.

DESCRIPTION AND COMMENTS The first feature you encounter on entering the park is the 300,000-gallon Hawaiian Reef Tank, filled with more than 2,000 species of reef fish, rays, hammerhead sharks, and other colorful marine life. From there, head to the Rocky Shores exhibit, which provides above- and below-water views of marine life in a tidal zone, and then the Sea Turtle Lagoon, where you'll get an up-close look at Hawaii's protected green sea turtles. Children especially will want to drop by the Discovery Pool, where they can hold tiny sea critters, like sea cucumbers and spiny sea stars.

Other don't-miss exhibits include the Sea Lion Pool (you can purchase fish to feed the sea lions), Sea Bird Sanctuary, and Penguin Habitat (home to a successful breeding colony of Humboldt penguins). At Whaler's Cove, you can view the park's performing dolphins, whales, and Kekaimalu, the world's only known "wholphin" (half false killer whale, half dolphin).

The park offers three live shows. The Hawaii Ocean Theater, a 400-seat amphitheater, features performances by bottlenose dolphins, sea lions, and penguins. Whaler's Cove is the site of a show built around the amazing leaps and flips of the bottlenose dolphins. And the Kolohe Kai Sea Lion Show, in Makapuu Meadow, spotlights a group of delightful sea lions and their trainers.

Also on site are the Sea Lion Café and Rabbit Island Bar and Grill. Two gift shops—the Sea Life Park General Store and Little Treasures—offer an assortment of T-shirts, souvenirs, and park-related merchandise.

The special program Dolphin Adventures is offered three times daily. Dolphin Adventures lets you learn how the trainers use positive reinforcement to teach the dolphins. Better yet, you'll have an opportunity to get in the water and interact with specially trained dolphins. The cost is $165 per person, and participants must be at least 13 years of age. Dolphin Royal Swim—the most popular activity here—gets you a dolphin kiss and a thrill ride while you cling to the dorsal fin of two dolphins that take off across the pool with you; $215 per adult or child.

Splash University, meanwhile, also gives you an insider's look at how these friendly mammals are trained. You'll learn a few signals that dolphins respond to and participate in training sessions during shallow-water interaction. The cost is $104 for adults and $72 for children ages 4–12 (children under age 12 must be accompanied by an adult). Splash University is held four times daily.

The Hawaiian Ray Encounter program offers participants an opportunity to swim with rays and learn their eating habits. The cost is $15 per person.

Tuition costs include general admission into Sea Life Park. Each program lasts approximately one hour. Be sure to bring swimwear and a towel. Call ☎ 808-259-2500 for more information or to make a reservation.

TOURING TIPS The Hawaiian Reef Show begins at 9:50 a.m.; Hawaii Ocean Theater at 10 a.m.; Kolohe Kai Sea Lion Show at 11 a.m.; and Whaler's Cove at 11:15 a.m. The show rotation continues throughout the day, with the final set starting at 2:45 p.m.

OTHER THINGS TO DO NEARBY Sandy Beach and Makapuu Beach are just a few minutes away by car.

Senator Fong's Plantation and Gardens WINDWARD OAHU

APPEAL BY AGE	PRESCHOOL ★★	GRADE SCHOOL ★★½	TEENS ★★★
YOUNG ADULTS ★★★	OVER 30 ★★★★	SENIORS ★★★★	

47-285 Pulama Road, Kaneohe; ☎ 808-239-6775; www.fonggarden.com

Admission $14.50 for adults; $13 for seniors; $9 for children ages 5–12. **Hours** Daily, 10 a.m.–4 p.m. **When to go** Anytime. **How much time to allow** 90 minutes. **Author's rating** ★★★; a Windward Oahu outing featuring family-style aloha spirit.

DESCRIPTION AND COMMENTS Hiram Fong was the first Asian-American to serve in the U.S. Senate, retiring in 1977. Fong's family runs this 725-acre private estate, with tropical flower gardens, more than 100 different fruits and nuts, and scenic views of Windward Oahu. Hands-on activities here include lei-making lessons using flowers picked from nearby gardens. A 50-minute tram tour takes visitors through valleys and tropical forests. A snack bar, fruit stand, and gift shop are on site.

TOURING TIPS Narrated tram tours are scheduled frequently throughout the day; reservations are not needed.

Tropic Lightning Museum CENTRAL OAHU

APPEAL BY AGE	PRESCHOOL ★	GRADE SCHOOL ★	TEENS ★★
YOUNG ADULTS ★★	OVER 30 ★★	SENIORS ★★★★	

Schofield Barracks; ☎ 808-655-0438

Admission Free. **Hours** Tuesday–Saturday, 10 a.m.–4 p.m. **When to go** Anytime. **How much time to allow** 30 minutes. **Author's rating** ★★½; an attraction strictly for military buffs.

DESCRIPTION AND COMMENTS This cozy museum documents the history of Schofield Barracks and the famed "Tropic Lightning" 25th Infantry Division, which fought in World War II, the Korean War, and the Vietnam War.

U.S. Army Museum WAIKIKI

APPEAL BY AGE	PRESCHOOL ★	GRADE SCHOOL ★★	TEENS ★★
YOUNG ADULTS ★★★	OVER 30 ★★★½	SENIORS ★★★★	

Battery Randolph, Fort DeRussy, at the intersection of Kalia and Saratoga roads, next to the Hale Koa Hotel; validated parking available in Fort DeRussy's Saratoga parking lot; ☎ 808-438-2821

Admission Donations accepted. **Hours** Tuesday–Sunday, 10 a.m.–4:30 p.m. **When to go** Anytime. **How much time to allow** 1 hour. **Author's rating**

★★★½; a wealth of war memorabilia, and you can't beat the price.

DESCRIPTION AND COMMENTS Built in 1909, the Battery Randolph served as an imposing military fortress, ready to defend Waikiki from attacking battleships. (It was a part of the military's "Ring of Steel" that encircled Oahu.) However, when it outlived its usefulness, officials faced a dilemma: the structure was nearly impossible to tear down. Its walls were 22 feet thick (solid concrete) and built to withstand a direct hit from a 2,000-ton artillery shell. Any attempt to bring it down with explosives would undoubtedly cause damage in the surrounding areas of Waikiki. In 1976, the battery was transformed into the 13,500-square-foot U.S. Army Museum, recalling the history of the American army in the Pacific.

Included here are more than 2,000 artifacts and 1,900 photographs tracing the U.S. military's presence in Hawaii. The artifacts range from small (medals and tags) to huge (a Japanese battle tank). One popular exhibit pays tribute to the 100th/442nd Regimental Combat Team, a unit made up of local and mainland Japanese-American men who overcame prejudice to enlist in the U.S. Army during World War II. They became the most highly decorated unit in the war, living up to their battle cry of "Go for broke." A gift shop is available on the premises.

USS *Arizona* Memorial CENTRAL OAHU

APPEAL BY AGE	PRESCHOOL ★½	GRADE SCHOOL ★★★	TEENS ★★★½
YOUNG ADULTS ★★★½	OVER 30 ★★★★½	SENIORS ★★★★★	

1 Arizona Memorial Place; ☎ 808-422-0561 or 808-422-2771; www.arizonamemorial.org

Admission Free. **Hours** Daily, 7:30 a.m.–5 p.m.; program runs 8 a.m.–3 p.m., weather permitting (shuttle boats to the memorial leave every 15 minutes). **When to go** Anytime. **How much time to allow** Between 2 and 4 hours; due to the popularity of this attraction (estimated 4,500 visitors a day), you are likely to wait in line for an hour or more. The program itself lasts about 75 minutes. **Author's rating** ★★★★; a solemn, moving experience.

DESCRIPTION AND COMMENTS The museum exhibits historic photos and touching memorabilia from December 7, 1941, the day Japanese warplanes bombed Pearl Harbor. You can see a 23-minute film depicting the attack as well as events that led to it. Then you are transported to the memorial via shuttle boat. The memorial is a white structure that sits over the sunken *Arizona,* where 1,102 men went down with the ship and remain entombed. A marble wall pays tribute to the 1,177 sailors and marines who perished during the surprise attack. The memorial, designed by a Honolulu architect, was made possible after a benefit concert staged in Honolulu in 1961 by an ex-G.I. by the name of Elvis Presley.

TOURING TIPS Tickets are issued on a first-come, first-served basis. Each guest must pick up his or her own ticket in person at the ticket office. An audio headset is available for a nominal fee.

OTHER THINGS TO DO NEARBY The USS Battleship *Missouri* and USS *Bowfin* Submarine and Park are both in the immediate vicinity.

USS Battleship *Missouri* Memorial CENTRAL OAHU

APPEAL BY AGE	PRESCHOOL ★½	GRADE SCHOOL ★★★	TEENS ★★★½
YOUNG ADULTS ★★★½	OVER 30 ★★★★½		SENIORS ★★★½

Ford Island, Pier Fox Trot 5; ☎ 808-423-2263 or 877-MIGHTY-MO; www.ussmissouri.com

Admission General admission: $16 for adults; $8 for children ages 4–12. **Hours** Daily, 9 a.m.–5 p.m. **When to go** Anytime. **How much time to allow** 90 minutes–2 hours. **Author's rating** ★★★★; forms an appropriate bookend to the USS *Arizona* Memorial.

DESCRIPTION AND COMMENTS One of America's most storied battleships now calls Pearl Harbor home as an interactive museum and memorial. The 45,000-ton "Mighty Mo" is the last of four Iowa-class battleships built during World War II. It was on the deck of the *Missouri* that Japan officially surrendered to the allied forces, marking the end of World War II in the Pacific theater. The *Missouri* earned three battle stars for missions in Iwo Jima, Okinawa, and Japan during that war, then five more while serving in the Korean War. The *Missouri* also served during the Persian Gulf War. In 1986, it became the first battleship to circumnavigate the world.

Buses transport visitors to Ford Island, where the ship is anchored. Touring Mighty Mo, which is nearly three football fields long, you'll be able to view documents and photographs and hear a portion of a speech made by General Douglas MacArthur.

TOURING TIPS The "Chief's Guided Tour" includes an hour-long tour led by a crew member: $22 for adults; $14 for children ages 4–12. A recorded "AcoustiGuide" tour, with nearly two hours of recorded information, is available for the same prices. Tickets must be purchased before 4 p.m.

OTHER THINGS TO DO NEARBY The USS *Arizona* Memorial and USS *Bowfin* Submarine Museum and Park.

USS *Bowfin* Submarine Museum and Park CENTRAL OAHU

APPEAL BY AGE	PRESCHOOL ★½	GRADE SCHOOL ★★★	TEENS ★★★½
YOUNG ADULTS ★★★½	OVER 30 ★★★★		SENIORS ★★★★½

11 Arizona Memorial Drive; ☎ 808-423-1341; www.bowfin.org

Admission Entry to both the museum and submarine: $10 for adults; $6 for seniors and military personnel; $3 for children ages 4–12. (Children under 4 are not allowed on the sub but can visit the museum free) Entry to museum only: $4 for adults; $2 for children ages 4–12. **Hours** Daily, 8 a.m.–5 p.m. **When to go** Anytime. **How much time to allow** 1–1½ hours. **Author's rating** ★★★½; excellent for military-history buffs.

DESCRIPTION AND COMMENTS Nicknamed the "Pearl Harbor Avenger," the *Bowfin* is credited with sinking 44 enemy ships on nine patrols. It is one of only 15 remaining World War II U.S. submarines. Visitors can check out the interior of the vessel and examine defused torpedoes. The park houses a museum filled with submarine history, featuring outdoor exhibits and a minitheater.

OTHER THINGS TO DO NEARBY The USS *Arizona* Memorial and USS Battleship *Missouri* Memorial.

kids Waikiki Aquarium WAIKIKI

APPEAL BY AGE	PRESCHOOL ★★★★	GRADE SCHOOL ★★★★½	TEENS ★★★★
YOUNG ADULTS ★★★★½	OVER 30 ★★★★½		SENIORS ★★★★½

2777 Kalakaua Avenue; ☎ 808-923-9741; www.waquarium.org

Admission $9 for adults; $6 for seniors, military personnel, and college students; $4 for children ages 13–17 and people with disabilities; $2 for children ages 5–12. **Hours** Daily, 9 a.m.–5 p.m. **When to go** Anytime. **How much time to allow** 1 hour. **Author's rating** ★★★★½; excellent small aquarium by the sea.

DESCRIPTION AND COMMENTS The Waikiki Aquarium's history is no mere fish story. Built in 1904, it is the third-oldest public aquarium in the United States and has distinguished itself as a living classroom for anyone interested in Hawaii ocean life. The aquarium is one of the first facilities in the world to successfully breed mahimahi (also known as dolphin fish), and the first in the United States to breed the chambered nautilus. Although not very large, the facility houses more than 2,500 ocean creatures representing some 420 different species, and it's very accessible in Kapiolani Park, a short walk or number 2 TheBus ride from central Waikiki. Here you can learn about endangered species, like the Hawaiian monk seal, and threatened species, like the Hawaiian green sea turtle. A gallery of aquariums display colorful reef fish, coral, a giant clam, jellyfish, and mahimahi. It's a great companion experience for your snorkeling adventures. In addition to the live exhibits, several educational classes focus on Hawaii's marine environment.

TOURING TIPS Live 24-7 cameras let you tune in via the Internet to watch sharks and other hunters in their tank, coral-reef creatures doing their thing and Hawaiian monk seals lazing around. More Webcasts are planned.

OTHER THINGS TO DO NEARBY The Honolulu Zoo is within walking distance.

Waimea Valley Audubon Center NORTH SHORE

APPEAL BY AGE	PRESCHOOL ★★	GRADE SCHOOL ★★★	TEENS ★★★★
YOUNG ADULTS ★★★★	OVER 30 ★★★★		SENIORS ★★★★

59-864 Kamehameha Highway, Waimea; ☎ 808-638-9199

Admission $8 for adults; $5 for seniors, military, and children ages 4–12. **Hours** Daily, 9:30 a.m.–5 p.m.; closed Christmas and New Year's Day. **When to go** Anytime. **How much time to allow** 2 hours plus lunch. **Author's rating** ★★★★; magical valley is your tropical-forest fantasy come true.

DESCRIPTION AND COMMENTS This former theme park has returned to the botanical garden and nature walk it always was underneath the mountain biking, ATV rides, and narrated wagon tours of yesteryear. It's an ancient place, and on the 0.75-mile walk up to the waterfall pool, you will pass historic village ruins of a former time in Hawaii, along with gigantic gingers and other plants in 32 botanical collections that thrive in this fecund environment. At the pool you can swim; a lifeguard is on duty. There's no finer way to cool off after a steamy and possibly buggy uphill trek. If you forgot your suit, sit and dangle your toes in the water. But don't drink it—here or anywhere animals may live and graze uphill—because you don't want leptospirosis for the rest of your vacation.

OTHER THINGS TO DO NEARBY Watch winter waves at Waimea Bay from a safe perch, admire expert bodysurfers and surfers take on the dangerous pipeline curl at Pupukea Beach, poke through the shops of Haleiwa, and generally, enjoy the "country."

MAUI

Alexander and Baldwin Sugar Museum CENTRAL MAUI

APPEAL BY AGE	PRESCHOOL ★½	GRADE SCHOOL ★★	TEENS ★★½
YOUNG ADULTS ★★★	OVER 30 ★★★½		SENIORS ★★★½

3957 Hansen Road, Puunene; ☎ 808-871-8058; www.sugarmuseum.com

Admission $5 for adults; $2 for children ages 6–17. **Hours** Monday–Saturday, 9:30 a.m.–4:30 p.m. **When to go** Anytime. **How much time to allow** 45 minutes. **Author's rating** ★★★; a look at Maui's sugar-plantation history.

DESCRIPTION AND COMMENTS Formerly the residence of a factory superintendent, this museum houses a number of artifacts, photographs, and a working scale model of sugar-processing machinery.

Bailey House Museum CENTRAL MAUI

APPEAL BY AGE	PRESCHOOL ★½	GRADE SCHOOL ★★★	TEENS ★★½
YOUNG ADULTS ★★★	OVER 30 ★★★½		SENIORS ★★★½

2375-A Main Street, Wailuku; ☎ 808-244-3326; www.mauimuseum.org

Admission $5 for adults; $4 for seniors; $1 for children ages 7–12. **Hours** Monday–Saturday, 10 a.m.–4 p.m. **When to go** Anytime. **How much time to allow** 1 hour. **Author's rating** ★★★; worth a stop for history buffs and a look through the shop.

DESCRIPTION AND COMMENTS The Bailey mission home, built in 1833 of lava rock and native woods, sits on land given to the missionaries by Hawaiian chiefs. Hawaiians attended reading and writing classes here, using Hawaiian-language books printed on Maui. Today the Bailey House houses the Maui Historical Society and displays Hawaiian artifacts, including *tapa,* weaving, featherwork, and tools made out of stones, shells, and bones. A gallery of paintings from the late 1800s portrays the beauty of the Valley Isle, and the outside gardens reveal rare native plants, a koa-wood canoe, and a surfboard once used by legendary surfer-swimmer Duke Kahanamoku. A gift shop offers crafts, apparel, Hawaiian music, and books.

The Bailey House Museum is one of the few places where you can see a Maui *oo,* an extinct bird last seen alive on Molokai in 1904. The black bird with bright-yellow wing feathers lies in a glass case with its little feet crossed as if it has just dropped out of the sky. It became extinct

100 years ago. The Kauai *oo* (*Moho braccatus*) was last seen in the Alakai Swamp in 1986. The *oo* trophy is so rare that curators of the Bernice Pauahi Bishop Museum of Natural Science in Honolulu keep a solitary taxidermy specimen in a dark safe. If you happen to be in London, you may see a cape once worn by Hawaiian kings made of 20,000 bright-yellow *oo* thigh feathers at the Pitt-Rivers Museum at the University of Oxford. Writer Simon Winchester called the *oo* cape "certainly one of the most remarkably lovely things in any museum in England."

OTHER THINGS TO DO NEARBY Wailuku shops and restaurants and the Hawaii Nature Center and Kepaniwai Park are a short drive away.

Baldwin Home Museum WEST MAUI

APPEAL BY AGE	PRESCHOOL ★½	GRADE SCHOOL ★★	TEENS ★★★
YOUNG ADULTS ★★★	OVER 30 ★★★½		SENIORS ★★★½

120 Dickenson Street, Lahaina; ☎ 808-661-3262; www.lahainarestoration.org

Admission $5 for families; $3 for adults; $2 for seniors. Hours Daily, 10 a.m.–4 p.m. When to go Anytime. How much time to allow 1 hour. Author's rating ★★★; a peek into Maui's missionary era.

DESCRIPTION AND COMMENTS This two-story structure was the home of Reverend Dwight Baldwin, a Protestant medical missionary, from 1838 to 1871. Today the home and grounds, lovingly restored by the Lahaina Restoration Foundation, give visitors a glimpse of what life was like for 19th-century missionary families in Lahaina. On display are various household items and furniture, photographs, and other historic artifacts. Ask for a free self-guided-tour map of Lahaina's other restored treasures.

OTHER THINGS TO DO NEARBY Located at Dickenson and Front Streets, the Baldwin Home is one of several historic sights in Lahaina, restored and maintained by the foundation. The Wo Hing Temple is within easy walking distance.

Haleakala National Park UPCOUNTRY MAUI

APPEAL BY AGE	PRESCHOOL ★★	GRADE SCHOOL ★★★	TEENS ★★★½
YOUNG ADULTS ★★★★	OVER 30 ★★★★		SENIORS ★★★★

The park extends from the 10,023-foot summit of Haleakala down the southeast flank of the mountain to the Kipahulu coastline near Hana. The summit area is accessible from Kahului via Roads 37, 377, and 378. The Kipahulu area, at the east end of the island between Hana and Kaupo, can be reached via Highway 36. Driving time is about 3–4 hours each way. ☎ 808-572-9306; www.haleakala.national-park.com

Admission $10 per vehicle, good for 7 days. Hours Park Ranger Headquarters is open daily, 9 a.m.–4 p.m.; the visitor center is open daily, sunrise–3 p.m. (Overnight camping is permissible. The Hosmer Grove Campground in the summit area, located just inside the park's entrance, can be used without a permit; all other camping areas require permits.). When to go Anytime. Haleakala Summit is renowned for its dramatic sunrises and sunsets, although most people come for sunrise; be sure to arrive at least 30 minutes before either event. **How much time to allow** Half a day or more, depending on whether you plan to spend time hiking or taking part in one of the park's programs. **Author's rating** ★★★★★; one of the great natural wonders of the world.

DESCRIPTION AND COMMENTS Haleakala ("House of the Sun"), a dormant volcano that last spilled lava a bit more than 200 years ago, was designated as a national park in 1961. The park consists of nearly 29,000 acres, most of it wilderness. In the summit area, see the Park Ranger Headquarters and Haleakala Visitor Center, which houses a variety of cultural and natural-history exhibits. Rangers are on duty and can be a tremendous help in making the most of your visit. Each facility has a selection of books, maps, postcards, and other souvenirs for sale.

TOURING TIPS Check the park bulletin board for a schedule of daily programs and guided hikes. Keep an eye out for the rare spiky silversword plants and the endangered Hawaii state bird, the nene goose (a relative of the Canadian goose, but with claw feet for walking on cinders). Obey all posted warning signs. It can be cold at the summit, so dress accordingly. Due to the high elevation and reduced oxygen at the park, anyone with heart or respiratory conditions is advised to check with a doctor before visiting.

Hana Cultural Center UPCOUNTRY MAUI

| APPEAL BY AGE | PRESCHOOL ★★ | GRADE SCHOOL ★★½ | TEENS ★★½ |
| YOUNG ADULTS ★★★ | OVER 30 ★★★ | | SENIORS ★★★ |

4974 Uakea Road, Hana; ☎ 808-248-8622; www.planet-hawaii.com/hana

Admission Donations accepted. **Hours** Monday–Friday, 10 a.m.–4 p.m. **When to go** Anytime. **How much time to allow** 1 hour. **Author's rating** ★★★; a reward after the long journey to Hana.

DESCRIPTION AND COMMENTS This cultural center is home to a quaint museum that features more than 500 artifacts, 600 books, 5,000 historic photographs of the Hana district, and, oddly enough, 680 Hawaiian bottles. Opened in 1983, the nonprofit museum houses Hawaiian quilts, *poi* boards, stones, *kapa*, ancient tools, fishhooks, gourd bowls, stone lamps, and a century-old fishing net. Also featured are tributes to some of Hana's most notable personalities. The cultural center also includes a series of old Hawaiian *hale* (houses), the historic Hana courthouse, and a jailhouse.

kids Hawaii Nature Center CENTRAL MAUI

| APPEAL BY AGE | PRESCHOOL ★★★ | GRADE SCHOOL ★★★★ | TEENS ★★★★ |
| YOUNG ADULTS ★★★★ | OVER 30 ★★★★ | | SENIORS ★★★★ |

875 Iao Valley Road, Wailuku; ☎ 808-244-6500; www.hawaiinaturecenter.org

Admission $6 for adults; $4 for children ages 4–12. **Hours** Daily, 10 a.m.–4 p.m. **When to go** Anytime. **How much time to allow** 1 hour. **Author's rating** ★★★★; good hands-on learning experience about the nature of Hawaii.

DESCRIPTION AND COMMENTS The Nature Center's Interactive Science Arcade features more than 30 interactive exhibits celebrating Maui's natural environment. The main exhibit hall features an amazing 10-foot-high, 30-foot-long, three-dimensional replication of four streams that feed into the Iao Stream. Aquariums, rain-forest explorations, arcade games, telescopes, and live insect and animal exhibits are among the other highlights. The gift shop features an extensive selection of nature-themed merchandise. All proceeds go to environmental-education programs for Maui elementary school children.

TOURING TIPS Guided nature walks are offered twice daily for $29.95 for adults and $19.95 for children 5 and older. Call for reservations.

OTHER THINGS TO DO NEARBY Visit Kepaniwai Cultural Park and the Bailey House Museum.

Hui Noeau Visual Arts Center UPCOUNTRY MAUI

| APPEAL BY AGE | PRESCHOOL ★★ | GRADE SCHOOL ★★½ | TEENS ★★★ |
| YOUNG ADULTS ★★★ | OVER 30 ★★★½ | | SENIORS ★★★½ |

2841 Baldwin Avenue; ☎ 808-572-6560; www.huinoeau.com

Admission Donations accepted. Hours Monday–Sunday, 10 a.m.–4 p.m. When to go Anytime. How much time to allow 1 hour. Author's rating ★★★; a haven for art lovers.

DESCRIPTION AND COMMENTS Housed on a beautiful nine-acre estate in Makawao, this nonprofit art center features works by both local and international artists. The estate itself is a historic landmark (built in 1917 for Harry and Ethel Baldwin), dotted with pine and camphor trees and adorned with an immaculate formal garden and reflecting pool. The arts center features classes and workshops for aspiring artisans, including some for visitors, and exhibits are open to the public. The gift shop offers a selection of original artwork, note cards, books, and other gift items.

kids Kahanu Garden
(National Tropical Botanical Garden) HANA

| APPEAL BY AGE | PRESCHOOL ★★ | GRADE SCHOOL ★★★★ | TEENS ★★★ |
| YOUNG ADULTS ★★★★ | OVER 30 ★★★★ | | SENIORS ★★★★ |

Mile Post 31, Hana Highway, Hana (turn ma kai on Ulaino Road at the sign for the garden near Mile Post 31 and go about 1.5 miles); ☎ 808-248-8912; www.ntbg.org

Admission $10 for adults. Hours 10 a.m.–2 p.m. for self-guided tours. When to go Anytime. How much time to allow 2 hours (not including the drive). Author's rating ★★★★★; if you care about Pacific culture, this is way more than a welcome diversion on the curvy road to Hana.

DESCRIPTION AND COMMENTS Hana's "Power of Place" calls undeniably to you here through two marvelous features: Piilanihale Heiau, believed to be the largest sacrificial *heiau* archeological site in all of Polynesia (nearly four acres, walls 42 feet high and stepped up a hill) and a National Historic Landmark, and Kahanu Garden, 427 acres of Pacific Island plant collections. The garden boasts the world's largest collection of breadfruit varieties. Breadfruit, a staple of tropical-island life, figured into the ill-fated voyage of the Bounty and of Captain Cook's travels. The garden is surrounded by a forest of native pandanus or *lauhala* trees; the tour route is about half a mile long. The view of wild coastline and surf crashing on lava is awesome.

TOURING TIPS If you want to see Maui for real, plan to drive the Hana Highway early or late, to avoid most of the competing drivers; wear bathing suits and stop at waterfall pools and botanical gardens; and spend the night in Hana. Then you can slow down and see the place at a Hawaiian pace, meet people, and let the Hana magic take you. Bring sun and bug protection, picnic lunch, and drinking water. Remember that all *heiau* are religious sites, to be respected, not climbed.

OTHER THINGS TO DO NEARBY Wainapanapa State Park, with camping and glistening black-sand beaches.

Kepaniwai Cultural Park   CENTRAL MAUI

| APPEAL BY AGE | PRESCHOOL ★★ | GRADE SCHOOL ★★½ | TEENS ★★★ |
| YOUNG ADULTS ★★★ | OVER 30 ★★★½ | | SENIORS ★★★½ |

Iao Valley Road, Wailuku; ☎ 808-243-7389

Admission Free. **Hours** Daily, 7 a.m.–7 p.m. **When to go** Anytime. **How much time to allow** 1 hour. **Author's rating** ★★★; a pleasant stop when you're visiting Iao Valley.

DESCRIPTION AND COMMENTS Picturesque gardens and architectural pavilions representing five different ethnic groups who lived and worked on Maui plantations. Good spot for a picnic. Ironically, one of Maui's bloodiest ancient battles occurred near this peaceful place.

OTHER THINGS TO DO NEARBY Iao Valley, Hawaii Nature Center, and Bailey House Museum.

Kula Botanical Garden   UPCOUNTRY MAUI

| APPEAL BY AGE | PRESCHOOL ★★ | GRADE SCHOOL ★★½ | TEENS ★★½ |
| YOUNG ADULTS ★★½ | OVER 30 ★★★ | | SENIORS ★★★½ |

On Kekaulike Avenue (Highway 377), 0.7 mile from Kula Highway, Kula; ☎ 808-878-1715

Admission $10 for adults; $3 for children ages 6–12. **Hours** Daily, 9 a.m.–4 p.m. **When to go** Anytime. **How much time to allow** 90 minutes. **Author's rating** ★★★; a great place to see the exotic, other-worldly flowers called proteas for which Upcountry Maui is famous (although they're South African natives).

DESCRIPTION AND COMMENTS Kula, blessed with a mild, cool climate and fertile soil, is the home of this six-acre wonderland originally owned by Princess Kekaulike. The upcountry climate allows tropicals and semi-tropicals both to flourish. Opened in 1969, the garden today features nearly 2,000 tropical plants, including 60 types of proteas, as well as heliconias, orchids, anthuriums, and gingers.

kids Lahaina Kaanapali Railroad, Kaanapali
WEST MAUI

APPEAL BY AGE	PRESCHOOL ★★★½		GRADE SCHOOL ★★★★	TEENS ★★
YOUNG	ADULTS ★★	OVER 30 ★★		SENIORS ★★½

975 Limahana Place, Suite 203. Lahaina; ☎ 808-667-6851 or 800-499-2307; www.sugarcanetrain.com

Admission $22.50 for adults; $15.50 for children ages 3–12 (round-trip); sunset barbecue dinner and show train, $76 for adults and $43 for children. **Hours** 4 rides daily, beginning at 10:15 a.m., plus 5 p.m. dinner train on Thursday nights. **When to go** Anytime. **How much time to allow** 90 minutes. **Author's rating** ★★★; it's a cute train ride with fine views of the West Maui coastline (look for whales in winter).

DESCRIPTION AND COMMENTS The "Sugar Cane Train," with its 1890s locomotive and distinctive whistle, was used by the Pioneer Mill to transport sugar crops until the early 1950s. Today, the train does tourist duty, shuttling visitors between Lahaina and the resort area of Kaanapali. The six-mile route through an upland cane field lasts about 40 minutes each way. A friendly conductor shares the history of Maui's sugar industry.

kids Maui Ocean Center SOUTH MAUI

APPEAL BY AGE	PRESCHOOL ★★★★½	GRADE SCHOOL ★★★★★	TEENS ★★★★★
YOUNG	ADULTS ★★★★★	OVER 30 ★★★★★	SENIORS ★★★★½

Maalaea Harbor Village, 192 Maalaea Road, Maalaea; ☎ 808-270-7000; www.mauioceancenter.com

Admission $25 for adults; $22 for seniors; $18 for children ages 3–12. **Hours** Daily, 9 a.m.–5 p.m. (July and August, open to 6 p.m.). **When to go** Anytime. **How much time to allow** 2 hours. **Author's rating** ★★★★; a must for understanding island marine life.

DESCRIPTION AND COMMENTS The star attraction is the 600,000-gallon ocean aquarium tank with a walk-through acrylic tunnel so that you can get a good view of the inhabitants, including a six-foot tiger shark and other sharks, spotted eagle rays, mahimahi, triggerfish, sea turtles, eels, and a dazzling array of colorful reef fish. You can also elect to dive the shark tank and get a closer look at the 20 shark species and other marine life there. The 2½-hour orientation and dive, for certified divers 15 and older, costs $199 or more, which includes equipment and admission for one viewing guest. Reservations are required. Other exhibits include a supervised touch pool for kids, allowing them to hold sea critters; interactive displays about the humpback whale; and smaller aquariums that provide a close look at eels, shrimp, coral, and other sea life. The Reef Café and Seascape Maalaea Restaurant provide food and drinks, and the large gift shop carries logo and ocean-themed goods.

OTHER THINGS TO DO NEARBY The center overlooks busy Maalaea Harbor, where tour and whale boats come and go. It's easy to combine a trip to the aquarium with a snorkeling or whale-watching tour to see sea creatures in the wild.

Maui Tropical Plantation and Country Store
CENTRAL MAUI

APPEAL BY AGE	PRESCHOOL ★	GRADE SCHOOL ★	TEENS ★
YOUNG ADULTS ★★	OVER 30 ★★		SENIORS ★★

1670 Honoapiilani Highway; ☎ 808-244-7643

Admission Free; 40-minute tram tours cost $9.50 for adults and $3.50 for children ages 3–12. **Hours** Daily, 9 a.m.–5 p.m.; tours start at 10 a.m. **When to go** Anytime. **How much time to allow** 75 minutes. **Author's rating ★**; when you want to know more about tropical crops, this is the place. You can buy fresh fruit at the country store.

DESCRIPTION AND COMMENTS The 50-acre garden is filled with tropical plants, including pineapple, sugarcane, papaya, guava, star fruit, anthuriums, and protea, and also features a restaurant and plant nursery.

Tedeschi Winery SOUTH MAUI

APPEAL BY AGE	PRESCHOOL ★½	GRADE SCHOOL ★	TEENS ★★½
YOUNG ADULTS ★★★	OVER 30 ★★★		SENIORS ★★★

Ulupalakua Ranch, about 10 miles past the junction of Highways 377 and 37 in Kula; ☎ 808-878-6058; www.mauiwine.com

Admission Free. **Hours** Daily, 9 a.m.–5 p.m.; free guided tours of the facilities and the historic ranch headquarters are held at 10:30 a.m. and 1:30 p.m. **When to go** Anytime. **How much time to allow** 1 hour or more. **Author's rating ★★★**; worth a taste for wine lovers, and a beautiful picnic spot for all.

DESCRIPTION AND COMMENTS Tedeschi Vineyards is known for its fruity wines, particularly Maui Blanc pineapple wine. Wines are available for tasting and purchase at the tasting room in the King's Cottage, once used as a retreat by King Kalakaua. The 18-foot-long bar is cut from a single mango-tree trunk. You'll have a choice of Ulupalakua Red, a blend of Cabernet and Syrah grapes; sparkling wines that include Maui Brut, made the classic way; Framboise de Maui, a raspberry dessert wine; a blush, pineapple wine, and pineapple–passion fruit wine. The Tedeschi labels of upcountry scenes are so artful that you can buy larger versions at the label art gallery.

TOURING TIPS The tour explains how the wines are processed and bottled. But it's not necessary to take a tour to enjoy sampling the wines and walking through the shady lawns and gardens.

Whalers Village Museum WEST MAUI

APPEAL BY AGE	PRESCHOOL ★★	GRADE SCHOOL ★★½	TEENS ★★½
YOUNG ADULTS ★★½		OVER 30 ★★½	SENIORS ★★½

**Whalers Village, 2435 Kaanapali Parkway, Kaanapali Beach Resort;
☎ 808-661-5992; www.whalersvillage.com/museum**

Admission Free. **Hours** Daily, 9:30 a.m.–10 p.m. **When to go** Anytime. **How much time to allow** 1 hour. **Author's rating** ★★½; displays and historic artifacts about whaling will entertain the family if they get restless shopping.

DESCRIPTION AND COMMENTS This museum traces the history of Lahaina's colorful whaling era, roughly from 1825 to 1860. Among more than 100 items on exhibit are a six-foot model of a whaling ship, harpoons, maps, logbooks, and an extensive collection of scrimshaw.

Wo Hing Temple Museum WEST MAUI

APPEAL BY AGE	PRESCHOOL ★	GRADE SCHOOL ★★	TEENS ★★
YOUNG ADULTS ★★½		OVER 30 ★★½	SENIORS ★★★

858 Front Street; ☎ 808-661-3262; www.lahainarestoration.org/temple

Admission Donations accepted. **Hours** Daily, 10 a.m.–4 p.m. **When to go** Anytime. **How much time to allow** 30 minutes. **Author's rating** ★★½; good for historians; young kids will be bored.

DESCRIPTION AND COMMENTS A Buddhist shrine is the centerpiece of this restored Chinese temple, which provides a revealing look at how early Chinese settlers lived in Lahaina. Old photographs and artifacts are also on exhibit. A cookhouse (built separately from the main building to reduce the risk of a house fire) sits just to the right of the building. Two Hawaii films shot in 1898 and 1906 by Thomas Edison are among the highlights. The temple is affiliated with Chee Kung Tong, a Chinese fraternal society with branches throughout the world.

OTHER THINGS TO DO NEARBY The Baldwin Home Museum is nearby.

THE BIG ISLAND OF HAWAII

After Dark in the Park HILO AND VOLCANO

APPEAL BY AGE	PRESCHOOL ★	GRADE SCHOOL ★★	TEENS ★★★
YOUNG ADULTS ★★★★		OVER 30 ★★★★★	SENIORS ★★★★★

**Hawaii Volcanoes National Park, Volcano (see separate listing page 251);
☎ 808-985-6000; www.nps.gov/havo**

Admission $1 donation and park-entrance fees apply. **Hours** Tuesday, 7 p.m. **When to go** Tuesday evening. **How much time to allow** 2 hours. **Author's rating** ★★★★★; it's the next best thing to seeing Pele's lava eruptions.

DESCRIPTION AND COMMENTS After Dark in the Park attracts locals and visitors curious about the natural and supernatural facets of Hawaii's culture. The once-a-week program features Hawaiian musicians, storytellers, artists, scientists, historians, and local authors who offer insights on everything from lava flows and Madame Pele to hula. Hawaiian elders and other Pacific Islanders perform chants, songs, and dance. The variety of topics is as big as the park: Pacific humpback whales, *limu* (seaweed), hurricanes and tsunamis, fishing (ancient and modern), the alien species found in submarine volcanoes, shipwrecks, coral reefs, Pacific migrations, the gooney birds of Midway Island, tiger sharks, marine archaeology, endangered Hawaiian monk seals, and the revival of arts like celestial navigation and ocean sailing brought about by the Hokulea outrigger canoe voyages. The program is offered at 7 p.m. two or three Tuesdays a month at Kilauea Visitor Center Auditorium, Hawaii Volcanoes National Park.

TOURING TIPS After a day in the park, go to After Dark in the Park, then head down Chain of Craters Road to watch the lava flow. Bring a windbreaker, water, and a flashlight.

OTHER THINGS TO DO NEARBY America's most exciting national park (the only one with a live volcano) is right outside your door.

Ahuena Heiau   KONA

APPEAL BY AGE	PRESCHOOL ★	GRADE SCHOOL ★★	TEENS ★★
YOUNG ADULTS ★★½	OVER 30 ★★★		SENIORS ★★★

Next to Kamakahonu Beach, fronting the King Kamehameha's Kona Beach Hotel; ☎ 808-329-2911 (hotel)

Admission Free. Hours Always open. When to go Anytime, except luau nights at the hotel, when the area is not accessible to non-luau guests. How much time to allow Up to 1 hour. Author's rating ★★½; one of Hawaii's most treasured *heiau*.

DESCRIPTION AND COMMENTS Rebuilt by King Kamehameha I, this historic *heiau*—a temple of peace dedicated to Lono, the god of fertility—is part of a free walking tour offered at the King Kamehameha's Kona Beach Hotel. The *heiau* was used by ancient Hawaiians to pray for bountiful harvests, healthy children, and good weather. The tallest structure is the *anuu* (oracle tower), where the *kahuna* (priest) received messages from the gods. Kamehameha spent the last seven years of his life in this area. Many Hawaiians still believe the *heiau* is a site of great spiritual significance, so access to the temple's platform is strictly forbidden. The grounds surrounding the platform are open to the public.

TOURING TIPS Guided tours held Monday through Friday at 1:30 p.m. Tour time often changes, so call the hotel to confirm.

OTHER THINGS TO DO NEARBY Hulihee Palace is just minutes away by car.

Akatsuka Orchid Gardens   HILO AND VOLCANO

APPEAL BY AGE	PRESCHOOL ★	GRADE SCHOOL ★★½	TEENS ★★½
YOUNG ADULTS ★★★½	OVER 30 ★★★		SENIORS ★★★½

Off Highway 11, just north of Volcano Village (on the way to Hawaii Volcanoes National Park); ☎ 888-967-6669; www.akatsukaorchid.com

Admission Free (self-guided tours). Hours Daily, 8:30 a.m.–5 p.m. When to go Anytime. How much time to allow 45 minutes. Author's rating ★★★; the variety of orchids is astounding.

DESCRIPTION AND COMMENTS This six-acre garden is recognized as a world leader in the hybridization of orchids, nurturing more than 400,000 plants. Many of the latest varieties were developed by noted horticulturist Mori Akatsuka. A gift shop offers orchids that can be shipped home.

OTHER THINGS TO DO NEARBY Hawaii Volcanoes National Park is minutes away by car.

Amy B. H. Greenwell Ethnobotanical Garden KONA

APPEAL BY AGE	PRESCHOOL ★★	GRADE SCHOOL ★★	TEENS ★★½
YOUNG ADULTS ★★½		OVER 30 ★★½	SENIORS ★★★★

**82-6188 Mamalahoa Highway, off Highway 11 in Captain Cook;
☎ 808-323-3318; www.bishopmuseum.org/greenwell**

Admission $4 suggested donation. Hours Monday–Friday, 8:30 a.m.–5 p.m. When to go Anytime. How much time to allow 1 hour. Author's rating ★★½; an interesting garden with a cultural focus.

DESCRIPTION AND COMMENTS Owned by the Bishop Museum, this 12-acre ethnobotanical garden features more than 200 species of plants, including ten native varieties that are on the endangered species list. These plants were used by ancient Hawaiians for food, medicine, and other daily necessities. Some of the crops on display include banana, breadfruit, sugarcane, and taro.

TOURING TIPS A guided tour is offered for $5 per person at 1 p.m. Wednesdays and Fridays and for free at 10 a.m. on the second Saturday of every month. Helpful information for self-guided tours is provided.

kids Astronaut Ellison S. Onizuka Space Center KONA

APPEAL BY AGE	PRESCHOOL ★★	GRADE SCHOOL ★★★★	TEENS ★★★½
YOUNG ADULTS ★★★		OVER 30 ★★★	SENIORS ★★★

Keahole-Kona International Airport; ☎ 808-329-3441; www.planet-hawaii.com/astronautonizuka

Admission $3 for adults; $1 for children under age 12. Hours Daily, 8:30 a.m.–4:30 p.m. When to go While waiting for your flight out of Kona (arrive a half hour early at the airport). How much time to allow 30 minutes. Author's rating ★★★½; a hands-on attraction with equal parts fun and education.

DESCRIPTION AND COMMENTS This space museum features ten interactive exhibits and more than a dozen audiovisual displays, including an authentic Apollo 13 space suit and a Space Theater showing NASA videos. You can launch a miniature space shuttle, log on to the space shuttle's computer program to learn about the system's components, and even attempt a "rendezvous" with an object in outer space. Proceeds from the gift shop help maintain the center, which is named in honor of Hawaii's first astronaut, Ellison S. Onizuka. Born and raised in the Kona area, Onizuka was among the shuttle crew members who perished in the *Challenger* explosion as it launched on January 28, 1986.

Hawaii Tropical Botanical Garden   HILO AND VOLCANO

APPEAL BY AGE	PRESCHOOL ★★	GRADE SCHOOL ★★½	TEENS ★★½
YOUNG ADULTS ★★★	OVER 30 ★★★½	SENIORS ★★★★	

27-717 Old Mamalahoa Highway, Onemea, 7 miles north of Hilo; watch for a sign along Highway 19 that announces a scenic route 4 miles long; turn *ma kai*, then drive to the garden's headquarters and registration area; ☎ 808-964-5233; www.htbg.com

Admission $15 for adults; $5 for children ages 6–16. **Hours** Daily, 9 a.m.–5 p.m. **When to go** Last admission is at 4 p.m. **How much time to allow** 90 minutes. **Author's rating** ★★★½; one of the most beautiful spots in the state.

DESCRIPTION AND COMMENTS   In this 40-acre nature preserve, you can wander through supersize torch gingers and giant tropical shade trees bordering a stream, and suddenly you'll find yourself right at the sea watching waves crash on lava rocks. The gardens and wild growth flourish in the steamy atmosphere, as is true in the valleys all along the Hilo-Hamakua coast, but this is a rare chance to appreciate their beauty up close. Visitors are shuttled to the valley and provided with trail maps, mosquito repellent, and umbrellas. A 500-foot-long boardwalk leads through a steep ravine filled with banana, bamboo, ferns, and other tropical plants. From there, other trails bring you to a scenic triple waterfall, lily pond, stream, aviary, and more than 2,000 plant species, including some 200 species of palms, as well as orchids, bromeliads, heliconia, and fruit trees collected from around the world. Upon your return, drop by the gift shop to browse through local arts and crafts, books, and other items. Proceeds go toward the preservation of the garden, opened to the public in 1984.

kids Hawaii Volcanoes National Park
HILO AND VOLCANO

APPEAL BY AGE	PRESCHOOL ★★★★★	GRADE SCHOOL ★★★★★	TEENS ★★★★★
YOUNG ADULTS ★★★★★	OVER 30 ★★★★★	SENIORS ★★★★★	

About 30 miles from Hilo, traveling up Highway 11 (follow the road signs and turn left into the park entrance); ☎ 808-985-6000; www.nps.gov/havo

Admission $10 per vehicle; admission is good for 7 days. **Hours** The park is open 24 hours a day year-round; the visitor center is open daily, 7:45 a.m.– 5 p.m. **When to go** Anytime; the best time of day to view eruption activity is after sunset. **How much time to allow** At least half a day. **Author's rating** ★★★★★; Hawaii's premier attraction; don't expect up-close views of fountaining lava, however.

DESCRIPTION AND COMMENTS   The 377-acre Hawaii Volcanoes National Park, established in 1916 by the National Park Service, is certainly one of the world's top wonders. Kilauea Volcano has been spewing lava continuously since 1983. Begin at the visitor center, which houses a gallery of volcano exhibits and a 200-seat minitheater showing a terrific 23-minute film about the history of Hawaii's volcanoes and their significance to the Hawaiian culture. Park rangers are on hand to answer any questions and offer suggested itineraries at the park.

Next door, the Volcano Art Center offers a wide range of creative works by some of Hawaii's top artists. Drive on into the park to find the Thomas A. Jaggar Museum, which features exhibits spotlighting Hawaii's volcanic history, current seismic activity (you can watch a seismograph at work), land formations, and a profile of Madame Pele, the goddess of fire, whose home is Halemaumau Crater and whose handiwork is evident in the eruptions of Kilauea.

From the museum, you can drive to any and all public trails in the park. Be respectful of the surroundings, which native Hawaiians regard as sacred to their culture. (See separate listing for After Dark in the Park, page xref.)

OTHER THINGS TO DO NEARBY The tranquil village of Volcano is located a mile from the park.

Hulihee Palace KONA

APPEAL BY AGE	PRESCHOOL ★★	GRADE SCHOOL ★★½	TEENS ★★★
YOUNG ADULTS ★★★½	OVER 30 ★★★★		SENIORS ★★★★

75-5718 Alii Drive; ☎ 808-329-1877; www.huliheepalace.org

Admission $6 for adults; $4 for seniors; $1 for children under age 18. **Hours** Monday–Saturday, 9 a.m.–4 p.m.; Sunday, 10 a.m.–4 p.m. **When to go** Anytime. **How much time to allow** 45 minutes. **Author's rating** ★★★; a historic treasure in the heart of Kailua-Kona.

DESCRIPTION AND COMMENTS Operated by the Daughters of Hawaii, this handsome Victorian structure was built in 1838 out of lava rock, coral, koa, and ohia wood for Governor John Kuakini. It later served as a vacation retreat for Hawaiian royalty. Among the treasures here are *kahili* (feathered staffs), stone tools, *tapa,* jewelry, and a collection of javelins that once belonged to Kamehameha I. *Note:* Photography and videotaping are not allowed inside the palace.

TOURING TIPS Due to earthquake-repair efforts, tours are currently offered on a limited basis. Contact the palace for the latest tour details.

OTHER THINGS TO DO NEARBY Ahuena Heiau and the Kailua Candy Company are among the notable stops located in Kailua-Kona. A ten-minute drive from Kailua-Kona leads you to Holualoa, a town of artists' studios and boutique coffee farms.

Kaloko-Honokohau National Historical Park KONA

APPEAL BY AGE	PRESCHOOL ★★	GRADE SCHOOL ★★½	TEENS ★★½
YOUNG ADULTS ★★★	OVER 30 ★★★		SENIORS ★★★½

Situated at the base of Hualalai Volcano, 3 miles north of Kailua-Kona and 3 miles south of Kona International Airport at Keahole (along Highway 11); ☎ 808-329-6881; www.nps.gov/kaho

Admission Free. **Hours** Daily, 8:30 a.m.–4 p.m. **When to go** Anytime. **How much time to allow** 1 hour. **Author's rating** ★★★; worthwhile stop for anyone interested in Hawaiian history.

DESCRIPTION AND COMMENTS This 1,300-acre lava-field park by the sea features more than 200 archaeological sites, including *heiau,* petroglyphs, fishing shrines, *holua* (stone slides), and fishponds. Several species of endangered animals and plants live here. Picnicking, fishing, snorkeling, swimming, bird-watching, and hiking are among the activities you can enjoy. Overnight camping is not permitted.

Kamuela Museum KONA

APPEAL BY AGE	PRESCHOOL ★½	GRADE SCHOOL ★★½	TEENS ★★½
YOUNG ADULTS ★★★	OVER 30 ★★★		SENIORS ★★★

Waimea, at the intersection of Highways 250 and 19; ☎ 808-885-4724

Admission $5 for adults; $2 for children under age 12. **Hours** Daily, 8 a.m.–5 p.m. **When to go** Anytime. **How much time to allow** 1 hour. **Author's rating** ★★½; not worth going out of your way to see, but it has several intriguing exhibits.

DESCRIPTION AND COMMENTS This cozy museum features an eclectic collection of island artifacts. Among the historical prizes are antique American furniture and Chinese porcelain.

Lyman Museum & Mission House HILO AND VOLCANO

APPEAL BY AGE	PRESCHOOL ★★	GRADE SCHOOL ★★	TEENS ★★½
YOUNG ADULTS ★★★	OVER 30 ★★★		SENIORS ★★★★

Hilo, 276 Haili Street, a few blocks up from Hilo Bay; ☎ 808-935-5021; www.lymanmuseum.org

Admission $10 for adults; $6 for seniors; $3 for children ages 17 and under. **Hours** Monday–Saturday, 9:30 a.m.–4:30 p.m. **When to go** Anytime. **How much time to allow** 90 minutes. **Author's rating** ★★★; good small museum focusing on Hawaii's natural history, culture, missionary era, and plantation life.

DESCRIPTION AND COMMENTS The mission house was built in 1839 for David and Sarah Lyman, the first Christian missionaries to Hilo. This well-preserved 1839 New England–style home is the oldest wooden-frame structure on the island and houses missionary-era furnishings, clothing, photographs, and other artifacts that can be seen on a 25-minute docent-led tour. The exhibits show what life was like for these transplanted New Englanders and those whose lives they changed. The adjacent two-story museum, built in 1973, showcases Hawaii's natural and cultural history. Exhibits here include one of the top-ten mineral and gem collections in the United States, original documents, historic photographs, and period pieces reflecting the many people who immigrated to the Islands.

OTHER THINGS TO DO NEARBY The Pacific Tsunami Museum is a few minutes away on Kamehameha Avenue.

Mauna Loa Macadamia Nut Visitor Center
HILO AND VOLCANO

| APPEAL BY AGE | PRESCHOOL ★★ | GRADE SCHOOL ★★★½ | TEENS ★★★½ |
| YOUNG ADULTS ★★★½ | OVER 30 ★★★½ | SENIORS ★★★½ |

On Highway 11, 5 miles south of Hilo; turn onto Macadamia Road and drive to the road's end (you'll pass through Mauna Loa's 2,500-acre orchard); ☎ 808-966-8618 or 888-628-6556; www.maunaloa.com

Admission Free. **Hours** Daily, 8:30 a.m.–5:30 p.m. **When to go** Anytime. **How much time to allow** 1 hour. **Author's rating** ★★★½; life story of everyone's favorite nut, complete with free samples.

DESCRIPTION AND COMMENTS Head to the visitor center first and enjoy a free taste of Mauna Loa's macadamia-nut products, then head outside and watch a brief video presentation about Mauna Loa and the macadamia-nut industry. A minifactory shows how macadamia-nut chocolates are made. Adjacent to the visitor center is the company's nut-processing plant, where you can watch the proceedings through large viewing windows (helpful signs explain the process). Also on the premises is a snack shop serving macadamia-nut ice cream, soft drinks, Kona coffee, and other treats.

OTHER THINGS TO DO NEARBY Nani Mau Gardens and Panaewa Rainforest Zoo are just minutes away by car.

Nani Mau Gardens **HILO AND VOLCANO**

| APPEAL BY AGE | PRESCHOOL ★½ | GRADE SCHOOL ★★ | TEENS ★★★ |
| YOUNG ADULTS ★★★ | OVER 30 ★★★½ | SENIORS ★★★½ |

421 Makalika Street (from Hilo, drive about 3 miles south on Highway 11 and turn left onto Makalika Street); ☎ 808-959-3500;

Admission $10 for adults; $5 for children ages 6–18; a $25 fee for adults includes admission and lunch buffet from 10:30 a.m. to 1:30 p.m. **Hours** Daily, 9 a.m.–4 p.m. **When to go** Anytime. **How much time to allow** 1 hour. **Author's rating** ★★; the price is a little steep for our tastes, but Nani Mau lives up to its name, which means "forever beautiful."

DESCRIPTION AND COMMENTS This 20-acre botanical garden, established in 1970, includes more than a hundred varieties of tropical-fruit trees and some 2,000 varieties of tropical flowers, including anthuriums, orchids, and bromeliads. A handy map is provided. Highlights include the Orchid Walkway, Hibiscus Garden, Bromeliad Garden, Lily Pond, Polynesian Garden, European Garden, Fruit Orchard, and Annual Garden. A restaurant and gift shop are also on the premises. The garden is under new ownership, and guided tours, previously available on trams, are no longer offered.

TOURING TIPS Self-guided tour. Visitors can opt to combine a garden visit with lunch.

OTHER THINGS TO DO NEARBY Mauna Loa Macadamia Nut Visitor Center and Panaewa Rainforest Zoo.

Ocean Rider Seahorse Farm   KONA

Turn *ma kai* off Queen Kaahumanu Highway onto Natural Energy Lab Road, 1.2 miles south of the airport (heading toward Kailua-Kona), then follow the signs to Ocean Rider; ☎ 808-329-6840; www.seahorse.com

Admission $35 for adults, $25 for children age 4–7. **Hours** Guided tours Monday–Friday, 10 a.m., 12 p.m., and 2 p.m. **When to go** You must be on a guided tour to explore the facility and see Hawaii's seahorses. **How much time to allow** 90 minutes. **Author's rating ★★★★**; pricey, but the tickets support the farm's continuing research and conservation efforts; a fascinating tour, and probably the only chance you'll ever have to actually hold a live, pregnant male seahorse. (Honestly!) This one-hour, personally guided, interactive event is $150.

DESCRIPTION AND COMMENTS This three-acre oceanfront facility breeds more than 18 species of seahorses and is the only seahorse farm in the United States. More than 30 million seahorses are taken from the wild each year for medicinal use and personal aquariums, and many of the species are now endangered, bordering on extinction. Wild seahorses, which mate for life, do not adapt well to aquariums, and nearly three-quarters die almost immediately. The Ocean Rider aquafarm is helping to reduce the threat to wild seahorses by raising and selling captive seahorses— sold in pairs and accustomed to tank living. The farm has the world's largest collection of seahorses, numbering more than 20,000, from microscopic newborns to full-grown adults. The interactive guided tour, led by a biologist, takes visitors through the facility and the various stages of seahorse development, ending with an opportunity to reach into a seahorse tank and hold one of the creatures.

TOURING TIPS Arrive at least 15 minutes before the tour begins, as participants are required on-site to scrub both arms up to the elbows before starting the tour. The walk is not difficult, but much of it is outdoors on gravel, so wear comfortable shoes, sunscreen, and a hat. Advance reservations are highly recommended.

OTHER THINGS TO DO NEARBY Kaloko-Honokohau National Historic Park is less than two miles away, on the way to Kailua-Kona.

Onizuka Center for International Astronomy and Mauna Kea Observatory   HILO AND VOLCANO

Take Highway 200 to the Visitor Information Station, at the 9,200-foot elevation level on Mauna Kea; ☎ 808-961-2180; www.ifa.hawaii.edu/info/vis

Admission Free. **Hours** Visitor Information Station: Daily, 9 a.m.–10 p.m. **When to go** Anytime; nights for stargazing, weekends for summit visits. **How much time to allow** Half a day or night. **Author's rating ★★★★½**; an out-of-this-world experience for visitors who are able to ascend to Mauna Kea's summit, and a fascinating day or night at the visitor station below for those who can't comfortably go higher.

DESCRIPTION AND COMMENTS The Onizuka Center at the 9,200-foot level offers fascinating displays covering the observatory's history, programs, and accomplishments. Specially equipped telescopes are set up for sunspot viewing. The Visitor Information Station offers free tours to the 13,796-foot summit of Mauna Kea every Saturday and Sunday from 1 to 5 p.m. (weather permitting). Visitors should arrive promptly by 1 p.m., as participants are required to spend an hour of acclimation time here before ascending to higher elevations.

Every night, the Visitor Information Station holds a stargazing program from 6 to 10 p.m. The program begins with an astronomy video, followed by a discussion of astronomy and Mauna Kea, then moves outside to observe celestial delights through two large telescopes: star clusters, double stars, white dwarfs, planetary nebulas, star-forming nebulas, supernova remnants, supernovas, planets, galaxies, and all of the constellations visible in Hawaii. The Visitor Information Station enjoys clear, dark skies at a higher elevation than most other major telescopes on the planet. Bring binoculars and flashlights with red filters. Most important, dress warmly—temperatures up there can drop to the 40s on summer nights and the 20s on winter nights.

TOURING TIPS For trips to the summit, participants in their own four-wheel-drive vehicles (regular rental cars cannot do this trek; check with your car-rental agency about a four-wheel-drive vehicle) are led to the summit, perhaps the finest spot on Earth for stargazing. The clear, dark skies allow astronomers in observatories from 11 countries to peer into deep space. *Important note:* Be sure that you have a full tank of gas before driving up Mauna Kea. The steep grade and low oxygen level make engines run inefficiently. Fuel is not available on Mauna Kea. For current road conditions, call ☎ 808-935-6268.

Children under age 16, pregnant women, and those with respiratory, heart, and severe-obesity conditions are not allowed to travel to the summit. Be aware that the weather conditions at Mauna Kea can be quite severe, including freezing temperatures, snow, and high winds. Scuba divers must wait at least 24 hours after their last dive before ascending to the summit.

Pacific Tsunami Museum HILO AND VOLCANO

| APPEAL BY AGE | PRESCHOOL ★★ | GRADE SCHOOL ★★★ | TEENS ★★★★ |
| YOUNG ADULTS ★★★★ | OVER 30 ★★★★½ | SENIORS ★★★★ | |

130 Kamehameha Avenue in downtown Hilo; ☎ 808-935-0926; www.tsunami.org

Admission $8 adults; $7 seniors; $4 children ages 6–17. **Hours** Monday–Saturday, 9 a.m.–4 p.m. **When to go** Anytime. **How much time to allow** 30 minutes–1 hour. **Author's rating** ★★★; sad but riveting reminder of the power of tidal waves and an important chapter in Hilo's history; will make you look twice at that calm bay.

DESCRIPTION AND COMMENTS The Pacific Tsunami Museum pays tribute to the hundreds of Hilo residents who perished during the horrific tsunamis that struck the city in 1946 and 1960. It also educates today's residents about what to do when the next tsunami hits. Exhibits include informative video presentations and startling photographs.

OTHER THINGS TO DO NEARBY Browse downtown Hilo; the Lyman Museum & Mission House is a few blocks away.

kids Panaewa Rainforest Zoo HILO AND VOLCANO

APPEAL BY AGE	PRESCHOOL ★★★	GRADE SCHOOL ★★★★	TEENS ★★★
YOUNG ADULTS ★★★½	OVER 30 ★★★½		SENIORS ★★½

Mamaki Street, off Highway 11 south of Hilo; ☎ 808-959-9233; www.hilozoo.com

Admission Free. **Hours** Daily, 9 a.m.–4 p.m. **When to go** Anytime. **How much time to allow** 1 hour; longer if you want to include a picnic lunch. **Author's rating** ★★★½; the kids will love it.

DESCRIPTION AND COMMENTS This 12-acre zoo in the Panaewa Rainforest Reserve is the only tropical-rain-forest zoo in the United States. It spotlights the world's rain-forest animals, reptiles, and birds, including a white Bengal tiger, water buffalo, pygmy hippos, spider monkeys, deer, iguanas, feral goats, tapirs, and vultures—most of which can't be seen in the Islands—as well as some native birds, including the endangered nene, Hawaii's state bird. Picnic tables and rain shelters are provided. The county-operated zoo is well kept, with lovely grounds and lots of shade providing a pleasant place for a picnic and leisurely stroll.

TOURING TIPS The tiger feeding is at 3:30 p.m. every day.

OTHER THINGS TO DO NEARBY The Mauna Loa Macadamia Nut Visitor Center and Nani Mau Gardens are minutes away by car.

Parker Ranch Visitor Center and Historic Homes KONA

APPEAL BY AGE	PRESCHOOL ★★½	GRADE SCHOOL ★★★½	TEENS ★★★½
YOUNG ADULTS ★★★★	OVER 30 ★★★★		SENIORS ★★★★

Parker Ranch Shopping Center, 67-1185 Mamalahoa Highway; ☎ 808-885-7655; www.parkerranch.com

Admission Visitor center: $7 for adults (children and seniors discount); historic homes: $9 for adults (children and seniors discount); both attractions: $15 for adults, $13 for seniors, $12 for children. **Hours** Monday–Saturday, 9 a.m.–4:45 p.m. **When to go** Anytime. **How much time to allow** 2 or more hours. **Author's rating** ★★★★; worth the time and money to learn about this ranch and sample the Hawaiian *paniolo* (cowboy) way of life; this is about as west as you can get, and you'll never see another ranch like it.

DESCRIPTION AND COMMENTS One of the larger private ranches in the United States, the 150,000-acre Parker Ranch owns the town of Waimea (also known as Kamuela), in the heart of Big Island *paniolo* country. The Parker Ranch Visitor Center traces the storied history of the Parker family through a variety of displays, photographs, artifacts, and a 20-minute video. In 1809, John Palmer Parker, a sailor from Massachusetts jumped ship in the Islands, befriended King Kamehameha I, and married a Hawaiian princess. At the king's behest, Parker began rounding up wild horses and cattle that had been given to the Hawaiian royals years before and left to roam free. Their hooves and grazing were harming the fragile slopes of Mauna Kea. In thanks, Parker was given a two-acre land grant. In the 1850s, Parker began purchasing more land in the area, laying the foundation for Parker Ranch. Today, tours reveal Puuopelu, a handsome ranch home with a fine-art collection, and a replica of Mana Hale, the Parker family homes compound located about three-fourths of a mile from the visitor center. The Parker Ranch Store carries an assortment of *paniolo* apparel, hats, boots, buckles, music, artwork, greeting cards, and books.

TOURING TIPS Four-wheel-drive, ATV, wagon, and horseback rides across the vast ranch are now available at various prices. A one-hour guided tour is offered for children, including pony rides and supervised access to a petting zoo. Cost is $25 per child. Hunters will be delighted to find that hunts of big game or birds can be arranged year-round (☎ 808-885-7311 for details).

Puuhonua O Honaunau National Historical Park KONA

| APPEAL BY AGE | PRESCHOOL ★ | GRADE SCHOOL ★★ | TEENS ★★½ |
| YOUNG ADULTS ★★½ | OVER 30 ★★★ | | SENIORS ★★★★ |

Approximately 22 miles south of Kailua-Kona; from Highway 11, turn onto Highway 160 at the Honaunau Post Office near Mile Marker 103; follow the road for about 3.5 miles to the park's entrance.;
☎ 808-328-2288; www.nps.gov/puho

Admission $5 per car. **Hours** Visitor center: daily, 8 a.m.–5 p.m. Park: daily, 7 a.m.–8 p.m. **When to go** Anytime; if you visit during the weekend closest to July 1, you can take part in the park's annual cultural festival, featuring Hawaiian games, hula performances, and arts-and-crafts demonstrations. **How much time to allow** 1–2 hours. **Author's rating** ★★★½; one of Hawaii's most sacred cultural-historic sites.

DESCRIPTION AND COMMENTS In ancient Hawaii, this area, flanked by huge (1,000 feet long, 17 feet wide, 10 feet high) lava rock walls set precisely, with no mortar, served as a place of refuge or sanctuary where minor offenders and refugees of war could seek safety and redemption. You'll find self-guided tour brochures and maps at the park visitor center. You can listen to an audio message along the center's mural wall or sit in on an orientation discussion in the amphitheater. Then explore Hale O Keawe

Heiau, built in 1650, as well as wooden *kii* images, canoe sheds, and other ancient artifacts and structures. Stop and observe cultural demonstrators working at their crafts; they are friendly and eager to share their knowledge of Hawaiiana. Hikers can follow a mile-long trail that hugs the Kona coastline and is dotted with several archaeological sites, including *heiau*.

TOURING TIPS Orientation talks at the visitor center are scheduled on a frequent basis.

OTHER THINGS TO DO NEARBY Kealakekua Bay, where Captain Cook landed and met his death, is a five-minute drive north.

Puukohola Heiau KONA

APPEAL BY AGE	PRESCHOOL ★	GRADE SCHOOL ★★	TEENS ★★½
YOUNG ADULTS ★★½	OVER 30 ★★★	SENIORS ★★★★	

On the north end of the Kohala Coast near Kawaiahae Harbor; from the intersection of Route 270 and Highway 19, drive a quarter-mile north on Route 270 to the park access road; ☎ 808-882-7218; www.nps.gov/puhe

Admission Free. Hours Daily, 7:30 a.m.–4 p.m. When to go Anytime; in mid-August, the park stages a cultural festival featuring Hawaiian food and games, hula performances, a royal-court procession, and arts-and-crafts demonstrations. How much time to allow 1 hour. Author's rating ★★★; the unification of the Islands into a kingdom began here.

DESCRIPTION AND COMMENTS Two historic *heiau*—Puukohola and Mailekini—are within a short walk of the visitor center. Puukohola, with its huge stone walls facing the sea, looks like the war temple it was. The site was originally constructed in 1550 and rebuilt by Kamehameha I in 1790 when he launched his efforts to unite the Islands into a kingdom. (There is, in fact, a third *heiau*, Hale O Kapuni, which rests underwater and is not visible.) Hiking and tours of the park are available here.

OTHER THINGS TO DO NEARBY Spencer Beach Park is within walking distance.

Sadie Seymour Botanical Gardens KONA

APPEAL BY AGE	PRESCHOOL ★★	GRADE SCHOOL ★★½	TEENS ★★½
YOUNG ADULTS ★★★	OVER 30 ★★★½	SENIORS ★★★★	

76-6280 Kuakini Highway; located *ma kai* of the intersection of Kuakini and Highway 11; look for the "Kona Outdoor Circle Educational Center" sign; ☎ 808-329-7286

Admission Donations accepted. Hours Daily, 9 a.m.–4 p.m. When to go Anytime. How much time to allow 1 hour. Author's rating ★★★; a beautifully kept Eden for nature lovers.

DESCRIPTION AND COMMENTS Maintained and operated by the Kona Outdoor Circle, this international garden features beautiful landscapes and exotic flora representing areas from throughout the globe, including Hawaii, the Pacific, Asia, Central America, South America, and Africa. Brochures for self-guided tours are available.

Suisan Fish Market and Auction   HILO AND VOLCANO

APPEAL BY AGE	PRESCHOOL ★	GRADE SCHOOL ★★★	TEENS ★★★
YOUNG ADULTS ★★★½		OVER 30 ★★★	SENIORS ★★★

Hilo, 85 Lihiwai Street, at the corner of Banyan Drive; ☎ 808-935-9349

Admission Free. **Hours** Monday–Saturday, opens at 7 a.m. **When to go** Early. **How much time to allow** 30 minutes. **Author's rating** ★★½; for early risers with an appreciation of "fishy" business.

DESCRIPTION AND COMMENTS The public is invited each morning to watch brokers representing restaurants and markets from around the state bid on the day's fresh catch, including ahi (yellowfin tuna), mahimahi, snappers, marlin, swordfish, and squid. Consumers may purchase fresh fish at the market next door.

OTHER THINGS TO DO NEARBY Visit downtown Hilo, walk through the Japanese garden.

Volcano Winery   HILO AND VOLCANO

APPEAL BY AGE	PRESCHOOL ★	GRADE SCHOOL ★★	TEENS ★★
YOUNG ADULTS ★★½		OVER 30 ★★★	SENIORS ★★★

Off Highway 11, 30 miles south of Hilo; turn onto Pii Mauna Drive and follow the road (also called Golf Course Road on some maps); ☎ 808-967-7772; www.volcanowinery.com

Admission Free. **Hours** Daily, 10 a.m.–5:30 p.m. **When to go** Anytime. **How much time to allow** 30 minutes. **Author's rating** ★★½; a great stop for sweet-wine lovers on the way to (or from) Hawaii Volcanoes National Park.

DESCRIPTION AND COMMENTS The southernmost winery in the United States, this 18-acre vineyard, at the 4,000-foot elevation mark, produces 100% tropical-honey and tropical-fruit-blend (half-grape, half-fruit) wines. Visit the tasting room and sample unique flavors including Macadamia Nut Honey Wine, Lehua Blossom Honey Wine, Guava Chablis, Passion Chablis, and Volcano Blush.

OTHER THINGS TO DO NEARBY Winery borders Hawaii Volcanoes National Park.

KAUAI

Grove Farm Homestead   KAUAI

APPEAL BY AGE	PRESCHOOL ★½	GRADE SCHOOL ★★	TEENS ★★½
YOUNG ADULTS ★★★		OVER 30 ★★★	SENIORS ★★★½

Just off Nawiliwili Road outside Lihue; ☎ 808-245-3202; www.hawaiimuseums.org/mc/isKauai_grove.htm

Admission Donations of $5 for adults and $2 for children ages 12 and under are requested. **Hours** Monday, Wednesday, and Thursday, guided tours at 10 am. and 1 p.m.; reservations required. **When to go** Anytime. **How much time to allow** 90 minutes. **Author's rating** ★★½; a good visit if you're interested in the island's plantation history.

DESCRIPTION AND COMMENTS This peaceful 80-acre homestead, owned by a prominent plantation family, provides a revealing glimpse of plantation life during the 19th century. The complex encompasses a museum, washhouse, teahouse, and other plantation buildings.

OTHER THINGS TO DO NEARBY Kauai Museum is a short drive away on Rice Street in Lihue, and Kilohana Plantation is nearby on the highway.

Kauai Museum KAUAI

APPEAL BY AGE	PRESCHOOL ★★	GRADE SCHOOL ★★★	TEENS ★★★
YOUNG ADULTS ★★★	OVER 30 ★★★½		SENIORS ★★★★

4428 Rice Street, Lihue; ☎ 808-245-6931; www.kauaimuseum.org

Admission $10 for adults; $8 for seniors; $3 for children ages 13–17; $1 for children ages 6–12. Hours Monday–Friday, 9 a.m.–4 p.m.; Saturday, 10 a.m.–4 p.m., closed Sunday. When to go Anytime. How much time to allow 75 minutes. Author's rating ★★★½; history museum with a slightly different take on the past.

DESCRIPTION AND COMMENTS This compact little museum in a coral-block building in downtown Lihue says as much as most schoolchildren or people on vacation can absorb at one time about Hawaii's mysterious history. Some of its exhibits of treasured artifacts and written legends are presented along a curving ramp like a timeline. It dates the earliest migrations of Polynesian voyagers from about 200 AD, a few centuries earlier than the commonly accepted theory. Kauai, always the independent kingdom, is said to have been the home of ancient Tahitian chiefs who settled along the Wailua River and left behind many signs of their residence—temples, birthing stones, and house sites. Kauai was never conquered by Kamehameha I like the other islands, but joined the kingdom voluntarily, after all the rest were conquered. The Hawaiian sugar industry was born in Koloa. This particular history of the Garden Isle, within the overall history of Hawaii, comes to life through the extensive collection of displays and artifacts.

Kilauea Point National Wildlife Refuge KAUAI

APPEAL BY AGE	PRESCHOOL ★★	GRADE SCHOOL ★★★	TEENS ★★★½
YOUNG ADULTS ★★★½	OVER 30 ★★★★		SENIORS ★★★★

Turn ma kai off Highway 56 at the entrance to the town of Kilauea and follow the signs to Kilauea Lighthouse; the refuge is at the end of Light-house Road; ☎ 808-828-1413; www.fws.gov/pacificislands/wnwr/kkilaueanwr.html

Admission $5 for adults; free for children age 16 and under. Hours Daily, 10 a.m.–4 p.m. When to go Anytime. How much time to allow 75 minutes. Author's rating ★★★★; the views from Kilauea Point are breathtaking, and the pelagic wildlife is rarely seen this close.

DESCRIPTION AND COMMENTS A variety of wildlife can be viewed after a short walk to Kilauea Point, including more than a dozen species of seabirds, spinner dolphins, Hawaiian green sea turtles, Hawaiian monk seals, and, during the winter months, humpback whales. A 52-foot-high lighthouse, built in 1913, once boasted the largest lens of its kind in the world. It was deactivated in 1976 and is now listed on the National Register of Historic Places.

OTHER THINGS TO DO NEARBY The Kong Lung store is a short drive away in Kilauea.

Kilohana Plantation KAUAI

APPEAL BY AGE	PRESCHOOL ★★½	GRADE SCHOOL ★★★	TEENS ★★★
YOUNG ADULTS ★★★½		OVER 30 ★★★	SENIORS ★★★

3-2087 Kaumualii Highway, Puhi; ☎ 808-245-5608; carriage information ☎ 808-246-9529; train information ☎ 808-245-7245; www.kilohanakauai.com

Admission Free to the estate; the carriage ride costs $12 for adults and $6 for children under age 12; the wagon tour costs $29 for adults and $15 for children; the train ride costs $18 for adults and $14 for children age 2–12. **Hours** Monday– Saturday, 9:30 a.m.–9:30 p.m; Sunday, 9:30 a.m.–5 p.m. A 20-minute carriage ride is available (no reservations required), and a 1-hour horse-drawn wagon tour of the cane fields is offered at 11 a.m. and 2 p.m. Monday, Tuesday, and Thursday. Train rides operate every hour from 10 a.m. to 2 p.m. daily, except Sunday. **When to go** Anytime. **How much time to allow** 1–2 hours. **Author's rating ★★★**; shoppers will like the boutiques and galleries; kids will enjoy the carriage and train rides.

DESCRIPTION AND COMMENTS This 35-acre estate, owned by the Wilcox sugar-plantation family, was built in 1935 and today features a wealth of agricultural displays, antiques, and other treasures from Kauai's plantation era. Shops, galleries, and Gaylord's restaurant are located inside the beautiful restored home. The Kauai Plantation Railway is a new attraction at Kilohana, providing a 10-minute train ride through the 70-acre plantation that surrounds the estate.

Kokee Natural History Museum KAUAI

APPEAL BY AGE	PRESCHOOL ★½	GRADE SCHOOL ★★½	TEENS ★★½
YOUNG ADULTS ★★★		OVER 30 ★★★½	SENIORS ★★★★

Kokee State Park; ☎ 808-335-9975; www.kokee.org

Admission Free; donation appreciated. **Hours** Daily, 10 a.m.–4 p.m. **When to go** Anytime. **How much time to allow** 1 hour. **Author's rating ★★★**; a surprisingly good museum worth a visit if you're in the area.

DESCRIPTION AND COMMENTS This is an intimate museum focusing on the island's ecology, geology, and climatology. Featured are stone artifacts, shells, samples of native Hawaiian woods, and an informative display about weather systems in the Pacific region (including information on Hurricane Iniki, which devastated Kauai in September 1992). The museum gift shop has an impressive selection of Hawaiian books, maps, and hiking guides.

OTHER THINGS TO DO NEARBY Kokee is the location of Waimea Canyon, one of Kauai's most popular natural attractions.

Limahuli Garden and Preserve
(*part of the National Tropical Botanical Garden*) KAUAI

APPEAL BY AGE	PRESCHOOL ★	GRADE SCHOOL ★½	TEENS ★★
YOUNG ADULTS ★★½	OVER 30 ★★★	SENIORS ★★★	

5-8291 Kuhio Highway (56) in Haena, near the end of the road, a quarter mile before Kee Beach; ☎ 808-826-1053; www.ntbg.org

Admission Guided tours are $30 for adults and $15 for children age 13–18 (reservations required); self-guided tours are $15 (no reservations needed); children age 12 and under, free. **Hours** Tuesday–Saturday, 9:30 a.m.–4 p.m. for self-guided tour; 10 a.m. for guided tour. **When to go** Anytime. **How much time to allow** 1½ hours for self-guided tour; 2½ hours for guided tour. **Author's rating** ★★★★; photographers, gardeners, and those who just want to walk in the rain forest will find few places more appealing than this.

DESCRIPTION AND COMMENTS This award-winning 17-acre garden and 990-acre forest preserve—it was named America's Natural Botanical Garden of the Year in 1997 by the American Horticultural Society—features ancient terraced taro patches, native plants, gardens, and a lush rain-forest walk. Three distinct ecological zones are found within the garden.

TOURING TIPS The garden tour involves a 0.75-mile walk, with some steep areas. Wear good walking shoes. Long pants or mosquito repellent recommended. Umbrellas and walking sticks provided.

Moir Gardens KAUAI

APPEAL BY AGE	PRESCHOOL ★★	GRADE SCHOOL ★★	TEENS ★★
YOUNG ADULTS ★★½	OVER 30 ★★½	SENIORS ★★½	

Kiahuna Plantation, 2253 Poipu Road; ☎ 808-742-6411; www.plantationgardens.net

Admission Free. **Hours** Daily, 24 hours. **When to go** Anytime. **How much time to allow** 30 minutes. **Author's rating** ★★½; an unusual garden for Hawaii, emphasizing cacti and succulents.

DESCRIPTION AND COMMENTS Nearly 4,000 varieties of plant life are featured in this garden, which surrounds the former home of Koloa Plantation Company's last plantation manager (now the site of Plantation Gardens Restaurant). Lagoons, lily ponds, trees, and flowers provide photo opportunities. A highlight here is one of the finest cactus gardens in the world.

OTHER THINGS TO DO NEARBY McBryde and Allerton Gardens are a short drive away in Lawai.

National Tropical Botanical Garden–
McBryde and Allerton Gardens KAUAI

APPEAL BY AGE	PRESCHOOL ★	GRADE SCHOOL ★½	TEENS ★★★
YOUNG ADULTS ★★★½	OVER 30 ★★★★½	SENIORS ★★★★½	

Located in Lawai Valley; all tours (guided and self-guided) depart via tram from the visitor center across from Spouting Horn in Poipu, 4425 Lawai Road; ☎ 808-742-2623, tour information and reservations; www.ntbg.org

Admission Allerton Garden guided tours (reservations required): $35 for adults (age 13 and over), $20 for children age 10–12; children under age 10 not allowed on tour. McBryde Garden self-guided tours (reservations not required): $20 for adults, $10 for children age 6–12; children under age 6, free. **Hours** The visitor center is open daily, 8:30 a.m.–5 p.m. **When to go** Anytime. **How much time to allow** 2½ hours for Allerton Garden guided tours; 1½ hours for doing it on your own at McBryde Garden. **Author's rating** ★★★★½; research gardens meet formal estate gardens in a serene tropical environment

DESCRIPTION AND COMMENTS The National Tropical Botanical Garden (NTBG) headquarters in Lawai boasts one of the world's largest collections of rare and endangered tropical flora, including palms, heliconia, orchids, and other plants that have been collected from tropical regions throughout the world. Made up of several gardens in Hawaii and one in Florida, NTBG is the only national research garden chartered by Congress. McBryde Garden, formerly named Lawai Garden, is primarily a research, education, and conservation garden featuring 171 acres of native and exotic plants, including rare and endangered Hawaiian species. In contrast to McBryde Garden's natural landscape, neighboring 10-acre Allerton Garden, once a retreat of Hawaii's Queen Emma, boasts immaculately groomed formal gardens, including waterfalls, gazebos, and a bamboo jungle. A gift shop at the visitor center offers island gift items.

TOURING TIPS McBryde Garden self-guided tour trams depart hourly (on the half-hour) from 9:30 a.m. to 2:30 p.m., daily. Allerton Garden offers guided tours Monday–Saturday at 9 and 10 a.m. and 1 and 2 p.m. Wear comfortable shoes, as you will walk about a mile on either tour. Check in for both tours at least 15 minutes ahead of time.

Waioli Mission House Museum, Hanalei KAUAI

APPEAL BY AGE	PRESCHOOL ★½	GRADE SCHOOL ★★	TEENS ★★½
YOUNG ADULTS ★★½	OVER 30 ★★★	SENIORS ★★★½	

Hanalei, behind Mission Hall and Waioli Church; ☎ 808-245-3202; www.hawaiimuseums.org/mc/iskauai_waioli.htm

Admission Free. **Hours** Tuesday, Thursday, and Saturday, 9 a.m.–3 p.m. Guided tours are available. **When to go** Anytime. **How much time to allow** 30 minutes–1 hour. **Author's rating** ★★½; recommended for anyone interested in Hanalei history and the missionary era.

DESCRIPTION AND COMMENTS Built in 1837, this structure was the home of missionaries Lucy and Abner Wilcox. The New England–style Waioli Mission Hall and Waioli Huiia Church are located on adjoining grounds. What brings it to life are docents in period dress who act the part. You get a sense of what life was like for the missionaries who landed in exotic, faraway, and impossibly scenic Hanalei.

OTHER THINGS TO DO NEARBY Limahuli Garden and Preserve is located just 10 minutes north on the highway.

MOLOKAI

Molokai Museum and Cultural Center MOLOKAI

APPEAL BY AGE	PRESCHOOL ★★½	GRADE SCHOOL ★★	TEENS ★★½
YOUNG ADULTS ★★★	OVER 30 ★★★		SENIORS ★★★½

On Kalae Highway, just west of Kaunakakai; ☎ 808-567-6436

Admission $2.50 for adults; $1 for students ages 5–18. **Hours** Monday–Saturday, 10 a.m.–2 p.m. **When to go** Anytime. **How much time to allow** 1 hour. **Author's rating** ★★½; not terribly exciting, but filled with history.

DESCRIPTION AND COMMENTS The museum is a restored sugar mill established in 1878 by Rudolph Wilhelm Meyer, an engineer and surveyor who arrived on Molokai in 1851 and married a Hawaiian princess. Now listed on the National Register of Historic Places, the mill houses original machinery and other artifacts from sugar-plantation days. Guided tours and Hawaiian cultural programs are offered.

PART EIGHT

GREAT OUTDOORS

OUTDOOR HAWAII IS WHAT THE ISLANDS ARE ALL ABOUT. The weather seldom intrudes, the scenery lures you, no snakes or toxic plants block your path, and you have abundant choices, from lolling on hundreds of beaches to climbing Diamond Head Crater, from plunging in waterfall pools to learning to surf. Golf is so popular that we've devoted a lengthy section to various courses (see page 329). Activities and guided tours can be arranged by a concierge or hotel activity desk, or you can arrange many on your own.

HAWAII *by* SEA: *Get Wet*

THE BEACH EXPERIENCE

A SWIMMING POOL MAY LOOK INVITING, but head for the beach first. The Hawaiian Islands boast some of the world's finest beaches on 180 collective miles of sandy shoreline—243 beaches, all open to the public. Sands come not only in traditional gold but also in black, green, or red. Some beaches have natural splendor (such as Hanalei or Lanikai) or resort action (like Waikiki or Kaanapali), but we're confident you will find beaches in Hawaii that meet your every need: strolling, water sports, or just lying around.

Hawaii's beaches often top the "Best Beach in America" list compiled by geologist Stephen Leatherman ("Dr. Beach") of Florida International University, who rates beaches on environmental quality, aesthetics, water safety, and amenities (visit **www.topbeaches.com** to learn more).

Beaches may not be exactly the same from visit to visit. Beaches that are big in winter can be small in summer; the reverse is also true. Kilauea Volcano is still building beaches on the southeast shoreline of the Big Island, which is the youngest and least eroded in the chain and consequently has the fewest beaches. Kauai, oldest of the major islands, is ringed with scenic strands of sand in all shapes and sizes. Storms rage in every decade or so to remodel island sands, and human-caused coastal erosion is as much a problem in the Aloha State as it is anywhere else. Some beaches vanish overnight under high tides, like White Sands Beach, also known as Disappearing Sands, on the Kona coast.

Lucky beachcombers can find treasures like shells and glass fishing floats on certain beaches, including those on north and east shores of Kauai and Oahu. We have also found shells on Kihei beaches. People-watchers are endlessly entertained at crowded beaches, such as Waikiki. Seekers of solitude can leave resort beaches and easily find remote strands, where the only footprints are their own. But the resorts are located on certain beaches because the sands are superlative, so plenty of residents take advantage of public access to use them, and so can you.

Many resorts have public trails to walk or jog while you're checking out the beach action and perhaps looking for whales, like Wailea and Kaanapali resorts on Maui or Mauna Lani and Mauna Kea on the Big Island. Several also maintain publicly accessible historic sites. The public is welcome in hotel restaurants, spas, stores, and bars.

unofficial **TIP**
All Hawaiian resorts are required to provide public beach access, so look for beach-access signs and pathways nearby.

Though the beaches are grand, the water is even better. Even the most devoted sun-seeking beachgoers who don't want to get their hair wet can't resist a refreshing dip in the ocean. The seawater is clear, ideal in temperature, and salty enough to make you quite buoyant. To swim easily in the ocean is a joyous experience and one of the most special aspects of Hawaii.

The same mid-Pacific location that keeps Hawaii's waters clean and warm demands great respect for the sea. Like any other natural environment, Hawaii's seas are not entirely hazard-free. The biggest dangers are seasonal surf and currents, posted on most park beaches. Heed lifeguards and warning signs, and never turn your back on the ocean. Many Hawaiian beaches are sheltered by reefs, but those that are not get pounded, usually in winter, by relentless waves that slap the shore with such force that they can knock the unwary off their feet and send them out to sea.

Kauai's scenic Lumahai Beach, where Mitzi Gaynor "washed that man right out of her hair" in the movie *South Pacific,* is notorious for the number of newlyweds and others swept away while posing for photos at the shoreline with their backs to big waves.

You can see and hear rising surf; it's an awesome phenomenon, best observed safely from shore. When the surf comes up, village stores may even shut down while local surfers head out to catch some waves. But novices are wise to consider big-wave surfing strictly a spectator sport. Swimming is out of the question. By the same token, most bodysurfers have heard of fabled Sandy Beach on Oahu's south shore, a pinnacle challenge for that sport. But when the water is

Oahu Beaches and Outdoor Activities

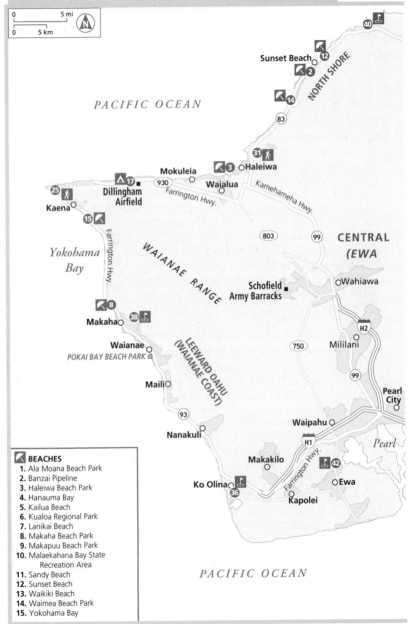

0   5 mi
0   5 km

PACIFIC OCEAN

NORTH SHORE

Sunset Beach

Mokuleia
Waialua
Haleiwa

930

Farrington Hwy.

Kamehameha Hwy.

**Dillingham
Airfield**

Kaena

803   99

**CENTRAL
(EWA**

*Yokohama
Bay*

WAIANAE RANGE

**Schofield
Army Barracks**

Wahiawa

Farrington Hwy.

Makaha

Waianae
POKAI BAY BEACH PARK

LEEWARD OAHU
(WAIANAE COAST)

750

H2

Mililani

Maili

99

**Pearl
City**

93

Waipahu

Nanakuli

H1

Pearl

Makakilo

Farrington Hwy.

42

Ko Olina
36

Ewa

Kapolei

PACIFIC OCEAN

⬈ BEACHES
1. Ala Moana Beach Park
2. Banzai Pipeline
3. Haleiwa Beach Park
4. Hanauma Bay
5. Kailua Beach
6. Kualoa Regional Park
7. Lanikai Beach
8. Makaha Beach Park
9. Makapuu Beach Park
10. Malaekahana Bay State
    Recreation Area
11. Sandy Beach
12. Sunset Beach
13. Waikiki Beach
14. Waimea Beach Park
15. Yokohama Bay

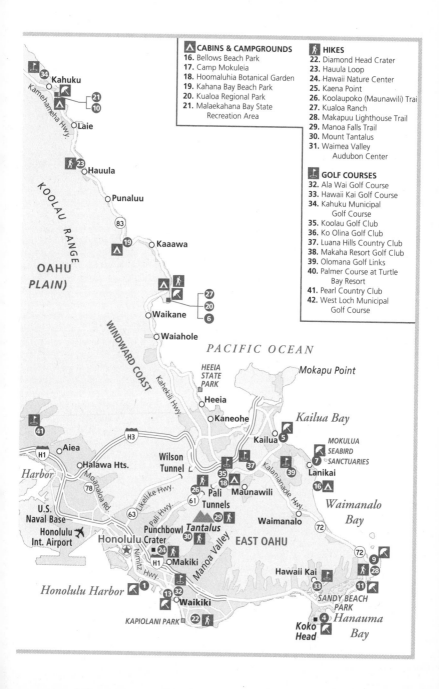

CABINS & CAMPGROUNDS
16. Bellows Beach Park
17. Camp Mokuleia
18. Hoomaluhia Botanical Garden
19. Kahana Bay Beach Park
20. Kualoa Regional Park
21. Malaekahana Bay State
    Recreation Area

HIKES
22. Diamond Head Crater
23. Hauula Loop
24. Hawaii Nature Center
25. Kaena Point
26. Koolaupoko (Maunawili) Trail
27. Kualoa Ranch
28. Makapuu Lighthouse Trail
29. Manoa Falls Trail
30. Mount Tantalus
31. Waimea Valley
    Audubon Center

GOLF COURSES
32. Ala Wai Golf Course
33. Hawaii Kai Golf Course
34. Kahuku Municipal
    Golf Course
35. Koolau Golf Club
36. Ko Olina Golf Club
37. Luana Hills Country Club
38. Makaha Resort Golf Club
39. Olomana Golf Links
40. Palmer Course at Turtle
    Bay Resort
41. Pearl Country Club
42. West Loch Municipal
    Golf Course

Kahuku

Kamehameha Hwy.

Laie

Hauula

KOOLAU RANGE

Punaluu

OAHU PLAIN)

Kaaawa

Kahekili Hwy.

Waikane

Waiahole

WINDWARD COAST

PACIFIC OCEAN

HEEIA STATE PARK

Mokapu Point

Heeia

Kaneohe

Kailua Bay

Kailua

MOKULUA SEABIRD SANCTUARIES

H3

Aiea

Halawa Hts.

Harbor

Wilson Tunnel

Moanalua Rd.

Likelike Hwy.

Lanikai

Kalanianaole Hwy.

Pali Tunnels

Maunawili

Waimanalo Bay

U.S. Naval Base

Honolulu Int. Airport

Punchbowl Crater

Tantalus

Waimanalo

EAST OAHU

Manoa Valley

Nimitz Hwy.

Makiki

Hawaii Kai

Honolulu Harbor

Waikiki

SANDY BEACH PARK

KAPIOLANI PARK

Koko Head

Hanauma Bay

Big Island Beaches and Outdoor Activities

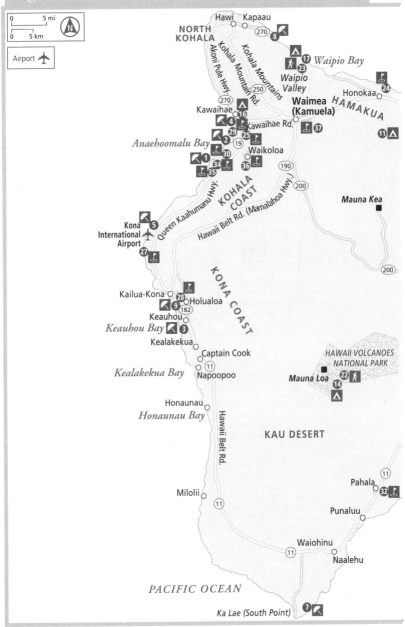

0 5 mi
0 5 km

Airport

Hawi   Kapaau
NORTH   270   8
KOHALA
Waipio Bay
17
23   Waipio
Valley
250   Honokaa   24
Kawaihae   HAMAKUA
16   Waimea
270   4   (Kamuela)
Kawaihae Rd.
29   37
2
Anaehoomalu Bay   25   11
19
30   Waikoloa
1   36
34   190
35   KOHALA
COAST   200
Mauna Kea
Kona   5
International   Queen Kaahumanu Hwy.
Airport   Hawaii Belt Rd. (Mamalahoa Hwy.)
27
KONA COAST
Kailua-Kona   28
9   Holualoa
Keauhou   182
Keauhou Bay   3
Kealakekua
Captain Cook   200
11
Kealakekua Bay
Napoopoo   HAWAII VOLCANOES
NATIONAL PARK
Honaunau   22
Honaunau Bay   Mauna Loa   14
KAU DESERT
Hawaii Belt Rd.
11
Pahala
Milolii   32
11   Punaluu
Waiohinu
11   Naalehu

PACIFIC OCEAN

Ka Lae (South Point)   7

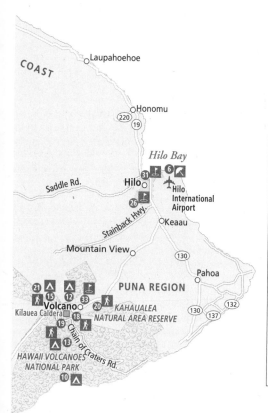

BEACHES
1. Anaehoomalu Beach (A-Bay)
2. Hapuna Beach County Park
3. Kahaluu Beach Park
4. Kaunaoa (Mauna Kea) Beach
5. Kekaha Kai State Park
6. Leleiwi Beach Park
7. Papakolea Green Sand Beach
8. Pololu Beach
9. White Sands Beach

CABINS & CAMPGROUNDS
10. Halape Shelter
11. Kalopa State Recreation Area
12. Kilauea State Recreation Area
13. Kulanaokuaiki Campground
14. Mauna Loa Summit Cabins
15. Namakani Paio Campground
16. Spencer Beach Park
17. Waimanu Valley Campground

HIKES
18. Devastation Trail
19. Halemaumau Trail
20. Kilauea Iki Trail
21. Kipuka Puaulu (Bird Park) Trail
22. Mauna Loa Trail
23. Waimanu Valley's Muliwai Trail

GOLF COURSES
24. Hamakua Country Club
25. Hapuna Golf Course
26. Hilo Municipal Golf Course
27. Hualalai Golf Club
28. Kona Country Club
29. Mauna Kea Golf Course
30. Mauna Lani Resort Frances
   I'i Brown Championship
   Courses
31. Naniloa Volcanoes Golf Club
32. Sea Mountain Golf Course
33. Volcano Golf and Country Club
34. Waikoloa Beach Course
35. Waikoloa Kings' Course
36. Waikoloa Village Golf Course
37. Waimea Country Club

Hawaii Volcanoes National Park

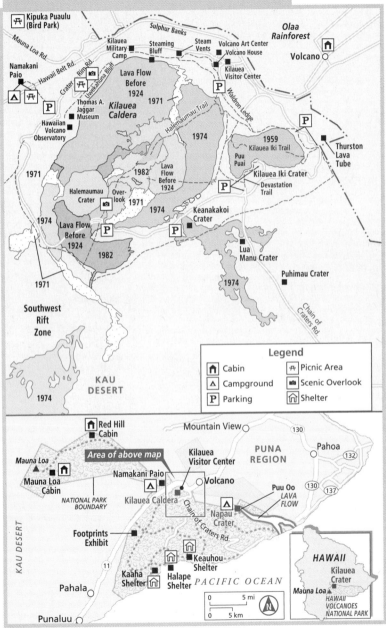

Kipuka Puaulu (Bird Park)
Mauna Loa Rd.
Olaa Rainforest
Sulphur Banks
Kilauea Military Camp
Steaming Bluff
Steam Vents
Volcano Art Center
Volcano House
Volcano
Namakani Paio
Hawaii Belt Rd.
Crater Rim Rd.
Uwekahuna Bluff
Kilauea Visitor Center
Lava Flow Before 1924
1971
Thomas A. Jaggar Museum
Kilauea Caldera
Waldron Ledge
Hawaiian Volcano Observatory
Halemaumau Trail
1974
1959
Kilauea Iki Trail
Thurston Lava Tube
1971
Puu Puai
1982
Lava Flow Before 1924
1971
Kilauea Iki Crater
Devastation Trail
Halemaumau Crater
Overlook
1974
Keanakakoi Crater
1974
Lava Flow Before 1924
1982
Lua Manu Crater
1971
Puhimau Crater
Southwest Rift Zone
1974
Chain of Craters Rd.

KAU DESERT

1974

Legend

Cabin		Picnic Area	
Campground		Scenic Overlook	
Parking		Shelter	

Red Hill Cabin
Mountain View
130
PUNA REGION
Pahoa
Mauna Loa
Area of above map
Kilauea Visitor Center
132
Mauna Loa Cabin
NATIONAL PARK BOUNDARY
Namakani Paio
Volcano
Puu Oo LAVA FLOW
130
Kilauea Caldera
137
Chain of Craters Rd.
KAU DESERT
Napau Crater
Footprints Exhibit
11
Keauhou Shelter
Kaaha Shelter
Halape Shelter
PACIFIC OCEAN
Pahala
0   5 mi
0   5 km
N
Punaluu

HAWAII
Kilauea Crater
Mauna Loa
HAWAII VOLCANOES NATIONAL PARK

rampaging, the wicked shore break can break necks too. It's Hawaii's most dangerous beach.

Currents are insidious, because you can't always tell when and where they are. The major Hawaiian Islands are sunken mountains with deep, steep sides and resulting strong currents. Kealaikahiki Channel, off the south coast of Lanai, is famous for a powerful current that leads straight to Tahiti, 1,500 miles away. (That's what "Kealaikahiki" means—"the way to Tahiti.") Should you get carried out by a rip current, don't panic. Figure out which direction is perpendicular to the current and also leads toward shore, and swim across the current toward safety.

Shark attacks are rare in Hawaiian waters, but sharks themselves are not. Don't swim or surf alone at sunset or in murky waters when the predators feed. Most hazardous are invasions of jellyfish—box jellyfish, which appear often at Waikiki and Ala Moana beaches nine or ten days after the full moon, and are nasty enough that lifeguards issue warnings and supply soothing vinegar to treat the stings.

unofficial **TIP**
The greatest health hazard is the jellyfish. Treat the stings of the box jellyfish with vinegar; treat the burns of the blue-bottle jellyfish with blue aloe vera gel.

You might also encounter the milder Hawaiian version of Portuguese man-of-war, known as blue bottles, which float in from time to time. Your first clue to their presence might be stepping on a small, blue balloon that pops along the debris line onshore. On the water's surface, this jellyfish appears as an innocent floating bubble, but the unseen trailing blue tendril leaves a burn that stings like a knife blade. Our hint for a quick antidote is the blue-colored aloe vera gel widely sold in Hawaii as a sunburn soother. Be sure to keep a bottle in your beach bag. A dab on a blue-bottle sting will extinguish the fire for most victims. More extreme allergic reactions may require quick and expert medical care.

Swimmers and snorkelers sometimes run into coral heads and find later that they got cut or scraped in the process. Coral cuts tend to infect quickly, and the antidote in this case is hydrogen peroxide, the WD-40 of tropical living. Put that in your beach bag, too.

Obviously, a foremost beach-bag item should be sunscreen. No pale-skinned visitor wants to return home from the Islands without a golden Hawaiian tan. But go easy—this tropical sun is strong, the ocean air is clear, and burns happen very quickly, particularly on children. Don't go out without sunscreen in Hawaii—it's that simple. Apply it before you go outside; reapply it after swim-

unofficial **TIP**
Coral scrapes and cuts infect quickly—treat with hydrogen peroxide as soon as you come out of the water.

ming, snorkeling, or sweating a lot; and try to avoid midday exposure. You can get a great tan at 9 a.m. or after 3 or 4 in the afternoon, even with SPF 15 sunscreen. If skin cancer doesn't scare you, maybe wrinkles will (take a good look at the skin on senior surfers).

Maui Beaches and Outdoor Activities

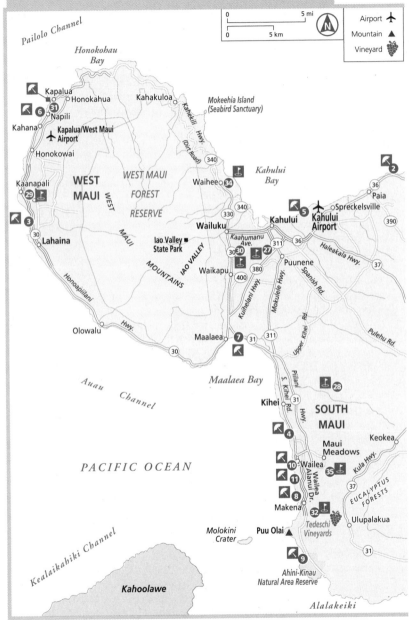

0   5 mi
0   5 km

N

Airport ✈
Mountain ▲
Vineyard 🍇

Pailolo Channel

Honokohau Bay

Honokohau
Kapalua
Honokahua
Kahakuloa
Mokeehia Island
(Seabird Sanctuary)

Napili
Kahana
Kapalua/West Maui Airport

Honokowai

WEST MAUI

WEST MAUI FOREST RESERVE

Waihee
Kahului Bay

Kaanapali

WEST MAUI MOUNTAINS

Wailuku
Kahului
Kahului Airport
Spreckelsville
Paia

Lahaina

Iao Valley State Park
IAO VALLEY

Waikapu

Puunene

Haleakala Hwy.

Kaahumanu Ave.

Olowalu

Maalaea

Maalaea Bay

Pulehu Rd.

Kihei

SOUTH MAUI

Keokea

Maui Meadows

Wailea

Makena

Tedeschi Vineyards

Ulupalakua

EUCALYPTUS FORESTS

PACIFIC OCEAN

Molokini Crater
Puu Olai

Ahini-Kinau
Natural Area Reserve

Kealaikahiki Channel

Kahoolawe

Alalakeiki

Auau Channel

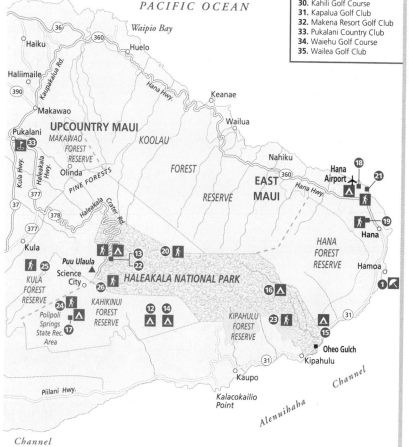

BEACHES
1. Hamoa Beach
2. Hookipa Beach Park
3. Kaanapali Beach
4. Kamaole III Beach Park
5. Kanaha Beach Park
6. Kapalua Beach
7. Maalaea Beach
8. Maluaka (Makena) Beach State Park
9. Oneloa Beach (Big Beach)
10. Ulua Beach
11. Wailea Beach

CABINS & CAMPGROUNDS
12. Holua Cabin & Campground
13. Hosmer Grove
14. Kapalaoa Cabin
15. Kipahulu Campground
16. Paliku Cabin & Campground
17. Polipoli Springs State Recreation Area Campground
18. Waianapanapa State Park

HIKES
19. Fagan's Cross
20. Halemauu Trail
21. Hana-Waianapanapa Coastal Trail
22. Hosmer Grove Nature Trail
23. Kaupo Gap
24. Polipoli Loop
25. Skyline Trail
26. Sliding Sands Trail

GOLF COURSES
27. Dunes at Maui Lani
28. Elleair Maui Golf Course
29. Kaanapali Gulch Courses
30. Kahili Golf Course
31. Kapalua Golf Club
32. Makena Resort Golf Club
33. Pukalani Country Club
34. Waiehu Golf Course
35. Wailea Golf Club

Haleakala National Park

Legend

🛈 Ranger Station	♿ Handicap Access	▲ Mountain Peak
ⓘ Information	⌂ Picnic Area	■ Point of Interest
	Scientific Research Reserve	⋯ Hiking Trail
⌂ Shelter Cabin		
⌂ Campground		

Kukui Bay

To Hana→ (31)

Oheo Gulch

Kipahulu Area

Makahiku Falls

Kipahulu Valley

Kipahulu Campground

Palikea

Waimoku Falls Trail

SCIENTIFIC RESEARCH RESERVE
(Closed to Entry)

Kaupo Trail

Kalapawili Ridge

Paliku Cabin & Campground

Kaupo Gap

Hanakauhi ▲

Kapalaoa Cabin

Silversword Loop

Halemauu Trail

HALEAKALA CRATER AREA

Bottomless Pit

Sliding Sands Trail

Koolau Gap

Hosmer Grove

Holua Cabin & Campground

Leleiwi Overlook

Kalahaku Overlook

Haupaakea Peak ▲

Haleakala ▲ Haupaakea Peak

Park Headquarters

To Kahului ← (378)

Visitor Center

Puu-Ulaula Overlook

MAUI

Hana

HALEAKALA NATIONAL PARK

N

1 mi
1 km

0
0

Kauai Beaches and Outdoor Activities

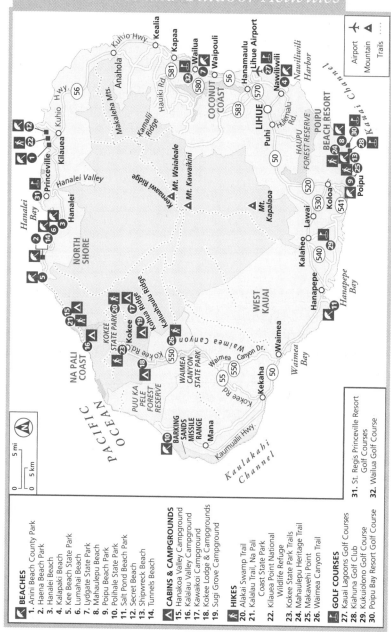

BEACHES
1. Anini Beach County Park
2. Haena Beach Park
3. Hanalei Beach
4. Kalapaki Beach
5. Kee Beach State Park
6. Lumahai Beach
7. Lydgate State Park
8. Mahaulepu Beach
9. Poipu Beach Park
10. Polihale State Park
11. Salt Pond Beach Park
12. Secret Beach
13. Shipwreck Beach
14. Tunnels Beach

CABINS & CAMPGROUNDS
15. Hanakoa Valley Campground
16. Kalalau Valley Campground
17. Kawaikoi Campground
18. Kokee Lodge & Campgrounds
19. Sugi Grove Campground

HIKES
20. Alakai Swamp Trail
21. Kalalau Trail, Na Pali Coast State Park
22. Kilauea Point National Wildlife Refuge
23. Kokee State Park Trails
24. Mahaulepu Heritage Trail
25. Makawehi Point
26. Waimea Canyon Trail

GOLF COURSES
27. Kauai Lagoons Golf Courses
28. Kiahuna Golf Club
29. Kukuiolono Golf Course
30. Poipu Bay Resort Golf Course
31. St. Regis Princeville Resort Golf Courses
32. Wailua Golf Course

One other precaution about your beach bag: Leave your most valuable belongings in your room or in a safe when you head for the beach. If you carry a good camera or money, don't leave it unattended. You wouldn't tempt fate at home; don't do it in Hawaii, either.

HAWAII'S TOP BEACHES

OAHU

 ### Ala Moana Beach Park GREATER HONOLULU
**1201 Ala Moana Boulevard,
directly across from Ala Moana Center**

ACTIVITIES Swimming, surfing, bodyboarding, scuba diving, fishing

SPECIAL APPEAL Safe swimming, good for kids, nearness to Waikiki and Ala Moana Center, park facilities, shade

COMMENTS This shoreline oasis, stretching for more than a mile between Waikiki and Honolulu, is one of America's best urban beach parks and the most popular with local families. The beach is a narrow half-mile stretch of white sand with a deep swimming channel. Thanks to light surf, it's considered one of the most swimmable beaches in Hawaii and one of the best for children.

Lifeguards are on duty daily. Magic Island, a 30-acre man-made extension at the eastern end of the park, is a popular spot for picnicking and jogging. The facilities include softball fields, tennis courts, a lawn-bowling area, food concessions, showers, restrooms, the McCoy Pavilion, and more than 100 acres of picnic areas. Parking is limited but is available on the road between the park and beach and in a lot near Magic Island.

 ### Kailua Beach Park WINDWARD OAHU
450 Kawailoa Road, Kailua

Activities Swimming, surfing, windsurfing, bodyboarding, bodysurfing, canoeing, kayaking, beachcombing, sailing, boating

SPECIAL APPEAL Good walking, gentle waves, scenery, occasional brisk trades, shade, dunes, picnic areas

COMMENTS "Best Beach in America" winner. The crescent-shaped, golden-sand beach is more than two miles long. The waters are ideal for swimming, surfing, and sailing. This is one of Hawaii's best-known windsurfing and kayaking areas. Inexperienced surfers, bodyboarders, and bodysurfers will find waves they can handle. Facilities include restrooms, showers, a snack stand, equipment rentals, and picnic areas. Lifeguards are on duty daily.

Lanikai Beach WINDWARD OAHU
Fronting Mokulua Drive, Lanikai

ACTIVITIES Swimming, kayaking, canoe paddling, snorkeling, windsurfing, surfing, sailing, fishing

SPECIAL APPEAL Beauty, some shade, safe for small kids and swimmers, uncrowded on weekdays

COMMENTS One of Oahu's best family beaches. This scenic, mile-long stretch of golden beach with a vivid aqua-and-green lagoon bordered by photogenic islets is Hawaii's best for swimming. Waves are docile, thanks to the sheltering reef, and thus offer safe swimming for children, the handicapped, and the elderly. It's a favorite spot for paddlers and for kayakers who head out to the Mokulua, two islets about three-fourths of a mile offshore. Both are state seabird sanctuaries, but the larger, more accessible Moku Nui is a popular target for boaters and swimmers. Human access is restricted to its beaches. The Mokulua, particularly at sunrise, frame a breathtaking scene often used in ads and TV commercials, so it may look familiar to you. This neighborhood beach lacks public facilities or lifeguards. The beach is widest at the middle and northern ends. The southern end has been experiencing severe erosion due to seawalls. Public access is marked with signs on Mokulua Drive.

For a terrific view of the Windward Coast and passing whales in winter, hike up Ka Iwa Ridge behind the community. As you drive into the one-way Lanikai loop, take the first right on Kaelepulu, park near the cul de sac, and go uphill next to the fence. This is not for people afraid of narrow-ridge heights, but it's an easy climb to the concrete World War II bunkers and back.

Sandy Beach GREATER HONOLULU
8800 Kalanianaole Highway, Hawaii Kai, south shore

ACTIVITIES Bodyboarding, bodysurfing, skimboarding, fishing

SPECIAL APPEAL Daredevil bodysurfing

COMMENTS Great local atmosphere. The 1,000-foot-long beach at the base of Koko Crater is known for its challenging shore break and feats of daring performed by local experts in wave riding. Some of Oahu's best bodysurfers, skimboarders, and bodyboarders strut their stuff here, and it's worth a visit to see them in action. Because the beach is subject to treacherous surf throughout the year, you should swim only when the waves are flat. Lifeguards are on duty daily. Restrooms, showers, and picnic areas are available.

Sunset Beach THE NORTH SHORE
59-100 Kamehameha Highway, Sunset Beach

ACTIVITIES Surfing, bodysurfing, bodyboarding, summer swimming

SPECIAL APPEAL Big-wave surfing, scenic beauty

COMMENTS Some of the biggest winter waves in the world pound ashore along the coast from here to Haleiwa. This is the fabled North Shore, nirvana for surfers. This mile-long beach and its neighbors draw expert surfers from all parts of the world. In summer, the golden sands stretch to a strand of more than 200 feet in width, popular with swimmers and bodysurfers. But the beach narrows in winter, when waves rise ten feet or more and the pounding surf sometimes forces evacuations. The annual Triple Crown of Surfing professional events are held here. Lifeguards are on duty daily. Portable restrooms are available.

Neighboring North Shore beaches include Ehukai Beach, home of the world-renowned Banzai Pipeline, a curling wave that skilled surfers ride through, and Waimea Bay Beach, whose most famous wave is the 30-foot signature monster wave that introduced the television show *Hawaii 5-0.*

Waikiki Beach WAIKIKI
Fronting Waikiki resort area

ACTIVITIES Swimming, surfing, bodyboarding, snorkeling, outrigger-canoe riding, sailing, kayaking, fishing

SPECIAL APPEAL Beachgoers of all ages, from the old-timers who play chess and cards in the sidewalk pavilions to the bikinied multitudes bronzing in the sand and the surfers offshore

COMMENTS The world's most famous beach is a two-mile stretch of imported golden sand, from Hilton Hawaiian Village on one end to the cluster of high-rises at the base of Diamond Head at the other. Great for strolling the new beachside walkway, swimming, sunbathing, water sports, and people-watching. The average water temperature ranges from 77°F to 82°F, depending on the season. Beachgoers are most concentrated in front of four neighboring hotels—Sheraton Waikiki, Royal Hawaiian, Outrigger Waikiki Beach, and Sheraton Moana Surfrider—and least crowded in the Kapiolani Park beach areas, such as Queen's Surf Beach (by the aquarium) and Sans Souci Beach (by the New Otani Kaimana Beach Hotel).

Waikiki Beach is an amalgam of several beaches (in order from *Ewa* to *Diamond Head*): Duke Kahanamoku Beach, Fort DeRussy Beach, Gray's Beach, Kuhio Beach, Queen's Surf Beach, and Sans Souci Beach. Sans Souci is our favorite—it's low-key and safe for swimming. Public facilities and services throughout Waikiki include restrooms, showers, equipment rentals, snacks, and surfing lessons. Lifeguards are on duty daily. Free parking is limited to the streets of Kapiolani Park.

MAUI

Kaanapali Beach WEST MAUI
Honoapiilani Highway, fronting Kaanapali Beach Resort

ACTIVITIES Swimming, bodysurfing, bodyboarding, snorkeling, scuba diving, windsurfing, kayaking, sailing, fishing

SPECIAL APPEAL   Places to hang for teens and young people, coastal walkway, boats that cruise from beach landings

COMMENTS   This is a popular resort beach. Swimming conditions are good when the surf is flat; otherwise, strong currents, undertow, and a drop-off make this a "swim at your own risk" beach. The base of Black Rock, a volcanic cinder cone jutting up at the center of the four-mile beach, is a protected and crowded snorkeling site. A lifeguard is on duty at the Lahaina end. Beach concessions and outdoor showers are available at various points along the walkway that links Kaanapali's neighboring hotels and condos.

 Kapalua Beach WEST MAUI
Lower Honoapiilani Highway, Kapalua Resort

ACTIVITIES   Swimming, snorkeling, scuba diving, sailing, kayaking

SPECIAL APPEAL   Quiet atmosphere, good swimming, safe for kids

COMMENTS   This secluded strand on the Napili end of Kapalua Resort is one of Maui's best-looking and best-swimming beaches. Lava promontories protect both sides of the beach from rough water. Public facilities are available, but no lifeguards are on duty. The sunset is often spectacular, spotlighting Molokai across the channel.

Makena State Park SOUTH MAUI
Makena Alanui, Makena

ACTIVITIES   Swimming, surfing, snorkeling, bodysurfing, bodyboarding, fishing

SPECIAL APPEAL   Scenic beauty, undeveloped nature, walking (Big Beach)

COMMENTS   Makena State Park at Maui's southern end has two scenic golden-sand beaches: Big Beach and Little Beach. Big Beach, 3,300 feet long, is Maui's longest beach and a favorite spot for experienced bodyboarders and bodysurfers. Little Beach, meanwhile, is a small cove with gentler ocean conditions, a good prospect for novice wave riders. No lifeguards are on duty, nor are there public restrooms or showers. Secluded Little Beach is one of Hawaii's most popular "unofficial" nude beaches, even though public nudity is prohibited by law.

kids **Wailea Resort Beaches** SOUTH MAUI
On Wailea Alanui, Wailea

ACTIVITIES   Swimming, bodysurfing, bodyboarding, snorkeling, scuba diving, windsurfing, kayaking, sailing, fishing

SPECIAL APPEAL   Scenic beauty, resort surroundings, public-access facilities

COMMENTS   Wailea Resort has five golden-sand beaches: Polo, Wailea, Ulua, Mokapu, and Keawakapu. Wailea Beach—shared by the Four Seasons Maui, Grand Wailea, and the public—is an appealing golden crescent about 1,000 feet long and a "Best Beach in America" winner. The waters are clear, with gentle waves to ride and a singular view dotted with neighboring islands. Snorkel along the rocky promontory that defines one side of the beach, where green sea turtles frequent the waters.

Ulua is the centermost beach, 1,000 feet long and 200 feet wide, between the Renaissance Wailea and Outrigger Wailea beaches. Locals regard the offshore reef here as one of Maui's best snorkeling spots. A deeper reef, excellent for scuba diving, is about 100 yards out.

Wailea Resort's 1.5-mile coastal trail links public accessways to all the beaches and private hotel and condo properties. The southern end of the trail, between the Four Seasons and Kea Lani, features a showcase Hawaiian native-plant garden and historic house.

Public facilities include restrooms and showers. Beach concessions offer surfboard rentals and instruction. No lifeguards are on duty.

BIG ISLAND OF HAWAII

kids Anaehoomalu Beach KONA
Queen Kaahumanu Highway, Waikoloa Beach Resort, south shore of Anaehoomalu Bay, by historic fishponds and Marriott Waikoloa Beach Resort

---

ACTIVITIES Swimming, surfing, snorkeling, scuba diving, windsurfing, and kayaking

SPECIAL APPEAL Scenic setting, historic features

Comments This beach is a picture-perfect finger of golden sand with palms for shade, on a bay where ancient kings played. Suitable for a wide range of ocean activities, this beach is favored for windsurfing. Novices can frolic in the calmer waters near shore, which they may share with sea turtles. Expert riders enjoy the more-challenging wave conditions farther offshore. Public restrooms and showers are available. No lifeguards are on duty.

Papakolea Green Sand Beach KONA
Mamalahoa Highway near Naalehu at the southern tip of the island; turn off on South Point Road to Ka Lae (South Cape). The paved road ends at Kaulana Boat Ramp. This beach is about 2.5 miles east via a dirt road. You can park at the ramp and hike in or use a four-wheel-drive vehicle.

ACTIVITIES Beachcombing, fishing

SPECIAL APPEAL Green sand

COMMENTS An off-the-beaten-path beach for active adventurers, but perhaps a bit rugged for little kids. The sand is green, with fragments of olivine rock. High surf throughout the year can pose danger. No lifeguards are on duty. Beachcombers can hunt for gemstone-sized lumps of pale green olivine, a volcanic phenomenon.

This is the most famous green-sand beach, but if your kids are pining to see green sand, try searching the shore from the public beach park at Kaupulehu between Kona Village Resort and Four Seasons Hualalei. We have found green mixed with white-coral and black-lava sands there.

kids Hapuna Beach State Park KONA
Queen Kaahumanu Highway, Kohala Coast; look for a highway sign for the entrance to the park

---

ACTIVITIES Swimming, surfing, bodyboarding, bodysurfing, snorkeling, camping

SPECIAL APPEAL Biggest Big Island strand, the only one with camp cabins

COMMENTS Hapuna Beach is a gold-sand jewel stretching more than half a mile and more than 200 feet across. It is very popular with bodyboarders and bodysurfers, and can get crowded on weekends and holidays. Public restrooms, showers, camping shelters, and picnic pavilions are available. Lifeguards are on duty daily and can inform you of current ocean conditions, which are often rough during the winter. Walk up the coastal path in front of the Westin Hapuna Beach Prince a short distance, and you'll discover a hidden snorkeling cove teeming with fish.

Kaunaoa Beach KONA
Queen Kaahumanu Highway, fronting the Mauna Kea Beach Hotel within Mauna Kea Resort, Kohala Coast

ACTIVITIES Swimming, surfing, bodyboarding, bodysurfing, snorkeling

SPECIAL APPEAL Great protected swimming, friendly waves, scenic setting

COMMENTS There's no finer way to begin your day than with a morning swim on this beach, the Big Island's best. The water is clear, calm enough to swim across from one side of the 2,500-foot strand to the other, and sends waves that roll you lazily to shore. The neighboring hotel is one of the oldest and most venerated, and this beach is one good reason why. The water is inviting to ocean enthusiasts of all types, from snorkelers to bodysurfers. No lifeguards are on duty, but hotel beach attendants know current ocean conditions. Public facilities are available. If you stay after dark, stroll along the coastal walk to a floodlit platform to watch the manta rays that come to shore to feed on smaller creatures drawn to the light.

Pololu Beach KONA
Highway 270, North Kohala; park at the end of the road and take the 15-minute hike down an ancient switchback trail from the Pololu Lookout

ACTIVITIES Beachcombing, surfing, bodyboarding, fishing

SPECIAL APPEAL Scenic beauty, hiking, beachcombing

COMMENTS A scenic black-sand beach with plenty of photo ops. No lifeguards or public facilities are provided. Because this remote beach is exposed to treacherous surf throughout the year, do not swim here unless the ocean is flat. This is a favored site for beachcombers, who scour the shoreline for treasures blown in by storms or high surf.

KAUAI

Hanalei Bay KAUAI
Weke Road, Hanalei Pavilion Beach Park, behind the village of Hanalei on Kauai's north shore

ACTIVITIES Swimming, surfing, bodyboarding, bodysurfing, snorkeling, windsurfing, sailing, fishing, canoeing

SPECIAL APPEAL Spectacular scenic setting, seasonally gentle bodysurfing waves, walking, winter surfing

COMMENTS Hanalei Bay is a dream come true. The golden sands extend about two miles around the scenic bay. On one side, the clear waters stretch out toward Japan; on the other is a bowl of lush, green mountains ribboned with waterfalls and capped with jagged volcanic peaks. The bay shore is bordered by private homes with public access via walkways and a trio of beach parks—Black Pot Beach Park, Waioli Beach Park, and Hanalei Pavilion Beach Park—in the center. Restrooms and showers are available at each. In summer, visiting yachts moor in the calm waters. In winter, the boats head for safer shelter because the surf can exceed ten feet, making Hanalei popular with the best surfers. Lifeguards are stationed at Black Pot Beach Park by the pier at the mouth of the Hanalei River.

kids Kalapaki Beach KAUAI
Fronting Kauai Marriott Resort on Nawiliwili Bay in Lihue

ACTIVITIES Swimming, surfing, bodyboarding, bodysurfing, snorkeling, windsurfing, sailing, fishing

SPECIAL APPEAL Walking, safe swimming for kids, passing ships, restaurants and bars close by

COMMENTS One of Kauai's busiest beaches, this strand is protected by cliffs and a seawall. The inlet between the cliffs leads to Nawiliwili's natural harbor and the Huleia River and Menehune Fish Pond behind it. While picnicking or playing on the beach, you may see large ships cruise by on their way into the harbor. Kalapaki is a safe playground for young children and a training ground for novice surfers. Showers and restrooms are provided for the public courtesy of the Kauai Marriott. Picnic facilities are available at Nawiliwili Park, adjacent to Kalapaki. No lifeguards are on duty.

kids Kee Beach KAUAI
End of Kuhio Highway, Haena State Park, North Shore; park along the road or in the small lot

ACTIVITIES Swimming, snorkeling, fishing

SPECIAL APPEAL Movie-set beauty (parts of *The Thorn Birds* were filmed here), views of Na Pali Coast, near-shore snorkeling

COMMENTS The reef surrounding Kee Beach breaks the waves, except for the giants of winter, and provides excellent snorkeling conditions. The shallow, protected lagoon is home to several species of rainbow-colored fish and offers safe swimming. No lifeguards are on duty, but public restrooms, outdoor showers, and some parking are provided. This area is the staging point for hikers bound for the Kalalau Trail, 12 miles along the precipitous Na Pali wilderness coast to Kalalau State Park beach, a true hiking commitment. Less-devoted hikers will enjoy the scenic first two miles of the (often muddy) trail to Hanakapiai Valley, where a stream littered with boulders runs from a scenic inland waterfall to the sea. The surf is rough there, so save the swim for your return to Kee Beach.

Lumahai Beach KAUAI
Kuhio Highway, at the foot of Lumahai Valley, North Shore; on the Hanalei end, park along the highway, then follow the trail down to the beach; on the far end, park in a grove of ironwood trees

ACTIVITIES Surfing, bodyboarding, bodysurfing, snorkeling, windsurfing, sailing, fishing

SPECIAL APPEAL Scenic splendor, walking

COMMENTS Some 4,000 feet long, this beautiful strip of shoreline was made famous in the movie *South Pacific*. It remains one of the most photographed beaches in the state. This beach is great for appreciating wild beauty from shore, but with no protective reef, swimming or even wading can be very risky. No lifeguards are on duty.

Poipu Beach Park KAUAI
Hoowili Road, just off of Poipu Beach Road, Poipu Beach Resort, South Shore

ACTIVITIES Swimming, bodysurfing, bodyboarding

SPECIAL APPEAL Kids' tide pool, resort beach

COMMENTS More than 1,000 feet long, Poipu Beach is a popular playground shared by public parks and accessways, and private hotels, restaurants, and condo resorts. Portions are sheltered enough for safe swimming by young children. Restrooms, showers, and picnic tables are available; lifeguards are on duty daily. Wave riders should avoid the area past Brennecke's, a rocky and hazardous point.

Polihale State Park (Barking Sands) KAUAI
Kaumualii Highway, Kekaha, end of the road on the west shore

ACTIVITIES Surfing, bodyboarding, windsurfing, summer swimming, camping

SPECIAL APPEAL Wide expanses of wild beauty at the foot of Na Pali

COMMENTS Polihale, 17 miles long and 300 feet wide, is Hawaii's biggest beach. The "Barking Sands" are dunes that squeak and bark under your feet when walked on, special effects thanks to the composition of the coral sands. Hawaiians named such sites ke one kani (musical sands). In summer, the reef protects a plunge known as Queen's Pond. Facilities include restrooms, showers, parking, and a pavilion. No lifeguards are on duty.

Secret Beach KAUAI
Kuhio Highway, near Kalihiwai Road, Kilauea, between Kilauea Point and Kalihiwai Bay; public access via a dirt road

ACTIVITIES Swimming, surfing, bodyboarding, bodysurfing, snorkeling, windsurfing, sailing, fishing

SPECIAL APPEAL Long stretch of golden beach, but beware: it has also gained a reputation as the island's best-known nude beach.

COMMENTS This 3,000-foot-long golden beach is called "secret" because it's not visible from any roads, not just because it is a favorite nude beach.

From land, it can be seen only from the Kilauea Point National Wildlife Refuge. A haven for hippies in the early 1970s, Secret Beach is now a popular summer swimming spot. Winter surf, however, poses danger for swimmers. There are no public facilities or lifeguards here. *A reminder:* Nude sunbathing is technically against the law in Hawaii, but certain beaches are so remote that nobody seems to mind. If you're offended, opt for another beach—there are plenty on Kauai.

Shipwreck Beach KAUAI
Fronting the Grand Hyatt Kauai Resort and Spa in Poipu Beach Resort, South Shore

ACTIVITIES Surfing, bodysurfing, windsurfing, fishing

SPECIAL APPEAL Coastal trail, dunes walk

COMMENTS Shipwreck Beach got its name from an unidentified wooden boat that lay crashed onshore for years until Hurricane Iwa washed it away in 1982. Low-lying rocks keep this golden-sand beach from being good for swimming, but bodysurfers and bodyboarders love it, especially in summer. The beach's most interesting sunbathers are often endangered Hawaiian monk seals or green sea turtles that surf the waves between the Hyatt and nearby Embassy Vacation Resort. Public restrooms and showers are available. A coastal walkway, about a mile long along the cliffs, leads to sand dunes that once served as a Hawaiian burial site. No lifeguards are on duty, but ocean conditions are posted.

kids Tunnels Beach KAUAI
Kuhio Highway, about a half mile beyond Haena Beach Park, North Shore

ACTIVITIES Surfing, bodyboarding, snorkeling, scuba diving, windsurfing, beachcombing, fishing

SPECIAL APPEAL Scenic splendor, seasonal shells, shade, near-shore reef tunnels

COMMENTS Tunnels is a grainy, gold-sand beach with good summer snorkeling around reefs and coral heads close to shore. Its name refers to the "tunnels" found in Makua Reef's lagoon, a popular scuba-diving spot. When the surf's up, Tunnels is one of Kauai's best surfing spots for expert wave riders. Restrooms and showers are available at the public beach park. No lifeguards are on duty.

MOLOKAI

Papohaku Beach MOLOKAI
Kaluakoi Road, just beyond defunct Kaluakoi Resort

ACTIVITIES Surfing, bodyboarding, bodysurfing, snorkeling

SPECIAL APPEAL Broad strand, wild beauty, shady picnics, great sunset views of Oahu

COMMENTS Two miles long and 400 feet wide, Papohaku Beach is the biggest beach on Molokai and one of the only sandy Molokai beaches that is easily accessible for families. However, since Molokai Ranch shut down the west end of the island you may find a *kapu* (prohibited) sign on the road to this beach. This isn't a swimming beach, but more a wilderness strand with good paved-road access and public-beach park facilities—restrooms, showers, parking, and camping sites sheltered in the shoreline *kiawe* forest. Dangerous swimming conditions exist because the beach is fully exposed to the forces of the sea and surf. High-surf conditions can occur any time of year. No lifeguards are on duty.

Sandy Beach MOLOKAI
**Kamehameha V Highway, 7 miles past the Wave Crest Resort,
Kaunakakai, at Mile Marker 21, East End**

ACTIVITIES Swimming, bodysurfing, snorkeling, diving

SPECIAL APPEAL Good swimming, views of Maui

COMMENTS It's not easy to find a swimming beach on Molokai, which has rough open seas, sheer cliffs, and muddy fishponds. This small, reef-sheltered pocket beach is a rare exception. Soft, golden sands and gentle waters make it great for kids. Don't stub your toes on the rocky bottom while admiring the West Maui Mountains across the channel. Restrooms are available, but no lifeguards are on duty. Good swimming conditions also prevail at nearby Waialua Beach, just before Mile Marker 19.

LANAI

 ## Hulopoe Beach Park LANAI
**Route 440, Manele Road near Manele Bay Hotel,
8 miles from Lanai City**

ACTIVITIES Swimming, surfing, bodyboarding, bodysurfing, snorkeling, fishing, picnicking, camping

SPECIAL APPEAL Kids' tide pool, shade, scenic features

COMMENTS This is the only beach park on Lanai, a former pineapple plantation transformed into a luxury resort enclave. But it's a fine one, another Hawaii strand recognized as a "Best Beach in America." It features a large tide pool carved into a lava cliff with all-season swimming for children. Palms offer shade along the golden beach, which is 1,500 feet long and 200 feet wide. Swimming is subject to wave action, but it's usually calm enough inshore. Snorkeling is rewarding along the sheltering lava headland, a place to explore on shore, too. Public restrooms, showers, picnic areas, and campsites are provided by the private owner. Tent camping at the six campsites, limited to six people each, costs $5 per person per night for a maximum of three nights and requires a $20 permit from Castle & Cooke Resorts. Write Attn: Camping Permits, P.O. Box 630310, Lanai City 96763, or ☎ 808-565-2970. Facilities include restrooms, showers, picnic tables, grills, and drinking water.

KAYAKING: *Different Strokes*

SINCE THE FIRST VOYAGERS LANDED IN HAWAII from the South Pacific, paddling the seas has been a way of life. Outrigger-canoe paddling is a fiercely competitive local sport. You'll often see paddlers practicing offshore. Today's Hawaiian kayaks are made of fiberglass and come in a variety of shapes and sizes.

The biggest kayak contest, the annual World Championship Kayak Race, takes off from Kepuhi Beach on Molokai each May with solo paddlers who run across the dunes and beach carrying their kayaks, jump in when they hit water, and paddle to Oahu 32 miles away.

For expert ocean kayakers, we recommend a summertime trip along Kauai's picturesque Na Pali Coast, when the sea is calm. In summer, the eastern Molokai shore from Halawa to Kalaupapa also offers wilderness kayaking and beach camping. (Read *Paddle Your Own Canoe*, by solo kayaker Audrey Sutherland.)

Novices can rent a kayak in Kailua and head out for the Mokulua islets off Oahu's Lanikai Beach. On Kauai, paddle down the peaceful Huleia, Wailua, and Hanalei rivers. Maui kayakers may find themselves whale-watching closer than most in winter, when the humpbacks loll around quiet inshore waters. On the Big Island, tranquil Hilo Bay is perfect for kayaking. Try riding gentle waves to shore for a thrill, or maybe a splash, in Kauai's Hanalei Bay, Oahu's Mamala Bay, or Maui's Wailea Bay.

Rentals for single-person kayaks are $30 to $35 for a full day; for tandem kayaks, about $42 to $50 per day. A short lesson is usually

Kayak Rentals

OAHU

Go Banana Kayaks	Kapahulu	☎ 808-737-9514
Kailua Sailboards and Kayaks	Kailua	☎ 808-262-2555
Twogood Kayaks	Kailua	☎ 808-262-5656

MAUI

Maui Ocean Activities	Kaanapali Beach	☎ 808-667-2001
South Pacific Kayaks	Kihei	☎ 808-875-4848

BIG ISLAND

Adventures in Paradise Scuba Adventure	Kealakekua	☎ 808-323-3005
Hawaii Pack and Paddle	Captain Cook	☎ 808-328-8911

KAUAI

Kayak Kauai	Hanalei	☎ 800-826-9844
Kayak Wailua	Kapaa	☎ 808-822-3388
Outfitters Kauai	Poipu Beach	☎ 808-742-9667

included in the price, and all kayaking equipment can be transported to the beach for you. Any of the following outfitters can rent equipment and teach you how to use it. Kayak Kauai Outbound in Hanalei and Outfitters Kauai in Poipu Beach have rental equipment and guides for Na Pali Coast outings. The listed firms offer paddles on the Huleia, Wailua, and Hanalei rivers.

SCUBA: *Dive, Dive, Dive*

A GROWING SEGMENT OF DIVING ENTHUSIASTS has discovered Hawaii's particular underwater treasures—lava caverns, reefs full of fish, humpbacks, and other sea life.

Most dive excursions require participants to be certified by a scuba-training organization, such as the Professional Association of Diving Instructors (PADI), the National Association of Underwater Instructors (NAUI), the National Association of Scuba Diving Schools (NASDS), and the World Association of Scuba Instructors (WASI). Specialized dives—including explorations of wrecks and caves, and night diving—require more-advanced training.

Most divers arrive certified, but certification courses are offered at dive shops throughout the Islands. Rates range from $75 for a beachside lesson to $300 or more for full open-water instruction and certification (plus an additional $10 to $20 for a scuba-certification card). Equipment is provided.

Scuba-diving Outfitters

OAHU		
Aaron's Dive Shops	Kailua	☎ 808-262-2333
Aloha Dive Shop	Hawaii Kai	☎ 808-395-5922
Clark's Diving Tours	Honolulu	☎ 808-923-5595
MAUI		
Ed Robinson's Diving Adventures	Maui	☎ 808-879-3584
Lahaina Divers	Maui	☎ 808-667-7496
Maui Dive Shop	Five offices	☎ 800-542-3483
Mike Severns Diving	Kihei	☎ 808-879-6596
BIG ISLAND		
Big Island Divers	Kailua-Kona	☎ 808-326-3827
Nautilus Dive Center	Hilo	☎ 808-935-6939
KAUAI		
Dive Kauai Scuba Center	Kapaa	☎ 808-822-0452
Fathom Five Divers	Poipu Beach	☎ 808-742-6991
Seasport Divers	Poipu Beach	☎ 808-742-9303

Would-be divers can see how it feels by way of introductory dives, usually conducted in a pool. Participants receive basic instruction, get fitted for scuba gear, and dive with the instructors. The entire experience lasts two to four hours, with rates ranging from $100 to $150.

Dive-tour rates range from $75 to $250, depending on the size of the boat, the equipment, and the number of dives included on the trip. Booking deposits are usually required, and are refundable if you cancel in advance. Expect to spend at least half a day for a guided scuba adventure. The actual time you spend in the water will vary—the deeper the water you're in, the faster you use your air supply—but usually it's between 90 minutes and 2 hours. The diver-to-guide ratio has a legal maximum of six-to-one. A few tips:

- In choosing a dive operator, ask about his or her experience in the business, safety expertise, type of boat, type of dive destination, and so on to make sure he or she meets your expectations and needs.

- Be careful where you put your hands and feet underwater. Some marine life—such as eels, jellyfish, and scorpion fish—can bite or sting. Do not touch any animal you don't recognize. Try to avoid touching or crushing coral, which will leave a permanent dent in the underwater environment.

- Never dive alone.

- If you're attempting underwater photography for the first time, shoot from within four feet. For best results, use an underwater camera with a 15 mm or 20 mm lens.

A fun alternative in the sea is a "snuba" tour, where snorkelers can go underwater tethered by a breathing tube to an air-supply float on the surface. Snuba of Oahu (☎ 808-396-6163) offers shallow-water diving for people age eight and older on three bays; Snuba Big Island (☎ 808-326-7446) guides snuba dives in Kailua-Kona. Snuba Kauai (☎ 808-823-8912) offers snuba on Kauai.

Hawaii has more than 250 diving sites, with depths ranging from 20 to 150 feet. The most popular and one of the best is Molokini, a crescent-shaped sunken cinder cone about three miles off the coast of South Maui, near Kahoolawe. Molokini, a Marine Life Conservation District, has high visibility and thriving ocean life, including reef fish, sea turtles, and manta rays. But it gets swamped with snorkelers and tour boats as the day goes on. One solution is to book one of the boats that leave early directly from the nearest Maui beach, at Makena or Wailea, rather than those that depart from Maalaea Harbor.

A favorite South Maui site is La Perouse Pinnacle, in the middle of picturesque La Perouse Bay beyond Makena. The pinnacle rises 60 feet from the sea floor to about 10 feet below the ocean's surface and is exceptional for snorkeling as well as shallow dives. Look for brilliant damselfish, triggerfish, puffers, and wrasses.

Divers of all skill levels probe Five Caves in Makena. Lava ridges and small pinnacles provide food and shelter for anglerfish, sea turtles, eels, and white-tipped sharks. The waters here are around 30 to 40 feet deep and can be accessed from shore as well as boat.

Lanai's deep, clear waters (there is little runoff on this dry island) draw divers from around the world. At Cathedrals, off the south shore, a stained-glass effect occurs when sunlight pours through the holes in twin underwater caves. This dive is for experienced divers only.

If diving with giant wintering whales is your dream, sign up with Captain Ed Robinson on Maui, who knows how to find them. Nautilus Dive Center in Hilo offers divers a chance to see the underwater lava flow from Kilauea Volcano. Kona Aggressor II offers weeklong luxury diving excursions aboard a yacht (☎ 800-329-8182). Mana Divers in Port Allen, Kauai (☎ 808-335-0881), offers trips to dive off the private island of Niihau. See dive-company recommendations on page 289.

SNORKELING:
Exploring the Undersea World

ALTHOUGH NOT AS "DEEP" AN EXPERIENCE AS SCUBA DIVING, snorkeling is an underwater adventure anyone can do. Just wade in backward in your flippers, look through your face mask, and breathe through your J-tube.

Some practical snorkeling tips:

- Know how to swim. Although some snorkeling spots are shallow, being able to swim is the best way to ensure your own safety in the water.
- Novices should practice in shallow water.
- Always snorkel with a buddy or in groups.
- Don't stray too far from shore or the boat.
- Check your snorkel gear carefully before entering the water. Popular wisdom requires you to spit on your mask and rub it around the lens before dunking it in saltwater and then putting it on. Make sure the mask fits, airtight, to your face.

The most famous snorkeling spot is Oahu's Hanauma Bay, the best place for novice snorkelers. Huge schools of friendly reef fish populate this picturesque bay, which often seems overpopulated by snorkelers. Here are some excellent snorkeling beaches:

Hanauma Bay Nature Preserve   WAIKIKI
7455 Kalanianaole Highway, at Koko Head Regional Park, Hawaii Kai, South Shore. Head east on the H-1 Freeway, which turns into Kalanianaole Highway, and go up the hill just beyond Hawaii Kai; ☎ 808-396-4229, ext. 42

ACTIVITIES Snorkeling, scuba diving

COMMENTS Just wade in and look down: you are surrounded by glamorous tropical fish that teem in this too-tame bay. By day Hawaii's most popular dive spot teems with people peeking at tropical fish; on Saturday nights there are more fish than folks. Now open for night divers from 6 to 10 p.m. Saturday nights only, Hanauma Bay attracts the brave and curious who probe shadows in search of nocturnal creatures like hawks-bill turtles, polka-dotted moray eels, and big-eyed (the better to see you with) yellowfin goatfish. Bring your own dive light or rent one.

This U-shaped bay aquarium in a broken crater, one third of a mile point to point, has near-shore reefs ideal for novice snorkelers and more-challenging reefs farther out. Lifeguards are on duty daily. Facilities include restrooms, showers, picnic areas, a snack bar, and snorkel rent-als. Ask at the beach desk about free educational tours of the bay. The parking fee is $1 per vehicle, and admission is $3 for all nonresidents over age 12. Hanauma Bay is open six days a week (closed on Tuesday) from 6 a.m. to 7 p.m. Smoking is prohibited. Feeding reef fish—once a favorite pastime—is now *kapu* (prohibited). Go early, before 8 a.m. if possible, as incoming vehicles are turned away when the parking lot is full.

Ahihi-Kinau Preserve SOUTH MAUI
On remote south shore of Maui, beyond Makena, at end of a dirt road

ACTIVITIES Snorkeling

COMMENTS Black, barren lava reefs reach into aquamarine pools full of tropical fish. The best snorkeling on Maui is in this scenic 2,000-acre nature preserve on the rugged south coast, where Haleakala last spilled red-hot lava into the sea in 1790. It's difficult to reach but easy to enjoy. No facilities.

Kealakekua Bay KONA
On Kona coast of the Big Island, south of Kailua-Kona and downhill from Captain Cook

ACTIVITIES Snorkeling, scuba diving

COMMENTS An octopus's garden is shared by free-swimming moray eels, parrotfish, and, once in a while, a pod of spinner dolphins in this deep blue, mile-wide bay that's the Big Island's best snorkeling spot. Coral heads, lava tubes, and underwater caves provide an excellent habitat for Hawaii's tropical fish, and the warm, clear water is a natural attraction for snorkelers. Snack bar, bathroom, and showers are available.

Kee Beach KAUAI
End of Kuhio Highway, Haena State Park, North Shore; park along the road or in small lot

ACTIVITIES Swimming, snorkeling, fishing

COMMENTS Here you can float like a leaf on a pond, sucking air through a snorkel and watching little yellow fish dart here and there in crystal-clear water. You can float face-up, staring at green-velvet cathedral cliffs, under a blue sky with long-tailed tropical birds riding trade winds. Palms rustle, a wave breaks. If this isn't perfection, what is? Bathrooms, showers, and parking are available. Nearby Tunnels Beach also offers exceptional snorkeling.

Five Needles LANAI
Off remote south shore of Lanai

ACTIVITIES Snorkeling, swimming

COMMENTS Spiky sea stacks dominate an almost-secret snorkel spot on Lanai's rugged, seldom-seen south side. Go there only by kayak, sailboat, or launch, mostly by tours departing from Maui. Take *Navatek II* or *Trilogy* from Maui's Maalea Harbor for this unforgettable outing (see information on guided tours below). Clarity of water and abundant sea life make this snorkel site excellent. No facilities.

GUIDED TOURS

GUIDED SNORKELING ADVENTURES are available on every island, priced from $35. In addition, many shops rent snorkeling equipment, including fins, masks, snorkels, and gear bags. Most snorkel and dive shops accept major credit cards. Guided snorkel tours take about half a day. Instruction for beginners is available. Snorkel outings are weather dependent.

Snorkel Bob's, one of the most popular outfits, has locations on Oahu (☎ 808-735-7944); Maui (☎ 808-879-7449, ☎ 808-669-9603, or 808-661-4421); the Big Island (☎ 808-329-0770); and Kauai (☎ 808-823-9433 or 808-742-2206). Here are our favorite guided snorkel tours.

Maui

Navatek II, an 82-foot, 149-passenger SWATH (Small Waterplane Area Twin Hull) vessel—it's a smooth cruiser—sails from Maalaea Harbor to Lanai's remote south shore on the "Voyage of Discovery," the best family-snorkel adventure because of its high-tech boat. It's stable to calm queasy stomachs, easy to get on and off in deep water, and the crew grills hamburgers to order for lunch. *Navatek II* and several other snorkel sail cruises are operated by Royal Hawaiian Cruises. ☎ 800-852-4183.

Trilogy, a 64-foot cutter-rigged sailing catamaran operated by brothers Jim and Rand Coon and their families, takes blue-water sailors on six-hour snorkel excursions to Lanai, Molokini, or Kaanapali. Trilogy Excursions is the veteran operator for Maui-to-Lanai sails with a well-deserved reputation for delivering a superior experience. ☎ 888-MAUI-800, or visit **www.sailtrilogy.com.**

The Big Island of Hawaii

Fair Wind II, a 60-foot catamaran operated by Puhi and Mendy Dant since 1971, delivers 100 snorkelers to Kealakekua Bay every morning for a four-and-a-half-hour snorkel excursion. The big, safe boat is a solid favorite of families. Call ☎ 800-677-9461, or visit **www.fair-wind.com.**

Kauai

Hold on for a wet, bumpy ride to Kauai's remote beaches, sea caves, and waterfalls with a picnic and snorkeling stop. Captain Zodiac pioneered rides on 15-passenger, 24-foot rigid-hull rubber rafts along the Na Pali Coast in the 1970s and is still going strong, only now Captain Andy's at the helm. ☎ 800-535-0830, or **www.napali.com.**

Molokai
Walter Naki of Molokai Action Adventures takes four snorkelers on four- or six-hour dives in seldom-explored coastal coves and reefs aboard his 21-foot Boston whaler. ☎ 808-558-8184.

SURFING: *Catch a Wave*

HAWAII'S OWN KINGS PERFECTED SURFING, and no place does it better. Hawaii offers the most consistent surf, biggest waves, and deepest tubes. The best big-wave surfers test their skills here in the winter when Oahu's North Shore turns into the world's surfing capital and the setting for annual professional competitions. No one knows exactly when surfing originated, but many historians believe Polynesians were already well-versed in the sport when they migrated to the Hawaiian Islands nearly 2,000 years ago. Big Island petroglyphs depict board-riding figures. Ancient Hawaiians called surfing *hee nalu* (wave sliding). Only the high chiefs enjoyed access to the best surf spots. King Kamehameha I was said to be an avid surfer.

Today, waves are shared according to skill. Beginning surfers can get quick lessons from Waikiki beach boys or sign up for more formal training with an expert instructor, such as Hans Hedemann, a veteran pro and former surfing champion. **Hans Hedemann Surf School** (☎ 808-924-7778) offers lessons on the beach at Waikiki. Equipment is provided.

Lessons for one or two students or groups up to five per instructor are conducted in areas where the waves are small and the beach relatively crowd-free. Students learn the basics on the beach, including ocean safety and how to paddle a surfboard, how to get up and stand on the board, proper foot placement, and where to shift body weight. Next they get in the water to do it again, and then catch a real wave and ride it. Once you get the hang of it, you'll learn other basic maneuvers, such as turning your board to move in a certain direction.

Surfers come in all shapes, sizes, and ages. You should know how to swim and expect to do a lot of paddling and kicking in the water. Most schools have a minimum age of five to seven years for surfing lessons. "If you think you can do it, you probably can," said one instructor. Hedemann said almost everyone is "up and riding" on their first lesson. Then you may be hooked for life, because the feeling of being one with the sea, flying in on a cresting wave, is a thrill like no other.

Other recommended surfing schools include **Hawaiian Watersports** (☎ 808-255-4352; **www.hawaiianwatersports.com**) on Oahu, **Hawaiian Surfing Adventures** (808-482-0749; **www.hawaiiansurfingadventures**

.com) on Kauai, and **Buzzy Kerbox Surf School** (☎ 808-573-5728; kerbox@aol.com) and the **Nancy Emerson School of Surfing** (☎ 808-244-7873) on Maui. Surfing instruction is available year-round.

Group rates range generally from about $60 for one-hour lessons to $225 to $250 for all-day lessons. Private lessons are about $85 to $125 for one-hour lessons and $425 to $450 for all-day lessons. Multiday and weeklong rates are also available. Book at least a day in advance, although most surf schools will try to accommodate last-minute students.

For experienced surfers able to deal with surfing etiquette and crowds, Oahu is the place to be, with the widest choice of good-quality surf spots in the state. Surf conditions are good somewhere on the island nearly year-round, and plenty of surf breaks are just right for less-than-expert surfers. Weather forecasters routinely report surf conditions on radio and television. Maui has some great surf spots near Lahaina and just past Paia. Kauai has excellent surf spots at Hanalei, Princeville, and elsewhere on its north shore and at Poipu and south-shore locales. Big Island has a few good surfing areas, like Anaehoomalu at Waikoloa Resort, although many are inaccessible by car. A helpful book on the best surf spots is the *Surfer's Guide to Hawaii* by Greg Ambrose (published by Bess Press), which includes tips, descriptions, and maps.

Keep in mind the following safety and etiquette tips before heading out to ride Hawaiian waves:

- Check with lifeguards first. They can point out the hazardous rip currents, jagged reefs, and tricky waves to avoid. Obey posted warnings.
- Never surf alone, and always make sure someone on shore knows where you are.
- Be considerate of other surfers. Don't drop in on someone else's wave.
- Don't surf after dark.
- Use leg ropes to control your board, for your safety and the safety of fellow surfers.
- If you get in trouble, don't panic. Signal for help by raising one arm vertically.

WINDSURFING: *Ride the Wind*

A WHOLE DIFFERENT SPORT seeks to challenge the wind as well as the waves—the combination of sailing and surfing known as windsurfing or board sailing. A day of brisk trade winds prompts a hatch-out of butterfly-like sails as windsurfers zip here and there across the water, enjoying the pure sensation of natural speed. In Hawaii, where water sports are a way of life, many ocean devotees surf when the waves are right, windsurf when the winds are right, and kayak when it's calm. Expert windsurfers will want to try their hands or just watch the pros at **Kanaha Beach** and **Hookipa Beach** on Maui's North Shore, known as "the Aspen of windsurfing," where the world's top wave riders gather to take advantage of strong winds and optimum waves. **Diamond Head Beach Park** near Waikiki is favored for wave-jumping, quite a spectacle to watch. Windsurfers fly up the face of a wave and soar, sometimes doing somersaults and other feats before returning to water.

To learn to windsurf on Oahu, cross the Koolau to **Kailua** and **Lanikai** beaches on Windward Oahu for scenic rides and gentle seas, although periodic blustery trade winds will sideline the beginners and bring out the experts. Robbie Naisch was one of the early stars of windsurfing, and **Naish Windsurfing Hawaii** in Kailua (☎ 808-261-6067; **www.naishsails.com**) is the oldest windsurf shop in the state. There you can buy or rent gear and accessories and sign up for lessons at all skill levels. Private lessons are $75; lessons for two are $100, including equipment rental. Naish also pioneered the new spinoff sport of kitesurfing—windsurfing with the extra speedy lift of a hang-gliding kite attached, popular on Kailua Bay. $120 for private lessons.

Ocean Sports Waikoloa provides windsurfing services at **Anaeho-omalu Bay** at Waikoloa Beach Resort on the Big Island (☎ 888-SAIL-234; **www.hawaiioceansports.com**). On Kauai, **Anini Beach** on the North Shore near Princeville is a good place to learn the sport.

Windsurf Kauai (☎ 808-828-6838) offers a three-hour lesson for $75. Sailboard rentals are $25–$40 for a full day. **Alan Cadiz's HST** (☎ 808-871-5423; **www.hstwindsurfing.com**) on Maui offers two-and-a-half-hour lessons for $69.

CHARTER SPORTFISHING:
Reely Big Ones

IF YOU'VE EVER DREAMED OF HOOKING a 1,000-pound "grander" Pacific blue marlin, go to the Kona Coast, the best place to land the fish of a lifetime.

The giants, lesser marlin, and desirable food fish roam the seas off all islands, but the best chance of hooking a trophy fish is off Kona, considered the big-game-fishing capital of the world. Kona has an optimal fishing environment, thanks to the seas that plunge to great depths right outside the mouth of Honokohau Harbor and to the hulking volcanoes that tend to block onshore winds and high seas. A charter boat may chase a fish on a line for many miles and hours (or days), but it rarely has to go farther than five or six miles out to sea to hook one.

About 100 charter boats operate out of Honokohau Harbor. Contact one of the charter-boat associations to choose yours. They handle plenty of boats and customers, and can connect you with people who want to share a charter, put you on a tag-and-release boat, or connect you with a crew that will give you a share of your edible catch. Most captains have commercial-fishing licenses and keep the food fish caught on their boat to sell, sharing proceeds with the crew. Marlin over 50 pounds are not considered good to eat, particularly after they have been dragged all over the sea. **Kona Charter Skippers Association** (see contact info below) also offers fishing-trip packages and group bookings.

We suggest browsing the Internet, asking other fishermen, and checking activity guides to familiarize yourself with your fishing options. Experience and frequency of trips, plus electronic gear, help your captain know where the fish are biting. Most charters offer fishing adventures that last four, six, and eight hours. Departures are usually at 7 a.m., with half-day charters returning by noon and full-day charters returning by 4 p.m. Prices vary according to the size and amenities of the boat, among other factors.

To maximize your chances of landing a big-game fish, book a full-day charter. It can take an hour or more to catch live bait—usually an *aku,* a skipjack tuna of up to 20 pounds—and when you add the time required to handle lines and tackle for both small bait and big game, you won't have much time left for fishing on a half-day excursion. Half-day charters often use lures as a result, and big marlin seem to prefer live bait.

Walk-up bookings are available, but it's better to make your reservations in advance so you can get the type of boat you want and,

Hawaii Ocean-Sportfishing Charters

OPERATOR	PHONE/WEB SITE
STATEWIDE	
Sportfish Hawaii	☎ 877-388-1376; www.sportfishhawaii.com
BIG ISLAND, KONA	
Bite Me Sportfishing	☎ 808-936-3442; www.bitemesportfishing.com
Kona Charter Skippers Association	☎ 800-7-MARLIN (762-7546); 808-936-4970 www.konabiggamefishing.com
Kona Activities Center	☎ 808-329-3171
OAHU	
Maggie Joe Sportsfishing	☎ 877-806-FISH (3474); www.maggiejoe.com
MAUI	
Fish Maui	☎ 877-889-7035; www.fishmaui.com
KAUAI	
Anini Fishing Charters	☎ 808-828-1285
Kai Bear Sportfishing	☎ 808-652-4556; www.kaibear.com
Deep Sea Fishing Kauai	☎ 808-634-8589; www.deepseafishingkauai.com
Captain Don's Sportfishing	☎ 808-639-3012; www.captaindonsfishing.com
MOLOKAI	
Alyce C Sport Fishing	☎ 808-558-8377; www.alycecsportfishing.com

if you choose, share a charter with someone. A deposit is usually required (up to half the charter cost) and is refundable up to 48 hours prior to the fishing date. Most charters accept major credit cards and personal checks.

Most boats are licensed to hold six passengers, plus the captain and two deckhands, but four passengers is a more comfortable crowd. The crew provides instruction and equipment. You don't need a fishing license for offshore fishing. Bring your own food and drinks (liquor is allowed) for the ice chest, and sun and seasickness protection. Shorts, swimsuits, and T-shirts are appropriate wear, plus a sweatshirt or light jacket as needed.

Charter boats range in size from 25 to 58 feet, with the average being 33 to 35 feet. If you're new to sportfishing, you may want to splurge on a midsize or larger boat so that you can enjoy the experience of luxuriating on the water, even if the fish aren't biting that day. But remember—the size of the boat doesn't guarantee the catch. The fish don't care how much you spend or how big your boat is.

Three types of marlin roam Hawaiian waters: black, blue, and striped. Though the chances are good that a marlin will strike your bait, the odds of actually landing one of the tenacious fighters are about one in three. With luck, you might catch one of the "granders"—a trophy marlin of 1,000 pounds or more. You can see what one looks like on the wall of the King Kamehameha Beach Hotel in Kailua-Kona.

You won't need the strength of an Olympian to land a giant marlin. If you're using up to 130-pound test line, the drag is about 40 or 50 pounds, meaning the most you have to worry about pulling in is between 40 and 50 pounds. If you can pull 20 pounds around for a while, you can reel in a marlin. What you may need is staying power. Some big-game fish fight for hours before exhausting themselves. Other fish in the sea you might want to meet are ahi (yellowfin tuna) and other tuna species, ono (wahoo), mahimahi (dolphin fish), and other billfish and spearfish. Some Kona boats go after snappers, onaga, opakapaka, and other bottom fish using a rigorous Asian fishing method called jigging. The **Sea Strike** is one (☎ 800-264-4595; **www.kona-fishing.com**).

Mahimahi, ono, and marlin are present throughout the year, except for striped marlin, which is a winter fish. Spearfish are also more abundant in the winter months, and ahi are more numerous in summer. Or you might want to try some inland bass fishing on Kauai's South Shore freshwater reservoirs. **Cast & Catch Freshwater Bass Guides** (☎ 808-332-9707) will take you there.

WHALE WATCHING

TWO-THIRDS OF THE PACIFIC HUMPBACK whale population migrates to warm Hawaiian waters each winter to breed, bear, and nurse their young. Few sights match the spectacle of a whale leaping out of the sea.

Whales cruise so close to shore, you can often see them from coastal roads and hotel *lanai* (patios). For a closer look, take a whale-watching cruise if you are in Hawaii between mid-December and mid-April. Whale-watching excursions are offered throughout Hawaii, but are mainly concentrated off the south and west coasts of Maui, the heart of the whale migration.

Luck plays a big role in seeing action by large creatures on the move, but some tours offer substantial expertise and special equipment, such as state-of-the-art hydrophones that let you hear whale songs, and support marine-conservation nonprofits like the Pacific Whale Foundation and Whales Alive.

Experience makes a big difference between whale watching and whale "glimpsing," as federal law requires boats to stay at least 100 yards away from the whales. Some cruises guarantee sightings by giving you a rain check if you don't actually see a whale.

Whale-watching boats come in all sizes, from rubber rafts that bounce through the surf to large, motorized catamarans and sleek sailing sloops, and offer a wide range of comforts, such as shaded decks, beverages, and marine heads.

Daily humpback whale–watching cruises cost $20 to $60 for adults and $12 to $30 for children ages 11 and under. Book your tour

Whale-watching Cruise Operators

OPERATOR	PHONE / WEB SITE
MAUI	
Maui Princess	☎ 808-661-8397, 800-275-6969
Pacific Whale Foundation	☎ 808-249-8811, 800-942-5311; www.pacificwhale.org
America II Sailing	☎ 808-667-2833 or 888-667-2133
BIG ISLAND	
Dan McSweeney's Year-round Whale Watch	☎ 808-322-0028; www.ilovewhales.com
Red Sail Sports	☎ 808-886-2876
Captain Zodiac Raft Expeditions	☎ 808-329-3199; www.captainzodiac.com
OAHU	
Honolulu Sailing Co.	☎ 808-239-3900, 800-829-0114; www.honsail.com
Royal Hawaiian Cruises	☎ 808-848-6360; www.atlantisadventures.com
KAUAI	
Capt. Andy's Sailing Adventures	☎ 800-535-0830; www.napali.com
Kauai Sea Tours	☎ 800-733-7997; www.kauaiseatours.com

several days in advance during holiday periods. Most tours last two to three hours and provide snacks and juice. Some tours offer hotel transportation. Wear swimsuits or casual attire, and bring binoculars and cameras.

Tip: To see whales best from shore, get to an elevated viewing post that gives you a better perspective. Look for whale spouts, geysers of sea spray that shine in the sun and seem to disappear into thin air. Look for large black bodies poking their noses above water as they "spy-hop," possibly to get a better look at you.

If you're in the resort area of Wailea, Maui, check the telescope in front of the Marriott Wailea Beach. The first person to report a whale sighting to the cafe each day gets a free breakfast.

Though humpbacks visit the Islands only in winter, Hawaii has five other whale species that can be viewed throughout the year—sperm whales, pilot whales, melon-headed whales, false killer whales, and beaked whales. Big Island boat captain Dan McSweeney, based in Kailua-Kona, is one of the few operators who offers year-round whale-watching adventures spotlighting these lesser-known marine mammals, with tours out of Honokohau Harbor three times a week.

Some informative Web sites on humpback whales include **www .pacificwhale.org** and **www.ilovewhales.com.** A list of some whale-watching tour operators appears above.

SHARK WATCHING

YOU'VE SEEN IT ON TV: A big shark, jaws wide, lunges at the human diver in the submerged steel cage. Now, you can experience a real-life close encounter with a shark in Hawaii. A 26-foot launch takes you three to four miles off Oahu's North Shore to the deep-blue sea, where big tiger sharks roam crystal-clear waters looking for lunch. You get locked in a "shark-proof" cage and lowered into the 200-foot depths while scores of 15-foot sharks come in close to see if you are something to eat. You can stay in the cage until you scream, or conquer your fear of sharks. Either way, you leave with great awe and respect. Thrill seekers from England, Ireland, Canada, New Zealand, Australia, Japan, and nearly every U.S. state have survived the encounter. Odds are you will, too. The two-hour adventure departs at 7 a.m. from Haleiwa Small Boat Harbor on Oahu's North Shore. Bring a swimsuit, T-shirt, sunscreen, snorkel and mask, and your underwater camera. Cost is $120 a person. Contact North Shore Shark Adventure at Haleiwa Small Boat Harbor (☎ 808-228-5900; **www.sharktour hawaii.com; hawaiisharktourhawaii.copms.com**).

While sharks abound in Hawaiian waters, they are seldom seen. Most attacks tend to occur offshore of Olowalu Beach in the West Maui resort area. On that reef-fringed coast, the Islands' first permanent shark warnings now stand, posted after a rash of shark attacks—several fatal—on snorkelers, divers, and surfers. Eight signs are now posted along a one-mile stretch of Olowalu Beach. Hawaii averages three or four shark attacks annually.

HAWAII *by* LAND

HIKING: TAKE TO THE TRAILS

HIKING IS THE MOST POPULAR off-beach outdoor activity in Hawaii. Conditions are generally fine for meeting the natural environment face-to-face, and the natural environment is extraordinary. There's something Garden of Eden–like about walking on a forest trail edged with leaves bigger than your head and seeing tropical fruit like mountain apple, guava, wild mango, and avocado, surrounded by jungle greenery and waterfall streams—especially when it's within minutes of downtown Honolulu and Waikiki. Waterfall trails lead to waterfall pools, ideal spots to cool off after a tropical trek. There's a certain historic continuity to hiking on trails that were carved by ancient trekkers and smoothed by generations' footsteps long before other means of land travel were available in the Islands. The experience is truly rewarding, with few dangers.

About those dangers: Rain forest means slippery, muddy trails and mosquitoes (take bug repellent). Waterfall valleys are steep and narrow and can flash-flood quickly after cloudburst deluges upstream, with frightening and sometimes fatal results. Dry hikes on lumpy lava and steep, crumbly dirt trails require paying close attention to your footing and drinking lots of water. No matter what the locals do, don't hike in rubber slippers (beach thongs). Use supportive footwear suitable for Hawaiian red-dirt treks, muddy-forest jaunts, or rough lava trails. Don't let the views keep you from watching where you put your feet. It is *Blue Lagoon* and *Castaway* rolled into *Lost*, but stand still while you admire the scenery. Stick to the trails. Rain-forested mountains swallow up injured or missing hikers from sight almost instantly. If possible, carry a charged cell phone on remote ventures.

> *unofficial* **TIP**
> To keep safe, use bug repellent, don't hike in rubber slippers, watch your steps, stick to the trails, carry a cell phone, and drink lots of water.

Inviting though the streams may be, don't drink the water or swim with open cuts and risk getting leptospirosis, a wild pig–related bacterial fever. You can get that within minutes of downtown Honolulu, too (at Kapena Falls, a swimming hole wildly popular with kids, despite the danger of disease).

Easy-to-reach hiking spots on Oahu include **Manoa Falls,** a highly traveled trail directly behind Waikiki in upper Manoa Valley. The hike is about 1.5 miles round-trip through a rain forest, with a waterfall. Park near the trailhead off Upper Manoa Road.

The arid, south-shore area around Makapuu Head includes a series of trails with fantastic views of Windward Oahu and the sea. **Mount Tantalus,** on the Honolulu side of Manoa Valley, has several well-marked trails off Round Top Drive, flourishing with guava, bamboo, *lilikoi* (passion fruit), and other tropical vegetation. In upper Makiki, the **Hawaii Nature Center** operates exhibits and guides hikes aimed at helping children discover the outdoors.

For a moderately strenuous Oahu hike, tackle all or part of **Koolaupoko Trail,** a recent, well-maintained option. Park at the hairpin curve on the windward side of the Pali Highway and walk back behind Mount Olomana through the mountain rain forest, past waterfalls, down to Waimanolo, eight miles. If the round-trip is too much, do it one way and get someone to meet you at the other end. Or hike partway and turn around.

Clubs such as Hawaiian Trail and Mountain and student groups from Chaminade University and other local colleges also post helpful information and maps for Oahu and Neighbor Islands hiking. **Kapalua Nature Center** is Kapalua Resort's ecotourism arm. The resort offers guided hiking tours in its 17,000 acres of upcountry watershed and pineapple-plantation lands. Once a year by lottery, a dozen hikers are dropped off by helicopter with a guide at the top of Puu Kukui to walk on a boardwalk through high-country bogs to see rare and endangered species of plants and birds.

Experienced hikers on Kauai can retrace the footsteps of early Hawaiians along the **Kalalau Trail** that traverses the stunning Na Pali Coast, or explore the many trails of Kokee. An easy hike is offered from the **Kilauea Point National Wildlife Refuge** on the North Shore, where knowledgeable guides recount area history and information on a variety of seabirds that nest in the refuge and other wildlife. The Mahaulepu Heritage Trail on Kauai's South Shore provides an easy-to-moderate four-mile coastal hike (**www.hikemahaulepu.org**).

If you are not a hiker but want to walk through the lush Kauai countryside, go to Limahuli Gardens, a small branch of the National Tropical Botanical Gardens, near the north end of Kuhio Highway. It features native Hawaiian plants and trees along a hilly one-mile loop path through a small scenic valley.

Guided hiking tours can be booked throughout Hawaii, to bring the countryside to life as only personal experience can. This is the best way for visitors to see private and inaccessible country; discover shy, indigenous creatures; and understand the context of what they see.

The newest guided hike on Windward Oahu is a **Kualoa Ranch** trek over a ridge connecting two wild valleys that goes down to the shoreline at Milolii Fishpond (☎ 808-237-7321; **www.kualoa.com**). Our suggestions for hiking guides include **Oahu Nature Tours** (☎ 808-924-2473; **www.oahunaturetours.com**) and, on the Big Island, experts Rob Pacheco and the staff of **Hawaii Forest and Trail** (☎ 808-331-8505 or 800-464-1993; **www.hawaii-forest.com**) and Hugh Montgomery and staff of **Hawaiian Walkways** (☎ 808-775-0372; **www.hawaiian walkways.com**).

The Big Island's Warren Costa operates a homegrown company specializing in guided hikes and driving tours conducted by a native-Hawaiian guide (☎ 808-982-7575; **www.nativeguidehawaii.com**). On Kauai, the Kokee Natural History Museum offers a varying schedule of guided hikes in Kokee State Park (☎ 808-335-9975; **www.kokee.org**).

Island bookstores and the Internet offer a wealth of information about island hikes. For free trail maps, call the Department of Forestry and Wildlife at ☎ 808-587-0166. Several books are available for those hoping to discover more of Hawaii on foot.

▌**NATIONAL** *and* **STATE PARKS**

HAWAII'S 2 NATIONAL PARKS and 52 state parks encompass more than 50,000 acres on Oahu, Maui, the Big Island, Kauai, and Molokai. In addition, a number of federal and state historic parks and monuments designate cultural sites worthy of your attention.

Hawaii Volcanoes National Park, home to the world's most active volcano, is one of the nation's oldest and best national parks and a must-see for Big Island visitors. If you're traveling with children, you owe it to yourself and them to discover this park together, particularly if Pele, the fire goddess who lives in Halemaumau Crater, is producing any spectacular eruptions during your trip. (Call for eruption updates, ☎ 808-985-6000, or check the Web site at **hvo.wr.usgs.gov.**) Your best chance of seeing red-lava flows is after sunset at the end of Chain of Craters Road. Park rangers are posted there from 2 p.m. to 8 p.m. daily. (See the next page for details.)

Also on the Big Island, **Puuhonua O Honaunau,** the Place of Refuge on the South Kona Coast, is a national historic park on the site of an ancient waterfront sanctuary. A temple has been reconstructed there, within the remaining lava-rock walls built centuries ago. The place has an air of peace you can't miss even on a quick walk-through. It's worth the time to watch local people demonstrate ancient skills and games and help you understand something about old Hawaiian life. There's an annual summer cultural festival in late June or early July.

On the north end of the Kona-Kohala Coast, **Puukohola National Historic Site** is an archaeological monument by the sea. This is the preserved temple from which King Kamehameha I set out to conquer the other islands and unite them into a kingdom in the 1700s. And an annual cultural pageant is held here in August.

On Maui, **Haleakala National Park's** 10,023-foot summit is a great place for watching the sun rise, hiking in the vast caldera, and marveling at the claw-footed native-Hawaiian nene geese. These endangered state birds of Hawaii evolved special feet for life on cinders. You can also see silversword plants, which are found nowhere else.

Four state parks are especially noteworthy: **Kakaako Waterfront Park** along the downtown-Honolulu shoreline, on Oahu; **Iao Valley State Park** on Maui; and **Kokee State Park** and **Waimea Canyon State Park** on Kauai. Each provides scenic settings, exceptional views, and activities for young and old. Information on these parks is included below.

For more information and permits on Hawaii's state parks, write to the Division of State Parks, 1151 Punchbowl Street, Room 310, Honolulu 96813, or call ☎ 808-587-0300.

OVERALL SAFETY TIPS AND PARK REGULATIONS

- Guard against tropical sunburn.
- Do not drink from streams and ponds or expose an open cut or abrasion to the water. Harmful bacteria may pose a serious health risk.
- Never leave your valuables unattended in a car at a scenic lookout.
- Drinking or possession of alcoholic beverages is prohibited in parks.
- Build fires only in fireplaces and grills. Portable stoves and other warming devices may be used in designated picnicking and camping areas.
- Do not disturb any plants or any geological, historical, or archaeological features.
- Skating and skateboards are prohibited where posted.

NATIONAL PARKS

 Hawaii Volcanoes National Park
HILO AND VOLCANO
Highway 11, about 30 miles from Hilo; follow the road signs and turn left into the park entrance; ☎ 808-985-6000; www.nps.gov/havo

Hours Daily, 7:45 a.m.–5 p.m.; once you are admitted, the park is open all day, every day. **Admission** $10 per vehicle, good for a week; $5 per person for people hiking or biking in; $25 for a yearlong pass; $10 for a seniors' lifetime pass. **When to go** Anytime; the best time to see red lava is after sunset. **How much time to allow** At least half a day, including early evening if the lava is flowing.

COMMENTS The 377-acre Hawaii Volcanoes National Park was established in 1916, but the mighty spectacle of Kilauea in action has drawn visitors since the 1800s. Then, hardy adventurers were housed in a grass shack on the rim of Halemaumau Crater, fire goddess Pele's legendary home. Now the Volcano House lodge stands on the rim and is an interesting spot for sunset cocktails.

Kilauea Volcano has been erupting in its current phase since 1983. It runs on its own schedule, sometimes fuming quietly, rarely fountaining, more usually spilling fire and liquid rock down its slopes, creating new real estate and black-sand beaches. Live volcanic action is not guaranteed during your visit, but the park features are well worth the trip even when the volcano is quiet. A variety of natural "attractions" compete for attention; we suggest that you don't miss the Thomas A. Jaggar Museum, an excellent interpretive center where seismographs and easy-to-understand exhibits help illustrate the scientific theories of volcanic works, and where Hawaiian artist Herb Kane's murals illustrate the Hawaiian theory, the legend of Pele.

Just outside the museum is one of several overlooks along the trail to view Halemaumau Crater—2.5 miles wide and more than 400 feet deep—within Kilauea Caldera. Halemaumau means "house of ferns," named for greenery that once grew there between eruptions. Now it looks like a cinder pit. That must be the way Pele likes it, and many islanders still believe she lives there, causing eruptions when she is displeased. Her fiery temper is said to be appeased by gifts of gin, a modern embroidery on the legend. Pele is also said to direct her wrath, in the form of really bad luck, on anyone who steals her rocks. The post office and Volcano House are deluged with tons of rocks each year sent back by hapless miscreants. If you want our advice, leave the lava alone.

Start your park tour at the visitor center, which houses volcano exhibits and a 200-seat minitheater showing a terrific 23-minute film about the history of Hawaii's volcanoes and their significance to the Hawaiian culture. Park rangers can answer questions, suggest itineraries, and conduct an introductory hike from the center. Next door, the Volcano Art Center offers a good selection of works by some of Hawaii's top artists, including Herb Kane, Peggy Chun, Rocky Jensen, and Dietrich Varez.

Guide map in hand, drive into the park, where you'll soon find the Jaggar Museum and other features. A word of caution: Sulfuric fumes from the craters and steamy fumaroles may be hard on pregnant women, small children, and people with breathing problems. If this includes you, roll the windows up and head for less-fumy features. Otherwise, drive across the caldera floor and stop to look into the yawning fire pit, a ten-minute walk from the parking area. This is the world's only drive-in volcano, predictable enough to observe up close.

The park includes 150 miles of trails of varying difficulty. For an easy walk, Devastation Trail is a good choice that illustrates some of the havoc caused by volcanic action. It is a mile round-trip, paved and wheelchair accessible, through an area that was devastated by the hot fallout from lava fountains from a 1959 Kilauea Iki eruption. Look for golden strands in the *pahoehoe* lava called Pele's hair, as well as "lava tree" molds formed when hot lava surrounded a tree trunk and burned the tree but left the round form of rock cooling on the outside.

Chain of Craters Road will take you down to the sea, about half an hour's drive through a moonscape of smooth, ropy *pahoehoe* lava (one of two kinds of lava—the other is *aa*, the rough clumps seen on the Kona Coast). The road once traversed the region, but now it dead-ends in more lava. It has been revised many times by recent flows and could be changed again at any time. Watch the coastline for a telltale plume of white smoke—that's where the lava meets the sea.

For a moderate-to-challenging hike, try the four-mile loop of Kilauea Iki Trail, which descends 400 feet through rain forest; crosses the Kilauea Iki crater floor, which might still feel warm under your feet;

Madame Pele's Rock Garden

IF YOU TAKE MADAME PELE'S LAVA ROCKS HOME, even by mistake, something awful could happen to you. That's the threat of Pele's Curse, which *akamai* Hawaii folks know is a myth fabricated by a Big Island tour guide in the 1950s. Yet, each year thousands of hot rocks come back to Hawaii from around the world, returned by folks with hard-luck tales of woe—personal calamities, accidents, injuries, and death. In case you've been snorkeling, Madame Pele is the goddess of fire and volcanoes in ancient Hawaiian mythology. She is revered as one of the most powerful Hawaiian deities. Traditional Hawaiian culture maintains that rocks are conductors of many forms of *mana* (spiritual energy) found in nature. For decades, rangers at Hawaii Volcanoes National Park and other recipients of rock returns tossed the rocks with little or no ceremony back on the black-lava beds. Now, the rocks are welcomed home by a Hawaiian *kahuna* at Ka Ahu Paepae o Hoaka Hoomalu, a special rock garden at the Marriott Waikola Beach Hotel on the Big Island's Kohala Coast.

The new garden sits at the center of a sacred crescent of five volcanic summits: Haleakala, Mauna Kea, Mauna Loa, Kohala, and Hualalai. Everyone who returns a rock receives a personal letter from the resort's Hawaiian cultural affairs office informing them that their rock is now safe in "a sheltered resting place where a sense of care will prevail." Anyone may attend the ceremony, held at high noon on the first Wednesday of each month, in the garden area south of the Queen Kaahumanu wing.

and returns via the crater rim. Look for birds, insects, steam vents, and cinder cones. Allow two or three hours, and bring water. Be prepared for wet weather and steep, rocky terrain. The trail begins at the Lava Tube parking area.

Stop at Thurston Lava Tube on the way out. The 20-minute walk through lush tree ferns leads into a large, cavelike (and lighted) tube formed by a long-ago lava river.

To get a closer view of the current interaction of lava and ocean, drive to the opposite side of the lava flow, near Kalapana, and take advantage of an access added in 2001. Kilauea's active flow left the park boundaries to ooze over county jurisdiction areas where former flows buried subdivisions, beaches, graveyards, and the road. Hawaii County officials rebuilt the end of Highway 130 so that viewers can park and walk a short coastal trail to a viewing area, rather than the former, challenging six-mile hike from the other side of the older flow that trespassed on buried property. Reach the new access by turning off the Hilo-Volcano road, Highway 11, at Keaau and taking Highway 130 through Pahoa.

At the end of the road, park and follow signs to the nearest designated lookout, currently a bluff over the place where molten magma of some 2,000° F drips or rolls into the ocean in a billow of steam, sizzling and spitting and writhing like an agonized creature as fire battles water and eventually loses. The sight is mesmerizing and unforgettable. You are walking on the newest land on Earth. You are witnessing creation.

But stay on the bluff, away from the fragile beach shelf that could crack off and fall in any time. County rescue squads are churlish about saving witless tourists and might charge you for the privilege. Overnight camping is available at the park via free permit (see "Camping in the Wilds," page 311).

Overall, be respectful of the park's surroundings, which Hawaiians regard as sacred to their culture, and the buried neighborhoods, still people's homes.

After Dark in the Park, an award-winning interpretative program, features Hawaiian musicians, storytellers, artists, scientists, historians, and local authors who share knowledge of Hawaii's rich natural and supernatural culture. The program is offered at 7 p.m. on Tuesdays at Kilauea Visitor Center, Hawaii Volcanoes National Park (see page 248 for details).

Haleakala National Park UPCOUNTRY MAUI

The park extends from the top of Haleakala ("House of the Sun") down the southeast flank of the mountain to the sea at Kipahulu near Hana, including scenic waterfall pools at Oheo Gulch. The summit area is accessible via Roads 37, 377, and 378 up the mountain through Kula, a 3-hour round-trip drive from the Kahului area below. Add more time to get to and from resort areas. Kipahulu, at the east end of the island between Hana and Kaupo, can be reached via Hana Highway. Driving time is 3–4 hours each way between Kahului and Kipahulu; ☎ 808-572-9306; www.nps.gov/hale

Hours Park Ranger headquarters open daily, 7:30 a.m.–4 p.m.; the visitor center is open daily, sunrise–3 p.m. **Admission** $10 per vehicle, good for a week; $5 per person not in vehicles. **When to go** Anytime. Haleakala is renowned for dramatic sunsets and sunrises, a mystic experience that draws people from slumber in the middle of the night to be there on time. Be sure to arrive at least 30 minutes early. It's also well worth the 3-hour round-trip drive (from Kahului) at other times of day—including after dark, when it is a fabulous place for stargazing. **How much time to allow** Up to half a day, depending on whether you take part in park programs. Rangers offer guided hikes on all Haleakala's trails, at the cindery summit, in the cloud forest, or down below in the lush tropical forests of Kipahulu. This is a good option. Take your pick of environments.

COMMENTS Haleakala, a dormant volcano, became a separate national park in 1961. The park consists of 29,000 acres, most of it wilderness. At the summit, the park headquarters and visitor center house cultural and natural-history exhibits.

In the Kipahulu area, trails begin at the Ranger Station–Visitor Center. The Kuloa Point Trail is an easy half-mile loop toward the ocean that affords a look at the pools and waterfalls, as well as the sea and the Big Island, but go early or late if you want to avoid crowds. Enjoy a picnic on the grass next to the remnants of an ancient fishing shrine and house site.

Check the park bulletin board for a schedule of daily programs and guided hikes. Obey posted warnings. Because the weather at the summit is unpredictable—temperatures range from 40°F to 65°F but with windchill factored in can dip below freezing—wear lightweight, layered clothing and comfortable, sturdy shoes. No restaurants or gas stations are available in the park. People with heart or breathing programs should use caution because of the high elevation and thin air.

Limited drive-in and wilderness overnight camping is permitted in the crater and below at Kipahulu. The Hosmer Grove Campground in the summit area is located just inside the park entrance (see "Camping in the Wilds," page 311, for details on Haleakala camping).

OAHU STATE PARKS

Diamond Head State Monument WAIKIKI
Diamond Head Road, between Makapuu and 18th avenues

Comments Woke up jet-lagged? Go climb Diamond Head! Early in the day when it's cool, you can make the moderate climb to the summit in about 45 minutes to enjoy panoramic views of Waikiki, Honolulu, mountains, and ocean. You can sign up for a guided walk sponsored by the Clean Air Team of Hawaii (☎ 808-948-3299) on Saturday mornings at 9 a.m.

Heeia State Park WINDWARD OAHU
46-465 Kamehameha Highway at Kealohi Point, Heeia

Comments Beautiful views of Kaneohe Bay, Mokolii (better known as Chinaman's Hat), and the majestic Koolau Mountains.

Kaena Point State Park LEEWARD OAHU
The end of the road, Farrington Highway, Makua

Comments A 778-acre park located at the northwest end of Oahu. Picnicking and shore-fishing are popular. You can view Kaneana, a large sea cave that is the legendary home of a shark-man. Bring drinking water.

Kakaako Waterfront Park GREATER HONOLULU
End of Ahui or Ohe Streets off Ala Moana Boulevard, Honolulu

Comments A little-known 35-acre waterfront park located in downtown Honolulu, favored by residents who come here during lunch and *pau hana* (after work). A waterfront promenade, amphitheater, and picnic areas highlight this scenic park.

MAUI STATE PARKS

Iao Valley State Park CENTRAL MAUI
End of Iao Valley Road (Highway 32) in Iao Valley, behind Wailuku

Comments The centerpiece is Iao Needle, a pinnacle that rises 1,200 feet from the forested valley floor. Be prepared to share it with tour buses that stop for photo ops. Take a look at the multicultural architectural-heritage village below. In 1790, King Kamehameha fought to gain control of Maui, and in the aftermath, so many bodies blocked Iao stream that they named the site Kepuniwai (damming of the waters).

Waianapanapa State Park UPCOUNTRY MAUI
End of Waianapanapa Road, off Hana Highway, Hana

Comments This remote, ocean-view campground features rustic cabins sleeping four to six at $55 per night, and free tent camping for up to five days in a grassy open field surrounded by trees. Seek reservations as far in advance as possible, as this is a prized spot. Permits can be obtained at any state parks office. Write to the Maui office at Division of State Parks, P.O. Box 1049, Wailuku, Maui 96793, or ☎ 808-984-8109.

Restrooms, outdoor showers, picnic tables, grills, and drinking water are available for tent campers. Each cabin has kitchen, living room, bedroom, and bathroom with bedding, linens, and utensils provided. Amenities include good hiking trails, native forest, cave, *heiau,* a black-sand beach sprinkled with tiny blue shells, and fishing. Ocean conditions are seldom safe for swimming.

BIG ISLAND STATE PARKS
Akaka Falls State Park HILO AND VOLCANO
End of Akaka Falls Road (Highway 220), Hilo

Comments Free and open year-round. Get off the highway and see some inland wonders now and then, like this sizable waterfall and its jungle valley. It's a short walk through the tropical vegetation to scenic points overlooking the falls; picnic facilities are available.

Kohala Historical Sites State Monument KONA
On a coastal dirt road to the left off Akoni Pule Highway, Hawi

Comments If you're going to pick one ancient temple site, visit Mookini Heiau, believed to be the oldest and largest sacrificial temple, with huge stone walls and a spooky atmosphere. Nearby is the reputed birth site of Kamehameha I, Hawaii's greatest king (☎ 808-974-6200).

Lapakahi State Historical Park KONA
Akoni Pule Highway, North Kohala

Comments This archaeological dig of an ancient Hawaiian fishing village is worth a stop while en route through Kohala District. Interpretive helpers will answer questions (☎ 808-889-5566).

Wailuku River State Park HILO AND VOLCANO
Off Waianuenue Avenue, Hilo

Comments Free and open year-round, this 16-acre park is the home of Rainbow Falls, named for the brilliant color bands that form through a misty waterfall. Boiling Pots, a series of pools that appear to "boil" after frequent rains, is nearby. The cave beneath the waterfall is said to be the home of Hina, mother of the demigod Maui.

KAUAI STATE PARKS
Kokee State Park KAUAI
High up Kokee Road, 15 miles from Kekaha. This park and Waimea Canyon State Park adjoin.

Comments Far from any beach, Kokee is a special place for its upcountry atmosphere and native plants and birds. Picnicking, camping, and hiking are the best ways to enjoy this 4,345-acre park, the site of a lookout with an arresting view of Kalalau Valley. Camp cabins are available with wood-stoves to ward off the upcountry chill. Trails of varying difficulty lead off through the woods; pick one that suits your time frame. Even the easy walks take you into native forest. The forest includes California redwoods among the ohia and koa trees. The Alakai Swamp is a boggy treasure for birders intent on seeing or hearing rare native species. The 11-mile Nualolo-Awaawapuhi Loop, with dramatic vistas of the Na Pali Coast, is one of Hawaii's best hikes. In summer, a very short trout season draws local anglers (☎ 808-245-6001 for weather info).

The adjoining 1,866-acre park overlooks spectacular Waimea Canyon, which you can explore on horseback or on foot. It's often likened to the Grand Canyon for its colorful striated geologic layers and steep walls.

Tent-camping is $5 per campsite per night at Kokee with a five-night limit, but it requires a permit. Permits can be obtained at any state-parks office or online at **www.hawaii.gov/dlnr/dsp/NaPali/prkprmt.** For more information, write to the Kauai office at Division of State Parks, 3060 Eiwa Street, Lihue 96766, or call ☎ 808-274-3444. Restrooms, showers, picnic tables, sinks, and drinking water are provided.

Kokee Lodge has a dozen cabins that sleep up to six people each. The older cabins have a large dormitory-style room, a bathroom, and a kitchen; newer cabins offer two bedrooms, a living room, a kitchen, and a bath-room. Rates are $45 per night for the two-bedroom cabins, $35 per night for the dorm-style ones. For cabin reservations, write to Kokee Lodge at P.O. Box 819, Waimea 96796, or call ☎ 808-335-6061.

For information, call the YWCA of Kauai (☎ 808-245-5959), Kokee Methodist Camp (☎ 808-335-3429), or Hongwanji Camp (☎ 808-335-3444). Rates are $40 to $96 per night.

A restaurant at the lodge offers breakfast and lunch daily. The Kokee Museum, located adjacent to the lodge, spotlights Kauai's natural history (see Part Seven, Attractions).

Neighboring Waimea Canyon State Park is located at the bottom of Waimea Canyon, along the Waimea River and Koaie and Waialae streams. Access is via the Kukui Trail, located 7.5 miles north on Waimea Canyon Road.

Tent-camping is available for up to five nights at five campsites on the canyon floor, with a permit. To get one, write the Division of Forestry and

Wildlife, 3060 Eiwa Street, Room 306, Lihue 96766; call ☎ 808-274-3444; or visit **www.hawaii.gov/dlnr/dsp/fees.html.**

The best is Lonomea Camp, located six miles from the Kukui trailhead. Lonomea has pit toilets, a picnic table, and roofed shelters. Wiliwili Camp, at the base of the trail, also has those facilities. Hipalau Camp has no toilets but offers a roofed shelter, picnic table, and two refreshing pools fed by waterfalls. Bring your own drinking water.

Wailua River State Park KAUAI
Along the banks of the Wailua River off Kuhio Highway, Wailua

Comments Historic 1,092-acre site within a river valley. Picnicking, boating, and fishing are available, along with paid boat tours to the much-ballyhooed Fern Grotto. Instead, you might want to search out the *heiau*, ancient refuge, and birthstones that are among the historic landmarks in this valley, which was once reserved for ancient chiefs.

MOLOKAI STATE PARKS

Palaau State Park MOLOKAI
End of Kalae Highway, Palaau

Comments This 230-acre park overlooks historic Kalaupapa, the place where people stricken with Hansen's disease (leprosy) were once banished. It's open 24 hours a day, and picnicking and camping are available. A short trail leads to aptly named Phallic Rock, a monolith reputed to enhance fertility among women who sleep beside it overnight. Donations accepted.

■ CAMPING *in the* WILDS

HAWAII HAS MORE THAN 120 CAMPSITES and campgrounds on six main islands, with sites ranging from beaches and open mountain terrain to lush green valleys and rain forests. Nearly all are within the jurisdiction of a county, state, or federal agency and require camping permits. Book as far ahead as possible, and be prepared to take part in a lottery-style competition to get permits, because residents like camping, too. It's an affordable way to vacation in the Islands.

Bring a tent with a rain flap or tarp, a ground pad, and lightweight sleeping bags to sleep on (more than in, unless you're headed for cool higher altitudes). You'll need bug repellent and your own drinking water, or you'll need to bring what's necessary to purify any water to drink by boiling it or adding some sort of purifier.

Hawaii has no animals to encounter in the wilds, except occasional feral pigs and goats. You can scare them away by shouting or making sudden movements. Otherwise, leave them alone, and they'll extend the same courtesy. No island plants are poisonous to the touch (except, for some people, mango, which is a relative of poison ivy), but some are poisonous if eaten. Hawaii does have some creepy bugs

Camping-equipment Rentals

BIG ISLAND

Hawaii Forest & Trail
74-5035B Queen Kaahumanu Hwy
Kailua-Kona 96740
☎ 808-331-8505 or
800-464-1993

OAHU

The Bike Shop
1149 South King Street
Honolulu 96814
☎ 808-596-0588

Omar the Tent Man
94-158 Leoole, Warehouse A
Waipahu 96797
☎ 808-677-8785 or
888-242-8556

KAUAI

Kayak Kauai
P.O. Box 508
Hanalei 96714
☎ 808-826-9844

MAUI

West Maui Sports & Fishing Supplies
1287 Front Street
Lahaina 96761
☎ 808-661-6252 or
888-498-7726

MOLOKAI

Molokai Off-road Tours & Taxi
P.O. Box 747
Kaunakakai 96748
☎ 808-553-3369 or 808-552-2218

of tropical proportions, capable of nasty stings—not the big German brown cockroaches that terrorize visitors, but giant centipedes that can be five inches or longer, scorpions in rocky areas, and black widow or brown recluse spiders under damp wood. Shake out your shoes and bed gear before using them, and wear shoes or use a flashlight to watch your step, even in soft grass at night.

If you want to camp without lugging all the gear from home, rent equipment from suppliers such as those listed above, most of which also rent kayaks, mountain bikes, and other outdoor equipment.

WHERE TO CAMP

HERE ARE SUGGESTED CAMPSITES, in addition to the state parks covered previously. A good resource to help you learn more is *Camping Hawaii* by resident camping expert Richard McMahon. Camping information is available on the Hawaii Visitors and Convention Bureau Web site (**www.gohawaii.com**).

OAHU

Bellows Beach Park WINDWARD OAHU

41-043 Kalanianaole Highway; located at Bellows Air Force Station, about 2.5 miles northwest of Waimanalo. On Kalanianaole Highway, turn right at the sign marking BAFS and follow the road to the park.

Type of camping Weekend tent camping only, Friday noon–Monday 8 a.m.
Permits Applications accepted no earlier than two Fridays before the requested camping dates. You must apply in person at any satellite city hall on Oahu or at

the Department of Parks and Recreation, 650 South Street, Honolulu; ☎ 808-523-4525. **Cost** Free.

COMMENTS Fifty campsites share an ironwood forest by the beach. Picnic tables, restrooms, drinkable water, and outdoor showers are available. Gentle bodysurfing waves make Bellows a favorite destination. Swimming and beachcombing are popular year-round.

Camp Mokuleia THE NORTH SHORE
Farrington Highway (Highway 930), about 4 miles west of Waialua (toward the ocean)

Type of camping Cabins, lodge, and tent sites. **Permits** Write to Camp Mokuleia at 68-729 Farrington Highway, Waialua 96791, call ☎ 808-637-6241, or e-mail info@campmokuleia.com. **Time limit** None. **Cost** Tent camping: $8 per person per night; cabins: $160 (14 beds) or $200 (22 beds) per night; lodge: $65 (rooms with shared bath), $65–$75 (with private bath), $100 (suites). Optional meal service ranges from $5 to $7 per meal.

COMMENTS The best of four campsites on Mokuleia Beach. Used primarily by groups. The area is peaceful, a sample of the rugged beauty of the North Shore. Swimming and snorkeling are good in summer, but the surf gets rough in winter. The tent area is sparse on facilities, but all campers may use the facilities at the main camp section.

Kualoa Regional Park WINDWARD OAHU
Kamehameha Highway, country end of Kaneohe Bay. From Honolulu, head west on the H-1 to the Likelike Highway exit; drive through the tunnel, turn on Kahekili Highway, and drive about 9 miles to the park entry on the right.

Type of camping Tents only. **Permits** Applications accepted no earlier than two Fridays before the requested camping dates. Group campers must apply for a permit in person at the City Department of Parks and Recreation, 650 South Street, Honolulu; ☎ 808-523-4525. Others can also apply at any satellite city hall on Oahu. **Time limit** 5 nights, from Friday at 8 a.m. to Wednesday at 8 a.m. **Cost** Free.

COMMENTS Facilities include restrooms, showers, picnic tables, sinks, a volleyball court, drinking water, and a public phone. Amenities include scenic views, a tranquil atmosphere, the beach, and a commanding photo op: Mokolii islet just offshore. Gates to the park close at 8 p.m. and reopen at 7 a.m.

MAUI
Haleakala National Park

Get groceries and gas before you get to the park, at Kula or lower communities. Three camping alternatives are available in the park, listed below.

Hosmer Grove UPCOUNTRY MAUI
6,800-foot level, just off Haleakala Crater Road; watch for the sign indicating Hosmer Grove, which is almost 10 miles from the Crater Road turnoff

Type of camping Tent and vehicle camping. Vehicles must stay in the parking lot. **Permits** None; the campground is limited to 25 people, with no more than 12 in a single group. **Time limit** 3 nights. **Cost** Free.

COMMENTS The campsite, a grassy clearing surrounded by trees, has a covered pavilion with two picnic tables and two grills, restrooms, and drinkable water. Hiking is the activity of choice. A half-mile loop nature trail begins at one end of the parking lot. Pick up hiking-trail information at the park's headquarters. Bring extra blankets—it can get cold at night.

Kipahulu Campground UPCOUNTRY MAUI
Hana Highway, about 10 miles past Hana

Type of camping Tent and vehicle camping. **Permits** None. Space is limited to 100 people, on first-come, first-served basis. On busy holiday weekends, arrive early to get your space. **Time limit** 2 consecutive nights. **Cost** Free.

COMMENTS Camping in this extraordinary spot, a grassy area overlooking the sea and the Oheo Gulch pools and waterfalls, is so memorable that even noncampers ought to get a tent and give it a try. Facilities include restrooms, picnic tables, and grills, plus the showers and pools provided by nature. Bring drinking water. No food or gas is available. Swimming and jungle hiking are right at hand.

Exploring the infamous curvy road to Hana and its real-Hawaii villages, swimmable waterfall pools, and botanical gardens can be one of Maui's finer nonresort experiences, when you combine the long drive with an overnight stay in the Hana area. Lodging is limited in Hana, and camping at Kipahulu or Waianapanapa (see page 309) is a great alternative.

Wilderness Cabins and Tent Campground
UPCOUNTRY MAUI
Inside Haleakala Crater, on the Halemauu Trail

Type of camping Tent and cabin camping. **Permits** Tent permits are issued at the park's headquarters on a first-come, first-served basis on the day of use. The campground is limited to 25 people, with no more than 12 in a single group. Reservations for Holua, Paliku, and Kapalaoa wilderness cabins must be made 3 months in advance. Be sure to include alternate dates. Write to Haleakala National Park, P.O. Box 369, Makawao 96768, or call ☎ 808-572-9306. **Time limit** 2 consecutive nights. **Cost** Free for tent campers. The 3 cabins are $40 (to accommodate 1–6 people) and $80 (7–12 people) per night.

COMMENTS Awe-inspiring views of Haleakala Crater, big enough to contain Manhattan with room to spare, are among the highlights here at the near-7,000-foot elevation. You are likely to meet the endangered nene goose, Hawaii's state bird. Facilities for tent camping are sparse, and the campground is rocky. Cabins contain bunks with mattresses (but no linens), table, chairs, cooking utensils, and a wood-burning stove with firewood.

THE BIG ISLAND OF HAWAII

Hawaii Volcanoes National Park

Two drive-in campgrounds (Namakani Paio and Kulanaokuaiki) are located within the national park. These facilities are free, once you pay the entry fee to the park, and are available on a first-come, first-serve basis, with no reservations, permits, or check-in required. Stays are limited to 7 days in a month, not to exceed 30 days per year. Get groceries and gas before you arrive. Volcano village has two small groceries (look for locally made Lilikoi curd for a tropical treat), and Hilo and Keaau have supermarkets.

Kalopa State Recreation Area HILO AND VOLCANO
Highway 19, Hamakua Coast, 5 miles from Honokaa

Type of camping Tent and group cabins up to 32 people. **Permits** Obtain at state-parks offices in the Islands. Write to the Big Island office at Division of State Parks, P.O. Box 936, Hilo 96721, or call ☎ 808-974-6200. **Time limit** 5 nights. **Cost** $5 per campsite per night for tent campers. Group cabins start at $8 per night per person and slide down to $2 per night when the maximum of 32 has been reached.

COMMENTS Located in a deep forest of ohia trees, this well-maintained park houses a campground, a picnic area, and group cabins. Facilities in a concrete-block building include restrooms, showers, sinks, and drinking water. The nearby picnic area features a covered pavilion with several tables. The cabins each contain beds and bedding, toilets, showers, and sinks. Cabin users share a dining hall with a fireplace and kitchen.

Kilauea State Recreation Area HILO AND VOLCANO
Kalanikoa Road, Volcano, a half mile from Hawaii Volcanoes National Park

---

Type of camping One cabin, sleeping up to 6. Always in high demand. **Permits** Seek reservations from any state-parks office; or write to the Big Island office at Division of State Parks, P.O. Box 936, Hilo 96721, or call ☎ 808-974-6200. **Time limit** 5 nights. **Cost** One person, $10 per night; 2 people, $7 each per night; 3 people, $6.50; 4 people, $6; 5 people, $5.50; 6 people, $5.

COMMENTS Count yourself lucky if you're able to stay at this two-bedroom cabin, which is comfortably nestled within a shady grove of trees and ferns, with a full kitchen, a combined living and dining room, and a bathroom. Blankets and linens are provided.

Kulanaokuaiki Campground HILO AND VOLCANO
Hawaii Volcanoes National Park, about 5 miles down Hilina Pali Road

---

Type of camping Tent and vehicle camping. **Permits** Not necessary; sites are first-come, first-served. **Time limit** 7 nights. **Cost** Free.

COMMENTS Located at 2,700-foot elevation. No drinking water is available at this new campground. It has three campsites, two of them wheelchair accessible. Facilities include barbecue grills, a vault-type toilet, and picnic tables. **www.hawaii.volcanoes.national-park.com/camping.htm.**

Mauna Loa Summit Cabins HILO AND VOLCANO

Eastern rim of Mauna Loa summit crater. Take Highway 11 to Mauna Loa Road; drive up the narrow road until it ends at a trailhead and parking lot. Hike the trail 7.5 miles to Red Hill Cabin. Mauna Loa Cabin is located 11.6 miles farther up the trail.

Type of camping High-altitude tent and cabin camping. **Permits** They are first-come, first-served at Hawaii Volcanoes National Park Visitor Center. Limited to 8 people per night per group. For more information, write to the Hawaii Volcanoes National Park, P.O. Box 52, Volcano 96718, or call ☎ 808-985-6000. **Time limit** 7 nights. **Cost** Free.

COMMENTS Used by die-hard hikers able to make the thin-air trek. Located at the 13,250-foot level, Mauna Loa Cabin is near the edge of Moku-aweoweo, Mauna Loa's breathtaking caldera. It offers 12 bunk beds and spare mattresses (so additional people can sleep on the floor). An enclosed pit toilet is behind the cabin. Bring your own stove and drinking water (the water here needs to be treated before use). Tent camping is allowed, but try to get the cabin if at all possible; temperatures can dip below freezing at night. Bring warm clothes. At this elevation, even snow is possible any time. Altitude sickness can pose another problem for lowlanders.

Namakani Paio Campground HILO AND VOLCANO

Hawaii Volcanoes National Park, 5 miles west of park entrance on Rte. 11

Type of camping Tent, vehicle, and rustic-cabin camping. **Permits** None. For cabin reservations, write Volcano House, P.O. Box 53, Volcano 96718, or call ☎ 808-967-7321. Reservations should be made as far in advance as possible for summer and holiday periods. **Time limit** 7 nights. **Cost** Cabins are $40 per night for up to 4 people; $8 for additional people.

COMMENTS Located at a 4,000-foot elevation, this scenic campground is surrounded by towering eucalyptus and native ohia trees. Tents are pitched on an open grassy field or under trees. Facilities include a large pavilion with two grills and a fireplace (pack your own firewood; it's not available in these woods), picnic tables, barbecue pits, restrooms, sinks, and potable water. Tent campers can rent showers from Volcano House, which operates ten cabins near the campground. Each cabin has a pair of single bunks and a double bed, picnic table, and outdoor barbecue grill. Toilets, sinks, and showers are provided in a separate building for cabin renters. Expect cool, damp weather. Bring warm clothing.

Spencer Beach Park KONA

Highway 19, Kohala Coast, south of Kawaihae

Type of camping Tent and vehicle camping. **Permits** Book your reservations early, particularly during the summer. Write to the Dept. of Parks and Recreation, County of Hawaii, 25 Aupuni Street, Hilo 96720, or call ☎ 808-961-8311. **Time limit** 1 week during the summer, 2 weeks during the rest of the year. **Cost** $5 per day for adults; $2 per day for children age 13–17; $1 per day for children ages 12 and younger.

COMMENTS Spencer Beach Park offers some of the best camping on the Big Island, with plenty of picnic tables and a large pavilion, restrooms, sinks, washrooms, changing areas, and showers. The water is drinkable. Swimming and snorkeling are popular here. The campground is located next to Puukohala Heiau National Historical Site.

KAUAI

Kalalau Valley, Na Pali Coast State Park KAUAI
End of Kalalau Trail, about 11 miles from Kee Beach. Experienced hikers walk in, but this precipitous trail, which has been subjected to 1,000 years of erosion since the ancient Hawaiians first used it, is not for novices.

Type of camping Tents only. **Permits** Camping in Kalalau is restricted to 60 people per day, so try to obtain a permit as far in advance as possible. For more information, write to the Division of State Parks, 3060 Eiwa Street, Lihue 96766, or call ☎ 808-241-3444. **Time limit** 5 nights. **Cost** $10 per person per night.

COMMENTS Kalalau has become too popular to feel alone in the jungle, but it still has appeal as a singular tropical fantasy come to life with magnificent golden-sand beach, waterfalls, and steep cliffs. The camping area stretches a half mile behind the beach. The only facilities are toilets and water from nearby Hoolea Falls. Pack your own drinking water. Safe swimming in summer only. Most of your fellow travelers in this isolated wilderness are likely to have shed their clothes, since the tradition is to go au naturel.

▌ BICYCLING: *Pedal Power*

EXPLORING HAWAIIAN ISLANDS BY BIKE puts you in touch with your surroundings at your own speed. Most of the islands have mountains in the middle, which add a challenging element.

A few biking tours are available. **Backroads,** the well-known bike-vacation agency in Berkeley, California (call ☎ 800-462-2848 or visit **www.backroads.com**), has inn-to-inn trips on the Big Island and multisport adventures on Maui and Lanai. **Bicycle Adventures** in Olympia, Washington (call ☎ 800-443-6060 or visit **www.bicycle adventures.com**) has six- and eight-day Big Island trips in winter combining biking and B&B stays.

Bike-path systems are still being developed in the place that needs them most: busy, trafficky Oahu. Kailua on the windward side recently

Bike-rental Shops

OAHU

Barnfield's Raging Isle Surf and Cycle	☎ 808-637-7707

MAUI

Haleakala Bike Co.	☎ 808-575-9575 or 888-922-2453
Island Biker	☎ 808-877-7744
South Maui Bicycles	☎ 808-874-0068
West Maui Bicycles	☎ 808-661-9005

BIG ISLAND

Bike Work	☎ 808-326-2453
Cycle Station	☎ 808-327-0087
Hawaiian Pedals	☎ 808-329-2294
Mauna Kea Mountain Bikes	☎ 808-883-0130 or 888-682-8687

KAUAI

Kauai Cycle & Tour	☎ 808-821-2115
Outfitters Kauai	☎ 808-742-9667

MOLOKAI

Molokai Bicycle	☎ 808-553-3931

added bike lanes through beach-park areas and up the Pali Highway. The City and County of Honolulu are developing a master plan for a bikeway system throughout the city. In the meantime, TheBus has free bike carriers on front; bikers can take the bus between biking points.

Ala Moana Beach Park in Honolulu and **Kapiolani Park** in Waikiki offer scenic, comfortable biking in late afternoon and around sunset. For fitness-minded cyclists, a grueling ride is the winding road up to the 2,013-foot summit of Mount Tantalus.

The roads on Neighbor Islands are more often traffic-free. The Big Island's wide-open spaces, decent roads, and challenging landscape have plenty of bike appeal. Maui has bike-friendly lanes, some with stunning views of neighboring Molokai, Lanai, and Kahoolawe. One candidate is the one-lane road around Maui's northwest end between Kahului and Kapalua. The scenery and the winding road slow everyone down. Stop and get a refreshing shave ice at Kahakuloa. Or drive up to Kula, on the 3,000-foot shoulder of Haleakala, and cruise along the hilly country road to Ulupalakua and back, through flower farms, jacaranda trees, botanical gardens, and pastures.

One popular cycling adventure is cruising down the steep and scenic slopes of Hawaii's volcanoes—best known on Maui, where several tour companies will outfit you with special bikes and gear, then take you to the top of 10,023-foot Haleakala and guide you safely down the mountain, 38 miles to the seashore past pasturelands, farms, and forests. Some companies also provide hotel transportation and a snack; others offer unguided tours, letting you set your own pace. Be forewarned—some deceptive grades and curves coming down the mountain have launched even experienced bikers over the side. If you elect to go on your own, take the curves more slowly than you normally would. Dress in layers; the top third of the ride is virtually alpine, while the bottom is tropical.

Hawaii is a terrific place for mountain biking, offering a wide range of terrain, scenic sites, and tracks.

The favorite Maui venue for mountain bikers is **Polipoli State Park,** where you'll find more than ten miles of singletrack that wind through thick forests of eucalyptus and redwood trees. On Oahu, other good trails are found in Mililani in central Oahu, at **Maunawili** in Windward Oahu, in **Pupukea** on the North Shore, and at **Kaena Point** in Leeward Oahu.

The Big Island offers a wide range of mountain biking experiences. Experts in the high-altitude sport can ride through a forest at **Mauna Loa,** pedal on the crater rim, cruise the green pastures in **North Kohala,** and more. A mountain biking trail map is available free of charge at most Big Island bike shops, or call the Big Island Visitors Bureau at ☎ 808-961-5797.

Kauai has five single-tracks and nine dirt roads open to mountain bikes. Coastal treks have numerous scenic stops and spectacular views among the rewards of biking at **Kokee State Park** and **Waimea Canyon.**

Plenty of dirt roads on Lanai call to mountain bikers, as well as the challenging climb to the summit of **Lanaihale,** the island's highest point at 3,370 feet.

Keep in mind these biking-safety tips:

- Wear a helmet, comfortable shoes, and close-fitting clothing.
- Carry a first-aid kit and cell phone, if possible, in case of emergency.
- Familiarize yourself with your rental bike and the tropical heat and humidity before riding.
- Ride with a partner or a group.
- Bring drinking water, sunscreen, and sunglasses.
- Keep at least five lengths between riders if traveling in a group.
- Don't use headphones or get distracted by views while riding.
- Avoid narrow, single-track trails, which sometimes skirt the edges of dangerous cliffs, if you are a novice mountain biker. Instead, ride on the dirt roads. Be careful on the Big Island, where rough and craggy lava rocks pose a shredding danger to tires and skin.

Hawaii Bicycling League (☎ 808-735-5756) issues a newsletter for local biking enthusiasts. A good resource is John Alford's *Mountain Biking the Hawaiian Islands.* The book features maps and photos, as well as detailed descriptions of Hawaii's best biking trails. You can order through **www.bikehawaii.com.**

Daily rentals run from $25 to $40 for a mountain bike and $20 for a road bike.

HORSEBACK RIDING:
Back in the Saddle

YOU MAY NOT THINK OF HAWAII as part of the Wild West, but there's no more western state. Horses were brought to the Islands more than a century ago, and a grateful populace, who had either walked or sailed everywhere, eagerly took to riding. Horseback riding is a great way to get off the roads and into the countryside of the vast ranches that invite visitors onto their lands for tropical trail rides. In the Islands, the wide-open spaces lead between volcanoes, along beaches and sea cliffs, and into jungled valleys with waterfalls. The horses are well trained and know their trails, leaving you free to enjoy the views.

Riding adventures are available on all islands, with colorful and personable guides to share local lore. Rates are reasonable, ranging from $55 per person for a one-hour ride to $85 to $100 for a two-hour trek. Call for age and weight restrictions if you're concerned: the minimum age for riders is usually 8 years old, and the maximum weight ranges to 275 pounds. Book your reservation at least a day in advance, or a week ahead if you have a group. Most rides are limited to 10 to 12 people. You can secure your reservation with a credit card, and most operators also accept traveler's checks or cash. Plan to call on the morning of your ride (or leave a phone number where you can be reached) to check on weather conditions. All riders must sign liability waivers.

A short orientation on horsemanship and safety precautions for island conditions precedes the tour. Previous riding experience is not a requirement; first-time riders are common. Operators will ask your experience level and match you to an appropriate horse. The group will go at the pace of the least-experienced rider. Certain ranches offer intermediate- and advanced-level rides. Most island stables use thoroughbreds and quarter horses.

Rides include stops for a picnic lunch or barbecue, a sampling of local fruit, or a cooling swim. Full-cover shoes are mandatory, long pants are suggested, and sun protection is recommended.

MAUI'S BEST HORSEBACK-RIDING ADVENTURES
Just Say Giddyup

If you wonder how to talk to a horse and make sense, or make a horse do what you want without a struggle, sign up for an **Adventure on Horseback** with wrangler Frank Levinson, also known as "the horse whisperer," on his 55-acre ranch in Haiku, on the way to Hana. He teaches you how to use the techniques made famous in Robert Redford's 1997 film *The Horse Whisperer,* to train horses with respect and understanding instead of fear and punishment. If

Horseback-riding Adventures

OAHU

Happy Trails Hawaii
North Shore ☎ 808-638-7433; www.happytrailshawaii.com

Kualoa Ranch
Windward Coast ☎ 808-237-7321; www.kualoa.com

MAUI

Makena Stables
South Maui ☎ 808-879-0244; www.makenastables.com

Mendes Ranch and Trail Rides
Northwest Maui ☎ 808-871-5222; www.mendesranch.com

Thompson Ranch Riding Stables
Kula ☎ 808-878-1910; www.thompsonranchmaui.com

THE BIG ISLAND

Paniolo Riding Adventures
North Kohala ☎ 808-889-5354; www.panioloadventures.com

Waipio Ridge Stables
Waipio Valley ☎ 808-775-1007 or 877-757-1414; www.waipioridgestables.com

KAUAI

CJM Country Stables
Poipu Beach ☎ 808-742-6096; www.cjmstables.com

Esprit de Corps Riding Academy
Kapaa ☎ 808-822-4688; www.kauaihorses.com

Princeville Ranch Stables
North Shore ☎ 808-826-6777; www.princevilleranch.com

LANAI

The Stables at Koele
☎ 808-565-4000; www.fourseasons.com/koele

you learn improved motivational skills or something else pertinent to your personal life as well as equine psychology, so much the better. In Levinson's The Maui Horse Whisperer Experience program, you don't even have to ride but can elect simply to learn more about horses and spend a day or half a day in the tropical ranch country. Naturally, participants can elect to ride and put their skills to use. Levinson offers a range of trail rides and a special program for families with teenagers, Horse Sense for Humans. You can talk, walk, and ride with horses, and private guided trail rides can be arranged. After you learn how to talk to your horse, go on a trail ride along the coast or through a rain forest to a tropical waterfall pool for lunch. Something to whisper about back home.

For details, contact **Adventures on Horseback** at P.O. Box 1419, Makawao; ☎ 808-572-6211 or visit **www.mauihorses.com.**

SAVE *the* ISLANDS: *Hunt Pig*

SINCE CAPTAIN COOK INTRODUCED the European boar (*Sus scrofa*) to Hawaii in 1776, the pig has served as the main entree in local luaus. But the porkers are also a public nuisance.

They root around in the rain forest gnawing rare silversword plants and other endangered tropical flora. Left unchecked they could eat the Islands right down to their waterlines.

You can help save the Islands by joining a "fair chase" pig hunt on more than 100,000 acres of private ranch land in remote Maui uplands above Haiku.

The hunt goes on year-round from sunrise to sunset on Maui, and everything's provided: a four-wheel drive, guns and ammo, meat storage and packing for shipping, even taxidermy service, if you bag a trophy.

For information, call Bobby Caires of Hunting Adventures of Maui at ☎ 808-572-8214, or write Caires at 645-B Kaupakalua Road, Haiku, Maui 96708.

HAWAII *by* SKY

HANG GLIDING: FREE AS A BIRD

IMAGINE SOARING HIGH ABOVE Hawaii's wilderness, mountain ridges, rain forests, azure bays, and jagged sea coasts. Hang gliding is growing in popularity in the Islands, and you can sign up for an instruction course followed by a memorable tandem flight with your instructor, using a traditional glider or a motor-powered glider.

Those of you who want to spread your kite and fly high can do it above Maui's most famous landmark: Haleakala Crater. You can sign up for an instruction course followed by a memorable tandem flight with your instructor, using a traditional glider or a motor-powered glider. Veteran pilot Armin Engert of **Hang Gliding Maui** offers a four-hour adventure from the top of Haleakala, with shorter excursions using a motorized glider. Call ☎ 808-572-6557 or visit **www.hanggliding maui.com** for more information.

SKYDIVING: A LEAP OF FAITH

WHETHER YOU'RE SEARCHING for the ultimate in aerial views or simply seeking thrills, skydiving may be for you. **Skydive Hawaii** (☎ 808-637-9700) provides skydiving experiences for novices and experts alike at Dillingham Airfield on the north shore of Oahu. The half-day experience includes training and instruction, 15 minutes of flight time to a cruising altitude of 13,000 feet, the jump (in tandem with a professional skydiver), a 5,000-foot free fall, and six or seven minutes of gliding down to Earth via parachute. The cost, $250 per person, includes transportation to and from Waikiki ($180 if you drive yourself).

BIPLANE RIDING: GET LOOPY

IF THE ROMANCE OF THE BIPLANE APPEALS, you can choose flightseeing—or, if you have a strong enough stomach, a heart-thumping aerobatic adventure that includes a dizzying repertoire of loops, spins, rolls, and hammerheads. **Stearman Biplane Rides** (☎ 808-637-4461) at Dillingham Airfield on the north shore of Oahu offers single-passenger rides aboard a restored 1941-vintage, open-cockpit Stearman N2S biplane. A 20-minute North Shore flight is $135; a 35-minute tour over historic Pearl Harbor is $205. Add $50 for an extra 10 minutes of aerobatic action.

Also at Dillingham Airfield, **Tsunami Aviation** (☎ 808-677-3404) features the state-of-the-art aerobatic sport biplane PITTS S2B, billed as the "Formula One racer of airplanes." **Glider Rides** (☎ 808-677-3404) offers an exciting 20-minute ($79) flight with all kinds of topsy-turvy maneuvers—it'll literally turn the island upside-down for you.

A BIRD'S-EYE VIEW

HOOKED IN A HARNESS TO A HIGH WIRE, you leap off a platform and go zipping over canyons like a bird at a top speed of 40 miles per hour from 40 to 200 feet off the ground. Not for everyone—Afraid of heights? Bad back? Beware—the new thrill on the hill on Maui puts you in virgin turf without leaving a footprint. Skyline Eco Adventure operates two lines, one on 10,000-foot Haleakala, the other in the West Maui Mountains above Kaanapali, each with spectacular Island views. Five lines (each named for a different native Hawaiian bird) skim over cliffs and valleys. Each zip is longer and faster; the last is 750 feet across a 125-foot-deep canyon. The two-hour adventure ends too soon. Safer (and swifter) than driving in Kihei, each harness is tested to 6,000 pounds; cables are rated at 14,500 pounds. Guides double-check your harness at each station. Zippers must be over age 10 and weigh between 80 and 260 pounds. Wear long pants, closed-toe shoes, and, if you go in the morning, layer up. It's chilly on Haleakala at 4,000 feet. Call ☎ 808-878-8400 or visit **www.zipline.com** for details.

SPAS: *For Your Health*

HEALTH, IN HAWAIIAN, TRANSLATES AS *hooponopono*—it means making things right. The very nature of the place—sun, sea, sky, and perfect weather—already makes you feel all right. A spa in Hawaii gilds the lily.

Health Clubs and Fitness Centers

OAHU

Spa Fitness Center	☎ 808-949-0026
24 Hour Fitness	☎ 808-923-9090 in Waikiki; 808-951-7677 in Honolulu; www.24hourfitness.com

MAUI

24 Hour Fitness	☎ 808-877-7474; www.24hourfitness.com

THE BIG ISLAND

The Club in Kona	☎ 808-326-2582; www.theclubinkona.com

KAUAI

Kauai Athletic Club	☎ 808-245-5381 or 808-246-0631; www.kauaiathleticclub.com
Kauai Gym	☎ 808-823-8210

Devoted to rejuvenation and pampering care, spas are open on all islands, at nearly every hotel and resort, and offer European, Asian, New Age, and other modern therapies. But while in the Islands, you should try Hawaii's own unique spa techniques.

Seek Hawaiian practitioners of ancient healing arts using Hawaiian medicinal plants, massage, and relaxation techniques.

Look for spas that use Hawaiian plants and seaweeds, ocean water in peaceful surroundings, and methods like *lomilomi,* a vigorous rubbing technique, or hot-lava-rock massage to relax sore muscles.

Several spas take advantage of Hawaii's great outdoors—you'll find private outdoor massage cabanas near the sea and open-air facilities at resorts. Spa treatments are affordable alternatives to a day in the surf (a natural massage preferred in the Islands), and it's easy to treat yourself to first-class therapeutic pampering. Hotel guests need only touch 9, as the bedside phone reminds. However, you don't have to be a resort guest to enjoy a resort spa. Spas now offer their own brands of soaps, oils, lotions, towels, and robes, and they offer services to non-guests as well.

Most hotels offer round-the-clock fitness centers with treadmills, spinners, and free weights. Those who go to health clubs to restore vigor will delight in new, improved facilities featuring waterfall showers and furo soaking tubs. In addition to hotel spas and fitness centers, there are health clubs and gyms across the Islands. Daily rates average around $15 to $20, with weekly and monthly rates available.

Here are our top spa choices:

OAHU
Halekulani Waikiki
☎ 808-931-5322

Hours Daily, 9 a.m.–8 p.m.

COMMENTS Leave it to Halekulani to introduce the healing traditions of the Pacific Islands, including Samoa, Tonga, and Tahiti. SpaHalekuani (it's one word like TheBus) fronts Gray's Beach, known to early Hawaiians for its healing waters, or *kawehewehe*. Just saying that makes your inner self glow.

This new high-end luxury spa offers three first-class package deals, of varying lengths and escalating prices, beginning with Elegant Passage, a 2.5-hour journey of relaxation that begins with a foot-pounding ritual and ends with a facial to wipe that silly grin off your face ($390).

Next is Grand Voyage, a four-hour odyssey with a light refreshment on the spa terrace plus manicure and pedicure ($490). But as long as you're here, why not go all the way and take Heavenly Journey? It's four hours of indulgent pampering complete with tropical treatments like hibiscus for cleansing, papaya pineapple for anti-aging, or coconut for nourishment; the price ($640) includes ritual foot pounding.

Couples can share a special spa package "designed to spark the bliss of romance"—foot pounding, couples massage, deluxe facials, a soak in the furo, champagne and decadent tasty treats on the terrace, plus manicures and pedicures ($1300 per couple).

Other body and facial experiences are offered, including Partnering with the Sun, important if you stayed too long under the tropic sun without SPF 16; Polynesian Steam Therapy; Hawaiian Pohaku with Pele's hot rocks; and Japanese-style Ton Ton Amma, followed by a deep soak in an authentic Japanese *furo*. There are special experiences for brides, grooms, pregnant women, and tweens (ages 11–15), who can sign up for a makeup lesson ($65), "Here's Looking at You, Kid" mini-facial and skin assessment ($75), or manicure and pedicure ($95). To get a facial, guests must be age 16 or older; a massage, 18 or older—unless an adult accompanies any younger guest in the treatment room. The spa prohibits cell phones and pagers.

Hilton Hawaiian Village Waikiki
☎ 808-945-7721 (Mandara Spa)

Hours Daily, 6 a.m.–9 p.m. (fitness); 9 a.m.–9 p.m. (spa)

COMMENTS Hilton's spa opened in 2001 on two floors of Kalia Tower at Hawaii's largest hotel with interesting innovations. It is a traditional spa and salon operated by Mandara Spa, which runs luxury spas worldwide.

Mandara Spa incorporates Balinese treatments in the mix of Hawaiian, European, and Asian techniques. It created some treatments based on Hawaiian ingredients, notably the chocolate–macadamia nut scrub and the vanilla-*pikake* (jasmine) facial. Hawaiian ingredients have been used in a variety of other treatments—ground Kona coffee, fresh coconut, sea salt, *limu kala* seaweed, *ti* leaves, and traditional protective plants. Or you could opt for the Kalia tropical *pikake*-papaya bath or chocolate scrub. Facilities include 25 private "wet and dry" and massage-treatment rooms and some spa suites for couples, friends, and families to share treatments; a private outdoor infinity pool, a whirlpool, and a sundeck; all the usual showers, lockers, fitness center, salon services, sauna, and steam rooms, as well as a cafe with spa cuisine and a boutique. Guests can also schedule massages in their rooms, between 9 a.m. and midnight.

Spa treatments can be reserved with a credit card; the fee will be forfeited in case of cancellations with less than two hours' notice before the appointment. Children can have spa services but must be accompanied by a parent or guardian for treatments unless they are age 16 or older. Hotel guests get a 20% break if they reserve spa services online prior to arrival: (**www.hiltonhawaiianvillage.com/resort_activities/ mandara_spa_and_fitness_center.cfm;** use code 20%WEB).

Massages start at $120; men's spa escapes, from $270. The full "Nirvana" package for more than five hours is $540. The two-and-a-half-hour indulgence called "Exploration in Chocolate" is $450 for two sharing a suite.

Service charges of 18% and 4% state taxes are added to the bill; tips are at your discretion.

J. W. Marriott Ihilani Resort and Spa Leeward Oahu
☎ 808-679-0079; www.ihilani.com

Hours Daily, 7 a.m.–7 p.m.

COMMENTS The 35,000-square-foot Ihilani Spa offers some 70 services and treatments, many based on distinctive Hawaiian products and ingredients, including piped-in seawater from the adjoining shore. The spa menu includes a wide range of hydrotherapies, fitness and relaxation programs, massage treatments, aromatherapies, skin-care treatments, and salon services.

Men's and women's lounges are equipped with steam room, sauna, Needle Shower Pavilion, Roman pool, and other amenities. Use fee for hotel guests—$20 between 7 and 11 a.m. and 2 and 7 p.m.—is waived if you purchase a spa treatment. The fee for others is $25, plus any treatment fees. The facility also has weight and cardiovascular-workout rooms, with classes led by trained staff. Proper athletic footwear is required.

Appointments are scheduled in advance, and patrons who are not hotel guests need a credit card to hold a reservation. Cancel or reschedule any appointment for a treatment at least four hours in advance to avoid being charged half of the treatment fee. No-shows will be charged the full fee. You can request a male or female therapist and alert the spa to any allergies or medical conditions.

Individual treatments range from $145 for a massage or $165 for an age-protection facial and body treatment. Half- and full-day treatment programs are available, ranging from $392 to $546. An 18% service charge is added for each treatment.

The Ihilani is one of two places in the United States to offer thalassotherapy, an underwater full-body massage using 180 pulsating jet streams of warm seawater that is pumped directly into the spa for each treatment. The massage lasts 25 minutes and costs $75. Contact the spa for a complete list of services.

MAUI

Spa Grande, Grand Wailea Resort Hotel and Spa
South Maui
☎ 808-875-1234; www.grandwailea.com

Hours Treatments, 8 a.m.–7 p.m.; fitness and workout rooms, 6 a.m.–8 p.m.; beauty salon, 8 a.m.–7 p.m.

COMMENTS The Grand Wailea's Spa Grande is Hawaii's largest at 50,000 square feet, a favorite with the spa-going world.

Spa Grande has an "East meets West" philosophy, mixing traditional Hawaiian healing techniques with European, American, Indian, and Asian spa therapies. Everything's here: massage treatments, aromatherapy, body treatments, facials, hair care, manicures, pedicures, waxings, yoga, meditation instruction, racquetball, basketball, and more. Prices range from $26 for a nail-polish change to $645 for a luxurious lavender package for two. Most soothing is the spa's Termé ala carte, a refreshing hour-long treatment. You begin with a quick shower, enjoy some quality time in a Roman bath, and visit the steam room and sauna before being escorted for a personalized loofah scrub, a cleansing treatment that exfoliates surface skin cells and produces healthier-looking skin. The treatment continues with your choice of specialty baths—Moor mud, *limu* and seaweed, aromatherapy, tropical enzyme, and mineral salt—followed by a Swiss jet shower. Sound invigorating? The cost is $55 for hotel guests and $80 for non–hotel guests.

Non–hotel guests pay a $30 surcharge added to the first spa treatment (salon and wellness services not included). The surcharge is waived if you book two or more spa treatments on the same day. Programs for children and teens (ages 6–17) include such tasty-sounding treatments as a chocolate coconut polish or a honey mango manicure. Non–hotel guests need a major credit card to reserve an appointment. A 50% charge is assessed for no-shows and cancellations less than two hours prior to your appointment. All spa and salon services are subject to an additional 15% service charge plus 4% tax.

Use of the cardiovascular and weight-training gyms and all fitness classes are complimentary for guests of the hotel.

THE BIG ISLAND OF HAWAII

Four Seasons Resort Hualalai Kona
☎ 808-325-8440; www.fourseasons.com/hualalai

Hours Daily, 6 a.m.–8 p.m.

COMMENTS "Starlight spa voyage" is the signature spa treatment—a massage by the King's Pond lava pool, followed by a float on a tethered raft on the pond, surrounded by candlelight as the stars begin to twinkle overhead ($750 per person for four hours). The Hualalai Spa has been expanded to encompass tropical gardens, including one with a waterfall and stream.

Pretreatment rituals to get you in the mood are complimentary. Your choice of more than 20 Hawaiian ingredients and waters are used to make the spa experience extra special. Other spa therapies (available to guests age 14 and older) include several types of massages and body treatments ($170 for 50 minutes, $225 for 80 minutes), and various combination packages. The ultimate pampering package is the endless spa journey, unlimited services for a day ($2,000). Fitness die-hards can sign on for climbs, hikes, paddling, surfing, ocean swimming, and a host of other adventures and classes. The sports club offers a variety of fitness classes, including high- and low-impact aerobics and aqua aerobics. Acupuncture, a session with a naturopath, and chiropractic care, as well as nutritional analysis, are also available.

Provide at least 4 hours' notice if you need to cancel or reschedule your appointment to avoid being charged in full (24 hours' notice is required from December 15 to January 3). Children under the age of 14 are not allowed into the spa. When making an appointment for a spa treatment, you'll be asked to arrive 30 minutes ahead of time to shower and enjoy the sauna, steam bath, whirlpool, and a cold dip.

KAUAI

Grand Hyatt Kauai Resort & Spa Kauai
☎ 808-240-6440; www.anaraspa.com

Hours Daily, 6 a.m.–8 p.m.

COMMENTS The hotel's ANARA Spa, considered state of the art when it opened in 1991, remains one of Hawaii's best spas—even more so after its recent expansion to 45,000 square feet, making it the second-largest spa in the state. New outdoor private *hale* (huts) provide protected areas for massages, and indoor treatment rooms overlook private gardens. Facilities include a 25-yard heated lap pool in the center of the courtyard, a Turkish steam room, a Finnish sauna, private outdoor soaking tubs, open-air relaxation lounge, and open-air "shower gardens" carved from lava rock. Combine all this with Kauai's natural therapeutic value, and you have a refreshing and invigorating experience.

Admission to the spa is $30 per day for hotel guests and $50 for non–hotel guests, and includes use of the fitness center. Admission is complimentary with any spa treatments. Appointments for treatments should be booked at least a day in advance (especially for treatment packages). Non–hotel guests must reserve their bookings with a major credit card. Cancellation notice must be given at least four hours in advance; otherwise, you'll be charged in full. No one under the age of 16 is allowed in the spa at any time.

Here's a sampling of ANARA Spa services and prices: 50-minute massage starts at $160; 50-minute body treatments are $165; 25-minute herbal wraps are $95; manicures are $60; and pedicures are $105. Salon-spa combination treatment packages range from $250 to $696. Private lockers are provided.

GOLF: *Tee Time*

IF YOU LOOK AT THE HAWAIIAN ISLANDS as a chain of golf courses in the middle of the Pacific Ocean, you'll begin to see the challenges they pose. Ninety courses on six islands, with exotic names like Hapuna, Ko Olina, Koolau, and Mauna Lani, are set like jewels by the sea, in black-lava beds, on turquoise lagoons, near volcanoes, beside lush rain forests, and deep in jungle valleys. Nowhere else on Earth can you tee off to whale spouts, putt under rainbows, or play around a live volcano. But be forewarned: Many of these courses feature hellish natural hazards—razor-sharp lava, gusty trade winds, distracting views, an occasional wild pig, and, always, the tropical heat.

There is one major handicap—that big blue ocean between you and the Islands poses a time and distance problem. It's impossible to play all of Hawaii's great courses unless you move here and take up golf full time (which some duffers do).

Ever since a Scotsman opened Oahu's first golf course in 1898, the game spread across the Islands like red-hot lava. Eight 18-hole golf courses blanket the Big Island's Kona-Kohala Coast alone, with another three located inland in West Hawaii. Golf is now an important attraction in Hawaii and serious business. Golf employs more people here than do sugar and pineapple—some 3,000 people in all, including 240 golf pros, thanks to visitors and residents who play some 5 million rounds of golf each year.

BEST AND MOST CHALLENGING COURSES IN HAWAII

Koolau Golf Course, Oahu

"The toughest golf course in America," according to *Men's Journal*, was originally built as a private club for Tokyo's high-rollers. But Koolau Golf Course on the windward side opened to the public after the global recession pinched Japan. The 7,310-yard, par 72 course with a slope rating of 155 was designed by Dick Nugent. It offers "demoralizing" hazards like ravines, monster bunkers, a jungle of foliage, and a lone mango tree that blocks the tiny landing approach to the 18th hole, a 474-yard par 4.

Ko Olina Golf Club, Oahu

The par 72, 18-hole Ted Robinson Ko Olina Golf Club course beckons at Ko Olina Resort on Oahu's western shore. This wide-open course abounds with lakes, ponds, brooks, and waterfalls. The par 5 fifth hole is rated most difficult. It plays 528 yards to a small narrow-neck green guarded by a pond full of black swans.

Gold Course at Wailea Resort, Maui

Three championship courses distinguish Wailea Resort in South Maui: the newer Gold and Emerald courses, as well as the par 72,

GREENS FEES

Based on one 18-hole round, with or without cart:

Resort courses, $110–$250	Semiprivate courses, $25–$135
Private courses, $50–$100	Public courses, $14–$135
Municipal courses, $42–$54	Military courses, $9–$40

18-hole Blue course, considered the Grand Lady of Wailea. *Golf for Women* magazine recently named the Wailea Golf Club one of the three most women-friendly golf facilities in the country. On this island already noted for great courses, nothing compares to the Gold course at Wailea. This Robert Trent Jones Jr. course is a rugged, natural-style 7,070-yard, par 72 layout that plays over the foothills of 10,023-foot Mount Haleakala.

Kapalua Resort, Maui

Surrounded by a pineapple plantation on Maui's northwest coast, Kapalua Resort's 1,500 tidy acres include two of the world's most beautiful and challenging 18-hole courses—the Bay and Plantation courses.

The par 3 fifth hole on the Bay course gives everyone butterflies; it's a 205-yard-long shot across Oneloa Bay from the back tees. With the nearly constant wind at your back, you may dodge the surf but hit the bunkers that shield the green's front, back, and right sides.

The Challenge at Manele and the Experience at Koele, Lanai

Lanai may have more deer than people, but it boasts two stunning resort golf courses—the Experience at Koele and the Challenge at Manele. The Jack Nicklaus–designed Challenge is a target-style course carved from lava cliffs by the sea. The water hazard on the par 3, signature 12th hole at Manele is a wave-lashed coast of jagged lava. This course on the south coast of Lanai will test your patience and increase your impolite vocabulary. Or face the Experience's signature hole, which plays into a ravine from a knoll 250 feet above the fairway of this upland course. The layout begins high on the slopes of 3,366-foot Mount Lanaihale, complete with Norfolk pine forest and a gallery of deer, pheasant, and wild turkey. Designed by Greg Norman and Ted Robinson, this course features the only bent-grass greens in Hawaii.

Hapuna Prince Course, The Big Island

Native grasslands and wildflowers cover old lava flows that rumple the layout of this environmentally aware 18-hole golf course above the Kohala Coast. Designed by Arnold Palmer and Ed Seay, Hapuna is a 6,875-yard, par 72 course that makes extensive use of the rugged terrain (it stretches from the shore to 700 feet above sea level). One of *Golf* magazine's top-ten new golf courses in the United States when it opened, Hapuna was cited for environmental sensitivity and called "the course of the future."

Hualalai Golf Course, Kaupulehu, The Big Island

Jack Nicklaus was among the first to tee off on Hualalai, his par 72, 18-hole PGA championship course carved out of black lava on the Kona Coast. He made it look so easy. You can play this course only if you are a guest at the Four Seasons Resort Hualalai or a resident of the neighboring exclusive golf retreat.

Mauna Lani, The Big Island

If the Smithsonian Institution ever seeks a golf course for its collection, Mauna Lani is a likely candidate. Set in black lava beside the blue Pacific, this course is, thanks to man and nature, a work of art. Carved from 19th-century lava flows, the two 18-hole Francis H. I'i Brown North and South courses feature two striking ocean holes that challenge pros and amateurs who try to beat the records of Arnold Palmer, Lee Trevino, and Raymond Floyd. The South Course's signature 15th hole, a 196-yard par 3, is a seascape portrait of lush greens, azure sea, charcoal lava, and gold sand, all under a vivid blue sky.

Princeville Resort, Kauai

When designer Robert Trent Jones Jr. first saw the plateau on Kauai's North Shore that would become Princeville's golf links, he said he became "truly nervous." It's a reaction most golfers have today when they tee off at Princeville. With its awesome setting above scenic Hanalei Bay and challenging holes (the 205-yard, par 3 seventh tee addresses a wide-mouthed gorge), the 18-hole Prince course is ranked as one of the most difficult in Hawaii and one of the top-100 courses in the United States. The famed 27-hole Makai course features three separate nines: the Ocean, the Woods, and the Lakes; the Ocean-Lakes combo is the most popular.

GOLF, YOUR WAY

HAWAII'S FAMOUS COURSES are high on the life lists of most players who plan their vacations around golf. It's a passion fanned by sunny scenes in televised winter tournaments from resorts like Kapalua, where the water feature might be a humpback in the background, or fabled Mauna Kea and Mauna Lani on the Big Island, with their implausible green-on-lava oases under the volcanoes. When you've got that dream, nothing else will satisfy it. However, golf in Hawaii isn't necessarily an expensive indulgence. Hawaii residents who can't afford world-class resort greens fees are equally hooked on the game, and they play golf year-round as often as possible. The Islands' resort, municipal, public, military, semiprivate, and private courses, running the gamut of designers, challenges, layouts, and expense, share a measure of distracting natural beauty.

Devoted golfers will no doubt have a course in mind when they choose where to stay. If you just want to play some golf in Hawaii and not base your vacation around it, be your own concierge and make your own arrangements, so that you can choose the time and place you want to play and the fees you want to pay. Hotels will recommend their neighboring courses to keep their guests close to home. That may be exactly what you had in mind, because fees are lower and tee times often more readily available to resort guests. Plenty of them offer package rates for room, car, and golf with other extras thrown in. If you want to roam, your options include some enticing public and municipal courses—the perennially top-ranked Wailua municipal course on Kauai, for instance—where great golf experiences may cost half the fees of resort courses. Imagine how top-this options, like the Volcano course at 4,000 feet on the edge of Kilauea or the historic jewel of a plantation course at Ironwood Hills on Molokai, will play later at your local clubhouse.

Tee times are usually easy to reserve; the busiest times are weekends and the winter tourist season. Oahu has the biggest crowd of golfers and the most competition for bookings. Your hopes may be dashed at that course right across the canal from Waikiki: Ala Wai Golf Course is the busiest in the nation. Koolau Golf Club, on the other side of the mountains, is considered the most difficult course in the nation, according to *Men's Journal*.

Most courses allow you to request a tee time at least a few days in advance. If you're looking for a last-minute tee time, try **Stand-By Golf** (☎ 808-922-2665), which gives visitors a discount. The company makes a small margin on each booking, you get discounted rates, and the course managers are happy to fill in empty time slots.

Shorts are acceptable attire on Hawaiian courses, but blue jeans are sometimes banned. Collared shirts are often required and a good idea anyway to avoid sunburn on the back of your neck. Spikeless golf shoes are now the standard.

Discover Hawaii's Best Golf, an 86-page book by golf writer George Fuller, is a helpful resource. Issued by Island Heritage Publishing, this volume provides vivid descriptions and photos of the state's top courses.

Oahu

Ko Olina Golf Club LEEWARD OAHU

ESTABLISHED: 1990 STATUS: RESORT, 18 HOLES, PAR 72

92-220 Aliinui Drive, Ewa Beach 96707 (Head west on H-1; take the Ko Olina exit. The exit loops around to the course.) ☎ 808-676-5300; www.koolinagolf.com

TEES *Championship:* 6,867 yards. *Men's:* 6,450 yards. *Ladies':* 5,392 yards
FEES $160; $140 for Ihilani Resort guests. Includes cart. Special twi-light rates

($100 for 18 holes, $80 for 9 holes) are available after 2:30 p.m. Club rentals: $50. Accepts tee times a week in advance. Accepts AE, D, MC, V.

FACILITIES Driving range, practice area, pro shop, restaurant, and a locker room with showers, steam rooms, and Jacuzzi.

COMMENTS Brisk winds make for challenging play. This course is considered one of Ted Robinson's best designs. Water hazards—including waterfalls, lakes, and ponds—pop up throughout the course. Greens are split-level and multitiered. The course's signature 18th hole—featuring a waterfall to the right of the tee area, which spills into a lake surrounding the green—is a tough finishing hole. Collared shirts required.

Koolau Golf Club WINDWARD OAHU

ESTABLISHED: 1992 STATUS: PUBLIC, 18 HOLES, PAR 72

45-550 Kionaole Road, Kaneohe 96744 (Take Pali Highway to-ward Kailua, turn left on Kamehameha Highway, then make a left on Kionaole Road. The entrance to the course is on the left.) ☎ 808-247-7088; www.koolaugolfclub.com

TEES *Tournament* (black tees): 7,310 yards. *Championship* (gold tees): 6,797 yards. *Men's* (blue tees): 6,406 yards. *Ladies'* (white tees): 5,102 yards.

FEES $89 daily. Special $65 twilight rate available after 1 p.m. Fees include cart. Club rentals: $40. Accepts tee times up to 30 days in advance. Accepts AE, MC, V.

FACILITIES Driving range, putting green, chipping range, snack bar, and pro shop.

COMMENTS This is considered the most difficult course in the United States, even though water comes into play on only one hole. The first hole is a 593-yard par 5. The 18th requires a tee shot over a wide ravine with a precipitous sand trap running the length of the fairway on the right. This is an exceptionally scenic course, in very high demand. Collared shirts required.

Luana Hills Country Club WINDWARD OAHU

ESTABLISHED: 1994 STATUS: SEMIPRIVATE, 18 HOLES, PAR 72

770 Auloa Road, Kailua 96734 (Pali Highway, toward Kailua; after the third stoplight, turn right onto Auloa and take an immediate left on the winding road to the course.) ☎ 808-262-2139; www.luanahills.com

TEES *Championship* (black tees): 6,595 yards. *Championship* (blue tees): 6,164 yards. *Men's* (white tees): 5,522 yards. *Ladies'* (yellow tees): 4,654 yards.

FEES Every day, $125 plus tax. Accepts MC, V.

FACILITIES Driving range, putting greens, pro shop, locker rooms with showers and Jacuzzi, restaurant, and cocktail lounge.

COMMENTS This course is a growing favorite among residents and visitors, and is so scenic that the city is talking about making it a park. The front nine is carved into the side of Mount Olomana, and the back nine take you through a tropical rain forest. The par 3 11th hole is a scenic masterpiece dominated by a picturesque pond.

Makaha Resort Golf Club LEEWARD OAHU

ESTABLISHED: 1969 STATUS: RESORT, 18 HOLES, PAR 72

84-626 Makaha Valley Road, Waianae 96792 (Head west on Farrington Highway, turn right at Makaha Valley Road, and turn left at the fork.) ☎ 808-695-9544; www.makaharesortgolfclub.com

TEES *Championship:* 7,077 yards. *Men's:* 6,414 yards. *Ladies':* 5,856 yards.

FEES $140; $115 for guests of Waikiki hotels. Includes cart. Special $95 twilight rate after noon. Club rentals: $40. Accepts tee times 14 days in advance. Accepts AE, D, MC, V.

FACILITIES Driving range, putting green, chipping area, clubhouse, and restaurant.

COMMENTS Formerly the Sheraton Makaha Golf Club. A favorite challenging course offering spectacular views, especially at sunset. Course overlooks the ocean; the back nine play into Makaha Valley. Winds blow down the valley toward the ocean. The par 4 18th hole is one of the most challenging holes on the island, with two bunkers to the left of the fairway, water on the right, and another water hazard fronting the green. Collared shirts are required; no denim. Bring a light jacket to be prepared for frequent rain drizzles in the valley.

The Palmer Course at Turtle Bay Resort THE NORTH SHORE

ESTABLISHED: 1992 STATUS: RESORT, 18 HOLES, PAR 72

57-049 Kuilima Drive, Kahuku 96731 (Head west on H-1, exit onto H-2 Freeway, and stay to the right. Take the Wahiawa exit and stay right to Kamehameha Highway; the course is about a half hour away.) ☎ 808-293-8574

TEES *Men's:* 7,200 yards. *Ladies':* 4,851 yards.

FEES $175 for 18 holes. Includes cart. Special $110 twilight rate available after 2 p.m. on weekdays. Club rentals: $55. Accepts tee times 14 days in advance. Accepts AE, D, MC, V.

FACILITIES Driving range, putting greens, pro shop, and snack bar.

COMMENTS Designed by golf legends Arnold Palmer and Ed Seay, this is a tough course because of strong trade winds and plentiful sand traps. Though the course is near the ocean, only one hole (the 17th) provides close views of the surf. Several holes skirt a marine-wildlife sanctuary. The back nine holes are the most scenic. *Golf Magazine* ranked the course as one of the top ten new courses in the United States; *Golf Digest* ranked it fourth among new resort courses when it opened. No tank tops or cutoffs allowed.

Pearl Country Club CENTRAL OAHU

ESTABLISHED: 1967 STATUS: PUBLIC, 18 HOLES, PAR 72

98-535 Kaonohi Street, Aiea 96701 (West on H-1, take Pearlridge exit, and make a right. Turn right on Kaonohi Street. The entrance is on the right.) ☎ 808-487-3802; www.pearlcc.com

TEES *Championship:* 6,787 yards. *Men's:* 6,232 yards. *Ladies':* 5,536 yards.

FEES Weekdays, $100; weekends, $110. Includes cart. Twilight rates: $48 2–3 p.m. and $30 after 3 p.m. Nine-hole twilight rate: $20. Club rent-als: $30. Accepts tee times 60 days in advance. Accepts AE, MC, V.

FACILITIES Driving range (lit at night), pro shop, and locker room with showers.

COMMENTS Older, hilly course that remains popular, especially among residents. Difficult lies provide a good challenge. Overlooks Pearl Harbor and the USS *Arizona* Memorial. No tank tops or cutoffs.

Maui

The Dunes at Maui Lani SOUTH MAUI

ESTABLISHED: 1999 STATUS: PUBLIC, 18 HOLES, PAR 72

1333 Mauilani Parkway, Kahului 96732 (From the Kahului Air-port, head toward Lahaina on Dairy Road until you hit Kuihelani Highway 380. The course is 1.5 miles off to the right. The entrance is marked by green flags.) ☎ 808-873-0422; www.dunesatmauilani.com

TEES *Championship* (black tees): 6,840 yards. *Championship* (blue tees): 6,413 yards. *Men's* (white tees): 5,833 yards. *Ladies'* (red tees): 4,768 yards.

FEES $100, includes cart; twilight fees, $60 after 2 p.m. Club rentals: $30. Accepts tee times up to three months in advance; check cancellation policy. Accepts AE, MC, V.

FACILITIES Driving range, 15-acre practice facility, putting greens, clubhouse, pro shop, and restaurant.

COMMENTS Maui's most surprising course is an Irish-links island-style course incorporating natural sand dunes, not on the coast where Maui has none, but inland where the sea left them a million or so years ago in a valley. Architect Robin Nelson took advantage of ancient dunes (up to 80 feet high) to provide drama on several holes. His layout is a true mental challenge. There is a peek of the sea now and then, but guests see mostly rolling terrain with a forest of thorny *kiawe* trees. Instead, the killer views are of towering Haleakala. The short par 3 third hole is a classic dune hole fashioned after the sixth at Lahinch in Ireland. The course anchors a residential development.

Elleair Maui Golf Course SOUTH MAUI

ESTABLISHED: 1987 STATUS: PUBLIC, 18 HOLES, PAR 71

1345 Piilani Highway, Kihei 96753 (*ma uka*, or uphill, side of Highway 31 in Kihei) ☎ 808-874-0777; www.elleairmauigolfclub.com

TEES *Championship:* 6,801 yards. *Men's:* 6,404 yards. *Ladies':* 6,003 yards.

FEES $100; twilight special after 1 p.m., $80. Cart included. Club rentals: $40. Accepts tee times 30 days in advance. Accepts MC, V.

FACILITIES Driving range, night lit, pro shop, and restaurant.

COMMENTS Morning and late-afternoon trade winds usually hit the course, and many holes bring the winds into play. Views of the sea are af-forded from most of the greens on this public course.

Kaanapali Golf Courses WEST MAUI

ESTABLISHED: 1962 (ROYAL KAANAPALI), 1997 (KAANAPALI KAI)
STATUS: RESORT, 18 HOLES, PAR 71 (FOR BOTH COURSES)

2290 Kaanapali Parkway, Kaanapali Resort, Lahaina 96761 (Take Highway 30 past Lahaina to Kaanapali Beach Resort. Turn left at the first entrance of the golf course.) ☎ 808-661-3691; www.kaanapali-golf.com

TEES *Men's:* North: 6,994 yards; South: 6,555 yards. *Ladies':* North: 5,417 yards; South: 5,485 yards.

FEES $195–$235; less for resort guests. Includes cart. Special $95 twilight rate (Kaanapali Kai only) noon–2:30 p.m. Twilight rate after 2 p.m., $85 (Royal Kaanapali); $75 (Kaanapali Kai). Repeat rounds, $49. Club rentals: $45 ($25 twilight rate). Accepts tee times two days in advance. Accepts AE, MC, V.

FACILITIES Driving range, putting green, pro shop, restaurant, and locker room with showers.

COMMENTS Two excellent 18-hole courses. The 18th on the Royal Kaanapali course is one of Hawaii's toughest finishing holes, with water hazards lined up on the right side and the kidney-shaped green bordered by two treacherous bunkers on the left. The shorter Kaanapali Kai course has more forgiving greens and wider fairways. The Royal hosts the annual Kaanapali Classic, a Senior PGA Tour event.

Kahili Golf Course SOUTH MAUI

ESTABLISHED: 1991   STATUS: RESORT, 18 HOLES, PAR 72

2500 Honoapiilani Highway, Wailuku 96793 (Turn uphill off Highway 30, just south of Wailuku.) ☎ 808-242-4653; www.kahiligolf.com

TEES *Championship:* 6,433 yards. *Men's:* 5,918 yards. *Ladies':* 5,162 yards.

FEES $95, cart included. Club rentals: $25. Accepts MC, V.

FACILITIES Driving range, pro shop, banquet facility, locker rooms, clubhouse, putting and chipping greens, and restaurant.

COMMENTS Robin Nelson and Rodney Wright designed this layout among sandalwood trees at Waikapu, nestled into the side of the West Maui Mountains overlooking Maui's green cane fields. Sloping fairways and hefty trade winds can make for a challenging day, along with a lot of elevated greens and par 4s that are long, straight, and into the wind.

Kapalua Golf Club WEST MAUI

ESTABLISHED: 1975 (BAY), 1991 (PLANTATION)   STATUS: RESORT
BAY COURSE: 54 HOLES, PAR 72; PLANTATION COURSE: 18 HOLES, PAR 73

300 Kapalua Drive, Kapalua 96761 (Take Highway 30 past La-haina and Kaanapali to Kapalua Resort; turn left at Kapalua Drive.) ☎ 808-669-8830 or 877-527-2582

TEES *Men's:* Bay: 6,600 yards; Plantation: 7,263 yards. *Ladies':* Bay: 5,124 yards; Plantation: 5,627 yards.

FEES Bay, $220; Plantation, $298. Includes cart. Twilight special after 2 p.m.:

Bay, $138; Plantation, $158. Club rentals: $65. Accepts tee times four days in advance. Accepts AE, D, MC, V.

FACILITIES Driving range, putting green, pro shop, clubhouse, restaurants.

COMMENTS These two courses are among Maui's best, providing gor-geous views at every turn. The Bay course's Hole 5 is one of the world's most dramatic signature holes, requiring a tee shot over Oneloa Bay. The links-style Plantation course, highly regarded by many pros, is the home of the PGA Tour's Mercedes Championships. No tank tops or cutoffs.

Makena Resort Golf Club SOUTH MAUI

ESTABLISHED: 1983 (SPLIT INTO TWO SEPARATE COURSES IN 1994)
STATUS: RESORT, 18 HOLES, PAR 72 (FOR BOTH COURSES)

5415 Makena Alanui, Makena 96753 (From Kahului Airport, take Dairy Road to Piilani Highway, turn right at the end, then left at the stop sign on Wailua Alanui and go south past Wailea. The entrance is on the left.) ☎ 808-879-3344; www.makenagolf.com

TEES *Championship:* North: 6,500 yards; South: 6,600 yards. *Men's:* North: 6,100 yards; South: 6,200 yards. *Ladies':* North: 5,300 yards; South: 5,500 yards.

FEES South, $149; North, $129. Includes cart. Special twilight rate available from 2 p.m. (South, $105; North, $95). Club rentals: $45. Accepts tee times three days in advance. Accepts AE, MC, V.

FACILITIES Practice range, putting green, pro shop, and locker room with showers.

COMMENTS Located by the Maui Prince Hotel. Both courses are among the state's best, with views of the ocean, Haleakala, Molokai, Lanai, and Kahoolawe. This course was designed by noted golf architect Robert Trent Jones Jr. Severe slopes and fast greens make for very challenging play. The lack of strong winds at Makena is a big plus. The South course's 15th and 16th holes are among Hawaii's most picturesque oceanfront holes. The North course is generally considered the more difficult of the two courses.

Waiehu Golf Course CENTRAL MAUI

ESTABLISHED: 9-HOLE COURSE OPENED IN 1933; BACK 9 ADDED IN 1966
STATUS: MUNICIPAL, 18 HOLES, PAR 7 (PAR 73 FOR WOMEN)

P.O. Box 507, Wailuku 96793 (From Highway 340, make a right just past Waihee Park. The entrance is on the right.) ☎ 808-244-5934

TEES *Men's:* 6,330 yards. *Ladies':* 5,555 yards.

FEES Weekdays, $40; weekends and holidays, $45. Cart: $16.60 per person. Club rentals: $15. Accepts tee times two days in advance. Accepts MC, V.

FACILITIES Driving range, putting green, pro shop, clubhouse, restaurant.

COMMENTS Maui's only municipal course. The front nine are relatively flat, whereas the back nine are hilly in spots. This course features one lake and more than 40 sand bunkers. Three holes front the ocean.

Wailea Golf Club SOUTH MAUI

ESTABLISHED: 1972 (BLUE), 1993 (GOLD), 1995 (EMERALD)
STATUS: RESORT, 18 HOLES, PAR 72 (ALL 3 COURSES)

100 Wailea Golf Club Drive, Wailea 96753 (From Kahului Air-port, take Dairy Road to Piilani Highway, drive to the southern end of the road, and turn right. At the stop sign, turn left on Wailea Alanui.) ☎ 808-875-7450 (Gold and Emerald courses); ☎ 808-875-5155 (Blue course)

TEES *Championship:* Gold: 7,078 yards; Emerald: 6,825 yards; Blue: 6,758 yards. *Men's:* Gold: 6,653 yards; Emerald: 6,407 yards; Blue: 6,152 yards. *Ladies':* Gold: 5,442 yards; Emerald: 5,268 yards; Blue: 5,291 yards

FEES Gold and Emerald: $225, $190 for Wailea Resort guests. Blue: $160, $190 for nonguests. Includes cart. Club rentals: $60. Accepts tee times five days in advance. Accepts AE, D, MC, V.

FACILITIES Driving range, putting greens, pro shop, and restaurant.

COMMENTS All three courses have breathtaking ocean and mountain views. The Blue course, with wide, open fairways, is the easiest, but it does have 74 bunkers and four water hazards. The Gold course, featuring ancient lava-rock walls, was ranked as one of *Golf Magazine*'s ten best new courses in 1993. The Emerald course offers stunning views of Haleakala and the Pacific, and is considered a friendlier course for high-handicap players. Its signature hole is the 18th, a 553-yard par 5 challenge with a downhill slope. Collared shirts required.

The Big Island of Hawaii

Hapuna Golf Course KONA

ESTABLISHED: 1992   STATUS: RESORT, 18 HOLES, PAR 72

62-100 Kaunaoa Drive, Kohala Coast 96743 (From Kona, drive north along Highway 19 past Waikoloa until you see the roads leading to the Hapuna Beach Prince Hotel on the left. Drive a bit farther; the golf course is on the right.) ☎ 808-882-5400

TEES *Tournament:* 6,875 yards. *Championship:* 6,534 yards. *Men's:* 6,029 yards. *Ladies':* 5,067 yards.

FEES $165; $125 for resort guests. Includes cart. Special twilight rate available after 3 p.m. Club rentals: $45. Accepts AE, MC, V.

FACILITIES Driving range, putting green, pro shop, clubhouse, restaurant.

COMMENTS This is a sister course to Mauna Kea Golf Course. The de-manding links-style course is set amid arid lava flows, natural vegetation, and spectacular scenery. Water hazards come into play on four holes. The front nine play into the winds that blow down from Mauna Kea. The 545-yard, par 5 third hole features wide expanses, an imposing ravine, a lake, and a series of bunkers. This is another Arnold Palmer–Ed Seay collaboration. Golfers share the course with several endangered bird species, including the nene goose, Hawaii's state bird. Unquestionably, this is one of the Big Island's best courses. Collared shirts required; no denim.

Hilo Municipal Golf Course HILO

ESTABLISHED: 1951   STATUS: MUNICIPAL, 18 HOLES, PAR 71

340 Haihai Street, Hilo 96720 (From Hilo, head south on Highway 11, past the Prince Kuhio Plaza. Turn right on Puainako Street, left on Kilauea Avenue, then right on Haihai Street.) ☎ 808-959-7711

TEES *Championship:* 6,325 yards. *Men's:* 6,006 yards. *Ladies':* 5,034 yards.

FEES Weekdays, $39; weekends, $44. Cart: $16 for 18 holes. Club rentals: $15. Accepts MC, V.

FACILITIES Driving range, pro shop, and restaurant.

COMMENTS The Big Island's municipal course features flat, tree-lined fairways with no sand traps but plenty of water hazards in the form of streams and lakes. This is a good course for average players. Light rains are frequent in Hilo, so pack an umbrella.

Hualalai Golf Club KONA

ESTABLISHED: 1996   STATUS: PRIVATE, 18 HOLES, PAR 72

100 Kaupulehu Drive, Kaupulehu 96740 (Take Mamalahoa Highway. Hualalai Resort and the golf course are just 5 minutes north of the airport.) ☎ 808-325-8480

TEES *Championship:* 7,117 yards. *Men's:* 6,632 yards. *Ladies':* 5,374 yards.

FEES $250, cart included. Only Hualalai homeowners or guests staying at the Four Seasons Resort Hualalai may play. Club rentals: $60. Accepts AE, D, MC, V.

FACILITIES Driving range, putting greens, practice area, clubhouse, snack bar, and restaurant.

COMMENTS Designed by Jack Nicklaus, this beautiful course is the home of the PGA Tour Champions Tour Mastercard Championship. Hole 17, a 172-yard par 3, is the signature hole, with an expansive green that demands precise pin placement. The golf club is the first in Hawaii to be designated an official PGA Tour facility.

Kona Country Club KONA

ESTABLISHED: 1985 (KONA), 1991 (ALII) STATUS: RESORT, 27 HOLES, PAR 72 (FOR BOTH COURSES)

78-7000 Alii Drive, Kailua-Kona 96740 (From the Kona Airport, drive south on Highway 11, then turn right down Alii Drive. The course is located near the end of the road.) ☎ 808-322-2595; www.konagolf.com

TEES *Championship:* Ocean course: 6,748 yards; Mountain course: 6,634 yards. *Men's:* Ocean course: 6,281 yards; Mountain course: 5,976 yards. *Ladies':* Ocean course: 5,436 yards; Mountain course: 5,038 yards.

FEES Ocean, $145; Mountain, $125. Includes cart. Special twilight rate available after 11 a.m.: Ocean, $107; Mountain, $97. Club rentals: $45. Accepts AE, MC, V.

FACILITIES Driving range, putting green, pro shop, restaurant, and lounge.

COMMENTS The Ocean course is a friendly place for golfers in need of a confidence boost, with wide fairways and easy greens. Much of the course hugs the Pacific, with particularly gorgeous vistas from Holes 11 to 13. The Mountain course, however, has more hazards and tricky hillside lies. The signature seventh hole is a downhill par 4 (446 yards) that plays straight into the wind and requires a tee shot over a water hazard.

Mauna Kea Golf Course KONA

ESTABLISHED: 1964 STATUS: RESORT, 18 HOLES, PAR 72

62-100 Mauna Kea Beach Drive, Kohala Coast 96743 (From Kona, drive north on Highway 19 to the Mauna Kea Resort entrance on the left.) ☎ 808-882-5400; www.maunakearesort.com

TEES *Tournament:* 7,124 yards. *Championship:* 6,737 yards. *Men's:* 6,365 yards. *Ladies':* 5,277 yards.

FEES $250; $225 for resort guests. Includes cart. Special twilight rate available seasonally. Club rentals: $45. Accepts AE, MC, V.

FACILITIES Driving range, putting green, pro shop, and restaurant.

COMMENTS The first course to be designed using a lava-strewn landscape, this Robert Trent Jones Sr. course is a perennial favorite, although it is quite demanding. The signature Hole 3, a 261-yard par 3, requires a tee shot over 180 yards of ocean to reach the green. Jones himself rated this hole as one of his all-time favorites. The course remains one of Hawaii's top layouts. Collared shirts required.

Mauna Lani Resort KONA

ESTABLISHED: 1981 (NORTH), 1991 (SPLIT INTO 2 COURSES, ADDING SOUTH)
STATUS: RESORT, 18 HOLES, PAR 72 (FOR BOTH COURSES)

68-1310 Mauna Lani Drive, Kohala Coast 96743 (From Kona, drive north on Highway 19 and turn left at Mauna Lani Drive. The golf course is on the left.) ☎ 808-885-6655; www.maunalani.com

TEES *Championship:* North: 6,913 yards; South: 6,938 yards. *Men's:* North: 6,601 yards (blue tees), 6,086 yards; South: 6,436 yards (blue tees), 5,940 yards. *Ladies':* North: 5,383 yards; South: 5,028 yards.

FEES $260; $160 for resort guests. Includes cart. Special $100 twilight rate available after 2 p.m. Club rentals: $45. Accepts AE, D, MC, V.

FACILITIES Driving range, putting green, pro shop, clubhouse, restaurant.

COMMENTS Both courses have spectacular visual appeal and play. The North course, blessed with rolling terrain and thickets of *kiawe* trees, is the longer course and requires more strategy off the tee. The 132-yard, par 3 Hole 17 is its signature hole, where your tee shot carries from an elevated tee to (hopefully) a green framed by black lava. The South's signature hole, the 196-yard, par 3 Hole 15, requires a bold tee shot over crashing surf. During the winter, the 15th may feature another distraction: humpback whales, often spotted in the deep waters. Collared shirts required.

Sea Mountain Golf Course HILO AND VOLCANO

ESTABLISHED: 1974 STATUS: RESORT, 18 HOLES, PAR 72

P.O. Box 190, Pahala 96777 (Drive south from Hilo on Highway 11 to Mile Marker 56. The course is on the left.) ☎ 808-928-6222

TEES *Championship:* 6,492 yards. *Men's:* 6,106 yards. *Ladies':* 5,663 yards.

FEES Weekdays, $46.50; weekends, $49.50. Guests of Sea Mountain Golf Course Colony Condominiums receive a $10 discount. Includes cart. Club rentals: $30. Accepts MC, V.

FACILITIES Driving range, putting green, pro shop, and restaurant.

COMMENTS The front nine here line a picturesque beach, and the back nine are set against a mountain. Beautiful views from everywhere on the course.

Volcano Golf and Country Club HILO AND VOLCANO

ESTABLISHED: 194 (AS 9-HOLE COURSE); EXPANDED AND REDESIGNED IN 1967 STATUS: PUBLIC, 18 HOLES, PAR 72

Hawaii Volcanoes National Park 96718 (From Hilo, drive past the Hawaii Volcanoes National Park, and look for Mile Marker 30. Turn right on Golf Course Road.) ☎ 808-967-7331; www.volcanogolfshop.com

TEES *Championship:* 6,547 yards. *Men's:* 6,180 yards. *Ladies':* 5,514 yards.

FEES $70. Twilight rate after 12 p.m. $56. Includes shared cart. Club rentals: $20. Senior discounts available. Accepts AE, D, DC, MC, V.

FACILITIES Driving range, putting green, pro shop, restaurant, and lounge.

COMMENTS Located beside Hawaii Volcanoes National Park, this course neighbors an active volcano. But the lava flow is a considerable distance away and won't pose a threat. A mostly flat course, except for some rolling hills. A pond and three ditches come into play on four holes. Nearly all the tees and some of the greens are elevated. No tank tops or cutoffs.

Waikoloa Beach Golf Course KONA

ESTABLISHED: 1981 STATUS: RESORT, 18 HOLES, PAR 70

1020 Keana Place, Waikoloa 96743 (From the airport, drive north on Highway 19. Turn left into Waikoloa Beach Resort.) ☎ 808-886-6060; www.waikoloabeachresort.com

TEES *Championship:* 6,566 yards. *Men's:* 5,958 yards. *Ladies':* 5,094 yards.

FEES $195; $130 for resort guests. Club rentals: $50. Accepts AE, D, MC, V.

FACILITIES Driving range, putting green, pro shop, and restaurant.

COMMENTS A challenging course with narrow fairways framed by rug-ged black lava. An ancient petroglyph field borders the sixth, seventh, and eighth holes, adding a unique sense of place. The 502-yard, par 5 Hole 12, meanwhile, leads to the ocean surf. It features a dogleg fairway and green bordered on the right by the Pacific. Collared shirts required.

Waikoloa Kings Course KONA

ESTABLISHED: 1990 STATUS: RESORT, 18 HOLES, PAR 72

600 Waikoloa Beach Drive, Waikoloa 96738 (From the airport, drive north on Highway 19. Turn left into Waikoloa Beach Resort, then make a right on Keana Place after the third stop sign.) ☎ 808-886-7888; www.waikoloabeachgolf.com

TEES *Championship:* 7,074 yards. *Men's:* 6,594 yards. *Ladies':* 5,459 yards.
FEES $195; $130 for resort guests. Twilight $75. Club rentals: $50. Accepts AE, D, MC, V.
FACILITIES Driving range, putting green, practice sand trap, and pro shop.
COMMENTS Designed by Tom Weiskopf and Jay Morrish, this links-style course was voted among *Golf Digest's* "Best New Resort Courses in America" when it opened. It has a challenging layout characterized by many sand bunkers and lava-rock formations with treacherous greens. The signature hole, the 327-yard, par 4 Hole 5, features a long bunker that stretches along the left side of the fairway, with two large boulders posing another threat for players trying to reach the green. The course is very playable when played from the regular tees. Collared shirts required.

Waikoloa Village Golf Course KONA

ESTABLISHED: 1972 STATUS: RESORT, 18 HOLES, PAR 72

68-1792 Melia Street, Waikoloa 96738 (From the Kona Airport, drive north along Highway 19. Turn right onto Waikoloa Road and look for the golf course on the left.) ☎ 808-883-9621; www.waikoloa.org

TEES *Championship:* 6,791 yards. *Men's:* 6,142 yards. *Ladies':* 5,558 yards.
FEES $80. Includes cart. Club rentals: $35. Accepts AE, D, MC, V.
FACILITIES Driving range, putting green, pro shop, and restaurant.
COMMENTS Oldest of the Waikoloa courses, this scenic layout takes you from ancient lava beds to raging surf. Layout features rolling terrain, dogleg fairways, and two lakes that come into play on three holes. No tank tops or cutoffs.

Waimea Country Club KONA

ESTABLISHED: 1994 STATUS: SEMIPRIVATE, 18 HOLES, PAR 72

P.O. Box 2155, Kamuela 96743 (east of Kamuela, also known as Waimea, on Mamalahoa Highway) ☎ 808-885-8053; www.waimeagolf.com

TEES *Championship:* 6,661 yards. *Men's:* 6,210 yards. *Ladies':* 5,673 yards.
FEES $95. Includes cart. Special $75 twilight rate available from 1:30 p.m. Club rentals: $35. Senior discounts available. Accepts AE, MC, V.
FACILITIES Driving range, putting green, and snack shop.
COMMENTS Built on open pasturelands, but features enough tall iron-wood trees to keep you honest. There are 28 sand bunkers, and water hazards come into play on five holes. Features large, unrelenting greens. All in all, this is a good course for players of all skill levels. No dress code, but bring a jacket or sweater, as weather conditions here are often cool and misty.

Kauai

Kauai Lagoons Golf Club KAUAI

ESTABLISHED: 1989 STATUS: RESORT, 18 HOLES, PAR 72 (BOTH COURSES)

3351 Hoolaulea Way, Lihue 96766 (From Lihue Airport, turn left on Ahu-kini Road, left again on Highway 51, and left again into the entrance of the Kauai Marrriott Resort. The golf clubhouse is past the hotel's porte cochere, on the right.) ☎ 808-241-6000; www.kauailagoonsgolf.com

TEES *Championship:* Kiele course: 7,070 yards; Mokihana course: 6,960 yards. *Men's:* Kiele: 6,674 yards (blue tees), 6,164 yards; Mokihana: 6,578 yards (blue tees), 6,136 yards. *Ladies':* Kiele: 5,417 yards; Mokihana: 5,607 yards.

FEES $125–$175. Includes cart. Club rentals: $55. Accepts AE, MC, V.

FACILITIES Driving range, putting and chipping greens, pro shop, locker rooms with showers, snack bar, and restaurant.

COMMENTS Both the Kiele and Mokihana (previously named the La-goon) courses here were designed by Jack Nicklaus. The Kiele course is the more difficult of the two, with the need to carry many tee shots over ravines. The Kiele course is one of Hawaii's best and *Golf Magazine* has named it a Gold Medal course. The Mokihana course is more favorable to players with higher handicaps. Collared shirts required; no cutoffs. *Note:* The back nine of the Kiele Course remains closed until the economy improves.

Kiahuna Golf Club KAUAI

ESTABLISHED: 1983 STATUS: RESORT, 18 HOLES, PAR 70

2545 Kiahuna Plantation Drive, Koloa 96756 (In Poipu, drive down Poipu Road and turn left on Kiahuna Plantation Drive at the entry to Poipu Shopping Village. The golf course entrance is on the left.) ☎ 808-742-9595; www.kiahunagolf.com

TEES *Championship:* 6,885 yards. *Men's:* 6,183 yards. *Ladies':* 5,560 yards.

FEES $99. Special $75 twilight rate available after 3 p.m. Includes cart. Club rentals: $40. Guests staying at selected hotels receive discounts. Accepts AE, D, MC, V.

FACILITIES Driving range, putting green, pro shop, and snack bar.

COMMENTS A challenging layout built around historic Hawaiian sites. The course features narrow fairways, water hazards, and plenty of trade winds. Designed by Robert Trent Jones Jr. Collared shirts required.

Poipu Bay Golf Course KAUAI

ESTABLISHED: 1991 STATUS: RESORT, 18 HOLES, PAR 72

2250 Ainako Street, Koloa 96756 (In Poipu, follow Poipu Road to Ainako Street and make a right. The course is just past the Grand Hyatt Kauai.) ☎ 808-742-8711; www.poipubaygolf.com

TEES *Championship:* 7,123 yards. *Men's:* 6,612 yards (blue tees), 6,127 yards. *Ladies':* 5,372 yards.

FEES $220 before noon, $135 after noon. Includes cart. Special twilight rate of $75 available after 2:30 p.m. Guests staying at the Grand Hyatt are eligible for discounts. Club rentals: $50. Accepts AE, MC, V.

FACILITIES Driving range, putting and chipping greens, practice sand bunkers, pro shop, locker room with showers, clubhouse, and restaurant.

COMMENTS Water hazards come into play on 11 holes at this immaculate course; more than 80 bunkers add to the challenge. The 501-yard, par 4 Hole 16 is lined by a lake on one side of the fairway and the ultimate water hazard—the ocean—on the other. The 201-yard, par 3 Hole 17 is the site of another spectacular setting. Collared shirts required.

St. Regis Princeville Resort Golf Courses KAUAI

ESTABLISHED: 1971 (MAKAI), 1990 (PRINCE) STATUS: RESORT,
MAKAI: 27 HOLES, PAR 36; PRINCE: 18 HOLES, PAR 72

Makai course: 4080 Lei O Papa Road, Princeville 96722 (From Kuhio Highway, turn right into the St. Regis Princeville Resort. The golf course is one mile away, on the left.) Prince course: 5-3900 Kuhio Highway, Princeville 96722 (From Kuhio Highway, drive past the Princeville Airport. The golf course is on the right.) ☎ 808-826-3581 (Makai course); ☎ 808-826-5001 (Prince course); www.princeville.com

TEES *Championship:* Makai: 3,430 yards (Ocean), 3,456 yards (Lakes), 3,445 yards (Woods); Prince: 7,309 yards. *Men's:* Makai: 3,157 yards (Ocean), 3,149 yards (Lakes), 3,208 yards (Woods); Prince: 6,960 yards (blue tees), 6,521 yards (white tees), 6,029 yards (gold tees). *Ladies':* Makai: 2,802 yards (Ocean), 2,714 yards (Lakes), 2,829 yards (Woods); Prince: 5,346 yards.

FEES Makai: $155; twilight rate after 2 p.m., $125; sunset rate after 3:30 p.m., $50. Prince: $200 before noon; $120 after 12 p.m.; twilight rate after 3 p.m., $70. Includes cart. Guests at Princeville area resorts receive discounts, with the lowest rate offered to guests of the Princeville Hotel. Club rentals: $45. Accepts AE, MC, V.

FACILITIES Makai: Driving range, putting and chipping greens, pro shop, and snack bar. Prince: All of the above plus a larger practice facility and spectacular clubhouse with a full-service spa and a restaurant.

COMMENTS The Makai course is made up of three separate 9-hole courses that combine to form three different 18-hole layouts. Lakes come into play on three holes on the Lakes course and one hole on the Woods course. The highly acclaimed Prince course provides more of a challenge with its rolling hills and multitude of ravines. You can see ocean views from every tee. *Golf Digest* has rated the Prince as Hawaii's number-one course.

Wailua Golf Course KAUAI

ESTABLISHED: 1930S (AS 6-HOLE COURSE); EXPANDED AND REDESIGNED IN 1961
STATUS: MUNICIPAL, 18 HOLES, PAR 72

3-5350 Kuhio Highway, Lihue 96746 (From Lihue on Kuhio Highway, drive 3 miles north toward Kapaa. The golf course is on the right.) ☎ 808-241-6666; www.kauai.gov/golf

TEES *Championship:* 6,991 yards. *Men's:* 6,585 yards. *Ladies':* 5,974 yards.

FEES Weekdays, $60; weekends and holidays, $70. Twilight rate after 2 p.m., 50% discount available. Cart: $18. Club rentals: $32. Accepts only traveler's checks or cash.

FACILITIES Driving range, putting green, pro shop, restaurant, and shower rooms.

COMMENTS Ranked as one of the best municipal courses in the United States. This is a challenging course with elevated tees and a lovely oceanfront location. It has served as the site of past USGA Amateur Public Links Championships. No tank tops or cutoffs.

Molokai

Ironwood Hills Golf Course MOLOKAI

ESTABLISHED: 1928   STATUS: PUBLIC, 18 HOLES; 9 HOLES, PAR 34

Kalae Highway, Kualapuu 96757; ☎ 808-567-6000

TEES *Championship:* 3,088 yards. Middle: 2,816 yards. Forward: 2,409 yards.

FEES $23 for 18 holes; $18 for 9 holes. Rental clubs and carts, $12 each for 9 holes. Tee-time reservations advised. Accepts MC, V.

FACILITIES Driving range, pro shop, and food service. Metal spikes allowed.

COMMENTS Historic upcountry course designed for Del Monte Plantation executives. One of the oldest courses in Hawaii, it has been preserved as a literal link to the past. Its rustic hilly layout set in the Molokai highlands is a challenging test, with brisk trade winds in the afternoons and fairways of tightly woven kukuya grass framed by tall stands of island pine, eucalyptus, and the ironwoods for which it is named. Golfers must drive through narrow shoots of trees, and battle long uphill holes into the wind. After teeing off on the sixth hole, those in the know take only the clubs they need to finish and a driver for the seventh, leaving the rest under a tree for the steep climb to the seventh. Views of this and neighboring islands are breathtaking.

Lanai

The Challenge at Manele LANAI

ESTABLISHED: 1993   STATUS: RESORT, 18 HOLES, PAR 72

P.O. Box 310, Lanai City 96763 (transportation via Lanai Resorts shuttle); ☎ 808-565-2222; www.fourseasons.com/manelebay/golf

TEES *Championship:* 7,039 yards. *Men's:* 6,684 yards. *Ladies':* 5,024 yards.

FEES $225; $210 for guests staying at the Lodge at Koele, Manele Bay Hotel, or Hotel Lanai. Club rentals: $70. Accepts AE, MC, V.

FACILITIES Driving range, putting and chipping greens, locker rooms, pro shop, and restaurant.

COMMENTS Designed by Jack Nicklaus. This is a links-style course that offers great ocean views from every hole. Fairways are open; greens are small and fast. Built on the side of a hill, the course features several changes of elevation and requires several blind tee and approach shots. Winds often come into play. Bring extra balls for Hole 12, a 202-yard par 3 that includes a tee shot across 200 yards of Pacific Ocean. The tee box area on a 150-foot cliff above crashing surf is the picturesque spot where Bill and Melinda Gates were married in 1994. Archaeological sites are among the features. Collared shirts required; no denim.

The Experience at Koele LANAI

ESTABLISHED: 1991 STATUS: RESORT, 18 HOLES, PAR 72

P.O. Box 310, Lanai City 96763 (transportation via Lanai Resorts shuttle); ☎ 808-565-4653; www.fourseasons.com/koele/golf

TEES *Championship:* 7,014 yards. *Men's:* 6,217 yards. *Ladies':* 5,425 yards.

FEES $225; $210 for guests of the Lodge at Koele, Manele Bay Hotel, or Hotel Lanai. Club rentals: $70. Accepts AE, MC, V.

FACILITIES Driving range, putting and chipping greens, executive putting course, clubhouse, and snack bar.

COMMENTS A magnificent course designed by golf greats Greg Norman and Ted Robinson. The front nine were carved from the side of a mountain, and the back nine are more open and flat. Water features are prominent, with seven lakes, streams, and waterfalls. Hole 8—a 444-yard par 4—is the signature, featuring a 250-foot drop from tee to fairway, with a lake bordering one side and thick shrubs and trees lining the other. Even Jack Nicklaus needed seven attempts to get the ball in play here. Hole 17 is surrounded by a lake. Collared shirts required; no denim.

▌▐ SPECTATOR SPORTS

EVEN WITHOUT A MAJOR PROFESSIONAL SPORTS FRANCHISE, the islands of Oahu, Maui, Hawaii, and Kauai host major sporting events throughout the year. If you're looking to augment your beach time, here's a game plan.

FOOTBALL

COLLEGE FOOTBALL ALL-STARS fly to Oahu each January for the annual **Hula Bowl.** After being held on Maui for eight years, this contest returned to Aloha Stadium in Honolulu for its 60th anniversary in 2006.

Call Ticketmaster at ☎ 877-750-4400 or go to **www.ticketmaster .com** for tickets.

GOLF

A HANDFUL OF MAJOR WINTER professional golf events brings Hawaii's gorgeous links into the snowbound homes of golf fans via television. In early January, the **Mercedes Championships** at Kapalua, Maui, features top players competing for more than $2.5 million in prize money. ☎ 808-669-2440.

Formerly the Hawaiian Open, the new **Sony Open** on Oahu draws the PGA's best to the Waialae Country Club in Kahala. This January tournament kicks off the official PGA Tour season, with another $2.5 million purse. ☎ 808-523-7888. Also in January is the **MasterCard Championship,** which gathers the winners from the previous year's Senior PGA Tour to the Hualalai Golf Club on the Big Island. This tournament, featuring more than $1 million in prize money, kicks off the Senior PGA Tour. ☎ 808-325-8480.

In February, the Kapolei Golf Course on Oahu hosts the annual **Sunrise Hawaiian Ladies Open,** a 54-hole medal play competition featuring top women's golfers from the United States and Japan. ☎ 808-674-2227.

OCEAN SPORTS

A SURF MEET PROVIDES A DIFFERENT kind of experience for sports fans. It's a good chance to see Hawaii's most prized individual sport at its finest while hanging out at the beach. Admission is always free.

Competitors take to the water in four-man heats, each lasting 20 to 30 minutes. The surfers ride as many waves as they can. A panel of five judges uses a point system to name the winners. Criteria include the size of the waves, length of the rides, board control, and creative maneuvers.

The most prestigious surfing competition is the **Triple Crown** of surfing, held in November and December. The best professional wave riders from around the world gather on Oahu's North Shore for the **Ocean Pacific Pro** at Alii Beach Park in Haleiwa, **World Cup of Surfing** at Sunset Beach, and Pipeline Masters at the famous Banzai Pipeline at Ehukai Beach Park. The events occur on the four days of best surf conditions during a period of about two weeks. Recently, a special longboard competition was launched at Alii Beach Park. Visit **www .triplecrownofsurfing.com.**

You won't be able to follow all the action of the annual **Bankoh Na Wahine O Ke Kai** and the **Bankoh Mokokai Hoe,** two 41-mile outrigger canoe races from Mokokai to Waikiki. (The women's *wahine* race is held in late September, while the men's race takes place in early October.) But you can watch the colorful finale as the six-member canoe teams paddle to a finish on the beach. Both events draw international outrigger canoe teams from Australia, Canada, and Tahiti, as well as Hawaii and other states.

TRACK

FEW EVENTS ARE AS PHYSICALLY DEMANDING as the zenith of all triathlons, the **Ford Ironman Triathlon World Championship** held each October on the Big Island, where the world's top triathletes plunge into a 2.4-mile ocean swim followed by a 112-mile bike race and a 26.2-mile marathon. Unless it's the annual **Ultraman,** which ups the ante to a 6.2-mile swim, 261.4-mile bike ride, and 52.4-mile run. Fair warning: The weekend of the Ironman is often Kailua-Kona's busiest of the year, and certain visitor necessities may be hard to come by. ☎ 808-329-0063.

COLLEGE BASKETBALL

COLLEGE BASKETBALL FANCIERS focus on Honolulu each year around Christmastime for the annual **Outrigger Hotels Rainbow Classic Basketball Tournament.** A tradition launched in the mid-1960s, the Rainbow Classic has a reputation for spotlighting future first-round NBA draft picks. Certainly enough scouts attend the tourney to find them. College teams compete with equal fervor in the annual women's **Asahi Rainbow Wahine** Classic staged in late November, also in Honolulu. Watch for college all-stars in the annual **Aloha Basketball Classic** tournament in Honolulu in mid-April, and you may be previewing more pro standouts of the future.

PART NINE

DINING *and* RESTAURANTS

EXPERIENCING HAWAII'S MULTICULTURAL CUISINE

ISLAND DINING SCENES

HAWAII HAS AN ASTONISHING ARRAY of restaurants for a state in which only a few decades ago most people ate at home. The choices range from lunch wagon takeout to world-class fine dining in breathtaking beachfront settings. Luxury hotels in the Island State are known for great, rather than dull, dining, and many of their former chefs have spread the joy by opening their own inspired restaurants on all major islands. The joke used to be that the best Hawaiian dining was the airplane food on the flight over. Now it's fair to say Hawaiian dining is a good reason to look forward to a trip to the Islands, right up there with beaches and tropical beauty.

Thanks to Hawaii's great multicultural magnet, Island cuisine is truly unlike food anywhere else. The Hawaiian table has roots dating to the earliest Polynesian voyagers, who brought taro, coconut, banana, yam, breadfruit, and other staples to their new home, along with a heritage of hospitality in which strangers and other visitors were always welcomed with food. Centuries later, missionaries, whalers, and plantation workers from Asia, the United States, and Europe added their own food traditions to the Hawaiian stew. Chinese, Japanese, Filipino, Portuguese, Puerto Rican, Korean, Southeast Asians, and others adapted their favorite dishes to ingredients available locally. In communal kitchens and plantation homes, they shared and borrowed from each other, building the foundation of a multicultural cuisine.

Local food in the plantation heyday was primarily home cooking and backyard barbecues, simple fare from the garden and from the company store, spiced with Hawaiian salt, ginger, soy, miso, lemongrass, fish sauce, achiote, sugar, hot sauces, and other condiments.

Restaurants tended to be quick-service lunchrooms and walk-up stands serving fast, hearty plate lunches to field workers. Visiting tourists, on the other hand, were treated to imported frozen entrees in hotel continental-dining rooms that Islanders thought they wanted. The twain began to meet in the steak houses that blossomed near beaches in the 1960s.

HAWAII REGIONAL CUISINE

HAWAII REGIONAL CUISINE was born in the 1980s, when the burgeoning luxury-hotel market drew bright young chefs from around the world to perk up hotel dining rooms. Even in this Eden where almost anything grows, the chefs found few fresh ingredients to work with, so they set about coaxing farmers and fishermen to produce the fresh fruits and vegetables, fish, and meats needed to create first-rate dining. They dared to experiment, mixing exotic local cooking methods they learned from their staffs and island families with their own classic training and experience in French, Mediterranean, Asian, and American kitchens. Then they spiced the rich local bounty of fish and flora with flavors from around the Pacific, and something new was born. In 1991, a dozen top chefs created a formal marketing organization bent on giving Hawaii a new food reputation to match its top ranking as a destination. They named their effort Hawaii Regional Cuisine.

Island farms grew along with the supportive restaurant industry, providing baby squash, tender meats, luscious berries, exotic mushrooms, vine-ripened tomatoes, spicy greens and herbs. Aquaculture, an ancient Hawaiian art, resumed centuries later. Strawberries, lobster and other shellfish, abalone, and salmon are grown with modern technology developed at Keahole on the Big Island, using cold, nutrient-rich waters piped ashore from deep-sea canyons. Kona coffee has been grown for generations in backyard groves, but now menus also boast Hawaii-grown chocolate and vanilla. Hawaii's chefs still import truffles, capers, olive oil, duck, Kobe beef, caviar, and the like, but they prefer to use them in combination with local treasures such as beef, lamb, fern shoots, or hearts of palm from the Big Island; fresh watercress and other produce, shrimp, and papaya from Oahu; strawberries, pineapple, herbs, and greens from Maui; or corn and purple sweet potatoes from Molokai.

Hawaii Regional Cuisine means creative, innovative dishes and fresh local ingredients, with the emphasis on flavor, excitement, and fun for chef and diner alike. This is not staid eating in stuffy rooms with snooty waiters. It is, however, often expensive, just as shoppers will find that local bananas, chicken, pork, and produce in the markets cost more than imported food. Most of the original Hawaii Regional Cuisine chefs are still in Hawaii, running their own restaurants, all worth seeking out and sampling, some at haute-cuisine prices and some not. The original chefs are Sam Choy, Roger Dikon, Mark Ellman, Bev Gannon, Jean-Marie Josselin, George Mavrothalassitis,

Peter Merriman, Amy Ferguson-Ota, Philippe Padovani, Gary Strehl, Alan Wong, and Roy Yamaguchi. The interesting twist of fate is that the sons and daughters of Hawaii's plantation workers, who grew up on (and still love) down-home local food, have also acquired increasingly sophisticated tastes in food and wine.

As island tastes grew more refined in recent years, so did local wine palates. Hawaii boasts many knowledgeable wine purveyors. Wines are increasingly popular and available, and many restaurants have extensive wine lists and wines by the glass (the Brasserie Du Vin, part of the lively Honolulu restaurant scene, has more than 200 wine choices). Several wine bars and restaurants feature by-the-glass lists with two-ounce pours as well as the standard five-ounce glass. Locally produced wine is mostly limited to the vintages of Tedeschi Vineyards in Upcountry Maui. The tiny vineyard on Ulupalakua Ranch has a tasting room and scenic picnic spots under the spreading avocado trees.

Chef's restaurants and five-star dining rooms may not fit everyone's daily budget. Visitors often wonder how Hawaii's people afford to eat in the islands. The answer is right before you, on many a side street in Waikiki, Kihei, Kailua-Kona, Lanai City, and Lihue: little hole-in-the-wall eateries, take-out counters, lunch wagons, ethnic delicatessens, and unassuming restaurants. Venture out of the resort and away from the fast-food chains, and eat where the local people go. That includes classy regional-cuisine restaurants, which depend heavily on their local base of customers who always have something to celebrate.

> *unofficial* **TIP**
> For affordable Hawaii Regional Cuisine, venture out of the resorts and eat where the locals do.

THE ULTIMATE BUFFET

ONE INEXPENSIVE PLACE to sample the tastes of plantation heritage is the *okazu-ya,* or Japanese delicatessen. It's an experience something like a Chinese take-out counter or a stand-alone food court. In addition to Japanese dishes, Hawaii's *okazu-ya* are likely to offer Filipino *adobo,* Puerto Rican *gandule,* Chinese chow mein, or Korean *kimchi* fried rice. Find these unassuming family-run places all over the state and be advised, they tend to run out of wares and close early. Consider it part of the adventure.

QUICK EATS

THE FASTEST LOCAL FOOD is found at the counter of the traveling plate-lunch wagon, or *manapua* truck (named for the Hawaiian version of *char siu bao,* the Chinese dim sum roll that is stuffed with barbecued pork and steamed). These quaint reminders of earlier days travel through sophisticated downtown Honolulu as well as to popular surfing-beach parks and other spots where hungry folks gather. They park only for a few minutes, usually well before noon, and dispense their foods hot from the back of the truck. You can get a fast fix of local food at plate-lunch diners, modeled after old-fashioned drive-ins. These establishments go far beyond burgers and fries, offering specialties such as *katsu* (fried pork or chicken cutlet), teriyaki (soy-marinated grilled pork, beef, or chicken), and island-style curry or beef stew. Order a combination, a mixed plate. Expect a yeoman's quantity of food, accompanied by two scoops of Japanese-style steamed white rice and one of macaroni salad. It's a carbo-loaders' dream. Favorite diners include Grace's Inn, L&L Drive-Inn (a chain of some 50 locations, including Seattle), Loco Moco Drive Inn, and Zippy's.

Ethnic restaurants, particularly Asian cuisines, abound throughout the islands, with various levels of price and decor. Local Korean chains, such as Yummy Bar-B-Q and Kim Chee, offer a cheap, tasty introduction to traditional Korean barbecue and other dishes. Japanese, Chinese, Thai, and Vietnamese noodle houses sell steaming bowls of *ramen, udon, soba, mein, pad,* and *pho.* Wonton *mein,* a noodle soup, is a soothing remedy for warding off colds and flu, kind of a local-style chicken soup. Hawaii has its own noodle dish, sold at restaurants and fast-food stands: *saimin,* a big soup bowl of thin noodles in fragrant broth with garnishes such as slivers of green onion, red-edged *char siu* barbecued pork, and pink-and-white pinwheels of fish cake, often topped with a tempura-fried shrimp. On Kauai, try Hamura's Saimin Stand in Lihue for some of the best. In Honolulu, go to Likelike Drive-In on Keeaumoku Street near Ala Moana Center. On Maui, Kitada's in Makawao has many devoted fans.

The ultimate island carry-out snack is Spam *musubi,* a fusion of American, Japanese, and local tastes, in which sushi rice is molded into a rectangle, topped with a slice of Spam luncheon meat, and wrapped in a sheet of *nori,* or fried seaweed. Find it in delis, supermarkets, convenience stores (7-Eleven is the biggest producer), and the sundries stores below Honolulu high-rise office buildings. Hawaii remains a major consumer of Spam, a canned holdover from prerefrigeration days, and is perhaps the only state where "spam" is more likely to refer to junk food than junk mail.

FISH FACTS

AT THE HEART OF HAWAIIAN CUISINE is the wealth of delicious fish harvested from Hawaii's deep middle-of-the-sea waters. In the past, mahimahi was Hawaii's best-known fish. These days, mahimahi, while still a favorite in the Islands and around the nation, shares top restaurant billing with a whole list of other fish, once caught only for home tables and known by Hawaiian, Japanese, and American names unfamiliar to many visiting diners.

Choosing a fish dish can be a challenge, with unfamiliar fish often served in a multitude of preparations. Checking out the daily fish specials is akin to picking new wines at fine-vintage prices, and asking your waiter to describe the fish doesn't always help. To allay confusion and encourage the use of lesser-known fish, the State Department of

Business, Economic Development, and Tourism sponsors a yearly Seafood Festival in July, markets Hawaiian fish around the world, and publishes a chart naming and describing various fish.

 Following is an abbreviated guide to help you choose a fish, and then you can decide how you want it prepared. Hawaii's people tend to love fish served raw, as sashimi or sushi, or marinated in *poke*. All these deep-sea fish are best when not overcooked. Hawaiian fish are rarely deep-fried in the East Coast tradition, but can be heavenly in light Japanese tempura.

AHI, YELLOWFIN TUNA Light, bright red flesh cooks to creamy white. High fat content makes this fish ideal to slice raw for sashimi. When cooked, it's best when only seared or grilled quickly and still rare in the middle, or at least undercooked and juicy.

AKU, SKIPJACK TUNA Deep-red translucent flesh turns to firm ivory color when cooked. The high fat content makes this fish also good sliced raw for sashimi.

BIGEYE AHI, BIGEYE TUNA Light-red flesh cooks to creamy white. The high fat content makes this fish good sliced raw for sashimi.

MAHIMAHI, DOLPHINFISH Light-pink flesh cooks to delicate, sweet white meat. It's excellent solo when fresh, but also goes well with trimmings, especially macadamia nuts and lemon-butter sauce.

ONO, WAHOO This is a firm-textured, mild-flavored flaky white fish often served grilled in thick steaks.

OPAH, MOONFISH Rich, large-grained flesh ranges from pink to orange to bright red throughout the fish. It cooks to a delicate white.

MOI, THREADFISH Islanders like the moist, mild white meat steamed, though some chefs prepare it crisp-fried with its edible scales intact.

MONCHONG, BIGSCALE, OR SICKLE POMFRET Mild-flavored, smooth, well-textured flesh cooks to moist white meat.

ONAGA, RUBY, OR LONG-TAILED SNAPPER The onaga's pale-pink, delicately flavored flesh is considered a good-luck food when served raw. This most prized snapper is also delicious when baked to white with a silky texture.

OPAKAPAKA, CRIMSON SNAPPER A favorite fish in Hawaii's restaurants, with a mild flavor and pink flesh that is good when crusted and sautéed, grilled, or baked, but also when steamed Chinese style.

SHUTOME, BROADBILL SWORDFISH Firm, well-textured, mild-flavored pinkish meat cooks to white. Hawaiian waters provide much of the nation's swordfish, but only recently have Hawaii residents begun eating it at home. Seems early fishermen began avoiding these billfish when the fish would ram and puncture their boats to avoid capture.

If there is a signature fish dish for Hawaii, it's ahi sashimi, served in restaurants of all persuasions, from bar appetizer to brunch buffet. Sashimi is a good-luck New Year's dish for local Japanese, and the price will skyrocket during the holidays when demand outstrips supply in restaurants and markets. Some chefs roll a block of ahi in spices and sear it, then slice it thin for blackened ahi, or sometimes the block is wrapped in *nori* seaweed, then fried quickly in light batter before slicing. But usually the buttery red fish is simply chilled, sliced, and served fresh and glistening, with slices of pink pickled ginger, a dab of green hot wasabi horseradish, and a dish of soy or shoyu sauce for dipping. Hawaii style is to mix some wasabi into the soy sauce before dipping.

LUAU LORE: TO GO OR NOT TO GO?

IF YOU HAVE NEVER BEEN TO A LUAU, you should go. The traditional feast is one of those events you'll remember most about Hawaii. Wear a smile, a flower behind your ear, and your favorite muumuu or aloha shirt. Be prepared to taste exotic foods, sip tropical drinks, and enjoy live music and dance. If you are lucky enough to get invited to a private or community luau, don't miss it. Otherwise, buy tickets to a commercial luau and have a good time. This is your chance to sample Hawaiian specialties, but, just in case, the commercial luau buffet lines often include items like teriyaki chicken or steak, sautéed fish, or salads, in addition to the more adventurous luau food.

The luau is a feast held to celebrate babies' first birthdays, graduations, weddings, life in general, and special guests such as you. What is served is a modern version of prehistoric food, seasoned with generations of tradition and mostly cooked together in a leaf-lined pit of hot stones in the ground called the *imu*. In old Hawaii, this was the most popular way to cook, and the soul of any luau is still the preparation and unearthing of the *imu*. Dishes include *kalua pig,* which is smoky pit-roasted pork that has been pulled into tender strips; yam; *laulau* (bundles of fish and pork steamed in taro leaves); *poi,* a paste pounded from taro root; a salted-salmon salad called *lomilomi*; rice; sometimes *poke* (a marinated raw-fish dish not unlike Mexican *ceviche*) or *opihi,* a shellfish plucked fresh off the beach rocks; concoctions like chicken long rice (chicken, ginger, green onion, and slithery rice noodles) and squid luau (bits of octopus mixed with cooked taro leaf and coconut milk, like creamed spinach); a beef jerky called *pipikaula;* tropical fruit; and *haupia* (a jelled coconut-milk pudding) for dessert, along with other sweets. It's all good, and you might even like it. Go with friends, or make friends with the folks across the table.

Visitors can experience a romantic luau on their hotel's grounds, or attend rollicking affairs on secluded beaches such as Paradise Cove or Germaine's on Oahu, where the party starts on the bus ride over from Waikiki; Old Lahaina Luau or Feast at Lele on Maui; Kona Village Resort's old-fashioned luau on a Big Island fishpond; or Kauai Paradise Garden on Kauai. Before dinner, guests can admire the fragrant baked pig as it is lifted from the *imu*. They might have a chance to wade into the sun-warmed ocean to help pull in the *hukilau* net filled with flopping fish.

All the commercial luau feature a lively Hawaiian or Polynesian music-and-dance show. The entertainment may include fire dances from Samoa, *poi*-ball dances from New Zealand, the rapid-fire drums and gyrating Tahitian dance *tamure,* and Hawaii's own haunting chants and hula, danced in everything from grass skirts to Victorian ball gowns. And yes, someone in your party is likely to get dragged onto the stage to try the dance, so take a camera and capture that Kodak moment, or maybe snap Mom digging into the *poi* bowl with two fingers, the traditional way to enjoy it.

TRENDS

TAPAS, ALSO KNOWN AS izakaya—"small plates" on many menus—are every bit as popular in Hawaii as elsewhere, just over a broader range of cultures. Some popular izakaya or Japanese-style pubs with excellent tapas-like bar food are Tokuri Tei and Nonbei, both in the Kapahulu neighborhood of Honolulu near Waikiki.

Microbreweries dot the casual dine-and-drink scene on several islands. Some are mainland imports, such as Gordon Biersch at Aloha Tower Marketplace; most are local endeavors, such as Kona Brewing Company with brew pubs on Oahu and on the Big Island. In all, you'll find beers made and named for their Island-grown ingredients and flavors, and contemporary food attractively served at reasonable prices.

THE MELTING POT IS SIZZLING

FOOD FESTIVALS HELD THROUGHOUT the Islands celebrate Hawaii's bounty in terms of both fresh produce and celebrated chefs. On Oahu, the Ko Olina Taste of Kapolei stars local chefs on the western side of the island, while on the Windward Coast, the I Love Kailua festivities each spring are a chance for Kailua chefs to show off their best. Kauai hosts the annual Taste of Hawaii each June. Maui hosts the Kapalua Food and Wine Festival, and Taste of Lahaina. The Big Island's Kona-Kohala Coast features the Kona Coffee Festival and a continuing round of upscale dining celebrations at various resorts.

The RESTAURANTS

OUR FAVORITE ISLAND RESTAURANTS: EXPLAINING THE RATINGS

WE HAVE DEVELOPED DETAILED PROFILES FOR THE BEST RESTAURANTS and for those that offer some special reason to visit, be it decor, ethnic appeal, or bargain prices. Each profile features an easily scanned heading that allows you quickly to check out the restaurant name, cuisine, overall rating, cost, quality rating, and value rating.

CUISINE In a place where food traditions meet and merge, and where Hawaii Regional Cuisine has existed as such only since 1992, categorizing restaurants is tricky. Hawaii Regional Cuisine is a blend of ethnic foods and cookery, with dishes that incorporate flavors and cooking methods from Asia, Hawaii and elsewhere in America, the Pacific Rim, the Mediterranean, Europe, and more. Many chefs prefer not to be categorized at all, but in most cases restaurant owners or chefs name their own categories. Fusion specialties are simply called contemporary cuisine. Even restaurants that once served classic French cuisine now prepare sauces with a lighter hand and use fresh, Island-grown ingredients, one of the prerequisites of Hawaii Regional Cuisine.

OVERALL RATING The overall rating encompasses the entire dining experience, including style, service, and ambience, in addition to the taste, presentation, and quality of the food. Five stars is the highest, best rating possible. Four-star restaurants are exceptional, three-star restaurants are well above average, and two-star restaurants are good. One star indicates an average restaurant that demonstrates an unusual capability in some area of specialization—for example, an otherwise unmemorable place that has great *saimin.*

COST Our expense description provides primarily a comparative sense of how much a meal will cost. A meal for our purposes consists of an entree with a vegetable or side dish, and a choice of soup or salad. Appetizers, desserts, drinks, and tips are not included. Categories and related prices are listed below:

Inexpensive	$14 or less per person
Moderate	$15–$30
Expensive	More than $30 per person

QUALITY RATING Food quality is rated on a scale of one to five stars, where 5 is the best rating attainable. It is based expressly on the taste, freshness of ingredients, preparation, presentation, and creativity of the food served. Price is not considered. If you want the best food available and cost is not an issue, you need look no further than the quality ratings.

VALUE RATING If, on the other hand, you are looking for both quality and value, then you should check the value rating. The perception of value can vary from place to place. Hawaii is a tourist destination, so restaurant prices probably compare favorably with prices in New York, San Francisco, and other major tourist destinations, but not so favorably with smaller towns. Because most people feel that hotel restaurants are universally overpriced (where else would you pay $4 to $6 for a glass of orange juice?), we have indicated restaurants of this sort with a two-star rating rather than a discouraging one-star rating. Two stars are meant to convey that yes, the restaurant charges more than you would pay for a similar entree somewhere else, but because the setting, service, and preparation are exceptional, it's worth the splurge. We wouldn't want to rate the restaurant with one star, causing a reader to reject a special dining experience. The value ratings are defined as follows:

★★★★★	Exceptional value; a real bargain
★★★★	Good value
★★★	Fair value; you get exactly what you pay for
★★	Somewhat overpriced
★	Significantly overpriced

LOCATING THE RESTAURANT On the far right is a designation for location; it will give you a general idea of where the restaurant is located. We've divided the six major islands into these geographic areas:

Waikiki	Central Oahu	Kona
Greater Honolulu	Central Maui	Hilo and Volcano
Windward Oahu	South Maui	Kauai
The North Shore	West Maui	Molokai
Leeward Oahu	Upcountry Maui	Lanai

PAYMENT We've listed the type of payment accepted at each restaurant using the following codes:

AE	American Express	DC	Diners Club	MC	MasterCard
CB	Carte Blanche	JCB	Japan Credit Bank	V	VISA
D	Discover				

WHO'S INCLUDED Restaurants open and close frequently, so we've included mostly those with a proven track record. However, some of the newest upscale restaurants run by local celebrity chefs have been included to keep the guide as up-to-date as possible. Local chains, such as Roy's, are included, as are a few franchises that have a distinctly Hawaiian look in food and decor. Also, the list is highly selective. Our leaving out a particular place does not necessarily mean that the restaurant is not good, only that we did not rank it among the best of its type. Detailed profiles of individual restaurants follow in alphabetical order at the end of this chapter. In the section titled "More Recommendations" below, we've named reputable restaurants that you might want to try for a specific reason—for pizzas, bagels, plate lunches—that don't otherwise merit a full description. These are listed according to their island location; an omitted island simply may not have a good restaurant in the category.

The Best Hawaii Restaurants

ISLAND CUISINE AND NAME	OVERALL RATING	PRICE	QUALITY RATING	VALUE RATING
OAHU				
CHINESE				
Little Village Noodle Shop	★★★★	Inexp/Mod	★★★★	★★★★
CONTEMPORARY				
Hoku's	★★★★	Exp	★★★★	★★★
Prince Court Restaurant	★★★★	Mod/Exp	★★★★	★★★
Tango Contemporary Café	★★★★	Mod	★★★★	★★★★
Duke's Canoe Club Restaurant	★★★	Mod	★★★½	★★★
CONTINENTAL				
Michel's at the Colony Surf	★★★★½	Exp	★★★★½	★★★
EURASIAN FUSION				
Indigo Eurasian Restaurant & Bar	★★★★½	Mod	★★★★½	★★★★
Hiroshi Eurasian Tapas/ Vino Italian Tapas & Wine Bar	★★★★	Mod	★★★★	★★★
Bali by the Sea	★★★½	Exp	★★★½	★★★
EUROPEAN				
Brasserie du Vin	★★★★★	Mod	★★★★★	★★★★★
FRENCH				
La Mer	★★★★★	Exp	★★★★★	★★★★★
FRENCH AND ITALIAN				
Elua Restaurant & Wine Bar	★★★★	Exp	★★★★½	★★★★
HAWAII REGIONAL				
Alan Wong's Restaurant	★★★★★	Mod/Exp	★★★★★	★★★★★
Roy's Restaurant Honolulu	★★★★★	Mod	★★★★★	★★★★
The Pineapple Room	★★★★½	Mod/Exp	★★★★	★★★
Helena's Hawaiian Foods	★★★★	Inexp	★★★★½	★★★★★
Don Ho's Island Grill	★★★	Inexp/Mod	★★★½	★★★
Sam Choy's Breakfast, Lunch, Crab, and Big Aloha Brewery	★★★	Mod/Exp	★★★½	★★★
Haleiwa Joe's Haiku Gardens	★★★	Mod	★★★	★★★
ITALIAN				
Sarento's Top of the "I"	★★★½	Exp	★★★★	★★★
JAPANESE CONTEMPORARY				
Nobu Waikiki	★★★★	Exp	★★★★½	★★★★
JAPANESE FUSION				
Sansei Seafood Restaurant and Sushi Bar/d. k. Steak House	★★★★★	Mod/Exp	★★★★★	★★★★

ISLAND CUISINE AND NAME	OVERALL RATING	PRICE	QUALITY RATING	VALUE RATING
OAHU (CONTINUED)				
PACIFIC RIM				
Chef Mavro Restaurant	★★★★★	Exp	★★★★★	★★★★★
3660 On the Rise	★★★★	Mod/Exp	★★★★½	★★★
Hau Tree Lanai	★★★	Exp	★★★½	★★★
SEAFOOD				
Orchids	★★★★½	Mod/Exp	★★★★½	★★★
STEAK AND SEAFOOD				
Hy's Steak House	★★★★½	Exp	★★★★	★★★
Buzz's Original Steak House	★★★½	Mod	★★★½	★★★
THAI				
Keo's Thai Cuisine in Waikiki	★★★★½	Mod	★★★★½	★★★★
Singha Thai Cuisine	★★★	Mod	★★★★	★★★★
MAUI				
AMERICAN				
Lahaina Grill	★★★★½	Exp	★★★★½	★★★
Stella Blues Cafe	★★★★½	Mod	★★★★	★★★★
CONTEMPORARY				
Gerard's	★★★★	Exp	★★★★	★★★★
Ko	★★★★	Exp	★★★★	★★★
Mala, An Ocean Tavern	★★★★	Mod/Exp	★★★★	★★★★★
Mala, Wailea	★★★★	Mod/Exp	★★★★	★★★★★
FRENCH				
Chez Paul's	★★★★½	Exp	★★★★★	★★★
HAWAII REGIONAL				
Haliimaile General Store	★★★★★	Mod/Exp	★★★★★	★★★★★
I'o	★★★★½	Exp	★★★★½	★★★
Pacific'O	★★★★½	Mod/Exp	★★★★½	★★★
Spago	★★★★½	Exp	★★★★½	★★★
Hula Grill Kaanapali	★★★★	Mod	★★★★	★★★★
Roy's Kahana Bar & Grill	★★★★	Mod/Exp	★★★★	★★★
Roy's Kihei Bar & Grill	★★★★	Mod/Exp	★★★★	★★★
Plantation House Restaurant	★★★½	Exp	★★★★	★★★
JAPANESE FUSION				
Sansei Seafood Restaurant and Sushi Bar	★★★★★	Mod/Exp	★★★★★	★★★★

The Best Hawaii Restaurants (continued)

ISLAND CUISINE AND NAME	OVERALL RATING	PRICE	QUALITY RATING	VALUE RATING
MAUI (CONTINUED)				
MEXICAN CONTEMPORARY				
Cilantro Grill	★★★	Inexp	★★★★	★★★
MEDITERRANEAN				
Longhi's	★★★½	Exp	★★★★	★★★
PACIFIC REGIONAL				
Banyan Tree	★★★★★	Exp	★★★★★	★★★★★
SEAFOOD				
Mama's Fish House	★★★★	Exp	★★★★½	★★★
Maalaea Waterfront Restaurant	★★★½	Mod/Exp	★★★★½	★★★
STEAK AND SEAFOOD				
Kimo's	★★★	Mod	★★★	★★★★
VIETNAMESE				
A Saigon Café	★★★	Inexp	★★★	★★★★★
THE BIG ISLAND				
CONTEMPORARY				
Café Pesto	★★★½	Mod	★★★★	★★★★
CONTINENTAL				
Kilauea Lodge Restaurant	★★★	Mod/Exp	★★★	★★★★
FRENCH/ASIAN				
Daniel Thiebaut Restaurant	★★★½	Mod	★★★★	★★★★
HAWAII REGIONAL				
Merriman's	★★★★★	Exp	★★★★★	★★★★★
Hualalai Grille by Alan Wong	★★★★½	Exp	★★★★★	★★★★
Brown's Beach House	★★★★	Mod/Exp	★★★★	★★★★
Pahuia at Four Seasons	★★★★	Exp	★★★★	★★★★
Roy's Waikoloa Bar & Grill	★★★★	Mod/Exp	★★★★	★★★★
CanoeHouse	★★★½	Exp	★★★★	★★★
O's Bistro	★★★½	Mod	★★★★	★★★★
JAPANESE FUSION				
Sansei Seafood Restaurant and Sushi Bar	★★★★★	Mod/Exp	★★★★★	★★★★★
PACIFIC RIM				
Coast Grille & Oyster Bar	★★★★½	Mod	★★★★½	★★★
Huggo's	★★★	Mod/Exp	★★★	★★★
THAI				
Royal Siam Thai	★★★½	Inexp	★★★	★★★★★

ISLAND CUISINE AND NAME	OVERALL RATING	PRICE	QUALITY RATING	VALUE RATING
KAUAI				
AMERICAN				
Duke's Kauai	★★★½	Mod	★★★½	★★★
CONTEMPORARY				
Postcards Café	★★★½	Mod	★★★★	★★★
Brennecke's Beach Broiler	★★★	Mod/Exp	★★★½	★★★
The Kauai Grill	★★★	Exp	★★★	★★★
HAWAII REGIONAL				
Roy's Poipu Bar & Grill	★★★★	Mod/Exp	★★★★	★★★
Plantation Gardens	★★★	Mod	★★★	★★★
HAWAIIAN LOCAL				
Hamura's Saimin Stand	★★	Inexp	★★★	★★★★★
ITALIAN				
Casa di Amici	★★★	Mod	★★★★	★★★
PACIFIC RIM				
The Beach House	★★★★	Mod	★★★★	★★★
Tidepools	★★★★	Exp	★★★½	★★★
STEAK AND SEAFOOD				
Keoki's Paradise	★★★½	Mod	★★★	★★★★
Shells Steak and Seafood	★★★	Exp	★★★½	★★★
THAI/CHINESE				
Mema Thai & Chinese Cuisine	★★½	Inexp/Mod	★★★	★★★★★
MOLOKAI				
PIZZA AND SANDWICHES				
Molokai Pizza Café	★★	Inexp	★★★½	★★★★
LANAI				
PACIFIC RIM				
Lanai City Grille	★★★	Mod	★★★★	★★★
CONTEMPORARY				
The Dining Room	★★★★★	Exp	★★★★★	★★★
ITALIAN				
Ihilani	★★★★½	Exp	★★★★½	★★★
HAWAII LOCAL				
Blue Ginger Café	★	Inexp	★★★	★★★★★

MORE RECOMMENDATIONS

BEST BAGELS
Oahu

- **Lox of Bagels** 111 Sand Island Access Road, Honolulu; ☎ 808-845-2855

BEST BAKERIES
Oahu

- **Agnes Portuguese Bake Shop** 46 Hoolai Street, Kailua; ☎ 808-262-5367;
  www.agnesbakeshop.com. It's a well-known Kailua secret . . . Agnes easily
  tops Leonard's in Honolulu for the best malasadas on Oahu—and if you call
  ahead, they'll make yours to order, ready when you arrive.
- **Grand Café & Bakery** 31 North Pauahi Street, Chinatown;
  ☎ 808-531-0001; **www.grandcafeandbakery.com.** Serves notable
  breakfasts and other meals as well.
- **Mary Catherine's Bakery** 2820 South King Street, Honolulu;
  ☎ 808-946-4333

Maui

- **T. Komoda Store & Bakery** 3674 Baldwin Avenue, Makawao;
  ☎ 808-572-7261. For breakfast doughnuts, cream puffs, and macadamia-
  nut cookies.

Big Island

- **Punaluu Bake Shop** Highway 11, Naalehu; ☎ 808-929-7343. Known for
  Hawaiian sweetbread.
- **Tex Drive In** Highway 19 at Pakalana Street, Honokaa, Hamakua Coast;
  ☎ 808-775-0598. For Portuguese malasadas, plain and filled.

Kauai

- **Kilauea Bakery and Pau Hana Pizza** Kong Lung Center, Kilauea;
  ☎ 808-828-2020

Molokai

- **Kanemitsu Bakery** 79 Ala Malama Street, Kaunakakai; ☎ 808-553-5855.
  For Molokai bread and lavosh.

BEST BREAKFASTS
Oahu

- **Boots & Kimos Homestyle Kitchen** 119 Hekili Street, Kailua;
  ☎ 808-263-7929. Local favorites.

Maui

- **Gazebo Restaurant** 5315 Lower Honoapiilani Road, Napili Shores Resort,
  Napili; ☎ 808-669-5621. Big breakfast with a bigger view.

The Big Island

- **Ken's House of Pancakes** 1720 Kamehameha Avenue, Hilo;
  ☎ 808-935-8711. Breakfast served 24-7.

Kauai

- **Eggbert's** 4-484 Kuhio Highway, Coconut Marketplace, Kapaa;
  ☎ 808-822-3787

BEST BREWPUBS

Oahu

- **Sam Choy's Breakfast, Lunch, Crab, and Big Aloha Brewery**
  580 North Nimitz Highway, Honolulu; ☎ 808- 545-7979

Maui

- **Maui Brews** 900 Front Street, Lahaina; ☎ 808-667-7794

The Big Island

- **Kona Brewing Company and Brew Pub** 75-5629 Kuakini Highway,
  Kailua-Kona; ☎ 808-334-2739

Kauai

- **Waimea Brewing Company** 9400 Kaumualii Highway, Waimea;
  ☎ 808-338-9733

BEST BURGERS

Oahu

- **Burgers on the Edge** 890 Kapahulu, Honolulu; ☎ 808-737-8866
- **The Counter Kahala** Kahala Mall, 4211 Waialae Avenue, Kahala;
  ☎ 808-739-5100
- **Kua Aina Sandwich** 66-160 Kamehameha Highway, Haleiwa;
  ☎ 808-637-6067
- **Teddy's Bigger Burgers** 539 Kailua Road, Kailua; ☎ 808-262-0820

Maui

- **Cheeseburger in Paradise** 811 Front Street, Lahaina; ☎ 808-661-4855

Kauai

- **Duane's Ono-Char Burgers** Kuhio Highway, Anahola; ☎ 808-822-9181

BEST DELI FOOD

Oahu

- **Brent's Restaurant & Delicatessen** 629A Kailua Road, Kailua;
  ☎ 808-262-8588. Deli, breakfast and lunch.

Maui

- **Caffe Ciao** Fairmont Kea Lani Maui, Wailea Alanui, Wailea;
  ☎ 808-875-4100. Italian taste treats.

Big Island

- **Merriman's Market Café** King's Shops, Waikoloa Beach Resort,
  ☎ 808-886-1700
- **Ocean Sushi Deli** 239 Keawe Street, Hilo; ☎ 808-961-6625. Fresh sushi
  and other Japanese favorites.

Kauai

- **Deli and Bread Connection** Kukui Grove Shopping Center, Lihue; ☎ 808-245-7115. Fresh baked bread.

Lanai

- **Pele's Other Garden** 811 Houston Street, Lanai City; ☎ 808-565-9628. Fresh salads, sandwiches, and pizza.

BEST DEPARTMENT STORE RESTAURANTS

Oahu

- **Mariposa, Nieman Marcus, Ala Moana** 1450 Ala Moana Boulevard, ☎ 2101, Honolulu; ☎ 808-951-3420
- **Pineapple Room by Alan Wong, Macy's Ala Moana** 1450 Ala Moana Boulevard, Honolulu; ☎ 808-945-6573

BEST FRESH FISH

Oahu

- **Roy's Restaurant** 6600 Kalanianiole Highway, Hawaii Kai; ☎ 808-396-7697
- **Uncle's Fish Market and Grill** Pier 38, 1135 North Nimitz Highway; ☎ 808-275-0063

Maui

- **Mama's Fish House** 799 Poho Place, Paia; ☎ 808-579-8488

The Big Island

- **Seaside Restaurant** 1790 Kalanianaole Avenue, Hilo; ☎ 808-935-8825 (order ahead if you want fish from the pond for dinner)

Kauai

- **Tidepools** Grand Hyatt Kauai, 1571 Poipu Road, Poipu Beach; ☎ 808-742-6260

BEST GOLF COURSE RESTAURANTS

Oahu

- **Bird of Paradise** Hawaii Prince Golf Course, Ewa Beach; ☎ 808-689-2270

Maui

- **Plantation House Restaurant** 2000 Plantation Club Drive, Kapalua Resort; ☎ 808-669-6299

The Big Island

- **Hualalai Grille by Alan Wong** Four Seasons Hualalai Resort, 100 Kaupulehu Drive, Kailua-Kona; ☎ 808-325-8525

Kauai

- **Poipu Bay Grill & Bar** Poipu Bay Clubhouse, 2250 Ainako Street, Poipu; ☎ 808-742-1515

Lanai

- **The Challenge at Manele Bay Clubhouse** Manele, Lanai;
  ☎ 808-565-2222

BEST HAWAIIAN FOOD
Oahu

- **Ono Hawaiian Foods** 726 Kapahulu Avenue, Honolulu; ☎ 808-737-2275
- **The Willows** 901 Hausten, Honolulu; ☎ 808-952-9200

Maui

- **Pukalani Country Club Restaurant** 360 Pukalani, Pukalani;
  ☎ 808-572-1325

The Big Island

- **Hawaiian Style Café** 64-1290 Mamalahoa Highway, Waimea;
  ☎ 808-885-4295
- **Kuhio Grille** 111 East Puainako, Prince Kuhio Plaza, Suite A106, Hilo;
  ☎ 808-959-2336

Kauai

- **Pono Market** 4-1300 Kuhio Highway, Kapaa; ☎ 808-822-4581

BEST ICE CREAM (LOCALLY MADE)

CALL LISTED NUMBERS FOR OTHER OUTLETS.

Oahu

- **Bubbie's Homemade Ice Cream and Desserts** Kahala Mall Shopping
  Center, Kahala; ☎ 808-739-2822; 1010 University Avenue, Honolulu;
  ☎ 808-949-8984
- **Dave's Ice Cream** 41-1537 Kalanianaole Highway, # 5, Waimanalo;
  ☎ 808-259-0356

Maui

- **Roselani Ice Cream** 918 Lower Main Street, Wailuku; ☎ 808-244-7951

The Big Island

- **Tropical Dreams Ice Cream** Kress Building, Kamehameha Avenue, Hilo;
  ☎ 808-935-9109; Kohala Coffee Mill, Akoni Puli Highway, Hawi;
  ☎ 808-889-5577

Kauai

- **Lappert's Ice Cream** 1-3555 Kaumualii Highway; ☎ 808-335-6121
  (also at Koloa, Coconut Marketplace, and Princeville)

BEST ITALIAN CUISINE
Oahu

- **Baci Bistro** 30 Aulike Street, Kailua; ☎ 808-262-7555
- **Vino Italian Tapas & Wine Bar** Restaurant Row; ☎ 808-524-8466

Maui

- **Penne Pasta** 180 Dennison Street, Lahaina; ☎ 808-661-6633

Big Island

- **Mi's Italian Bistro** 103 Mamalahoa Highway, Kealakekua;
  ☎ 808-323-3880

Kauai

- **Dondero's** Grand Hyatt Kauai; ☎ 808-240-6456

BEST JAPANESE TEAHOUSES

Oahu

- **Natsunoya Tea House** 1935 Makanani Drive, Honolulu;
  ☎ 808-595-4488. Minimum of ten people per party, except in new sushi
  bar Thursday–Sunday; walk-ins welcome.

Kauai

- **Hanamaulu Restaurant, Tea House and Sushi Bar**
  3-4291 Kuhio–Highway, Hanamaulu; ☎ 808-245-2511

BEST LOCAL ATMOSPHERE

Oahu

- **Buzz's Lanikai** 413 Kawailoa Road, Kailua; ☎ 808-261-4661;
  www.buzzsoriginalsteakhouse.com

Maui

- **Aloha Mixed Plate** 1285 Front Street, Lahaina; ☎ 808-661-3322;
  www.alohamixedplate.com

The Big Island

- **Bamboo Restaurant** Akoni Pule Highway, Hawi; ☎ 808-889-5555;
  www.bamboorestaurant.info/

Kauai

- **Tahiti Nui Restaurant** 5-5134 Kuhio Highway, Hanalei; ☎ 808-826-2677;
  www.thenui.com

Molokai

- **Hotel Molokai** Kamehameha Highway, Kaunakakai; ☎ 808-553-5347;
  www.hotelmolokai.com

BEST LUAU

Oahu

- **Paradise Cove** 92-1089 Alii Nui Drive, Kapolei; ☎ 808-842-5911,
  or toll-free, ☎ 800-775-2683

Maui

- **The Feast at Lele** 505 Front Street, Lahaina; ☎ 866-244-5353

The Big Island

- **Kona Village Resort** Queen Kaahumanu Highway, Kaupulehu-Kona;
  ☎ 808-325-5555

Kauai

- **Smith Family Garden Luau** Wailua Marina off Highway 56, Wailua;
  ☎ 808-822-4520

BEST MEXICAN CUISINE

Oahu

- **Cholo's Homestyle Mexican Restaurant** North Shore Marketplace,
  Haleiwa; ☎ 808-637-3059

Maui

- **Pollis** 1202 Makawao Avenue, Makawao; ☎ 808-572-7808

Kauai

- **La Bamba** 3-2600 Kaumualii Highway, Suite 3043, Lihue;
  ☎ 808-245-5972

BEST PIZZA

Oahu

- **Pizza Bob's Haleiwa** Haleiwa Shopping Plaza, Haleiwa; ☎ 808-637-5095

Maui

- **Pizza in Paradise** 60 East Wakea, Kahului; ☎ 808-871-8188

Kauai

- **Brick Oven Pizza** 2-2555 Kaumualii Highway, Kalaheo;
  ☎ 808-332-8561

Molokai

- **Molokai Pizza Café** Kaunakakai Place on Wharf Road, Kaunakakai;
  ☎ 808-553-5655

BEST PLACES TO HANG OUT

Oahu

- **Duke's Waikiki Barefoot Bar** Outrigger, Waikiki, 2335 Kalakaua Avenue;
  ☎ 808-922-2268
- **Gordon Biersch** Aloha Tower Marketplace, Honolulu; ☎ 808-599-4877

Maui

- **Hula Grill's Barefoot Bar on the beach** Whaler's Village, 2435 Kaanapali
  Parkway, Kaanapali; ☎ 808-667-6636

The Big Island

- **Kona Inn Restaurant** 75-5744 Alii Drive, Kailua-Kona; ☎ 808-329-4455

Kauai

- **Keoki's Paradise** Poipu Shopping Village, 2360 Kiahuna Plantation Drive, Poipu; ☎ 808-742-7534
- **Tahiti Nui Restaurant** 5-5134 Kuhio Highway, Hanalei; ☎ 808-826-2677

BEST PLATE LUNCHES

Oahu

- **Kakaako Kitchen** Ward Centre, 1200 Ala Moana Boulevard, Honolulu; ☎ 808-596-7488

Maui

- **Sam Sato's in Wailuku Millyard** 1750 Wili Pa Loop, Wailuku; ☎ 808-244-7124

The Big Island

- **Kona Mix Plate** 75-5660 Kopiko Street, Kopiko Plaza, Kailua-Kona; ☎ 808-329-8104

Kauai

- **Hanalei Mixed Plate** Ching Young Village, 5-5190 Kuhio Highway, 3E4, Hanalei; ☎ 808-826-7888
- **Koloa Fish Market** 5482 Koloa Road, Koloa; ☎ 808-742-6199

BEST ROMANTIC SEASIDE RESTAURANTS

ASK FOR A WATERFRONT TABLE.

Oahu

- **Orchids** 2199 Kalia Road, Waikiki; ☎ 808-923-2311

Maui

- **Maalaea Waterfront Restaurant** 50 Hauoli Street, Maalaea; ☎ 808-244-9028

The Big Island

- **Pahuia Restaurant at Four Seasons Hualalai** 100 Kaupulehu Drive, Kaupulehu-Kona; ☎ 808-325-8000

Kauai

- **Tidepools** Grand Hyatt Kauai Resort and Spa, 1571 Poipu Road, Poipu; ☎ 808-742-1234

BEST SEAFOOD BUFFETS

CHECK FOR TIMES AND DAYS.

Oahu

- **Plumeria Beach House at Kahala Hotel & Resort** 5000 Kahala Avenue, Honolulu; ☎ 808-739-8888
- **Prince Court at Prince Hotel Waikiki** 100 Holomoana Street, Waikiki; ☎ 808-944-4494

Big Island

- **Mauna Kea Clambake, Mauna Kea Beach Hotel** 62-100 Mauna Kea Beach Drive, Kohala Coast; ☎ 808-882-7222

Kauai

- **Naupaka Terrace at Hilton Kauai Beach Resort** 4331 Kauai Beach Drive, Lihue; ☎ 808-245-1955

BEST SHAVE ICE

Oahu

- **Matsumoto Shave Ice** 66-087 Kamehameha Highway, Haleiwa; ☎ 808-637-4827

Maui

- **Tobi's Ice Cream and Shave Ice** 1913 South Kihei Road, Kihei; ☎ 808-891-2440

Big Island

- **Scandinavian Shave Ice** 75-5699 Alii Drive, Kailua-Kona; ☎ 808-331-1626

Kauai

- **Jo Jo's Clubhouse** Mile Marker 23, Kaumualii Highway, Waimea; ☎ 808-635-7615

BEST STEAK HOUSES

Oahu

- **d. k. Kodama Steak House** Waikiki Beach Marriott Resort & Spa, 2552 Kalakaua Avenue, Waikiki; ☎ 808-931-6286

The Big Island

- **Big Island Steak House** Kings Shops, Waikoloa Beach Drive, Waikoloa; ☎ 808-886-8805

Kauai

- **Kalaheo Steak House** 4444 Papalina Road, Kalaheo; ☎ 808-332-9780

BEST SUNDAY BRUNCH

Oahu

- **Hoku's at Kahala Resort** 5000 Kahala Avenue, Honolulu; ☎ 808-739-8780
- **Orchids** 2199 Kalia Road, Waikiki; ☎ 808-923-2311

Maui

- **Grand Wailea Hotel** 3850 Wailea Alanui Drive, Wailea; ☎ 808-875-1234
- **Maui Prince Hotel** 5400 Makena Alanui, Makena; ☎ 808-874-1111

Big Island
- **Mauna Kea Beach Hotel** 62-100 Mauna Kea Beach Drive, Kohala Coast; ☎ 808-882-7222

Kauai
- **Gaylord's at Kilohana** 3-2087 Kaumualii Highway, Lihue; ☎ 808-245-9593

BEST SUSHI BARS
Oahu
- **Nobu Waikiki** Waikiki Parc Hotel, 2233 Helumoa Road, Waikiki; ☎ 808-924-3535

Maui
- **Sansei Seafood Restaurant & Sushi Bar** 600 Office Road, Kapalua Resort; ☎ 808-669-6286

The Big Island
- **Imari at Hilton Waikoloa Village** 69-425 Waikoloa Beach Drive, Waikoloa; ☎ 808-886-1234

Kauai
- **Kintaro Japanese Restaurant** 4-370 Kuhio Highway, Wailua; ☎ 808-822-3341

BEST THAI CUISINE
Oahu
- **Keo's in Waikiki** 2028 Kuhio Avenue, Waikiki; ☎ 808-922-9888

Maui
- **Royal Thai Cuisine** 1280 South Kihei Road, Kihei; ☎ 808-874-0813

The Big Island
- **Bangkok House** 75-5626 Kuakini Highway, Building 5, Kailua-Kona; ☎ 808-329-7764
- **Royal Siam Thai** 70 Mamo Street, Hilo; ☎ 808-961-6100

Kauai
- **Lemongrass** 4-885 Kuhio Highway, Kapaa; ☎ 808-821-2888

BEST VEGETARIAN CUISINE
Oahu
- **Chef Mavro** 1969 South King Street, Honolulu; ☎ 808-944-4714
- **Down to Earth Natural Foods and Lifestyle** 2525 South King Street, Honolulu; ☎ 808-947-7678

Maui
- **Down To Earth All Vegetarian Organic & Natural** 305 Dairy Road, Kahului; ☎ 808-877-2661

The Big Island

- **O's Bistro** 75-1027 Henry Street, Kailua-Kona; ☎ 808-327-6565

Kauai

- **Hanapepe Café & Espresso** 3830 Hanapepe Road, Hanapepe;
  ☎ 808-335-5011

Molokai

- **Outpost Natural Foods** 70 Makaena Place, Kaunakakai; ☎ 808-553-3377

BEST VIETNAMESE CUISINE

Oahu

- **A Little Bit of Saigon** 1160 Maunakea, Honolulu; ☎ 808-528-3663

Maui

- **A Saigon Café** 1792 Main Street, Wailuku; ☎ 808-243-9560

BEST VIEWS

Oahu

- **Hau Tree Lanai at New Otani Kaimana Beach** Waikiki; ☎ 808-923-1555
- **House Without a Key** Halekulani, Waikiki; ☎ 808-923-2311

Maui

- **Plantation House Restaurant** Kapalua Resort, 2000 Plantation Club
  Drive; ☎ 808-669-6299

The Big Island

- **Ka Ohelo Dining Room** Volcano House, Hawaii Volcanoes National Park;
  ☎ 808-967-7321

Kauai

- **Makana Terrace** St. Regis Princeville Resort, Princeville; ☎ 808-826-2746

Lanai

- **Manele Bay Clubhouse** Four Seasons Resort Lanai at Manele Bay;
  ☎ 808-565-2230

RESTAURANT PROFILES

OAHU

Alan Wong's Restaurant ★★★★★

HAWAII REGIONAL MOD/EXP QUALITY ★★★★★ VALUE ★★★★★ WAIKIKI

**1857 South King Street, 3rd floor, Waikiki/Honolulu; ☎ 808-949-2526;
www.alanwongs.com**

Reservations Highly recommended. **When to go** Anytime, but less crowded
5–6:30 p.m. **Entree range** $27–$52; 5-course prix fixe tasting menu and farmers

dinners, $75; $105 with wine pairings; 7-course dinner, $95, $135 with wine pairings. **Payment** AE, DC, JCB, MC, V. **Service rating** ★★★★★. **Parking** Valet in garage or limited on-street parking. **Bar** Full service. **Wine selection** Extensive, mostly domestic, good selection by the glass. **Dress** Dressy resort attire. **Disabled access** Good, via elevator. **Customers** Islanders and visitors. **Hours** Daily, 5–9 p.m.

SETTING AND ATMOSPHERE Located in an innocuous midrise building on South King Street a short drive or cab ride from Waikiki, Alan Wong's is hard to spot, but totally worth the search. Local artwork adorns the walls, and sparkly lights brighten interiors. An exhibition kitchen on one side of the comfortable restaurant showcases the action indoors, while glassed-in-lanai diners look across part of the city to the Koolau Mountains.

HOUSE SPECIALTIES One of the best steamed clams preparations anywhere is Wong's "Da Bag," an appetizer in a billowy foil pillow, pierced at the table to yield aromatic clams steamed with *kalua* pig, and shiitake mushrooms. Ginger-crusted onaga with a miso-sesame vinaigrette is a signature dish. Pacific flavors continue throughout the meal in desserts such as "The Coconut," an eye-catching ball of chocolate filled with *haupia* (coconut custard) sorbet, nestled in tropical fruits and *lilikoi* (passion fruit) sauce.

OTHER RECOMMENDATIONS Wong's light-hearted creativity keeps fine dining approachable and Island-style, but his consistently top-notch results keep him high on the list of the nation's best chefs. His ability to fuse Asian, Hawaiian, and American flavors while never forgetting his classic French training is evident in appetizers like "poki pines" (ahi tartare fried in a crispy, spiky shell), duck nachos (Chinese-style duck on tapioca-scallion chips with avocado salsa), and sautéed shrimp and clams with pasta (in a spicy lemongrass–black bean sauce), or entrees like macadamia nut–coconut crusted lamb chops with Asian ratatouille and roasted-garlic mashed potatoes. Diners who just can't choose can opt for a five-course ($65 per person) or seven-course ($85) tasting menu. Wong stages quarterly "Farmers Series" dinners ($75 prix fixe), which star local ingredients and bring farmers and fishermen into the restaurant to "talk story" with diners and staff about what and how they grew or caught their produce and seafood.

SUMMARY AND COMMENTS Alan Wong is one of Hawaii's most accomplished chefs, and is a James Beard Foundation winner known for artistry and hands-on care in his kitchen. His fans include President Barack Obama, who invited Wong to create a full-on luau at the White House in the summer of 2009 for members of Congress. Over the years, the Honolulu restaurant scene has exploded with talent, but Alan Wong's, the original of Wong's four restaurants, has withstood the competition and remains a perennial favorite .

Bali by the Sea ★★★½

EURASIAN EXPENSIVE QUALITY ★★★½ VALUE ★★★ WAIKIKI

Hilton Hawaiian Village Hotel, 2005 Kalia Road, Waikiki;
☎ **808-949-4321, restaurant** ☎ **808-949-4321, ext. 43;**
www.hiltonhawaiianvillage.com/dining

Reservations Highly recommended. **When to go** Sunsets. **Entree range** $31–$50; 5-course chef's tasting menu, $62; $87 with wine pairings. **Payment** All major credit cards. **Service rating** ★★★★★. **Parking** Free valet or hotel lot. **Bar** Full service. **Wine selection** Exceptional; the wine selection wins awards. **Dress** Business casual; no T-shirts, shorts, tank tops, or slippers. **Disabled access** Good. **Customers** Hotel guests and Islanders for special occasions. **Hours** Monday–Saturday, 6–9:30 p.m.

SETTING AND ATMOSPHERE White linens, candlelight, and fine china and crystal impart elegance to this romantic, open-air restaurant in the Hilton Rainbow Tower that overlooks both ocean and lagoon. Diamond Head looms on the far shore.

HOUSE SPECIALTIES Signature dishes include a surf-and-turf that features lobster poached in Hawaiian vanilla–and-butter sauce, paired with a filet mignon ($60). For a local fish treat, try orange miso-glazed Kona kampachi ($41).

OTHER RECOMMENDATIONS Rack of lamb comes in a mustard crust, and a light tempura batter masks scallion-crusted ahi tuna, served with Ponzu buerre blanc sauce. Among the appetizers are sugar cane–crusted scallops. The signature salad features roasted island beets with goat cheese, macadamia nuts, and dried pineapple over greens. Vegetarians will enjoy angel-hair pasta with wild mushrooms, local tomatoes, asparagus, and shaved Parmesan. The three-course Sunset Dinner special ($38) is a bargain.

SUMMARY AND COMMENTS Open-air dining with soft breezes and moonlit beach, great service, and fine food make this prize-winning restaurant a favorite of those ready to pop the question.

Brasserie du Vin ★★★★★

| EUROPEAN | MODERATE QUALITY ★★★★★ VALUE ★★★★★ | GREATER HONOLULU |

1115 Bethel Street, downtown Honolulu; ☎ 808-545-1115; www.brasserieduvin.com

Reservations Highly recommended. **When to go** Anytime, but less crowded 5–6:30 p.m. **Entree range** $16–$20; three-course prix fixe dinner, $25. **Payment** AE, DC, JCB, MC, V. **Service rating** ★★★★★. **Parking** Valet in garage or limited on-street parking. **Bar** Full service. **Wine selection** Extensive, mostly domestic, good selection by the glass. **Dress** Casual business attire. **Disabled access** Good. **Customers** Islanders and visitors. **Hours** Lunch, Monday–Saturday, 11:30 a.m.–4 p.m.; dinner, daily, 4–10 p.m., later on weekends or on demand.

SETTING AND ATMOSPHERE European-style brasserie in Chinatown right across from the Hawaii Theatre, a little bit French, a taste of tapas, a touch of Italian. Patrons have a choice of venue—a long stand-up bar, a farmhouse table in a rustic room, or tables for two in an open courtyard. Live music lends a festive note, but most people are already happy with the array of tasty, affordable dishes, hundreds of wine choices, and friendly setting.

HOUSE SPECIALTIES Appetizers include mussels steamed in wine broth and topped with crispy pommes frites; a cruet of mixed herbed olives;

brie baked in puff pastry; oysters on the half shell or baked; artisan cheeses such as manchego, gruyere, and taleggio, with dried fruits and nuts. Favorite entrees include grilled fish du jour with olive butter and Manchego cheese on a white-bean salad and grilled flat-iron steak with shallot aioli and pommes frites. Daily soups, such as cream of fennel, and antipasti-style salads vie for attention with escargot with green garlic butter.

OTHER RECOMMENDATIONS Lunch features include a daily risotto choice and a novel croque monsieur sandwich—grilled ham and Dijon mustard topped with a gratin of Swiss cheese and béchamel sauce. Monday-night wine dinners are worth checking out.

SUMMARY AND COMMENTS Chef Scott Nelson has a menu to match the wine collection. None of this is particularly Hawaiian, except for some of the fresh ingredients, but it certainly shows a true brasserie spirit—unpretentious atmosphere, simple good food, and a drink.

Buzz's Original Steak House, Lanikai ★★★½

STEAK AND SEAFOOD MODERATE QUALITY ★★★½ VALUE ★★★ WINDWARD   OAHU

413 Kawailoa Road, Kailua; ☎ 808-261-4661

Reservations Highly recommended. **When to go** Anytime. **Entree range** Lunch $7–$15; dinner, $15–$36. **Payment** No credit cards. **Service rating** ★★★. **Parking** Free in adjacent lot. **Bar** Full service. **Wine selection** Good, many by the glass. **Dress** Casual. **Disabled access** Good. **Customers** Islanders, tourists brought in by Islanders, lucky beachgoers. **Hours** Daily, 11 a.m.–3 p.m. and 4:30–9:30 p.m.

SETTING AND ATMOSPHERE Across from beautiful Kailua Beach and beside Kaelepulu Stream, Buzz's is the ideal Hawaii dining spot you may have been searching for on Oahu—kick-back atmosphere, good food and drinks, and lots of aloha, not to mention mile-high mud pie. More outdoors than in, this old-fashioned beach shack has the fragrance of the sea wafting through on sea breezes and the loyalty of more than one generation of devoted followers. Customers line up to sit at wooden tables and booths indoors and outdoors on a roofed lanai built around a tree, sipping excellent mai tais while they wait for a table. Inside, the polished koa bar is a local gathering spot in this windward town about 12 miles from Waikiki.

HOUSE SPECIALTIES Don't miss the melt-in-your-mouth calamari steak with caper lemon-butter sauce, or another favorite appetizer, a whole steamed "Artichoke Surprise" filled with a creamy garlic dipping sauce. Salad lovers prize Buzz's salad bar because it usually includes avocado among the fresh offerings. Buzz's, a pioneer in the salad bar–steak house trend (it's been there since 1962), still does it right, serving fresh fish, teriyaki and plain steaks and burgers, lobster and rack of lamb with salad bar and extras such as tempura fries or baked potato.

OTHER RECOMMENDATIONS Catch of the day Chinese-style is flavored with peanut oil, soy sauce, garlic, ginger, and cilantro. At lunch, try the excellent garden burger laden with avocado, cheese, sprouts, mushrooms, and sauces or one of the inventive, hearty salads. That will make you feel better about indulging in one of the mountainous ice-cream cakes from the dessert tray.

SUMMARY AND COMMENTS The most secluded table on the deck bears a little plaque proclaiming that former President and Mrs. Clinton dined there during an Island sojourn. Several celebrities live nearby and stop in from time to time. The only downer is inconsistent service that ranges from very good to very iffy, depending perhaps on whether owner Bobbi Lou Schneider Yaeckel is in town.

Chef Mavro Restaurant ★★★★★

PACIFIC RIM EXPENSIVE QUALITY ★★★★★ VALUE ★★★★★ WAIKIKI

1969 South King Street, Waikiki/Honolulu; ☎ 808-944-4714; www.chefmavro.com

Reservations Highly recommended. **When to go** Anytime. **Entree range** Seasonal prix fixe menus range from $69 to $165 per person or $260 with wines for a full tasting menu. **Payment** AE, DC, JCB, MC, V. **Service rating** ★★★★★. **Parking** Valet only. **Bar** Full service. **Wine selection** Fine. **Dress** Dressy resort attire. **Disabled access** Good. **Customers** Islanders and visitors. **Hours** Tuesday–Sunday, 6–9:30 p.m.

SETTING AND ATMOSPHERE Gleaming pink marble at the entry foretells the simple elegance of the interior. A graceful arch divides the dining area, with banquette seating beside two walls of etched glass windows. The intimate 68-seat restaurant is filled with sprays of orchids and lit with pinpoint lights suspended like stars from the ceiling. The restaurant is about a five-minute drive from Waikiki.

HOUSE SPECIALTIES Marseille, France–born chef-owner George Mavrothalassitis, a founding member of the Hawaii Regional Cuisine group, changes his menu to reflect the seasons. The emphasis is always on fresh ingredients, from Hawaii and elsewhere, assembled with genius and originality. A typical fall menu may begin with appetizers such as fresh scallops flavored with red bell pepper, proscuitto, cilantro, and ginger; Big Island maitake mushroom salad served with asparagus, braised salsify, and poached quail egg; or seared foie gras set off by oven-dried grapes and a pistachio-raisin-cardamon biscuit. Entrees might include Keahole lobster curry; roasted lamb loin with artichokes and cured olives; or fresh catch prepared with raite sauce of capers, anchovies, and wine reduction.

OTHER RECOMMENDATIONS Then there's dessert, ranging from Big Island goat-cheese mousse with a biscotti, white peach, and maple syrup on baby greens, to lilikoi *malassadas* (Portuguese doughnuts) with guava coulis and pineapple-coconut ice cream.

SUMMARY AND COMMENTS The essence of Chef Mavro is the pairings of food and wine, and the best way to appreciate his cuisine is through tasting menus. He offers a choice of prix fixe dinners, with or without wine pairings, ranging from $69 per person for three courses ($117 with wines) to $165 if your table of diners wants to taste everything ($260 with wines). Mavrothalassitis opened Chef Mavro in 1998 after an award-winning stint as executive chef of the Halekulani. In 2003, he won the James Beard Foundation Award as Best Regional Chef. Check out his Web site for current menus (in English and Japanese) and for messages from the chef, who conducts cooking classes from time to time.

Don Ho's Island Grill ★ ★ ★

HAWAII REGIONAL COMFORT FOOD INEXPENSIVE/MODERATE QUALITY ★ ★ ★ ½
VALUE ★ ★ ★   GREATER HONOLULU

Aloha Tower Marketplace, 1 Aloha Tower Drive, Honolulu;
☎ **808-528-0807; www.donho.com/grill**

Reservations Recommended. **When to go** Lunch or sunset for best harbor views. **Entree range** $9–$22. **Payment** AE, DC, JCB, MC, V. **Service rating** ★ ★ ★ ★. **Parking** Valet or in adjacent pay lot. **Bar** Full service, good selection of tropical drinks. **Wine selection** Adequate. **Dress** Casual. **Disabled access** Good if using valet. **Customers** Islanders and tourists. **Hours** Lunch and dinner, daily, 10 a.m.–9 p.m., Brunch, Sunday, 10 a.m.–2 p.m.

SETTING AND ATMOSPHERE This restaurant is a nostalgia trip back to the Hawaii depicted by Hollywood in the 1940s and 1950s. Walls are covered with surfboards, paddles, rattan, and memorabilia and pictures of the late Don Ho. The salad bar is nestled in an outrigger canoe. The restaurant opens to views of busy Honolulu Harbor on one side, and a thatched-roof bar just outside the confines of the restaurant also overlooks the harbor. Pillars decorated like palm trees and a bamboo-lined bar with stools covered in colorful aloha prints are all part of the yesteryear atmosphere.

HOUSE SPECIALTIES Most fun for sharing is the surfboard pizza with a variety of toppings, presented on a miniature surfboard atop two big pineapple cans. Substantial *pupu* include homemade coconut shrimp, calamari with passion-fruit cocktail sauce, barbecued ribs, teriyaki skewers, kulua pork quesadillas, and seared ahi. You can get a cheeseburger, but why not chance a blackened ahi, swiss cheese, and bacon sandwich with wasabi aioli?

OTHER RECOMMENDATIONS Fresh salads with Island touches like *li hing* or miso dressing and topped with sashimi or cooked ahi are tempting, along with a grilled veggie sandwich on focaccia bread for lunch. Try seafood curry Asian risotto, if you can get past a local food fix with the Hawaiian plate (*kalua* pig, *ahi poke*, *lomilomi* salmon, and *poi*) or Molokai lobster-fried rice. The fresh fish comes pan seared with *lomilomi* salmon butter. For dessert, the sweet potato–*haupia* pie in a macadamia-nut crust is memorable.

ENTERTAINMENT AND AMENITIES Musicians grace the stage Sunday to Wednesday, and on Thursday to Saturday nights, Don Ho's turns into a hot nightclub.

SUMMARY AND COMMENTS This is a pleasant place to meet for lunch or drinks, have a better-than-expected dinner, and hear some live Hawaiian music while watching the ships come and go.

Duke's Canoe Club Restaurant ★★★

CONTEMPORARY MODERATE QUALITY ★★★½ VALUE ★★★ WAIKIKI

Outrigger Waikiki Hotel, 2335 Kalakaua Avenue, Waikiki;
☎ **808-922-2268; www.dukeswaikiki.com**

Reservations Accepted. **When to go** Anytime. **Entree range** $18.95–$29.95.
Payment AE, D, DC, MC, V. **Service rating** ★★★. **Parking** Valet, hotel lot. **Bar**
Full service. **Wine selection** Good. **Dress** Casual. **Disabled access** Good if using
valet. **Customers** Tourists, Islanders, beach boys. **Hours** Daily, 7 a.m.–10 p.m. A
simpler menu is served in the Barefoot Bar 5 p.m.–midnight.

SETTING AND ATMOSPHERE *Pau hana* (after work) surfers, paddlers, and tourists hang out at the big wooden bar watching the sunset over Waikiki
Beach in this casual, oceanfront eatery. Historic photos, surfboards, and
saltwater aquariums bring back memories of the days when Duke Kahanamoku was an Olympic swimmer and surfer extraordinaire.

HOUSE SPECIALTIES At dinner try a huge slab of prime rib or awesome fresh
fish—ahi, mahimahi, ono, or opakapaka—available in five preparations:
baked, firecracker, Parmesan- and herb-crusted, hibachi-style teriyaki,
or simply grilled. A convenient lunch spot for anything from a burger to
huli huli (rotisserie) chicken to Thai-style seafood coconut curry.

OTHER RECOMMENDATIONS Breakfast and lunch buffets and a salad bar at
dinner are a good value. If you prefer table service, you might order
burgers, fries, pasta, and salads. For a splurge (in calories), finish with a
piece of hula pie.

ENTERTAINMENT AND AMENITIES From 4 to 6 p.m., thoroughly modern musicians play island sounds. On Friday, Saturday, and Sunday, dance bands
keep the lower lanai jumping.

SUMMARY AND COMMENTS Duke's is one of the most popular places to hang
out after a day on Waikiki Beach for both Islanders and tourists, partly
because it opens right onto the sand, but also because local surfers are
rightly proud of the great Hawaiian swimmer whom this restaurant
commemorates.

Elua Restaurant & Wine Bar ★★★★

**PROVENCAL FRENCH AND ITALIAN EXPENSIVE QUALITY ★★★★½ VALUE ★★★★
GREATER HONOLULU**

1341 Kapiolani Boulevard, Honolulu; ☎ 808-955-3582;
www.eluarestaurant.com

Reservations Recommended. **When to go** Anytime **Entree range** $28–$49.
Payment AE, DC, JCB, MC, V. **Service rating** ★★★★. **Parking** Complimentary
self-parking in garage. **Bar** Full service. **Wine selection** Good, many wines by
the glass. **Dress** Dressy casual. **Disabled access** Good, via elevator from parking
building. **Customers** Islanders and tourists. **Hours** Sunday–Thursday, 6–10 p.m.;
Friday and Saturday, 5:30–10 p.m.

SETTING AND ATMOSPHERE Elua ("two" in Hawaiian) features works by Hawaiian artists set off by dark-wood panels in an attractive setting. A big marble-topped bar near the entrance to the dining room is a good place to relax if you forgot to make reservations.

HOUSE SPECIALTIES Two fine chefs, one from Provence and one from Pugia, present two fine menus, one of French classics and one of Italian, changing with the seasons and the chefs' inclinations. Fans of Padovani, one of the dozen original Hawaii Regional Cuisine chefs and co-owner of Padovani Chocolates, will recognize his signature in dishes such as roast duck breast with sweet-and-sour ginger jus, a tart of foie gras with mushrooms and onion confit, an unusual Hawaiian salad of avocado, mango, papaya, hearts of palm, and macadamia nuts with balsamic vinaigrette, and , a veal chop bathed in a Madeira-truffle sauce.

OTHER RECOMMENDATIONS Fans of Donato, who also owns Pasta & Basta at Restaurant Row, will relish Italian classics such as fresh-made gnocchi in Tuscan ragout; crispy filet of moi fish, puttanesca-style; or lamb shank braised with porcini mushrooms.

SUMMARY AND COMMENTS This is not fusion or collaboration in terms of dishes—just two top local chefs, each doing his thing, side by side. The left side of the menu features Padovani's French dishes; the right, Donato's Italian entrees. Both are shortened versions of what each chef would feature on his own, and both include nightly specials and seasonal changes. This is the best-of-both-worlds solution for diners who can't decide whether they want French or Italian cuisine for dinner. Diners can choose from both menus, or a five-course tasting menu ($88, $118 with wines) that unites their individual efforts.

Haleiwa Joe's Haiku Gardens Restaurant ★★★

HAWAII REGIONAL MODERATE QUALITY ★★★ VALUE ★★★ WINDWARD OAHU

46-336 Haiku Road, Kaneohe; ☎ 808-247-6671

Reservations Recommended. **When to go** Anytime. **Entree range** $18.50–$28.50. **Payment** All major credit cards. **Service rating ★★★★**. **Parking** Adjacent lot. **Bar** Full service. **Wine selection** Good. **Dress** Casual. **Disabled access** Good. **Customers** Islanders, tourists. **Hours** Daily, 5:30–9:30 p.m. and Sunday brunch, 7:30 a.m.–2p.m.

SETTING AND ATMOSPHERE Anchored to the hillside by a lava-rock wall, this hideaway is one big open-air lanai with a soaring Polynesian roof, overlooking a garden in a grotto below. Once Haiku Gardens, a tropical park lushly landscaped around a steeply walled scenic pond, was the destination, as it still is if you're getting married. But these days it's more the restaurant and bar that lure people up residential Haiku Road to the secluded spot at the foot of the Koolau cliffs, where you're bound to be hungry and thirsty after going *holoholo* (island road trip) on the windward side.

HOUSE SPECIALTIES The focus is on lots of fresh fish fixed different ways—daily fresh catch baked with a macadamia crust, grilled and served in a crispy lumpia bowl with Asian slaw, or steamed Thai-style with coconut, onion, peanuts, and a side of red-curry sauce; spicy-seared ahi with udon noodles; salmon baked with citrus sauce. Shellfish include king crab and lobster, coconut-crusted shrimp, as well as spicy shrimp satay, one of several satay preparations; beef and chicken dishes are also available. Chocolate lovers may be unable to resist Kilauea Cake, a chocolate cake with hot cream cheese–and–chocolate filling, topped with raspberry sauce.

OTHER RECOMMENDATIONS Appetizers include Island favorites like ahi in many styles, Thai fried calamari with spicy dipping sauce, ceviche, and Kal bi ribs. Tough choice, so why not have the *pupu* platter and share several. For vegetarians, several salads, sizzling mushrooms, and a huge baked potato are tempting, along with vegetables in spicy green curry and stir-fried with tofu.

SUMMARY AND COMMENTS Haleiwa Joe's in Haiku Gardens and Haleiwa Joe's in the North Shore village of Haleiwa illustrate the Hawaiian concept of *ma uka* (toward the mountain) and *ma kai* (toward the sea). They have menus in common. But only at the Kaneohe location can you kick back in the bar and watch the homebound commuters, crawling down the Likelike Highway and wishing they were where you are.

Hau Tree Lanai ★★★

PACIFIC RIM EXPENSIVE QUALITY ★★★½ VALUE ★★★ WAIKIKI

New Otani Kaimana Beach Hotel, 2863 Kalakaua Avenue, Waikiki; ☎ 808-921-7066; www.kaimana.com/dining/hautree

Reservations Recommended, especially for dinner. **When to go** Anytime; sunset is exceptional. **Entree range** Lunch, $11.50–$18.50; dinner, $18.50–$35. **Payment** AE, D, DC, JCB, MC, V. **Service rating** ★★★★. **Parking** Valet or on-street meters. **Bar** Full service. **Wine selection** Good. **Dress** Casual for breakfast and lunch, resort attire at dinner. **Disabled access** Good, with ramp to the beach terrace. **Customers** Visitors, hotel guests, Islanders. **Hours** Monday–Saturday, 7–10:45 a.m., 11:45 a.m.– 2 p.m., and 5:30–9 p.m.; Sunday, 7–11:30 a.m., noon–2 p.m., and 5:30–9 p.m.

SETTING AND ATMOSPHERE This is one place where the setting outweighs other considerations, a beachfront terrace with a front-row seat for sunset. The Hau Tree Lanai's linen-draped tables are snuggled under a spreading *hau* tree on the beach under Diamond Head, said to be the same spot that writer Robert Louis Stevenson sat a century or so ago and made friends with Princess Kaiulani. If you want a beach-edge table, go about 5:30 p.m., and be sure to make reservations noting your request.

HOUSE SPECIALTIES Hau Tree Lanai's signature dishes include seafood mixed grill with lobster, shrimp, fish, and scallops with creamy sweet chili–Boursin sauce and grilled lamb. Other favorites include filet mignon in a green peppercorn and béarnaise sauce or pork chops, adobo style or with Madeira plum sauce. Or try something new, such as shrimp and scallops wrapped in phyllo dough, fried golden and served with curry sauce.

OTHER RECOMMENDATIONS Appetizers include a coconut-crusted soft-shell crab with greens and mango aioli, tempura ahi sushi California-style, which is ahi wrapped with crab and avocado in *nori*, battered and fried to medium rare, with balsamic soy syrup and wasabi aioli. Breakfast features several house variations on eggs benedict, *poi* pancakes and waffles, as well as cappuccino and lattes. Lunch could be an old favorite, chicken salad in a half papaya, mahimahi burger, or a variety of Malaysian curries.

SUMMARY AND COMMENTS Location, location, location, but the menu has vastly improved, as well.

Helena's Hawaiian Foods ★★★★

**TRADITIONAL HAWAIIAN INEXPENSIVE QUALITY ★★★★½ VALUE ★★★★★
GREATER HONOLULU**

1240 North School Street, Honolulu; ☎ 808-845-8044

Reservations None taken. Takeout is popular. **When to go** Anytime. **Entree range** Lunch or dinner, $6–$12. **Payment** No credit cards accepted. **Service rating** ★★★. **Parking** A few spots in a small lot. **Bar** None. **Wine selection** None. **Dress** Casual. **Disabled access** Two shallow steps up from the parking lot. **Customers** Locals. **Hours** Tuesday–Friday, 10 a.m.–7:30 p.m.

SETTING AND ATMOSPHERE Helena's is a down-to-earth, no-frills but clean eatery, with the door painted red for good luck. On the walls you will find lithographs by Jean Charlot, gifts from the late artist that were personally framed. Also on the wall: the late owner Helen Chock's James Beard Foundation Award. In 2000, the restaurant was named a Regional Classic, a special designation for locally owned neighborhood eateries.

HOUSE SPECIALTIES The menu is small and entirely devoted to traditional Hawaiian foods. It has remained unchanged for more than 50 years. The *pipikaula* short ribs are exceptional—chewy on the outside and pull-apart moist on the inside. The flavoring is one of a kind, drawn from Helena's grill, where the ribs hang to dry slightly before cooking. Butterfish collars, made from the sweet, delicate meat just behind the fish's gills, are served fried or stewed (fried is better, crunchy and flavorful). Salt beef with watercress, soft cubes of brisket in a mellow broth, is perfect comfort food.

OTHER RECOMMENDATIONS *Lomi* salmon, squid luau, and *kalua* pig are done well at Helena's. Refreshing squares of *haupia* (coconut pudding) are the perfect ending to the meal. You can order à la carte and assemble your own mixed plate. Whatever you have, don't forget a bowl of *poi*.

SUMMARY AND COMMENTS Helen Chock ran Helena's almost single-handedly for more than half a century, beginning in 1946, winning the hearts of an extremely devoted clientele. She died at age 89 in 2007. Her grandson, Craig Katuyoshi, is now the principal owner.

Hiroshi Eurasian Tapas/
Vino Italian Tapas & Wine Bar ★★★★

EURASIAN FUSION MODERATE QUALITY ★★★★ VALUE ★★★ GREATER HONOLULU

Restaurant Row, 500 Ala Moana Boulevard, Honolulu; ☎ 808-533-4476

Reservations Recommended. **When to go** *Pau hana,* early dinner. **Entree range** $8.50–$36.95. **Payment** All major credit cards. **Service rating** ★ ★ ★ ★. **Parking** Valet or validated garage. **Bar** Full service. **Wine selection** Extensive with many by the glass. **Dress** Casual, business. **Disabled access** Good. **Customers** Urbanites, movie-goers, tourists. **Hours** *Hiroshi:* appetizers and dinner, daily, 5:30–9:30 p.m. *Vino:* Wednesday and Thursday, 5:30–9:30 p.m.; Friday and Saturday, 5:30–10:30 p.m.

SETTING AND ATMOSPHERE   Cool, high-ceilinged rooms with a large, comfortable bar on one side, metro-chic table decor, and a view of the busy city street from the window wall.

HOUSE SPECIALTIES   The word *tapas* rarely describes Spanish bar food when used in Hawaii. At Hiroshi it means excellent small plates to share, with Japanese and other accents combined, as in Kona Kampachi carpaccio with ponzu vinaigrette ; or bacon-wrapped jumbo shrimp with ginger-scallion, sweet miso, and green-papaya salad. There's locally produced foie gras sushi with a teriyaki glaze and shiso essence, panko-encrusted, *nori*-wrapped ahi with trimmings, fresh moi in a bag with Hauula tomato concasse, chili-pepper water, *konbu* broth, and truffle butter . . . well, you get the idea: Japan meets Europe in Hawaii. Full-size dinner plates are also available, ranging from Chilean sea bass or wine-steamed veal cheeks to rib-eye steak. At neighboring Vino, a limited and more traditional array of small Italian plates includes homemade ravioli stuffed with seafood or sweet fennel sausage, spinach, and ricotta cheese; pizza; salads; antipasti; light seafood dishes; vegetable dishes (asparagus Milanese, eggplant Napoleon); and osso buco for those who want heartier fare.

OTHER RECOMMENDATIONS   Among other personal touches of genius, Chef Hiroshi Fukui likes foam—herbed-foam garnish; garlic chili foam; and guava foam on dessert. Foam is at the heart of a novel take on Caesar salad that takes the cliché right out of the dish: Baby hearts of romaine with curls of Parmesan-Reggiano cheese, rice-cake crispies, and Caesar dressing foam in which to dip the lettuce. Similarly, whoever invented crème brûlée would be surprised at how the dish changes with Asian flavors—*haupia* (coconut) and lemongrass give brûlée a whole new twist.

SUMMARY AND COMMENTS   Chef Fukui was trained in the Zen-inspired *kaiseki* tradition of formal Japanese dining, in which seasonal delicacies are served in elaborate presentations—works of art on the plate. Hiroshi plates are also very artful, with garnishes that complement the flavors. In some respects, this is dining for the 21st century—small servings of excellently prepared, healthful food that don't empty the wallet or stuff the diner. Fukui was executive chef at L'Uraku, where he honed his fusion reputation and made the restaurant a hit before leaving to join D. K. Kodama's Sansei Group from Maui. Hiroshi shares this space with another Kodama enterprise: Vino, which on Oahu is a wine bar serving Italian tapa-size plates and larger dishes designed to complement the selection of wines, many of them Italian. The wines, handpicked by Master Sommelier and co-owner Chuck Furuya, are offered in two- and five-ounce servings.

Hoku's ★★★★

Kahala Hotel & Resort, 5000 Kahala Avenue, Honolulu;
☎ **808-739-8780; www.kahalaresort.com**

Reservations Highly recommended. **When to go** Anytime. **Entree range** Dinner, $32–$55. **Payment** All major credit cards. **Service rating** ★★★★★. **Parking** Valet or validated in hotel garage. **Bar** Full service. **Wine selection** Extensive, including half a dozen ports. **Dress** Resort attire; long pants and collared shirts for men. **Disabled access** Good. **Customers** Hotel guests, Islanders. **Hours** Monday–Sunday, 5:30–10 p.m.; Sunday for brunch, 10:30–2 p.m.

SETTING AND ATMOSPHERE Hoku's is a stylish restaurant where every table has a panoramic vista of the Pacific. An open kitchen anchors one end of the dining room. A sushi bar offers additional tidbits.

HOUSE SPECIALTIES Appetizers include several ahi dishes, particularly ahi musubi, a concoction of ahi poke and sushi rice, fried crispy. Try the lobster thermidor with Maui goat cheese and mushrooms, or the crisped whole Island fish for two.

OTHER RECOMMENDATIONS Rack of lamb comes in a salt crust, roasted and carved tableside. Two diners can share a crispy whole fish with a trio of sauces. The Sunday brunch buffet ($58 adults, $29 children ages 5 to 12) includes an awesome array of chilled seafood, hot breakfast, lunch, and dinner-like dishes (rack of lamb, rib roast, roast chicken) finished off by a chocolate fountain with fruit.

SUMMARY AND COMMENTS Chef Wayne Hirabayashi has come into his own at Hoku's. Although the menu has retracted to more basic fare, the restaurant remains a favorite in a spectacular setting.

Hy's Steak House ★★★★½

Waikiki Park Heights Hotel, 2440 Kuhio Avenue; ☎ 808-922-5555;
www.restauranteur.com/hyshawaii

Reservations Recommended. **When to go** Anytime for dinner. **Entree range** $26.95–$65.95. **Payment** All major credit cards. **Service rating** ★★★★½. **Parking** Valet in garage. **Bar** Full service. **Wine selection** Award-winning, extensive and pricey, 16 by the glass. **Dress** Dressy attire to resort casual. **Disabled access** No ramp for stairs, but wheelchair lift available. **Customers** Islanders and tourists. **Hours** Monday–Friday, 6–10 p.m.; Saturday–Sunday, 5:30–10 p.m

SETTING AND ATMOSPHERE Diners enjoy formal candlelit ambience in a British old-boys' club atmosphere; one room is arranged around a glassed-in performance kitchen with a huge copper caldron in which the *kiawe* grilling occurs. Wood-paneled walls with heavily carved moldings, gleaming brass chandeliers, and a huge beveled mirror reflect tables dressed in pink cloths. The lighter-natured Emerald Garden room has tropical plants and art deco touches. Hy's spirit is Continental; tuxedoed waiters prep salads, carve Chateaubriand, and flame cherries jubilee and bananas Foster at your table, but proudly add some regional touches. You'll find blackened ahi sashimi and scallop katsu on the appetizers list, along with dearly market-priced Beluga caviar.

HOUSE SPECIALTIES There's a reason that Hy's steaks are so famously good: They are prime beef, aged on the premises and grilled on Hawaiian *kiawe* wood. Start with a garlicky Caesar salad fixed tableside, and proceed to your favorite beef—tender New York strip, filet mignon, or T-bone, prime rib, Delmonico, shish kebab, teriyaki steak, Chateaubriand, or filet of beef Wellington. The steak house, originally part of the Canadian chain, also serves lamb and veal, local fish (Chinese-style steamed opakapaka), and imported fish and shellfish. The signature dessert is bananas Foster, one of several flambéed desserts and other après-dinner choices, including a roster of dessert drinks and sweet wines, ports, Cognacs, and brandies.

OTHER RECOMMENDATIONS Chicken marsala, fish, seafood combos, scallops, Alaskan king crab, lobster, and scampi are also available. Vegetarians will be grateful for several salads, a vegetable plate, and steamed or roasted vegetables.

ENTERTAINMENT AND AMENITIES Audy Kimura, winner of eight local music awards, strums guitar and sings Wednesday through Saturday evenings.

SUMMARY AND COMMENTS Hy's, a beefy institution in Waikiki, has a loyal local following.

Indigo Eurasian Restaurant & Bar ★★★★½

| EURASIAN FUSION | MODERATE | QUALITY ★★★★½ | VALUE ★★★★ |
| GREATER HONOLULU | | | |

1121 Nuuanu Avenue, Honolulu; ☎ 808-521-2900; www.indigo-hawaii.com

Reservations Recommended. **When to go** Anytime. **Entree range** Lunch buffet, $16.95; Dinner, $22–$35; Vegetarian, $20. **Payment** D, DC, JCB, MC, V. **Service rating** ★★★★. **Parking** Valet, street, or nearby Gateway Plaza lot. **Bar** Full service. **Wine selection** Extensive and excellent, more than 30 by the glass. **Dress** Casual. **Disabled access** Good if using valet. **Customers** Islanders and businesspeople at lunch, pre- and post–Hawaii Theatre attendees, smart tourists. **Hours** Tuesday–Friday, 11:30 a.m.–2 p.m. and 6–9:30 p.m.; Saturday, 6–10 p.m. On weekends evening hours expand with Hawaii Theatre performances.

SETTING AND ATMOSPHERE Enter, and you trade a tattered street for a tropical Eurasian retreat in the heart of old Honolulu. Creative chef-owner Glenn Chu's imaginative restaurant is set in a historic 1903 building. With a high ceiling, suspended fans circling lazily overhead, antique carved panels from Indonesia, and big paintings of Chinese goddesses by local artist Pegge Hopper, you feel you've traveled to some exotic movie-set locale. The back of the building opens onto a lanai fronting Chinatown Gateway Park. Diners on the lanai are surrounded by lush greenery, with paper lanterns hung overhead and Balinese umbrellas placed here and there. The lanai bar, roofed with Indonesian ironwood shingles, is a fine place to sip a tropical drink while watching evening showers drip off the table umbrellas nearby.

HOUSE SPECIALTIES Appetizers are a spectrum of East-meets-West textures and flavors, from soft, steamed filled dumplings to crispy spring rolls, wonton, and shrimp lumpia, served with chipotle aioli and tangerine sauce. One favorite is goat cheese wontons with four-fruit sauce. At lunch, a dim sum buffet lets you taste several. Entrees include Emperor Po's braised pepper-and-ginger ham shanks, Shanghai mahogany duck with raspberry hoisin glaze, Sumatra peppered beef pendang curry, chicken with peanut sauce, and seared fresh catch with hints of Kaffir lime and coconut-chili sauce.

OTHER RECOMMENDATIONS Regulars won't let Chef Chu take the spicy roasted tomato–garlic–crab soup off the menu. You'll want to try the signature dessert: Madame Pele's chocolate volcano, a cone-shaped mound of mousse spouting raspberry coulis and crème anglaise, which arrives at the table amid a cloud of dry-ice smoke announced by a resonating gong. If not, you could have Indonesian coffee bread pudding or "warm soft chocolate cloud in high heaven," among others.

SUMMARY AND COMMENTS Indigo has been a pacesetter in the efforts to class-up Chinatown and to fuse European and Southeast Asian dishes and flavors, and Chu continues to keep it fresh. Located across the park from Hawaii Theatre, it's a perfect spot for a preshow dinner. Romantics might ask for the table screened by greenery and set near a bubbling waterfall. The Garden Bar and Green Room Lounge feature Indigo's famous appetizers from 4 p.m. to midnight.

ENTERTAINMENT AND AMENITIES Live events and music amp up the Green Room lounge and Opium Den on Tuesday through Saturday nights (cover on Saturday for dance bands). On Tuesdays, Wrath of Grapes Wine Club is an ongoing wine-tasting event with light *pupu;* monthly wine dinners are also presented.

Keo's Thai Cuisine in Waikiki ★★★★½

THAI/ISLAND MODERATE QUALITY ★★★★½ VALUE ★★★★ WAIKIKI

Ambassador Hotel, 2028 Kuhio Avenue; ☎ 808-951-9355; www.keosthaicuisine.com

Reservations Recommended. **When to go** Anytime. **Entree range** $12.95–$19.95, set dinners to $44.95. **Payment** All major credit cards. **Service rating** ★★★★½. **Parking** Valet. **Bar** Full service. **Wine selection** Adequate. **Dress** Resort attire. **Disabled access** Good. **Customers** Tourists and Islanders, American and Asian. **Hours** Daily, 4–10:30 p.m.

SETTING AND ATMOSPHERE Creative chef-owner Keo Sananikone designed and decorated this Keo's Waikiki in the same style as his earlier restaurants: teak furnishings, a profusion of Asian and Hawaii artwork, and Keo's signature forest of orchids. In the heart of Waikiki, the restaurant still delivers the peace of a quiet Asian refuge, with indoor and outdoor seating at linen-draped tables surrounded by art, potted palms, and blooms.

HOUSE SPECIALTIES Locally grown catfish, deep-fried crispy with a variety of toppings, and Evil Jungle Prince (Keo's own delicious concoction of shrimp, chicken, or beef in a spicy coconut sauce) are favorites. The menu also features Thai curries of every heat level and description and a full roster of traditional appetizers, such as crispy noodles (*mee krob*), a tangled cloud of fried rice noodles and seasonings; fried spring rolls to enclose in a lettuce leaf with cucumber and sauce; summer rolls in rice paper, with dipping sauce and stuffed Bangkok wings (chicken wings filled with veggies, rice noodles, and chicken, lightly fried), served with *sa-teh* sauce.

OTHER RECOMMENDATIONS Green-papaya salad is the ideal foil with rich curries and fried goodies—crunchy and tart with hot chilis, lime juice, fish sauce, and cold tomatoes. If you're heat sensitive or wary of exotica, try the grilled Cornish game hen, marinated in soy, lemongrass, shallots, garlic, ginger, and honey, just plain wonderful. You can hardly go wrong with any dishes that sound good, as the chef adapts Thai recipes to suit Western tastes, using prime meat, seafood, and poultry, and fresh herbs and produce grown on his own farm.

SUMMARY AND COMMENTS Keo Sananikone, who is actually Laotian and introduced northern Thai food to Hawaii in the early 1980s, might be responsible for the success of Thai restaurants in the Islands, at least, if not the whole U.S. Keo's has received numerous local and national awards, as well as endorsements from Hollywood stars and celebrities, whose pictures line his "Wall of Fame."

La Mer ★★★★★

FRENCH EXPENSIVE QUALITY ★★★★★ VALUE ★★★★★ WAIKIKI

Halekulani, 2199 Kalia Road, Waikiki; ☎ 808-923-2311; www.halekulani.com

Reservations Recommended. **When to go** Sunset for most romantic atmosphere. **Entree range** Prix fixe range $75–$190. **Payment** AE, DC, JCB, MC, V. **Service rating** ★★★★★. **Parking** Valet. **Bar** Full service. **Wine selection** Extensive. **Dress** Dressy attire. **Disabled access** Good, via elevator. **Customers** Hotel guests, Islanders for special occasions. **Hours** Daily, 6–10 p.m.

SETTING AND ATMOSPHERE Serenity and elegance focus your attention on spectacular views of Diamond Head and glowing sunsets over the ocean, interrupted only by the gracious service of haute cuisine prepared by the French chef de cuisine, Yves Garnier. Soft colors, reflecting mirrors, waiters in white dinner jackets, and the best beachfront views at this second-floor, open-air restaurant can keep you dallying over dinner for more than three hours, despite the fact that the service is the best in the Islands.

HOUSE SPECIALTIES Taste the refined power of the kitchen in seasonal dishes, such as a Chilean sea bass paired with pork confit on sauerkraut; roast goose breast with sea salt and lavender honey with butternut squash; and filet mignon of venison with poached pear and salsify croquettes, from a fall menu. La Mer's dinners are offered at set prices for two, three, or four courses plus dessert. A separate vegetarian menu of three courses plus dessert is $75, and a tasting menu is $150 per person for the whole table, available until 9 p.m. A signature appetizer is the trio of fish tartares, a combination of onaga, ahi, and salmon. An appetizer sampler for two is available for an additional $36, and diners can choose Caviar from Aquitaine and accompaniments for an extra $120.

OTHER RECOMMENDATIONS A port with a selection of French cheeses and walnut bread can finish the meal, if you can resist the "Symphonie La Mer" dessert assortment—an array that might include poached pear, almond Napoleon with hazelnut and coffee cream, or candied-chestnut nougat in a chocolate tower. La Mer's soufflés in five different flavors—*lilikoi*, Grand Marnier, banana, chocolate, and coconut—have gained regional fame.

ENTERTAINMENT AND AMENITIES Music drifts up from atrium and outdoor lanai below during dinner hour.

SUMMARY AND COMMENTS This is one of the few Hawaii restaurants where jackets or long-sleeved, collared shirts are required for men. On breezy winter nights when the windows are open, women might also want to bring a light wrap. The menus are written in two languages—English and French. La Mer is Hawaii's only perennial (since 1980) AAA Five Diamond Award restaurant.

Little Village Noodle House ★★★★

CHINESE INEXPENSIVE/MODERATE QUALITY ★★★★ VALUE ★★★★
GREATER HONOLULU

1113 Smith Street, Honolulu; ☎ 808-545-3008;
www.littlevillagehawaii.com

Reservations None. **When to go** Anytime. **Entree range** $9–$19; (print out a coupon from the Web site and take it to dinner for a 10% discount off the special of the week). **Payment** Major credit cards. **Service rating ★★★★.** **Parking** Nearby. **Bar** None. **Wine selection** None. **Dress** Casual, but presentable. **Disabled access** Good. **Customers** Hungry Chinese-food fans. **Hours** Daily, 10:30 a.m.–10:30 p.m. Takeout available.

SETTING AND ATMOSPHERE Clean and bright, with tablecloths and an open window to the kitchen, Little Village makes a rare and somewhat kitschy attempt to create ambience in a Chinese restaurant. The interior resembles a village courtyard, complete with thatched roof, bamboo-like table dividers, artificial willow tree, and a wind-up bird singing in a cage. The restaurant recently expanded next door, creating a private dining room fashioned after a miniature Chinese palace, linked by a footbridge to the original restaurant.

HOUSE SPECIALTIES Steaming hot pots and sizzling platters, such as butterfish with black-bean sauce, clamor for attention as they pass by your table while you're studying the menu and blackboard list of specials. Like heat? Try spicy garlic shrimp or volcano pork chops with a bit of fire in the salt-and-pepper seasoning. Little Village's version of pork and eggplant is augmented with curry and tofu. Chef's specialties include asparagus in black-bean sauce and "sizzling shrimp chili," not to mention sweet honey shrimp with fried walnuts. Classics such as roast duck and Peking duck are also available, in half or whole duck portions.

OTHER RECOMMENDATIONS Try fried rice seasoned with salty fish, or the garlic fried rice, both highly recommended; or especially on a rare wet and windy winter's day, cozy up with the stellar duck noodle soup. But who could pass up Chicken Chive Pot Stickers? For unusual drinks, try Hong Kong–style milk tea or milk coffee, or homemade soy milk.

SUMMARY AND COMMENTS Mandarin, Szechuan, and Cantonese dishes are all represented on this lengthy menu. Chefs will delete MSG at your request, use olive oil for some dishes, and make vegetarian substitutions. They add flavor and flair with spices such as anise, bean, and shrimp pastes.

Michel's at the Colony Surf ★ ★ ★ ★ ½

CONTINENTAL EXPENSIVE QUALITY ★ ★ ★ ★ ½ VALUE ★ ★ ★ WAIKIKI

Colony Surf Condominium, 2895 Kalakaua Avenue, Waikiki;
☎ **808-923-6552**

Reservations Highly recommended. **When to go** Sunset. **Entree range** $36–$49. **Payment** AE, DC, JCB, MC, V. **Service rating** ★ ★ ★ ★ ★. **Parking** Valet. **Bar** Full service. **Wine selection** Extensive, a dozen wines by the glass. **Dress** Resort casual. **Disabled access** Good. **Customers** Tourists, hotel guests, Islanders for special occasions. **Hours** Daily (except Christmas Day), 5:30–9 p.m.

SETTING AND ATMOSPHERE For the romantically inclined, the urban stressed, the business group, and anyone else yearning to breathe free, a table here at the ocean's edge can work magic, melting cares away while flickering torchlights cast shadows on surfers headed home and the lights of Waikiki twinkle all along the crescent of white sand. You may even see the famous green flash on the horizon as the sun sets on the ocean. And that's all before you get to the classic menu.

HOUSE SPECIALTIES Beef Wellington, steak Diane, garlicky escargots, baked lobster—Michel's serves traditional fine fare, in retro or updated versions. You may want to sip a perfectly iced cocktail while you choose between the Hudson Valley foie gras, sautéed and served with carmelized shallots and Armagnac, or frog's legs. Michel's is one of the few restaurants in Hawaii that prepare steak tartare tableside, where the waiters ceremoniously mix in capers and onions, Tabasco, pepper, and Worcestershire sauce, and serve the dish on toast points. Take your time: There's lobster bisque, flamed in Cognac tableside, or Caesar salad, unless you go straight to a rack of lamb cooked to order in a goat cheese and onion crust.

OTHER RECOMMENDATIONS Can't decide? Combination seafood dishes for two, offered iced (lobster, crab legs, sashimi and poke, oysters and shrimp) or steaming (Kona Kampachi, blackened ahi, oysters Rockefeller, prawns, lobster, and abalone). Don't miss the flambéed desserts for two to experience the waiters' tableside artistry one last time: Cherries jubilee, bananas in rum, and strawberries with balsamic vinegar, foie gras, and Cognac, all served with ice cream. White and dark chocolate mousse, *liliko'i* lemon sabayon, orange crème brûlée, sorbets, and tropical martinis are among the heavenly finales.

SUMMARY AND COMMENTS Plan on an extended dining experience; you may want to follow dinner with a snifter of good Cognac.

Nobu Waikiki ★★★★

CONTEMPORARY JAPANESE EXPENSIVE QUALITY ★★★★½ VALUE ★★★★ WAIKIKI

Waikiki Parc Hotel, 2233 Helumoa Road, Honolulu; ☎ 808-237-6999; www.noburestaurants.com

Reservations Recommended. **When to go** Anytime, late night (until midnight). **Entree range** Lunch, $18–$38; omakase tasting menu, $55–$65. Dinner, $32–$40; omakase tasting menu, $75–$95. **Payment** AE, DC, JCB, MC, V. **Service rating** ★★★★★. **Parking** Valet. **Bar** Full service. **Wine selection** Excellent. **Dress** Resort attire. **Disabled access** Good. **Customers** Tourists, Islanders, Nobu fans and occasional celebrities, hotel guests who can get Nobu treats by the pool or by room service. **Hours** Lunch, Monday–Friday, 11:30 a.m.–2 p.m. Dinner, nightly, 6–11 p.m. **Bar** lounge, 5 p.m.–midnight.

SETTING AND ATMOSPHERE "Waikiki chic" is the casual-but-toney decor, which is to say Italian onyx paneling, soaring artistic wall hangings, and splashes of light intended to make all 250 diners look their best. The beach across the street is not the focus here; attention is centered on food, albeit largely from the sea. Acclaimed celebrity Chef Nobu Matushisa of Beverly Hills and partners who include actor Robert DeNiro have expanded Nobu restaurants throughout the world now, including this stylish spot in Waikiki's newly redefined culinary heart—somewhere between the oceanfront Hawaiian elegance of Halekulani, parent of the Waikiki Parc and home of AAA Five-Diamond restaurant, La Mer, and the slick new neighboring Waikiki Beach Walk complex.

HOUSE SPECIALTIES Spectacularly fresh, top-quality sushi and sashimi will please discriminating sushi addicts—and raw fish this good is indeed addictive. However, the Nobu way is to hold back on the sushi and sashimi until after trying cold dishes and then hot dishes (including Washu beef priced by the ounce). Resident diners recognize plantation homestyle dishes such as "black cod saikyo miso" (also known as butterfish misoyaki, a local standard) on this world-class menu, but that's the point—to incorporate local influences and ingredients in Chef Nobu's repertoire, at a gourmet level. Then again, dishes such as duck breast with wasabi salsa, prepared in a brick oven, are brand-new acculturated creativity on the plate.

OTHER RECOMMENDATIONS Stop in for a drink and *pupu* (trio of appetizers) during Nobu's version of happy hour, Pau Hana Nobu, 5–7 p.m. weeknights; the full dinner menu is available at the bar at 5 p.m. for the jetlagged. Vegetarians will find a full selection of treats, such as hearts of palm, lotus root, or avocado tempuras, as well as vegetables or tofu skewered and grilled. The Emporio martini is one to add to your life list—Bombay gin, Hokusetsu sake, lychee, cranberry, and lime juice.

SUMMARY AND COMMENTS Local diners are already accustomed to excellence and creativity in fusion dining, having grown up with Roy Yamaguchi, Alan Wong, and other chefs who defined Hawaii Regional Cuisine. Nobu is not Hawaii Regional, but more Japanese-California fusion. The fun at Nobu is to sample lots of different tastes on small-portion plates izakaya-style, a Japanese version of tapas or pub dining.

Orchids ★★★★½

CONTEMPORARY SEAFOOD   MODERATE/EXPENSIVE   QUALITY ★★★★½
VALUE ★★★   WAIKIKI

Halekulani Hotel, 2199 Kalia Road, Waikiki; ☎ 808-923-2311; www.halekulani.com

Reservations Highly recommended. **When to go** Anytime, dine al fresco on the covered lanai. **Entree range** $23–$58. **Payment** AE, DC, JCB, MC, V. **Service rating** ★★★★. **Parking** Valet. **Bar** Full service. **Wine selection** Extensive. **Dress** Resort attire in daytime, collared shirts for men and evening attire for women at dinner. **Disabled access** Good. **Customers** Tourists, power lunchers, and Islanders. **Hours** Monday–Saturday, 7:30–11 a.m., 11:30 a.m.–2 p.m., and 6–10 p.m.; Sunday, 9:30 a.m.–2:30 p.m. (brunch) and 6–10 p.m.

SETTING AND ATMOSPHERE This lovely, light, and airy open-air setting, decorated profusely with orchids, has a great view of Diamond Head and the passing parade of beachgoers beyond the green lawn.

HOUSE SPECIALTIES Appetizers such as oyster-caviar shooters or Kona crab "cappuccino" with truffle and coconut cream top a menu studded with fresh fish dishes—herb-crusted opah with citrus curry butter; broiled ono with roast garlic, ginger, and soy vinaigrette; steamed onaga with sizzling sesame oil, shiitake mushrooms, green onion, ginger, cilantro, and soy sauce; salmon with edamame and tomato, tangerine, and ginger sauce. Meat dishes include filet mignon, charbroiled veal chop, duck breast with plum sauce, and lamb chops with artichoke hearts.

OTHER RECOMMENDATIONS At lunch, Peking duck and pear salad might catch your eye, or the lobster-crab sandwich with dill dressing on ciabatta bread. More substantial lunches include several fish preparations, Madras seafood curry, or a fancy burger on a brioche bun. Desserts include lemon curd tart or Halekulani's own sorbets in pineapple, guava, *lilikoi*, and lychee flavors. For breakfast, the choices are abundant, ranging from a chorizo-and-cheese omelet on a croissant to a *haupia* French toast sandwich with carmelized fresh pineapple; be sure to try the popovers baked on the premises. For a more moderately priced breakfast and lunch, visit the open-air House Without a Key next door.

ENTERTAINMENT AND AMENITIES For Sunday brunch, 9:30 a.m.-2:30 p.m., a harpist and a flutist play soft classical music in the atrium.

SUMMARY AND COMMENTS Sunset cocktails and live Hawaiian music on the terrace at House without a Key next door, then dinner on the Orchids lanai; that's an evening that's hard to top.

The Pineapple Room by Alan Wong ★★★★½

HAWAII REGIONAL MODERATE/EXPENSIVE QUALITY ★★★★ VALUE ★★★
GREATER HONOLULU

**Third floor of Macy's, Ala Moana Center, Honolulu; ☎ 808-945-6573;
www.alanwongs.com/pineroom**

Reservations Recommended. **When to go** Anytime; early for special rate.
Entree range Lunch, $13.50–$16.75; dinner, $27–$38. **Payment** All major
credit cards. **Service rating** ★★★★. **Parking** Free in the shopping-center lot.
Bar Full service. **Wine selection** Extensive. **Dress** Casual. **Disabled access** Good.
Customers Shoppers, business crowd, tourists. **Hours** Monday–Friday, 11 a.m.–
8:30 p.m.; Saturday, 8 a.m.–8:30 p.m.; Sunday, 9 a.m.–3 p.m.

SETTING AND ATMOSPHERE The Pineapple Room is a real restaurant located in
a department store, but in terms of design and menu, it challenges any
definition of a shopping restaurant. It has its own third-floor entrance at
Ala Moana Center but is also accessible through the store. The contemporary decor is bright and lively. A large exhibition kitchen fills one side
of the room; you can sit at a counter if the tables are full. At dinner, the
stakes rise to fine dining—sweet chili-glazed monchong or duck roasted
with soy and lemongrass, for instance.

HOUSE SPECIALTIES Wong's take on Hawaii Regional Cuisine, which he helped
create, is "comfort food with a local twist" and fresh Island ingredients,
and that's what you'll find here in dinner dishes like Chinese-style
steamed *onaga*, steak with garlic butteryaki fries, and a pork chop or
loin with mango chutney and macadamia-nut crust, apple curry glaze,
and purée of kabocha pumpkin and marscapone cheese.

OTHER RECOMMENDATIONS At lunch, when shopping has sharpened your
appetite, try the *kalua* pig "BLT"; crispy calamari with somen and macadamia nuts; local-style Caesar with Kalua pig or huli-spiced chicken and
lomi tomatoes on top; kim chee Reuben; tempura-fried mahi sandwich;
or locally raised beef burgers. Whatever you eat here, leave room for
dessert. Pastry chef Mark Okumura's chocolate crunch bars, *lilikoi*
cheesecake, homemade tropical ice cream, and *haupia* tapioca halo-halo
are worth it.

SUMMARY AND COMMENTS The Pineapple Room is casual and affordable at
lunch, a good spot to take a break while shopping, but also a pricier dinner destination for diners attracted by the food and willing to eat early.

Prince Court Restaurant ★★★★

CONTEMPORARY ISLAND MODERATE/EXPENSIVE QUALITY ★★★★ VALUE ★★★
WAIKIKI

**Hawaii Prince Hotel, 100 Holomoana Street; ☎ 808-956-1111 or
944-4494; www.princehawaii.com**

Reservations Highly recommended; required for Chef's Studio. **When to go**
Anytime, especially sunset. **Entree range** $37–$57. **Payment** AE, DC, MC, V.
Service rating ★★★★. **Parking** Valet or self-parking in hotel garage. **Bar** Full

service. **Wine selection** Extensive, 20 by the glass. **Dress** Resort attire. **Disabled access** Good, via elevator. **Customers** Islanders, hotel guests, tourists. **Hours** Monday–Saturday, 6–10:30 a.m., 11:30 a.m.–2 p.m., and 5:30–9:30 p.m.; Sunday, 10 a.m.–1 p.m. (brunch) and 5:30–9:30 p.m.

SETTING AND ATMOSPHERE Views through the floor-to-ceiling windows reveal yachts bobbing lazily at the Ala Wai Boat Harbor and sometimes a rainbow over nearby Magic Island. It's reason enough to come for lunch or Sunday brunch.

HOUSE SPECIALTIES Dinner is a choice of three prix fixe menus or an extravagant seafood buffet with separate stations for sushi, soba, and prime rib as well as a full array of cold seafood, fruits, and salads and hot appetizers and entree dishes. The fixed-menu dinners include entrees such as a seafood combo of grilled snapper, prawns, scallops, and lobster with a coconut- saffron sauce, and (its almost equal) poached opakapaka with green grapes and Champagne sauce. Items change frequently, but one dessert standby is chocolate soufflé with vanilla ice cream and crème Anglaise.

OTHER RECOMMENDATIONS Baked crab hash–crusted salmon and a trio of Indian-, Thai-, and Hawaiian-style curries might tempt you for lunch, if not a grilled prawn salad with avocado, papaya, and herb vinaigrette. Buffet and à la carte breakfasts offer a choice of Continental, Japanese, and American classics. Sunday brunch buffets ramp it up with another station or two, adding waffles, omelets, sushi, and soba.

SUMMARY AND COMMENTS Prince Court offers spectacular buffets for breakfast, Sunday brunch, and dinner. Seniors get a periodic break on prices.

Roy's Restaurant Honolulu ★★★★★

**HAWAIIAN FUSION MODERATE/EXPENSIVE QUALITY ★★★★★ VALUE ★★★★
GREATER HONOLULU**

Hawaii Kai Corporate Plaza, 6600 Kalanianaole Highway; ☎ 808-396-7697; www.roysrestaurant.com (Also Roy's Waikiki Beach, 226 Lewers Street, Waikiki Beach Walk; ☎ 808-923-7697; and Roy's Ko Olina, 92-1220 Aliinui Drive, Kapolei; ☎ 808-676-7697)

Reservations Highly recommended. **When to go** Anytime. **Entree range** $25–$33; $35 for seasonal prix fixe menus. **Payment** All major credit cards. **Service rating** ★★★★½. **Parking** Free in adjacent lot. **Bar** Full service. **Wine selection** Extensive, many wines by the glass. **Dress** Casual. **Disabled access** Good, via elevator. **Customers** Islanders and tourists. **Hours** Monday–Thursday, 5:30–9:30 p.m.; Friday, 5:30–10 p.m.; Saturday, 5–10 p.m.; Sunday, 5–9:30 p.m. at Hawaii Kai. Daily, 11 a.m.–11 p.m. at Waikiki Beach Walk. Sunday–Thursday, 11 a.m.–9:30 p.m.; Friday and Saturday, 11 a.m.–10 p.m. at Ko Olina Resort.

SETTING AND ATMOSPHERE At Roy's Restaurant in Hawaii Kai, the original in what is now an international chain, the best tables are those that are farthest from the exhibition kitchen and closest to the floor-to-ceiling windows, which look out over Maunalua Bay and fabulous sunsets nightly. This high-ceilinged restaurant is generally a full and vibrant (translate: noisy) place, a sign, says Chef Roy Yamaguchi, that people are having a good time. Soft pink walls decorated with artwork by Island artists, white tablecloths, and fresh flowers on the table complete the picture.

HOUSE SPECIALTIES An extensive menu of up to 25 daily special items is where Roy's shines brightest. However, it is the classic dishes on the regular side of the menu that underscore Roy's rank at the top of the fusion lineup. Eight to ten different fresh fish in myriad preparations are available nightly, including Roy's signature classics: the original blackened ahi with a spicy soy-mustard-butter sauce and the macadamia nut–crusted mahimahi with lobster-butter sauce. Salmon never ran in local waters, but hibachi-style grilled Roy's salmon is among the best anywhere. Grilled Szechuan baby back pork ribs are definitely worth getting your fingers saucy. Crispy Thai chicken stuffed with Chinese noodles and exotic mushrooms, served with chutney and macadamia-nut curry sauce, is also a favorite. You can't leave without a melting-hot chocolate soufflé—outside crispy, inside molten like lava—with ice cream and raspberry coulis.

OTHER RECOMMENDATIONS Don't miss Roy's Canoe, an ample chef's choice appetizer sampler that changes every day and is presented in a canoe—unless you simply can't pass up the "poketini," ahi *poke* in a 'tini glass with wasabi aioli, avocado, and *tobiko*. Heavier entrees include braised short ribs or wood-roasted rack of lamb. Some diners like to confine themselves to the appetizers, perhaps a cassoulet of escargot or teriyaki-glazed duck breast in Chinese black-bean sauce, so they'll have room for dessert.

ENTERTAINMENT AND AMENITIES Various musical entertainers perform in the downstairs lounge on weekends.

SUMMARY AND COMMENTS Chef Roy Yamaguchi can lay claim to starting the Hawaiian fusion trend in 1988, blending European techniques with fresh local ingredients and the bold flavors of Asia and the Pacific Rim. A member of the first Hawaii Regional Cuisine chefs, he is also a genius at creating and running a restaurant chain. This is the first of James Beard Award-winning Chef Roy Yamaguchi's 34-plus restaurants. Yamaguchi, in partnership with Outback Steakhouse, now has outlets across the country, throughout Hawaii and in other countries, yet the restaurant never feels like part of a chain. To Roy's way of thinking, the true fusion is good food with "aloha style of service." Yamaguchi has an unerring sense of flavor and has trained his staff well in maintaining his exceptional standards when he is away tending to his empire.

Sam Choy's Breakfast, Lunch, Crab, and Big Aloha Brewery ★★★

HAWAII REGIONAL   MODERATE/EXPENSIVE   QUALITY ★★★½   VALUE ★★★
WAIKIKI AND GREATER HONOLULU

580 North Nimitz Highway, Honolulu; ☎ 808-545-7979; 449 Kapahulu Avenue, 2nd level, Waikiki (Diamond Head); ☎ 808-732-8645; www.samchoy.com

Reservations Recommended for dinner. **When to go** Anytime, especially en route from the airport. **Entree range** Breakfast, $8–$15; lunch, $11–$36; dinner, $12–$47. **Payment** All major credit cards. **Service rating** ★★★½. **Parking** Valet or nearby lot. **Bar** Full service; a brewmaster at Choy's Big Aloha Brewery within the spacious BLC turns out five special varieties of beer. **Wine selection** Good. **Dress** Casual. **Disabled access** Good. **Customers** Tourists and Islanders, business breakfast and lunch patrons, large family groups. **Hours** Monday–Thursday, 7 a.m.–3 p.m. and 5–9:30 p.m.; Friday and Saturday, 7 a.m.–4 p.m. and 5–10 p.m.; Sunday, 7 a.m.–4 p.m (brunch) and 5–9:30 p.m.

SETTING AND ATMOSPHERE Breakfast, Lunch, and Crab has a lively, happy atmosphere, with an exhibition kitchen, showcases full of fresh seafood, and stainless-topped tables. It's a big restaurant with fun touches, like a fishing *sampan* with tables in it, and a fountain or two in the middle of the dining room so you can rinse your hands conveniently after ripping into cracked crab legs.

HOUSE SPECIALTIES The focus is on seafood, with oysters on the half shell, half a dozen preparations for the daily catches, massive portions of Alaskan king crab legs and several imported crab varieties, and lobster served steamed, roasted with garlic, or as part of a clambake. Steaks, ribs, and other meats are also available.

OTHER RECOMMENDATIONS Try the *poke*, a traditional Hawaiian appetizer of marinated cubes of raw fish served with onions, soy sauce, or seaweed, and various seasonings and oils. Choy, an expert at *poke*, offers it in many preparations—even fried, a different but wonderful dish, especially for those who just can't handle it raw.

SUMMARY AND COMMENTS Nothing says "Aloha!" after a long flight quite as well as stopping at Choy's BLC on the way in from the airport. It's an instant immersion in the Hawaiian way, from the smiling attendant who takes your car to the fruity iced tea or fresh beer, to the *poke* and fried rice and all those Island tastes you've been missing. Larger-than-life chef-owner Sam Choy has become an industry in himself, with television shows, cookbooks, and lines of food products.

Sansei Seafood Restaurant and Sushi Bar/
d. k. Steak House ★★★★★

**JAPANESE FUSION MODERATE/EXPENSIVE QUALITY ★★★★★ VALUE ★★★★★
WAIKIKI**

**Waikiki Beach Marriott Resort & Spa, 2552 Kalakaua Avenue, Waikiki;
☎ 808-931-6286 www.sanseihawaii.com**

Reservations Recommended for dinner. **When to go** Anytime. **Entree range**
$16–$42 at Sansei; $19–$33 at d. k. Steak House. **Payment** All major credit
cards. **Service rating** ★★★½. **Parking** Street; valet. **Bar** Full service. **Wine
selection** Extensive list of wines by the glass and premium sakes. **Dress** Dressy
casual. **Disabled access** Good. **Customers** Tourists, Sansei devotees, late-night
club crowd. **Hours** *Dinner:* Daily, 5:30–10 p.m. *Pupu and sushi:* Sunday–Thursday,
5–10 p.m.; Friday and Saturday, 5 p.m.–2 a.m.

SETTING AND ATMOSPHERE   Owner D. K. Kodama divided a large space (formerly Acqua and, before that, Third Floor) into two 130-seat restaurants
separated by a bar. He moved his Sansei restaurant and sushi bar from
its former location at Restaurant Row into one half and opened d. k.
Kodama Steak House in the other—alter egos in a sense, because Sansei
presents hip, creative, futuristic East-meets-West dishes, and the steak
house has a retro approach, bringing back the classics of the genre.

HOUSE SPECIALTIES   Appetizers and New Wave Sushi are designed for sharing and illustrate the Sansei philosophy that dining should be fun.
Award winners include rock shrimp cake with ginger-lime-chili butter
and cilantro pesto, mango salad crab roll, and calamari salad in a crispy
wonton basket with a sweet, spicy sauce. Panko-crusted ahi sashimi,
with arugula wrapped around the ahi instead of dried *nori* seaweed,
comes with wasabi-soy butter sauce. "New Looks" include tempters
like moi sashimi rolled around sweet Maui onion and pickled gobo with
aioli, topped with flying-fish roe and a hint of habanero.

OTHER RECOMMENDATIONS   Sweet plates include macadamia-nut tempura
fried ice cream and hot apple tart. d. k. Steak House features dry-aged
beef in seven different steaks in various sizes and sauces, a fresh catch
and other seafood entrees and appetizers such as a shrimp cocktail,
cheesy garlic focaccia bread, and desserts that include homemade
banana bread pudding.

SUMMARY AND COMMENTS   Kodama is one of Hawaii's most charismatic and
ambitious chefs. His original Maui restaurant perfected his formula of
bold, colorful dishes that invite smiles.

Sarento's Top of the "I" ★★★½

ITALIAN EXPENSIVE QUALITY ★★★★ VALUE ★★★ WAIKIKI

**Renaissance Ilikai Waikiki Hotel, 1777 Ala Moana Boulevard, Waikiki;
☎ 808-955-5559; www.ilikaihotel.com/sarentos.html**

Reservations Recommended. **When to go** Anytime you can see the view. **Entree
range** $27–$39. **Payment** AE, D, DC, JCB, MC, V. **Service rating** ★★★★. Valet or

self-park in garage. **Bar** Full service. **Wine selection** Extensive. **Dress** Dressy resort attire. **Disabled access** Adequate, via elevator. **Customers** Tourists and Islanders. **Hours** Sunday–Thursday, 5:30–9 p.m.; Friday and Saturday, 5:30–9:30 p.m.

SETTING AND ATMOSPHERE The ride in the glass-sided elevator is just a sample of the view from the top in your private booth–a panorama of the sea, Ala Wai Boat Harbor, Waikiki lights, and the beach and Diamond Head.

HOUSE SPECIALTIES The signature dish is veal osso buco, but seafood lovers will be interested in the shellfish cioppino.

OTHER RECOMMENDATIONS Homemade pastas, particularly the lobster ravioli, and pizza from a wood-burning oven are enticing.

SUMMARY AND COMMENTS Part of a local chain, Sarento's offers a fine wine cellar to complement dinner.

ENTERTAINMENT AND AMENITIES Live piano music Tuesday–Saturday; late-night bar until midnight on weekends.

Singha Thai Cuisine ★★★

THAI MODERATE QUALITY ★★★★ VALUE ★★★★ WAIKIKI

Canterbury Place, 1910 Ala Moana Boulevard, Waikiki; ☎ 808-941-2898; www.singhathai.com

Reservations Highly recommended. **When to go** Anytime. **Entree range** $16–$32. **Payment** AE, DC, JCB, MC, V. **Service rating** ★★★★½. **Parking** Free with validation in Canterbury Place lot. **Bar** Full service. **Wine selection** Extensive. **Dress** Casual. **Disabled access** Good. **Customers** Tourists. **Hours** Daily, 4–10 p.m.

SETTING AND ATMOSPHERE After dark Singha's exotic magic emerges. During dinner, lights twinkle on the restaurant's mirrors and golden Buddha, and a fountain splashes in the open-air patio dotted with orchids. Outdoor patio seating at umbrella tables is right next to the street but set at a lower level and surrounded by a wall so that it feels like a private garden.

HOUSE SPECIALTIES One of Chef Chai's original recipes from Bangkok is the spicy Siamese fighting fish (not the betas of your fish tank) fried whole and served with chili-lime sauce. Blackened ahi summer rolls with a soy-ginger-sesame dipping sauce and shredded green mango successfully combine Hawaii regional and Thai cuisine. Seafood lovers go for the grilled jumbo black tiger prawns with Thai peanut sauce, or lobster tail with Singha's signature Thai chili, ginger, and light black-bean sauce.

OTHER RECOMMENDATIONS Sampling menus for two to five people are composed of an appetizer sampler plus an ample variety of entrees and rice, plus dessert, for $34.95 per person.

ENTERTAINMENT AND AMENITIES Thai dancers in extravagant headdresses and colorful silk costumes perform on a tiny stage nightly, while rose petals float through the air.

SUMMARY AND COMMENTS Award-winning cuisine blends Hawaii Regional elements with Bangkok-style dishes. The food of celebrity chef-owner Chai Chaowasaree is a work of art (melons might be carved into flower shapes, for example) that balances fresh Island ingredients and flavors with Thai spices, fresh herbs, and reduced sauces. While the prices are steep at his other restaurant—Chai's Island Bistro at Aloha Tower Marketplace—Singha is a relative bargain.

Tango Contemporary Café ★★★★

**CONTEMPORARY MODERATE QUALITY ★★★★ VALUE ★★★★
GREATER HONOLULU**

**Hokua Building, 1288 Ala Moana Boulevard, Greater Honolulu;
☎ 808-593-7288; www.tangocafehawaii.com**

Reservations Recommended for dinner and holidays. **When to go** Anytime. **Entree range** Lunch, $5.50–$13.50; Dinner, $14.50–$23.50. **Payment** AE, D, DC, JCB, MC, V. **Service rating** ★★★★. **Parking** Garage, validated. **Bar** Limited. **Wine selection** Good. **Dress** Resort or business attire. **Disabled access** Good. **Customers** Islanders and visitors. **Hours** Monday–Friday, 7–10 a.m., 11 a.m.–2 p.m., 5–9:30 p.m.; Saturday–Sunday, 8–10:30 a.m., 11 a.m.–4:30 p.m., 5–9:30 p.m.

SETTING AND ATMOSPHERE Tango's cool, spare Scandinavian design—a row of faux birches and reeds to divide diners, Marimekko fabric wall panels—is as refreshingly untropical as an ice sculpture in this small (55 seats), tall space in a swanky new condominium tower complex.

HOUSE SPECIALTIES Crispy duck breast in a spiced wine sauce, sautéed moi with tomato-fennel coulis over ratatouille, sirloin steak on a smoky cedar plank, and five-spice braised beef are among the offerings. One dish celebrates the chef's Finnish heritage: a silky house-cured gravlax, served either with mustard-dill sauce and potato salad or as an openfaced sandwich on Finnish rye bread with Boursin, egg, tomato, and cucumber and mustard-dill sauce. Also available is a roasted beet salad with goat cheese, eggs cucumber, greens, and vinaigrette served with rye bread. Tempura and sushi rolls, among other choices, celebrate Honolulu's heritage.

OTHER RECOMMENDATIONS For an extra $6.50, patrons can opt to add soup or salad and *lilikoi* sorbet to their dinners. Similarly, diners can select a classic hamburger or a Portobello mushroom on a whole wheat–brown rice roll with lettuce, tomato, and onion, or they can pay a little more and add avocado, bacon, cheese, mushrooms, and grilled onions.

SUMMARY AND COMMENTS Partners Tami Orozco and Chef Goran Streng, both alumnae of the Hawaii Prince Hotel where Streng was executive chef, have created a hit the old-fashioned way—by offering straightforward, well-prepared food for reasonable prices.

3660 On The Rise ★★★★

**PACIFIC RIM MODERATE/EXPENSIVE QUALITY ★★★★½ VALUE ★★★
GREATER HONOLULU**

3660 Waialae Avenue, Kaimuki; ☎ 808-737-1177; www.3660.com

Reservations Highly recommended. **When to go** Anytime, except Monday. **Entree range** $24.50–$59. **Payment** AE, D, JCB, MC, V (no checks). **Service rating**

★★★★½. **Parking** Free in garage. **Bar** Full service. **Wine selection** Award-winning, with many by the glass and some great matches for the cuisine. **Dress** Resort or business attire. **Disabled access** Good. **Customers** Islanders and visitors. **Hours** Tuesday–Sunday, 5:30–9 p.m.; closed Monday.

SETTING AND ATMOSPHERE Jade green marble floors, black marble bar, frosted glass panels, and light wood accents set a cool backdrop for this busy restaurant, but don't dampen the din when repeat customers table-hop, chatting with friends.

HOUSE SPECIALTIES Ahi *katsu,* wrapped in *nori,* lightly battered and deep-fried to medium rare, served with wasabi-ginger-butter sauce, is a signature appetizer, but you'll also find ahi poke paired with escargots and served in a wonton basket with onion, tomato, and crunchy seaweed. Entrees include flaky tempura catfish with *ponzu* sauce, rack of lamb with a macadamia nut crust, duck with duck confit spring rolls and orange-hoisin sauce, Chinese steamed snapper, or Angus New York steak. Vegetarians will find daily chef's choice appetizers and entrees. A four-course tasting menu is $40; with wine pairings, $55.

OTHER RECOMMENDATIONS Desserts beckon: warm chocolate soufflé cake with mocha sauce and ice cream or mile-high Waialae pie (vanilla and coffee ice cream, macadamia brittle, caramel, and chocolate sauce). Banana Napoleon features caramel marscapone mousse and sliced bananas between layers of chocolate phyllo. Or try sorbets with fruit and Champagne or a tasty bread pudding du jour.

SUMMARY AND COMMENTS Chef Russell Siu's chic restaurant has won countless awards, yet retains the friendly feel of a neighborhood restaurant. It's outside Waikiki, but the service and food make it worth the trip.

MAUI

Banyan Tree, Ritz-Carlton, Kapalua ★★★★★

PACIFIC REGIONAL EXPENSIVE QUALITY ★★★★★ VALUE ★★★★★ WEST MAUI

One Ritz-Carlton Drive, Kapalua, West Maui; ☎ 808-669-6200; www.ritzcarlton.com

Reservations Highly recommended. **When to go** Sunset. **Entree range** $35–$45. **Payment** AE, D, DC, MC, V. **Service rating** ★★★★★. **Parking** In lot or valet. **Bar** Full service. **Wine selection** Excellent. **Dress** Resort attire. **Disabled access** Adequate. **Customers** Hotel guests, other visitors, and Islanders. **Hours** Tuesday–Saturday, 5:30–9:30 p.m.

SETTING AND ATMOSPHERE Romantic terrace overlooking the sea with extraordinary views; choose between an outdoor lanai with a canopy of stars or tables under a roof, with no walls unless weather demands.

HOUSE SPECIALTIES Cuisines of the Pacific meet in dishes such as chorizo-crusted *opah* with cauliflower, yellow curry, and oyster mushrooms; or Kobe beef rib-eye steak with *kobocha* squash, *mizuna* salad, and sage and rosemary demiglace. The "50-50" features a three-course prix fixe meal with select bottles of wine.

OTHER RECOMMENDATIONS The acculturated theme continues in a pasta dish—house-smoked salmon ravioli with *tobiko* creme. For starters, try one of the dishes with Maui cheeses—goat cheese with lavender strawberries, for example, or roasted beets with feta and quinoa salad. But keep in mind desserts like the chocolate-tasting trio (dark fudge cake, milk-chocolate molten cake, and white chocolate-vanilla sorbet) or pineapple-caramel cake with lavender sorbet and roasted-pineapple carpaccio. An array of tropical sorbets and gelatos is created in-house.

SUMMARY AND COMMENTS Banyan Tree is all you'd expect Ritz-Carlton's five-diamond top dining spot to be—beautiful, romantic, well served, excellent.

Chez Paul's ★★★★½

FRENCH EXPENSIVE QUALITY ★★★★★ VALUE ★★★ CENTRAL MAUI

Highway 30 (6 miles south of Lahaina), Olowalu Village;
☎ **808-661-3843; www.chezpaul.net**

Reservations Highly recommended. **When to go** Dinner seatings. **Entree range** $34–$49. **Payment** AE, D, MC, V. **Service rating** ★★★★★. **Parking** Free in adjacent lot. **Bar** Full service. **Wine selection** Good; wine cellar in restaurant; several ports. **Dress** Resort attire. **Disabled access** Good. **Customers** Celebrities, Islanders, tourists. **Hours** Daily, seatings at 6 p.m. and 8:30 p.m.

SETTING AND ATMOSPHERE "Centrally located in the middle of nowhere," says chef-owner Patrick Callerac, and he's right. But in truth it's just a few miles to Lahaina from this little blink-and-you'll-miss-it roadside restaurant at Olowalu. Classical French Provençal cuisine, but with an Island touch, is served in a cozy setting, just 14 tables and banquettes plus a private room.

HOUSE SPECIALTIES Dishes change seasonally, but several will be fish, such as Pacific salmon carmelized with soy and Grand Marnier, or the fresh catch poached in Champagne with leeks and capers. Duck roasted in black currant sauce and fresh Kona lobster are typical entrees.

OTHER RECOMMENDATIONS Homemade country-style duck pâté is a must-taste appetizer, along with other French classics such as escargots, classic French onion soup, and fresh duck foie gras. Desserts you don't want to miss are crème brûlée served in a Maui pineapple shell and local-banana clafouti (cobbler) with coconut ice cream. Crêpes Suzette are prepared at the table. Cheeses, fresh fruits with crème fra"che and Grand Marnier, and hot, runny chocolate cake might also tempt you.

SUMMARY AND COMMENTS It's absolutely worth the drive, from Maalaea, Wailea or Lahaina, or wherever you are on Maui, to savor the award-winning talent of Callerac, a bright, personable chef, in this cozy (14 tables plus banquettes and a private room) and comfortable spot.

Cilantro Grill ★★★

CONTEMPORARY MEXICAN INEXPENSIVE QUALITY ★★★★ VALUE ★★★ WEST MAUI

170 Papalaua Avenue, Lahaina; ☎ **808-667-5444; www.cilantrogrill.com**

Reservations None **When to go** Anytime **Entree range** Under $10–$14. **Payment** MC, V. **Service rating** ★★★ **Parking** Free lot. **Bar** None **Wine selection** None **Dress** Casual. **Disabled access** Good. **Customers** Islanders and tourists. **Hours** Monday–Saturday, 11 a.m.–9 p.m.; Sunday, 11 a.m.–8 p.m.

SETTING AND ATMOSPHERE Casual and colorful restaurant is located in Old Lahaina Center a block from Front Street. Chef-owner Paris Nabavi left the world of high-toned hotel dining rooms some years back to launch his own creative endeavors—such as this dine-in or take-out Mexican restaurant. "A fresh take on Old Mexico" is the goal, and it is met with fresh, healthy, flavorful dishes with roots not in TexMex but in Mexico's more traditional dishes and delicious handmade street food.

HOUSE SPECIALTIES Lemon-herb-chipotle marinated rotisserie chicken is the signature product—take it home whole or find it tucked into burritos or tacos made to order with fresh corn tortillas. Cilantro pesto and a variety of housemade salsas spice things up. The chunky salsa is called "tom tom"—tomatoes and tomatillos chopped together with avocadoes and onions. For dessert, try Tres Leches—a moist vanilla cream cake with peaches and cinnamon.

OTHER RECOMMENDATIONS Other ingredients for tacos, burritos, salads, and tortas include adobo-roasted pork, margarita shrimp, carne asada (beef), and grilled or battered ono (aka wahoo)—accompanied by Mexican cheeses, pepitos (pumpkin seeds), beans (black, ranchero, or refried), jicama slaw, and pico de gallo.

SUMMARY AND COMMENTS Chef Nabavi was looking for a challenge when he went to Mexico to find out how cooks there produced the tasty dishes of Jalisco and Yucatan. Then he returned home to Maui and set about making authentic dishes affordable and accessible. Cilantro is the result.

Gerard's ★★★★

CONTEMPORARY ISLAND/FRENCH EXPENSIVE QUALITY ★★★★ VALUE ★★★★
WEST MAUI

Plantation Inn, 174 Lahainaluna Road, Lahaina; ☎ 808-661-8939; www.gerardsmaui.com

Reservations Recommended. **When to go** Anytime. **Entree range** $32.50–$46.50. **Payment** All major credit cards. **Service rating** ★★★★★. **Parking** In nearby lot. **Bar** Full service. **Wine selection** Award-winning, excellent, many wines by the glass. **Dress** Casual resort attire. **Disabled access** Good for garden-level dining, adequate via back entry for in-house dining. **Customers** Tourists and Islanders for special occasions. **Hours** Daily, 6–8:30 p.m.

SETTING AND ATMOSPHERE Located in a plantation-style inn, Gerard's has the feel of a gracious old home, with flowered wall paper, stained-glass windows, and tables are lit with candle lamps. You can also sit outside on a lanai or garden patio screened with plants.

HOUSE SPECIALTIES Classic French touches include fresh snapper quenelles in sorrel sauce and bistro dishes such as cassoulet and coq au vin, while local influences are evident in the ahi tartare with taro chips and shiitake and oyster mushrooms in puff pastry. Though chef-owner Gerard Reversade changes the menu annually, some constants are the confit of duck with green peas and white beans, as well as the roasted snapper with star anise and savory and fennel fondue in an orange-ginger emulsion.

OTHER RECOMMENDATIONS Girard celebrates "Hawaiian success" by layering macadamia nut meringue with chocolate genache. Weigh that against chocolate mousse profiteroles with raspberry sabayon or (with a day's notice) the pièce de résistance, a baked Kilauea volcano. An eight-course tasting menu for the whole table is available for $95 per person.

SUMMARY AND COMMENTS In the years since Girard's opened in 1982, Riversade has incorporated lighter sauces and tropical ingredients into traditional dishes, creating his own Hawaiian-French blend. He was an innovator long before Hawaii Regional Cuisine came into being.

kids Haliimaile General Store ★★★★★

**HAWAII REGIONAL MODERATE/EXPENSIVE QUALITY ★★★★★ VALUE ★★★★★
SOUTH MAUI**

**900 Haliimaile Road, Haliimaile; ☎ 808-572-2666;
www.haliimailegeneralstore.com**

Reservations Highly recommended for dinner; required for six or more at lunch. **When to go** Anytime Monday–Friday. **Entree range** $22–$39. **Payment** D, DC, JCB, MC, V. **Service rating** ★★★½. **Parking** In adjacent lot. **Bar** Full service. **Wine selection** Good, many by the glass. **Dress** Casual. **Disabled access** Adequate, via ramp. **Customers** Islanders and tourists. **Hours** Monday–Friday, 11 a.m.–2:30 p.m. and 5:30–9:30 p.m.; Saturday-Sunday, 5:30–9 p.m.

SETTING AND ATMOSPHERE Chef-owner Bev Gannon's Hawaii Regional Cuisine is famous throughout the Islands, but you'll still feel as if you've made a discovery when you search out the restaurant, located in the middle of sugarcane and pineapple fields, partway up the slope of Haleakala. Once a 1920s plantation store, the large, airy, casual and occasionally noisy rooms are now a creative dining destination.

HOUSE SPECIALTIES The crab pizza is legendary for appetizers or lunch. For dinner, check the fish preparations, as they vary every night—blackened ahi with sweet Thai-chili sauce, for instance, or baked wild salmon with spicy tobiko aioli. Seared scallops come with goat cheese cannelloni and lemon cream sauce. As an appetizer, sashimi Napoleon—a crispy wonton layered with smoked salmon, ahi tartare, and sashimi and served with a spicy wasabi vinaigrette—is always in demand. But try a sashimi pizza for a change—a thin flour crust spread with edamame hummus and topped with ahi sashimi, sesame seeds, and a drizzle of soy-sesame aioli. Hunan-style rack of lamb keeps Islanders coming back for more.

OTHER RECOMMENDATIONS *Paniolo* ribs done with a secret lime barbecue sauce and coconut seafood curry are also popular. For dessert, what could be better, in the middle of a pineapple field, than pineapple upside-down cake, unless it's *liliko'i* brulèe in an almond-brittle cup over fresh berries. Not only is there a special menu for kids, but the kids get a special cocktail menu, too. How about a Green Gecko (kiwi soda) or a Baby Blue Whale (lemonade with blue oranges)?

SUMMARY AND COMMENTS Gannon was one of two women among the founding members of the Hawaii Regional Cuisine movement. The award-winning chef also runs a catering service, two Wailea restaurants— Seawatch at the Wailea Golf Club and Joe's Place at the Wailea Resort tennis complex, and has a hand in Lanai City Grille on neighboring Lanai.

Hula Grill Kaanapali ★★★★

HAWAII REGIONAL MODERATE QUALITY ★★★★ VALUE ★★★★   WEST MAUI

Whalers Village, 2435 Kaanapali Parkway, Kaanapali; ☎ 808-667-6636; www.hulagrill.com

Reservations Recommended for dinner. **When to go** Anytime, but especially sunset on the lanai. **Entree range** Barefoot Bar, $9.50–$18; Dining room, $18–$30. **Payment** AE, D, DC, MC, V. **Service rating** ★★★★. **Parking** Validated, in shopping center garage. **Bar** Full service. **Wine selection** Good, many wines by the glass. **Dress** Casual. **Disabled access** Good. **Customers** Tourists and Islanders. **Hours** Daily, 11 a.m.–10:30 p.m. (pizzas, salads, and sandwiches served through the day in the casual Barefoot Bar area); dinner, 5–9:30 p.m.

SETTING AND ATMOSPHERE Hula Grill is oceanfront and center at Whaler's Village in the Kaanapali Beach Resort. Charming and comfortable, it brings to mind a 1930s-style Hawaiian plantation home, with an open-air lanai on the beach and the interior dining room in nostalgic decor, the entry done up like a library in warm koa wood paneling and filled with Hawaiian memorabilia. An exhibition kitchen allows you to watch the chefs if there's a wait for a table. The Barefoot Bar outdoors serves drinks, lunch, and light dinner at a bar and some lanai tables under roof, plus some tables with umbrellas set right in the sand.

HOUSE SPECIALTIES Chef Peter Merriman makes certain that even the cheeseburgers are special at Hula Grill. For starters you can order a shrimp cocktail with Thai lemongrass, lime, and ginger; dim sum, such as scallop and lobster pot stickers, served in bamboo steamer baskets; sashimi or *poisson cru*. Dinner entrees include macadamia nut–roasted fresh mahimahi or other fresh catch, which also can be prepared tandoori style with raita and kiawe grilled with pineapple salsa. Other choices include lemon-ginger roasted chicken, coconut seafood chowder, a Thai curried vegetarian entrée, and a variety of steaks.

OTHER RECOMMENDATIONS At lunch this is a great place to cool off and enjoy a casual lunch, maybe a warm focaccia chicken sandwich with Monterey Jack cheese, roasted poblano pepper, avocado, and tomato–chili pepper aioli. Try an Indonesian *gado gado* salad, with chilled vegetables and brown rice in a Thai peanut dressing or Island-style fish and chips. Pizzas topped with Puna goat cheese, spinach, tomato, and mushrooms come hot from the *kiawe* wood–fired oven. You might not want to share your order of Hula Grill's famous dessert—a homemade vanilla ice-cream sandwich, made with two chocolate macadamia-nut brownies.

ENTERTAINMENT AND AMENITIES It's easy to slip off the beach for a Lava Flow, a piña colada–like drink made with fresh coconut, pineapple juice, and rum, and topped with a strawberry "eruption," during happy hour, when a guitarist and vocalist entertain from 3 to 5 p.m. Hawaiian musicians return during dinner hour from 6:30 to 9 p.m., joined by hula dancers around 7 p.m.

SUMMARY AND COMMENTS Merriman is a founder of Hawaii Regional Cuisine, and his expertise is reflected in Hula Grill. The restaurant, a tasty combination of Maui casual and beachfront fine dining, can accommodate parties of up to 350 people. You will eat well here.

I'o ★★★★½

HAWAII REGIONAL EXPENSIVE QUALITY ★★★★½ VALUE ★★★ WEST MAUI

505 Front Street, Lahaina; ☎ 808-661-8422; www.iomaui.com

Reservations Recommended. **When to go** Sunset for great views. **Entree range** Dinner $30–$39. **Payment** AE, DC, JCB, MC, V. **Service rating** ★★★★½. **Parking** Free in lots. **Bar** Full service. **Wine selection** Carefully chosen to complement the food; suggested pairings by the glass. **Dress** Casual. **Disabled access** Adequate. **Customers** Tourists and Islanders. **Hours** Daily, 5:30–10 p.m.

SETTING AND ATMOSPHERE Sunset views are exceptional from the outdoor tables set amid tropical plants on a beachfront lanai. But the three-island ocean vista is also fine from the airy interior: A small, bright, modern setting of pale-blond woods and stainless steel, fanciful light fixtures that resemble bouquets of multicolored flowers, concrete floors, and aqua trim reflecting the artful focus of the decor. Two huge sea-scene murals of etched pale-aqua glass appear to be aquariums. One allows a glimpse of chefs at work on the other side.

HOUSE SPECIALTIES East meets West in dishes such as the I'o crab cake, made with crab and goat cheese, crusted with panko crumbs and served with red beet pepper and a miso aioli with green papaya slaw. Several Island fish are featured daily in a variety of preparations, including one that delivers pan-roasted fish with lemongrass pesto and tomato over sautéed cucumber and dill, with truffle oil and goat-cheese fondue sauce.

OTHER RECOMMENDATIONS A cut beyond the steak house, I'o's grilled filet mignon comes with Maui onions and Asian mushroom in a veal demiglace sauce. Vegetarians will delight in the sesame-crusted tofu with polenta and root vegetables.

ENTERTAINMENT AND AMENITIES Live jazz is featured at 505 Front Street, Thursday–Saturday nights, 9 p.m.–midnight.

SUMMARY AND COMMENTS Executive chef–owner James McDonald, voted best chef on Maui, also owns and operates Pacific'O next door, reviewed on page 408, and the Feast at Lele, a gourmet luau held beachfront at sunset, with food prepared at I'o. McDonald's eight-acre vegetable farm in Kula supplies the eateries with some of their fresh green ingredients.;

Kimo's ★★★

STEAK AND SEAFOOD MODERATE QUALITY ★★★ VALUE ★★★★ WEST MAUI

845 Front Street, Lahaina; ☎ 808-661-4811; www.kimosmaui.com

Reservations Recommended for dinner. **When to go** Anytime; early, if you want to sit outside upstairs—it's first come, first seated. **Entree range** Lunch, $8–$13; dinner, $18–$35. **Payment** AE, D, DC, JCB, MC, V. **Service rating** ★★★½. **Parking** Limited on-street or use Lahaina Center lot and walk a couple of blocks. **Bar** Full service. **Wine selection** Good. **Dress** Casual. **Disabled access** Access to the main dining room upstairs is inadequate for wheelchairs, but seating is available downstairs in a dining area near the bar. **Customers** Tourists, some Islanders **Hours** Daily, 11 a.m.–3:30 p.m., 3:30–5 p.m. (*pupu*), and 5–10:30 p.m. The bar is open until 1:30 a.m.

SETTING AND ATMOSPHERE This two-level restaurant is a casual place where it's easy to drop by for lunch or a cocktail downstairs at sunset, then find your way upstairs for dinner. Kimo's takes full advantage of its ocean's-edge setting, with an open lanai perched one story above the rocks and lapping waves. Signal flags lend a sailing motif, and tropical foliage adds an Island touch. At night, flaming torches cast flickering shadows on the spreading limbs of a monkey pod tree. You can order from the full menu or a lighter menu at the bar, which seats 22 downstairs.

HOUSE SPECIALTIES Kimo's fresh fish might be ono, ahi, onaga, au, mahi, opah, or opakapaka, depending on what comes in. Of four preparations, Kimo's Style—baked in garlic, lemon, and sweet basil glaze—has widespread approval.

OTHER RECOMMENDATIONS Meat eaters swear by the prime rib, but fence-sitters are likely to choose the top sirloin and Tahitian shrimp (touched up with a bit of garlic and cheese) combination. Consider a light lunch, such as the Wo Hing Salad with wontons, peanuts, and sesame dressing, plus chicken or fish, and then you can top it off with the dessert that sailors swim to shore for—the original hula pie, a wedge of vanilla–macadamia nut ice cream in an Oreo-cookie crust.

ENTERTAINMENT AND AMENITIES Kimo's is the place to be Friday and Saturday nights from 10 p.m. to midnight, for live rock and roll. Live Hawaiian music sets the mood Monday through Friday, from 7 to 8 p.m.

SUMMARY AND COMMENTS Kimo's, in the heart of touristy Lahaina, delivers just what many people are looking for on Maui—good, fresh fish and steaks, a drop-dead view, fun drinks, and music. Kimo's entrees come with Caesar salad, carrot muffins, sour cream rolls, and steamed herb rice.

Ko ★★★★

CONTEMPORARY HAWAIIAN EXPENSIVE QUALITY ★★★★ VALUE ★★★ SOUTH MAUI

Fairmont Kea Lani, 4100 Wailea Alanui, Wailea, South Maui;
☎ 808-875-4100; www.fairmont.com/kealani

Reservations Recommended. **When to go** Anytime. **Entree range** $31–$50. **Payment** AE, DC, MC, V. **Service rating** ★★★★. **Parking** Valet or hotel lot. **Bar**

Full service. **Wine selection** Good. **Dress** Resort wear. **Disabled access** Good. **Customers** Visitors, hotel guests. **Hours** Wednesday–Monday, 5:30–9 p.m.

SETTING AND ATMOSPHERE Alfresco tables are tucked into quiet corners of the Fairmont Kea Lani's expansive outdoor decks and pools, and under a keawe tree and a sky full of stars with tiki torches flickering.

HOUSE SPECIALTIES Maui's plantation legacy is celebrated with refined versions of original classics that the sugarcane workers brought from their Hawaiian, Chinese, Filipino, Portuguese, Korean, and Japanese cultures. (*Ko* is Hawaiian for cane.) For instance, offerings include coconut-curry lamb chops, grilled and served with mango mint salsa, or lobster tempura with a trio of sauces—spicy sesame, pineapple sweet chili garlic, and grapefruit soy.

OTHER RECOMMENDATIONS Try "ahi on the rock," a cake of ahi and peppery shichimi spices wrapped with strips of velvety ahi, served with a big, hot rock on which you can sear it to taste, and orange-ginger miso sauce. The recipe for *lumpia* (a thin, crispy spring roll) comes from Chef Pang's own Filipino family cooks. The "*mauka* harvest" salad features treasures of the uplands as residents might have gathered them—fern shoots, hearts of palm, baby lettuce, macadamia nuts, and *lilikoi* vinaigrette.

SUMMARY AND COMMENTS This is a noble effort to present dishes that are true to the heritage or at least the spirit of the Island, but prices are substantially loftier than those of some similar dishes at less romantic local restaurants on all the islands.

Lahaina Grill ★★★★½

CONTEMPORARY AMERICAN EXPENSIVE QUALITY ★★★★½ VALUE ★★★
WEST MAUI

Lahaina Inn, 127 Lahainaluna Road, Lahaina, West Maui;
☎ **808-667-5117; www.lahainagrill.com**

Reservations Highly recommended. **When to go** Early or late to avoid the 7 p.m. rush. **Entree range** $29–$48. **Payment** AE, DC, MC, V. **Service rating** ★★★★★. **Parking** On street or in adjacent lot. **Bar** Full service. **Wine selection** Extensive, many by the glass. **Dress** Resort wear. **Disabled access** Good, separate wheelchair access. **Customers** Islanders and tourists. **Hours** Daily, 6–10 p.m.

SETTING AND ATMOSPHERE This lively bistro, located in Lahaina action central, has two dining rooms plus an intimate room for up to eight people for Chef's Table dinners. Diners may also eat at the bar. Soft pastels and fresh flowers add a measure of calm to the slightly hectic atmosphere of this popular, consistent award-winner.

HOUSE SPECIALTIES Signature dishes like tequila shrimp with firecracker rice, kalua duck, or appetizer Kona crab cakes compete with the macadamia-nut smoked pork chop for your attention at dinner. Kona coffee–roasted rack of lamb, Chef Arnie's meatballs on penne pasta, and Keahole lobster are among the choices. Vegetarian entrees include four-cheese manicotti and grilled polenta with vegetables.

OTHER RECOMMENDATIONS Starters like king crab ravioli with mascarpone tomato sauce and crispy-fried chile rellenos stuffed with prawns, cheese, and scallops will challenge your ability to save room for dessert—a luscious triple-berry pie of raspberries, blueberries, and black currants topped with whipped cram, perhaps, or lime tart, or the sunken chocolate cake with coffee ice cream. A tasting menu is offered for two or more ($76 per person). Bring the kids—they can choose gourmet corn dogs, pasta, veggies, fish and shrimp, and burgers, before sweet-treat desserts.

SUMMARY AND COMMENTS If you'd like a quiet little table for a romantic dinner, ask for tables 28, 29, or 34. These tables for two are tucked into an out-of-the-way corner of the restaurant, where you can check out the action in the dining room, but the action can't check you out.

Longhi's ★★★½

MEDITERRANEAN/ITALIAN   EXPENSIVE   QUALITY ★★★★   VALUE ★★★
WEST MAUI AND SOUTH MAUI

800 Front Street, Lahaina; ☎ 808-667-2288; The Shops at Wailea,
☎ 808-891-8883; www.longhi-maui.com

Reservations Recommended for dinner. **When to go** Anytime. **Entree range** Lunch, $9–$35; dinner, $26–$120 ($40 per pound of lobster). **Payment** AE, D, DC, JCB, MC, V. **Service rating** ★★★. **Parking** Valet at dinner, self-parking in adjacent lot. **Bar** Full service. **Wine selection** Extensive. **Dress** Casual. **Disabled access** Good for downstairs. **Customers** Tourists and Islanders. **Hours** Daily, 7:30–11:30 a.m., 11:45 a.m.–4:45 p.m., and 5–10 p.m.

SETTING AND ATMOSPHERE Both Maui Longhi's have open-air settings with ocean views and casual surroundings. The upper floor in Lahaina has additional tables fanned by trade winds.

HOUSE SPECIALTIES Tempting appetizers include grilled portobello mushrooms with goat-cheese pesto. Follow up with Shrimp Longhi, a classic first served on opening night more than 20 years ago. Plump white shrimp are sautéed in butter, lemon juice, and white wine, then simmered with fresh Maui basil and tomatoes and served on garlic toast. Fresh fish prepared with white wine and grapes is another specialty.

OTHER RECOMMENDATIONS The in-house bakery prepares pastries and breads. House-made pastas, sandwiches like the Peking duck (duck and hoisin sauce on a scallion roll), and fresh salads are available at lunch and dinner. Desserts include macadamia-nut pie à la mode or chocolate soufflé with a hot flowing center.

ENTERTAINMENT AND AMENITIES Live bands play music for dancing upstairs on Friday nights in Lahaina, from 9:30 p.m. until closing.

SUMMARY AND COMMENTS Created in 1976 by Bob Longhi, "a man who loves to eat," Longhi's finally succumbed to customer pressure and put some of its offerings on a printed menu as well as the traditional verbal menu recited by servers. At Lahaina the adjacent street scene gets a little trafficky; at Wailea, surroundings are more refined.

Maalaea Waterfront Restaurant ★★★½

SEAFOOD/CONTINENTAL MODERATE/EXPENSIVE QUALITY ★★★★½ VALUE ★★★
CENTRAL MAUI

50 Haouli Street, Maalaea; ☎ 808-244-9028;
www.waterfrontrestaurant.net

Reservations Highly recommended. **When to go** Anytime. **Entree range** $26–$38, not including market-priced fish and game. **Payment** AE, D, DC, JCB, MC, V. **Service rating** ★★★½. **Parking** Free in adjacent condominium garage. **Bar** Full service. **Wine selection** Extensive. **Dress** Resort attire. **Disabled access** Adequate, via elevator. **Customers** Islanders and tourists. **Hours** Daily, 5 p.m.–closing.

SETTING AND ATMOSPHERE This oceanfront restaurant has Island landscape paintings on the walls and outdoor dining on the deck.

HOUSE SPECIALTIES Depending on what the fishermen bring in at the neighboring harbors, a dozen different kinds of Island fish are served daily in your choice of nine preparations. This means plenty of choices to make while you nibble on homemade Maui onion bread spread with special beer-cheese. You might start with lobster chowder.

OTHER RECOMMENDATIONS Prime rib and rack of lamb share the meaty menu with game meats, with a changing chef's choice of venison, pheasant, or ostrich. For dessert, the award-winning white chocolate–blueberry cheesecake tops the rich selections, all made at the restaurant.

SUMMARY AND COMMENTS Maalaea Waterfront Restaurant, opened in 1990, is a family endeavor.

Mala, An Ocean Tavern and Mala Wailea ★★★★

CONTEMPORARY MODERATE/EXPENSIVE QUALITY ★★★★ VALUE ★★★★★
WEST MAUI AND SOUTH MAUI

1307 Front Street, Lahaina ☎ 808-667-9394; www.malaoceantavern
.com; Mala Wailea at the Wailea Beach Marriott Resort, 3700 Wailea
Alanui, Wailea, ☎ 808-875-9394; www.malawailea.com

Reservations Suggested. **When to go** Anytime. **Entree range** Dinner, $21–$38. **Payment** All major credit cards. **Service rating** ★★★★. **Parking** Tavern, adjacent lot or across the street at Lahaina Cannery Mall; hotel valet or lot, Wailea. **Bar** Full service. **Wine selection** Awesome, extensive by the glass. **Dress** Casual. **Disabled access** Adequate. **Customers** Tourists and Islanders. **Hours** Monday–Friday, 11 a.m–10 p.m.; 9 a.m.–10 p.m. Saturday, 9 a.m.–9 p.m. Sunday.

SETTING AND ATMOSPHERE The Tavern is an unpretentious, hip plantation-style waterfront wine bar eatery celebrating the genius of one of the original Hawaii Regional Cuisine chefs, Mark Ellman. At Wailea, every seat in the house or out on the lanai has an ocean view, and sunsets, framed by Lanai and Kahoolawe, are magnificent. Did we mention whales? They hang out around here too in winter.

HOUSE SPECIALTIES Many small plates allow you to sample the chefs' considerable talent. The menu changes frequently and emphasizes organic, healthy dishes and local ingredients prepared with Latin, Mideastern, or Asian flavors. Look for steamed clams with ginger–garlic–black bean sauce, or spicy lamb in a pita, or miso-glazed opakapaka with pickled ginger. Cheeseburgers are made of Kobe beef. For dessert, hail the return of the real Caramel Miranda, a dessert platter stacked with macadamia-nut ice cream, piled with tropical fruit and drizzled with caramel.

OTHER RECOMMENDATIONS Vegetarians will be pleased to find on the Wailea menu vegan items such as white bean soup with white truffle oil and flaxseed lavosh or gado gado salad with coconut-peanut sauce. Crunchy calamari with aioli, seared sashimi with shiitake ginger sauce, and rich potato soup are among the offerings at the Tavern, along with flatbread, a thin crust bearing shrimp, cilantro pesto, and grape tomatoes. Sweets include the Key lime martini and *lilikoi* panna cotta with figs.

SUMMARY AND COMMENTS Ellman also runs Penne Pasta, an excellent inexpensive pasta house in Lahaina, with dinner nightly and lunch on weekdays, 180 Dickenson Street, ☎ 808-661-6633. At Wailea, executive chef Corey Waite oversees the kitchen, and the wine list is not to be believed, with great choices ranging from a bubbly $25 kava to a breathtaking $2,700 1980 La Tache. Celebrity backers such as Clint Eastwood and Alice Cooper increase the chances of seeing someone enchanting across the crowded room.

Mama's Fish House ★★★★

SEAFOOD EXPENSIVE QUALITY ★★★★½ VALUE ★★★   WEST MAUI

799 Poho Place, Kuau; ☎ 808-579-8488; www.mamasfishhouse.com

Reservations Highly recommended. **When to go** Anytime, but sunset is most romantic. **Entree range** Lunch $28–$54, dinner $34–$115. **Payment** AE, D, DC, JCB, MC, V. **Service rating** ★★★★. **Parking** Valet or adjacent lot. **Bar** Full service. **Wine selection** Award-winning, extensive. **Dress** Casual resort wear. **Disabled access** Good, but it's a walk from the lot. **Customers** Tourists and Islanders **Hours** Daily, 11 a.m.–2 p.m. and 4:45–9:30 p.m.; *pupu,* 12:30–4:30 p.m.; closed Christmas Day.

SETTING AND ATMOSPHERE Mama's is a rambling, open-air beach house on Maui's North Shore, beside the ocean, with cool green lawns and shady coconut palms to frame the vista. The bar and paneling inside are tropical almond, monkey pod, and mango wood. It's a place to while away an afternoon over a Mai Tai Roa Ae—a fresh fruit–and–rum concoction like that originated by Trader Vic years ago—or to sample other oldfashioned tropical drinks, like Singapore Slings of Raffles Hotel fame.

HOUSE SPECIALTIES In Mama's proud tradition, fresh catches of the day are identified by the fishermen who caught them and where and how they were caught, and the fish is always top-notch. Preparations include sautéed with garlic butter, white wine, and capers; grilled with Thai red curry; fried with Maui onion, chili pepper, and avocado; or served with honey-roasted macadamia nut–lemon sauce. A signature dish, Pua me hua Hana, features sautéed fish with fresh coconut milk and lime juice served surrounded by tropical fruit and Molokai sweet potatoes.

OTHER RECOMMENDATIONS For dinner, the *laulau* is non-traditional but delicious, a bundle of mahimahi baked in *ti* leaves with mango and coconut milk and served with tender *kalua* pig, *lomilomi* salmon, and *poi*. Another imaginative entree with local flair is crispy *kalua* duck with mango-*mui* glaze. Local lobster tails, bouillabaisse, and New York steak, cut from beef raised on the Big Island, are also served.

SUMMARY AND COMMENTS The open-air, old Hawaii–style area near the entrance called "Grandma's Living Room" is a popular spot to listen to music and nibble on appetizers. This prize-winning restaurant, situated near the world-class windsurfing destination Hoopika Beach, serves what is reputedly Maui's most expensive fish dinners. But a lot of patrons seem to feel it's worth the tab to eat here.

Pacific'O ★★★★½

HAWAII REGIONAL MODERATE/EXPENSIVE QUALITY ★★★★½ VALUE ★★★
WEST MAUI

505 Front Street, Lahaina; ☎ 808-667-4341; www.pacificomaui.com

Reservations Recommended. **When to go** Anytime. **Entree range** Lunch, $9.50–$15.50; dinner, $30–$40. **Payment** AE, DC, JCB, MC, V. **Service rating** ★★★★. **Parking** Free in lot across the street. **Bar** Full service. **Wine selection** Excellent. **Dress** Casual. **Disabled access** Adequate, but it's a long way from the parking lot. **Customers** Tourists and Islanders. **Hours** Daily, 11:30 a.m.–4 p.m. and 5:30–10 p.m.

SETTING AND ATMOSPHERE This is a pleasant spot for indoor or outdoor dining at shaded tables set a stone's throw from the ocean. Inside, ceiling fans stir the air above a long bar, and tables by big windows open wide to the ocean breezes and three-island view.

HOUSE SPECIALTIES You'll see why chef-owner James McDonald has won awards for his appetizers of prawns and basil wontons served with a spicy sweet-and-sour sauce and Hawaiian salsa; and for crispy coconut rice rolls with seared scallops, arugula pesto, and yuzu lime sauce. And also for hapa-hapa tempura—two hunks of ahi wrapped in nori, tempura fried medium rare and served with miso sauce and lime-basil dressing.

OTHER RECOMMENDATIONS Roast rack of lamb is flavored with tahini, tamarind, and mint and served with roasted garlic aioli. The mixed grill is a pork chop and scallops done with oyster garlic sauce and arugula pesto. *Vegetarian alert:* The Leaning Tower of Tofu features organic tofu grilled with spicy soy sauce, stir-fried greens, salsa, rice, wasabi aioli, and ginger *ponzu* sauce.

ENTERTAINMENT AND AMENITIES Friday and Saturday nights, 9 p.m.–midnight, the indoor-outdoor restaurant at ocean's edge attracts jazz aficionados with live jazz performances.

SUMMARY AND COMMENTS McDonald also owns I'o, an artfully hip modern restaurant next door (see page 402), and The Feast at Lele, a luau production and beachfront neighbor. McDonald's own farm provides greens, herbs, fruits, and vegetables for the restaurants.

Plantation House Restaurant ★★★½

HAWAII REGIONAL EXPENSIVE QUALITY ★★★★ VALUE ★★★   WEST MAUI

**Kapalua Resort, Plantation Course Clubhouse, 2000 Plantation Club Drive;
☎ 808-669-6299; www.theplantationhouse.com**

Reservations Recommended for dinner. **When to go** Anytime you can see the smashing view. **Entree range** Lunch, $10–$18; dinner, $27–$42. **Payment** AE, DC, MC, V. **Service rating ★★★**. **Parking** In adjacent lot. **Bar** Full service. **Wine selection** Extensive. **Dress** Casual. **Disabled access** Good, drop off at front door. **Customers** Golfers, tourists, and Islanders. **Hours** Daily, 8 a.m.–3 p.m., 3–5 p.m. (light menu), and 5:30–9 p.m.

SETTING AND ATMOSPHERE Location, location: high above the shoreline, diners in this not-your-average-golf-club restaurant can admire sweeping views of moody Molokai, wind-whipped blue ocean, green fairways and the rest of Kapalua Resort through windows open to cool upland breezes. The decor is a blend of swanky and casual, as befits the well-heeled golfers, with lots of rattan and tropical woods setting off a large mural of pineapple workers in the Kapalua fields. A double-sided fireplace creates a warm glow to ward off any evening chill up on the lower slope of Puu Kukui.

HOUSE SPECIALTIES Fresh fish comes dressed for dinner in many styles, including an Oscar with asparagus, crabmeat, and lemon-butter sauce and an Italian-style ahi with arugula, cannellini bean, and cucumber salad, olives, and caper salsa. Diners can substitute tofu for fish in any of the featured preparations or request other meatless entrees. A full roster of eggs Benedicts tops the breakfast-lunch menu, including one that could stretch your fusion limits—Cajun-style ahi sashimi Benedict with wasabi hollandaise.

OTHER RECOMMENDATIONS Hearty fare like lamb shanks and mashed potatoes, Australian lobster and filet mignon, and pork tenderloin with port wine and caramelized Maui onion, along with pasta, chicken piccata, vegetarian entrees made to order and weekly market specials round out the dinner selections.

SUMMARY AND COMMENTS Chef Alex Stanislaw created an innovative menu deserving of the spectacular setting, merging Mediterranean flavors and island ingredients. It's a refreshing alternative to the other resort restaurants down below. Kapalua Resort operates a free shuttle to the restaurant.

Roy's Kahana Bar & Grill and
Roy's Kihei Bar and Grill ★★★★

**HAWAII REGIONAL   MODERATE/EXPENSIVE QUALITY ★★★★   VALUE ★★★★
SOUTH AND WEST MAUI**

**Kahana Gateway Shopping Center, 4405 Honoapiilani Highway, Kahana;
☎ 808-669-6999; Piilani Village Shopping Center, 303 Pilikea Street, Kihei;
☎ 808-891-1120; kahana@roysrestaurant.com;
kihei@roysrestaurant.com**

Reservations Highly recommended. **When to go** Anytime. **Entree range** $25–$35. **Payment** AE, D, DC, JCB, MC, V. **Service rating** ★★★★½. **Parking** Free in shopping center lot. **Bar** Full service. **Wine selection** Excellent, 10–15 by the glass. **Dress** Casual. **Disabled access** Good. **Customers** Tourists and Islanders. **Hours** Daily, 5:30–10 p.m. (Kahana); 5:30–9:30 p.m. (Kihei).

SETTING AND ATMOSPHERE Maui's two Roy's both offer the same creative fare, with little difference except geography and setting. (The Kahana restaurant is on the second floor of a small shopping complex; the Kihei restaurant is a new separate building in a small shopping center.) Both are guided by corporate chef Jacqueline Lau with 20 to 25 specials nightly.

HOUSE SPECIALTIES Since specials change so rapidly, you never know what you'll find, but everything is made with the freshest local ingredients, with Eurasian, American, and Hawaiian flavors. Appetizers like Szechuan baby-back ribs or Roy's shrimp-and-pork spring rolls with hot sweet mustard and black-bean sauce set a spicy scene. The lemongrass-crusted *shutome* (swordfish) reflects a touch of Thailand, with sticky rice and basil-peanut sauce.

OTHER RECOMMENDATIONS The left side of the menu is made up of Roy's signature dishes, prepared the same throughout the chain, including standards like hibachi-grilled salmon and slow-braised short ribs. These dishes are proven hits and tend to be less expensive, as well as reliably available. The right side reflects the chefs' daily inspirations, which lean toward Hawaiian.

SUMMARY AND COMMENTS You really can't go wrong with Roy's fusion brand of Hawaiian Regional Cuisine, dishes that are exciting and rarely disappointing. Master chef Roy Yamaguchi is himself a genius in the kitchen, but he has the even rarer skill of picking and training other chefs to guide his far-flung restaurants. His plaudits include countless awards, including that of the James Beard Foundation, and his television cooking show airs in 60 nations.

A Saigon Café ★★★

VIETNAMESE INEXPENSIVE QUALITY ★★★ VALUE ★★★★★ CENTRAL MAUI

1792 Main Street, Wailuku; ☎ 808-243-9560

Reservations Recommended, especially for dinner. **When to go** Anytime. **Entree range** $7–$20. **Payment** AE, D, DC, JCB, MC, V. **Service rating** ★★★★. **Parking** In lot. **Bar** Full service. **Wine selection** Limited. **Dress** Casual. **Disabled access** Good. **Customers** Islanders, celebrity chefs on their days off, a few tourists. **Hours** Monday–Saturday, 10 a.m.–9:30 p.m.; Sunday, 10 a.m.–8:30 p.m. Takeout is available.

SETTING AND ATMOSPHERE Sit at the low wooden bar with rolling chairs, or choose a Formica-topped table or booth in this basic restaurant minimally decorated with Vietnamese carved and lacquered art. A gold statue of Buddha greets guests at the door, ceiling fans whir overhead, and the TV might be on at the bar. It's a low-key hideaway that can be difficult to find because there is no sign. (As you enter Wailuku from Kahului, cross the bridge, take the first right onto Central Avenue, then the first right onto Nani Street, and at the next stop sign look for an "open" sign on a small bungalow with trees in pots flanking the doorway.

HOUSE SPECIALTIES Start with *cha gio* (fried spring rolls), deep-fried bundles of ground pork, rice noodle, carrot, and onion wrapped in rice paper; the waiter will show you how to eat them in leaves of romaine lettuce with mint leaves and vermicelli, then dip them in sweet-sour garlic sauce. A favorite is the *banh hoi chao tom*, known as "shrimp pops burritos" (marinated shrimp, ground, steamed, and grilled on a stick of sugarcane). With 135 items on the menu, it's hard to make a choice, but yours could be the crispy spiced Dungeness crab. Vegetarians will be happy with tofu stuffed with mushrooms and sprouts or rice-paper rolls created at the table from a platter of tofu, noodles, and vegetables.

OTHER RECOMMENDATIONS For lunch, any of the noodle soups—seafood and chicken, calamari and shrimp, wonton, and others—provide a big bowl of steaming goodness. Several rice-in-a-clay-pot dishes are done with chicken, catfish, shrimp, or pork. Among the Vietnamese entrees, garden-party shrimp lightly battered, deep fried, and served with sautéed ginger and green onions on bean sprouts and lettuce is most popular.

SUMMARY AND COMMENTS Proprietor Jennifer Nguyen opened the restaurant in January 1996, but the identifying sign is still in a box somewhere because she's been too busy to put it up.

Sansei Seafood Restaurant and Sushi Bar ★★★★★

JAPANESE FUSION MODERATE/EXPENSIVE QUALITY ★★★★★ VALUE ★★★★
SOUTH MAUI

Kapalua Resort, 600 Office Road, Lahaina; ☎ 808-669-6286;
Kihei Town Center, 1881 S. Kihei Road, Kihei; ☎ 808-879-0004;
www.sanseihawaii.com

Reservations Highly recommended. **When to go** Anytime, early and late for specials. **Entree range** $16–$43. **Payment** AE, D, JCB, MC, V. **Service rating** ★★★★. **Parking** In adjacent lots. **Bar** Full service. **Wine selection** Extensive. **Dress** Resort attire. **Disabled access** Adequate. **Customers** Islanders and tourists. **Hours** Daily, 5:30–10 p.m.; late-night specials, Thursday–Saturday, 10 p.m.–1 a.m.

SETTING AND ATMOSPHERE Booths and tables fill up fast in this intimate restaurant, which includes a sushi bar and cocktail lounge.

HOUSE SPECIALTIES Try several dishes and share. Sansei offers creative sushi ranging from the nearly traditional to crab and mango salad hand roll, spider rolls with soft-shell crab, and bagel rolls with smoked salmon, Maui onion, and cream cheese. Entrees range from Japanese jerk chicken to ginger-hoisin smoked duck breast, grilled ahi and Asian rock-shrimp cake, or *nori* ravioli of shrimp and lobster.

OTHER RECOMMENDATIONS Pay attention when the waiter describes nightly specials like asparagus tempura or choose a simple grilled fresh catch on Kula greens with plum vinaigrette. Granny Smith baked-apple tart is a pure American finish to any meal.

SUMMARY AND COMMENTS Sansei is fun and a gustatory experience to antici-
pate beyond hunger. Maui fans of the Sansei restaurant experience have
embraced the Kihei location, as well as the original Kapalua restaurant,
now housed in a new building near the Honolua Store.

kids **Spago at Four Seasons Resort Maui at Wailea** ★★★★½

HAWAII/CALIFORNIA EXPENSIVE QUALITY ★★★★½ VALUE ★★★ SOUTH MAUI

**Four Seasons Resort Maui at Wailea, 3900 Wailea Alanui, Wailea;
☎ 808-874-8000; www.fourseasons.com**

Reservations Highly recommended. **When to go** Sunset is spectacular. **Entree range** $38–$125; tasting menus, $78–$145. **Payment** AE, D, DC, JCB, MC, V. **Service rating** ★★★★★. **Parking** Complimentary valet or self-parking in covered hotel lot. **Bar** Full service. **Wine selection** Extensive. **Dress** Resort attire, jackets optional. **Disabled access** Good, via elevator. **Customers** Hotel guests and Islanders for special occasions. **Hours** Daily, 6–9 p.m.; bar, 6–11 p.m.

SETTING AND ATMOSPHERE Spago enjoys a spectacular setting, with sweeping
ocean vistas along virtually the entire length of the Wailea coastline, plus
glimpses of Kahoolawe through the coconut palms. The interiors are contemporary Asian in design, focusing on wood, stone, and Asian art.

HOUSE SPECIALTIES Rave notices abound for the ahi poke cone appetizer—spicy
ahi tartare with chili aioli in a sesame-miso cone. Roasted opakapaka with
lobster sauce and grilled mahimahi with pineapple-ginger barbecue sauce
demonstrate Spago's skills with Island fish. The carmelized pork chop
arrives with lomilomi tomatoes, greens, and polenta.

OTHER RECOMMENDATIONS Thai coconut soup with Big Island lobster and
Thai flavors of Kaffir lime, galangal ginger, and chili is a superb starter;
for dessert, who could resist the macadamia-nut ice cream or Maui
mango upside-down cake with *lilikoi* sorbet? Puck's first children's
menu is bound to be a hit with visiting kids: chicken fingers and pizza,
spaghetti, or a classic grilled cheese with fries.

ENTERTAINMENT AND AMENITIES A Hawaiian trio serenades diners with traditional sounds of Hawaii from 7 to 10 p.m. nightly, and a dance floor
beckons romantics. In the adjacent lobby lounge, a guitarist strums
contemporary tunes from 8:30 to 11 p.m.

SUMMARY AND COMMENTS Master chef–owner Wolfgang Puck and his wife
and partner, Barbara Lazaroff, brought their signature style to the
Hawaiian cornucopia in this fine-dining room of a hotel especially popular with southern Californians.

Stella Blues Cafe ★★★★½

AMERICAN MODERATE QUALITY ★★★★ VALUE ★★★★ SOUTH MAUI

**1279 Kihei Road, Azeka II Mall, Kihei; ☎ 808-874-3779;
www.stellablues.com**

Reservations Recommended. **When to go** Anytime. **Entree range** Lunch, $6–$13; dinner, $16–$28. **Payment** Cash, no credit cards. **Service rating** ★★★.

Parking Shopping-center lot. Bar Full service. Wine selection Good. Dress Casual. Disabled access Good. Customers Residents, visitors. Hours Daily, 7:30 a.m.– 11 p.m.

SETTING AND ATMOSPHERE Stella Blues grew from a little vegetarian lunchroom to a large, modern space with curving walls and warm Mediterranean colors, with an exhibition kitchen and bar, where diners can watch chefs at work, and an outdoor lanai. The menu grew, too, to three meals of "new American comfort food."

HOUSE SPECIALTIES The menu takes a something-for-everyone approach with an extensive list of "small plates" ranging from hummus to crab cakes, served from 5 p.m. to midnight; plus pastas, pizzas, fresh fish, and Maui-grown beef, in burgers, steak sandwiches, and steak and eggs. Stella Blues' roots are still evident in dishes such as vegetarian shepherd's pie and tofu curry. For dessert, go light with tropical sorbets or rich with mud pie or *lilikoi* cheesecake.

OTHER RECOMMENDATIONS If you're hungry for breakfast that doesn't cost $20 at the same daily hotel buffet, hop in the car and head here for smoothies and espresso drinks, lox and bagels, or the choice of hungry dawn-patrol surfers—loco moco (a hamburger patty with two eggs, rice, and gravy over all). You can build your own omelet or savor tofu scramble, not to mention eggs with cheese and jalapeños.

SUMMARY AND COMMENTS Takeout and catering are also available. Stella's is an affordable, attractive, and popular spot, known for its list of martinis along with its Grateful Dead posters. Live music happens weeknights at happy hour, from 4 to 6 p.m.

THE BIG ISLAND

Brown's Beach House ★★★★

HAWAII REGIONAL   MODERATE/EXPENSIVE   QUALITY ★★★★   VALUE ★★★★
KONA

**The Fairmont Orchid Hotel, 1 North Kaniku Drive, Kohala Coast;
☎ 808-887-7368; www.fairmont.com/orchid**

Reservations Recommended. When to go Sunset, for the view and dinner special. Entree range $28–$49. Payment All major credit cards. Service rating ★★★★★. Parking Valet or hotel lot. Bar Full service. Wine selection Extensive. Dress Casual resort attire. Disabled access Good, via elevator. Customers Hotel and resort guests, Islanders. Hours Daily, 5:30–8:30 p.m.

SETTING AND ATMOSPHERE Open-air lanai with palms framing the beach-level view of the sea. When you've got a setting like this, it's a shame to be indoors.

HOUSE SPECIALTIES Fresh fish dishes are the draw. Ahi poke, prepared tableside, combines fresh raw tuna, shredded green papaya, teardrop tomatoes, crunchy *ogo* seaweed and a dressing of *yuzu* chili-garlic soy sauce. Ahi and imagination are paired again in the seared ahi entree, which comes with rice and Portuguese sausage, bok choy, and a touch of tropical chili. Crispy Kona kampachi is accompanied by edamame and corn curried couscous and tomato sambal.

OTHER RECOMMENDATIONS Braised short ribs over tomato risotto and crispy curry tofu with eggplant, asparagus, shiitakes, and Thai curry sauce are among the starters.

SUMMARY AND COMMENTS Fine dining at this resort has lightened up substantially in an effort to present healthy, tasty dishes with flair while using local ingredients, which reflects Fairmont's corporate "sustainability" goal.

Café Pesto ★★★½

CONTEMPORARY MODERATE QUALITY ★★★★ VALUE ★★★★
KONA, HILO AND VOLCANO

Wharf Road and Mahukona Highway, Kawaihae Center, Kawaihae; ☎ 808-882-1071; 308 Kamehameha Avenue, Hilo; ☎ 808-969-6640; www.cafepesto.com

Reservations Recommended. **When to go** Anytime. **Entree range** $17–$35. **Payment** All major credit cards. **Service rating** ★★★. **Parking** Adjacent parking lot. **Bar** Full service. **Wine selection** Good. **Dress** Casual. **Disabled access** Good. **Customers** Islanders and tourists. **Hours** Sunday–Thursday, 11 a.m.– 9 p.m.; Friday and Saturday, 11 a.m.–10 p.m.

SETTING AND ATMOSPHERE Here's a chance to leave the rarified resort atmosphere behind and go someplace fun for lunch or dinner. Café Pesto in Hilo and at Kawaihae Harbor on the Kohala coast share a bright, cheerful approach, with white wicker chairs, black-and-white floors, and big windows. Kawaihae is intimate, while the Hilo restaurant, in the restored historic S. Hata Building, retains the high ceilings of former glory days.

HOUSE SPECIALTIES Sip a *lilikoi* margarita or passion-berry martini, and contemplate the list of ten gourmet pizzas, or the menu stressing fresh Island ingredients. The fresh catch might come grilled or sautéed, with soba noodles, sugar snap peas, and Vietnamese coriander pesto at Kawaihae or accompanied with white-truffle mashed potations, leek cream sauce, and tomato caprese at Hilo.

OTHER RECOMMENDATIONS Pastas are great, including a wonderful smoked salmon Alfredo; or try the market-priced seafood risotto made with Keahole lobster, prawns, scallops, and grilled local fish. Appetizers include coconut-crusted calamari on a slaw of arugula, won bok, and pickled ginger, with a honey-mustard-mango dipping sauce.

SUMMARY AND COMMENTS Café Pesto spans the gap between the rarefied resort dining rooms and local lunchrooms, and is worth a short drive north from the Kohola resorts or a stop en route from the volcano in Hilo.

CanoeHouse ★★★½

HAWAII RREGIONAL EXPENSIVE QUALITY ★★★★ VALUE ★★★ KONA

Mauna Lani Resort, 68-1400 Mauna Lani Drive, Kohala Coast; ☎ 808-885-6622; www.maunalani.com

Reservations Highly recommended. **When to go** Sunset. **Entree range** $28–$75. **Payment** All major credit cards. **Service rating** ★★★★. **Parking** Valet or hotel lot. **Bar** Full service. **Wine selection** Good. **Dress** Resort attire. **Disabled access** Adequate, but some distance from parking. **Customers** Resort and hotel guests and Islanders. **Hours** Daily, 6–9 p.m.

SETTING AND ATMOSPHERE Follow the torchlit path over a little bridge spanning a koi-filled stream with waves lapping on the beach a few steps away to find your way to a romantic evening. The lanai is one of Hawaii's prime sunset-watching perches. Inside, a huge koa canoe serves as the namesake. You can choose semi-privacy in a raised booth, or be in the middle of things at a table, or join the convivial folks at the bar.

HOUSE SPECIALTIES Chef Dee Ann Tsurumaki, back home in Hawaii after a stint at Hong Kong's Peninsula Hotel, carries on Hawaii Regional traditions with east-west entrees such as seared mahimahi with macadamia-nut crust, sun-dried tomato, lemon cream, and gold rice. Seared rare ahi is paired with sautéed scallops, nori, black sesame, and mustard Port sauce. Wasabi *ponzu* sauce dresses Wagyu strip loin beef.

OTHER RECOMMENDATIONS Start with coconut-crusted crab cakes, or an ahi poke-tini (ahi poke, avocado, ginger marinade, and wonton crisp). For dessert, Hawaiian vanilla (grown right up the road) flavors crème brûlée and homemade ice cream. For a tropical twist on a classic, try the mango shortcake, or chocolate-*lilikoi* cake with coconut sorbet.

SUMMARY AND COMMENTS The food is innovative, the setting lovely, and the beach trail is right there for a stroll after dinner.

Coast Grille & Oyster Bar ★★★★½

PACIFIC RIM MODERATE QUALITY ★★★★½ VALUE ★★★ KONA

Hapuna Beach Prince Hotel, 62-100 Kaunaoa Drive, Kohala Coast; ☎ 808-880-3023; www.princeresortshawaii.com

Reservations Recommended. **When to go** Sunset. **Entree range** $14–$29. **Payment** AE, DC, JCB, MC, V. **Service rating** ★★★★. **Parking** Valet or hotel lot. **Bar** Full service. **Wine selection** Extensive. **Dress** Resort wear. **Disabled access** Adequate, via elevator. **Customers** Hotel and resort guests, and Islanders for special occasions. **Hours** Saturday–Thursday, 6–9 p.m.

SETTING AND ATMOSPHERE At this spacious restaurant, you can sit at a table inside the soaring multilevel dining room, although it's a waste of an exhilarating view, or eat out on the deck, or choose banquettes that face the ocean when the breeze is chilly.

HOUSE SPECIALTIES Freshness is the imperative here, and dishes change accordingly. The approach is also fresh: shrimp cocktail, for instance, features grilled and chilled shrimp with pepper-olive salad, and Keahole clams are flavored with pancetta, summer peas, chili, and garden mint. Ono "fish and chips" are presented with pickled vegetable remoulade, fried lemon, and Hawaiian chili pepper vinegar.

OTHER RECOMMENDATIONS Celebrate the land of perpetual summer with a salad of tomatoes, watermelon, feta, and arugula with a honey-sherry vinaigrette. For dessert, consider the bittersweet chocolate "Budino" tart with baby fennel jam, olive oil, and Maldon sea salt.

SUMMARY AND COMMENTS Brett Vallarmia, the chef de cuisine, has simplified the menu, but not at the expense of flavor. Sit outside at sunset on warm Hawaiian evenings to appreciate fully the view of a turquoise ocean and white sand.

Daniel Thiebaut Restaurant ★★★½

FRENCH ASIAN MODERATE QUALITY ★★★★ VALUE ★★★★ KONA

65-1259 Kawaihae Road, Kamuela; ☎ 808-887-2200; www.danielthiebaut.com

Reservations Suggested. When to go Anytime. Entree range Dinner $21–$32. Payment All major credit cards. Service rating ★★★★. Parking Free, on site. Bar Full service. Wine selection Extensive. Dress Casual. Disabled access Good. Customers Locals, tourists. Hours Monday–Saturday, 11:30 a.m.–9 p.m. and Sunday, 10 a.m.–1:30 p.m and 11:30 a.m.–9 p.m.

SETTING AND ATMOSPHERE Located in a historic yellow building, Daniel Thiebaut is set in the century-old former Chock Inn Store and Family Home. The character structure has been preserved in five dining rooms that reflect the rooms' original uses: a dress shop, general store, and family dining parlor. Wood floors and vintage Hawaiiana reflect old times, and brightly colored fabrics by Big Island designer Sig Zane add a cheerful contemporary note.

HOUSE SPECIALTIES Local produce is at its freshest in this cool, upland ranching community, and Thiebaut takes advantage of the bounty. French techniques are combined with Island ingredients and flavors. The chef's signature Hunan-style rack of lamb comes with an eggplant compote and goat cheese made nearby.

OTHER RECOMMENDATIONS Vegetarian entrees include avocado spring roll with smoked tomato coulis, and macadamia nut–crusted tofu with cilantro-tahini sauce. Particularly welcome on chilly Waimea evenings is lobster bisque with brandy, topped with cilantro-coconut cream.

SUMMARY AND COMMENTS Chef Daniel Thiebaut came to the Kohala Coast from his native France by way of such diverse assignments as the Manila Hotel, Gleneagles Hotel in Scotland, and Switzerland's Winter Resort prior to becoming chef at the Mauna Kea down below.

Hualalai Grille by Alan Wong ★★★★½

HAWAII REGIONAL EXPENSIVE QUALITY ★★★★★ VALUE ★★★★ KONA

Four Seasons Resort Hualalai, Kaupulehu (north Kona Coast); ☎ 808-325-8525; www.hualalairesort.com

Reservations Recommended. When to go Anytime. Entree range Dinner, $35–$56. Payment All major credit cards Service rating ★★★★. Parking Valet or hotel lot. Bar Full service. Wine selection Extensive. Dress Casual resort attire, dressier for dinner. Disabled access Good (elevator). Hours Daily, 5:30–9 p.m. for dinner, 2:30–10 p.m. at the bar.

SETTING AND ATMOSPHERE Perched atop the golf clubhouse, with glass walls that disappear to allow the trades and breezes to blow through in a casual but refined atmosphere, with warm woods and tropical greens. This place with this food is enough to make one take up golf.

HOUSE SPECIALTIES Specialties include some of Alan Wong's best-known dishes, such as ginger-crusted onaga with miso vinaigrette, shiitake and enoki mushrooms, and corn; and some others, like locally raised rib-eye steak or soy-braised short ribs. At lunch, plain old "soup and sandwich" becomes chilled red-and-yellow tomato soup served with a foie gras, *kalua* pig, and grilled-cheese sandwich. Or try the clams steamed in sake with edamame and mushrooms. **OTHER RECOMMENDATIONS** The Korean hot pot with beef, cabbage, and savory broth is bound to be comforting, no matter how your golf day went. For dessert, savor roasted-local-banana tiramisù with macadamia nut–brittle ice cream, or indulge in the popular chocolate crunch bar—layers of milk chocolate, macadamia nut crunch, and dark chocolate mousse.

SUMMARY AND COMMENTS Hualalai's signature restaurant, Pahuia, built virtually in the beach sands, has the ocean-side setting and a respected fine-dining menu, but Hualalai Grille is a lot more culinary fun, led by the talented Wong and his creative staff. And with menu items relying heavily upon fresh, organic ingredients from local ranchers and farmers, the quality is tops.

Huggo's ★★★

PACIFIC RIM MODERATE/EXPENSIVE QUALITY ★★★ VALUE ★★★ KONA

75-5828 Kahakai Road, Kailua-Kona; ☎ 808-329-1493; www.huggos.com

Reservations Recommended. **When to go** Sunset or moonlight. **Entree range** $22–$37. **Payment** D, DC, JCB, MC, V. **Service rating** ★★★. **Parking** Adjacent lot. **Bar** Full service. **Wine selection** Adequate, a dozen by the glass. **Dress** Casual. **Disabled access** Good. **Customers** Islanders and tourists. **Hours** Daily, 11:30 a.m.–midnight.

SETTING AND ATMOSPHERE At Huggo's, waterfront dining means you could get splashed if the waves kicked up on the rocks below. With open-air tables set just above water's edge, Huggo's has been a landmark since 1969. The decor runs to marine memorabilia, big anchors, ships' lamps, rope, and natural wood.

HOUSE SPECIALTIES Fresh local seafood and natural beef draw Huggo's dedicated following. Even the tofu is locally made. Fresh oysters on the half shell, grown right up the road, are topped with a citrus mignonette sauce and wasabi *tobiko*. House-made kabocha squash gnocchi with local greens, mushrooms, and edamame could tempt you, or go directly to the signature dish of teriyaki steak with a secret-recipe sauce, greens, and rice.

OTHER RECOMMENDATIONS A juicy cut of certified Angus prime rib, rosemary-garlic grilled chicken, and a variety of pasta dishes provide other options. Plentiful small plates range from tempura fern shoots to slow-roasted lamb shank spring rolls with pea shoots and minted sweet chili-lime sauce. Lunch and dinner at Huggo's on the Rocks features mahimahi tacos, fresh catch sandwich, and Kailua pig and tomatillo tostada, among many choices.

ENTERTAINMENT AND AMENITIES Live contemporary music nightly in the lounge.

SUMMARY AND COMMENTS Ask for a table by the window to savor Huggo's oceanfront appeal, especially at sunset.

Kilauea Lodge Restaurant ★★★

CONTINENTAL MODERATE/EXPENSIVE QUALITY ★★★ VALUE ★★★★
HILO AND VOLCANO

19-4055 Old Volcano Road, Volcano Village; ☎ 808-967-7366; www.kilauealodge.com

Reservations Highly recommended. **When to go** Anytime; especially after post-sunset lava-viewing. **Entree range** $20–$45. **Payment** MC, V. **Service rating** ★★½. **Parking** Adjacent lot. **Bar** Full service. **Wine selection** Good. **Dress** Casual. Bring a sweater; Volcano nights are cool. **Disabled access** Adequate, via lift. **Customers** Islanders and tourists. **Hours** Monday–Saturday, 7:30–10 a.m. and 5–8:45 p.m.; Sunday, 7:30 a.m.–2 p.m. and 5–8:45 p.m.

SETTING AND ATMOSPHERE This mountain lodge, surrounded by tree ferns in cool, remote Volcano, dates from 1938, when it was a scout retreat. The dining room has a massive stone fireplace, vaulted cedar ceiling, hardwood floors, local artwork, and rustic appeal.

HOUSE SPECIALTIES On chilly high-country evenings, this is a cozy place to sip a full-bodied red wine and nibble on an appetizer of Brie deep-fried in a coconut crust and served with brandied apples, papaya salsa, and bread. You're unlikely to encounter an antelope up in Volcano, unless it appears on your plate—one of Kilauea Lodge's game specials, along with ostrich schnitzel. Typical entrees include venison flamed with brandy, duck l'orange with red cabbage, or Seafood Mauna Kea, pasta with shellfish and a sauce of shiitake and shallots, crème fra"che and fresh basil. The signature dessert is Portuguese sweet bread pudding garnished with fruit sauces.

OTHER RECOMMENDATIONS The menu has a German accent, with hearty fare such as assorted German sausages with sauerkraut and fried potatoes, Koenigsberger Klopse (meatballs in a lemon caper sauce), and *hasenpfeffer* (braised rabbit in wine sauce). Fresh Island fish is also available.

SUMMARY AND COMMENTS Kilauea Lodge is the best place to eat in Volcano, and people from Hilo often drive the half hour from town to enjoy the "getting away from it all" feeling it provides.

Merriman's ★★★★★

HAWAII REGIONAL EXPENSIVE QUALITY ★★★★★ VALUE ★★★★★   KONA

Opelo Plaza II, Highway 19 and Opelo Road, Waimea; ☎ 808-885-6822; www.merrimanshawaii.com

Reservations Highly recommended. **When to go** Anytime for dinner. **Entree range** $20–$46. **Payment** AE, JCB, MC, V. **Service rating** ★★★★★. **Parking** In adjacent lot. **Bar** Full service. **Wine selection** Extensive. **Dress** Casual for lunch; resort attire for dinner. **Disabled access** Good. **Customers** Tourists and Islanders. **Hours** Monday–Friday, 11:30 a.m.–1:30 p.m. and 5:30–9 p.m.; Saturday and Sunday, 5:30–9 p.m.

SETTING AND ATMOSPHERE Set in the heart of Big Island cowboy country, Merriman's is a comfortably understated restaurant with a genius in the exhibition kitchen. Artwork for sale by local artists brightens the wall. Light colors and potted palms add to the ranch-house feel.

HOUSE SPECIALTIES Chef-owner Peter Merriman serves fresh, local meat, fish, and produce in dishes that reflect the cooking skills of Hawaii's various cultures. The signature dish is original wok-charred ahi, seared outside and rare inside, as an appetizer or an entree. New York steaks are from Parker Ranch, and the lamb from Kahua Ranch is prepared differently each day. You might find herb-roasted leg of lamb served with mango port wine jus, or a rack of lamb. Lokelani Farms grows special tomatoes just for Merriman's; organic spinach, grown at Honopua Farms, is tossed with hot balsamic vinegar and garnished with *pipikaula* (jerky) and crumbled bacon.

OTHER RECOMMENDATIONS Popular among the FOB (fresh off the boat) fish entrees is ponzu-marinated mahimahi. Other preparations include sautéed fish with shellfish and vegetables, grilled fish with wine butter sauce, and macadamia-nut and panko-crusted fish with spicy *lilikoi* sauce. Merriman's mixed plate includes a taste of three popular entrees: wok-charred ahi, steak medallion, and ponzu mahimahi. You can also choose a tasting plate of all the day's fresh vegetables. The coconut crème brûlée is a hit dessert, along with *lilikoi* mousse and warm-chocolate macadamia-nut cake with ginger ice cream.

SUMMARY AND COMMENTS This is probably the Big Island's best restaurant. Merriman was an initial force behind the Hawaii Regional Cuisine movement, and his dedication to fresh local produce is legendary. When he opened his first restaurant on the Big Island, the chef would climb coconut trees, dive for fresh shellfish, and make farmers deals they couldn't refuse so they would grow top-quality tomatoes for him. Merriman's reputation for the best food on the island is so widely known that diners, including celebrities like Robert Redford and Kevin Costner, drive many miles to get here.

Merriman offers a culinary and farm tour Monday through Thursday so that diners can meet farmers and see where the food comes from. Participants (with advance reservations) depart at 2:30 p.m. with Hawaii Forest & Trail for a visit to Kahua Ranch and Honopua Family Farm, on which produce is grown for the restaurant. They return to Merriman's for a special four-course dinner using products from the farms they toured.

O's Bistro ★★★½

HAWAII REGIONAL/SOUTHWEST FUSION MODERATE QUALITY ★★★★ VALUE ★★★★ KONA

Crossroads Shopping Center, 75-1027 Henry Street, Kailua-Kona; ☎ 808-327-6565; www.osbistro.com

Reservations Advised. **When to go** Anytime. **Entree range** Lunch or dinner, $21–$34; $10–$24 for the extensive vegetarian "food without faces" menu. **Payment** All major credit cards. **Service rating** ★★★. **Parking** Free in the adjoining shopping-center lot. **Bar** Full service. **Wine selection** Good, 18 wines by the glass. **Dress** Casual. **Disabled access** Good. **Customers** Locals, tourists. **Hours** Daily, 10 a.m.–9 p.m.

SETTING AND ATMOSPHERE Tucked away in a strip mall, O's is a refreshing surprise: chic and contemporary, with slate floors, warm woods, and local art. Better yet, it is the domain of a Hawaii Regional Cuisine founder and chef, Amy Ferguson-Ota, whose talents are spent turning out affordable and unforgettable pasta dishes from around the world with her own flair.

HOUSE SPECIALTIES You'll find Japanese udon and somen, Italian linguine, spaghetti, and orzo, Chinese chow fun, and Thai rice noodles, in seemingly endless presentations. Go simple with fettucine Alfredo or a steaming bowl of Hawaii's favorite *saimin,* made especially savory with duck broth and *lup cheong* (Chinese sausage). Or sample one of the Signature Noodles, such as Ferguson-Ota's wonderful version of tuna-noodle casserole: wok-seared fresh ahi with orecchiette pasta. Meat lovers will find ample selections for dinner, either with noodles or without.

OTHER RECOMMENDATIONS An extensive selection of salads and vegetarian entrees is also international in scope. Visit Asia through sweet-sour Thai salads topped with grilled fish or chicken and crispy noodles. Or go Mediterranean with linguine and kalamata olives, tomatoes, and roasted garlic. Fresh fish is also featured nightly, in a variety of preparations. Desserts include such delicacies as white-chocolate bread pudding or five-spice pineapple upside-down cake.

SUMMARY AND COMMENTS Ferguson-Ota is the former executive chef at the Ritz-Carlton Mauna Lani and one of the first women to hold that job with a luxury-hotel group. Now she runs her own restaurant, bringing her creativity to the universal favorite, noodles. Ferguson-Ota began her career in Texas and was influential in the development of a regional cuisine in the Southwest, before she helped do the same in Hawaii.

Pahuia at Four Seasons ★★★★

HAWAIIAN FUSION EXPENSIVE QUALITY ★★★★ VALUE ★★★★ KONA

Four Seasons Resort Hualalai, Kaupulehu; ☎ 808-325-8000; www.fourseasons.com/hualalai

Reservations Required for dinner. **When to go** Breakfast. **Entree range** Dinner, $32–$70. **Payment** AE, D, JCB, MC, V. **Service rating** ★★★★. **Parking** Valet or hotel lot. **Bar** Full service. **Wine selection** Extensive. **Dress** Resort wear. **Disabled access** Adequate, via paved pathways. **Customers** Hotel and resort guests. **Hours** Daily, 6:30–11:30 a.m. and 5:30–9:30 p.m.

SETTING AND ATMOSPHERE Spectacular indoor-outdoor architecture and beach location make Pahuia a magical place to dine, whether it's in the morning sunlight at breakfast or by torchlight at dinner. Outdoor floodlights at night illuminate the rhythmic surf. Cross a wooden bridge suspended across a rough, natural lava-rock fishpond to reach the mahogany-and-teak interior, where a huge aquarium displays colorful reef fish. Candles in black sand in hurricane lamps light individual tables. Check out the original hand-colored woodcuts by Charles Bartlett (circa 1922) displayed on restaurant walls: *Duke Kahanamoku, Surfing at Waikiki,* and *Hawaiian Fisherman.*

HOUSE SPECIALTIES At dinner, signature dishes include butter-poached Kona lobster or the day's catch with soy-ginger mushrooms, cilantro, and sizzling sesame oil. Scallops and shrimp are dressed with lomilomi tomato, hearts of palm, edamame puree, and poi vinaigrette.

OTHER RECOMMENDATIONS Appetizers include the "fire and ice," pepper-crusted Kona kampachi with icy cucumber sorbet and baby abalone grown nearby, grilled on the half shell with a coriander-chimichurri accent. Desserts include soufflé du jour and warm dark-chocolate lava cake with ice cream. On Saturdays, Pahuia stages the "surf, sand, and stars" barbecue on the beach, complete with grilled steak and lobster stations and an astronomer to help with amateur stargazing. A children's menu is available.

ENTERTAINMENT AND AMENITIES Island entertainers torch-dance nightly from 6:30 to 9:30 p.m.

SUMMARY AND COMMENTS This is the closest to the beach you could possibly sit without spreading a towel in the sand for a picnic.

Royal Siam Thai ★★★½

THAI INEXPENSIVE QUALITY ★★★ VALUE ★★★★★   HILO AND VOLCANO

70 Mamo Street, Hilo; ☎ 808-961-6100

Reservations Accepted. **When to go** Anytime. **Entree range** $9–$13. **Payment** AE, D, DC, MC, V. **Service rating** ★★★. **Parking** On street. **Bar** Full service. **Wine selection** Very limited. **Dress** Casual. **Disabled access** Adequate. **Customers** Islanders and some tourists. **Hours** Daily, 11 a.m.– 8:30 p.m.

SETTING AND ATMOSPHERE This neighborhood restaurant seats about 50 at booths and tables. Pictures of the king and queen of Thailand, the Buddha, and Thai dancers hang on the walls. Sprays of orchids and potted trees add a colorful touch.

HOUSE SPECIALTIES Start with deep-fried spring rolls served in the traditional way, with mint and lettuce leaves in which to roll the hot, crispy treats and a sweet-and-sour sauce for dipping. The most popular entree is Buddha rama, chicken prepared with spinach and peanut sauce. Thai curries can be ordered mild, medium, or hot.

OTHER RECOMMENDATIONS The chef's favorites are Thai garlic shrimp and cashew chicken with Thai sticky rice.

SUMMARY AND COMMENTS Though it's certainly not fancy, Royal Siam has a following in Hilo.

kids Roy's Waikoloa Bar & Grill ★★★★

HAWAII REGIONAL MODERATE/EXPENSIVE QUALITY ★★★★ VALUE ★★★★ KONA

Kings Shops, 250 Waikoloa Beach Drive, Waikoloa; ☎ 808-886-4321; www.roysrestaurant.com

Reservations Highly recommended. **When to go** Early to avoid crowds. **Entree range** $25–$35. **Payment** All major credit cards. **Service rating** ★★★★★. **Parking** Shopping-center lot. **Bar** Full service. **Wine selection** Very good, some by the glass. **Dress** Casual, no tank tops for men, no swimwear. **Disabled access** Good. **Customers** Islanders and tourists. **Hours** Daily, 5:30–9:30 p.m.

SETTING AND ATMOSPHERE This Roy's, with green carpets, a green marble bar, an exhibition kitchen, and window tables that overlook a golf-course lake, is the most handsome of Roy Yamaguchi's popular restaurants in Hawaii. The menu is the same combination of reliably excellent standard entrees (at every Roy's) on one side and unpredictable, but inspired daily specials on the other.

HOUSE SPECIALTIES You might find grilled Szechuan-style baby-back ribs or Thai noodle peanut chicken salad at dinner, or *imu*-roasted pork *laulau*, pizza, or sweet sake-glazed shrimp. Blackened Island ahi, served in spicy hot soy-mustard-butter sauce, is a Roy's standby. Fresh fish and preparations change nightly, as do appetizers, pizzas, pastas, salads, and soups.

OTHER RECOMMENDATIONS The seasonal prix fixe dinner is a deal at $35— three appetizers to sample, macadamia-nut crusted local catch with lobster sauce, and molten chocolate soufflé for dessert.

SUMMARY AND COMMENTS Youngsters are welcome; Roy's offers a children's menu and crayons. Like all the Roy's, some 30 menu items may change nightly, according to the chef's mood and the available fresh ingredients.

Sansei Seafood Restaurant and Sushi Bar/ Waikoloa Beach Resort ★★★★★

JAPANESE FUSION MODERATE/EXPENSIVE QUALITY ★★★★★ VALUE ★★★★★ KONA

Queens Market Place, 201 Waikoloa Beach Drive, Waikoloa Beach Resort; ☎ 808-885-6286; www.sanseihawaii.com

Reservations Recommended for dinner. **When to go** Early, for the specials. **Entree range** $16–$42. **Payment** All major credit cards. **Service rating** ★★★★. **Parking** Resort lot. **Bar** Full service. **Wine selection** Extensive list of wines by the glass and premium sakes. **Dress** Dressy casual. **Disabled access** Good. **Customers** Tourists, Sansei devotees, nightcappers, and karaoke crowd. **Hours** Dinner, daily, 5:30–10 p.m. Pupu and sushi, Friday and Saturday, 10 p.m.–1 a.m.

SETTING AND ATMOSPHERE Lines form early at the door to get the 25–50% off specials that end at 6 p.m. Once inside, the crowded, lively, and hip atmosphere becomes the décor.

HOUSE SPECIALTIES Miso butterfish is a melt-in-your-mouth Sansei way to begin, but the award-winning panko-crusted ahi tuna roll and mango crab roll with greens and crunchy peanuts, served with sweet Thai chili vinaigrette will beckon as well. Shrimp dynamite are crispy tempura shrimp with creamy garlic aioli and an *unagi* glaze.

OTHER RECOMMENDATIONS Entrees can be as plain as grilled chops with garlic mashed potatoes and sautéed spinach. Sansei's version of seafood pasta consists of tiger prawns, scallops, and vegetables tossed in a wok with chow funn rice noodles and served in spicy black-bean chili butter.

SUMMARY AND COMMENTS The Big Island resort scene is far richer for having a Sansei to spice up the fare.

KAUAI

The Beach House ★★★★

PACIFIC RIM MODERATE QUALITY ★★★★ VALUE ★★★ KAUAI

5022 Lawai Road, Poipu; ☎ 808-742-1424; www.the-beach-house.com

Reservations Highly recommended. **When to go** Sunset. **Entree range** $26–$40. **Payment** AE, DC, MC, V. **Service rating** ★★★★. **Parking** Valet or street. **Bar** Full service. **Wine selection** Extensive. **Dress** Resort wear. **Disabled access** Good; valet parking is free for disabled. **Customers** Tourists and Islanders. Dinner April–September: daily, 6–10 p.m.; October–March: daily, 5:30–10 p.m.

SETTING AND ATMOSPHERE A spectacular oceanfront location and a sparky Pacific Rim menu make this a natural choice for dinner in the Poipu area. Floor-to-ceiling windows reveal surfers and waves, whales and spouts, ships and the restless sea.

HOUSE SPECIALTIES For starters, contemplate the shiitake-crusted mussels with ginger-lime butter sauce and black-bean sauce, the crispy crab-stuffed ahi roll, or a seafood corn chowder with crab and sherry. A *kiawe* wood–burning grill adds a flavorful touch to the mint-coriander marinated lamb rack, filet mignon, and hoisin plum chicken breast. Imaginative and spicy fish dishes include wasabi-crusted snapper with *lilikoi* lemongrass beurre blanc and Kaffir lime–crusted sea scallops with chili aioli.

OTHER RECOMMENDATIONS Roast duck with cranberry Port sauce will take you in a different direction. For dessert, tropically flavored sorbets will cool you, but a "molten chocolate desire" (hot chocolate tart with ice cream and chocolate-caramel sauce) may have the opposite effect.

SUMMARY AND COMMENTS Make reservations early and request a seat by the window for the full effect of the stunning views.

Brennecke's Beach Broiler ★★★

CONTEMPORARY MODERATE/EXPENSIVE QUALITY ★★★½ VALUE ★★★ KAUAI

2100 Hoone Road, Poipu Beach; ☎ 808-742-7588;
www.brenneckes.com/restaurant

Reservations Recommended. **When to go** Sunset. **Entree range** Dinner, $20–$40. **Payment** All major credit cards. **Service rating** ★★★. **Parking** In adjacent lots. **Bar** Full service. **Wine selection** Limited. **Dress** Casual. **Disabled access** Poor, but staff will carry wheelchairs up the stairs. **Customers** Tourists and Islanders. **Hours** Daily, 11 a.m.–10 p.m.

SETTING AND ATMOSPHERE Eat well without a lot of fuss and enjoy the expansive vista in this second-floor restaurant in a landmark blue building across from Poipu Beach Park. Aim for seats by an open window to enjoy sunsets, surfers, palms, waves breaking, and golden sands beyond the window boxes.

HOUSE SPECIALTIES Fresh Island fish, steaks, grilled shrimp skewers, and prime rib arrive sizzling from the *kiawe* charcoal broiler for hungry diners who spent the day at the beach working up an appetite.

OTHER RECOMMENDATIONS Brennecke's signature scampi platter is a saute of shrimp and veggies over pasta, competing for your fancy with ginger-sesame crusted opah or king crab legs.

SUMMARY AND COMMENTS Brennecke's is handy when you want a cool beach-side place to enjoy a burger (beef, teriyaki chicken, or veggie) or dig into a fresh fish taco, salad, pizza, or quesadilla for lunch. Sea breezes blowing through the windows and a varied menu of *pupu,* including fresh sashimi caught by local fishermen, make this a great spot for a glass of wine or one of Brennecke's mai tais. For casual snacks, Brennecke's Deli downstairs serves shaved ice and sandwiches.

Casa di Amici ★★★

ITALIAN/INTERNATIONAL MODERATE QUALITY ★★★★ VALUE ★★★ KAUAI

2301 Nalo Road, Poipu; ☎ 808-742-1555

Reservations Requested. **When to go** Anytime. **Entree range** $20–$30. **Payment** AE, V. **Service rating** ★★★. **Parking** In adjacent lot. **Bar** Full service. **Wine selection** Excellent. **Dress** Casual. **Disabled access** Good. **Customers** Islanders and tourists. **Hours** Daily, 6–9 p.m.

SETTING AND ATMOSPHERE Windows open to the balmy air around this comfortable Poipu restaurant. Casa di Amici means "house of friends," and with rattan furnishings under ceiling fans inside and sweeping views to the ocean on the comfortable deck outside, it feels friendly, like the old Hawaii home it once was.

HOUSE SPECIALTIES You have the option to mix and match your favorite pasta and sauce, perhaps a *salsa arrabiatta*—spicy tomato with sautéed pancetta and chilis. The most popular item is a porcini-crusted chicken breast in a sun-dried-cherry, port-wine, and mushroom sauce. If you like bold flavors, try Japanese mahogany-glazed salmon served on frijole choritos and black beans, or salmon steak painted with soy sauce, sprinkled with Japanese *furukake* seasoning, baked and garnished with jalapeño-tequila aioli and served on a corn husk.

OTHER RECOMMENDATIONS Picatta (as in veal picatta) and marsala sauces are particularly flavorful and rich. Chef Randall Yates loves Mexican and Southwestern food, and is proud of his chili-verde risotto, not to mention classic four-cheese risotto, Indian curried lamb, *kalua* (usually pork), and other variations. One dessert you won't want to miss is the baked Hawaii—a chocolate–macadamia nut brownie topped with coconut and passion fruit sorbet and Italian meringue, flambéed.

ENTERTAINMENT AND AMENITIES Live classical piano music softens the mood on Friday and Saturday nights.

SUMMARY AND COMMENTS A big menu (including 24 pastas) and big portions set the pace. Some entrees are available in light portions, but once you taste the house scampi with a good red wine, you may want more. Because of the variety of the ethnic preparations, the French-trained chef-owner describes his restaurant as "the most un-Italian Italian restaurant you'll ever be in."

 **kids** **Duke's Kauai** ★★★½

AMERICAN MODERATE QUALITY ★★★½ VALUE ★★★ KAUAI

Kauai Marriott Resort and Beach Club, Kalapaki Beach, Lihue;
☎ **808-246-9599; www.dukeskauai.com**

Reservations Recommended. **When to go** Anytime. **Entree range** $19–$29 (fish and lobster, market priced). **Payment** AE, D, MC, V. **Service rating** ★★★½. **Parking** In adjacent lot or valet. **Bar** Full service. **Wine selection** Adequate. **Dress** Casual. **Disabled access** Adequate. **Customers** Tourists and Islanders. **Hours** Daily, 11:30 a.m.–10 p.m. (restaurant); 11:30 a.m.–11:30 p.m. (bar).

SETTING AND ATMOSPHERE At this casual open-air restaurant with awesome views onto Kalapaki Beach, diners can sit downstairs at the Barefoot Bar for lunch, snacks, afternoon cocktails, live entertainment, and people-watching, or amble upstairs for dinner. A stream and waterfall, edged by lush plantings, create an outdoor garden effect even in the cool interior.

HOUSE SPECIALTIES Steak or fresh fish is the name of the dinner game after a trip to Duke's all-you-care-to-eat salad bar. Best of the five preparations for fish is "Duke's Style," baked in garlic, lemon, and sweet-basil glaze.

OTHER RECOMMENDATIONS Macadamia-nut-and-crab wontons with mustard plum sauce are so delicious that you might be tempted to limit dinner to appetizers and the salad bar. At lunch, you can try stir-fried cashew chicken, a fresh mahi sandwich, or the fish tacos.

ENTERTAINMENT AND AMENITIES A strolling trio of guitar and ukulele players performs Hawaiian music in the restaurant upstairs. Downstairs on Thursday and "Tropical Friday" afternoons, a band entertains, and tropical drinks are happy-hour priced.

SUMMARY AND COMMENTS A collection of memorabilia about Olympic surfer Duke Kahanamoku, along with a 30-foot waterfall and pool, add interest to an already stunning setting. This is a casual place to grab a hamburger as you come off Kalapaki Beach for lunch or enjoy a mai tai at sunset, and then climb the stairs for a pleasant dinner.

Hamura's Saimin Stand ★★

HAWAIIAN LOCAL INEXPENSIVE QUALITY ★★★ VALUE ★★★★★ KAUAI

2956 Kress Street, Lihue; ☎ 808-245-3271

Reservations None. **When to go** Early lunch. **Entree range** $5–$15. **Payment** Cash. **Service rating** ★★. **Parking** Limited in lot and on street. **Bar** None; diners can bring their own. **Wine selection** None. **Dress** Casual. **Disabled access** Accessible, but there is no ramp. **Customers** Islanders and adventuresome tourists. **Hours** Monday–Thursday, 10 a.m.–10 p.m.; Friday–Saturday, 10 a.m.–midnight; Sunday, 10 a.m.–9:30 p.m.

SETTING AND ATMOSPHERE   Ready to leave your rarefied resort life behind and get down with the real Hawaii? This is down-home Hawaii on a dusty side street in Lihue, in a plantation-style building with louvered windows that let in a breath of air on muggy summer days. Old-fashioned U-shaped Formica counters fill the center of the restaurant, but there are a few tables.

HOUSE SPECIALTIES   Don't miss going to Hamura for a big steaming bowl of *saimin* that's especially good on a wet, windy day. You can watch the kitchen staff cook noodles and broth by the huge potfuls. The *saimin* special bowl has a little bit of everything: noodles garnished with vegetables, wontons, fish cake, chopped boiled egg, sliced pork, green onion, and sliced luncheon meat or a tempura shrimp. If something's ailing your stomach, saimin could be the remedy.

OTHER RECOMMENDATIONS   Soup is the reason people stand in line to eat at Hamura, but grilled chicken skewers and teriyaki beef sticks are also available, along with fresh *manapua,* steamed doughy buns with a savory filling. Have some *lilikoi* chiffon pie for dessert.

SUMMARY AND COMMENTS   Hamura Saimin is a Lihue institution. Don't expect to be blown away by fancy food or service; just enjoy the fun of having a local experience. This little cafe is always busy, but right after opening there might be a lull. If not, just line up and wait.

The Kauai Grill ★★★

CONTEMPORARY EXPENSIVE QUALITY ★★★ VALUE ★★★ KAUAI

St. Regis Princeville Resort, 5520 Ka Haku Road, Princeville; ☎ 808-826-9644; www.princevillehotelhawaii.com

Reservations Recommended. **When to go** Sunset. **Entree range** $50. **Payment** Major credit cards. **Service rating** ★★★★. **Parking** Valet. **Bar** Full service. **Wine selection** Excellent. **Dress** Casual sophisticated. **Disabled access** Good. **Customers** Tourists and Islanders. **Hours** Tuesday–Saturday, 6–10 p.m.

SETTING AND ATMOSPHERE   Kauai's breathtaking North Shore seascape, immortalized in the 1958 film *South Pacific,* has always been the star attraction at this cliffside resort. Now, with the arrival of chef Jean-Georges Vongerichten, reputed to be "one of the most celebrated chefs on the planet," the Island's natural beauty has a rival in the kitchen.

HOUSE SPECIALTIES Vongerichten, who earned his third Michelin star at his namesake (JeanGeorges) New York restaurant, creates Asian-inspired French cuisine full of flavor: grilled octopus and Maui onion salad, beet carpaccio with Kauai goat cheese, salmon tartare with avocado, pan-roasted foie gras with caramelized Meyer lemon, and young-ginger *onaga* in a warm sesame vinaigrette with water chestnuts, sea asparagus, and lavender. The coconut curry *onaga* is served over sesame spinach and rice. Kaffir-lime crème brûlée with spiced mango addresses the need for dessert. The steak comes from Princeville Ranch's own pampered organic herd.

OTHER RECOMMENDATIONS The Romantic Dinner ($850 a couple plus tip and taxes, with two days' advance notice) offers a lei greeting; escort to a secluded outdoor candle and torch-lit table; a consult with the chef on food tastes and dietary restrictions; a chilled bottle of Champagne; a dedicated private server; four-course custom feast; amuse-bouche and intermezzo; wine pairings by the sommelier; a table set with Rosenthal china, Spiegelau stemware, designer flatware, and botanicals; and, of course, the awe-inspiring beauty of Hanalei Bay. For al fresco breakfast, lunch, and a somewhat less costly dinner, it's hard to beat the adjacent Makana Terrace with its infinity pools seeming to drop off into Hanalei Bay below.

SUMMARY AND COMMENTS Over the years, some fine chefs have made it to faraway Kauai, and then left again with the tides. Vongerichten, the most exalted chef yet to wash ashore, heads an international restaurant empire that includes Bora Bora, Shanghai, Vancouver, Las Vegas, New York, London, and Paris. He's also set to open 50 more new restaurants in the next five years. So long as this high-flying star chef stays focused on this end-of-the-road island resort, The Kauai Grill may yet outshine the view.

Keoki's Paradise ★★★½

STEAK AND SEAFOOD MODERATE QUALITY ★★★ VALUE ★★★★ KAUAI

Poipu Shopping Village, Poipu; ☎ 808-742-7534; www.keokisparadise.com

Reservations Recommended. **When to go** Anytime. **Entree range** $19–$35, or market price. **Payment** Major credit cards. **Service rating** ★★★. **Parking** In adjacent lot. **Bar** Full service. **Wine selection** Good. **Dress** Casual. **Disabled access** Good. **Customers** Tourists and Islanders. **Hours** Daily, 11 a.m.–1:30 p.m. and 5:30–10 p.m.

SETTING AND ATMOSPHERE From the busy resort shopping center, you wouldn't expect to find a pleasant, cool boathouse-style restaurant set on a peaceful lagoon with tropical foliage and a thatched-roof bar, à la Elvis Presley in *Blue Hawaii*.

HOUSE SPECIALTIES If you've never tried it, you won't believe how addictive silky, raw, fresh ahi can be. Find out with the *maka ia* plate for two—raw tuna cut in cubes and sliced in sashimi, served wok-charred in *shoyu* poke. Fresh catch, prepared in five different ways and sauces, tops the menu. At lunch, a grilled-ahi sandwich or fish tacos will fill the bill. For dessert, it's hard to top the hula pie (ice cream pie with an Oreo-cookie crust), featured throughout this small chain's island restaurants.

OTHER RECOMMENDATIONS For a taste of local flavor, order Koloa pork ribs glazed with plum sauce or coconut-crusted chicken, or try both in a combination plate.

SUMMARY AND COMMENTS Live Hawaiian music performed on weeknights.

Mema Thai & Chinese Cuisine ★★½

THAI/CHINESE INEXPENSIVE/MODERATE QUALITY ★★★ VALUE ★★★★★
KAUAI

4–369 Kuhio Highway, Kapaa; ☎ 808-823-0899

Reservations Accepted. **When to go** Anytime. **Entree range** $9–$18. **Payment** AE, D, DC, MC, V. **Service rating** ★★★. **Parking** In adjacent lot. **Bar** Bring your own. **Wine** None. **Dress** Casual. **Disabled access** Good. **Customers** Islanders and tourists. **Hours** Monday–Friday, 11 a.m.–2 p.m. and 5–9:30 p.m.; Saturday and Sunday, 5–9:30 p.m.

SETTING AND ATMOSPHERE Set in a strip mall, Mema Thai & Chinese Cuisine is surprisingly attractive, with lots of statues, pink linens, and rosewood chairs.

HOUSE SPECIALTIES Thai curries—red, green, yellow, and house-style—are made with your choice of vegetables, chicken, pork, beef, shrimp, fish, or other seafood.

OTHER RECOMMENDATIONS There's plenty to satisfy vegetarians; many dishes can be ordered with tofu instead of meat, such as rice noodles with cabbage, mushrooms, and carrots, or stir-fried broccoli with oyster sauce.

SUMMARY AND COMMENTS *Thai Scene* magazine once named Mema Thai & Chinese "one of the ten best Thai restaurants outside Thailand."

Plantation Gardens Restaurant and Bar ★★★

HAWAII REGIONAL MODERATE QUALITY ★★★ VALUE ★★★ KAUAI

Kiahuna Plantation, 2253 Poipu Road, Poipu; ☎ 808-742-2121; www.pgrestaurant.com

Reservations Recommended. **When to go** Anytime. **Entree range** $21–$31. **Payment** AE, DC, MC, V. **Service rating** ★★★½. **Parking** In adjacent lots. **Bar** Full service. **Wine selection** Excellent. **Dress** Resort casual. **Disabled access** Good. **Customers** Tourists and Islanders. **Hours** Daily 5:30–9 p.m.

SETTING AND ATMOSPHERE Lush tropical gardens with torchlit paths, lava-rock walls, a rich wood interior, and tables on a gracious veranda overlooking a pond offer a lovely setting in a historic sugar-plantation manager's home.

HOUSE SPECIALTIES Seafood *laulau* features fresh fish, shrimp, and scallops, julienne vegetables and spinach all wrapped up in a *ti* leaf and steamed. Specials change often, but Plantation Gardens is known for its fresh fish and steaks. Fish of the day might be ahi, ono, or others, depending on what the fishermen bring to the door. A *kiawe* broiler gives pork tenderloin, steaks, and fish that special smoky flavor.

OTHER RECOMMENDATIONS Coconut-curry seafood stew includes fresh fish and shellfish, potatoes, and tomatoes. Try the local *lilikoi* cheesecake or tropical crème brûlée sampler for a sweet finale.

SUMMARY AND COMMENTS Fresh herbs are picked from the garden out back. This is an oasis of serenity in busy Poipu.

kids Postcards Café ★★★½

CONTEMPORARY MODERATE QUALITY ★★★★ VALUE ★★★ KAUAI

**5-5075 A Kuhio Highway, Hanalei; ☎ 808-826-1191;
www.postcardscafe.com**

Reservations Highly recommended. **When to go** Anytime for dinner. **Entree range** $19–$31. **Payment** AE, MC, V. **Service rating** ★★½. **Parking** In adjacent lot. **Bar** None. **Wine selection** Bring your own. **Dress** Casual. **Disabled access** Adequate. **Customers** Islanders and tourists. **Hours** Daily, 6–9 p.m.

SETTING AND ATMOSPHERE Set in a restored plantation house with a front porch, the restaurant has the charm of an earlier era.

HOUSE SPECIALTIES Gourmet vegetarian cuisine and savory seafood dishes draw raves from repeat visitors. Dishes that are gluten-free or vegan are so noted. Start with a Hanalei taro fritter (which is both) served with pineapple-ginger chutney, then plunge into saffron risotto with shellfish, mushrooms, and pesto—or with tofu and vegetables if you prefer. A kids' menu includes pasta and cheese quesadillas.

OTHER RECOMMENDATIONS Other highlights include seafood pasta with sun-dried tomatoes, greens, and goat cheese in Chardonnay sauce; fresh-fruit smoothies; seafood lumpia; and a hibiscus cooler.

SUMMARY AND COMMENTS Guests sign the guest book with notes like "We ate here three nights in a row" and "The best seafood in the Islands."

Roy's Poipu Bar & Grill ★★★★

HAWAII REGIONAL MODERATE/EXPENSIVE QUALITY ★★★★ VALUE ★★★
KAUAI

**Poipu Shopping Village, 2360 Kiahuna Plantation Drive, Poipu Beach;
☎ 808-742-5000; www.roysrestaurant.com**

Reservations Highly recommended. **When to go** Early for a quieter dinner, later for a livelier crowd. **Entree range** $20–$30. **Payment** AE, D, DC, MC, V. **Service rating** ★★★★. **Parking** In shopping-center lot. **Bar** Full service. **Wine selection** Excellent, many wines by the glass. **Dress** Resort casual. **Disabled access** Good. **Customers** Tourists and Islanders. **Hours** Daily, 5:30–10 p.m.

SETTING AND ATMOSPHERE Chef-owner Roy Yamaguchi's sleek shopping-center restaurant is a magnet for fans of Euro-Asian Pacific cuisine. The restaurant has an airy feeling, with windows that open to let in the night air. The exhibition kitchen is enclosed in glass.

HOUSE SPECIALTIES Hibachi-style salmon and oven-roasted pot roast have emerged from a long list of specials as steady favorites. Seafood lovers might choose fresh catch seared and served with orange shrimp butter and Chinese black-bean sauce. Volcanic puffed pastry filled with caramelized apple is a dessert winner.

OTHER RECOMMENDATIONS It's fun to go for dim sum and appetizers followed by a pizza from the wood-fired oven, so that you have a chance to sample more of the culinary creations. Or share appetizers like lobster pot stickers with spicy miso butter sauce as you sip on mango mojitos or Hawaiian martinis (vodka, coconut rum, and pineapple).

SUMMARY AND COMMENTS Diners return again and again to this popular restaurant in Poipu, so Roy's chefs make sure they will never get tired of the menu by offering 25 or more specials nightly.

Shells Steak and Seafood ★★★

STEAK AND SEAFOOD EXPENSIVE QUALITY ★★★½ VALUE ★★★ KAUAI

Sheraton Kauai Hotel, 2440 Hoonani Road, Poipu Beach; ☎ 808-742-1661; www.sheratonkauai.com

Reservations Recommended. **When to go** Early, for sunset. **Entree range** $25–$40. **Payment** AE, D, DC, JCB, MC, V. **Service rating** ★★★. **Parking** Valet or hotel lot. **Bar** Full service. **Wine selection** Good. **Dress** Resort wear. **Disabled access** Good. **Customers** Tourists. **Hours** Daily, 6:30–10:30 a.m. and 5:30–9:30 p.m.

SETTING AND ATMOSPHERE Floor-to-ceiling windows let in the trade winds, and the sound of the waves drift off the ocean to diners on the lanai and inside this high-ceilinged restaurant.

HOUSE SPECIALTIES The spice-brined pork chops are *ono* (delicious), but so is the lemon spice-rubbed grilled ahi.

OTHER RECOMMENDATIONS Appetizer crab cakes are a perennial favorite, but the restaurant is really known for a dessert called Mount Waialeale, a mountain of chocolate-mousse cake piled with sorbet and Island fruit.

SUMMARY AND COMMENTS Stop first at The Point lounge overlooking the sea, a great spot for predinner cocktails indoors or outdoors.

kids Tidepools ★★★★

PACIFIC RIM EXPENSIVE QUALITY ★★★½ VALUE ★★★ KAUAI

Grand Hyatt Kauai Resort & Spa, 1571 Poipu Road, Poipu Beach; ☎ 808-240-6456; Kauai.hyatt.com

Reservations Highly recommended. **When to go** Anytime. **Entree range** $23–$78. **Payment** AE, JCB, MC, V. **Service rating** ★★★★. **Parking** Valet or hotel lot. **Bar** Full service. **Wine selection** Adequate. **Dress** Resort casual. **Disabled access** Make advance arrangements. **Customers** Tourists, hotel guests, honeymooners. **Hours** Daily, 5:30–10 p.m.

SETTING AND ATMOSPHERE A romantic tropical atmosphere makes Tidepools extra-special. Torchlit paths lead to the restaurant, which appears to float on a fish-filled lagoon; open-air dining *hale* (huts) with thatched roofs are scattered around the edges like a small dining village. Some *hale* shelter individual candlelit tables.

HOUSE SPECIALTIES Tidepools serves interesting appetizers, like crab cakes with Thai-spiced aioli, tomato-ginger relish, and avocado; and entrees such as macadamia-crusted ono stuffed with crab; grilled *shutome* (swordfish) with hearts of palm, bacon, watercress, red pepper coulis, and tomato marmalade; and garlic-peppercorn-rubbed prime rib. A nightly selection of Island fish is offered in preparations such as sautéed with *lilikoi* butter, grilled with papaya-and-mango relish, steamed with sweet chili-and-lime sauce, or blackened with rum-pineapple sauce.

OTHER RECOMMENDATIONS Don't miss the triple chocolate bomb—chocolate mousse, chocolate pate, and dark choclate granache—unless you'd prefer bananas Foster bread pudding.

SUMMARY AND COMMENTS You needn't be afraid that Tidepools will be too toney for the kids. They can select from a children's menu of pasta, hamburgers, and chicken nuggets, and they will be enchanted by the surrounding lagoon.

MOLOKAI

Molokai Pizza Café ★★

AMERICAN INEXPENSIVE QUALITY ★★★½ VALUE ★★★★ MOLOKAI

15 Kaunakakai Place, on Wharf Road, Kaunakakai; ☎ 808-553-3288

Reservations None. **When to go** Anytime. **Entree range** $14–$24. **Payment** Cash only. **Service rating** ★★. **Parking** Adjacent lot. **Bar** None. **Wine selection** None. **Dress** Casual. **Disabled access** Good. **Customers** Locals and tourists. **Hours** Monday–Thursday, 10 a.m.–10 p.m.; Friday and Saturday, 10 a.m.–11 p.m.; Sunday, 11 a.m.–10 p.m.

SETTING AND ATMOSPHERE This is a clean, air-conditioned cafe with booths and tables in a spacious room. It's a family kind of place, often decorated with artwork and thank-you cards by schoolkids. Some of the Formica-topped tables are set in a smaller, quieter area at the front and some on an outside lanai, where guests are welcome to bring their own wine or beer.

HOUSE SPECIALTIES Pizzas and sandwiches are fresh and tasty. Daily specials include Hawaiian plates on Thursdays. Fresh fish is served at market price whenever available. Other classics like chicken and ribs add to the variety. Breads and pizza dough are homemade. Theme nights include Mexican food on Wednesdays, Hawaiian food on Thursdays, and a prime rib dinner on Sunday nights.

OTHER RECOMMENDATIONS You can order pizza by the piece, a Molokini pizza for a single person, or a big one to eat there or to go. Pasta, salads, and frozen yogurt are also on the menu.

SUMMARY AND COMMENTS Eventually everyone stops by the Pizza Café. Kids hang out here after school, and tourists come for a slice of pizza or dinner, as it's one of the few places open until 10 p.m. nightly.

LANAI

Blue Ginger Café ★

HAWAII LOCAL INEXPENSIVE QUALITY ★★★ VALUE ★★★★★ LANAI

409 Seventh Avenue, Lanai City; ☎ 808-565-6363

Reservations Needed only for large parties. **When to go** Anytime. **Entree range** $6.50–$14.95. **Payment** No credit cards. **Service rating** Self-serve. **Parking** Street. **Bar** Full service. **Wine selection** Limited. **Dress** Casual. **Disabled access** Good. **Customers** Islanders, visitors. **Hours** Daily, 6 a.m.–8 p.m. (9 p.m. on weekends).

SETTING AND ATMOSPHERE Set in a plantation building in Lanai City's main square, Blue Ginger diners order and pick up food at the counter and eat at tables with plastic cloths in this plain and simple restaurant and bakery, one of the few alternatives to Lanai's costly hotel dining rooms.

HOUSE SPECIALTIES Try the tasty vegetarian breakfast omelet that comes with rice, or order fresh-baked apple turnovers or cinnamon rolls. For lunch, the bacon-cheddar cheeseburgers are better than Big Macs, but you might want to try the *saimin,* a generous steaming bowl of noodle soup. At dinner, sautéed mahimahi with capers, onions, and mushrooms is the signature dish.

OTHER RECOMMENDATIONS Banana or blueberry pancakes accompanied by cappuccino make a tasty breakfast. For dinner, try a local plate of teriyaki beef, *katsu* chicken, or hamburger steak with gravy.

SUMMARY AND COMMENTS This has been a Lanai hangout owned by the same family since long before Lanai lost its pineapple fields and gained luxury resorts.

The Dining Room ★★★★★

CONTEMPORARY EXPENSIVE QUALITY ★★★★★ VALUE ★★★ LANAI

Four Seasons Resort Lanai, The Lodge at Koele, Keomuku Drive, Lanai City; ☎ 808-565-4000; www.fourseasons.com/koele

Reservations Highly recommended. **When to go** Anytime. **Entree range** $35–$75. **Payment** AE, DC, JCB, MC, V. **Service rating** ★★★★★. **Parking** Valet, hotel lot. **Bar** Full service. **Wine selection** Excellent. **Dress** Resort attire; collared shirts and closed shoes for men. **Disabled access** Adequate. **Customers** Hotel guests, other tourists, and visiting Neighbor Islanders. **Hours** Daily, 6–9:30 p.m.

SETTING AND ATMOSPHERE The mood is refined in this feasting room, which looks out onto the Lodge's expansive backyard acres of green lawns, reflecting pool, and a forested slope beyond. A fire in the hearth lends a romantic touch and a bit of warmth to soften the formality, and profuse orchid sprays remind you where you are. But the emphasis is on enjoying a fine dinner at the place some patrons consider the best in Hawaii.

HOUSE SPECIALTIES The kitchen works magic with fresh local ingredients in imaginative dishes such as these starters: lava rock–seared Lanai venison with celery and Granny Smith apple salad, and cranberry relish; or quail, prepared two ways—seared breast with golden raisin and fava beans, and macadamia-nut-crusted confit leg with artichoke purée and orange-balsamic glaze. Roast lamb loin is accompanied with roasted baby artichokes and tomato confit with olive tapenade.

OTHER RECOMMENDATIONS Save room for dessert: Perhaps the chocolate ice cream truffle with chocolate cookie, a milk chocolate Bailey's shooter, or halzelnut financier with chocolate-orange cream. Or lighten up with a concoction of roasted pineapple and coconut-rum ice cream parfait.

ENTERTAINMENT AND AMENITIES Dinner music, often traditional Hawaiian melodies, piano, or classical musical scores, drifts in from the adjoining Great Hall, where you can extend what is sure to be an expensive evening by relaxing after dinner with a brandy in front of a crackling fire in either of two massive fireplaces. Or if you didn't get enough chocolate at dessert, indulge in a selection from the hot-chocolate menu, a delicious choice of chocolates (dark, white, or milk chocolate), milks, toppings, and extras. The Great Hall Favourite is a mixture of dark chocolate, milk, whipped cream, nutmeg, and shaved chocolate.

SUMMARY AND COMMENTS The Dining Room at the Lodge at Koele provides an exquisite experience for the senses—fine food and drink, soft music, and an elegant setting. Make your reservation in advance, as The Dining Room seats only 60 people and fills up fast.

Ihilani ★★★★½

ITALIAN EXPENSIVE QUALITY ★★★★½ VALUE ★★★ LANAI

Four Seasons Resort Lanai at Manele Bay, 1 Manele Road, Lanai City; ☎ 808-565-2000; www.fourseasons.com/manelebay

Reservations Highly recommended. **When to go** Anytime. **Entree range** $32–$45. **Payment** AE, DC, JCB, MC, V. **Service rating** ★★★★★. **Parking** Valet. **Bar** Full service. **Wine selection** Extensive. **Dress** Resort attire. **Disabled access** Good. **Customers** Tourists and visitors. **Hours** Tuesday–Saturday, 6–9:30 p.m.

SETTING AND ATMOSPHERE Fine china, silver, and lace-bedecked tables under hand-blown Italian crystal chandeliers set the elegant mood in this formal dining room, with views of the pool and ocean.

HOUSE SPECIALTIES It's only right that a fine-dining palace perched on a cliff above the sea would have a menu dominated by seafood. Ihilani features contemporary Italian cuisine capitalizing on the island's fresh seafood and produce. Start with appetizers like baked scallops with wilted spinach and Muscato zabaglione sauce or bean and white truffle soup with fusili and Jerusalem artichokes. Move on to wild mushroom-ricotta-stuffed cannelloni with creamy truffle sauce, or Hawaiian sea bass with tomatoes, fennel, Galliano, preserved lemon, and sausage.

OTHER RECOMMENDATIONS Desserts include Grand Marnier tiramisu, warm almond soufflé cake with fresh apple compote, or zucotto—a praline-and-milk-chocolate mousse with carmelized bananas and hazelnut sponge cake. For a lighter finish, the dessert menu features a selection of house-made gelatos in various tantalizing flavors.

SUMMARY AND COMMENTS Ihilani offers a beautiful setting and a memorable experience. Besides, it's the only Italian restaurant on Lanai.

Lanai City Grille ★★★

PACIFIC RIM MODERATE QUALITY ★★★★ VALUE ★★★ LANAI

**Hotel Lanai, 828 Lanai Avenue, Lanai City; ☎ 808-565-2000;
www.hotellanai.com**

Reservations Recommended. **When to go** Dinner. **Entree range** $12–$28.
Payment AE, MC, V. **Service rating** ★★★★. **Parking** Free. **Bar** Full service. **Wine
selection** Extensive. **Dress** Resort casual. **Disabled access** Good. **Customers**
Resort guests, Island residents. **Hours** Wednesday–Sunday, 5–9 p.m.

SETTING AND ATMOSPHERE Renovated in bright, white old-plantation style,
the cozy restaurant seats 125, including a new 50-seat rear outdoor
lanai for music and dancing, with heaters to ward off the upcountry
chill. The little bar on the front lanai accommodates 10 to 15 and boasts
a flat-screen TV for sportscasts.

HOUSE SPECIALTIES Maui celebrity chef Bev Gannon's famous meat loaf,
cowboy ribs, and steaks join rotisserie chicken on the simple comfort-
food menu. Gannon remains an advisor, but executive chef Mike Davis
presides over the kitchen, adding his own creative flair with dishes
such as seared venison over mushroom risotto with a cherry-Port wine
reduction and pecan-crusted fresh catch with chipotle honey butter.

SUMMARY AND COMMENTS Even the captains of industry and Hollywood stars
who can readily afford the exclusive Four Seasons Lanai resorts appreciate another good dining choice and a break from the hotel atmosphere.
That's why hotel guests often pack the shuttle for Lanai City at night
and join those who live in the swanky new resort homes that now edge
the golf courses in search of tasty treats. Chances are Lanai City Grille
has just what they want, including live music on Friday and Saturday
nights. It's sure to be the brightest light on quiet Lanai.

PART TEN

SHOPPING

IN HAWAII, WHEN THE SUN GETS TOO HOT, the sunburned go shopping. And what a bazaar they'll find—everything from funky T-shirts to worldly imports and a growing selection of made-in-Hawaii clothing, art, sports gear, and jewelry.

Because the Islands have attracted an increasingly international crowd—particularly free-spending young Japanese and Koreans for whom Hawaii has become a cheap ticket to European as well as U.S. designer boutiques—retail prospects have soared from dismal to extraordinary in recent years.

Smart-shopping Americans found they could bargain for the best selection this side of Hong Kong in Asian pearls, jewelry, antiques, and other imports. The trickle-down effect also lured American discount stores that in turn brought everyday prices down in other Island stores. When sugar plantations shut down, the company-owned stores, where so many workers shopped exclusively, soon followed. The Island economy changed dramatically. That meant a lot of young people pursued better jobs and bigger dreams, with more money to spend than their immigrant field-worker parents ever had. Retail makes up a large and booming share of the Hawaiian economy, with plenty of new investment in both new retail development and renovations.

The Aloha State is known for high costs, understandable because most of the goods—and every piece of glass, nail, and board in the buildings that contain them—are imported. But the low sales tax of 4%, charged at 4.712% on Oahu and 4.166% on other islands, makes purchases more palatable, and some items just can't be found anywhere else. Besides, there's no going home empty-handed after an enviable trip to Hawaii, so bring an extra suitcase and get ready to shop! Here are suggestions to maximize the experience.

BUY HAWAIIAN

LOCAL ARTS AND CRAFTS ARE FLOURISHING. Finding them is often as much fun as giving them for gifts. Local wares sold by their makers dominate the frequent arts-and-crafts fairs held throughout the Islands. Particularly fine are the **Pacific Handcrafters Guild** fairs held periodically on Oahu. Hawaiian product stores have sprung up everywhere (see our recommendations beginning on page 437). Occasionally you'll find local things among the cheap imports in tourist-zone kiosks and souvenir stores. You can find local books, Hawaiian music, aloha wear, and other goods at favorable prices in local stores and the national chain stores, such as **Costco, Longs, Tower Records, Sears,** and **Borders,** and in the local chain **ABC** stores.

Hawaii's indigenous products range from inexpensive to very dear. They include foods (macadamia nuts, coffees, teas, wines, tropical jams, syrups, honeys, candies, and real Maui potato chips); soaps and cosmetics with tropical ingredients and fragrances; fiber arts made of coconut leaf, *lauhala,* or pandanus and other natural materials; aloha-print fabrics made into shirts, baby clothes, totes, dresses, glasses cases, and even golf bags; Hawaiian books and music; warm-weather designer and sports clothing; hand-painted clothing; surfboards and windsurfing equipment; furniture and boxes handmade from tropical woods; one-of-a-kind Hawaiian appliquéd quilts, sewn only with permission of the family that created the design; and gold heirloom jewelry, Niihau shell jewelry, and all kinds of artwork.

unofficial **TIP**
If you want to fit in with the Hawaiian *wahine,* choose an oval solid-gold bracelet bearing your name in black enameled script.

When it comes to clothing, Hawaiian style is a unique blend of local design and tropical-weight fabrics with a nod to mainland, Pacific, and Asian style. The fashion police live a long way away, and Islanders tend to wear what they want whenever possible. Boutiques throughout the Islands are filled with interesting, imaginative clothes and accessories for women, aloha shirts from ancient collectibles to modern silks and other sleek or sporty attire for men, plenty of beachwear, nearly-nothings, and surfer duds for kids.

Hawaiian heirloom gold jewelry, including monogrammed Victorian-style pieces in an arcane style created for 19th-century royals, is the precious gift of choice for special occasions in the Islands. Most women in Hawaii wear at least one oval solid-gold bracelet, ornately patterned and bearing their name in Hawaiian in black enameled script. Mothers may wear their daughters' bracelets until the girls are older. Many bracelets never come off. Many women wear them by the armload in Hawaii, where it is safe enough and the local style. Admiring them is an effective way to start a conversation and get some hints on designs.

unofficial **TIP**
If you buy a bracelet, shop early in your trip to allow time for sizing and engraving.

Heirloom jewelry has branched out to include medallions, pendants, watchbands, bracelets, rings, and earrings for men as well as women. It is sold at jewelry shops throughout the Islands and at jewelry counters in other stores, including the Japanese chain **Daiei.**

Jewelry prices vary by gold weight and creative design. A bracelet might cost anywhere from $350 for a simple pattern on a thin band to $1,500 or more for a complex design on a larger band. This is a subjective purchase based on design, but do shop around enough to satisfy yourself that the price is fair for what you want. Shop for a bracelet early in your trip, to allow time for sizing and name engraving. The case samples are inscribed *kuuipo,* or "my sweetheart."

Niihau shells are exquisite and extraordinarily expensive if you view them as just another shell necklace. After all, a strand of dyed "coral" costs $10, while a strand of the least expensive Niihau shells costs more than $100, and fancy museum-quality ones can run into the thousands of dollars. Consider that each nearly microscopic Niihau shell is picked off the beach on the private ranch island of Niihau by one of its few inhabitants and then sorted, pierced, and strung into a traditional design. Visitors to Kauai, Niihau's neighbor island, are most likely to learn to appreciate the beauty of these treasures and to see a variety displayed in shops and museums. You may even find some shells on a West Kauai beach.

SPECIALTY SHOPPING

IT'S HARD TO AVOID PLACES TO SHOP, beginning with lobby stores in hotels, where stylish, good-quality resort clothing and swimsuits can often be found. In Waikiki, you can run the full gamut by strolling through shops at a luxury hotel like **Halekulani** and then rambling through the varied boutiques of **Royal Hawaiian Shopping Center** and new Waikiki Beach Walk or to the colorful jumble of kiosks at the **International Market Place.** Walk out the back to Kuhio Avenue, jump on TheBus and get off at **Ala Moana Center,** which reinvented itself to cater to high-end shoppers on its upper floors with Nordstrom, Neiman Marcus, and Macy's, plentiful designer boutiques, in addition to its wild assortment of international department stores, Island stores, and restaurants.

Farther up Ala Moana Boulevard, **Ward Center** and **Ward Warehouse** offer boutique collections of Island-style clothes, gifts, and restaurants. Up the street on the left at the harbor, find **Aloha Tower Marketplace,** a harborfront complex of shops, food, and entertainment with the added amusement of container ships bringing more goods, passenger liners, and other cruisers in the active harbor. Shoppers can prowl while mates down a freshly brewed beer at Gordon Biersch and watch the ships in the harbor. If you're looking for national-brand outlet shops, you'll find them at **Waikele Centre,** west of the airport on H-1. As you explore the rest of Oahu, you'll find smaller communities like Kailua (over the Pali on the windward side) and Haleiwa (surfing capital of the North

Shore) with great stores to investigate; antiques, local arts, handicrafts, gifts, decor and clothing boutiques, and sports gear for surfing, windsurfing, and kayaking. Along the way you can stop at roadside stands for tropical fruit, shrimp, and handmade baskets.

You should expect slightly higher prices on some items in familiar chain stores, even at Wal-Mart. **Hilo Hattie's** matching aloha wear and Hawaiian goods are everywhere, and they will find you if you don't find them. But that's not all there is. Here are our recommendations for some places to find local arts and crafts and Hawaiian goods. Hours of operation are subject to change.

OAHU

Alii Antiques of Kailua
21 Malunui Avenue, Kailua; Windward Oahu; ☎ 808-261-1705; www.aliiantiques.com

HOURS Monday–Saturday, 10:30 a.m.–4:30 p.m.
DESCRIPTION Alii has a separate building filled with Hawaiian kitsch and many treasures, including jewelry. Great place to prowl the island past.

Crazy Shirts
International Market Place, Waikiki (more than 20 locations throughout the state); Waikiki; ☎ 808-922-4791; www.crazyshirts.com

HOURS Daily, 8 a.m.–11:30 p.m.
DESCRIPTION Hawaii's homegrown T-shirt shop, featuring hundreds of colorful, local-themed designs, is ubiquitous, but the International Market Place location is the biggest of the line, and the Waikiki Beach Walk store is among the newest.

Fighter's Corner
405 North King Street, downtown Honolulu; Greater Honolulu; ☎ 808-599-4448; www.fighterscorner.net

HOURS Monday–Friday, 10 a.m.–7 p.m.; Saturday, 10 a.m.–6 p.m., Sunday, 11 a.m.–6 p.m.
DESCRIPTION Martial-arts gear, training equipment, clothing, and DVDs for kickboxers, jujitsu practitioners, and martial-arts fans.

Harry's Music Store
3457 Waialae Avenue, Honolulu; Greater Honolulu; ☎ 808-735-2866

HOURS Monday–Friday, 9:30 a.m.–5:30 p.m.; Saturday, 9 a.m.–5 p.m.
DESCRIPTION Old Hawaiian records, sheet music, and ukuleles are among the vintage items offered at this small but famous stop for Hawaiian music aficionados.

Hawaiian Ukulele Company
Aloha Tower Marketplace, Honolulu; Greater Honolulu; ☎ 808-536-3228; www.thehawaiianukulelecompany.com

HOURS Monday–Saturday, 9 a.m.–9 p.m.; Sunday, 9 a.m.–6 p.m.

DESCRIPTION Specializes in hand-crafted Hawaiian ukulele and other instruments, plus accessories, songbooks, and instruction booklets.

Into Inc.

40 North Hotel Street, Chinatown; Greater Honolulu; ☎ 808-536-2211; www.intohonolulu.com

HOURS Tuesday–Saturday, 10 a.m.–6 p.m.

DESCRIPTION Stylish, bold, and fun home accessories, such as throw pillows, bar accessories, travel candles in scents like fig or Champagne, lamps, rugs, specialty books, ceramics, and glassware.

Island Treasures Gallery

629 Kailua Road, Kailua; Windward Oahu; ☎ 808-261-8131

HOURS Monday–Saturday, 10 a.m.–6 p.m.; Sunday, 10 a.m.–4 p.m.

DESCRIPTION Artwork, Hawaiian-style crafts, gifts with flair created locally.

Islands' Best

Ala Moana Center, Honolulu; Greater Honolulu; ☎ 808-949-5345

HOURS Monday–Saturday, 9:30 a.m.–9 p.m.; Sunday, 10 a.m.–7 p.m.

DESCRIPTION Wide range of Hawaiian gifts and souvenirs, including soaps, crafts, stationery, and arts.

Montsuki

1148 Koko Head Avenue, Honolulu; Greater Honolulu; ☎ 808-734-3457

HOURS Monday–Saturday, 9:30 a.m.–5 p.m.

DESCRIPTION Stylish apparel fashioned from vintage silk kimonos.

Native Books Na Mea Hawaii

Ward Warehouse and Hilton Hawaiian Village, Honolulu; Greater Honolulu and Waikiki; ☎ 800-887-7751; Ward ☎ 808-596-8885; www.nativebookshawaii.com

HOURS Hilton Hawaiian Village: Daily, 8:30 a.m.–9 p.m.; Ward: Monday–Saturday, 10 a.m.–9 p.m.; Sunday, 10 a.m.–6 p.m.

DESCRIPTION Fine collection of Hawaiian books, crafts, artworks, apparel, and gifts.

Nohea Gallery

Ward Warehouse, Honolulu; Greater Honolulu (also at Sheraton Moana Surfrider in Waikiki and 767 Kailua Road, Kailua); ☎ 808-596-0074, 808-262-2787 (Kailua); www.noheagallery.com

HOURS Monday–Saturday, 10 a.m.–9 p.m.; Sunday, 10 a.m.–5 p.m. at Ward; 8 a.m.–10 p.m. daily at Moana; Monday–Saturday, 10 a.m.–6 p.m. and Sunday 10 a.m.–4 p.m. at Kailua.

DESCRIPTION One of the best galleries for Island arts and fine crafts in all media.

Oogenesis Boutique
66-249 Kamehameha Highway, Haleiwa; ☎ 808-637-4422

HOURS Daily, 10 a.m.–6 p.m.

DESCRIPTION Owner and designer Inga Himmelmann has sewn, painted, and designed clothes since 1970. At this gaily painted green-and-pink plantation-style storefront with the big pink cat on front, dresses hang from a rafter and flutter in the wind, waving you inside to see more. Wares run the gamut from inexpensive baubles to costly treasures.

Silver Moon Emporium
66-250 Kamehameha Highway (North Shore Marketplace shopping center), Haleiwa; ☎ 808-637-7710

HOURS Daily, 10 a.m.–6 p.m.

DESCRIPTION Stuffed with chic, this boutique specializes in women's clothes with flair that suit the climate and island lifestyles, ranging from fairly conservative to out-and-outrageous. Kino, Citron, Flax, and other lines that cross age and size groups fight for attention with jewelry, accessories, scarves, bags, hats, some footwear, and lotions and perfume. Silk, cotton, linen, and rayon predominate in women's clothes for work and leisure, parties, and weddings.

Tapestries by Hauoli
1450 Ala Moana Boulevard (Ala Moana Center, 1026, street-level near Post Office), Honolulu; Greater Honolulu; ☎ 808-973-0566

HOURS Monday–Saturday, 9:30 a.m.–9 p.m.; Sunday, 10 a.m.–7 p.m.

DESCRIPTION Professional women shop for designer accents from East and West, cotton, silk, rayon, lace, and linen clothes for office, special occasion, and light-hearted leisure. With wide-ranging choices, you're bound to find something nobody at home has: elegant evening cover-up jackets designed locally and made from old kimonos or fashioned in silk with intricate patterns to set off a black outfit, Thai indigo prints, Asian prints on silk and linen, silk patchwork jackets, plus jewelry, dressy tees and accessories.

Welcome to the Islands
Ward Center, 1200 Ala Moana Boulevard, Honolulu; Greater Honolulu; ☎ 808-593-2035; www.welcometotheislands.com

HOURS Monday–Saturday, 10 a.m.–9 p.m.; Sunday, 10 a.m.–5 p.m.

DESCRIPTION Island gifts for folks back home, from jellies and tropically scented bath products to art glass and home decor.

MAUI

Dolphin Galleries
The Shops at Wailea and Whalers Village, Kaanapali; ☎ 808-891-8000 and 808-661-5115; www.dolphingalleries.com

HOURS Daily, 9:30 a.m.–9 p.m.

DESCRIPTION Jewelry and art, some familiar, some extraordinary, in well-designed galleries where "just looking" is a pleasure. Modern cloisonne set in gold, kinetic gemstone rings, and dolphins galore are among the works.

Hana Coast Gallery
Hotel Hana-Maui, Hana Highway, Hana; ☎ 808-248-8636; www.hanacoast.com

HOURS Daily, 9 a.m.–5 p.m.

DESCRIPTION Visit to see the exquisite collection of Maui artists' works as you might in a museum, because it's that committed to the culture and it's that good. Oil, watercolors, woods, feathers, stone, prints, glass, and fibers are among the media used to interpret the beauty of Hana and Maui by famous and lesser-known artists in artworks, furniture, and jewelry. If you want to purchase some excellent local pieces for your collection, don't miss this gallery.

Hasegawa General Store
5165 Hana Highway, Hana; Upcountry Maui and Beyond; ☎ 808-248-8231

HOURS Monday–Saturday, 7 a.m.–7 p.m.; Sunday, 8 a.m.–6 p.m.

DESCRIPTION An old-fashioned general merchandise store, so beloved that a song was written about it. Founded in 1910, this family-run store sells the necessities and some frills for residents and visitors to faraway Hana.

Hawaiiana Arts & Crafts
Wharf Cinema Center, Lahaina; West Maui; ☎ 808-661-9077

HOURS Daily, 10 a.m.–8 p.m.

DESCRIPTION Handmade arts and crafts by some of Maui's best artisans, including *raku* pottery, woodcrafts, and woven baskets.

Honolua Store
Office Road, Kapalua Resort; West Maui; ☎ 808-669-6128

HOURS Daily, 6 a.m.–8 p.m.

DESCRIPTION Historic plantation grocery store features books, gifts, and clothing, along with groceries, prepared food (hot breakfasts, plate lunch, and deli) and beverages.

Hui Noeau Visual Arts Center
2841 Baldwin Avenue, Makawao; ☎ 808-572-6560; www.huinoeau.com

HOURS Monday–Saturday, 10 a.m.–4 p.m.

DESCRIPTION This beautiful old ten-acre estate with its 1917 mansion is the heart of Maui's art colony. Devoted to art education with classes, demonstrations, and exhibitions, the Hui provides studios for artists and a fine shop for their wares.

Kaukini Gallery
Kahakuloa Head, northwest coast; ☎ 808-244-3371

HOURS Daily, 10 a.m.–5 p.m.
DESCRIPTION More than 100 local artists' paintings, prints, jewelry, sculpture, woodworks, fabric arts, and ceramics sold in a handsome yellow gallery in the middle of nowhere at Kahakuloa (but within half an hour's drive north of Kapalua).

Maui Hands
84 Hana Highway, Paia; 3620 Baldwin Avenue, Makawao; 612 Front Street, Lahaina; and Hyatt Regency Hotel, Kaanapali Beach Resort; ☎ 808-579-9245; www.mauihands.com

HOURS Monday–Saturday, 10 a.m.–7 p.m.; Sunday, 10 a.m.–6 p.m.
DESCRIPTION Works by more than 250 Maui artists, designers, and artisans are featured, including fine arts, wood bowls and sculptures, home furnishings, jewelry, glass and pottery, baskets, and accessories. Prices range from $2 to $10,000.

Moonbow Tropics
Locations 300 Maalaea Road, Maalaea; 612 Front Street, Lahaina; 36 Baldwin Avenue and 20 Baldwin Avenue, Paia; ☎ 808-243-9577 (Maalaea); 808-667-7998 (Lahaina); 808-579-8775 or 808-579-8592 (Paia)

HOURS Monday–Saturday, 10 a.m.–7 p.m; Sunday, 10 a.m.–6 p.m.
DESCRIPTION Men find comfortable shopping here, browsing through classy aloha shirts and other clothes for men and women, as well as appointments of the tropical good life, including CDs. Stores include one by the Maui Ocean Center, one in central Lahaina, and two on Paia's main shopping street, Baldwin Avenue.

Tropo/Hurricane Ltd.
3643 and 3639 Baldwin Avenue, Makawao; ☎ 808-573-0356 and 572-5076

HOURS Daily, 10 a.m.–6 p.m.
DESCRIPTION Guy things are featured at Tropo—men's designer aloha shirts of silk and other fine fabrics, name-brand tropical wear, and tasteful informal clothing; also books, jazz CDs, Swiss Army knives, binoculars, accessories, and Crabtree and Evelyn cosmetics. Hurricane carries tasteful women's wear by famous designers and local artists, perfumes, and accessories for the home.

THE BIG ISLAND

Big Island Candies
585 Hinano Street, Hilo; Hilo and Volcano; ☎ 808-935-8890; www.bigislandcandies.com

HOURS Daily, 8:30 a.m.–5 p.m.

DESCRIPTION Locally made chocolates, chocolate-dipped cookies, and candies. Large windows let you watch confections being made in the adjoining factory.

CC Whisper
Kona Alii Condos, Alii Drive, Kailua-Kona; Kona; ☎ 808-329-3726; www.ccwhisper.com

HOURS Daily, 9 a.m.–5 p.m.
DESCRIPTION Exquisite, life-like orchid plants crafted from clay by artist Darunee Fasano, a native of Thailand. She has also replicated roses, irises, gardenias, and various other flowers.

Harbor Gallery
Kawaihae Harbor Shopping Center, Kawaihae; Kona; ☎ 808-882-1510; www.harborgallery.com

HOURS Daily, 11:30 a.m.–8:30 p.m.
DESCRIPTION Diverse collection of Island art, including koa wood, furniture and art objects, sculptures, paintings, ceramics, and jewelry.

Phoenix Rising
25 Waianuenue Aveneue, Hilo; Hilo and Volcano; ☎ 808-934-7353

HOURS Monday–Friday, 9 a.m.–6 p.m.; Saturday, 9 a.m.–4 p.m.
DESCRIPTION Asian and contemporary decor, gifts, designer dog carriers, everything from wine glasses to Japanese swords, with a black-feather floor lamp for good measure.

Sig Zane Designs
122 Kamehameha Avenue, Hilo; ☎ 808-935-7077; www.sigzane.com

HOURS Monday–Friday, 9:30 a.m.–5 p.m.; Saturday, 9 a.m.–4 p.m.
DESCRIPTION Zane's bold graphic interpretations of Hawaiian flora and culture make striking Hawaiian prints in fabric, wall hangings, dresses, shirts, and pareos.

KAUAI

Kong Lung Trading Co.
2484 Keneke Street, Kilauea; Kauai; ☎ 808-828-1822

HOURS Daily, 11:30 a.m.–6:30 p.m.
DESCRIPTION Set in a historic stone building, this is one of Kauai's most famous shops. Collectibles, housewares, jewelry, apparel, and fine gifts make it a worthwhile stop on your way to the North Shore.

Ola's Hanalei
Hanalei Trader Building, 5-5016 Kuhio Highway, Hanalei; Kauai; ☎ 808-826-6937; olashanalei.com

HOURS Daily, 10 a.m.–9 p.m.
DESCRIPTION Jewelry, glassware, woodcrafts, soaps, and other handcrafted goods are for sale at this fun-to-browse shop.

Yellowfish Trading Company
Hanalei Center, Hanalei; Kauai; ☎ 808-826-1227

HOURS Daily, 10 a.m.–8 p.m.

DESCRIPTION Antiques and knickknacks, vintage aloha shirts, photographs and posters, Hawaiian furniture, and kitchenware.

MOLOKAI

Big Wind Kite Factory
120 Maunaloa Highway, Maunaloa; Molokai; ☎ 808-552-2364

HOURS Monday–Saturday, 8:30 a.m.–5 p.m.; Sunday, 10 a.m.–2 p.m.

DESCRIPTION Hula dancers, pirate ships, and happy dragons are among the artful kites of all shapes, sizes, and designs offered here. Some made on site; imported gifts. The friendly owner provides free kite-flying lessons (at an adjacent open field) with "no strings attached."

LANAI

Akamai Trading
408 Eighth Street, Lanai City; Lanai; ☎ 808-565-6587

HOURS Monday–Friday, 9 a.m.–6 p.m.; Saturday, 9 a.m.–5:30 p.m.; Sunday, 9 a.m.–4:30 p.m.

DESCRIPTION General store with an interesting selection of Island necessities, including furniture and appliances, as well as souvenirs, gifts, and locally made jams and jellies.

Gifts with Aloha
Corner of Ilima and Seventh Street, Lanai City; Lanai; ☎ 808-565-6589; www.giftswithaloha.com

HOURS Monday–Saturday, 9:30 a.m.–6 p.m.

DESCRIPTION Made-in-Hawaii gifts, including resort wear, koa-wood products, scented candles, books, and hand-quilted pillow covers.

SHOPPING CENTERS

OAHU

kids Ala Moana Shopping Center
Ala Moana Boulevard, next to Waikiki; Greater Honolulu; ☎ 808-955-9517; www.alamoanacenter.com

HOURS Monday–Saturday, 9:30 a.m.–9 p.m.; Sunday, 10 a.m.–7 p.m.

NUMBER OF STORES AND RESTAURANTS More than 200

DESCRIPTION Department stores, upscale European and American boutiques, jewelry, gifts, outdoor gifts and gear, drugstore, supermarket, shoes, cartoon art, candy, software, sandals and slippers, swimwear and beachwear, toys, sports gear, and Tahitian and Hawaiian fabrics. This is one of the largest shopping centers in the United States and the most lucrative, producing three times the average sales per square foot of malls nationwide. And it's certainly one of the most pleasant, too, with its open-air tropical gardens and ponds. Another expansion is underway to add a new Nordstrom store. Free entertainment daily on the stage in the middle of the Center, usually music and/or dance.

Aloha Tower Marketplace
1 Aloha Tower Drive, at the foot of Bishop Street downtown; Greater Honolulu; ☎ 808-528-5700; www.alohatower.com

HOURS Monday–Saturday, 9 a.m.–9 p.m.; Sunday, 9 a.m.–6 p.m.
NUMBER OF STORES AND RESTAURANTS About 75
DESCRIPTION Hawaiian woodcrafts, furniture, gifts, swimwear, coffee, candies, cartoon art, tropical apparel, cigar shop, shoes, magnets, and perfumes; plus changing goods, imports, and clothing in numerous kiosks. Stores are arrayed at the foot of historic ten-story Aloha Tower, where you can take the elevator to the top, enjoy panoramic views, and imagine the scene when this was the tallest building in town.

International Market Place
2330 Kalakaua Avenue, Waikiki; Waikiki; ☎ 808-971-2080; www.internationalmarketplacewaikiki.com

HOURS Daily, 10 a.m.–10:30 p.m.
NUMBER OF STORES AND RESTAURANTS About 150
DESCRIPTION Outdoor maze of kiosks features jewelry, T-shirts, pareo, handbags, touristy souvenirs, and imported knickknacks. Bargain like crazy to improve the prices—everybody here wants to sell.

North Shore Marketplace
66-250 Kamehameha Highway, Haleiwa; North Shore; ☎ 808-637-4416

HOURS Daily, 10 a.m.–6 p.m.
NUMBER OF STORES AND RESTAURANTS 25
DESCRIPTION Shaded by huge monkey pod trees, this small center with plantation-style architecture and lots of parking has surf shops, boutiques, eateries, and the North Shore Surf and Cultural Museum, which includes a timeline on the development of surfboards and how Haleiwa came to be the "Surf Capital of the World." The museum is usually open in the afternoons, depending on the surf conditions. For more information on the museum, call ☎ 808-637-8888 or visit www.captainrick.com/surf_museum.htm.

kids Pearlridge Shopping Center
231 Pearlridge Center, Honolulu; Central Oahu; ☎ 808-488-0981

HOURS Monday–Saturday, 10 a.m.–9 p.m.; Sunday, 10 a.m.–6 p.m.
NUMBER OF STORES AND RESTAURANTS More than 170
DESCRIPTION Department stores, electronics, outdoor goods, toys, books, drugstores, apparel, candy, lingerie, men's wear, videos, stationers, shoes, glasses, and movies. The most interesting thing about this suburban center

is the monorail linking two complexes, which was built so that development would not imperil the prized Sumida watercress farm below. (The superlative watercress is sold in huge bunches at Island markets.)

Royal Hawaiian Shopping Center
2201 Kalakaua Avenue, Waikiki; Waikiki; ☎ 808-922-0588

HOURS Daily, 10 a.m.–10 p.m.
NUMBER OF STORES AND RESTAURANTS More than 110
DESCRIPTION Upscale designer boutiques, biker logos, jewelry factory, sports apparel, collectibles, and Island wear. Frequent free Hawaiian entertainment at the central Kalakaua entrance of this sprawling mall, nearly 300,000 square feet of space, refreshed by a $110-million renovation in 2008.

kids Waikiki Beach Walk
Lewers Street at Kalia Road; office, 227 Lewers Street, Suite 150; Waikiki; ☎ 808-931-3593

HOURS Daily, generally 10 a.m.–11 p.m.
NUMBER OF STORES AND RESTAURANTS About 60
DESCRIPTION Brand-new half-a-billion-dollar hotel-restaurant-shopping complex has replaced a tacky section of Waikiki, just off the beach behind the Halekulani and the Outrigger Reef hotels. Shops include beach and surfing togs and tropical clothes, jewelry, art, and other gallery wares. Historical displays, cultural programs, free hula and contemporary Hawaiian music performances weekly and monthly throughout the year.

kids Ward Center/Ward Warehouse
1050–1240 Ala Moana Boulevard, Honolulu; Greater Honolulu; ☎ 808-591-8411 or 808-593-2376; www.victoriaward.com

HOURS Monday–Saturday, 10 a.m.–8 or 9 p.m.; Sunday, 10 a.m.–6 p.m.
NUMBER OF STORES AND RESTAURANTS 100 (restaurants mostly at Ward Center; mostly shops at Warehouse)
DESCRIPTION Books and music, gifts, gadgets, stationery, Island ceramics, University of Hawaii gear, chocolates, tropical wear, tropical home furnishings, art galleries, bath shop, shoes, crafts, holiday ornaments, sandals and shoes, apparel, toys, and perfumes. Free band concerts, shows, and exhibits throughout the year. Services include valet, car detailing, and concierge as well as conference rooms available for rent.

MAUI

505 Front Street
Front Street, Lahaina; West Maui; ☎ 808-667-2514; www.lahainarestaurants.com

HOURS Monday–Saturday, 10 a.m.–9 p.m.; Sunday, 10 a.m.–6 p.m.
NUMBER OF STORES AND RESTAURANTS More than 25

DESCRIPTION Oceanfront boutique mall at the quiet southern end of Lahaina. Unusual shops include Hawaiian products, spa goods, clothing, souvenirs, gifts. Live jazz outdoors at Pacific'O restaurant on Thursday, Friday, and Saturday nights.

kids Lahaina Center

900 Front Street, Lahaina; West Maui; ☎ 808-667-9216; www.lahainacenter.com

HOURS Generally, Monday–Saturday, 9 a.m.–10 p.m., Sunday; 9 a.m.– 6 p.m.

NUMBER OF STORES AND RESTAURANTS 30

DESCRIPTION Aloha wear, gifts, sundries, apparel, T-shirts, swimwear, jewelry, children's shop, microbrewery. Free hula shows Wednesday and Friday, 2 and 6 p.m.

kids Queen Kaahumanu Center

275 Kaahumanu Avenue, Kahului; Central Maui; ☎ 808-877-3369; www.queenkaahumanucenter.com

HOURS Monday–Saturday, 9:30 a.m.–9 p.m.; Sunday, 10 a.m.–5 p.m.

NUMBER OF STORES AND RESTAURANTS More than 100

DESCRIPTION Department stores, books, gifts, toys, cards, jewelry, cartoon logos, dime store, coffee, shoes, apparel, photo processing, movies, and community events.

kids The Shops at Wailea

Wailea Resort, 3750 Wailea Alanui Drive, Wailea; South Maui; ☎ 808-891-6770; www.shopsatwailea.com

HOURS Daily, 9:30 a.m.–9 p.m.

NUMBER OF STORES AND RESTAURANTS About 70

DESCRIPTION Resort wear, upscale designer boutiques, gifts, galleries, woodcrafts and furniture, toys, camera shops, sundries, ice cream, and swimwear and beachwear. Frequent events and food festivals.

Whalers Village

Kaanapali Beach Resort, 2435 Kaanapali Parkway, Lahaina; West Maui; ☎ 808-661-4567; www.whalersvillage.com

HOURS Daily, 9:30 a.m.–10 p.m.

NUMBER OF STORES AND RESTAURANTS 60

DESCRIPTION Upscale boutiques, jewelry, scrimshaw, Hawaiian koa furniture, gifts, art galleries, Island apparel, whalers museum and general goods. Free hula performances 7 p.m. nightly, except Tuesday and Thursday.

THE BIG ISLAND OF HAWAII

Keauhou Shopping Center

78-6831 Alii Drive, Keauhou; Kona; ☎ 808-332-3000

HOURS Monday–Saturday, 9 a.m.–6 p.m.; Sunday, 10 a.m.–5 p.m.

NUMBER OF STORES AND RESTAURANTS 40
DESCRIPTION Supermarket, drugstore, post office, hardware, coffee, art gallery, and movies. Craft demonstrations, talk story sessions, and various other activites are presented Fridays, 10 a.m.–2 p.m. Free Polynesian show Fridays, 6 p.m.–7 p.m.

Kings' Shops
Waikoloa Beach Resort, Kohala Coast; Kona; ☎ 808-886-8811

HOURS Daily, 9:30 a.m.–9:30 p.m.
NUMBER OF STORES AND RESTAURANTS About 40
DESCRIPTION Souvenirs, jewelry, art gallery, clothing, accessories, gifts, and sunglasses. Free entertainment and activities throughout the week.

Prince Kuhio Plaza
111 East Puainako Street (off Highway 11, near Hilo airport), Hilo; Hilo and Volcano; ☎ 808-959-3555

HOURS Monday–Friday, 10 a.m.–9 p.m.; Saturday, 9:30 a.m.–7 p.m.; Sunday, 10 a.m.–6 p.m.
NUMBER OF STORES AND RESTAURANTS Over 75
DESCRIPTION Department stores, books, videos, drugstore, apparel, swimwear.

Waikoloa Queens' Marketplace
Waikoloa Beach Resort (off Mamalahoa Highway), Kohala Coast; Kona; ☎ 877-WAIKOLOA

HOURS Daily, 9:30 a.m.–9:30 p.m.
NUMBER OF STORES AND RESTAURANTS 36 and counting
DESCRIPTION A gourmet food market is the centerpiece of this newly constructed complex across the Kings Trail from King's Shops. Other features include a food pavilion, clothing, jewelry and gift shops, and a day spa, as well as a Starbucks and the Big Island's first Sansei Seafood Restaurant & Sushi Bar, the acclaimed Eurasian fusion restaurant from Maui. The ethnobotanical cultural garden and entertainment center will spotlight Hawaiian cultural events and lore.

KAUAI
Coconut MarketPlace
484 Kuhio Highway, Wailua; Kauai; ☎ 808-822-3641

HOURS Monday–Saturday, 9 a.m.–9 p.m.; Sunday, 10 a.m.–6 p.m.
NUMBER OF STORES AND RESTAURANTS More than 70
DESCRIPTION Gifts, music, jewelry, clothing, Hawaiian products, swimwear. Free entertainment (including hula) Wednesdays at 5 p.m.

Kukui Grove Center
3-2600 Kaumualii Highway, Lihue; Kauai; ☎ 808-245-7784

HOURS Monday–Thursday and Saturday, 9:30 a.m.–7 p.m.; Friday, 9:30 a.m.–9 p.m.; Sunday, 10 a.m.–6 p.m.

NUMBER OF STORES AND RESTAURANTS Over 60
DESCRIPTION Department stores, Kauai products, clothing, shoes, jewelry, grocery, drug store, dining. Kauai's major shopping mall.

Poipu Shopping Village
Poipu Beach Resort, 2360 Kiahuna Plantation Drive, Poipu; Kauai;
☎ **808-742-2831**

HOURS Monday–Saturday, 10 a.m.–9 p.m.; Sunday, 10 a.m.–6 p.m.
NUMBER OF STORES AND RESTAURANTS About 20
DESCRIPTION T-shirts, art galleries, swimwear, gifts, sandals, sunglasses, cosmetics, and clothing. Free Polynesian shows Tuesdays and Thursdays at 5 p.m.

SWAP MEETS *and* FLEA MARKETS

BARGAIN HUNTERS ON OAHU should check out the major swap meet, the **Aloha Stadium Swap Meet** held in the parking lot surrounding Aloha Stadium on Wednesday, Saturday, and Sunday (and some holidays) from 6 a.m. to 3 p.m. You'll find an astounding variety of new and used merchandise, treasures and trash, eelskin leathers, imports, baskets, fresh produce, plants, and even fresh fish. Feel free to bargain; it's part of the fun. Admission is 50 cents a head for people over age 12. The sun can be relentless, so go early and dress casually for shopping with the local folks. Call ☎ 808-486-6704 for more information.

PART ELEVEN

ENTERTAINMENT *and* NIGHTLIFE

HAWAII NIGHTLIFE

LIVE ENTERTAINMENT IN HAWAII offers plentiful choices for all ages, from Honolulu dance clubs for 20-somethings to the ubiquitous and mesmerizing Hawaiian music and dance that define the Island State. No other American place has such a distinct culture, expressed on the air, in free public shows in Waikiki and resort hotels on all islands, in community pageants, backyard parties, outdoor concerts or fancy theater shows, and performed by players, singers, and dancers of any age from 6 to 80. You can also find the kinds of entertainment you know from home. (In need of a big screen to watch a big game? Try Murphy's Bar & Grill, 2 Merchant Street in downtown Honolulu.) But where else can you experience a luau (**Paradise Cove** or **Germaine's** on Oahu, **Old Lahaina Luau** on Maui, **Paradise Gardens** luau on Kauai or **Kona Village Resort** luau on the Big Island are top choices for commercial luau) or fall in love with a slack-key guitarist or a hula dancer while sipping your mai tai? Or watch a spectacular tropical sunset punctuated by whale spouts? When you're on Maui, don't miss *Ulalena* in Lahaina. *Ulalena* is the best live show in Hawaii, telling the story of the Islands in a haunting *Cirque du Soleil*–type production.

Hawaiian music is alive and well throughout the Islands, at places like **Duke's Canoe Club** in Waikiki or **Don Ho's Island Grill, Chai's Island Bistro,** and at Aloha Tower Marketplace. Hawaiian concerts are frequently billed at the beautifully renovated 1922 Hawaii Theatre in Chinatown. You can see Jerry Santos and Olomana at the **Paradise Lounge** at Hilton Hawaiian Village. After a long absence, popular contemporary Hawaiian musicians are again playing Waikiki.

The Islands are full of gifted musicians and singers, such as Kealii Reichel, Hookena, Willie K., Amy Hanaialii Gilliom, her brother Eric Gilliom and Barry Flanagan performing as Hapa, Makaha Sons of Niihau, the Peter Moon Band, Robbie Kahakalau, and Na Leo

Pumehana, to name a few. They appear on all islands, so check the local papers' entertainment sections.

Oahu is Hawaii's after-dark club hub with dance clubs, swanky cocktail lounges, local bars, karaoke clubs, adult-entertainment clubs, and hostess bars. Grown-ups in search of live jazz and specialty after-dinner drinks will feel at home in the Lewers Lounge at Halekulani. But more adventurous fun seekers can venture downtown to a somewhat cleaned-up Chinatown to prowl galleries or perhaps to find the former peep-show dive now reborn as a loft lounge and lanai, **thirtyninehotel** (39 Hotel Street).

If you're staying on a Neighbor Island, bring your iPod and a good book—folks may well draw their shades early. Only a few spots, like Kihei and Lahaina on Maui, stay open after dark and have crowds who linger past midnight. Otherwise, nightlife may be limited to hotel-lounge acts, some of which are quite good. You came to the Islands to relax, remember?

PERFORMING ARTS

SOONER OR LATER, EVERYONE PLAYS HONOLULU. The beach city attracts worldly entertainers who regularly perform at Neal Blaisdell Center, Waikiki Shell, and elsewhere. If your timing's good, you may see the Bolshoi Ballet, the Beach Boys, or even the Rolling Stones (who played Aloha Stadium) for a lot less than on the mainland. Jazz singer Diana Krall and Sir Elton John appeared one night in adjoining concert halls.

Major Concert and Performing-arts Venues

Check *Honolulu Weekly* or the local dailies for appearances and dates. Here are some contact numbers and general locations for public concert venues in Hawaii.

OAHU

Aloha Stadium	☎ 808-486-9300
Hawaii Theatre Center	☎ 808-528-0506
Neal Blaisdell Center Arena	☎ 808-591-2211
Neal Blaisdell Concert Hall	☎ 808-591-2211
Waikiki Shell	☎ 808-591-2211

MAUI

Maui Arts & Cultural Center	☎ 808-242-7469

◼ DINNER SHOWS

WAIKIKI ISN'T LAS VEGAS, nor does it want to be, so don't expect extravaganzas. You can choose among a few entertaining dinner shows. Here are seven worth a look because they can only be seen in the Islands, the dinner entrees will satisfy even picky eaters, and, in most cases, the price of admission won't cause sticker shock.

OAHU

kids Creation: A Polynesian Journey
120 Kaiulani Avenue, Ainahau Showroom, Sheraton Princess Kaiulani Hotel, Waikiki; ☎ 808-931-4660

Showtimes Shows Tuesday, Thursday–Sunday. Dinner seating at 6 p.m.; cocktail seating at 7 p.m. **Length** 90 minutes. **Cost** Premium dinner: $135 adults, $100 children ages 7–12; standard dinner: $85 adults, $63.75 children; cocktail show: $49 adults, $36.75 children. **Discounts** Discount coupons available inside "Best of Oahu" booklets. Hotel guests receive a two-for-one coupon. **Type of seating** Long tables facing the stage. First come, first served. **Menu** All-you-can-eat buffet. Prime rib, chicken, chow mein noodles with vegetables and char siu, beef curry stew, mahimahi, sushi rolls, fresh salad, fruits, cakes, and ice cream. The premium Alii Dinner is a sit-down meal featuring lobster and filet mignon, salad, rice or potato, dessert, and two drinks. **Vegetarian alternative** Salads at buffet. **Beverages** Mai tai, draft beer, soft drinks, juice, and coffee.

DESCRIPTION AND COMMENTS High-tech stage show follows Polynesian voyagers with vivid sound and light effects. Good choice for young families.

Magic of Polynesia
2300 Kalakaua Avenue, Ohana Waikiki Beachcomber Hotel, Waikiki; ☎ 808-971-4321

Showtimes Tuesday–Saturday, 8 p.m. Dinner seating at 7 p.m.; cocktail seating at 8 p.m. **Length** 75 minutes. **Cost** Deluxe dinner (featuring steak and lobster): $139 adults, $68 children ages 4–11; standard dinner: $85 adults, $57 children; cocktail show: $52.50 adults, $35 children. **Discounts** Book online to save 20%; Entertainment Book coupons offer buy one, get one free for the cocktail show. **Type of seating** Table seating. A seat toward the back gives better overall view. **Menu** Sit-down dinner of salmon, chicken, mashed potatoes, steamed vegetables, and cake. **Vegetarian alternative** Request in advance. **Beverages** Tropical drinks, wine, beer, soft drinks, juice, coffee.

DESCRIPTION AND COMMENTS John Hirokawa, a local boy taught by David Copperfield, delivers illusionist skills with Polynesian themes in family-oriented magic show. Reserve your seats 24 hours ahead of time, if possible.

Society of Seven

2335 Kalakaua Avenue, Main Outrigger Showroom, Outrigger Waikiki Beach Hotel, Waikiki; ☎ 808-922-6408; www.angelfire.com/hi/societyofseven

Showtimes Wednesday–Sunday, 8:30 p.m. **Length** 90 minutes. **Cost** Show only: $37.25 adults, $23.88 children ages 4–20; 3-course dinner at Hula Grill and show: $75 per person. **Discounts** None. **Type of seating** Cabaret-style table seating. **Beverages** Tropical drinks, beer, wine, mixed drinks, soft drinks, juice, and coffee.

DESCRIPTION AND COMMENTS Hawaii's longest running show (35 years and counting), for one reason: It's good fun. Comedy, Broadway tunes, musical skits, impressions, oldies, contemporary hits, and audience participation make for an entertaining evening.

MAUI

Masters of Hawaiian Slack Key Guitar Concert Series

Ritz-Carlton, Kapalua Hotel amphitheater, 1 Kapalua Drive, Kapalua; ☎ 808-669-3858; www.slackkey.com

Showtimes (*Note:* Check with the hotel or Web site for details. Shows were suspended during hotel renovations and resume in January 2010.) Food Hotel restaurants. **Beverages** Available at small wet bar or hotel lounge and bar.

DESCRIPTION AND COMMENTS Series spotlights virtuosos picking guitar in the elaborate slack-key style that sounds like musical lace. Hosted by George Kahumoku Jr. and sometimes by his son Keoki Kahumoku, who both play "talk story" with the audience, along with the other artists. Hawaiian music won its first Grammy award in 2005.

Ulalena

Maui Myth and Magic Theater, 878 Front Street, Lahaina; ☎ 877-688-4800 or 808-661-9913; www.ulalena.com

Showtimes Tuesday, Wednesday, Friday, and Saturday, 6:30 p.m. **Length** 75 minutes. **Cost** $59.50–$129.50 adults, depending on seating and dinner; children 3–12, $39.50–84.50. **Discounts** None. **Type of seating** $10-million, high-tech theater with stadium seating; features live Hawaiian chant and music with 8-channel surround sound. Food Dinner at Ruth's Chris Steakhouse; bar in lobby. **Beverages** Beer, wine, soft drinks, juice, and coffee.

DESCRIPTION AND COMMENTS Best original, creative show in Hawaii. A *Cirque du Soleil* production by the Montreal troupe blends Island myth and fact in culturally keen theatrical performance.

Warren & Annabelle's

900 Front Street, Lahaina; ☎ 808-667-6244

Showtimes One or two shows, Monday–Saturday, 5 p.m. and 7:30 p.m. **Length** 120 minutes. **Cost** $58.33. Guests must be age 21 or older. Special *pupu* (hors d'oeuvres) packages are available: $98.19 includes show, appetizer platter, dessert, and two drinks; Prices include tip, but tax is added. **Type of seating** Table seating for *pupu* and cocktails. Intimate 78-seat theater (stadium seating). First come, first served. **Menu** Unless you order *pupu*, everything is à la carte. *Pupu* menu includes spicy crab cakes, coconut- battered shrimp, shrimp cocktails, chicken satay, and kalua-pork wraps. Desserts include chocolate pots de crème, crème brûlée, apple pie, Key lime pie, and cheesecake. **Vegetarian alternative** Spinach and cheese ravioli; request in advance. **Beverages** Tropical drinks, specialty drinks, beer, wine, soft drinks, juice, and coffee.

DESCRIPTION AND COMMENTS Magician Warren Gibson performs sleight-of-hand tricks in the cozy theater with Annabelle, a piano-playing ghost who takes requests.

BEFORE- *and* AFTER-DINNER LOUNGES

MAJOR RESORT HOTELS on all the islands offer good live music and a place to dance or relax with an after-dinner drink and enjoy the evening. Here are some of the best.

OAHU

- **Duke's Canoe Club, Outrigger Waikiki** ☎ 808-922-2268 Open-air beach club full of young couples full of beer and mai tais jiving to Hawaiian music.
- **House without a Key, Halekulani** ☎ 808-923-2311 Elegant open-air setting ideal for sunset cocktails, with live music and hula against a Diamond Head backdrop.
- **Lewers Lounge, Halekulani** ☎ 808-923-2311 When you want the most romantic hideaway, come hear late-night jazz in the finest hotel.
- **Mai Tai Bar, Royal Hawaiian Hotel** ☎ 808-923-7311 Beach bar nonpareil. Sip a cool one in your swimsuit and watch babes and hunks go by.
- **Paradise Lounge, Hilton Hawaiian Village** ☎ 808-949-4321 The living-room setting is a cozy venue for weekend-night appearances by Olomana, one of Hawaii's best-loved contemporary Hawaiian groups.

MAUI

- **Lagoon Bar, Sheraton Maui** ☎ 808-661-0031 Outdoors, surrounded by the pool, this is the place to sip a sunset cocktail while observing the nightly torch lighting and Hawaii's only cliff-diving ceremony.

BIG ISLAND OF HAWAII

- **Honu Bar, Mauna Lani Resort** ☎ 808-885-6622 A favorite Kohala Coast nightspot, this chic wine bar full of couples offers dinner, jazz, and dancing.
- **Shipwreck Bar, Kona Village Resort** ☎ 808-325-5555 Lift a mai tai toast to Johnno Jackson, who hit the reef in 1959 aboard his 42-foot schooner (the hull forms the bar) and founded Kona Village. No music, just ocean breezes and drinks.

KAUAI

- **Duke's Canoe Club, Kauai Marriott Resort & Beach Club** ☎ 808-246-9599 Beachside shrine to Duke Kahanamoku, Hawaiian band on Fridays.
- **Stevenson's Library, Grand Hyatt Kauai Resort & Spa** ☎ 808-742-1234 Koa wood–paneled old boy's club (ladies welcome) lined with books and vintage art. Live jazz in the evenings.

DANCE CLUBS *and* NIGHTSPOTS

ANYONE WHO WANTS TO WHOOP IT UP in the tropical night should plan to do it on Oahu, although Maui shows some signs of nightlife. You can find late-night amusement on Lahaina's Front Street or the Kihei main drag on Maui and the waterfront bars of Kailua-Kona on the Big Island, but don't expect a scene elsewhere. The legal drinking age is 21, but some allow age 18-and-older patrons on certain nights. Clubs come and go; schedules, prices, and formats change often. Check with your hotel concierge or phone the club for details.

Nightclubs by Location

WAIKIKI

Coconut Willy's Bar & Grill Hang-loose older Waikiki fave, live music, dancing
Fusion Waikiki Alternative (gay) club
Hard Rock Cafe nternationally known rock-themed restaurant
Nashville Waikiki Waikiki country-music watering hole

GREATER HONOLULU

Mai Tai Bar Honolulu Live music atop Ala Moana Center
Rumours Oldies disco and nightclub
thirtyninehotel Modern art meets live jazz and DJ dances

OAHU

Coconut Willy's Bar & Grill

TWO CHOICES: NEW BEACHWALK CLUB WITH LIVE MUSIC AND DANCING, OR WAIKIKI INTERNATIONAL MARKETPLACE OPEN-AIR FAVORITE FOR HANG-LOOSE TROPICAL ATMOSPHERE AND DANCING

222 Lewers Street (CW on Lewers, Waikiki Beachwalk) and 2330 Kalakaua Ave #71 (International Marketplace), Waikiki; ☎ **808-921-2000 and 808-923-9454**

Cover None. **Minimum** None. **Mixed drinks** (try the Long Island iced tea), wine, and beer $3 and up. **Dress** Casual (shorts and sandals okay). **Specials** Mai tais. **Food available** Burgers and bar food. **Hours** Daily, 11 a.m.–4 a.m.

WHO GOES THERE WHO GOES THERE 30 and older crowd favors Coconut Willy's at the Marketplace, locals and tourists, some dapper ballroom dancers; 21 and up at CW on Lewers, tourists and locals.

WHAT GOES ON Dancing to live and DJ music.

SETTING AND ATMOSPHERE Tiki bar with small wooden dance floor that gets busy after 1 a.m. on Lewers, when crowds merge here after going elsewhere. Open-air tropical atmosphere at the Marketplace.

IF YOU GO Pick Beachwalk if you're in a clubby mood, or hang loose in the open air at the Marketplace.

Fusion Waikiki

ALTERNATIVE CLUB

2260 Kuhio Avenue, second floor, Waikiki; ☎ 808-924-2422

Cover $5 except free karaoke on Mondays. **Minimum** None. **Mixed drinks,** wine, and beer $3 and up. **Dress** Casual **Specials** DJs and drink specials nightly; Kids Club on 1st and 3rd Sundays (on the lower level) drops the minimum age for entry to 18. **Food available** None. **Hours** Sunday–Thursday, 8 p.m.–4 a.m.; Friday and Saturday, 10 p.m.–4 a.m.

WHO GOES THERE Gays and others who enjoy gay shows.

WHAT GOES ON Dancing nightly. Drag shows and male strippers on Fridays and Saturdays. Occasional other live entertainment and special events.

SETTING AND ATMOSPHERE Up a narrow staircase, a small, dark club full of couples.

IF YOU GO Be prepared to stay late; the serious action starts after midnight.

Hard Rock Cafe

INTERNATIONAL ROCK MUSIC–THEMED CHAIN RESTAURANT

1837 Kapiolani Boulevard, Waikiki; ☎ 808-955-7383

Cover Varies. **Minimum** None. **Mixed drinks,** wine, and beer $4 and up. **Dress** Casual. **Specials** Happy-hour drinks and *pupu* specials, daily 4–7 p.m. **Food available** Ahi sandwiches, Hard Rock burgers, barbecue-pig sandwiches, pot roast, grilled fajitas, and barbecue chicken. **Hours** Dining: daily, 11 a.m.–11 p.m.; bar: daily, 11 a.m.–midnight.

WHO GOES THERE 18–60 crowd; tourists, music lovers, T-shirt collectors.

WHAT GOES ON DJs; live entertainment for special events.

SETTING AND ATMOSPHERE Same place, different artifacts. Honolulu has Eddie Van Halen's guitar, a bust of Mick Jagger, and an outfit worn by No Doubt's Gwen Stefani, not to mention Hawaii touches such as an outdoor lanai garden for toasting the sunset.

IF YOU GO Get a table outside to avoid conversation-killing decibel levels in main room.

Mai Tai Bar Honolulu

LIVE LOCAL MUSIC *PAU HANA* **(AFTER WORK) AND LATE NIGHT, PLUS MAI TAIS GALORE**

1450 Ala Moana Boulevard, Ala Moana Shopping Center, Hookipa Terrace, Honolulu; ☎ 808-947-2900; www.maitaibar.com/honolulu

Cover None. **Minimum** None. **Mixed drinks**, wine, and beer $3 and up. **Dress** Whatever. **Specials** Daily award-winning Hang Ten Happy Hour features $5 *pupu* and $4 drinks, plus beer specials. **Food available** Tasty appetizers such as coconut shrimp, calamari, shrimp ceviche. Special drinks include the mai tai tini, li hing mui tini, and local Kona Longboard beer. **Hours** Monday–Saturday, 11 a.m.–1 a.m.; Sunday, 8 a.m.–1 a.m., 7 a.m. in football season.

WHO GOES THERE Young locals after work, visitors who linger after shopping.

WHAT GOES ON *Pau hana* (after work) cocktails and live music; later, more happy hour specials and live music by local groups with dancing; and in season, early-morning Sunday football.

SETTING AND ATMOSPHERE Part pub, part club, this large lanai is roofed but open to the tropical breezes and ocean views (and cooled by misters when it gets crowded at night). Plentiful free parking.

IF YOU GO Get your pro football fix before lunch and head for the beach—only in Hawaii.

Nashville Waikiki

WAIKIKI COUNTRY-MUSIC WATERING HOLE

2330 Kuhio Avenue, Waikiki; ☎ 808-926-7911

Cover None. **Minimum** None. **Mixed drinks**, wine, and beer $2.75 and up. **Dress** Blue jeans to shorts, boots to sandals; shirts and footwear are required; 10-gallon hats are optional. **Specials** Happy-hour prices, 4–8 p.m.; line-dancing lessons offered Wednesdays, 7–9 p.m. **Food available** Chips and popcorn. **Hours** Daily, 4 p.m.–4 a.m.

WHO GOES THERE 21–30 crowd; college cowpokes, country bumpkins, and the occasional curious visitor.

WHAT GOES ON Music provided nightly by country DJs.

SETTING AND ATMOSPHERE Two-step in hula land at Waikiki's only country-and-western bar. This joint has bullhorns, saddles, copper paneling, drink specials, and a posse-sized dance floor.

IF YOU GO If you're not into line dancing, try Casino Night on Wednesdays with blackjack and pool. Call for live music events ☎ 808-955-7494.

Rumours

OLDIES DISCO AND NIGHTCLUB

Ala Moana Hotel, 410 Atkinson Drive, Honolulu; ☎ 808-955-4811

Cover Varies. **Minimum** 2 drinks. **Mixed drinks**, wine, and beer $4 and up. **Dress** Long pants and shirts with collars for men; no beachwear, tank tops, or sandals.

Food available Nachos, steak strips, veggie platters, pizzas, burgers, wontons, and cheesecake. **Hours** Friday, 5 p.m.–3:30 a.m.; Saturday, 9 p.m.–3:30 a.m.; closed Sunday–Thursday, but available for private parties.

WHO GOES THERE 30–50s crowd; tourists and locals; trannys and straights.

WHAT GOES ON DJs and dancing.

SETTING AND ATMOSPHERE Waiters and waitresses decked out in formal black-and-white attire. Old-style lounge chairs, two-story club. Huge TV screen flanks dance floor.

IF YOU GO Bring your dancing shoes and be prepared to strut your stuff. People will be watching.

thirtyninehotel

GALLERY CLUB CREATING THE MOST BUZZ IN TOWN IN THE LEAST LIKELY SETTING

39 Hotel Street, Honolulu; ☎ 808-599-2552; www.thirtyninehotel.com

Cover Varies. **Minimum** None. **Mixed drinks**, wine, and beer $4 and up. **Dress** Whatever. **Food available** None. **Hours** Tuesday, 9 p.m.–2 a.m. with live jazz; Saturday, 9 p.m.–2 a.m., dancing to DJs at Live Tiger party, special events; gallery with changing modern exhibits, Tuesday–Saturday, noon–6 p.m.

WHO GOES THERE 21–38 crowd; hipsters, music connoisseurs, professionals, art lovers, and the curious.

WHAT GOES ON Art gallery by day, recorded and live music and cultural events by night.

SETTING AND ATMOSPHERE Multimedia loft with couches for lounging and outdoor lanai in gentrifying but still somewhat-dicey Chinatown.

IF YOU GO In Chinatown at night, you can expect a neighborhood of seedy as well as trendy bars, transvestite hookers, and drugs in dark doorways. The old taxi-dancing halls have vanished, but dancing is on the comeback at this and a few other brave new bars.

ADULT ENTERTAINMENT

SINCE WORLD WAR II, when prostitution was legal and soldiers and sailors queued up for Hotel Street hookers in Chinatown, Honolulu nightlife has been famous for its X-rated component. Streetwalkers still work Waikiki boulevards after dark, leaving the corners of Chinatown to their transvestite counterparts. And strippers tease in clubs near the convention center. Korean bars, adult clubs, and adult services are advertised in the daily newspapers and the Honolulu phone book. Oahu's best-known establishments, like **Femme Nu,** are located on Kapiolani Boulevard near the Hawaii Convention Center and on Keeaumoku Street, near Ala Moana Center.

unofficial **TIP**
Avoid clubs on Hotel Street in Chinatown, where transsexual hookers work street corners, and drugs (mostly crack) are readily available despite police presence.

ACCOMMODATIONS INDEX

RESTAURANT INDEX

SUBJECT INDEX

Unofficial Guide Reader Survey

If you would like to express your opinion in writing about Hawaii or this guidebook, complete the following survey and mail it to:

Unofficial Guide Reader Survey
P.O. Box 43673
Birmingham, AL 35243

Inclusive dates of your visit:_____

Members of your party:	Person 1	Person 2	Person 3	Person 4	Person 5
Gender:	M F	M F	M F	M F	M F
Age:					

How many times have you been to Hawaii? _____
On your most recent trip, where did you stay?_____

Concerning your accommodations, on a scale of 100 as best and 0 as worst, how would you rate:

The quality of your room?   The value of your room?
The quietness of your room?   Check-in/checkout efficiency?
Shuttle service to the airport?   Swimming pool facilities?

Did you rent a car?   From whom?

Concerning your rental car, on a scale of 100 as best and 0 as worst, how would you rate:

Pickup-processing efficiency?   Return-processing efficiency?
Condition of the car?   Cleanliness of the car?
Airport-shuttle efficiency?

Concerning your dining experiences:

Estimate your meals in restaurants per day? _____
Approximately how much did your party spend on meals per day? _____
_____
Favorite restaurants in Hawaii: _____
_____

Did you buy this guide before leaving?   while on your trip?

How did you hear about this guide? (check all that apply)

Loaned or recommended by a friend ☐   Radio or TV ☐
Newspaper or magazine ☐   Bookstore salesperson ☐
Just picked it out on my own ☐   Library ☐
Internet ☐

What other guidebooks did you use on this trip?_____

_____

_____

_____

On a scale of 100 as best and 0 as worst, how would you rate them?

_____

_____

_____

Using the same scale, how would you rate the *Unofficial Guide*(s)?

_____

Are *Unofficial Guides* readily available at bookstores in your area? _____

Have you used other *Unofficial Guides*? _____

Which one(s)? _____

_____

_____

Comments about your Hawaii trip or the *Unofficial Guide*(s):

_____

_____

_____

_____

_____

_____

_____

_____

_____

_____

_____

_____

_____

_____

_____

_____

_____

_____

_____

_____